Worlds of Music

AN INTRODUCTION TO THE MUSIC OF THE WORLD'S PEOPLES

Fourth Edition

Jeff Todd Titon
General Editor

Linda K. Fujie
David Locke
David P. McAllester
David B. Reck
John M. Schechter
Mark Slobin
R. Anderson Sutton

SCHIRMER
™
THOMSON LEARNING

Australia · Canada · Mexico · Singapore · Spain
United Kingdom · United States

SCHIRMER

THOMSON LEARNING™

Music Editor: Clark Baxter
Assistant Editor: Jennifer Ellis
Editorial Assistant: Jonathan Katz
Technology Project Manager: Steve Wainwright
Executive Marketing Manager: Diane McOscar
Marketing Assistant: Kasia Zagorski
Advertising Project Manager: Brian Chaffee
Project Manager, Editorial Production: Teri Hyde
Print/Media Buyer: Karen Hunt
Permissions Editor: Joohee Lee

Production Service: Greg Hubit Bookworks
Text Designer: Harry Voigt
Copy Editor: Molly Roth
Cover Designer: Laurie Anderson
Cover Image: Laguna © Alexander Couwenberg,
    Courtesy NextMonet.com, San Francisco, CA
Cover Printer: Phoenix Color Corp. (MD)
Compositor: TBH Typecast, Inc.
Printer: Quebecor World (Taunton)

Printed in the United States of America
1 2 3 4 5 6 7 05 04 03 02 01

For permission to use material from this text, contact us by:
Web: http://www.thomsonrights.com **Fax:** 1-800-730-2215
Phone: 1-800-730-2214

Wadsworth Group/Thomson Learning
10 Davis Drive
Belmont, CA 94002-3098
USA

For more information about our products, contact us:
Thomson Learning Academic Resource Center
1-800-423-0563
http://www.wadsworth.com

International Headquarters
Thomson Learning
International Division
290 Harbor Drive, 2nd Floor
Stamford, CT 06902-7477
USA

UK/Europe/Middle East/South Africa
Thomson Learning
Berkshire House
168–173 High Holborn
London WC1V 7AA
United Kingdom

Asia
Thomson Learning
60 Albert Street, #15-01
Albert Complex
Singapore 189969

Canada
Nelson Thomson Learning
1120 Birchmount Road
Toronto, Ontario M1K 5G4
Canada

Library of Congress Cataloging-in-Publication Data

Worlds of music : an introduction to the music of the world's
peoples / Jeff Todd Titon, general editor.—4th ed.
    p. cm.
  Includes bibliographical references and index.
  Contents: The music-culture as a world of music / Jeff Todd
Titon and Mark Slobin—North America/Native America /
David P. McAllester—Africa/Ewe, Mande, Dagamba, Shona,
BaAka / David Locke—North America/Black America /
Jeff Todd Titon—Bosnia and Central/Southeastern
Europe : musics and musicians in transition / Mark Slobin—
India/South India / David B. Reck—Asia/Indonesia /
R. Anderson Sutton—East Asia/Japan / Linda K. Fujie—Latin
America/Ecuador / John M. Schechter—Discovering and
documenting a world of music / Jeff Todd Titon, David B.
Reck, and Mark Slobin.
  ISBN 0-534-59103-5
  1. World music—History and criticism. 2. Ethnomusicology.
I. Titon, Jeff Todd.
  ML3545.W67 2002
780'.9—dc21   2001044676

Contents

3 Africa/Ewe, Mande, Dagbamba, Shona, BaAka 87

7 *Asia/Indonesia* 279

R. ANDERSON SUTTON

8 *East Asia/Japan* 331

LINDA FUJIE

9 Latin America/Ecuador 385

JOHN M. SCHECHTER

10 Discovering and Documenting a World of Music 447

JEFF TODD TITON, DAVID B. RECK, AND MARK SLOBIN

Recorded Selections

CD 1

1. Postal workers canceling stamps at the University of Ghana post office (2:59). The whistled tune is the hymn "Bompata," by the Ghanaian composer W. J. Akyeampong (b. 1900). Field recording by James Koetting. Legon, Ghana, 1975. Used by permission of the artists.

2. Songs of hermit thrushes (0:31). Field recording by Jeff Todd Titon. Little Deer Isle, Maine, 1999.

3. Grass Dance (1:51). Traditional Sioux War Dance. Field recording by Ray Boley, n.d. *Sioux Favorites.* Canyon Records Productions CR-6054. Phoenix, Arizona.

4. Lullaby (0:58). Traditional Zuni. Performed by Lanaiditsa. Field recording by David McAllester. White Water, New Mexico, 1950.

5. "Gadasjot" (0:47). Iroquois Quiver Dance or Warrior's Stomp Dance song. Twenty Jacobs of Quaker Ridge. Performed by Joshua Billy Buck and Simeon Gibson. Field recording by William Fenton, c. 1942. *Songs from the Iroquois Longhouse.* Archive of Folk Song of the Library of Congress AFS L6. LP. Washington, D.C. Used by permission of collector.

6. Yeibichai (2:15). Navajo dance song from Nightway. Led by Sandoval Begay. Field recording by Willard Rhodes, n.d. Archive of Folk Song of the Library of Congress AFS L41. LP. Washington, D.C. Used by permission of collector.

7. "Folsom Prison Blues" (2:50). Johnny Cash. Published by Hi-Lo Music. Performed by the Fenders. *The Fenders, Second Time Roun'.* LP. Thoreau, New Mexico, 1966. Used by permission The Harry Fox Agency, Inc.

8. "Shizhané'é" ("I'm in Luck") (1:20). Navajo Circle Dance song from Enemyway. Performed by Albert G. Sandoval, Jr., and Ray Winnie. Field recording by David P. McAllester.

Sedona, Arizona, 1957. Used by permission Albert G. Sandoval and Ray Winnie.

9. Navajo Sacred Prayer (0:59). Episode from Navajo Shootingway ceremony. Led by Dinet Tsosie. Field recording by David P. McAllester. Lukachukai, Arizona, 1958. Used by permission Dinet Tsosie.

10. Hymn of the Native American Church. (1:14). Navajo Peyote song. Performed by George Mitchell and Kaya David. Field recording by Willard Rhodes, n.d. Archive of Folk Song of the Library of Congress AFS 14. LP. Washington, D.C. Used by permission Willard Rhodes.

11. "Clinging to a Saving Hand" (3:42). Traditional Christian hymn. Performed by the Chinle Galileans. *Navajo Country Gospel* LPS 909. LP. Chinle, Arizona, n.d. Used by permission Roland Dixon.

12. "Mother Earth" (2:57). Sharon Burch. *Yazzie Girl*, by Sharon Burch. Canyon Records CR-534. © 1989 Sharon Burch. Courtesy Canyon Records Productions, Phoenix, Arizona.

13. "Proud Earth" (3:32). Arliene Nofchissey Williams. Performed by Arliene Nofchissey Williams and Chief Dan George. *Proud Earth.* Salt City Records SC-80. LP. Provo, Utah, n.d. © Arlienne Nofchissey Williams. Used by permission.

14. "Origins" (4:00). R. Carlos Nakai. *Cycles: Native American Flute Music.* Canyon Records Productions CR614-C 1985. Used by permission Canyon Records Productions, Phoenix, Arizona.

15. *Agbekor* (5:35). Traditional music of the Ewe people. Field recording by David Locke. Anlo-Afiadenyigba, Ghana, 1976. Used by permission of the artists.
    a. Three slow-paced songs (0:00–2:52)
    b. One song in free rhythm (3:02–4:20)
    c. One fast-paced song (4:27–5:35)

16. Demonstration: *Agbekor* (3:54). Performed by David Locke. You will hear the bell by itself, followed by each instrument with the bell (*axatse, kaganu, kidi, kloboto,* and *totodzi),* and finally, the polyrhythm of all the parts.

17. "Lambango" (3:02). Mande song. Mariatu Kuyateh. Performed by Mariatu Kuyateh, Kekuta Suso, and Seni Jobateh. Field recording by Roderic Knight. The Gambia, 1970. Used by permission Roderic Knight.

18. "Nag Biegu" ("Ferocious Wild Bull") (2:08). Traditional Praise Name Dance song of Dagbon. Performed by *lunsi* drummers of the Dagbamba people. Field recording by David Locke. Ghana, 1984. Used by permission of the artists.

19. "Nhemamusasa" (lit. "cutting branches for shelter"), *kushaura* section (2:39). Traditional Shona. Field recording by Paul Berliner. Zimbabwe, 1971. Used by permission Paul Berliner.

20. "Nyarai" ("Be Ashamed"), excerpt (2:29). Thomas Mapfumo. Performed by Thomas Mapfumo and Blacks Unlimited. *Thomas Mapfumo: The Chimurenga Singles, 1976–1980.* Gramma Records Zimbabwe. Shanachie CD 43066.

21. "Makala" (name of unknown person) (2:20). Traditional BaAka song. Field recording by Michelle Kisliuk. Central African Republic, 1988. Used by permission Michelle Kisliuk.

22. "Amazing Grace" (2:36). Traditional. Performed by deacon and congregation of the New Bethel Baptist Church. Field recording by Jeff Todd Titon. Detroit, Michigan, 1977. Used by permission.

23. "Amazing Grace" (2:52). Traditional. Performed by the congregation of the Fellowship Independent Baptist Church, led by Rev. John Sherfey. Field recording by Jeff Todd Titon. Stanley, Virginia, 1977. Used by permission.

24. Field Holler (0:43). Traditional solo work song. Performed by Leonard "Baby Doo" Caston. Field recording by Jeff Todd Titon. Minneapolis, Minnesota, 1971. (Background noise from the apartment is audible.) Used by permission of the artist.

1. "Rosie" (2:50). Traditional work song. Performed by prisoners at Mississippi State Penitentiary. Field recording by Alan Lomax. Parchman, Mississippi, 1947. © Alan Lomax. Used by permission Alan Lomax.

2. "Poor Boy Blues" (3:16). Performed by Lazy Bill Lucas Trio. Field recording by Jeff Todd Titon, Minneapolis, Minnesota, 1970. Used by permission of the artists.

3. "She Got Me Walkin'" (3:01). William "Lazy Bill" Lucas. Performed by Lazy Bill and His Blue Rhythm: Lazy Bill

Lucas, piano and vocal; Louis Myers, guitar; Elga Edmonds, drums. Chance 10" 78-rpm record. Chicago, Illinois, 1954. Used by permission of William Lucas.

4. "I Need $100" (2:59). Performed by One-String Sam, c. 1956. Detroit, Michigan. Reissued on *Detroit Blues: The Early 1950s.* Blues Classics LP, BC-12.

5. "Kokomo Blues" (2:40). Fred McDowell. Performed by Fred McDowell, vocal and guitar; Jeff Todd Titon, guitar; Mitchell Genova, drums. Field recording by Michael Justen. Minneapolis, Minnesota, July 1970. © Tradition Music, BMI; administered by BUG. Used by permission.

6. "From Dark Till Dawn" (3:29). John Ned "Johnny" Shines. Performed by Johnny Shines, vocal and guitar. Field recording by Jeff Todd Titon. Beloit, Wisconsin, March 1970. (Background noise from the audience is audible.) Used by permission of the artist and the copyright holder, Uncle Doris Music, ASCAP.

7. "You Don't Love Me" (3:35). Willie Cobbs. Performed by Magic Sam (Sam Maghett), vocal and guitar; Sam Lay, drums; unknown bass player. Field recording by Jeff Todd Titon. Ann Arbor, Michigan, August, 1969. Used by permission of the artists and the copyright holder, Embassy Music Corp., BMI.

8. "Ain't Enough Comin' In" (5:53). Otis Rush. Performed by Otis Rush on *Otis Rush: Ain't Enough Comin' In.* Mercury CD 314518769-2. 1994. © 1994 OTIS RUSH MUSIC, administered by BUG. Used by permission.

9. "Paparudele" ("Come, little rain") (0:27). Traditional. Performed by Gypsy children in Găşteşti village, Romania. *World Library of Folk and Primitive Music 17: Romania.* Rounder 11661-1759-2. Used by permission Alan Lomax Archives.

10. "Sisters, Hold on to Your Chastity" (0:40). Traditional women's *ganga* song of the Muslim highlands. Performed by Azra Bandić, Luckin Mevla, and Emsija Tatarović. Field recording by Mirjana Laušević. Umoljani village, Bosnia, 1990. Used by permission Mirjana Laušević.

11. "What Lifts the Heart of a Rascal?" (1:24). Traditional men's *ganga* song of the Muslim highlands. Performed by Safet Elezovic, Muhamed Elezovic, Zejnil Maslesa. Field recording by Mirjana Laušević. Gornji Lukomir village, Bosnia, 1990. Used by permission Mirjana Laušević.

12. "O šargija." (1:06). Traditional Muslim lowlands song with *šargija* lute. Performed by Skiba and friends. Field recording by Mirjana Laušević. Bosnia, 1989. Used by permission Mirjana Laušević.

13. "Trepetljika trepetala" ("That which trembles"), excerpt (1:17). Himzo Polovina. Lowlands *sevdalinka* song with *tamburitza* orchestra. Live radio performance. Sarajevo, Yugoslavia, 1986. Used by permission Edmir Polovina.

14. "Zadnja Stanica Brčko" ("Last Stop Brčko") (3:33). Mensur Hatić. Performed by Mensur Hatić. Field recording by Mark Slobin. Detroit, Michigan, 1994. Used by permission of the artist.

15. "Klaro del dija" ("Break of Day") (1:52). Traditional Sephardic Jewish song of Bosnia. Performed by Flory Jagoda, vocal and guitar, with Howard Bass and The Hesperus. Field recording by Abby Sternberg, Institute of Musical Traditions Concert. Silver Spring, Maryland, 2000. Used by permission Flory Jagoda and Abby Sternberg.

16. "Sisters, Hold on to Your Chastity" (1:06). As sung in 2000 by the same singers on CD 2, Track 10. Field recording by Mirjana Laušević. Umoljani village, Bosnia, 2000. Used by permission Mirjana Laušević.

17. "What Do You Love the Best, Little Devil?" (1:02). Contemporary women's *ganga* song. Performed by Azra Bandić, Luckin Mevla, and Emsija Tatarović. Field recording by Mirjana Laušević. Umoljani village, Bosnia, 2000. Used by permission Mirjana Laušević.

18. "Jel' Sarajevo gdje je nekad bilo" ("Is Sarajevo Still Where It Was?") (4:19). Dino Merlin. *Dino Merlin Live.* In Takt Records. Sarajevo, Bosnia, 1998. Used by permission of the artist.

19. *Hristianova kopanitsa* (dance) (3:26). Ivo Papazov. Performed by Ivo Papazov and Trakiya. *Balkanology.* Rykodisc CD HNBC 1363. Bulgaria, 1991.

20. "Engal Kalyanam" ("Our Wedding"), cinema song (3:25). Music by M. S. Viswanathan, lyrics by Vali. Performed by P. Susheela, T. M. Soundararajan, P. B. Sreenivos, and L. R. Eswari. From *Hits from Tamil Films*, Vol. 6. EMI Odeon (India) 3AECS 5519. LP. Calcutta, India, 1969. Published and copyrighted to The Gramophone Company of India, Ltd. Used by permission.

21. "Devi Niye Tunai" ("O Devi! with Fish-Shaped Eyes") (4:37), by Papanasan Sivan. Performed by Shobha Vasudevan, vocal, and David Nelson, *mridangam.* Recorded for author by recording engineer Owen Muir. Amherst, Massachusetts, January, 2001. Used by permission of the artists.

CD 3

1. "Sarasiruha" ("To the Goddess Saraswati") (22:32). *Kriti* in Natai *raga, Adi tala*, by Pulaiyur Doraismy Ayyar. Performed by Ranganayaki Rajagopalan, *veena;* Raja Rao, *mridangam.* Recorded for author by recording engineer Rahul K. Raveendran. Chennai, India, 2001. Used by permission of the artists.

2. *Bubaran* "Kembang Pacar" ("Red Flower"), *pélog pathet nem* (3:04). Central Javanese *gamelan* music in loud-playing style, performed by musicians affiliated with the royal palace in Yogyakarta. Field recording by R. Anderson Sutton. Yogyakarta, Java, Indonesia, 1980. Used by permission of the artists.

3. Demonstration: *Bubaran* "Kembang Pacar," *pélog pathet nem* (3:55). *Balungan* melody alone, followed by addition of other instruments one by one. Performed by University of Wisconsin–Madison Javanese *gamelan* ensemble, directed by R. Anderson Sutton. Recorded at the University of Wisconsin–Madison, December 2000.

4. *Ladrang* "Wilujeng" ("safe, secure"), *pélog pathet barang* (8:47). Central Javanese *gamelan* music in "soft-playing" style. Performed by musicians of Ngudya Wirama *gamelan* group under the direction of Ki Suhardi. Field recording by René Lysloff. Yogyakarta, Java, Indonesia, 1980.

5. *Playon* "Lasem," *sléndro pathet nem,* Rendition 1 (1:20). Central Javanese *gamelan* music for shadow puppetry. Performed by *gamelan* group of Ki Suparman. Field recording by R. Anderson Sutton. Yogyakarta, Java, Indonesia, 1974. Used by permission of the artists.

6. *Playon* "Lasem," *sléndro pathet nem,* Rendition 2 (0:33). Central Javanese *gamelan* music for shadow puppetry. Performed by *gamelan* group of Ki Suparman. Field recording by R. Anderson Sutton. Yogyakarta, Java, Indonesia, 1974. Used by permission of the artists.

7. "Kosalia Arini" (10:48), by Wayan Beratha. *Gamelan gong kebyar.* Performed by STSI (Sekolah Tinggi Seni Indonesia) *gamelan* musicians, directed by Nyoman Windha and Pande Gde Mustika. Recorded by Michael Tenzer and Ketut Gde Asnawa, with Yong Sagita. STSI campus, Denpasar, Bali, August, 1998.

8. *Gendang keteng-keteng,* two excerpts (1:58). Traditional Batak music. Performed by ensemble led by Tukang Ginting on *kulcapi.* Field recording by R. Anderson Sutton. Karo Batak highlands of North Sumatra, 1980. Used by permission of the artists.

9. "Begadang II" ("Staying up All Night") (3:33), by Rhoma Irama. Popular *dangdut* music. Performed by Rhoma Irama and his Soneta Group. *Begadang II.* Yukawi Indomusic. 1978. Used by permission.

10. "Shufflendang-Shufflending" (4:11). Ethno-jazz fusion, Sundanese. Performed by Krakatau: Dwiki Dharmawan, keyboard; Pra Budidharma, fretless bass; Budhy Haryono, Western drum set ("traps"); joined by Yoyon Darsono, *rebab* and flute; Adhe Rudiana, *kendang;* Elfik Zulfiqar and Tudi Rahayu, *saron;* Zainal Arifin, *bonang. Magical Match.* Kita Music. 2000.

11. "Distorsi" ("Distortion") (5:19). Dhani Ahmad Manaf. Indonesian rock music. Performed by Ahmad Band: Dhani, vocal; Andra Ramadhan, guitar; Bimo, drum; Bongky, bass; Pay, guitar. *Ideologi Sikap Otak.* Aquarius P 9173. 1998.

CD 4

1. "Tsuru no sugomori" ("Nesting Cranes") (3:41). Performed by Kawase Junsuke, *shakuhachi* (flute), and Kawase Hakuse, *shamisen* (lute). Field recording by Linda Fujie. Tokyo, Japan, 1989. Used by permission of the artists.

2. "Hakusen no" ("A White Fan") (3:23). Performed by Shitaya Kotsuru for Nippon Columbia WK-170. Used by permission.

3. "Nikata-bushi" ("Song of Nikata") (5:08). Performed by Asano Sanae, vocal; Asano Umewaka, *shamisen* (lute). Field recording by Karl Signell. Washington, D.C., 1986. Used by permission of performer and collector.

4. "Yatai" ("The Festival Wagon"), excerpt from *Kiri-bayashi* (1:18). Performed by Ueno Shachu. Field recording by Linda Fujie. Tokyo, Japan, 1981. Used by permission of the artist.

5. "Nonki-bushi" ("Song of the Lazy Man") (2:37). *Enka* song. Music by Soeda Azembo, lyrics by Ishida Ichimatsu. Performed by Ishida Ishimatsu for Nippon Columbia SP-ban fukugen. Used by permission.

6. "Naite Nagasaki" ("Crying Nagasaki") (3:35). Performed by Kanda Fukumaru for Nippon Columbia AH-210. Used by permission.

7. "Pajarillo" ("Little Bird") (2:31). *Joropo* of Venezuela. Recorded by Isabel Aretz, Luis Felipe Ramón y Rivera, and Álvaro Fernaud. Song 5 "Golpe (Joropo)." Barinas State, 1968. *Música Folklórica de Venezuela*. Disques Ocora OCR 78/Ocora Radio France. LP. Distribution Harmonia Mundi.

8. "El lazo" ("The Lasso") (3:53). Chile. Composed and performed by Víctor Jara. n.d. *Víctor Jara: Desde Lonquén hasta siempre*. Monitor Music of the World, vol. 4. Monitor Records MFS 810.

9. "Kutirimunapaq" ("So That We Can Return") (3:52). *K'antu* of Bolivia. Performed by Ruphay. Jach'a Marka, 1982. *Ruphay*, Discos Heriba SLP 2212. Heriba Ltda. La Paz, Bolivia. Used by permission.

10. "Cascarón" ("thick peel, rind, or eggshell—especially a broken one") (3:25). *Sanjuán* of Ecuador. Performed by Quichua harpist Efraín. Field recording by John Schechter, outside Cotacachi, Ecuador, April, 1980. Used by permission of the artist.

11. "Rusa María wasi rupajmi" ("Rosa Maria's House A-Burning") (2:28). *Sanjuán* of Ecuador. Performed by Quichua musicians Gerónimo, vocal; Sergio, harp; and his father, Miguel Armando, *golpe*. Field recording by John Schechter, outside Cotacachi, Ecuador, January, 1980. Used by permission of the artists.

12. "Ilumán tiyu" ("Man of Ilumán") (3:23). Composed by Segundo "Galo" Maigua Pillajo. *Sanjuán* of Ecuador. Performed by "Galo," guitar and vocal, with the Quichua ensemble Conjunto Ilumán. Field recording by John Schechter. Ilumán, Ecuador, October 1990. Used by permission of the artists.

13. "Amor imposible" ("Impossible Love") (2:35). Traditional Peruvian *wayno*. Performed by Chaskinakuy. *Chaskinakuy, Music of the Andes: Cosecha*. CD engineered and mixed by Joe Hoffmann and remastered by Brian Walder at Hoffmann Studios. Occidental, California, 1991. Used by permission.

14. *Vacación* (1:23). Performed by Quichua harpist Sergio, at a child's wake. Field recording by John Schechter, outside Cotacachi, Ecuador, February 1980. Used by permission of the artist.

15. Ecuadorian Quichua mother's lament to her deceased two-year-old girl, the morning after the child's wake (preceded by fifteen seconds of Sergio's *Vacación*) (3:07). Field recording by John Schechter, outside Cotacachi, Ecuador, January 1980. Used by permission.

16. "Toro barroso" ("Reddish Bull") (3:32). *Albazo* of Ecuador. Performed by Don César Muquinche. Field recording by John Schechter, outside Ambato, Ecuador, 1980. Used by permission of the artist.

17. "Vamos pa' Manabí" ("Let's Go to Manabí") (3:01). *Bomba* of Ecuador. Traditional text, music by the Congo brothers. Performed by Fabián Congo, guitar and vocal; Eleuterio Congo, guitar. Field recording by John Schechter. Chota Valley, Ecuador, March 1980. Used by permission of the artists.

Preface

*W*hy study music? There are many reasons, but perhaps the most important are pleasure and understanding. We have designed this book and its accompanying CDs to introduce undergraduates to the study of music the world over. Although *Worlds of Music* contains musical notation, the package may be used by students who do not read music. The only prerequisites are a curious ear and an inquisitive mind.

University courses in music of the world's peoples have increased dramatically since 1984, when the first edition of this book was published. It is easy to understand why. Students who love music are alive to all music. So are composers, and many use musical resources from throughout the world in their newest works. This breadth is an important feature of today's music, and the people who listen to it—now and in the future—will want to keep their musical horizons broad as well. Another reason for the recent interest in all kinds of music is an upsurge in ethnic awareness. As modern people try to locate themselves in a world that is changing with bewildering speed, they find music especially rewarding, for music is among the most tenacious of cultural elements. Music symbolizes a people's way of life; it represents a distillation of cultural style. For many, music *is* a way of life.

Interest in and appreciation of world music has grown enormously just in the past ten years. World music has also become a significant part of the concert world. Further, more recordings and videos are available than ever before, world music is now a part of the cable television mix, and many students actively seek world music on the World Wide Web. Musicians from all over the globe now appear on college and university campuses. World music is now important in the mass media, and multiculturalism—the celebration of the multiethnic heritage of North America—has brought a flood of ethnic festivals, always featuring music. Many younger people searching for musical roots have looked into their ethnic pasts and chosen to learn the music of their foreparents, while others view the variety of musics in the world as a vast resource to be drawn on in creating their own sounds.

The authors of this book are ethnomusicologists; our field, *ethnomusicology,* is usually defined as the study of music in culture. Some ethnomusicologists define it as the study of music *as* culture, underlining the fact that music is a way of organizing human activity. By culture we do not mean "the high arts." Rather, we use the term as anthropologists do: Culture is a people's way of life, learned and transmitted through the centuries of adapting to the natural and human world. Ethnomusicology is the study of music in the context of human life.

I like to think of ethnomusicology as the study of people making music. People "make" music in two ways: They make or construct the *idea* of music—what it is (and is not) and what it does—and they make or produce the *sounds* that they call music. Although we all experience music as something "out there" in the world, our response to music depends on the ideas we associate with that music, and those ideas come from the people (ourselves included) who carry our culture. In other words, people "make" music into a cultural domain, with associated sets of ideas and activities. We could not even pick out musical form and structure, how the parts of a piece of music work together to form a whole, if we did not depend on the idea that music must be organized rather than random and if we had not learned to make music that way. Analyzing form and structure is characteristic of some cultures, including Western ones, but in other areas of the world people do not habitually break a thing down into parts to analyze it.

As students of music in culture, ethnomusicologists have every reason to investigate Western art music—that is, the tradition of Palestrina, Bach, Beethoven, Verdi, Stravinsky, and the like. But with some recent exceptions, ethnomusicologists in North America have specialized in music outside this tradition. They know the Western classics well, but their interest embraces all music. Indeed, many have devoted years to performing music outside the Western mainstream. Further, because ethnomusicologists study more than the "music itself" (and some even deny that such a thing exists), they are not satisfied merely to analyze and compare musical forms, structures, melodies, rhythms, compositions, and genres. Instead, they borrow insights and methods from anthropology, sociology, literary criticism, linguistics, and history to understand music as human expression. In fact, until the 1950s, ethnomusicology courses in U.S. universities were more likely to be found in anthropology departments than music departments, and some nineteenth-century founders of ethnomusicology were psychologists. Ethnomusicology is therefore interdisciplinary, combining elements of the arts, humanities, and social sciences. Because of its eclectic methods and worldwide scope, ethnomusicology is well suited to students seeking a liberal arts education.

The number of world-music textbooks in print is quite small. Most offer broad surveys, but we think there are good reasons to avoid a survey course at the beginning level. In its broad sweep a survey offers only a passing acquaintance with the music of many peoples. Too often a survey turns into a superficial musical tour: If today is Tuesday, this must be India. The inevitable result is musical overkill; by the term's end, students are so overloaded they can barely recognize different musics of the world, let alone understand any one.

Instead of surveying the whole world of music, then, we explore in depth the music of a small number of representative human groups. This approach is not new; it adapts to ethnomusicology the case method in anthropology, the touchstone approach in literature, and the problems approach in history. Its main object is not to pile up factual knowledge about various musical worlds, though certainly this approach offers many facts. Rather, the point is to experience something of what it is like to be an ethnomusicologist puzzling out his or her way toward understanding an unfamiliar music. This process, we believe, is the best foundation for either future coursework (including surveys and seminars) or self-directed study and enjoyment of world music after college.

For *Worlds of Music* we decided on a relatively small number of case studies, because that is how we teach the introductory-level world-music course at our universities. We thought also that by writing about music in societies we know firsthand, we could write an authoritative book. Each chapter, then, reflects our own choice of subject. It also reflects our different ways of approaching music, for we agree that music cannot be "caught" by one method only. Still, we organized the chapters on six guiding principles. First, we think a textbook in world music should go beyond merely avoiding elitism and ethnocentrism. From the start, students need to understand an unfamiliar music on its own terms—that is, as the people who make the music understand it. Second, in order to know music as a human activity, not just a sequence of organized sound, we need to ask what the life of a musician is like in different societies and find answers in life histories and autobiographies. Third, we single out the words of songs for special attention because they often convey the meaning and purposes of musical performances as the music makers comprehend them. Fourth, we regard the musical examples not just as illustrations but as points of departure; therefore, most of them can be heard on the compact discs accompanying this book. Fifth, student music-making projects—singing, building, and playing instruments—can, if properly directed and seriously approached, greatly increase appreciation of a musical style. Sixth, and most important, we believe that an introduction to world music should provide pleasure as well as knowledge.

For this fourth edition, the first chapter has been extensively rewritten to introduce the elements of world music in greater detail. It now has many more illustrations and cross-references to musical examples in the various parts of the book keyed to an expanded, accompanying CD set. Using as illustrations the popular Ghanaian postal workers' stamp-canceling music and the song of the hermit thrush, Chapter 1 asks students how one draws the line between music and nonmusic. Using everyday ideas of rhythm, meter, melody, and harmony, it sharpens these rudimentary concepts and shows how they can help in understanding the various musics presented in this book. In an ethnomusicological context, rudiments include not only the familiar elements of musical organization but also a basic approach to music's place in human life. For that reason we introduce a performance model showing how music relates to communities and their history; we also introduce a component model that includes musical sound and structure as well as other elements of a music-culture, including ideas, social behavior, and material culture.

Chapters 4, 5, 6, 7, and 9 have been revised and updated, with several new musical examples. Expanding to a four-CD set has enabled us to include a new, outstanding performance of *karnataka sangeeta.* The CD set also features several new examples of African-American music and Javanese popular music, as well as a new Andean ensemble that reflects the popularity of this music in North America. The Balinese *gamelan* example has been updated. The CD set now includes a Javanese *gamelan* demonstration in which the orchestral layers are gradually incorporated, thereby showing how the ensemble's parts relate to the whole. We have also included the same kind of demonstration featuring the component parts of the drum ensemble that performs *Agbekor.* This will make it easier for students to understand the way these complex ensembles function.

We suggest that students begin with Chapter 1. The case studies, Chapters 2 through 9, make be taken in any order. In our experience, about two weeks per case study is about right; we encourage instructors to add or substitute a case study based on their own research. Because any fieldwork project should begin well before the end of the term, we suggest that Chapter 10 be read just after the first case study and that students begin fieldwork immediately afterward. Many students say the field projects are the most valuable experiences they take away from this course, particularly when they must make sense of what they document in the field. The field project encourages original research. Students find it attractive and meaningful to make an original contribution to knowledge. For instructors who find the fourth edition of *Worlds of Music* more than they need, a Shorter Version is also available from the publisher and can be ordered from the www.wadsworth.com Web site.

We have appreciated the assistance, over the years, of several editors at Schirmer Books and now Wadsworth—Maribeth Anderson Payne, Ken Stuart, Richard Carlin, Robert Axelrod, Jonathan Wiener, Clark Baxter, and Molly Roth—in seeing this project through production. We remember the contributions of the late James T. Koetting, my predecessor at Brown, who authored the Africa chapter through the first two editions of this book and whose field recording of the Ghanaian postal workers will always remain in it. We are grateful to Henrietta Mckee Carter who was in Ghana when Jim made that recording and who supplied us with additional information about it for this edition.

We would be pleased to hear from our readers, and we may be reached by writing the publisher or any of us at our respective universities.

Jeff Todd Titon
General Editor

The Authors

Linda K. Fujie received the Ph.D. in ethnomusicology from Columbia University, where she was a student of Dieter Christensen and Adelaida Schramm. She has conducted field research in Japan, mainly concerning urban festival and popular music, under grants from the National Endowment for the Humanities, Columbia University, and Colby College. Her interest in overseas Japanese culture has also resulted in research on Japanese-American and Japanese-Brazilian communities, the latter funded by the German Music Council. Her research has been published in the *Yearbook for Traditional Music,* in publications on popular music, and in Japanese journals. Other research interests, on which she has also written articles and delivered papers at European conferences, include the music of the Shaker community in Maine and folk music in Germany. She has taught at Colby College as Assistant Professor and at the East Asian Institute of the Free University of Berlin. She regularly writes and delivers radio programs on topics related to traditional music on German radio. She also lectures on ethnomusicology at the University of Bamberg.

David Locke received the Ph.D. in ethnomusicology from Wesleyan University in 1978, where he studied with David McAllester, Mark Slobin, and Gen'ichi Tsuge. At Wesleyan his teachers of traditional African music included Abraham Adzinyah and Freeman Donkor. He conducted doctoral dissertation fieldwork in Ghana from 1975 to 1977 under the supervision of Professor J. H. K. Nketia. In Ghana his teachers and research associates included Godwin Agbeli, Midawo Gideon Foli Alorwoyie, and Abubakari Lunna. He has published numerous books and articles on African music and regularly performs the repertories of music and dance about which he writes. He teaches at Tufts University, where he currently serves as the director of the master's degree program in ethnomusicology and as a faculty advisor in the Tufts-in-Ghana Foreign Study Program. His current projects include an ethnomusicological study of the music-culture of Dagbon, the documentation and analysis of repertories of African music, and the preparation of multimedia materials on music and culture. He is active in the Society for Ethnomusicology and has served as the president of its Northeast Chapter.

David P. McAllester received the Ph.D. in anthropology from Columbia University, where he studied with George Herzog. A student of American Indian music since 1938, he has undertaken fieldwork among the Comanches, Hopis, Apaches, Navajos, Penobscots, and Passamaquoddies. He is the author of such classic works in ethnomusicology as *Peyote Music, Enemy Way Music, Myth of the Great Star Chant,* and *Navajo Blessingway Singer* (with coauthor Charlotte Frisbie). He is one of the founders of the Society for Ethnomusicology, and he has served as its president and the editor of its journal, *Ethnomusicology.* He is professor emeritus of anthropology and music at Wesleyan University.

David B. Reck received the Ph.D. in ethnomusicology from Wesleyan University, where he studied under Mark Slobin and David P. McAllester. He has studied and traveled in India, Southeast Asia, and the Far East under grants from the American Institute of Indian Studies, the Rockefeller Foundation, the John Simon Guggenheim Memorial Foundation, and the JDR IIIrd Fund. A senior disciple of the legendary Ranganayaki Rajagopalan, he is an accomplished musician on the South-Indian *veena* and has performed in the United States, Europe, and India as a soloist, an accompanist, and a member of the group Kirtana. During his "fifteen minutes of fame" as a composer, he performed at Tanglewood, Town Hall, Lincoln Center, Carnegie Hall, and various universities and international music festivals. The author of *Music of the Whole Earth,* his research and publications include work on India's music, U.S. popular styles, J. S. Bach, the Beatles, and cross-influences between the West and the Orient. Currently he is Professor of Music and of Asian Languages and Civilizations at Amherst College.

John M. Schechter received the Ph.D. in ethnomusicology from the University of Texas at Austin, where he studied ethnomusicology with Gérard Béhague, Andean anthropology with Richard Schaedel, and Quichua with Louisa Stark and Guillermo Delgado. Following his Peace Corps volunteer service in Colombia during the 1960s, he pursued ethnomusicological fieldwork in the Andes of Ecuador in 1979–1980 and 1990. He is the author of *The Indispensable Harp: Historical Development, Modern Roles, Configurations, and Performance Practices in Ecuador and Latin America.* He is the general editor of, and a contributing author to, *Music in Latin American Culture: Regional Traditions,* a volume examining music-cultural traditions in distinct regions of Latin America, with chapters by ethnomusicologists specializing in those regions. Schechter's other recent publications have explored formulaic expression in Ecuadorian Quichua *sanjuán;* recent evolution in the *bomba,* a focal African-Ecuadorian musical genre; the syncretic nature of the Andean Corpus Christi celebration; and the ethnography and cultural history of the Latin American/Iberian child's wake music-ritual. He is Associate Professor of Music at the University of California, Santa Cruz, where he teaches ethnomusicology and music theory, directs two Latin American Ensembles, and serves as the provost of the campus's Merrill College.

Mark Slobin received the Ph.D. in musicology at the University of Michigan. He is the author, editor, or translator of many books, some on the music of Afghanistan and Central Asia and others on Jewish music in Europe and the United States, eastern-European music, and the theory and method of studying subcultural musics in Euro-America. *Tenement Songs: The Popular Music of the Jewish Immigrants* won the ASCAP–Deems Taylor Award. He is a past president of the Society for Ethnomusicology and of the Society for Asian Music, having edited the latter's journal, *Asian Music,* from 1971 to 1987. He teaches at Wesleyan University as Professor of Music and chairs the music department; he has also served as visiting professor at Harvard, Berkeley, and New York University.

R. Anderson Sutton received the Ph.D. in musicology from the University of Michigan, where he studied with Judith Becker and William Malm. He was introduced to Javanese music while an undergraduate at Wesleyan University, and he made it the focus of his master's study at the University of Hawaii, where he studied *gamelan* with Hardja Susilo. On numerous occasions since 1973 he has conducted field research in Indonesia, with grants from the East-West Center, Fulbright-Hays, Social Science Research Council, National Endowment for the Humanities, Wenner-Gren Foundation, and American Philosophical Society. He is the author of *Traditions of Gamelan Music in Java, Variation in Central Javanese Gamelan Music,* and numerous articles on Javanese music. He has recently completed a book on music and cultural politics in South Sulawesi, Indonesia, and his current research concerns music and the Indonesian media. Active as a *gamelan* musician since 1971, he has performed with several professional groups in Indonesia and directed numerous performances in the United States. He has served as the first vice president and a book review editor for the Society for Ethnomusicology, and as a member of the Working Committee on Performing Arts for the Festival of Indonesia (1990–1992). He has taught at the University of Hawaii and the University of Wisconsin–Madison, where he is Professor of Music and a past director of the Center for Southeast Asian Studies.

Jeff Todd Titon received the Ph.D. in American Studies from the University of Minnesota, where he studied ethnomusicology with Alan Kagan and musicology with Johannes Riedel. He has done fieldwork in North America on religious folk music, blues music, and old-time fiddling, with support from the National Endowment for the Arts and the National Endowment for the Humanities. For two years he was rhythm guitarist in the Lazy Bill Lucas Blues Band, a group that appeared in the 1970 Ann Arbor Blues Festival. The author or editor of seven books, including *Early Downhome Blues,* which won the ASCAP–Deems Taylor Award, and *Powerhouse for God,* he is also a documentary photographer and filmmaker. In 1991 he wrote a hypertext multimedia computer program about old-time fiddler Clyde Davenport that is regarded as a model for interactive representations of people making music. Smithsonian Folkways recently published a CD from his field recordings of Old Regular Baptists in eastern Kentucky; an anthology of old-time fiddle tune transcriptions is forthcoming in 2001 from the University Press of Kentucky; and he is coeditor of the forthcoming five-volume *American Musical Traditions,* a production of Schirmer Books with the Smithsonian Institution. He developed the ethnomusicology program at Tufts University, where he taught from 1971 to 1986. From 1990 to 1995 he served as the editor of *Ethnomusicology,* the journal of the Society for Ethnomusicology. A Fellow of the American Folklore Society, since 1986 he has been Professor of Music and the director of the Ph.D. program in ethnomusicology at Brown University.

CHAPTER 1

The Music-Culture as a World of Music

Jeff Todd Titon and Mark Slobin

The world around us is full of sounds. All of them are meaningful in some way. Some are sounds you make. You might sing in the shower, talk to yourself, shout to a friend, whistle a tune, beep the horn in your car, sing along with a song on your Walkman or CD player, practice a piece on your instrument, play in a band or orchestra, or sing in a chorus or an informal group on a street corner. Some are sounds from sources outside yourself. If you live in the city, you hear a lot of sounds made by people. You might be startled by the sound of a police siren or a car alarm. The noise of the garbage trucks for an early morning pickup or the drone of a motor in a parked truck might irritate you, but you usually block out the usual traffic noise. In the country you can more easily hear the sounds of nature. In the spring and summer you might hear birds singing and calling to each other, the snorting of deer in the woods, or the warning bark of a distant dog. By a river or the ocean you might hear the sounds of surf or boats loading and unloading or the deep bass of foghorns. Stop for a moment and listen to the sounds around you. Become alive to the soundscape.

Just as landscape refers to land, *soundscape* refers to sound: the characteristic sounds of a particular place, both human and nonhuman (The Canadian composer R. Murray Schafer developed this term; see Schafer 1980). The examples so far present present-day soundscapes, but it is also interesting to think about what they were like in the past. What kinds of sounds did the dinosaurs make? With our wristwatches we can always find out what time it is, but in medieval Europe people told time by listening to the bells of the local clock tower. Today we take the sounds of a passing railroad train for granted, but people found its sounds quite arresting when first heard.

The American naturalist Henry David Thoreau was alive to the soundscape when he lived by himself in a cabin in the woods at Walden Pond 150 years ago. As he wrote in *Walden,* "The whistle of the steam engine penetrated my woods summer and winter—sounding like the scream of a hawk sailing over some farmer's yard." After this ominous comparison—the hawk is a bird of prey—Thoreau describes the train as an iron horse

The Soundscape

1

(a common comparison at the time) and then a dragon, a threatening symbol of chaos rather than industrial progress: "When I hear the iron horse make the hills echo with his snort like thunder—shaking the earth with his feet, and breathing fire and smoke from his nostrils, what kind of winged horse or fiery dragon they will put into the new mythology I don't know." Writing about his wilderness soundscape, Thoreau first made sure his readers knew what he did *not* hear: the crowing of the rooster, the sounds of animals—dogs, cats, cows, pigs—the butter churn, the spinning wheel, children crying, the "singing of the kettle, the hissing of the urn": This was the soundscape of a farm in 1850, quite familiar to Thoreau's readers. We might stop and notice which of these sounds have disappeared from the soundscape altogether, for who today hears a butter churn or spinning wheel? What Thoreau heard instead in his wilderness soundscape were "squirrels on the roof and under the floor; a whippoorwill on the ridge-pole, a bluejay screaming in the yard, a hare or woodchuck under the house, a screech-owl or a cat-owl behind it, a flock of wild geese or a laughing loon in the pond, a fox to bark in the night"; but no rooster "to crow nor hens to cackle in the yard— no yard!" In Thoreau's America you could tell, blindfolded, whether you were in the wilderness, on a farm, or in a town or city. How have those soundscapes changed since 1850? What might Thoreau have written about automobiles in the countryside, tractors on the farms, trucks on the interstate highways, and jet planes everywhere?

Listen now to CD 1, Track 1. The soundscape is a post office, but it is unlike any post office you will likely encounter in North America. You are hearing men canceling stamps at the University of Accra, in Ghana, Africa. Two of the men whistle a tune while three make percussive sounds. A stamp gets canceled several times for the sake of the rhythm. You will learn more about this example shortly. For now, think of it as yet another example of a soundscape: the acoustic environment where sounds, including music, occur.

CD I/I

The Music-Culture

Every human society has music. Although music is universal, its meaning is not. For example, a famous musician from Asia attended a European symphony concert approximately 150 years ago. He had never heard Western music before. The story goes that after the concert, his hosts asked him how he had liked it. "Very well," he replied. Not satisfied with this answer, his hosts asked (through an interpreter) what part he liked best. "The first part," he said. "Oh, you enjoyed the first movement?" "No, before that." To the stranger, the best part of the performance was the tuning-up period. His hosts had a different opinion. Who was right? Different cultures give music different meanings. Recall from the preface that culture means the way of life of a people, learned and transmitted from one generation to the next. The word *learned* is stressed to differentiate a people's cultural inheritance from what is passed along biologically in their genes. From birth people all over the world absorb the cultural inheritance of family, community, schoolmates, and other larger social institutions such as the mass media—

magazines, movies, television, and computers. This cultural inheritance tells people how to understand the situations they are in (what the situations mean) and how they might behave in those situations. It works so automatically that they are aware of it only when it breaks down, as it does on occasion when people misunderstand a particular situation. Like the people who carry them, cultures do not function perfectly all the time.

Musical situations and the very concept of music mean different things and involve different activities around the globe. Because music and all the beliefs and activities associated with it are a part of culture, we use the term *music-culture* to mean a group's total involvement with music: ideas, actions, institutions, material objects—everything that has to do with music. In our example, the European music-culture dictates that the sound made by symphony musicians tuning up is not music. But to the stranger from Asia, it was music. Within their own cultural contexts, both the stranger and his hosts were correct.

People may be perplexed by music outside their own music-culture. They may grant that it is music but find it difficult to hear and enjoy. In Victorian England, for example, people said they had a hard time listening to the strange music of the native peoples within the British Colonial Empire. For example, the expansive and exciting improvisations of India's classical music were ridiculed because the music was not written down "as proper music should be." The subtle tuning of Indian *raga* scales was considered "indicative of a bad ear" because it did not match the tuning of a piano (see Chapter 6). What the British were really saying was that they did not know how to understand Indian music on its own cultural terms. Any music sounds out of tune when its tuning system is judged by the standards of another.

A person who had grown up listening only to Armenian music in his family and community recently wrote about hearing European classical music for the first time:

> I found that most European music sounds either like "mush" or "foamy," without a solid base. The classical music seemed to make the least sense, with a kind of schizophrenic melody—one moment it's calm, then the next moment it's crazy. Of course there always seemed to be "mush" (harmony) which made all the songs seem kind of similar. (posted to SEM public listserver 9 July 1998)

Because this listener had learned what makes a good melody in the Armenian music-culture, he found European classical melodies lacking because they changed mood too quickly. Unused to harmony in his own music, the listener responded negatively to it in Western classical music. Further, popular music in the United States lacked interesting rhythms and melodies:

> The rock and other pop styles then and now sound like music produced by machinery, and rarely have I heard a melody worth repeating. The same with "country" and "folk" and other more traditional styles. These musics, while making more sense with their melody (of the most undeveloped type), have killed off any sense of gracefulness with their monotonous

droning and machine-like sense of rhythm. (posted to SEM public list-server 9 July 1998)

You might find these remarks offensive or amusing—or you might agree with them. Like the other examples, they illustrate that listeners all over the world have prejudices based on the music they know and like. Listening to music all over the planet, though, fosters an open ear and an open mind. Learning to hear a strange music from the viewpoint of the people who make that music enlarges our understanding and increases our pleasure.

S ound is anything that can be heard, but what is music? As we have seen, not all music-cultures have the same idea of music; some music-cultures have no word for it, while others have a word that roughly translates into English as "music-dance" because to them music is inconceivable without movement. Writing about Rosa, the Macedonian village she lived in, Nahoma Sachs points out that "traditional Rosans have no general equivalent to the English 'music.' They divide the range of sound which might be termed music into two categories: *pesni*, songs, and *muzika*, instrumental music" (Sachs 1975:27). Of course, this distinction between songs and music is found in many parts of the world, even in North America. Old-time Baptists in the southern Appalachian Mountains (see Figure 1-1) sometimes say, "We don't have music in our service," meaning they do not have instrumental music accompanying their singing.

Other music-cultures have words for song types (lullaby, epic, historical song, and so on) but no overall word for music. Nor do they have words or concepts that directly correspond to what Euro-Americans consider the elements of music: melody, rhythm, harmony, and so forth. Most of the readers of this book (and its authors) have grown up within the cultures of Europe and North America. Consciously and unconsciously our approaches and viewpoints reflect this background. However, we must "get out of our cultural skins" as much as possible in order to view music through cultural windows other than our own. We may even learn to view our own music-culture from a new perspective. Today, because of the widespread distribution of music on radio, television, film, video, sound recordings, and computers, people in just about every music-culture are likely to have heard some of the same music. Although the local is emphasized throughout this book, music-cultures should not be understood as isolated and untouched but rather as ways of life that resist homogenization. In particular, thinking about the interaction between the local and the global can help us appreciate music-cultures, including our own.

If we want to understand the different musics of the world, then, we need to understand them on their own terms—that is, as the various music-cultures themselves do. We also need a way to talk about music as a whole without imposing our ideas of music inappropriately. To start, we can ask whether there is something about music common to all music-cultures, whether the people in those cultures are aware of it or not. If we

Music or Nonmusic?

Figure 1-1
Song leader Russell Jacobs leading the singing at the Left Beaver Old Regular Baptist Church in eastern Kentucky, 1979.

Jeff Todd Titon

CD 1/2
Songs of hermit thrushes (0:31). Field recording by Jeff Todd Titon. Little Deer Isle, Maine, 1999.

determine what that something is, then we can use it to guide our study of all music.

To approach this question, we might ask whether certain sounds are music. The answer does not involve simple disagreements over whether something people call "music" is truly music. For example, some people say that rap is not music, but what they mean is that they think rap is not good or meaningful music. Rather, there are difficult cases that test the boundaries of what differentiates sound from music, such as the songs of birds or dolphins or whales—are these music?

Consider bird songs. Everyone has heard birds sing, but not everyone has paid attention to them. Try it for a moment: Listen to the songs of a hermit thrush at dusk in a spruce forest (CD 1, Track 2). At Walden Pond, Thoreau heard hermit thrushes that sounded like these.

Many think that the hermit thrush has the most beautiful song of all the birds native to North America. Most bird songs consist of a single phrase, repeated, but the hermit thrush's melody is more complicated. You hear a vocalization (phrase) and then a pause, then another vocalization and pause, and so on. Each vocalization has a similar rhythm and is composed of five to eight tones. The phrase is a little higher or lower each time. If you listen closely, you also hear that the thrush can produce more than one tone at once, a kind of two-tone harmony. This is the result of the way his syrinx (voice box) is constructed.

Is bird song music? The thrush's song has some of the characteristics of music. It has rhythm, melody, repetition, and variation. It also has a function: Scientists believe that birds sing to announce their presence in a particular territory to other birds of the same kind, and that they sing to attract a mate. In some species one bird's song can tell another bird which bird is singing and how that bird is feeling. Bird song has inspired Western classical music composers. Some composers have taken down bird songs in musical notation, and some have incorporated, imitated, or transformed bird song phrases in their compositions. Bird song is also found in Chinese classical music. In Chinese compositions such as "The Court of the Phoenix," for sona (oboe) and ensemble, extended passages are a virtual catalog of bird calls and songs imitated by instruments.

Yet, people in the Euro-American music-culture hesitate to call bird songs music. Because each bird in a species sings the same song over and over, bird songs appear to lack the creativity of human expression. Bird songs do not seem to belong to the human world, whereas music is regarded in Euro-American culture as a human expression. By contrast, people in some other music-cultures think bird songs do have human meaning. For the *Kaluli* people of Papua New Guinea, bird songs are the voices of their human ancestors who have died and changed into birds. These songs cause humans grief, which expresses itself in weeping (Feld 1990). The *Kaluli* give a different meaning to bird songs than Euro-Americans do. Does this mean it is impossible to find a single idea of what music is? Not really. Euro-Americans may disagree with the *Kaluli* over whether bird songs have human meaning, but they both agree that music has human meaning. Our thought-experiment with bird song and its meanings in different music-cultures suggests that music has something to do with the human world. We can go further and say that music is sound that is humanly patterned or organized (Blacking 1973).

Let's take another example of a sound that tests the boundary between music and nonmusic. Listen again to CD 1, Track 1. Throughout the life of *Worlds of Music,* listeners have found the Ghanaian postal workers' sounds especially intriguing. Recently we learned a little more about the circumstances of the recording. Henrietta Mckee Carter (personal communication to Jeff Todd Titon, July 2000) wrote as follows:

> Sometime in 1975, Bill Carter and I were sitting in Jim and Ernestina Koetting's quarters at the University of Ghana chatting with Ernestina, while awaiting dinner. Jim came in excitedly, picked up his recording equipment and disappeared, saying on his way out that he had just heard something he wanted to record. He came back a while later and described the scene.

These postal workers hand-canceling stamps at the post office of the University of Ghana are making drumming sounds, and two are whistling;

CD I/I
Postal workers canceling stamps at the University of Ghana post office (2:59). The whistled tune is the hymn "Bompata," by the Ghanaian composer W. J. Akyeampong (b. 1900). Field recording by James Koetting. Legon, Ghana, 1975.

but there are no drums, and the workers are just passing the time. How, exactly?

Koetting (Titon 1992:98–99) wrote as follows:

> Twice a day the letters that must be canceled are laid out in two files, one on either side of a divided table. Two men sit across from one another at the table, and each has a hand-canceling machine (like the price markers you may have seen in supermarkets), an ink pad, and a stack of letters. The work part of the process is simple: a letter is slipped from the stack with the left hand, and the right hand inks the marker and stamps the letter. . . .
>
> This is what you are hearing: the two men seated at the table slap a letter rhythmically several times to bring it from the file to the position on the table where it is to be canceled. (This act makes a light-sounding thud.) The marker is inked one or more times (the lowest, most resonant sound you hear) and then stamped on the letter (the high-pitched mechanized sound you hear). . . . The rhythm produced is not a simple one-two-three (bring forward the letter—ink the marker—stamp the letter). Rather, musical sensitivities take over. Several slaps on the letter to bring it down, repeated thuds of the marker in the ink pad and multiple cancellations of single letters are done for rhythmic interest. Such repetition slows down the work, but also makes it much more interesting.
>
> The other sounds you hear have nothing to do with the work itself. A third man has a pair of scissors that he clicks—not cutting anything, but adding to the rhythm. The scissors go "click, click, click, rest," a basic rhythm used in [Ghanaian] popular dance music. The fourth worker simply whistles along. He and any of the other three workers who care to join him whistle popular tunes or church music that fits the rhythm.

Work song, found in music-cultures all over the world, is a kind of music whose function ranges from coordinating complex tasks to making boring and repetitive work more interesting. In this instance the workers have turned life into art. Writing further about the postal workers' recording, Koetting says,

> It sounds like music and, of course it is; but the men performing it do not quite think of it that way. These men are working, not putting on a musical show; people pass by the workplace paying little attention to the "music." (Titon 1992:98)

Even though the postal workers do not think of this activity as a musical performance, we have presented it as music here because it is humanly patterned sound and the whistled melody is a hymn tune written by a Ghanaian composer. Even so, not all humanly patterned sound is music. For example, although speech sometimes has musical attributes, we do not claim that speech is music. Whether canceling stamps at the University of Ghana post office is "really" music is a philosophical question. What do you think?

People in various music-cultures pattern sounds differently. What patterns do musical sounds follow? Several aspects of musical sound that our music-culture recognizes and talks about in ordinary language should be familiar to most readers of this book: rhythm, meter, melody, and harmony. These are ways of describing patterns or structure (form) in sound. It will be interesting to see what happens to these Western (but not exclusively Western) ideas when for better or worse they are applied to every music-culture throughout this book. Here we briefly review these ideas. Next we turn our attention to how music becomes meaningful in performance. Finally we consider the four components of a music culture, which in music textbooks are not usually considered rudiments but are no less a part of humanly organized sound: ideas, activities, repertories, and the material culture of music.

Rhythm and Meter

Structure in Music

In ordinary language we say "rhythm" when we refer to the patterned recurrence of events, as in "the rhythm of the seasons," or "the rhythm of the raindrops." As Hewitt Pantaleoni writes, "Rhythm concerns time felt as a succession of events rather than as a single span" (1985:211). In music, we hear rhythm when we hear a time-relation between sounds. In a class-room you might hear a pen drop from a desk and a little later a student coughing. You do not hear any rhythm, because you hear no relation between the sounds. But when you hear a person walking in the hall out-side, or when you hear a heartbeat, you hear rhythm.

If we measure the time-relations between the sounds and find a pat-tern of regular recurrence, we have metrical rhythm. Think of the soldiers' marching rhythm: HUP-two-three-four, HUP-two-three-four. This is a metered, regularly recurring sound pattern. The recurring accents fall on HUP. Most popular, classical, and folk music heard in North America today has metered rhythm. Of course, most of those rhythms are more complex than the march rhythm. If you are familiar with Gregorian chant, of the Roman Catholic Church, you know musical rhythm without meter. Although not music, ordinary speech is a common example of nonmetrical rhythm, whereas poetic verse is metrical (unless it is free verse). Think of the iambic pentameter in Shakespeare's plays, for example. Most of the musical examples in this book, including the postal workers' canceling stamps (CD 1, Track 1), are examples of metrical rhythm. In a metrical rhythm you feel the beat and move to it. The song of the hermit thrush is both metrically rhythmic and not (CD 1, Track 2). You can find a beat while the thrush sings a phrase, but after he stops you cannot predict exactly when the bird will start again.

"Tsuru no sugomori," the Japanese *shakuhachi* piece (CD 4, Track 1), lacks a steady, dancelike beat. Its rhythm is flexible and related to the per-former's breath. That it is unmetered does not mean that it is undisciplined. On the contrary, the uneven pulsation makes it harder for the student learning *shakuhachi* to convey the required precision in the sounds and silences that enhance one another (see pp. 338–343).

CD 4/1

On the other hand, the rhythm of *karnataka sangeeta* (CD 3, Track 1) is intricate in another way. The opening *alapana* section has a flexible, non-metered rhythm, but the following sections are metrically organized. This classical music of South India divides a metrical rhythm into long, complex,

CD 3/1

Figure 1-2
T. Viswanathan, flute, Ramnad V. Raghavan, *mridangam.*

improvised accent patterns based on various combinations of rhythmic figures. The *mridangam* drummer's art (see Figure 1-2) is based on fifteen or more distinct types of finger and hand strokes on different parts of the drumheads. Each stroke has its own *sollukattu,* or spoken syllable that imitates the sound of the drum stroke. Spoken one after another, they duplicate the rhythmic patterns and are used in learning and practice.

Although most North Americans may not be aware of it, the music they listen to usually has more than one rhythm. The singer's melody falls into one pattern, the guitarist's into another; the drummer usually plays more than one pattern at once. Even though these rhythms are usually tied to the same overall accent pattern, the way they interact with each other sets our bodies in motion as we move to the beat. Still, to a native Armenian who grew up on a diet of more intricate rhythms, this monometer is dull. Rhythm in the postal workers' canceling stamps (CD 1, Track 1) emphasizes the tugs of different rhythmic patterns. (For a detailed analysis, see Chapter 3.) This simultaneous occurrence of several rhythms with a shifting downbeat is called *polyrhythm.* Polyrhythm is characteristic of the music of Africa and wherever Africans have carried their music on the globe. In Chapter 3 you will learn to feel yet a further layer of complexity, *polymeter,* or the simultaneous presence of two different metrical systems, as you "construct musical reality in two ways at once" while playing an *Ewe* (pronounced *eh*-way) bell pattern in *Agbekor* (see pp. 94–113).

Melody

In ordinary language we say "melody" when we want to refer to the tune—the part of a piece of music that goes up and down, the part that most people hear and sing along with. It is hard to argue that melody and rhythm are truly different qualities of music, but it helps our understanding if we consider them separately. When we say that someone has a high-pitched or a low-pitched (deep) voice, we are calling attention to a musical quality called *pitch,* which refers to how high or low a sound is. When a sound is made, it sets the air in motion, vibrating at so many cycles per second. This vibrating air strikes the ear drum, and we hear how high or low pitched it is depending on the speed of the vibrations. You can experience this yourself if you sing a tone that is comfortable for your voice and then slide the tone down gradually as low as you can go. As your voice goes down to a growl, you can feel the vibrations slow down in your throat. Pitch, then, depends on the frequency of these sound vibrations. The faster the vibrations, the higher the pitch.

Another important aspect of melody is *timbre,* or tone quality. Timbre is caused by the characteristic ways different voices and musical instruments vibrate. Timbre tells us why a violin sounds different from a trumpet when they are playing a tone of the same pitch. We take the timbre of our musical instrument palette for granted, but when we encounter an instrument with a timbre that we may never have heard before, such as the Australian *didgeridoo,* we sit up and take notice. Some music-cultures, like the European, favor timbres that we may describe as smooth or liquid; others, like the African, favor timbres that are buzzy; others, like the Asian, favor timbres that we might describe as focused in sound. Other important aspects of melody, besides pitch and timbre, include volume—that is, how melodies increase and decrease in loudness. The Navajo Yeibichai song (CD 1, Track 6) begins at the loudest possible volume.

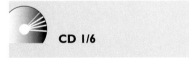

CD 1/6

Another critical aspect of melody to pay attention to in world music is emphasis: the way the major tones of the melody are approached (by sliding up or down to them in pitch, as some singers do; by playing them dead on, as a piano does; by "bending" the pitch, as a blues guitarist (Figure 1-3) does when pushing the string to the side and back (CD 2, Tracks 7 and 8). Figure 6-8 (p. 257) contrasts notes and melodies on the piano with their counterparts in Indian music.

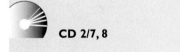

CD 2/7, 8

Yet another way to emphasize a point in a melody is to add decorative tones or what are called *ornaments* in classical music. These, too, occur in many of the musics of the world. See if you can find them as you listen to the CD set. Concentrate on the way the singers and musicians do not simply sing or play tones, but play *with* tones.

Finding how different music-cultures organize sounds into melodies is one of the most fascinating pursuits for the student of music. If we sing the melody of the Christmas carol "Joy to the World," we hear how Westerners like to organize a melody. Try it:

> Joy to the world, the Lord has come!
> (do ti la   so, fa   mi   re   do!)

This is the familiar do-re-mi *(solfège)* scale, in descending order. Try singing "Joy to the World" backwards, going up the do-re-mi scale and using the syllables in this order: "come has Lord the world the to joy."

Figure 1-3
Blues guitarists Johnny Winter (left) and Luther Allison, Ann Arbor (Michigan) Blues Festival, August 1970.

Jeff Todd Titon

You might find it difficult! But if you first sing the do-re-mi scale using the solfège syllables, and then replace do-re-me with "come has Lord," and so forth, you will be able to do it more easily.

The white keys of the piano show how most melodies in European and Euro-American music have been organized since the eighteenth century. Do-re-mi (and so forth) represent a major scale. Notice that these pitches are not equally spaced. Try singing "Joy to the World" starting on "re" instead of "do." You will see that it throws off the melody. If you are near a keyboard, try playing it by going down the white keys, one at a time. Only one starting key (C) gives the correct melody. This indicates that the intervals between pitches are not the same.

The Euro-American culture prefers the major scale, and Euro-Americans set up many instruments, such as the piano or the flute, so that they can easily play the pitch intervals of this scale. But other music-cultures set up their instruments and their scales differently. For example, Javanese musical gongs organize the octave (the solfège interval between one "do" and another) into five nearly equidistant intervals in their *sléndro* scale. The Javanese have a second scale, *pélog*, which divides the octave into seven tones, but the intervals are not the same as those in any Western scales (see Transcription 7-1, p. 283). The sounds of their *gamelan*, or orchestra, reflect these different tunings (for example, CD 3, Track 3, is in the *pélog* scale). Japanese music also employs two scales, the *in* and *yo*, which differ from the Javanese scales; the *yo* is a pentatonic scale that is

CD 3/3

also heard in European folk music (Transcription 8-1b, p. 335). In the classical music of South India, known as *karnatic* music, each melody conforms to a set of organizing principles called a *raga*. Although each *raga* has its own scale (based on one of seventy-two basic scale patterns), it also has its own characteristic melodic phrases, intonation patterns, and ornaments as well as a mood or feeling. A *raga* is an organized melodic matrix inside of which the south Indian singer or musician improvises melodically in performance (see Chapter 6, pp. 261–264).

Harmony

Most readers of this book use the word *harmony* to describe something that can happen to a melody: It can be harmonized. You sing a melody and someone else sings a harmony, a part different from the melody, at the same time (see Figure 1-4). You hear the intervals between the tones not only in a sequence, as in a melody, but also simultaneously. These simultaneously sounding tones are called *chords*. Western music theory is not always useful in describing music outside the Euro-American traditions, but in this case *texture,* a word borrowed from fabrics to describe the interweaving of fibers, helps describe how melody and harmony interact in various musics throughout the world. Just as threads weave together to make cloth, so melodies can intertwine to make a multimelodic musical whole. *Texture* refers to the nature of these melodic interrelationships.

When the musical texture consists of a single melody only—for example, when you sing by yourself, or when several people sing the same melody in unison—we call the texture *monophonic* ("mono" meaning "single," "phono" meaning "voice"). If you add one or more voices doing different things, the melodic texture changes, and we describe the way the voices relate. The classical music of India commonly includes a drone, an unchanging tone or group of tones sounding continuously, against which the melody moves (see Chapter 6). European bagpipes also include drones.

Russell Lee. Courtesy of the Library of Congress.

Figure 1-4
Teenagers harmonizing gospel music. Bristow, Oklahoma, 1938.

CD 4/1

CD 1/7 and 4/10

When two or more voices elaborate the same melody in different ways at roughly the same time, the texture is *heterophonic.* Although infrequent in Western music, it is typical of melodic organization in Japanese traditional music. CD 4, Track 1, shows heterophony among the voice and *shamisen* parts.

When two or more distinct melodies are combined, the texture is *polyphonic.* Polyphony can also be heard in New Orleans–style jazz from the first few decades of the twentieth century: Louis Armstrong's earliest recordings offer good examples in which several melodic lines interweave. Javanese *gamelan* and other ensemble music of Southeast Asia (Chapter 7) consists of many layers of melodic activity that some scholars have described as polyphony. Polyphony is characteristic of European classical music in the Renaissance period (roughly 1450 to 1600) and the late Baroque (Bach was a master of polyphony).

When two or more voices are combined in a such way that one dominates and any others seem to be accompanying the dominant voice—or what most people mean when they say they hear a harmony (accompaniment)—the texture is *homophonic.* Homophony is typical of folk and popular music throughout the world. A homophonic texture characterizes country music in the United States, such as the Fenders' Navajo rendition of "Folsom Prison Blues" (CD 1, Track 7) and Efraín's performance of the Quichua *sanjuán* "Cascarón" on the harp, which is an example of an instrument that can play a melody and an accompaniment simultaneously (CD 4, Track 10). Piano playing in jazz, rock, and other popular music is homophonic. The pianist usually gives the melody to the right hand and an accompaniment to the left. Sometimes the pianist plays only accompaniment, as when "comping" behind a jazz soloist. Blues guitarists such as Blind Blake and Mississippi John Hurt developed a homophonic style in the 1920s in which the fingers of the right hand played melody on the treble strings while the right-hand thumb simultaneously played an accompaniment on the bass strings.

Form

The word *form* has many meanings. From your writing assignments you know what an outline is. You might say that you are putting your ideas in "outline form." By form, here, you call attention to the way the structure of your thoughts is arranged. Similarly, in music, painting, architecture, and the other arts, *form* means structural arrangement. To understand form in music, we look for patterns of organization in rhythm, melody, and harmony. Patterns of musical organization involve, among other things, the arrangement of small to medium-sized musical units of rhythm, melody, and/or harmony that show repetition or variation. Just as a sentence (a complete thought) is made up of smaller units such as phrases, which in turn are made of individual words, so a musical thought is made up of phrases that result from combinations of sounds. Form can also refer to the arrangement of the instruments, as in the order of solos in a jazz or bluegrass performance, or the way a symphonic piece is orchestrated. Form refers to the structure of a musical performance: the principles by which it is put together and how it works.

Consider the pattern of blues texts (lyrics). The form often consists of three-line stanzas: A line is sung ("Woke up this morning, blues all around my bed"), the line is repeated, and then the stanza closes with a different line ("Went to eat my breakfast and the blues were in my bread"). Blues melodies also have a particular form, as do the chord changes (harmony) in blues (see Chapter 4). The form of traditional Native-American melodies (Chapter 2) involves the creative use of small units and variation. This form is not apparent to someone listening to the music for the first time or even the second, which is one of the reasons we pay careful attention to it (see pp. 38–39).

Structural arrangement is an important aspect of the way music is organized. It operates on many levels, and it is key to understanding not only how music-cultures organize music but also how various cultures and subcultures think about time and space in general. For these reasons musical form is an important consideration in all the chapters that follow.

Our understanding of rhythm, meter, melody, and harmony is greatly enriched when we consider how these organizing principles of human sound are practiced in music-cultures throughout the world. Much of the interest in the following chapters lies in seeing how these principles work in different circumstances. But there is more to music than the structure of sounds. When people make music, they do not merely produce sounds—they also involve themselves in various social activities and express their ideas about music. To ethnomusicologists considering music as a human phenomenon, these activities and ideas are just as important as the music's structure. In fact, the activities and ideas are also part of the human organization of the sound. In other words, ethnomusicologists strive for a way to talk about *all* the aspects of music, not just its sound. Where, for example, is there room to talk about whether musicians are true to an ideal or whether they have "sold out" to commercial opportunity? This book presents music in relation to individual experience, to history, to the economy and the music industry, and to each music-culture's view of the world, which includes ideas about how human beings ought to behave.

A Music-Culture Model: Affect, Performance, Community, and History

Even when we are curious about the music of the world's peoples and want to understand more about it, confronting a new music can be daunting. When watching a live performance, for example, our first impulse might be simply to listen to it, to absorb it, to see whether we like it or whether it moves us. Our next impulse may be to let our bodies respond by moving to the music. But soon we ask questions about it: What is that instrument that sounds so lovely? How does one play it? Why are the people dancing? (Or are they dancing?) Why is someone crying? Why are the musicians in costume? What do the words mean? What kind of a life does the head musician lead? To formulate and begin to answer these questions in a comprehensive way, we need to have some kind of systematic outline, or model, of any music-culture or subculture that tells us how it might work and what its components might be.

In this book we propose a music-culture model that is grounded in music as it is performed (Titon 1988:7–10). To see how this model works, think back to a musical event that has moved you. At the center of the event is your experience of the music, sung and played by performers (perhaps you are one of them). The performers are surrounded by their audience (in some instances, performers and audience are one and the same), and the whole event takes place in its setting in time and space. We can represent this by a diagram of concentric circles (Figure 1-5).

Figure 1-5
Elements of a musical performance.

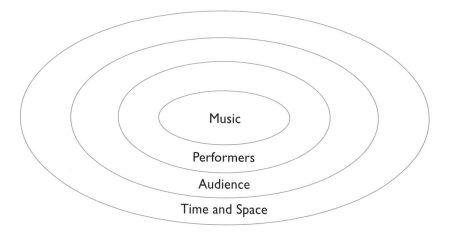

Now we transpose this diagram into four circles representing a music-culture model (Figure 1-6).

Figure 1-6
A music-culture model
(after Titon 1988:11)

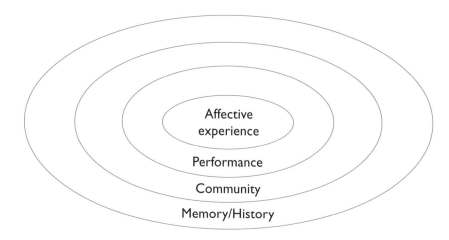

At the center of the music (as you experience it) is its radiating power, its emotional impact—whatever makes you give assent, smile, nod your head, sway your shoulders, dance. We call that music's *affect,* its power to move, and place affective experience at the center of the model.

Performance brings music's power to move into being, and so we move from performers in Figure 1-5 to *performance* in Figure 1-6. Performance involves many things. First, people mark performances, musical or otherwise, as separate from the flow of ordinary life: "Have you heard the story about . . ." or "Now we're going to do a new song that one of the members of the band wrote while thinking about. . . ." When performance takes place, people know the difference. Sammy Davis, Jr., told an interviewer, "Once I get outside my house in the morning, I'm *on*." We often mark endings of performances with applause. Second, performance has purpose. The performers intend to move (or not move) the audience, to sing and play well (or not well), to make money, to have fun, to learn, to advance a certain rite or ceremony. The performance is evaluated partly on how well those intentions have been fulfilled. Third, a performance is interpreted as it goes along, by the audience, who may cry out, applaud, or hiss, and by the performers, who may smile when things are going well or wince when they make a mistake.

The most important thing to understand about performance is that it moves along on the basis of agreed-on rules and procedures. These rules enable the musicians to play together and make sense to each other and to the audience. The performers usually do not discuss most of the rules; they have absorbed them and agreed to them. Starting at the same time, playing in the same key, playing in the same rhythmic framework, repeating the melody at the proper point—these are a few of the many rules that govern most of the musical performances that Westerners experience. Even improvisation is governed by rules. In a rock concert, for example, guitarists improvise melodic "breaks," but they usually do not use all twelve tones of the chromatic scale; instead they almost always choose from the smaller number of tones represented by the blues scale (see Chapter 4). Rules or accepted procedures govern the audience, too. In some situations shouting is not only permitted but expected. What to wear, what to say—these, too, are determined by spoken or unspoken rules at any musical performance. Sometimes musicians try to break these rules or expectations, as in a ritual destruction of their instruments at the close of the concert, which in turn can become an expectation.

The music-culture model presented here defines music in performance as meaningfully organized sound that proceeds by rules. Finding out those rules or principles becomes the task of analysis. These rules include (but are not limited to) what is usually covered under musical analysis: mode, motif, melody, rhythm, meter, section, and so forth. Beyond that, the task in exploring music-cultures is to discover the rules covering ideas about music and behavior in relation to music, as well as the links between these rules or principles and the sound that a group of people calls "music." You may resist the notion that music, which you think should be free to express emotion, is best thought of as governed by rules. The point is not that musical performance is predetermined by rules, but that it proceeds according to them. In this view, music is like a game or a conversation: Without rules we could not have a game, and without agreement about what words are, what they mean, and how they are used, we could not hold a meaningful conversation. Nonetheless, just as meaningful conversations can express emotion, so meaningful music can do so, though not, of course, in exactly the same way. Further, if a listener does not understand the rules, he or she can understand neither the composer's or musician's intention nor the music's structure.

The circle corresponding to audience in Figure 1-5 becomes *community* in the music-culture model (Figure 1-6). The community is the group (including the performers) that carries on the traditions and norms of performance. Performance is situated in community and is part of a people's culture. The community pays for and supports the music, whether directly with money or indirectly by allowing the performers to live as musicians. Community support usually influences the future direction of a particular kind of music. In a complex society such as the United States, various communities support different kinds of music—classical, rock, jazz, gospel—and they do so in different ways. Classical music, for example, gets its strongest boost from middle-class people climbing the social and economic ladder. When music becomes a mass-media commodity, then packaging, marketing, and advertising are as crucial to the success of musicians as they are to the popularity of a given perfume.

How the community relates to the music makers also has a profound effect on the music. Among the folk music-cultures of nonindustrial village societies, the performers are drawn from the community; everyone knows them well, and communication takes place face-to-face. At the other end of the spectrum is the postindustrial music-culture celebrity who guards his or her private life, performs from a raised platform, offers a disembodied voice coming through a machine, and remains enigmatic to the audience.

How the community relates to itself is another important aspect of performance. For example, do men, women, old people, and young people experience music differently? We will consider this issue later in this chapter.

Time and space, the fourth circle in Figure 1-5, becomes *memory and history* in our music-culture model (Figure 1-6). The community is situated in history and borne by memory, official and unofficial, whether remembered or recorded or written down. Musical experiences, performances, and communities change over time and space; they have a history, and that history reflects changes in the rules governing music as well as the effect of music on human relationships. For example, the development of radio, recordings, and television meant that music did not need to be heard in the performer's presence. This took the performer out of the community's face-to-face relationships and allowed people to listen to music without making it themselves. Today music is an almost constant background to many people's lives, but the musicians are largely absent.

Music historians also alter the effect of music by affecting the stock of ideas about music. When white America became interested in blues music in the 1960s and began presenting blues concerts and festivals (see Chapter

4), magazine and newspaper writers began asking blues singers questions about their music and its history. Knowing they would be asked these questions, the blues singers prepared their answers, sometimes reading and then repeating what writers had already said about blues, sometimes having fun with their questioners and deliberately misleading them, and sometimes answering truthfully based on their experiences.

Many times the subject of music is history itself. The Homeric poets sang about Odysseus; Serbian *guslars* sang about the deeds of their heroes; European ballads tell stories of nobles and commoners; African *griots* (see Chapter 3) sing tribal genealogies and history. Today, digital recorders, computers, and multimedia programs are revolutionizing community music history in the West, for they empower musicians and audience alike to record what they want to hear, represent it as they wish, and listen to it again and again; in this way they gain a kind of control over their history never before experienced. In studying the history of a music-culture, or some aspect of it, you need to know not only what that history is but also who tells or writes that history and what stake the historian has in it.

As you read through each of the case studies in the following chapters, bear this underlying music-culture model in mind. Because each of the case studies focuses on music and performance, you can use this model to understand how each chapter moves among experience, performance, community, memory, and history. Musical analysis—that is, finding patterns in the sound by breaking the music into parts and determining how the parts function in the whole—is an important part of this procedure. Unlike the analyst who investigates Western classical music by looking at the composer's written score, ethnomusicologists must usually deal with music that exists only in performance, without notation or instructions from a composer. The ethnomusicologist usually transcribes the music— that is, *notates* it—and then analyzes its structure. But it is impossible to understand structure fully without knowing the cultural "why" as well as the musical "what." A music-culture ultimately rests in the people themselves—their ideas, their actions, and the sound they produce (Merriam 1964:32–33). For that reason, we now introduce another way of talking about all these aspects of music—a component model of a music-culture. This model is divided into four parts: ideas about music, activities involving music, repertories of music, and the material culture of music (Table 1-1).

Ideas About Music
Music and the Belief System

What is music, and what is not? Is music human, divine, or both? Is music good and useful for humankind or is it potentially harmful? These questions reach into a music-culture's basic ideas concerning the nature of human society, art, and the universe. Cultures vary enormously in their answers to these questions, and the answers often are subtle, even paradoxical; they are embodied in rituals that try to reconcile love and hate, life

The Four Components of a Music-Culture

Table 1-1   The four components of a music culture.

I. Ideas about music
    A. Music and the belief system
    B. Aesthetics of music
    C. Contexts for music
    D. History of music
II. Activities involving music
III. Repertories of music
    A. Style
    B. Genres
    C. Texts
    D. Composition
    E. Transmission
    F. Movement
IV. Material culture of music

and death, the natural and the cultural. Even within one music-culture, the answers may change over time. For example, a medieval Christian would have trouble understanding one of today's folk masses.

Throughout the book you will see many examples of how belief systems and music-cultures interact. You will see in Chapter 2 that music is a major part of Navajo ceremonies to cure disease. Navajos understand the medical theories of the Euro-American world, and they use Western medicine. But they also believe that certain kinds of illness, such as depression, indicate that the person's relationship to the natural world is out of balance. Further, Navajos view nature as a powerful force capable of speaking directly to humans and teaching them the songs and prayers for the curing rituals that restore harmony. Music is so important to Native Americans that their stories of the creation of the universe are expressed traditionally in ceremonial chants (see Figure 1-7).

In Chapter 3 you will see that among the *Ewe* of Ghana, funerals feature singing, dancing, and drumming because the ancestral spirits, as well as their living descendants, love music and dance. Similarly, in Chapter 9 you will find that among the Quichua of Ecuador, as well as other Roman Catholic cultures of Latin America, music and dance are integral to the child's wake, a ceremony that takes place when a baptized infant dies. Joyous singing and dancing in the presence of death is understood as an affirmation of life. The *ragas* of India, considered in Chapter 6, are thought to have musical personalities, to express particular moods. As you read through the chapters in this book, see how each music-culture relates music to its worldview.

Aesthetics of Music

When is a song beautiful? When is it beautifully sung? What voice quality is pleasing, and what grates on the ear? How should a musician dress? How long should a performance last? Not all cultures agree on these ques-

Figure 1-7
Mr. and Mrs. Walker Calhoun, holding eagle feathers. Big Cove, near Cherokee, North Carolina, 1989. The Calhouns are leaders in preserving traditional songs and dances among the east coast Cherokee.

Jeff Todd Titon

tions about what is proper and what is beautiful. Some people in the United States find Chinese opera singing strained and artificial, but some Chinese find the European bel canto opera style imprecise and unpleasant. Music-cultures can be characterized by preferences in sound quality and performance practice, all of which are aesthetic discriminations.

Javanese *gamelan* music (Chapter 7) is not featured in concert the way we hear classical music in the West; rather, it is usually performed to accompany dance or theater. *Gamelan* music also accompanies a family's celebration of a birth, wedding, or other event, but people are expected to mingle and talk while the music takes place in the background. The aesthetics of Japanese *shakuhachi* flute music (Chapter 8) revolve around the breath, which produces a variety of timbres on the same instrument. Among Zen Buddhists, the *shakuhachi* is regarded more as a spiritual tool, a means toward enlightenment, than as a musical instrument.

Contexts for Music

When should music be performed? How often? On what occasions? Again, every music-culture answers these questions about musical surroundings differently (see Figure 1-8).

In the modern world, where context can depend on the mere flip of an on-off switch and a portable mp3 player, it is hard to imagine the days when all music came from face-to-face performances. Our great-grandparents had to sing or play music or hear it from someone nearby; they could not produce it on demand from the disembodied voice of a radio, television, CD player, or computer. How attentively you would have

Figure 1-8

Gospel singers at a Pentecostal revival in the Southeastern United States. Guitars, banjos, and camp-meeting songs that would be out place in some U.S. churches, such as the one in Figure 1-1, are appropriate in this context.

Jeff Todd Titon

listened to a singer or a band a hundred years ago if you had thought that the performance might be the only time in your life you would hear that music!

Even though much of the music around the globe today comes through mass media, people in music-cultures still associate particular musics with particular contexts. Navajo ceremonial music is appropriate in certain ceremonial contexts but not others. As we shall see in Chapter 2, these ceremonies have names such as Enemyway and Blessingway, and each has a specific music that must be performed properly for the ceremony to be effective. *Vacación* is a special symbolic composition for the harp that is performed at the start of the Quichuan child's wake, at the late-evening adorning of the corpse, and at the closing of the casket at dawn (Chapter 9). The usual context for blues is a bar, juke joint, dance hall, or blues club (Chapter 4). This is a far cry from the concert halls that provide the context for symphony orchestra performances. For many centuries in India the courts and upper classes supported the classical music that we shall consider in Chapter 6. But concerts of classical music in India are more relaxed and informal than in Europe, where the patronage of the courts and the aristocracy, as well as the Church, traditionally supported classical music.

Today in Europe and North America the government, the wealthy classes, and the universities supply this patronage. Classical music in various parts of the world, then, is usually associated with patronage from the elite classes, and it is performed in refined contexts that speak of its supporters' wealth and leisure.

Sometimes governments intervene to support other kinds of music. For example, during the twentieth century the Soviet Union and other

Communist states encouraged a certain kind of folk music, or workers' music, thought to inspire solidarity. Typically, under government management what had been a loose and informal village musical aesthetic was transformed into a disciplined, almost mechanized, urban expression of the modern industrial nation-state (see Chapter 5). Folk festivals, supported by Communist governments, showcased this music. In the United States, the last few decades have also witnessed the rise of government-supported folk festivals. Here, though, the diversity of ethnic musics is celebrated, and the government encourages the most traditional expressions within the music-cultures that are represented. Folk festivals provide an artificial context for traditional music, but the hope is that in a world where young people are powerfully attracted to new, mass-mediated, transnational popular music, folk festivals will encourage this local music in its home context.

History of Music

Why is music so different among the world's peoples? What happens to music over time and space? Does it stay the same or change, and why? What did the music of the past sound like? Should music be preserved? What will the music of the future be? Some cultures institutionalize the past in museums and the future in world's fairs; they support specialists who earn their living by talking and writing about music. Other cultures pass down knowledge of music history mainly by word of mouth through the generations. Recordings, films, videotapes, CDs, DVDs, and now the Internet allow us to preserve musical performances much more exactly than our ancestors could—but only when we choose to do so. For example, one ethnomusicologist was making tapes as he learned to sing Native-American music. His teacher advised him to erase the tapes and reuse them, but he decided to preserve his lessons.

Questions about music history may arise both inside and outside a particular music-culture. Most music-cultures have their own historians or music authorities, formally trained or not, whose curiosity about music leads them to think and talk about music in their own culture, ask questions, and remember or write down answers. In some music-cultures, authority goes along with being a good musician; in others, one need not be a good musician to be a respected historian. Historians usually are curious about music outside their own cultures as well, and they often develop theories to account for musical differences.

The four categories of ideas about music that we have just discussed—music and the belief system, aesthetics, contexts, and history—overlap. Though we separate them here for convenience, we do not want to suggest that music-cultures present a united front in their ideas about music or that a music-culture prescribes a single aesthetic. People within a music-culture often differ in their ideas about music. Ragtime, jazz, rock and roll, and rap were revolutionary when they were introduced in the United States. They met (and still meet) opposition from some within the U.S. music-culture. This opposition is based on aesthetics (the music is thought to be loud, awful noise) and context (the music's associated lifestyles are thought to involve narcotics, violence, free love, radical politics, and so forth).

When organized divisions exist within a music-culture, we can talk about music-subcultures, worlds within worlds of music. In fact, most music-cultures in the modern world may be divided into several subcultures, some opposed to each other: classical versus rock, for example, or (from an earlier era) sacred hymns versus dance music and drinking songs. Many Native-American music-cultures in the northeastern United States, for example, have a subculture of traditionalists interested in older musics that are marked as Native American, while other subcultures are involved more with the music of the Catholic Church, and yet others with forms of contemporary popular music (rock, jazz, country) that they have adapted to their needs and desires. Sometimes the subcultures overlap: The performance of a hymn in a Minnesota church may involve region (the upper Midwest), ethnicity (German), and religion (Lutheranism)—all bases for musical subcultures. Which musical subcultures do you identify with most strongly? Which do you dislike? Are your preferences based on contexts, aesthetics, or the belief system?

Activities Involving Music

People in a music culture do not just *have* ideas about music, of course; they put those ideas into practice in a variety of activities—everything from making the sounds to putting music up on the Internet, from rehearsing in their rooms alone to playing in a band to managing a concert to making recordings and marketing them. More and more people are becoming active consumers of music, carefully selecting the music they want to experience from the great variety available.

Human activities involving music also include the way people divide, arrange, or rank themselves in relation to music. Musical ideas and performances are unevenly divided among the people in any music-culture. For example, some perform often, others hardly at all. Some musicians perform for a living, while others play for little or no payment. People sing different songs and experience music differently because of age and gender. Racial, ethnic, and work groups also sing their own songs, and each group may develop or be assigned its own musical role. All of these differences have to do with the social organization of the music-culture, and they are based on the music-culture's ideas about music. We may ask, "What is it like in a given music-culture to experience music as a teenage girl, a young male urban professional, a rural grandmother of Swedish ethnic heritage who lives on a farm?"

Sometimes the division of musical behavior resembles the social divisions with the group and reinforces the usual activities of the culture. The Vienna Philharmonic was in the news in recent years because until 1997 it had no women in its orchestra. In many traditional ceremonies throughout the world, men and women congregate in separate areas; some ceremonies center exclusively on men and others on women. On the other hand, music sometimes goes against the broad cultural grain, often at carnival time or at important moments in the life cycle (initiations, weddings, funerals, and so forth). Then people on the cultural fringe become important when they play music for these occasions. In fact, many music-cultures assign a low social status to musicians but also acknowledge their power and sometimes even see magic in their work. The most important features of music's social organization are status and role: the prestige of the music-makers and the different roles assigned to people in the music-culture.

Many of the musical situations in this book depend on these basic aspects of social organization. The most spiritual and meditative Japanese *shakuhachi* music was the result of *samurai* (warriors) who became Buddhist priests during the Tokugawa period (1600–1867). Japanese *kouta* is closely linked to the participation of women (Chapter 8). When blues arose early in the twentieth century, middle-class African Americans associated it with the black underclass and tried to keep their youngsters away from it. Blues musicians were assigned a low social status (Chapter 4). Neither the Argentine *tango* nor the Trinidadian steelband were considered respectable when they arose. Only after they gained popularity abroad and returned to their home countries did they become respectable to the point of becoming national symbols of music in their respective countries.

Increasingly, ethnomusicologists have turned to the ways in which race, ethnicity, class, gender, region, and identity are embedded in musical activities. When people in a music-culture migrate out of their region, they often use music as a marker of ethnic identity. Flory Jagoda and Mensur Hatić (Chapter 5) are Bosnians who have found an audience for their traditional music among Bosnians who have come to the United States. Throughout North America, ethnic groups perform and sometimes revive music that they consider to be their own, whether Jewish *klezmer* music, Andean panpipe music, central-European polka, or Peking Opera.

In the twentieth century, the music industry has played an especially important role in various music-cultures. Music is packaged, bought, and sold. How does a song commodity become popular? When is popularity the result of industry hype and when does it come from a groundswell of consumer interest? How do new kinds of music break into the media? Why do certain kinds of music gain (or fall) in popularity? What makes a hit song? Fortunes are gained and lost based on music producers' abilities to predict what will sell—yet most of the music released commercially does not sell. How should a group of musicians deal with the industry? How can they support themselves while remaining true to their musical vision? What constitutes "selling out"? The roles of musicians, consumers, and producers in the popular music industry throughout the world have drawn closer in the last few decades as markets have expanded and musicians from all over the globe now take part. Music has become an enormously important aspect of the global economy. The current struggles over the future of music delivery on the Internet alone involve profits and losses in the billions of dollars.

Repertories of Music

A *repertory* is a stock of music that is ready to be performed, and a music-culture's repertory is what most of us think of as the "music itself." It consists of six basic parts: style, genres, texts, composition, transmission, and movement. Think of a music that you are familiar with and see if you can understand it using the following terms.

Style

Style includes everything related to the organization of musical sound itself: pitch elements (scale, melody, harmony, tuning systems), time elements (rhythm, meter), timbre elements (voice quality, instrumental tone color), and sound intensity (loudness/softness). All depend on a music-culture's aesthetics.

Together, style and aesthetics create a recognizable sound that a group understands as its own. For example, the fiddle was the most popular dance instrument in Europe and North America from about the eighteenth century until the turn of the twentieth century. In many areas it is still popular; in others, such as Ireland, it is undergoing a revival. Old-time fiddlers in Missouri prefer their regional dance and contest tunes to the bluegrass tunes of the upper South. Old-time fiddlers in the upper South, on the other hand, prefer their own repertory of breakdown tunes. People new to these repertories do not hear significant differences between them. Are they alike? Not entirely, because each group can distinguish its own music. People learning fiddle tunes know they are getting somewhere when they can recognize the differences in national and regional styles and put those differences into words—or music.

Genres

Genres are the named, standard units of the repertory, such as "song" and its various subdivisions (for example, lullaby, Christmas carol, wedding song) or the many types of instrumental music and dances (jig, reel, waltz, schottische, polka, *hambo,* and so forth). Most music-cultures have a great many genres, but their terms do not always correspond to terms in other music-cultures. Among the *Yoruba* in the African nation of Nigeria, for example, powerful kings, chiefs, and nobles retained praise singers to sing praises to them (Olajubu 1978:685). The praise songs are called *oriki.* Although we can approximate an English name to describe them (praise songs), no equivalent genre exists today in Europe or America. In Japan, the labels identifying popular music include *gunka* (military songs), *foku songu* (contemporary folk songs, distinguished from *minyō,* or the traditional folk songs of the countryside), *nyu myushiku* (new music), and *pops* (see Chapter 8). In North America, blues is one genre, country music another. Subdivisions of country music include rockabilly and bluegrass. If you listen to country music stations on the radio, you will see that some identify themselves as "real country" (along with the latest hits, more of a mix of oldies and southern-oriented country music) and others as "hard country" (more of a mix of rock-oriented country music). Consider electronic dance music and some of its subdivisions; the Web site mp3.com lists the following: ambient, breakbeat, dance, down tempo, drum 'n' bass, electronica, experimental, game soundtracks, house, industrial electronic, techno, and trance. Subgenres have proliferated as marketing has grown more sophisticated. How many subgenres can you name in your favorite kind of music?

Texts

The words to a song are known as its *text*. Any song with words is an intersection of two very different and profound human communication systems: language and music. A song with words is a temporary weld of these two systems, and for convenience we can look at each by itself.

Every text has its own history; sometimes a single text is associated with several melodies. On the other hand, a single melody can go with several different texts. In blues music, for example, texts and melodies lead independent lives, coupling as the singer desires (Chapter 4). *Pop berat* ("heavy pop") compositions fuse Indonesian patriotic texts, traditional Indonesian musical instruments, and electric guitars and synthesizers (see Chapter 7). Navajo ritual song and prayer texts often conclude by saying that beauty and harmony prevail (see Chapter 2).

Composition

How does music enter the repertory of a music-culture? Is music composed individually or by a group? Is it fixed, varied within certain limits, or improvised spontaneously in performance? Improvisation fascinates most ethnomusicologists: Chapters 3, 4, and 6 consider improvisation in African, African-American, and South-Indian music. Perhaps at some deep level we prize improvisation not just because of the skills involved but because we think it exemplifies human freedom.

The composition of music, whether planned or spontaneous, is bound up with social organization. Does the music-culture have a special class of composers, or can anyone compose music? Composition is related as well to ideas about music: Some music-cultures divide songs into those composed by people and those "given" to people from deities, animals, and other nonhuman composers.

Transmission

How is music learned and transmitted from one person to the next, from one generation to the next? Does the music-culture rely on formal instruction, as in South India (Chapter 6)? Or is music learned chiefly through imitation (Chapter 4)? Does music theory underlie the process of formal instruction? Does music change over time? How and why? Is there a system of musical notation? Cipher (number) notation in Indonesia did not appear until the twentieth century (Chapter 7). In the ancient musical notation for the *ch'in*, the Chinese writing indicates more than what note is to be played, because the Chinese pictograms (picture writing) suggest something in nature. For example, the notation may suggest a duck landing on water, telling the player to imitate the duck's landing with the finger when touching the string. Such notation can also evoke the feeling intended by the composer.

Some music-cultures transmit music through apprenticeships lasting a lifetime (as in the disciple's relation to a *guru,* Chapter 6). The instructor becomes a parent, teaching values and ethics as well as music. In these situations music truly becomes a way of life and the apprentice is devoted to the music and the teacher. Other music-cultures have no formal instruction, and the aspiring musician learns by watching and listening, often over many years. In these circumstances growing up in a musical family is helpful. When a repertory is transmitted chiefly by example and imitation rather than notation, we say the music exists in oral tradition rather than written. Blues (Chapter 4) is an example of music in oral tradition; so is the *sanjuán* dance genre of highland Ecuadorian Quichua (Chapter 9). Music in oral tradition varies more over time and space than does music tied to a printed musical score. Sometimes the same music exists both in oral and written traditions. At gatherings called singing conventions, people belonging to Primitive Baptist denominations in the upper South sing hymn tunes from notation in tune books such as *The Sacred Harp.* Variants of these hymn tunes also exist in oral tradition among the Old Regular Baptists (see Figure 1-1), who do not use musical notation but who rely instead on learning the tunes from their elders and remembering them.

Movement

A whole range of physical activity accompanies music. Playing a musical instrument, alone or in a group, not only creates sound but also literally moves people—that is, they sway, dance, walk, work in response. Even if we cannot see them move very much, their brains and bodies are responding as they hear and process the music. How odd it would be for a rock band to perform without moving in response to their music, in ways that let the audience know they were feeling it. This was demonstrated several years ago by the new-wave rock band Devo when its members acted like robots. In one way or another movement and music connect in the repertory of every culture. Sometimes the movement is quite loose, suggesting freedom and abandon, and at other times, as in Balinese dance, it is highly controlled, suggesting that in this culture controlling oneself is beautiful and admirable.

Material Culture of Music

Material culture refers to the material objects that people in a culture produce—objects that can be seen, held, felt, and used. This book is an example of material culture. So are dinner plates, gravestones, airplanes, hamburgers, pocket calculators, and school buildings. Examining a culture's tools and technology can tell us about the group's history and way of life. Similarly, research into the material culture of music can help us to understand music-cultures. The most important objects in a music-culture, of course, are musical instruments (see Figure 1-9). We cannot hear the actual sound of any musical performances before the 1870s, when the phonograph was invented, so we rely on instruments for information about music-cultures in the remote past. Here we have two kinds of evidence: instruments preserved more or less intact, such as Sumerian harps over 4,500 years old, and instruments pictured in art. Through the study of instruments, as well as paintings, written documents, and other sources, we can explore the movement of music from the Near East to China over a thousand years ago, we can trace the Guatemalan marimba to its African roots, or we can outline the spread of Near-Eastern musical influences to Europe, which resulted in the development of most of the instruments in the symphony orchestra.

Figure 1-9
Young man playing a one-stringed diddly-bow. Missouri, 1938. (Instructions for making and playing a similar instrument are given in Chapter 4.)

We can also ask questions of today's music-cultures: Who makes instruments and how are they distributed? What is the relation between instrument makers and musicians? How do this generation's musical instruments reflect its musical tastes and styles, compared with those of the previous generation? In the 1950s electric instruments transformed the sound of popular music in the United States, and in the 1960s this electronic musical revolution spread elsewhere in the world. Taken for granted today, electric instruments—guitars, basses, pianos, pedal-steel guitars—represented a musical revolution in the 1950s. The computer is the most revolutionary musical instrument today. Computer-assisted composition, incorporating sound sampling and other innovations, empowers a new generation of composers to do things they had otherwise been unable to accomplish, while computer-assisted distribution of music through the Internet may be the wave of the future.

Musical scores, instruction books, sheet music—these too are part of the material culture. Scholars once defined folk music-cultures as those in which people learn to sing music by ear rather than from print, but research shows mutual influence among oral and written sources during the past few centuries in Europe, Britain, and America. Because they tend to standardize songs, printed versions limit variety, but paradoxically they stimulate people to create original songs. Also, the ability to read music notation has a far-reaching effect on musicians and, when it becomes widespread, on a music-culture as a whole.

One more important part of a music's material culture should be singled out: the impact of electronic media—phonographs, radios, tape recorders, CDs, televisions, videocassettes, DVDs, and computers. This technology has facilitated the information revolution, a twentieth-century phenomenon as important as the industrial revolution was in the nineteenth. Electronic media have affected music-cultures all over the world. They are one of the main reasons many now call our planet a global village.

Ecological Worlds of Music

In the eighteenth century, when Europeans began collecting music from the countryside and from faraway places outside their homelands, they thought that "real," traditional music was dying out. From then on, each time a new music-culture was discovered, European and American collectors took the music of its oldest generation to be the most authentic, conferring on it a timeless quality and usually deploring anything new. This neither reflected the way music-cultures actually work nor gave people enough credit for creative choice. At any given moment, three kinds of music circulate within most communities: (1) music so old and accepted as "ours" that no one questions (or sometimes even knows) where it comes from, (2) music of an earlier generation understood to be old-fashioned or perhaps classic, and (3) the most recent or current musics, marketed and recognized as the latest development. These recent musics may be local, imported, or a combination of both. The last is most likely, because today the world is linked electronically; musics travel much more quickly than they did a hundred years ago.

Music-cultures, in other words, are dynamic rather than static. They constantly change in response to inside and outside pressures. It is wrong to think of a music-culture as something isolated, stable, smoothly operating, impenetrable, and uninfluenced by the outside world. Indeed, as we shall see in Chapter 4, the people in a music-culture need not share the same language, nationality, or ethnic origin. At the turn of the twenty-first century, blues is popular with performers worldwide. People in a music-culture need not even share all of the same ideas about music—as we have seen, they in fact do not. As music-cultures change (and they are always changing) they undergo friction, and the "rules" of musical performance, aesthetics, interpretation, and meaning are negotiated, not fixed. Music history is reconceived by each generation.

Music is a fluid, dynamic element of culture, and it changes to suit the expressive and emotional desires of humankind, perhaps the most changeable of the animals. Like all of culture, music is a peculiarly human adaptation to life on this earth. Seen globally, music operates as an ecological system. Each music-culture is a particular adaptation to particular circumstances. Ideas about music, social organization, repertories, and material culture vary from one music-culture to the next. It would be unwise to call one music-culture's music "primitive," because doing so imposes one's own standards on a group that does not recognize them. Such ethnocentrism has no place in the study of world musics.

In this book we usually describe the older musical layers in a given region first. Then we discuss increasingly more contemporary musical styles, forms, and attitudes. We wish to leave you with the impression that the world is not a set of untouched, authentic musical villages, but rather a fluid, interactive, interlocking, overlapping soundscape in which people listen to their ancestors, parents, neighbors, and personal CD and cassette machines all in the same day. We think of people as musical "activists," choosing what they like best, remembering what resonates best, forgetting what seems irrelevant, and keeping their ears open for exciting new musical opportunities. This happens everywhere, and it unites the farthest settlement and the largest city.

In the chapters that follow, we explore the acoustic ecologies of several worlds, and worlds within worlds, of music. Although each world may seem strange to you at first, all are organized and purposeful. Considered as an ecological system, the forces that make up a music-culture maintain a dynamic equilibrium. A change in any part of the acoustic ecology, such as the invention of the electric guitar or the latest computer music technology, may have a far-reaching impact. Viewing music this way leads to the conclusion that music represents a great human force that transcends narrow political, social, and temporal boundaries. Music offers an arena where people can talk and sing and play and reach each other in ways not allowed by the barriers of wealth, status, location, and difference. This book and CD set can present only a tiny sample of the richness of the world's music. We hope you will continue your exploration after you have finished this book.

References

Blacking, John. 1973. *How Musical Is Man?* Seattle: Univ. of Washington Press.

Feld, Steven. 1990. *Sound and Sentiment: Birds, Weeping, Poetics and Song in Kaluili Expression.* 2nd ed. Philadelphia: Univ. of Pennsylvania Press.

Merriam, Alan P. 1964. *The Anthropology of Music.* Evanston, Ill.: Northwestern Univ. Press.

Olajubu, Chief Oludare. 1978. "Yoruba Verbal Artists and Their Work." *Journal of American Folklore* 91:675–90.

Pantaleoni, Hewitt. 1985. *On the Nature of Music.* Oneonta, N.Y.: Wellkin Books.

Sachs, Nahoma. 1975. "Music and Meaning: Musical Symbolism in a Macedonian Village." Ph.D. diss., Princeton Univ.

Schafer, R. Murray. 1980. *The Tuning of the World: Toward a Theory of Soundscape Design.* Philadelphia: Univ. of Pennsylvania Press.

Titon, Jeff Todd. 1988. *Powerhouse for God: Speech, Chant, and Song in an Appalachian Baptist Church.* Austin, TX: Univ. of Texas Press.

———, ed. 1992. *Worlds of Music.* 2nd ed. New York: Schirmer Books.

Additional Reading

Barz, Gregory, and Timothy J. Cooley. 1997. *Shadows in the Field.* New York: Oxford Univ. Press.

Berliner, Paul. 1994. *Thinking in Jazz.* Chicago: Univ. of Chicago Press.

Crafts, Susan D., Daniel Cavicchi, Charles Keil, and the Music in Daily Life Project, 1993. *My Music.* Hanover, N.H.: Univ. Press of New England.

Hamm, Charles, Bruno Nettl, and Ronald Byrnside. 1975. *Contemporary Music and Music Cultures.* Englewood Cliffs, N.J.: Prentice-Hall.

Hood, Mantle. 1982. *The Ethnomusicologist.* 2nd ed. Kent, Ohio: Kent State Univ. Press.

May, Elizabeth, ed. 1981. *Musics of Many Cultures.* Berkeley: Univ. of California Press.

McAllester, David R. 1949. *Peyote Music.* New York: Viking Fund Publications in Anthropology no. 13.

———, ed. 1971. *Readings in Ethnomusicology.* New York: Johnson Reprint Corp.

Merriam, Alan. 1967. *Ethnomusicology of the Flathead Indians.* Chicago: Aldine.

Myers, Helen. 1992. *Ethnomusicology: An Introduction.* New York: Norton.

———. 1993. *Ethnomusicology: Historical and Regional Studies.* New York: Norton.

Nettl, Bruno. 1964. *Theory and Method in Ethnomusicology.* New York: Free Press.

———. 1983. *The Study of Ethnomusicology: Twenty-Nine Issues and Concepts.* Urbana: Univ. of Illinois Press.

———. 1985. *The Western Impact on World Music: Change, Adaptation, and Survival.* New York: Schirmer Books.

———. 1995. *Heartland Excursions: Ethnomusicological Reflections on Schools of Music.* Urbana: Univ. of Illinois Press.

Reck, David. 1977. *Music of the Whole Earth*. New York: Scribner.

Rice, Timothy. 1994. *May It Fill Your Soul: Experiencing Bulgarian Music.* Chicago: Univ. of Chicago Press.

Shelemay, Kay Kaufman. 1998. *Let Jasmine Rain Down.* Chicago: Univ. of Chicago Press.

Turnbull, Colin. 1962. *The Forest People.* New York: Clarion Books.

CHAPTER

2

North America / Native America

David P. McAllester

American Indian music is unfamiliar to most non-Indian Americans. Accordingly, this chapter first presents an overall perspective by contrasting three of the numerous different Native-American musical styles. Then we shall look in detail at some of the many types of music being performed today in just one tribe, the Navajos. Their musical life will be studied in relation to their traditional culture and their present history. Learning about the Navajos' cultural setting will greatly enhance your understanding of their music.

Sioux Grass Dance

Three Different Styles

The essence of music is participation, either by listening or, better still, by performing. We shall start with the sound likely to be the most "Indian" to the non-Indian American–a Sioux War Dance (Figure 2-1). This is also called a Grass Dance, from the braids of grass the dancing warriors used to wear at their waists to symbolize slain enemies. It is also called the Omaha Dance, after the Indians of the western plains, who originated it.

Listen for a moment to the recording of a Sioux Grass Dance (CD 1, Track 3, Transcription 2-1). When European scholars first heard this kind of sound on wax cylinder field recordings brought back to Berlin in the early 1900s, they exclaimed, "Now, at last, we can hear the music of the true savages!" For four hundred years European social philosophers had thought of Americans Indians as noble wild men unspoiled by civilization, and here was music that fitted the image.

CD 1/3
Grass Dance (1:51). Traditional Sioux War Dance. Field recording by Ray Boley, n.d. *Sioux Favorites*. Canyon Records Productions CR-6054. Phoenix, Arizona.

Nothing known to Europeans sounded like this piercing falsetto, swooping down for more than an octave in a "tumbling strain" that seemed to come straight from the emotions. The pulsating voices with their sharp emphases, the driving drumbeat with its complex relation to the vocal part, the heavy slides at the ends of phrases–what could better portray the warlike horsemen of the limitless American plains? Another feature that intrigued Europeans was the use of vocables (nonlexical or "meaningless" syllables) for entire texts of songs, as in this Grass Dance.

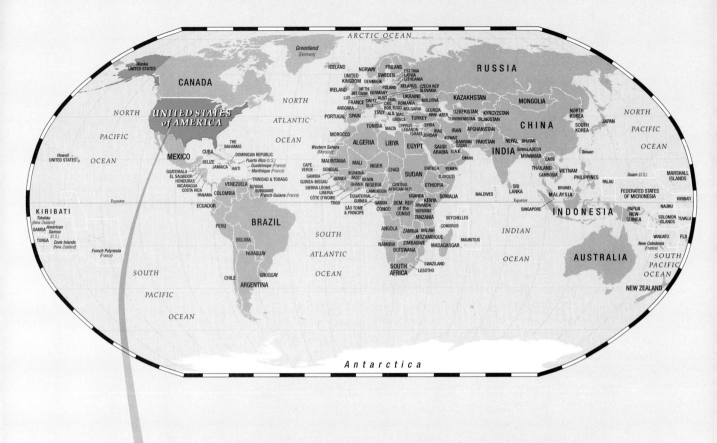

Figure 2-1
War dancers at a Michigan powwow.

Douglas Fulton. Courtesy of Gertrude Kurath.

Curt Sachs cited this as another reason for labeling this music pathogenic (arising from the emotions), as contrasted with logogenic music, in which translatable words are the basis of the song (Sachs 1962:51–58). Sachs theorized that one would find pathogenic music in the early stages of a culture's evolution. He may have wondered when listening to Native-American music whether his own Paleolithic ancestors sang like that when they were hunting wild horses across the plains of Europe and had not yet discovered agriculture.

Another supposed proof that American Indians belonged to an early stage of musical evolution was the relatively few kinds of musical instruments they used. From north of Mexico to the Arctic the music was almost entirely vocal and the instruments were chiefly rattles and drums used to accompany the voice. However, the varieties of rattles and drums invented by North American Indians are legion. To name a few, there are rattles made from gourds, tree bark, carved wood, deer hooves, turtle shells, spider nests, and, recently, tin cans. There are frame drums and barrel drums of many sizes and shapes, and the water drum (described in detail on pp. 74–75), with its wet membrane, is unique. There are a few flutes and flageolets, and one-stringed fiddles played without the voice, but these are rare. Instrumental ensembles such as Western classical orchestras are unknown in traditional North American Indian music.

In Central and South America, on the other hand, the native high civilizations did have orchestras before the Europeans came. They readily added European instruments to their ensembles and blended their music with new ideas from Portugal and Spain. Only in the last forty or fifty years has this mingling of musics begun to happen on any large scale in native North American music. The vast majority of traditional songs are still accompanied by only drum or rattle or both.

Clearly, the once-popular Euro-American theories just described did not take into account the actual diversity within Native-American cultures. Few scholars today find that a notion of "delayed evolution" explains the so-called simpler cultures of the world. In fact, they turn out not to be simple at all. Survival, whatever the climate, requires encyclopedic knowledge. A language never expressed in writing may contain the most complex grammatical structures known to linguists. Folk music with no harmonies may contain melodic, modal, and rhythmic sophistication unattainable in harmonic music.

Listen again to the Sioux Grass Dance song and see if you can sing along with it. You may think it is impossible, especially if you are a man and have never tried to sing in falsetto before. You might find it easier at first to try singing the song an octave lower. Transcription 2-1 will help you with the words and melody.

If you cannot read notes, think of the transcription as a kind of graph tracing the line of the melody. Even with no musical training you can see patterns of movement from high to low and back up again. The sections of the song that sound alike have been labeled with the same letter of the alphabet to help you see where similar musical ideas are repeated. The overall structure of phrases in this song may be represented as shown here.

$$\tfrac{1}{2}\,A\,A\,B\,B$$
$$\tfrac{1}{2}\,A\,A\,B\,B$$
$$\tfrac{1}{2}\,A\,A\,B\,B\,B$$

The song starts with an A phrase, sung by a leader, but before he can finish it the other male singers break in with the same phrase, repeated, and he joins them to sing it all the way through. The leader's first, uncompleted phrase is represented here as ½ A. Most of the melodic movement takes place in the B phrase. Here is where the melody drops a full octave below the tonal center established in the A phrase. In fact, the lower part of B is almost an exact repeat of A, performed twice and an octave lower. In Transcription 2-1, the points where this transposition begins and repeats are marked by (A_8). After three repeats of the whole melody, there is a pause; then B is repeated one last time to end the song. Indian singers often call that last brief section the "tail" of the song, which is also what the European musical term *coda* means.

Transcription 2-1
Sioux Grass Dance song. (All musical transcriptions in this chapter are by David P. McAllester.)

With permission of Canyon Records.

Although the song's overall structure is easy to understand, you will probably find it difficult to sing. It goes fast and does not have a regular meter. Most of it follows three-beat patterns, but every now and then the singers introduce a four-beat phrase (marked by horizontal brackets in the transcription). Notice that the melody makes the same downward dip wherever the meter breaks into four. Another difficulty is that the song's meter (about 200 beats per minute) does not seem to coincide with that of the drum (about 192 beats per minute). "C = B♭" means that I have transposed the melody level up a whole step so that it will be easier to read.

The best way to sing this is to relax and not try to count it out mechanically. Concentrate on the excitement that has made this kind of music the most popular Native-American style all over the country where there are Indian fairs, rodeos, and powwows. Like the Plains Indians' eagle-feather war bonnet and their stately, beautifully decorated tepees, the War Dance symbolizes "American Indian" throughout the world. Though Indian singing styles differ from region to region, many non-Plains Indians, especially young people, have learned this style so well that they have been able to compete with Plains singers in song contests. There are non-Indians, also, who have risen to the challenge of this music and have won prizes for their singing, costumes, and dancing at powwows. In singing this song, pay particular attention to the sharp emphases, the pulsations, and the glides. These are not mere "ornamentation" but an important part of the special art of Plains singing.

The dancing that goes with this song style is based on a toe-heel movement first with one foot and then with the other, as follows:

Foot:	left	right	right	left	left	right
Movement:	step	toe-heel,	change	toe-heel,	change	toe-heel, . . .

Each male dancer creates many personal variations and provides a solo display of his virtuosity. His body dips and bends, but his head is quite erect, sometimes nodding in time to the drumbeat and turning this way and that. His eyes are fixed on space, and the expression is rapt and remote. Often he carries a decorated stick or other object in one hand; during the dance he may manipulate it with all the subtlety a Japanese dancer uses a fan. Every dancer must stop precisely on the last beat at the rhythmic break before the "tail." Then the dancing resumes with all its intensity for the last few moments and must stop exactly on the last beat of the song. One extra step disqualifies a dancer from the competition.

The movement and sound of the costume is an essential part of the Grass Dance and its music. Bells are often tied around the legs; today they are sleigh bells, often quite large, mounted on a leather strap. These resound with every step. Ribbons sway, feathers and porcupine-hair roaches (see the heads of the dancers in Figure 2-1) quiver, beads and small mirrors gleam and flash. The costume is as elaborate as the vocal style.

Women participate by either using a subdued version of the dance step or simply walking around the edge of the dance area. They wear shawls with long fringes that sway in time to their movements. In recent years women's "jingle dancing" has become a competitive event. Wearing a dress decorated with scores of cone-shaped metal jingles, younger women leap and step, filling the air with glitter and tintinnabulation. Some women stand behind the male singers, who are seated around a bass drum, and enter the song an octave higher than the men, often on the B phrase when it starts down. In the recording heard here, their voices do not come in until the first point marked A_8 in the transcription.

Zuni Lullaby

CD 1/4

Lullaby (0:58). Traditional Zuni. Performed by Lanaiditsa. Field recording by David McAllester. White Water, New Mexico, 1950.

The next song (CD 1, Track 4, Transcription 2-2) provides a contrast with Plains singing and helps demonstrate that there is no single "Indian" musical style. It is a lullaby recorded in 1950 by a grandmother, Lanaiditsa, on the Zuni Reservation in western New Mexico. You will have little difficulty joining in with the song. The meter is rather free, and the whole gentle song has only two pitches.

Transcription 2-2
Zuni lullaby.

♪ = 92

① hm at - se - ki__ ok-shit - s'a - na__ po-ket - s'a - na po-ket - s'a - na

② hm at - se - ki__ ok - shit - s'a - na__ ko - chit - s'a - na__

③ at - set - s'a-na at - set - s'a-na hm at - se - ki__ po - ket-s'a - na__

④ ok-shit - s'a - na ok - shit - s'a - na hm at - se - ki __

po - ket - s'a -na__ ok - shit - s'a - na ko - chit - s'a - na

⑤ ko - chit-s'a - na hm at - se - ki__ po - ket - s'a - na__

(last verse three times)

ok-shit - s'a - na__ ko - chit - s'a - na ko - chit - s'a - na

In this case the text is in translatable words instead of vocables. The singer's affection for the child is expressed in the repetition of the word *little* and pet names, which seem to be interchangeable in the first half of the song but then settle into the same sequence.

Text, Zuni Lullaby

Hm atseki	my boy
okshits'ana	cottontail little
pokets'ana	jackrabbit little
kochits'ana	rat little

1. My boy, little cottontail,
   Little jackrabbit, little jackrabbit;
2. My boy, little cottontail,
   Little rat, little boy, little boy;
3. My boy, little jackrabbit,
   Little cottontail, little cottontail;
4. My boy, little jackrabbit,
   Little cottontail, little rat, little rat.
5. My boy, little jackrabbit,
   Little cottontail, little rat, little rat. (3 times)

Figure 2-2
Zuni mother and child, showing the costume and hairstyle of the early twentieth century.

Neg. no. 121630. Courtesy American Museum of Natural History. (Photo: Coles/Bierwert)

Repetition is a prominent feature in most North American Indian music: in the vocables, in the lexical texts (where they occur), and in the melodic and rhythmic patterns. This is not because Indians cannot create text and music with a "fuller" content, in a Western sense, but because their aesthetic taste delights in repetitions with slight variations that are sometimes too subtle for the ears of outsiders to detect. In Lanaiditsa's song each textual phrase can be used with either of the two musical phrases except for "my boy," which is always on an A. She settles on "my little rat" for the ending of verse 4 and the three repeats of verse 5, which suggests that she finds it the most endearing of the diminutives.

This love of repetition shows in Indian folk tales and other narratives and is very much a part of the way the Navajo singer or "medicine man," Frank Mitchell, tells the story of his life (see pp. 64–71).

Iroquois Quiver Dance

The Quiver Dance song, "Gadashot," illustrates still another of the many different musical styles in North American Indian singing (CD 1, Track 5, Transcription 2-3). Another name for it is Warrior's Stomp Dance song. This was recorded in 1941 by Joshua Buck and Simeon Gibson at the Six Nations Reserve in Ohsweken, Ontario, but the song was made up years

CD 1/5

"Gadasjot" (0:47). Iroquois Quiver Dance or Warrior's Stomp Dance song. Twenty Jacobs of Quaker Ridge. Performed by Joshua Billy Buck and Simeon Gibson. Field recording by William Fenton, ca. 1942. *Songs from the Iroquois Longhouse.* Archive of Folk Song of the Library of Congress AFS L6. LP. Washington, D.C.

Transcription 2-3
Iroquois Quiver Dance song.

With permission of William N. Fenton.

before that by Twenty Jacobs of Quaker Bridge, on the Allegheny Reservation in western New York. Note the difference between the lyrics as they would be spoken and as they appear in the song.

The first thing that strikes the ear is the "call-and-response" form. One singer utters a phrase of lexical text (the "call") and the other answers him with a vocable pattern: "yowe hi ye ye!" This alternation continues through the song. Although quite common in the Eastern Woodlands, this pattern is rare elsewhere in North American traditional Indian singing. (Call-and-response singing can be heard in many world music cultures, as we shall see in later chapters.) William Fenton's translation of the text shows the jocular content often found in Stomp Dance songs.

Text, Iroquois Quiver Dance Song

'Tga na hóna' 'Ohswégen	*yowe hi ye ye!*
Filled is Ohsweken	
Dedjo dinyaakon' on	*yowe hi ye ye!*
With divorced women	
Wegah hano hiiyo	*yowe hi ye ye!*
With good looking ones	
We hoonon hiiyo	*yowe hi ye ye!*
Fine looking ones!	

With the permission of William N. Fenton.

The singing in this Iroquois song is relaxed compared with Plains singing. A characteristic of Iroquois singing style is a pulsation of the voice at the ends of phrases, indicated in the transcription by ♩♩ and ♩ ♩. In Plains singing, by contrast, pulsations occur all through the song.

The Stomp Dance is a favorite recreational dance among Woodland Indians in the eastern United States and Canada. Among the Iroquois it usually takes place in the longhouse, a meetinghouse with a stove at each end of the hall and benches along the sides. The participants form a line behind the leader. They imitate his "short jog step" (Fenton 1942:31) and any other turns and gyrations he may invent as they sing the responses to his calls. More and more of the audience joins the dance until the line is winding exuberantly all over the longhouse floor. Woodland tribes other than the Iroquois may not have longhouses and often do the Stomp Dance outdoors. The singers accompany themselves with a cowhorn rattle.

Making a "Cowhorn" Rattle

The adventure of Native American music involves not only singing but also making instruments to accompany the voice. Here are the steps for creating a serviceable imitation of a cowhorn rattle (Figure 2-3). A section of cow's horn is not easy for most of us to obtain; a small fruit juice can, open at one end, makes a good substitute.

1. Any small metal can, two or three inches tall and two to two and one-half inches in diameter, will do. Make a plug for the open end of the can out of a disk of soft wood slightly wider than the diameter of the can. With a sharp knife or a file, bevel one edge of the disc just enough so that it can be tightly wedged into the can.

2. Find a stick of hard wood, such as a straight tree branch, about three-fourths of an inch in diameter; cut a one-foot length. A piece of birch dowel will do. Whittle away one end of the stick to make a tapering spindle about an inch longer than the height of the can. At the base of the spindle, leave a shelf as shown in the drawing.

3. Drill a hole in the wooden plug so that it will fit snugly over the spindle and seat itself, beveled side up, on the shelf. Punch a smaller hole in the bottom of the can and slide it, open end down, over the spindle until the rim of the can fits over the beveled edge of the plug. The end of the spindle should project an inch beyond the bottom of the can. Mark the spindle at the point where it emerges from the hole in the can. The mark should be as close to the bottom of the can as possible.

4. Remove the can and plug and fasten the plug in the open end of the can with furniture tacks with shiny brass heads. Drop fifteen or twenty BBs or small pebbles into the can to produce the rattling sound.

5. Drill a small hole in the spindle at the marked place and find a nail or peg that will fit tightly in the hole and project on both sides of the spindle. Fit the can back into place, plug-end down, and wedge the

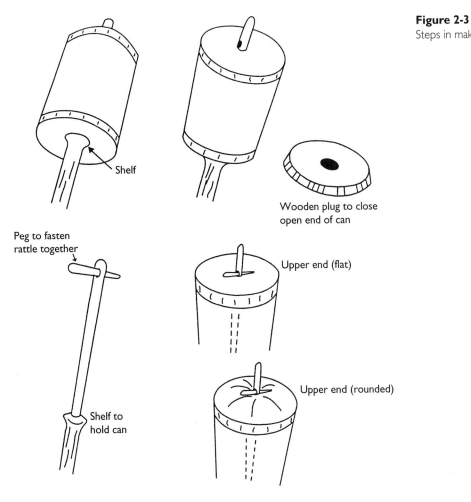

Figure 2-3
Steps in making a cowhorn rattle.

Shelf

Wooden plug to close
open end of can

Peg to fasten
rattle together

Upper end (flat)

Shelf to
hold can

Upper end (rounded)

nail or peg through the hole in the spindle. This should hold the can
firmly, supported by the shelf at the bottom end.

Extra Niceties

You could remove both ends of the can and have a wooden plug in each
end. This would give you two rows of ornamental tacks, holding in the
plugs. If you are good at woodworking you could turn the plug for the
upper end on a lathe so that it is rounded instead of being merely flat.

To make the can look like a cowhorn you could paint it dark brown
with cream-colored streaks or cream-colored with brown streaks. Figure
2-4 shows several cowhorn rattles. Notice the different ways the handle
can be carved to break the monotony of a straight stick. You can express
your own creativity in how you do it.

How to Play the Rattle

This kind of rattle may be struck against the user's thigh or palm to produce a sharp impact. At the beginning of a song a tremolo effect is often
produced by rapidly shaking the rattle, held high in the air.

Figure 2-4
Iroquois cowhorn rattles, showing a
variety of shapes and handles.

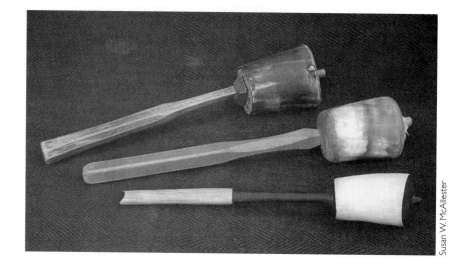

Susan W. McAllester

Music of the Navajos

Now that we have had a brief look at three of the many different North American Indian musical styles, we shall take a deeper look into the musical life of still another Indian group, the Navajos of the Southwestern desert. By studying their music in some detail we can see how many different kinds of music exist in just one Indian community. Examining the cultural context of the music will show us how closely music is integrated with Indian life. The autobiographical sketch of Frank Mitchell provides a firsthand account by a professional Navajo singer of how he learned his music and what it meant to him.

A Yeibichai Song from the Nightway Ceremony

To begin again with sound, we shall go first to one of the most exciting kinds of Navajo music, Yeibichai songs. *Yé'ii-bi-cháí* (gods-their-grand-fathers) refers to ancestor deities who come to dance at the major cere-monial known as Nightway. The masked dancers who impersonate the gods bring supernatural power and blessing to help cure a sick person.

Transcription 2-4
Navajo Yeibichai song.

* Repeat from A twice. High yell replaces 1st 2 notes of A on the first repeat; second repeat ends at "Fine".

Transcription by David P. McAllester from a field recording by Willard Rhodes.

CD 1/6

Yeibichai (2:15). Navajo dance song from Nightway. Led by Sandoval Begay. Field recording by Willard Rhodes, n.d. Archive of Folk Song of the Library of Congress AFS L41. LP. Washington, D.C.

With its shouts, ornamentation, and falsetto voices, this song (CD 1, Track 6, Transcription 2-4) makes one think of the Plains Indians. The tense energy of the singing also resembles that of the Plains style. However, the long introduction (phrases X, Y, and Z), sung almost entirely on the base note (the "tonic") of the song, differs strikingly from the Indian songs we have heard before. Then the melody leaps *up* an octave. In the first phrase, A, after the introduction, the song comes swooping briskly down to the tonic again to an ending I have labeled "e^1." This ending appears again later on in the song in two variations, "e^2" and "e^3." (Capital letters denote main phrases and small letters for motifs within the phrases.) The same descent is repeated (the second A and e^1) and then another acrobatic plunge takes place in B after two "false starts" (labeled $\frac{1}{2}$a) that each closely resemble the first half of A. The song then hovers on the tonic e^2 and e^3 and the phrase *hi ye, hi ye*, which also appears in Y and Z. I call it "z" because it has the weighty function of ending the introduction and, eventually, the song itself, in the Z phrase. After B, another interesting variation in the use of previous motifs occurs: the *second* half of A is sung twice, $a^{\frac{1}{2}}$ and $a^{\frac{1}{2}}$, followed by the first half of A, also repeated, $\frac{1}{2}$a and $\frac{1}{2}$a.

The Navajos are noted for their bold experiments in artistic form. This is true in their silversmithing, weaving, sandpainting, and their contemporary commercial painting. It is also true of their music, as the play of melodic and rhythmic motifs in the passage just heard suggests. Listen again, following the pattern of this complex and intriguing song, and try to sing it yourself along with Sandoval Begay and his group of Yeibichai singers.

Entirely in vocables, this song illustrates how far from "meaningless" vocables can be. Almost any Navajo would know from the first calls that this is a Yeibichai song; these and the other vocables identify what kind of song it is. Moreover, this song includes the call of the gods themselves:

Call of the Yei

Hi ye, hi ye, ho - ho ho ho!

Although there are hundreds of different Yeibichai songs, they usually contain some variation of this call of the Yei.

Yeibichai singers are organized in teams, often made up of men from one particular region or another. They create new songs or sing old favorites, each team singing several songs before the nightlong singing and dancing end. The teams prepare costumes and masks and practice a dance of the gods that proceeds in two parallel lines with reel-like figures. They also have a clown, who follows the dancers and makes everyone laugh with his antics: getting lost, bumbling into the audience, imitating the other dancers. The teams compete, and the best combination of costumes, clowns, singing, and dancing receives a gift from the family giving the ceremony. The representation of the presence of the gods at the Nightway brings god power to the ceremony and helps the sick person get well.

This dance takes place on the last night of a nine-night ritual that includes such ceremonial practices as purification by sweating and vomiting, making prayer offerings for deities whose presence is thus invoked, and sandpainting rituals in which the one-sung-over sits on elaborate designs in colored sands and other dry pigments. The designs depict the deities; contact with these figures identifies the one-sung-over with the forces of nature they represent and provides their protective power (see Figure 2-5). In the course of the ceremony hundreds of people may attend as spectators, whose presence supports the reenactment of the myth on which the ceremony is based. The one-sung-over takes the role of the mythic hero, and the songs, sandpaintings, prayers, and other ritual acts recount the story of how this protagonist's trials and adventures brought the Nightway ceremony from the supernatural world for the use of humankind (Faris 1990). Besides the Yeibichai songs there are hundreds of long chanted songs with elaborate texts of translatable ritual poetry (see pp. 60–64).

Such a ritual drama as Nightway is as complex as "the whole of a Wagnerian opera" (Kluckhohn and Leighton 1938:163). The organization

Neg. no. 2A 3634. Courtesy American Museum of Natural History. (Photo: Boltin)

Figure 2-5
Ceremonial practitioner making a sandpainting of a Lightning Deity in flint armor.

and performance of the whole event is directed by the singer or ceremonial practitioner, who must memorize every detail. Such men and women are among the intellectual leaders of the Navajo communities. The life story on pages 64–71 offers a rare glimpse into the mind of such a person.

Most readers find the Yeibichai song difficult to learn. The shifts in emphasis, the many variations, and the difficult vocal style demand hours of training before one can do it well. But there are many other kinds of Navajo music.

"Folsom Prison Blues"

You should be able to join in with the next song (CD 1, Track 7) right away, especially if you already listen to country and western music. This version of Johnny Cash's "Folsom Prison Blues" is played and sung by the Fenders,

CD 1/7

"Folsom Prison Blues" (2:48). Johnny Cash. Published by Hi-Lo Music. Performed by the Fenders. *The Fenders, Second Time Roun'*. LP. Thoreau, New Mexico, 1966.

Figure 2-6
Album cover of the Fenders, an early
Navajo country and western group.

an all-Navajo country band from Thoreau, New Mexico, who were popular
in the 1960s and 1970s (Figure 2-6). Country music has long been a great
favorite with Indian people, especially in the west. There are several
country and western bands on the Navajo reservation. Some, such as the
Sundowners and Borderline, have issued records that sell well in Indian
country. Even more popular are non-Indian country singers such as Garth
Brooks and Tim McGraw. The cowboy and trucker image appeals to most
people in the western states, including Indians, who identify with the open
life and the excitement of the roundup and the rodeo. The Fenders' liner
notes begin as follows:

> The five Fenders are genuine cowboys . . . as much at home on the back
> of a bucking rodeo bronc as behind the wild guitar at a good old rodeo
> dance. These boys believe that to be a No. 1, all-around cowboy, you
> must be able to play the guitar and sing just as well as you ride, rope
> and bull-dog.

The Navajo Way of Life

Who are these Navajos we have been listening to? Where and how do they
live? At more than 200,000, they are our largest Indian tribe. Descended
from Athabascan-speaking nomadic hunters who came into the Southwest

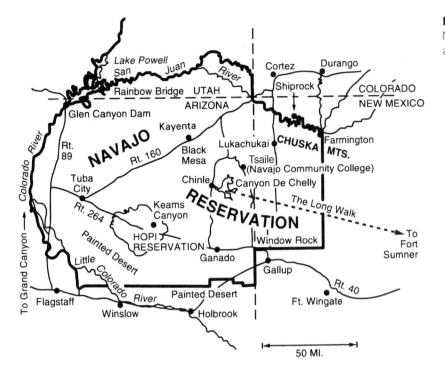

Figure 2-7
Map of the Navajo Reservation
and points of interest.

as recently as six or seven hundred years ago, they now live in scattered communities ranging from extended family groups to small towns on a reservation of 25,000 square miles (larger than West Virginia) spread over parts of New Mexico, Arizona, and Utah (see Figure 2-7). The exact census of the Navajos is uncertain, because thousands live off the reservation in border towns such as Farmington, Gallup, and Flagstaff and such cities as Chicago, Los Angeles, and San Diego. The reason for their move is largely economic: Their population has outgrown the support afforded by the reservation.

On the reservation the Navajos' livelihood is based, to a small but culturally significant degree, on farming, raising stock, weaving, and silversmithing (see Figure 2-8). The main part of their $110 million annual income, however, comes from coal, uranium, oil, natural gas, and lumber. Much of their educational and health care funds derive from the Department of the Interior, some of it in fulfillment of the 1868 treaty that marked the end of hostilities between the Navajos and the United States Army. Personal incomes range from the comfortable salaries of tribal administrative and service jobs to the precarious subsistence of marginal farmers. Many Navajos are supported on various kinds of tribal or government relief.

Although much of traditional Navajo culture remains intact, the People (*Diné*), as the Navajos call themselves, also welcome new ideas and change. Their scholarship funds enable hundreds of young people to attend colleges and universities around the country, including their own Navajo Community College on the reservation. A battery of attorneys and a Natural Resources Committee keep watch on the mining leases and

Figure 2-8
Navajos still travel on horseback in many parts of the reservation.

Neg. no. 335258. Courtesy American Museum of Natural History. (Photo: M. Raney)

lumber operations. The Navajos also operate motels, restaurants, banks, and shopping centers, and they encourage small industries to establish themselves on the reservation. Some Navajos jet to administrative and development conferences in Washington, D.C.; others speak no English and herd sheep on horseback or on foot miles from the nearest paved road.

The men dress in western style, and some of the women still wear skirts and blouses copied from the dresses worn by United States Army officers' wives in the 1860s, during the imprisonment of the Navajos at Fort Sumner, New Mexico. The skirts have shortened in recent years, and Navajo taste has always demanded the addition of buttons, rings, bracelets, necklaces, and heavy belts of silver set with turquoise. The men wear this jewelry, too, sometimes with the added panache of silver hatbands on big cowboy hats. Young people, male and female, are now usually seen wearing blue jeans like other young people anywhere in the country. Bright blankets from the Pendleton mills in Oregon used to be worn as an overcoat in cold weather. This garment is now so identified with traditional Navajo costume that it is often worn by the protagonist in ceremonials. The Navajos' own famous rugs are woven for cash income; most of them go to the local store, sometimes still called a trading post, to pay for food and other supplies. Some of these rugs are so finely designed and woven that they have brought $20,000 or more apiece in the world market for fine arts (see Figure 2-9).

Navajo houses range from the modern stucco ranch houses and large trailer homes of tribal officials, administrative staff, and school personnel to smaller one-room houses of every description. Some of the old-style circular log hogans (Navajo *hooghan,* "place home") can still be seen. Navajo ceremony requires a circular floor plan, and many adaptations of this well-loved and ceremonially important shape are designed into new kinds of structures. For example, the Tribal Council Building in Window Rock, Arizona, is a round sandstone structure with Navajo murals inside. It can accommodate the seventy-four council members, who gather there from all parts of the reservation. The Cultural Center at the Navajo Community College at Tsaile, Arizona, is six stories of concrete, steel, and glass, but it is octagonal, with a domed roof. Inside, at the heart of the building, stands a replica of a traditional log hogan with a dirt floor and a smoke hole that goes up four stories through a shaft to the open sky. It serves as a religious

Figure 2-9
Hand-weaving is a source of income for many Navajo women. This scene, from the 1920s, is still common today.

Neg. no. 14471. Courtesy American Museum of Natural History. (Photo: P.E. Goddard)

symbol and a meditation room. School buildings, chapter houses, information centers, and arts and crafts outlets exhibit other variations in size and design on the circular shape, which symbolizes the earth, and on the domed roof, which symbolizes both mountaintops and the vault of the sky.

Traditional Popular Music

Until the 1940s the most popular musics on the reservation were the different kinds of dance songs from the ceremonials. We have already studied a Yeibichai dance song from Nightway. Corral dance songs from several ceremonies were also popular, but the several different kinds of *Ndáá'* (war dance) songs from Enemyway made up the largest body of traditional popular music. These include Circle Dance, Sway, Two-step, Skip Dance, and Gift songs. Although country and western eclipsed them in the 1960s and 1970s, the traditional songs have found a renewed popularity on the reservation today.

In the 1990s a new recreational pastime called Song and Dance emerged. It makes use of Skip Dance and Two-step songs, and it can take place in any large hall. Couples of all ages, in traditional costumes, participate. Singers or tapes provide the music, and the dancers, identified by large numbered tags, circle the hall while judges note their costumes and dancing skill. Winners receive trophies, and entry fees and donations solicited during the dancing go toward the expenses of the Song and Dance Association hosting the event or for specified benefits such as school programs.

Some traditionalists have objected to *Ndáá'* songs being used in this new, secular context; however, this is only the latest in several new uses. Radio broadcasts have featured Ndáá' songs since the 1930s, and they found a new wave of radio popularity in the 1990s.

> Also known as Squaw Dance songs. Many Native Americans regard the word *squaw* as derogatory, so we use the Navajo term, *Ndáá'*.

The Circle Dance Song "Shizhané'é"

Ndáá' songs are the hit tunes of traditional Navajo life. Compared with the Yeibichai songs, *Ndáá'* songs are easy to sing, though for an outsider they can contain some surprises. Many of them are sung entirely with vocables, but the Circle Dance song "Shizhané'é" (CD 1, Track 8, Transcription 2-5) contains words that can be translated as well. If you play this song a few times and follow the words and music provided here, you should be able to get into the swing of this lively melody. Since you do not have to worry about producing the high falsetto sounds of the Yeibichai songs, you can concentrate on other fine points. Pay attention to the emphases marked with >. See if you can reproduce the nasal tone the Navajos enjoy in their singing. Every phrase ends with

he,   nai   ya

>
> **CD 1/8**
>
> "Shizhané'é" ("I'm in Luck") (1:20). Navajo Circle Dance song from Enemyway. Performed by Albert G. Sandoval, Jr., and Ray Winnie. Field recording by David P. McAllester. Sedona, Arizona, 1957.

This and the triple meter are characteristic of Circle Dance songs (Mc-Allester 1954:52). Notice how the A phrases introduce the melodic elements that are more fully developed in B and then even more so in C. The whole structure is too long to include on the sound recording.

With permission of Albert Sandoval, Jr. and Ray Winnie.

Transcription 2-5
"Shizhané'é." Navajo Circle Dance song.

The translatable portion of the text, in the C phrases, is like a nugget in the middle of the song, framed by a vocable chorus before and after it. This is a favorite principle of design in other Navajo arts as well as music. It is the dynamic symmetry discussed by Witherspoon (1977:170–74) and illustrated in weaving and silver jewelry designs. The brief, humorous text is, like many another in Navajo song, intended to make the girls laugh and pay attention to the (male) singers. Although the dance is part of a ceremony, it also offers courtship opportunities and serves as a social dance.

The text as it is sung:

Shizhané'é, shizhané'é, kiya sizini shika nóotaał, 'aweya he nai ya.

Free translation:

I'm in luck, I'm in luck!

She's leaning up against the store front,

Looking everywhere for me!

Text, "Shizhané'é" Navajo Enemyway Circle Dance Song. (See note on pronunciation on following page.)

With the permission of Albert Sandoval Jr. and Ray Winnie.

As the Navajo is spoken, with literal translation:

shizhané	me-good luck
kíyah	house-under/against
sizíní	standing-the one who
shíká	me-for/after (as in running after one)
nóotááł	searching for (3rd person)

Linger for a moment on the choices of expression that make the words so witty. The song begins with fatuous self-congratulation. But then we learn both from the form "yah" after "house" and from the neuter static form of *sizíní*, "the one who is standing," that the girl is really propped against the house. The suggestion is that she has had too much to drink and therefore is unable to be actively searching for ("running after") the singer at all, even though he claims she is. The irony of the situation combines with a jesting implication that women drink too much and chase after young men. Because it is actually the men who do most of the drinking and chasing after the opposite sex, the song is all the funnier. *Kiyah sizíní* also carries the meaning "prostitute." As in all clever poetry, the zest comes from the subtle shades of meaning.

Note on Pronunciation in Navajo

The ´ indicates a glottal stop, as in "oh-oh!" (ó-ó)

ł   is like the Welsh ll in Flloyd, unvoiced with the breath coming out on either side of the tongue.

aa   indicates a long "a"   likewise: oo and other vowels

ą   indicates a nasal "a"   likewise o and other vowels

é   indicates a high "e:"   Navajo has speech tones like Chinese.

ée   indicates a long "e" falling from high to low in tone

Vowels have "Continental values."

The Enemyway Ceremony

Religion is one of the keys to understanding culture. We can know the Navajos better if we take a closer look at the Enemyway ceremony in which "Shizhané'é" is used. Enemyway is one of the most frequently performed rites in traditional Navajo religion. Like Nightway, it is a curing ritual. In this case the sickness is brought on by the ghosts of outsiders who have died. Enemyway is often performed for a returned Navajo member of the United States Armed Forces or for others who have been away from home among strangers for a long time. A Navajo who has been in a hospital and returns home cured, in our sense, may have an Enemyway performed because of the inevitable exposure to the spirits of the many non-Navajos who have died in such a place (see Figure 2-10).

The ceremony involves two groups of participants, the "home camp" and the "stick receiver's camp." Members of the latter represent the enemy and are custodians of a stick decorated with symbols of the warrior deity,

Courtesy Andy Tsihnahjinnie.

Figure 2-10
This scene by the Navaho painter Andy Tsihnahjinnie shows drumming, singing, and dancing at the public part of an Enemyway ceremony.

Enemy Slayer, and of his mother, Changing Woman, who is the principal Navajo deity. The decorated stick is brought from the home camp along with gifts of many yards of brightly colored yarn. The first night of the ceremony consists of singing and dancing at the stick receiver's camp. This event offers the only time in traditional Navajo life that men and women dance together–a time for fun and courtship. Before the dancing starts a concert of Sway songs takes place. Although these may express the courtship theme, the majority of the Sway songs have texts entirely of vocables.

Text, Navajo Enemyway Sway Song

Heye yeye ya,
    Lonesome as I am,
    Lonesome as I am, *ha-i na,*
    Lonesome as I am,
    Lonesome as I am, *ha,*
    Lonesome as I am, *na'a- ne hana. . . .*

Text, Navajo Sway song. David P. McAllester, *Enemy Way Music,* pp. 29, 37. Papers of the Peabody Museum of Archaeology and Ethnology, vol. 41, no. 3. Copyright © 1954 by the President and Fellows of Harvard College.

After an hour or so, the singing shifts to dance songs and the women appear, looking for partners. That the women always choose perhaps reflects the powerful position of women in Navajo society. They own the household; the children belong to the mother's clan, not the father's; and when a couple marry the husband traditionally moves in with his wife's family.

In the dance the women tend to act bashful, but they find partners and the couples dance along together following other couples in a large circle. The dance is simply a light stepping along with a bounce on each step. When a woman wants to change partners, she lets the man know by demanding a token payment. Even some Navajos do not know that this is a symbol of the war booty brought back by Enemy Slayer from a mythical war and given away to Navajo women in the story in celebration of the victory. The song texts of the dance songs often poke fun at the women and sometimes refer to these payments.

Text, Navajo Enemyway Dance Song

He-ne, yane, yana-,
  Yala'e-le- yado'eya 'ana he,
  Yala'e-le- yado'eya ne. . . .

Your daughter, at night,
Walking around, *yado'eya yana hana,*
Tomorrow, money,
Lots of it, there will be, yana hana,

  Yala'e-le- yado'eya na'ana,
  Yala'e-le- yado'eya na'ana he. . . .

Text, Navajo Enemyway Dance song. David P. McAllester, *Enemy Way Music,* p. 45. Papers of the Peabody Museum of Archaeology and Ethnology, vol. 41, no. 3. Copyright © 1954 by the President and Fellows of Harvard College.

After a few hours of dancing, a Signal song indicates that the singing is to go back to Sway songs (McAllester 1954:27). The dancing stops, but the Sway songs may go on for the rest of the night. Again, the ceremony symbolizes war: The group of singers is divided into two halves, representing the home camp and the enemy, and the singers compete in vigor, repertory, and highness of pitch.

They stop at dawn, but after a rest and breakfast a new kind of singing, a serenade of Gift songs, takes place. The home camp people sing outside the main hogan of the stick receiver's camp; in exchange, small gifts such as oranges and boxes of Cracker Jack are thrown to the singers through the smoke hole. Larger gifts such as expensive blankets are brought out and handed to responsible members of the singing group; these presents will be reciprocated later in the ceremony. Most of the Gift songs are old and have text entirely in vocables, but a few of the newer ones have words concerning the hoped-for gifts.

Text, Navajo Enemyway Gift Song

Heye yeye yana,
Your skirts, how many? *yi-na,*
To the store I'm going, *'e hyana heye yeye ya,*
To Los Nores I'm going, *'e hya 'ena hya na. . . .*

'e-ye yeye yana,
Goats, I came for them, *yo'o'o 'ene hanena,*
Goats, I came for them, *yo'o'o 'ene hahe,*
Yo'o'o 'ena heye yeye yana. . . .

The gifts, like the payments during the dancing, represent war booty: The trip of the home party can be seen as a raid into enemy country and the gifts as the booty they take home with them. But reconciliation is symbolized at the same time, because the stick receiver's camp provides supper and camping facilities and because the meal and gifts will be returned in a similar exchange on the third morning.

After the breakfast and gift singing on the second day, the stick receiver's party prepares to move toward the home camp. Most of the home camp people leave early, but one of them remains as an official guide to lead the stick receiver to a good camping place a few miles from the home camp. They time their arrival to take place at about sundown, and another night of singing and dancing follows at this new camp.

Early the next morning the war symbolism of the ceremony is sharply emphasized with a sham battle. The stick receiver's people ride into the home camp with yells and rifle shots, raising a lot of dust and committing small depredations such as pulling down clotheslines. After four such charges they retire to a new campsite a few hundred yards away, where a procession from the home camp brings them a sumptuous breakfast. After the meal, the return gift singing takes place at the hogan of the one-sung-over.

Now comes further, heavy war drama. In a secret indoor ritual the afflicted person is given power and protection by sacred chanting and is dressed for battle. At the climax of the ceremony he goes forth and shoots at a trophy of the enemy, thus ritually killing the ghost. The songs used to prepare the warrior include long derisive descriptions of the enemy and praise of Navajo warriors (Haile 1938:276–84). If the person being sung over is a woman, a male proxy takes her place in shooting the enemy ghost.

In the late afternoon a Circle Dance is performed at the stick receiver's new camp. Men join hands in a circle, the two halves of which represent the two camps. At this point they compete with songs like "Shizhané'é" (CD 1, Track 8; Transcription 2-5). The two sides of the circle take turns singing to see who can sing the best songs most beautifully. As the songs alternate, so does the direction in which the Circle Dance moves. Most of the songs have no translatable words, and those that do are not overtly about war; however, the presence of the two competing sides is a reminder of conflict, and it is thought that every drumbeat accompanying the songs drives the enemy ghosts farther into the ground. After a while a girl carrying the stick and several other women may enter the circle and walk around, following the direction of the dancing men. The symbols of Changing Woman and her warrior son incised on the sacred stick remind participants further of the dance's meaning.

After the Circle Dance, another dramatic event takes place: The secret war name of the afflicted person is revealed. Members of the stick receiver's camp walk over to the home camp, singing as they go. Four times on the way, they stop and shout out the identity of the enemy. Then the stick receiver sits down in front of the ceremonial hogan and sings four songs that mention the name of the enemy and that of the one-sung-over. In traditional Navajo life it is impolite to address anyone by name and, in particular, by his or her war name. Polite address uses a kinship term, real or fictitious. Examples of war names are "She Went Among War Parties" and "He Ran Through Warriors" (Reichard 1928:98–99).

The songs describe battle with the enemy and refer to the anguish of the enemy survivors. The death of the enemy ghost is mentioned. Then, after a serenade of Sway songs, the stick receiver's party move back to the dance ground at their camp, and the last night of the ceremony begins with a further selection of Sway songs. After an hour or so the singing changes to dance songs and dancing, which, as on the previous two nights, may go on for several hours. Again the Signal song indicates the end of dancing, and the rest of the night is spent in Sway song competition between the two camps.

At dawn the ceremony ends with a brief blessing ritual conducted while participants face the rising sun. The stick receiver's party departs, and the afflicted person, now protected by the many symbolic ways in which the ghost has been eliminated, spends four days in rest and quiet while the effect of the ceremony settles into the entire household.

The "Classical" Music of the Navajos

We have listened so far to examples of the public or popular music in two Navajo ceremonials, as well as a relatively new kind of popular music, Navajo country and western. Next we shall consider the music at the core of Navajo traditional religious philosophy, the great ceremonial chants. These long series of songs accompany ritual procedures such as those for Nightway (purifications, prayer offerings, and sandpainting rituals) and Enemyway (preparation of the drum and decorated stick, dressing the one-sung-over, and giving him or her power and protection). Figure 2-11 shows yet another ceremonial chant, the Mountainway.

These chants are "classic" for several reasons. They represent a tradition generations old (no one knows how many). They also have enormous scope—one chant may contain over five hundred songs, and the texts comprise many thousands of lines of religious poetry. Finally, they contain in their prayers and songs, and in the related myths they present, the meaning the Navajos find in the natural and supernatural worlds.

Figure 2-11
Navajo fire dance from the Mountainway ceremony. The dancers represent fire deities who have come to help a sick person recover.

Neg. no. 127657, Courtesy American Museum of Natural History.

The performance of the chants may be brief or extended depending on the needs of the one-sung-over, the person to be cured. Excerpts of a few hours may suffice, but an extended version lasting as many as nine nights may be needed. To understand why, we need to consider the Navajo conception of illness.

The Navajos recognize the disease theory of the Euro-American world, and they gladly take advantage of hospitals, surgery, and antibiotics. In addition, however, they see bad dreams, poor appetite, depression, and injuries from accidents as results of disharmony with the world of nature. Although this view resembles Western psychiatry and psychosomatic medicine in many ways, the Navajos go still further. They see animals, birds, insects, and the elements of earth, water, wind, and sky as active potencies that directly influence human life. Each of these forces may speak directly to human beings and may teach them the songs, prayers, and ritual acts that make up the ceremonials. At the center of this relationship with the natural world is the concept of *hózhǫ́ǫ́* (beauty, blessedness, harmony), which must be maintained and which, if lost, can be restored by means of ritual. The prayers invoke this state over and over at their conclusions.

Hózhǫ́ǫ́ nahasdlíí',
Hózhǫ́ǫ́ nahasdlíí',
Hózhǫ́ǫ́ nahasdlíí',
Hózhǫ́ǫ́ nahasdlíí',!

Conditions of harmony have been restored,
Conditions of harmony have been restored,
Conditions of harmony have been restored,
Conditions of harmony have been restored!

Text, Concluding Phrase of Navajo Prayer

The ceremonial chants, some fifty of them, dramatize the Navajo creation story, an interlocking network of myths as long and complex as Greek mythology or the Vedas of India. No one person knows the entire story, but the tradition lives in the remarkable memories of several hundred ceremonial practitioners, men and women called "singers" (*hatáálí*) in Navajo. They direct the dance, art, and theater; chant the music; and recite the prayers that constitute these extraordinary achievements of the human spirit. They learn in the oral tradition as apprentices over many years. Some of these practitioners teach religion at such culturally oriented schools as the Rough Rock Demonstration School, near Chinle, Arizona, and the Navajo Community College at Tsaile, Arizona. One practitioner has dictated his life story, a narrative of over three hundred pages. Excerpts from this remarkable account are presented below.

No complete recording of a ceremonial is available on commercial discs or tapes, and there are very few commercial recordings of even one of the thousands of songs that make up this great literature of religious music. The main reason for the scarcity is that most singers feel these matters are too sacred to be made public. Often the concern is expressed that an uninitiated person might use one of these songs improperly, through ignorance, and cause great harm to the community or, worse yet, rob the song of its potency. Although the singers who recorded the next song (CD 1, Track 9) did not share this belief, out of respect for the feelings of those who do I present only a fragment of the song and give the text only in translation here.

CD 1/9

Navajo Sacred Prayer (0:59). Episode from Navajo Shootingway ceremony. Led by Dinet Tsosie. Field recording by David P. McAllester. Lukachukai, Arizona, 1958.

Text, Navajo Shootingway Song

I have been searching everywhere,
   Over the earth,
   That is what I was told to do,
I have been searching everywhere,
   Over the earth.

I have been searching everywhere,
   Over the mountains,
   That is what I was told to do,
I have been searching everywhere,
   Over the mountains.

I have been searching everywhere,
   Under the sun,
   That is what I was told to do,
I have been searching everywhere,
   Under the sun.

I have been searching everywhere,
   For the fire,
   That is what I was told to do,
I have been searching everywhere,
   For the fire.

I have been searching everywhere,
   With water,
   That is what I was told to do,
I have been searching everywhere,
   With water.

    The song form is characteristic of ceremonial music. There is an intro-
duction on the tonic, after which a chorus in vocables begins. The melody
may be restricted, as in this case, to only three or four notes, or it may move
about with a range of an octave or more. In any case, the interest of the
music is in the many subtle variations of a highly repetitive form. A section
of the chorus is usually repeated at the end of each verse in a kind of
refrain, adding still further to the feeling of repetition.

    Shootingway is a ceremonial that reenacts that part of the creation
myth in which a hero, Holy Young Man, goes in search of supernatural
power. Before his adventures end he has lived among snake people, fish
people, and buffalo people and has been carried up into the sky by thunder
people. In the sky he was taught the Shootingway ceremonial by the Sun
so that this knowledge might be brought back to earth for the protection
of humankind. The ceremony has many purposes, such as the restoration
of harmony between people, and snakes, water, and lightning. A person
suffering from snakebite might go to the hospital for treatment and later
undergo Shootingway in order to end the bad relations with the snake
people that led to the snakebite in the first place.

    The Shootingway song tells about Holy Young Man's journey to the
snake country. He is singing to the Sun, whom he met when he was in the
mountains, and he tells about a fire that he saw glimmering in the distance
at night when he was camping. Each day he tried to find the fire and this is
what led him at last into the snake country. He married four beautiful
snake wives and thus became related to these powerful creatures. During
his stay among them he was given their power to take back to earth. Today,
when someone is having trouble with the snake people, the restoration of
harmony can be achieved by the ceremonial reenactment of this episode in
Shootingway.

    Before the song begins, a fire is kindled in the ceremonial hogan and a
symbolic representation of the snake country prepared. To the east, south,
west, and north of the fire, images of snakes are laid out in colored pigments on the ground. A black, zigzag snake about three feet long faces the
fire from the east, and a blue one of the same shape faces the fire from the
south. On the west is a straight white snake and on the north a straight
pink one sprinkled with bits of glittering mica. As the song goes on, the
one-sung-over, in the role of Holy Young Man, walks around the fire stepping over the snakes, thus acting out the journey into the snake country.
The heat of the fire causes all the participants in the ceremony to sweat
profusely in a rite of purification, and a series of other acts also drives out

evil and further identifies the one-sung-over with the protagonist of the myth. To conclude this part of the ritual the singer cools off the people in the hogan by sprinkling them liberally with water shaken from a bundle of eagle feathers. This is the water mentioned in the last verse of the song.

Even this brief account of a fraction of one of the great ceremonials suggests how the music functions in support of an impressive drama. Shootingway is one of the ways the Navajos remind themselves of the sources of their means of dealing with the supernatural. The ceremony depicts the Navajos' view of themselves in relation to the natural world about them.

The beauty of the music, the poetry, the sandpaintings, and the myths that lie behind all of these has attracted the attention of scholars worldwide since the 1890s. Some representative examples of the many books written about Navajo myths and ceremonies are listed in the reference list at the end of this chapter: Matthews 1894, Kluckhohn and Wyman 1940, Haile 1947, Reichard 1950, Witherspoon 1977, McNeley, 1981, Wyman 1983, Farella 1984, and Griffin-Pierce, 1992.

The Life Story of a Navajo Ceremonial Practitioner

Frank Mitchell (Ółta'í Tsoh: "Big Schoolboy") was born near Wheatfields, Arizona, in 1881 (see Figure 2-12). Over the course of his eventful life he was a sheepherder, railroad worker, cook, handyman-interpreter, wagon freighter, headman, tribal council member, and tribal judge. In his early maturity he learned Blessingway, one of the most important Navajo ceremonies, from his father-in-law. How this affected his whole life is told in his autobiography.

There is no other full autobiography of a Navajo singer. The excerpts presented here illustrate the following aspects of Navajo life and music:

- *Repetitive narrative style:* Repetition has already been mentioned as a significant element in the form of Navajo music, narrative, and the other arts.

- *Importance of women:* In the opening we receive a glimpse of a matrilocal, matrilineal family. Traditional Navajo families live in the mother's household, and the children belong to the mother's clan. Women own their own property. It is not surprising that the principal deity is Changing Woman.

- *Traveling about:* The old nomadic lifestyle of the Navajos has not entirely disappeared. Mitchell's childhood memories show what it was like to follow the livestock a hundred years ago.

- *Navajo practicality:* Mitchell became a singer for practical as well as spiritual reasons. The spiritual dimension of his calling can be seen only between the lines.

Mable Bosch

Figure 2-12
Frank Mitchell, Navajo Blessingway singer. Chinle, Arizona, 1957.

- *The value of Navajo songs:* This is stated not in aesthetic terms but in terms of healing the sick, bringing prosperity, and enabling the possessor of certain songs to become a leader in the community.

- *Speech and leadership:* The word for "chief" in Navajo means "one who speaks." The voices of humans and all other creatures are the culminating point of sacred descriptions in prayers and songs. In Navajo thought, wind is the ultimate power and the voice is the wind made articulate.

- *Navajo humor:* The beloved jokester of his large family, Mitchell was known for his ability to keep up the spirits of the participants in a long ceremonial with his ready supply of jokes and funny comments.

Frank Mitchell died in the hospital at Ganado, Arizona, in 1968, a few weeks after he dictated his last paragraphs of the life story that he wanted to leave as a legacy to his children and grandchildren. (All excerpts reprinted with permission from Frisbie and McAllester 1978.)

I was just a small boy when I began to remember things. We happened to be living at a place called Tsaile; that is where I first began to remember things. I remember that I had a grandmother and my mother had some sisters besides herself. In those days a family like that used to stay close together. We moved around together; when we moved from one place to another, we always went in groups.

In those days the men who were singers and performed ceremonies were the only ones who went around and treated the sick. That is what they were occupied with. I had an uncle on my father's side who was very harsh. He would scold us all of the time. One time there was someone sick in the family and they were performing a ceremony. While that was going on we were told not to sleep. Whenever we fell asleep, they would wake us and make us stay awake. Finally I got so sleepy that I could not stay awake any more. I was sitting next to this uncle of mine who was pretty harsh, and I guess that I fell asleep and just rolled over right beside him. My uncle jumped up, grabbed me by the hair on the side of my head, and yanked me up, putting me back down in a sitting position. I could see he was pretty angry. Of course I did not look straight at him; I just glanced sideways over there every now and then to watch him. After that I did not go to sleep again; I just stayed awake for the rest of the ceremony until it was over. Then we were told, "Now you can go to sleep." That was something I remember very plainly because of course I was old enough to remember things then. . . .

The People traveled mostly on horseback; when we moved with the sheep we used horses to carry our belongings. We, being children, of course had to go along. Whenever the family started moving like that we children would sit in back of the rider. We were small and fell asleep sometimes, so they used to take anything they could find and tie us around the waist to the rider so we would not fall off. That is the way we moved around, tied to the riders so we could sleep sitting on those horses. The main reason for moving around like that was to look for new grazing ground and water for the sheep and horses. [pp. 29–30]

The leaders who went around recruiting children for school talked to the People about what the advantages would be in the future if they would put their children in school. The People would get angry and say, "No, absolutely not! I'm not going to give up my child; while I'm still alive I'm not going to turn my child over to those foreigners. Outsiders are not going to take my child away while I am still living." That's what they used to say. They would sometimes get out a butcher knife and toss it in front of those doing the recruiting and say, "Well, go ahead, cut my throat first; you'll have to do that before you can take my child." [p. 57]

At school we just went by the bell. It was a big bell like the one they have there by the cattleguard at the Franciscan church here in Chinle. At a certain hour we would go to bed. Every time that bell rang, it meant that we had to get in line, or go to bed, or get up and get ready for breakfast, or dinner, or supper. . . . [p. 63]

After awhile I thought I had had enough of school life so I took the first chance I got when I heard of some work that was available down on the railroad. The reason that I did not stay at school was because another boy, a schoolmate of mine, and I planned together to work on the railroad in the west somewhere. We planned this secretly, skipped out from school and went down on the railroad. The Navajos were already working on the railroad then, the railroad that was coming out of California, around Needles, and all down this way. So without telling my folks or his where we were going, we sneaked off. . . . [pp. 68–69]

Everybody at home started to get suspicious about where we were and my late uncle, my mother's brother whom we called Old Man Short Hair, inquired around and learned that it was likely we were with the railroad crew somewhere in the west. So he went in to Gallup and asked to work on the railroad. Of course he really did not want a job; he just wanted to look for us. . . . After my uncle overtook us and worked with us for a while, the railroad moved our crew back toward Flagstaff to a place called Seligman, Arizona, at the other side of Ash Fork. They had a railroad camp there where we all worked for a while. Then we were told, "You'll have to move now, go back to your country. There is no more work here. . . ." [pp. 80–81]

[Editor's note: Because Mitchell knows a little English he finds various jobs at trading posts, a mission, and a sawmill. He marries, obtains a wagon from the government, and becomes a freighter, hauling supplies from Gallup, New Mexico, to Chinle.]

Later on I came back over here because my wife's parents were getting pretty old and sick. I gave up hauling freight and started tending their farm and livestock. My father-in-law was a well-to-do man: he had cattle and sheep and horses and I just started taking care of them for him. Also, I knew that he was a Blessingway singer and I went out with him whenever he performed this ceremony. I noticed that the songs I learned from He Who Seeks War were the same as the ones my father-in-law was singing.

Before I began to learn these things, way back before that, I did not even think about life as being an important thing. I did not try to remember things or keep track of what happened at certain times. Nothing seemed to matter to me, I just didn't care about anything, so long as I kept on living. But then when I began to learn the Blessingway it changed my whole life. I began really thinking about ceremonies. I had heard singing before that but now I began to take it more seriously because I began to realize what life was and the kind of hardships we have to go through. Before I started learning Blessingway, the older people used to tell me that I should think about life more seriously. "If you don't know any songs you have nothing to go by. If a child grows up in a family like that he doesn't know where he is going or what he is doing." That is what the older people told me, that I should have something to live by. . . . I used to go out with my father-in-law, Man Who Shouts, whenever he was asked to perform the Blessingway. I went wherever he did. At first I just watched and then finally I had learned practically everything he was doing and before I knew it I was helping him with the ceremony. Finally I reached the point where I had learned it well enough so that I had a ceremony of my own. . . . [pp. 192–93]

[My father-in-law said to me,] "If you are a singer, if you remember your ceremonies really well even if you get old, even if you get blind and deaf, you'll still remember everything by heart, how each part of the ceremony is performed." He said to me, "Even though you are so old you can't ride a horse or you can't even see anymore, people will still have a use for you until old age finally finishes you off."

So that is why I chose that way of life. And I believe it now: it is true that even as old as I am now, unable to get around too much, people still come to have my ceremony done over them. I have it inside my head so well that I remember everything and even though I can't get around they come in a wagon or a car for me and take me over to where the ceremony is needed and then bring me back. So I think my father-in-law was right. If I had decided to be a farmer at that time I probably wouldn't have lasted very long. [pp. 193–94]

It is a custom with the People that, for instance, some family, even though everything may be going all right and nothing is wrong, still may say, "Well, let's have a Blessingway to freshen things up, to renew ourselves again." So they do. Or sometimes they might have acquired some valuable goods, if they have been off trading or something, and have brought them home. Then the things that they brought in from other places, well, it is on their minds that, "That's what we're blessed with in this family." They might feel they need the Blessingway because you do not wait until some misfortune happens before you have it. That is the reason it is called the peaceful way, the healing way, the blessing way. There is no specific time . . . it depends on the family. If they feel they should have it, then they do it, just an ordinary Blessingway.

Of course if you are able to have that ceremony, if you have the means to put it on, well, then you should do it. But if you have not, then in that case you just keep putting it off until you are able to bear the cost. . . .

Blessingway is used for everything that is good for a person, or for the people. It has no use other than that. For instance, when a woman is pregnant she has the Blessingway in order to have a good delivery with no trouble. It is also done so that she and her child may have a happy life. In case of bad dreams it is a kind of warning that there are some misfortunes ahead of you; in order to avoid that you have Blessingway so that you will have happiness instead. Or if you are worried about something, your family will want to get you back, to get that out of your mind, out of your system, so that you may have a good life. It is the same for any other things that could cause you to worry, to feel uneasy about yourself. That is the sort of thing it is used for. As for the prayers, you say, "Beauty shall be in front of me, beauty shall be in the back, beauty shall be below me, above me, all around me." On top of that you say about yourself, "I am everlasting, I may have an everlasting life with beauty." You end your prayers that way. . . . [pp. 218–19]

I remember all that I know about the Blessingway because I had those years of study to get it all in my head. And from my experience of learning I understand that it is not just my ability that makes it possible. I believe that there is a spirit that really is answering my prayers, because all these years I would not have been able to learn so much if I did not have such help. I could not do it by myself, so there must be something beyond human power helping me. . . . [pp. 237–38]

In Navajo religion there are prayers for certain purposes. I found out from my own father that in Blessingway there was a song for headman, and I learned that from him. I think that this is another reason why things came easily for me when I was talking to the People. It may be one reason that I was recognized for being a talker and a leader among the People, why I became well known as a headman and even eventually ended up in the Tribal Council. . . . [p. 241]

There are lots of songs that go with being a headman or leader. They start out from the beginning, way back with the first people. The story starts with how it was planned at first and how the first people decided who were to be the chiefs. After these chiefs were elected, the songs go along describing how they were dressed. They tell about all of the things they were wearing, their shoes, leggings, sash and skirts, belts, wristlets and beads, their head plumes and everything up to the last thing, that which is put in their mouths from which their speeches are known. That last thing is like the power to speak; it was put into their mouths so they could have the wisdom to say wise things and so the People could under-stand them. There are enough of those songs to sing them all night with-out sleeping. The songs are used in a series, but they are not just to be sung any place. You can only use them when someone is going to be a chief, a good leader; they can have the songs done for them. There are so many songs in that series that you could almost have a Blessingway done with them; there are just about as many songs involved in that as there are in the Blessingway itself. From the start to the end of that, the whole thing is like a Blessingway. The story of the songs are just like Blessingway right from the beginning: how the earth was first formed, how the mountains came up. The songs go on like that. It would probably take a little longer to do than the regular Blessingway; it is just like Blessingway when you do that except that the ceremony is mostly just singing. Almost all of what takes place is the singing of the Chief songs. . . . [p. 244]

Once I was placed there as one of the councilmen, I began to be asked to do different things. One of the things that there was a lot of talk about during this time was education and the need for building schools on the reservation. We also talked about hospitals and preventing outsiders from moving in with different things like industrial plants. We did a lot of work and I concerned myself with all those things. . . . [p. 256] We talked about that a lot on the Council, and we decided to ask for the schools and also hospitals and all of those things from Washington.

Several of us were then appointed to go to Washington to ask that these things be granted. I went over there with several other men. We went before those people and asked for a school and a hospital and other things. Henry Taliman, the tribal chairman, Howard Gorman, the vice-chairman, and Red Moustache's brother were some of the others who went over there, too. We were asked to fly there but most of the delegates were afraid of going in an airplane, so we went on the train. While we were there we were given sight-seeing tours around Washington. I got to see the White House, Arlington Cemetery, the Unknown Soldier's Tomb, and other places. One of the delegates got tired when we were near the Washington Monument. He wanted to rest but he could not find a place to sit down. So he took off his moccasins and laid down on the grass in front of the Monument. He was wearing half-socks like the ones I used to knit for myself. This man went to sleep and while he was sleeping a crowd gathered around looking at him. When he woke up he asked me, "What are all of these people standing around here looking at me for?" I said, "My younger brother, they are waiting for you to get up to see what kind of a creature you are. They are wondering whether or not when you get up you will crawl on all fours, like a bear." He replied, "You bear, you would say that." [pp. 257–58]

While I, myself, stand for the good of the People, right now I am just watching these things. I cannot step in there and try to do some of the things I used to do because I am getting pretty well along in years. So I just sit by and watch. I think about the future; of course I may never get to see it, but I just wonder how things will be in so many years, what improvements there will be for the benefit of the People. I wish I were young again, so I could see more of these things as time goes on. But those are just wishes and of course I do not expect to see those things. . . . [pp. 310–11]

In the early days, the old people were our teachers. They said that as long as we observed the rules laid down for us by the Holy People, everything was going to go along smoothly. But they said it would not last forever. Sooner or later we were going to start breaking the rules. Then that would lead us to ruin. It is like a seed of any kind, like corn, or beans, or anything that you put in the ground. You plant it, and it sprouts and bears fruit and grows to a certain extent. When it matures you harvest what it has produced; the stalks and leaves wither because their use is past. But you still have the seeds to continue planting and arriving at a new life. That is what the older people taught us. If you did not observe these things you are bound to ruin yourself. . . . [p. 311]

When you get put into a position of leadership, that teaches you to have some respect. Even if you have been irresponsible in the past, you now have to behave and lead a good life as an example to your people. [p. 315]

There are still lots of people coming around here wanting me to do Blessingway for them, but sometimes now because of my physical condition I have to refuse. When they come to ask, it just depends on how I feel. If I think that I can stand it, then I accept. . . . But a lot of the time now I'm not able to sing Blessingway. I can't stand the strain of being in a sitting position for that long, and my voice also gets tired. I especially feel the strain in the wintertime. The nights are long then, and performing that Blessingway is very strenuous even though we wait to start the all-night singing until pretty well on into the night. Of course in the summertime the nights are short. I will do Blessingway again when I get well and when I think that I am able to do it.

As you know, last fall I had my sacred bundle renewed and, of course, a Blessingway was used for that. But even though I had that and all of the other ceremonials I've been telling you about, right now my ailments are still hanging on. I still think we have not done the complete cure. The doctors do not seem to be able to tell me what the matter is, either. I went over to the Ganado hospital and they thoroughly examined my body. They could not find anything anywhere that could be causing my troubles. Finally they decided to take some tissue out of my stomach, just a small piece. I was not really operated on then. The doctor just said that there was no equipment there at Ganado to analyze what they had taken out of me, and that he would send it to Denver to find out what it was. They gave me some medicine and told me to go home. . . . [pp. 321–22]

While I was over at the Ganado hospital, and even before I went there, I had a lot of dreams and most of them were about dead people, those who had already passed away, even women. Those things were beginning to bother me; I was worrying about them. So I decided to have another ceremony. I also wanted to see if I could get some relief from the pains that I was feeling a lot of time. So I went and asked Black Sheep from Black Mountain to come over here and perform some of his small ceremonies for me to see if those could straighten out my dreams and give me some relief from those pains. He came down here and did some Ghostway rituals for me. He said prayers, cut prayersticks, bathed me and painted me with the blackening and reddening ceremonies. You can do those things to find out what effect they will have. If you feel a bit better after those, then you can go ahead and have the big ceremonial. After he did that I don't remember having any more dreams. I just forgot all about them. Before those things were done, as soon as I woke up, I would begin to think about what I had been dreaming about, but since then I do not do that any more. I still dream, but I do not remember what those dreams are about. I have felt a little better since Black Sheep performed all of those things for me, and right now I am thinking about calling him back again for a big, regular five-night Ghostway. Then, maybe I will go back to the hospital again. . . . [p. 323]

The Native American Church

In their comparatively recent history the Navajos have felt the call of two highly organized religious movements from outside their traditional culture. One is evangelical Christianity. The other is the Native American Church, an Indian movement with roots in ancient Mexico and recent development in Oklahoma. This religion established itself firmly in the United States in the nineteenth century and thereafter developed different perspectives and music from that which can still be seen among the Tarahumare and Huichol Indians of Mexico. It found its way into the Navajo country in the 1930s. By the 1950s it had grown in this one tribe to a membership estimated to be twenty thousand.

This music differs strikingly from traditional Navajo music. Let us listen to a hymn from the Native American Church and then consider the role of this music in contemporary Navajo life (CD 1, Track 10, Transcription 2-6).

What may strike you first is the quiet, introspective quality of the singing in this simple melody. Members of the Native American Church speak of their music as prayer. Although the text has no translatable words, the repetitive simplicity of vocables and music expresses a rapt, inward feeling. According to one theory, Native American Church hymns are derived from Christian hymnody. The quiet, slow movement and the unadorned voice, so unlike the usual boisterous, emphatic, out-of-doors

CD 1/10

Hymn of the Native American Church. (1:10). Navajo Peyote song. Performed by George Mitchell and Kaya David. Field recording by Willard Rhodes, n.d. Archive of Folk Song of the Library of Congress AFS 14. LP. Washington, D.C.

Transcription 2-6
Navajo Peyote song.

Transcription by David P. McAllester from field recording by Willard Rhodes. With permission of Willard Rhodes.

delivery in Indian singing, support this interpretation. On the other hand, the music shows many more features that are all Indian: the rhythmic limitation to only two note values, ♪ ♩ (a specialty of Navajo and Apache music), the descending melodic direction, the rattle and drum accompaniment, the pure melody without harmony, the use of vocables. These features are present in Native American Church music in many different tribes all across the continent to such a marked extent that one can identify a distinct, pantribal "Peyote style" (McAllester 1949:12, 80–82). In the present song, every phrase ends on "he ne yo," anticipating the "he ne yo we" of the last phrase. This ending, always sung entirely on the tonic, is as characteristic of Native American Church music as "Amen" is to Christian hymns and prayers.

True to its Oklahoma origin, the Native American Church ideally holds its meetings in a large Plains Indian tepee. This is often erected on Saturday evening for the all-night meeting and then taken away to be stored until the next weekend. Such mobility enables the meeting to move to wherever members want a service. Meetings are sometimes held in hogans because they, too, are circular and have an earth floor where the sacred fire and altar can be built.

The members of the Native American Church use a water drum and a rattle to accompany their singing. The drum is made of a small, three-legged iron pot with a wet, almost rubbery, buckskin drumhead stretched over the opening (see Figure 2-13). The pot is half full of water, which is splashed over the inside of the drumhead from time to time by giving the drum a tossing motion. This act serves to keep the drumhead moist and flexible while in use. The player kneels, holding the drum on the ground tipped toward his drumming hand. He controls the tone with pressure on the drumhead from the thumb of his holding hand. He strikes the membrane rapidly and rather heavily with a smooth, hard, slightly decorated drumstick. The water inside the pot most likely contributes to the strong resonance of this and other kinds of water drums, but no physical studies have yet been made to test the theory.

The peyote rattle is made with a small gourd mounted on a handle stick in much the same way as the cowhorn rattle of the Iroquois (see pp. 44–46. There is no carved shelf on the handle, however: Instead, the stick is merely wedged tightly into the gourd plug. The far end of the stick protrudes two or three inches beyond the gourd, and a tuft of dyed horse-hair is attached to it. This is often red to symbolize the red flower of the peyote cactus. Many Native American Church members hold a beautifully decorated feather fan during the service and use it to waft toward themselves the fragrant incense of cedar needles when these are put into the fire. The feathers of the fan are mounted in separate movable leather sleeves, like the feathers of the Plains war bonnet. This allows the user to manipulate the fan so that each feather seems to have a quivering life of its own.

The ritual consists of long prayers, many groups of four songs each (sung in turn by members of the meetings), a special water break at midnight, and a fellowship breakfast in the morning. At intervals, under the direction of the leader of the meetings, a Cedar Chief builds up the fire, puts cedar incense on the coals, and passes the cigarettes to make the sacred smoke that accompanies the prayers. He also passes small pieces of a cactus called *peyote* (from the Aztec *peyotl,* "wooly," describing the fine white hairs that grow in tufts on the cactus). When eaten, peyote produces a sense of well-being and, sometimes, visions in vivid color. The peyote is eaten as a sacrament, because Father Peyote is one of the deities of the religion. The Native American Church is sometimes called the Peyote Church.

A crescent-shaped earthen altar six or seven feet long lies west of the fire, and a large peyote cactus, symbolic of Father Peyote, is placed at the midpoint of the crescent. Prayers may be directed to Father Peyote, and some members can hear him responding to their pleas for help in meeting the difficulties of life. The intense feeling of dedication and piety at Peyote Meetings is expressed through prayers and testimonies, often with tears running down the cheeks of the speaker. Prayers include appeals to Jesus and God, as well as to Father Peyote. Peyotists consider the Native American Church to be hospitable to all other religions and include their ideas in its philosophy and beliefs. Members pray for friends and family members who are ill or otherwise in need of help. They also include leaders of the church, of the Navajo tribe, and of the country at large in their prayers.

In the past the Native American Church was bitterly opposed by the more tradition-minded Navajos; in the late 1940s meetings were raided by the police and church leaders were jailed. But the church constituency grew so large that the new religion had to be accepted, and today the tepees for peyote meetings can be seen in many Navajo communities. One of these tepees stands near the Cultural Center of the Navajo Community College, where participation in the Native American Church's meetings is a recognized student activity.

The Water Drum

Widespread in North and South America, the water drum is the only drum used in traditional Navajo and Apache music. The Navajos make theirs on a clay pot eight or ten inches high and use an unusual drumstick made of a twig bent around and tied in a loop at the far end. The Apaches use the same kind of drumstick but make the drum out of a large iron pot. The buckskin drumhead is stretched over an opening two or two-and-a-half feet across, and several of the singers beat the drum at the same time. A deep booming sound is produced, in contrast to the softer thump of the Navajo drum (see Figure 2-13).

The Iroquois and the Chippewas in the Eastern Woodlands make water drums using a hollowed-out log or a wooden keg. They do not have the looped drumstick but use a straight stick somewhat carved or, as in the case of the medicine drum of the Menomini, a somewhat elaborate curved stick. Eastern Woodland water drums range from five or six inches to two feet or more in height and from five or six inches across the drumhead to as many as fourteen inches or more.

The peyote drum seems to be an elaboration on the pot drum of the Navajos and Apaches. Nowadays the old-fashioned pot is hard to find, and members of the Native American Church can buy a specially manufactured aluminum replica that is much lighter to handle and gives the same sound. The church has also developed its own kinds of jewelry and costume and a genre of Indian painting depicting peyote meetings and peyote visions.

Because the water drum is so widespread in North and South America, students of Native-American music may find insight in making one. The peyote drum is difficult to assemble. It is also so intensely symbolic to members of the Native American Church that it might be in questionable taste for a nonmember to attempt to make this particular kind of water drum. However, the traditional Iroquois, Navajo, and Apache water drums

Figure 2-13
Two kinds of water drum. On the left is an Iroquois drum made from a short section of hollowed-out log. On the right is a Navajo pottery water drum, used only in the Enemyway ceremony.

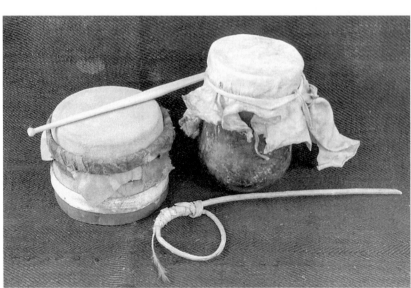

Susan W. McAllester

are used for social dancing and so do not have the same religious feelings associated with them.

Figure 2-14 contains the instructions for making a simple water drum. Iron pots or wooden kegs are hard to find, but a number ten tin can makes a good substitute. Buckskin is also difficult to obtain, but a piece of chamois from an auto supply store or a piece of rubber from an inner tube will work. Indians themselves sometimes use such materials if they cannot obtain the traditional ones.

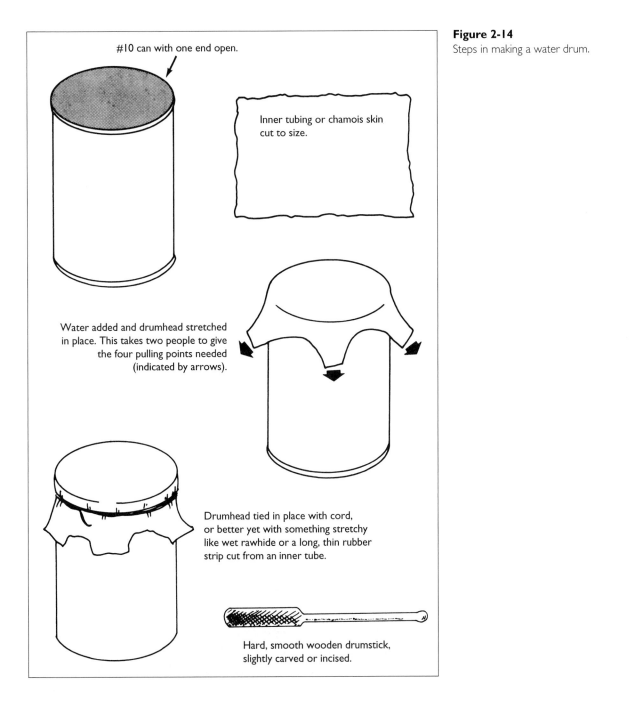

#10 can with one end open.

Inner tubing or chamois skin cut to size.

Water added and drumhead stretched in place. This takes two people to give the four pulling points needed (indicated by arrows).

Drumhead tied in place with cord, or better yet with something stretchy like wet rawhide or a long, thin rubber strip cut from an inner tube.

Hard, smooth wooden drumstick, slightly carved or incised.

Figure 2-14

Steps in making a water drum.

The Sun Dance

Another importation of a Native-American religion, the Plains Sun Dance, has occurred as recently as the 1980s on the Navajo reservation. This world renewal ceremony has undergone a revival on the Plains, and Sun Dance priests have been invited to Navajo communities to perform the ceremony and teach it to Navajo participants.

Navajo Hymn Music

Christian hymns share the popularity of peyote hymns, as evidenced by the requests that come in at the rate of several hundred a week at such radio stations as WGLF in Gallup, New Mexico. The Navajos who have joined the many Christian missions on the reservation appreciate them especially for their ministry. The hospitals, schools, and other services associated with the missions are a boon not only to church members but also to hundreds of other Navajos.

Navajo listeners make requests for particular hymns on the occasion of a birthday in the family, the anniversary of a death, or some other signal family event. When the request and the hymn are broadcast, the occasion is made known to hundreds of listeners. The hymns may be performed by nationally known gospel singers, but Navajo gospel singers as well have made records, and requests tend to favor these. One such group is the Chinle Galileans, a Navajo country gospel group. Their lyrics are in English, and their music is the familiar country combination of electric guitar and percussion (CD 1, Track 11, Transcription 2-7).

Interestingly, this music has few features that could be called traditionally Indian. Like the Fenders (p. 50), the Galileans have adopted a new style of music wholeheartedly. The clues that the performers are Navajos are the

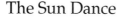

CD 1/11

"Clinging to a Saving Hand" (3:42). Traditional Christian hymn. Performed by the Chinle Galileans. *Navajo Country Gospel* LPS 909. LP. Chinle, Arizona, n.d.

Transcription 2-7
"Clinging to a Saving Hand."

With permission of Roland Dixon.

singers' Navajo accent and, in the case of the Fenders' CD selection, certain melodic and rhythmic shortcuts, compared with the Anglo original. This is what appeals to Navajo listeners and makes them feel that the performing groups are some of "their own."

New Composers in Traditional Modes

A recent genre of Navajo music comprises songs based musically on Enemyway style (usually Sway songs or Dance songs) but not intended for use in that ceremony. The texts are in Navajo, because the songs are intended for Navajo listeners, but they contain a different sort of social commentary from that in the popular songs of Enemyway. The new message is one of protest. For example, we can contrast the treatment of the use of alcohol in the old songs and the new. First we have a Skip Dance song from Enemyway, probably dating from the 1920s.

Text, Enemyway Skip Dance song

'E- ne- ya,

My younger brother,
My whiskey, have some! *Naŋa, he, ne-ye,*

My younger brother,
My whiskey, have some! *Naŋa, he, ne-ye,*

Your whiskey is all gone, *ne,*
My whiskey, there's still some, *wo,*

He yo-o-wo-wo, he yo-o-wo-wo,
Heya, we, heyana, he, nai-ya.

In contrast, "Navajo Inn" speaks of the damaging effects of drinking. It is a recent song by Lena Tsoisdia, who is a social service worker at Window Rock, the headquarters of the Navajo tribal government. The title takes its name from a drive-in liquor store that used to do a thriving business a few miles from Window Rock. The store was just across the reservation boundary and was thus outside the jurisdiction of the tribal prohibition laws. The lyrics refer to the inn and speak despairingly of women finding their husbands, unconscious, behind "the tall fence."

Such protests cover many topics, based on modern problems as well as historical injustice. Ruth Roessel, a prominent Navajo educator, has composed a song about the "Long Walk," when the Navajos were rounded up by Kit Carson and his troops in 1864 and forcibly removed to a large concentration camp at Ft. Sumner, New Mexico (see map, Figure 2-7). The hardships of the march, which preceded four years of captivity, and the Navajo love for their land are recounted here.

Text, "The Long Walk"

Long, long ago, our people,
Our grandfathers, our grandmothers,
Walking that long distance,

There was no food, there was no water,
But they were walking a long distance,
But they were walking a long distance!

At Fort Sumner, it was when they got there
They were treated badly,
They were treated badly.

"I wish I were still back in my own home,
I wish I were still back in my own home!
We shall never forget this,
The walk that we are taking now.
We shall never forget this,
The walk that we are taking now.
Even then, we still like our own land,
Even then, we still like our own land!"

With permission of Ruth Roessel. Translation by Ruth Roessel for David McAllester.

The two examples here have not been recorded commercially, but several Navajo composers of new songs in styles based on Enemyway popular songs have recorded their work on popular discs. Kay Bennett (Kaibah) has produced three records on her own label. Danny Whitefeather Begay, Cindy Yazzie, and Roger McCabe have released *My Beautiful Land* on the Canyon Records label with fifteen popular songs in this new genre. "Los Angeles Sweetheart" by Danny Whitefeather Begay gives an idea of how those songs go. It is in the Skip Dance style as indicated by the formula

he   ye,   ya - na

Text, "Los Angeles Sweetheart"

Heye, yaŋa, heye, yaŋa,

Awe 'a-no 'aweya'a heye, yaŋa,
Awe 'a-no 'aweya'a heye, yaŋa,

Hene ya'o wowo 'awe ya'a heye, yaŋa,
Hene ya'o wowo 'awe ya'a heye, yaŋa,

Oh, that girl, oh, that girl,
To a place called "L.A.," that's where she went,
She went, *aweya'a heye, yaŋa,*
To a place called "L.A.," that's where she went,
She went, *aweya'a heye, yaŋa,*
"All kinds of jobs for you," she wrote,
But she had another man, *'ano 'aweya'a heye, yaŋa,*

Hene ya'o wowo 'awe ya'a heye, yaŋa,
Hene ya'o wowo 'awe ya'a heye, yaŋa.

"Los Angeles Sweetheart" by Danny Whitefeather Begay, from *My Beautiful Land* (ARP-6078). Courtesy Canyon Records.

In this record many of the songs are nostalgic, about Navajos who have left the reservation to find work and wish they could go home again. Others are "flirting songs" referring to the courtship situation at a Ndáá' Dance. The mingling of the new experience in big cities and the traditional dance scene at an Enemyway ceremonial is reflected in the record's cover design, which combines the four sacred mountains, automobiles, hogans, and skyscrapers.

Music with Newly Created Navajo Texts and Melodies

Recently, Navajo music has seen a new genre: music with newly created Navajo texts and melodies. This genre is well-represented by Sharon Burch's "Mother Earth" (CD 1, Track 12) from her tape *Yazzie Girl* (1989). She accompanies herself on a guitar in a chantlike melody of her own composition. "She credits her inspiration as a songwriter to the songs, prayers and chants she recalls from her childhood" (Burch 1989).

CD 1/12

"Mother Earth" (2:57). Sharon Burch. *Yazzie Girl*, by Sharon Burch. Canyon Records CR-534.

Text, "Mother Earth"

Chorus:

Heiyee' t' áá aɬtso baa hózhǫ́ǫgo.	Heiyee' everything brings happiness.
Heiyee' t' áá aɬtso baa hózhǫ́ǫgo.	Heiyee' everything brings happiness.
Heineiyaa.	Heineiyaa.
Nahasdzáán bii' sézí,	I am part of Mother Earth.
Nahasdzáán bikee' shikee'.	Mother Earth's feet are my feet.
Nahasdzáán bijáád shijáád.	Mother Earth's legs are my legs.
Nahasdzáán bidziil shidziil.	Mother Earth's strength is my strength.
Nahasdzáán bigaan shigaan.	Mother Earth's arms are my arms.
Nahasdzáán bináá' hóló, shináá' hóló	Mother Earth has a vision, I have a vision.

(Chorus)

(first five lines of second verse, as in first verse)

Nahasdzáán binitsékees shinitsékees.	Mother Earth's consciousness is my consciousness.

(Chorus)

"Mother Earth," from *Yazzie Girl* (CR-534) by Sharon Burch. (P) © 1989 Sharon Burch. Courtesy Canyon Records Productions.

New Navajo Music with English Texts and Orchestral Accompaniment

Arliene Nofchissey Williams has been called "the Navajo nightingale." Her compositions stem from the Mormon sect of Christianity and express, musically and in words, both her religious perceptions and her Indian-ness. She wrote one of her songs, "Proud Earth" (CD 1, Track 13), when she was

CD 1/13

"Proud Earth" (3:32). Arliene Nofchissey Williams. Performed by Arliene Nofchissey Williams and Chief Dan George. *Proud Earth*. Salt City Records SC-80. LP. Provo, Utah, n.d.

a student at Brigham Young University. Musically, there are such Indian elements as the use of a steady, repetitive drumbeat and vocables, as well as Euro-American elements such as a string orchestra, harmonies, interpretive dynamics, and English text. The use of the voice of the late Chief Dan George, an Indian film star, as narrator adds to the richness of the production. The song has been a "hit" on the Navajo reservation and elsewhere among Indian people. It was produced in Nashville with all the musical technology that the name implies, and a more recent rendition can be heard on Williams (1989).

This song tells the world what the Native Americans feel they have to contribute to world culture from their mythopoeic philosophy of nature. The words reflect the Mormon respect for Native-American culture and the Indian closeness to nature. At the same time, the song conveys the aspiration of the Latter Day Saints to unite the Indian people under one God.

Text, "Proud Earth"
(The Song of the People)

The beat of my heart is kept alive in my drum,
And my plight echoes in the canyons, the meadows, the plains,
And my laughter runs free with the deer,
And my tears fall with the rain,
But my soul knows no pain.

I am one with nature,
Mother Earth is at my feet,
And my God is up above me,
And I'll sing the song of my People.

Come with me, take my hand, come alive with my chant *(heya, heya)*
For my life already knows wisdom, balance and beauty.
Let your heart be free from fear *(heya, heya)*
And your joy meet with mine,
For the peace we can find.

We are one with nature,
Mother Earth is at our feet,
And our God is up above us,
And we'll sing the song, the song of the people *(heya, heya)*,
And we'll sing the song, the song of the people.

"Proud Earth" by Arliene Nofchissey Williams. With permission of Arliene Nofchissey Williams.

The Native-American Flute Revival

The Native-American flute revival probably began in the 1970s in Oklahoma when "Doc Tate" Nevaquaya made the first commercial recording consisting entirely of music of the Plains courting flute (Smythe 1989:68). But it was a Navajo, R. Carlos Nakai, whose moving, improvisatory compositions, often with synthesizer or orchestral accompaniments, carried the instrument to worldwide popularity and created a large following of imitators, both Indian and non-Indian (McAllester 1994).

John Running

Figure 2-15
R. Carlos Nakai, Navajo flutist
and educator.

Nakai's first album appeared in 1982; since then he has made nineteen others to date, one of them in Germany and another in Japan. *Cycles* (1985) was chosen by the Martha Graham Dance Company to provide the music for their ballet *Nightchant.* Nakai has performed with several symphony orchestras and was awarded the Arizona Governor's Arts Award in 1992 and an honorary doctorate by Northern Arizona University in 1994. In that same year, *Ancestral Voices,* his third collaboration with the guitarist William Eaton, was a Grammy Awards finalist in Best Traditional Folk Music.

Here, we shall listen to "Origin," from *Cycles* (CD 1, Track 14). This piece offers an example of his synthesizer improvisation. Nakai comments in the liner notes: "My clan, Naashteezhi dine-e Taachiinii, allows me to be

CD 1/14
"Origins" (4:00). R. Carlos Nakai.
Cycles: *Native American Flute Music.*
Canyon Records Productions
CR614-C 1985. Phoenix, Arizona.

one of the People" (Nakai 1985). In all of his work the commentary accompanying the music stresses respect for the environment and a very Navajo celebration of tribal connections and harmony with nature.

In most of this chapter, we have explored the music of several generations and several religions in an effort to find clues to the thought of just one Indian tribe. Even so we have barely touched on the complexities of this rich and rapidly changing culture. One of the most powerful messages that reaches the outsider is that Indian traditional culture remains vital in its own ways even while Native-American people are adopting new ideas and technology from the Euro-American culture around them. This fact is clearly reflected in the many different kinds of music that co-exist on the Navajo reservation and in thousands of Navajo homes in Chicago, Los Angeles, San Francisco, and many other locations away from the reservation.

To varying degrees this picture of Navajo music exemplifies what is happening to other Indian communities around the country. The different Indian cultures have embarked on an adventure in which the larger population around them must inevitably share. Many Indian elements have already become part of the culture that is called "American." Some of these are relatively superficial: an Indian word such as *squash* or *moose,* or a bit of local legend. Other contributions have had an enormous economic effect, such as the corn and potatoes that feed much of the world. There is now evidence that some of the music and the other Indian arts, and the religious and philosophical ideas that lie beneath them, are becoming accessible to an increasingly sympathetic American public. No culture remains static, and the Indians will continue to contribute to other world cultures, which are themselves in the process of change.

References

Burch, Sharon. 1989. *Yazzie Girl.* Phoenix, Ariz.: Canyon Records CR534. Cassette.

Farella, John R. 1984. *The Main Stalk: A Synthesis of Navajo Philosophy.* Tucson: Univ. of Arizona Press.

Faris, James C. 1990. *The Nightway: A History and a History of Documentation of a Navajo Ceremonial.* Albuquerque: Univ. of New Mexico Press.

Fenton, William. 1942. *Songs from the Iroquois Longhouse.* Washington, D.C.: Smithsonian Institution Publication 369.

———. n.d. *Songs from the Iroquois Longhouse.* Library of Congress AFS L6.

Frisbie, Charlotte J., and David P. McAllester. 1978. *Navajo Blessingway Singer: Frank Mitchell, 1881–1967.* Tucson: Univ. of Arizona Press.

Gill, Sam D. 1981. *Sacred Words: A Study of Navajo Religion and Prayer.* Westport, Conn.: Greenwood Press.

Griffin-Pierce, Trudy. 1992. *Earth Is My Mother, Sky Is My Father: Space, Time, and Astronomy in Navajo Sandpainting.* Albuquerque: Univ. of New Mexico Press.

Haile, Berard. 1938. *Origin Legend of the Navajo Enemy Way.* New Haven, Conn.: Yale Univ. Press.

———. 1947. *Prayerstick Cutting in a Five Night Ceremonial of the Male Branch of Shootingway.* Chicago: Univ. of Chicago Press.

Kluckhohn, Clyde, and Dorothea Leighton. 1938. *The Navajo.* Cambridge, Mass.: Harvard Univ. Press.

Kluckhohn, Clyde, and Leland C. Wyman. 1940. *An Introduction to Navajo Chant Practice.* Menasha, Wis.: Memoirs of the American Anthropological Association, no. 53.

Matthews, Washington. 1894. "Songs of Sequence of the Navajos." *Journal of American Folk-Lore* 7:185–94.

McAllester, David P. 1949. *Peyote Music.* New York: Viking Fund Publications in Antropology, no. 13.

———. 1954. *Enemy Way Music.* Papers of the Peabody Museum of Archaeology and Ethnology, vol. 41, no. 5. Cambridge, Mass.: Harvard Univ. Press.

———. 1994. "The Music of R. Carlos Nakai." In *To the Four Corners: A Festschrift in Honor of Rose Brandel,* edited by Ellen C. Leichtman. Warren, Mich.: Harmonie Park Press.

McNeley, James K. 1981. *Holy Wind in Navajo Philosophy.* Tucson: Univ. of Arizona Press.

Nakai, R. Carlos. 1985. *Cycles: Native American Flute Music.* Phoenix, Ariz.: Canyon Records Productions CR614-C. Cassette.

Reichard, Gladys A. 1928. *Social Life of the Navajo Indians.* New York: Columbia Univ. Press.

———. 1950. *Navajo Religion.* New York: Bollingen Foundation.

Sachs, Curt. 1962. *The Wellsprings of Music.* The Hague: Martinus Nijhof.

Smythe, Willie. 1989. "Songs of Indian Territory." In *Songs of Indian Territory: Native American Music Traditions of Oklahoma.* Oklahoma City, Okla.: Center for the American Indian.

Witherspoon, Gary. 1977. *Language and Art in the Navajo Universe.* Ann Arbor: Univ. of Michigan Press.

Witmer, Robert. 1973. "Recent Change in the Musical Culture of the Blood Indians of Alberta, Canada." *Yearbook for Inter-American Musical Research* 9:64–94.

Wyman, Leland C. 1983. *Southwest Indian Drypainting.* Albuquerque: Univ. of New Mexico Press.

Additional Reading

Bailey, Garrick, and Roberta Glenn Bailey. 1986. *A History of the Navajos: The Reservation Years.* Santa Fe, N. Mex.: School of American Research Press.

Deloria, Vine, Jr. 1969. *Custer Died for Your Sins: An Indian Manifesto.* London: Collier-Macmillan.

Densmore, Frances. 1910. *Chippewa Music.* Washington, D.C.: Bureau of American Ethnology Bulletin 45.

Dyk, Walter. 1966. *Son of Old Man Hat.* Lincoln: Univ. of Nebraska Press.

Goodman, James B. 1986. *The Navajo Atlas: Environments, Resources, People, and the History of the Diné Bikeyah.* Norman: Univ. of Oklahoma Press.

Hadley, Linda. 1986. *Hózhǫ́ǫ́jí Hané' (Blessingway).* Rough Rock, Ariz.: Rough Rock Demonstration School. [In English and Navajo.]

Kurath, Gertrude P. 1966. *Michigan Indian Festivals.* Ann Arbor, Mich.: Ann Arbor Publishers.

Neihardt, John G. 1961. *Black Elk Speaks.* Lincoln: Univ. of Nebraska Press.

Underhill, Ruth M. 1953. *Red Man's America.* Chicago: Univ. of Chicago Press.

Additional Listening

Anilth, Wilson, and Hanson Ashley. 1981. *Navajo Peyote Ceremonial Songs.* Vol. 1. Taos, N. Mex.: Indian House 1541. LP.

Boniface Bonnie Singers. 1968. *Navajo Sway Songs.* Taos, N. Mex.: Indian House 1581. LP.

Boulton, Laura. 1957. *Indian Music of the Southwest.* Washington, D.C.: Smithsonian/Folkways 8850. LP. With 11-page booklet.

———. 1992. *Navajo Songs.* Recorded by Laura Boulton in 1933 and 1940. Annotated by Charlotte Frisbie and David McAllester. Washington, D.C.: Smithsonian/Folkways, SF 40403. CD, cassette.

Burch, Sharon. 1989. *Yazzie Girl.* Phoenix, Ariz.: Canyon Records CR534. Cassette and CD.

Burton, Bryan. 1993. *Moving Within the Circle: Contemporary Native American Music and Dance.* Danbury, Conn.: World Music Press. WMP 012. Cassette.

The Chinle Galileans. n.d. *Navajo Country Gospel.* Larry Emerson, Jerry Tom, Roland Dixon, Donnie Tsosie, Lee Begaye, Emerson Luther. Chinle, Ariz.: LPS 9039. LP.

DeMars, James. 1991. *Spirit Horses, Concerto for Native American Flute and Chamber Orchestra.* Composed for and performed by R. Carlos Nakai. Phoenix, Ariz.: Canyon Records Productions CR-7014. CD, cassette.

The Fenders. 1966. *Second Time 'Round.* Thoreau, N. Mex. LP. recording. Patrick Hutchinson made a careful study of "Folsom Prison Blues," noting interesting textual and rhythmic elisions and complications not found in the original Johnny Cash recording. These are similar to alterations noted by Robert Witmer in popular music performed by Blood Indians in Canada (1973:79–83).

Four Corner Yeibichai. 1988. Phoenix, Ariz.: Canyon Records Productions 7152. LP, cassette.

Iroquois Social Dance Songs. 1969. 3 vols. Ohsweken, Ontario, Canada: Iroqrafts QC 727. LP.

Isaacs, Tony. 1968. *Night and Daylight Yeibichai.* Taos, N. Mex.: Indian House IH 1502. LP.

My Beautiful Land and Other Navajo Songs. n.d. Danny Whitefeather Begay, Cindy Yazzi, and Roger McCabe. Phoenix, Ariz.: Canyon Records Productions ARP 6078. LP.

Nakai, R. Carlos. 1985. *Cycles: Native American Flute Music.* Phoenix, Ariz.: Canyon Records Productions CR614-C. Cassette and CD.

Rhodes, Willard. 1949. *Music of the Sioux and the Navajo.* Washington, D.C.: Smithsonian/Folkways 4401. LP. With 6-page pamphlet.

Rhodes, Willard, ed. n.d. *Navajo: Folk Music of the United States.* Washington, D.C.: Library of Congress, Division of Music, Archive of American Folk Song AFS L41.

———. n.d. *Puget Sound: Folk Music of the United States.* Washington, D.C.: Library of Congress, Division of Music, Archive of American Folk Song AAFS L34. With 36-page booklet on Northwest Coast culture (Erna Gunther) and music (Willard Rhodes).

Sioux Favorites. n.d. Phoenix, Ariz.: Canyon Records Productions ARP 6059. Cassette.

Smith Family Gospel Singers. 1987. *Touching Jesus.* Vol. 2. Phoenix, Ariz.: Canyon Records 620. Cassette.

Songs from the Navajo Nation. n.d. Recorded by Kay Bennet (Kaibah). Gallup, N. Mex.: K. C. Bennet (producer). LP.

Williams, Arliene Nofchissey. 1989. *Encircle . . . in the Arms of His Love.* Composed and performed by Arliene Nofchissey Williams, featuring flutist John Rainer, Jr. Blanding, Utah: Proud Earth Productions PE-90. Cassette.

———. *Proud Earth.* n.d. Performed by Chief Dan George, Arliene Nofchissey Williams, Rick Brosseau. Provo, Utah: Salt City Records SC-60. LP.

XIT. 1972. *Plight of the Red Man.* Detroit: Motown Record Corp. R536L. LP. Protest songs in rock style; XIT is an acronym for "Crossing of Indian Tribes," in reference to the pantribal makeup of the group.

Major Sources for Recordings

Canyon Records Productions, 3131 W. Clarendon Ave. Phoenix, Ariz. 85017-4513; (800) 268-1141. This is the main distributor of Native-American recordings. It not only stocks the large inventory under its own label but also keeps in print many of the recordings of smaller distributors, some of which might otherwise have gone out of business. It carries recordings of traditional music and also newer genres such as Indian rock, gospel, and country and western.

Indian House, Box 472, Taos, N. Mex. 87571; (505) 776-2953. This company specializes in traditional Indian music and typically devotes an entire recording to one genre such as Taos Round Dance songs or Navajo Yeibichai songs. The abundant examples and the excellent notes make these recordings valuable for scholars as well as other interested listeners.

Library of Congress. Archive of Folk Culture, Motion Picture, Broadcast, and Recorded Sound Division, Library of Congress, Washington, D.C. 20540; (202) 707-7833. This collection includes the Willard Rhodes recordings of Native-American music: excellent recordings and notes from all across the country.

Smithsonian/Folkways. The Folkways Collection, Smithsonian Institution, Washington, D.C. 20560; (202) 287-3262. The inventory of the Ethnic Folkways Records and Service Corp., formerly of New York City, has been preserved at the Smithsonian Institution and new recordings on a joint label are being produced. Their holdings include many early recordings of Native-American music.

CHAPTER

3

Africa/Ewe, Mande, Dagbamba, Shona, BaAka

David Locke

Consider a misleadingly simple question: Where is Africa's beginning and end? At first you might say that they lie at the borders that mark the continent. But musically, Africa spills over its geographic boundaries. Calling to mind the narrow Strait of Gibraltar, the recently dug Suez Canal, the often-crossed Red and Mediterranean Seas, and the vast Atlantic Ocean, we realize that people from Africa have always shaped world history. If we invoke images—Egypt, Ethiopia, the Moors, Swahili civilization, commerce in humans and precious metals—we know that Africa is not separate from Europe, Asia, and America. As pointed out in Chapter 1, music is humanly made sound; it moves with humankind on our explorations, conquests, migrations, and enslavements. This chapter, therefore, refers us not only to the African continent but also to the many other places we can find African music-culture.

Another question: What music is African music? We could be poetic and say, "Where its people are, there is Africa's music—on the continent and in its diaspora." The truth, however, is messier. Music is never pure; music-cultures are always changing and being shaped by many outside influences. From Benin and Luanda to Bahia, Havana, London, and Harlem, music-cultures blend along a subtle continuum. African-influenced music now circulates the planet by means of electronic media. After people learn new things about music, their own personal music-cultures adjust.

The African continent has two broad zones: (1) the Maghrib, north of the Sahara Desert, and (2) sub-Saharan Africa. North Africa and the Horn of Africa have much in common with the Mediterranean and western Asia; Africa south of the Sahara in many ways is a unique cultural area. Even so, history records significant contacts up and down the Nile, across the Sahara, and along the African coasts. Just as civilizations from the north (Greece, Rome) and east (Arabia, Turkey) have made an indelible impact on northern Africa, the south has influenced the Maghrib as well. Similarly, Africa south of the Sahara has never been isolated from the Old World civilizations of Europe and Asia. As this chapter will show, the history and cultural geography of sub-Saharan Africa vary tremendously (see Bohannan and Curtin 1995).

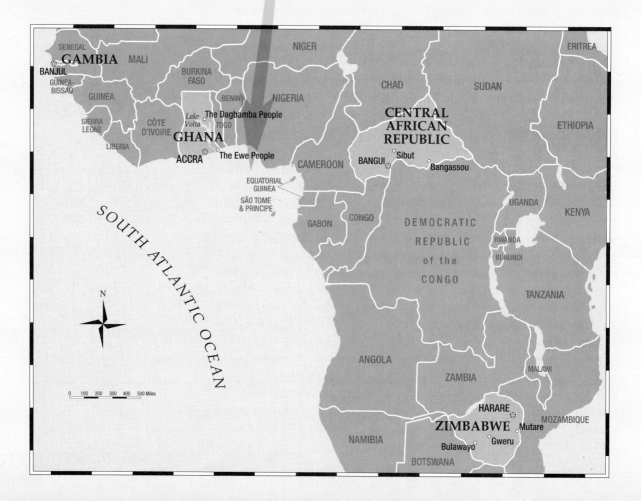

Permit an ungrammatical question: When is an African? In everyday circumstances, people in Africa do not usually think of themselves as "African" (Mphahlele 1962). Identity arises from local connections of gender, age, kinship, place, language, religion, and work. Ethnicity comes into play only in the presence of people from a different group. One "becomes" a Serer, so to speak, in the presence of a Wolof, an African when among the French, a White in the company of a Black, a Yellow, a Red (Senghor 1967). These terms suggest relationships among people more than they mark essential characteristics of individuals. Although physical appearance and genetic inheritance do not determine culture, the bogus concept of "race" persists, feeding the ignorance that spawns prejudice and the bigotry that fosters injustice (Appiah 1992). Such labels should therefore be marked: USE WITH CARE.

"Africa" serves as a resonant symbol for many people. People of African descent, wherever they are in the world, may regard Africa as the ancestral homeland, the place of empowerment and belonging (Asante 1987). Industrialized citizens of "information societies" may envision Africa as either a pastoral Eden or the impoverished Third World. Historically regarded as a land of "heathens" by Muslims and Christians, Africa is a fount of ancient wisdom for those who practice religions such as *santería* or *vodun*. Famine relief and foreign aid, wilderness safari and Tarzan, savage or sage—Africa is a psychic space, not just a physical place.

The sections that follow introduce six African music-cultures. They show Africa's diversity and some of its widely shared characteristics. Information for two of the sections comes from my own field research; other sections are based on the ethnomusicological scholarship of colleagues— Roderic Knight, Paul Berliner, Michelle Kisliuk, and the late James Koetting. The cooperative effort that underlies this chapter seems fitting, because one vital function of African music is to mold separate individuals into a group.

In Chapter 1, you first heard the sounds of African postal workers canceling stamps (CD 1, Track 1). As promised, we shall revisit this intriguing recording, this time examining how it reflects some of the general characteristics of African music-culture. To start, recall Koetting's description:

Postal Workers Canceling Stamps

> This is what you are hearing: the two men seated at the table slap a letter rhythmically several times to bring it from the file to the position on the table where it is to be canceled (this act makes a light-sounding thud). The marker is inked one or more times (the lowest, most resonant sound you hear) and then stamped on the letter (the high-pitched mechanized sound you hear). . . . The rhythm produced is not a simple one-two-three (bring forward the letter—ink the marker—stamp the letter). Rather, musical sensitivities take over. Several slaps on the letter to bring it down, repeated thuds of the marker in the ink pad and multiple cancellations are done for rhythmic interest. . . .
>
> The other sounds you hear have nothing to do with the work itself. A third man has a pair of scissors that he clicks—not cutting anything, but

adding to the rhythm. . . . The fourth worker simply whistles along. He and any of the other three workers who care to join him whistle popular tunes or church music that fits the rhythm. (Koetting 1992:98–99)

How does this musical event exemplify widely shared characteristics of African music-culture?

Generalizations About African Music-Culture
Music-Making Events

A compelling feature of this recording is its setting. Canceling stamps can sound like this? How marvelous! Obviously, the event was not a concert, and this most definitely is not art for art's sake. Like work music everywhere, this performance undoubtedly lifted the workers' spirits and enabled them to coordinate their efforts. The music probably helped the workers maintain a positive attitude toward their job. Music often helps workers control the mood of the workplace (B. Jackson 1972). (See "Music of Work" in Chapter 4.)

African music often happens in social situations where people's primary goals are not artistic. Instead, music is for ceremonies (life cycle rituals, festivals), work (subsistence, child care, domestic chores, wage labor), or play (games, parties, lovemaking). Music making contributes to an event's success by focusing attention, communicating information, encouraging social solidarity, and transforming consciousness.

Expression in Many Media

Just as Africans set music in a social context, they associate it with other expressive media (drama, dance, poetry, costuming, sculpture). Indeed, this example is unusual because it is a wordless instrumental. Although music making is usually not the exclusive purpose of an event, people do value its aesthetic qualities. Music closely associated with a life event is also enjoyed at other times for its own sake.

Musical Style

The whistled tune probably seems familiar to many listeners. The melody has European musical qualities such as duple meter, a major scale, and harmony (see Transcription 3-1). On the other hand, the percussion exhibits widespread African stylistic features such as polyrhythm, repetition, and improvisation (see Transcription 3-2).

History

These observations about genre and style lead to an important point about the history of music in Africa: The music-cultures of Europe, Asia, and the Americas have strongly affected those in Africa. Foreigners—Christians and Muslims, sailors and soldiers, traders and travelers—have brought to Africa their instruments, musical repertories, and ideas. Modern media technologies such as radio and audio recording only have increased the intensity of a very old pattern of border crossing. Like people everywhere, Africans have imitated, rejected, transformed, and adapted external influences in a complex process of culture change.

Although the concert music repertory of Europe has held little attraction for most Africans, many other musical traditions have affected African music making. Throughout Africa, Christian hymns and Muslim cantillation have exerted a profound influence on musical style. West Asian civilization has had an effect on African musical instruments such as the plucked lutes, double reeds, and goblet-shaped drums of the Sahel area. Euro-American influence shows up in the electric guitar and drum set, although East Asians manufacture many of these instruments. We hear the American influence of Cuban rumba on pop music from central Africa, and African-American spirituals on southern African religious music. From praise singers to pop bands, musical professionalism is an idea about music that developed in Africa by means of the intercultural exchange of ideas.

Participation

The postal workers join simple musical parts together to make remarkably sophisticated and satisfying music. This kind of musical design welcomes social engagement. Others could participate by adding a new phrase to the polyrhythm or cutting a few dance moves. Undoubtedly, Jim Koetting "got down" while picking up his mail! Much African music shares this generous, open-hearted quality that welcomes participation.

Training

We admire the postal workers because their music seems effortlessly beautiful. The genius we sense in this recording lies in the way the workers are musical together, in their sensitivity to a culturally conditioned musical style. Here, a musical education depends on a societywide process of enculturation, that is, the process of learning one's culture gradually during childhood. Babies move on the backs of their dancing mothers, youngsters play children's games and then join adults in worship and mourning, teenagers groove to pop tunes. Raised in this manner, Africans learn a way-of-being in response to music; intuitively, they know how to participate effectively. Genetic and sacred forces may shape musicality, but culture is the indispensable element in musical training.

Beliefs and Values

Often, Africans conceive of music as a necessary and normal part of life. Neither exalted nor denigrated as Art, music fuses with other life processes. Traditional songs and musical instruments are not commodities separable from the flux of life. In his book *African Music: A People's Art,* Francis Bebey quotes a musician who was asked to sell his instrument:

> He replied rather dryly that he had come to town to play his drum for the dancing and not to deliver a slave into bondage. He looked upon his instrument as a person, a colleague who spoke the same language and helped him create his music. (1975:120)

Intercultural Misunderstanding

These beliefs and attitudes about music make intercultural understanding a challenge, especially for scientifically minded persons from what might be called concert-music-cultures. What a non-African listener assumes is an item of music may be the voice of an ancestor to an African. When he recorded this example, Koetting found himself in this type of cross-cultural conundrum:

> It sounds like music and, of course, it is; but the men performing do not quite think of it that way. The men are working, not putting on a musical show; people pass by the work place paying little attention to the "music" (I used to go often to watch and listen to them, and they gave the impression that they thought I was somewhat odd for doing so). (1992:98)

Musical Analysis: Toward Participation

I too think this recording sounds like music, but I hesitate to say that it *is* music, because that would imply that the postal workers share my ideas about music. However, even though they do not "quite" regard this as music, what they are doing sounds great to me. I want to participate. In my music-culture, analysis can be an effective path toward active involvement, a bridge into the musical style of another culture. I use tools of musical analysis with caution, however, because music can never be pinned to cardboard like a lifeless butterfly. For many Africans, music is "a living thing ensouled by the spiritual energy that travels through it" (Amoaku 1985:37).

Melody: Tonality, Texture, Form, Rhythm

The postal workers' melody (see Transcription 3-1) uses a seven-note scale in a major mode (transcribed for convenience with the tonal center on G). The tune contains two melodic ideas: phrase A, which involves two shorter motives (Aa, Ab), and phrase B, which has three shorter motives (Ba, Bb, Bc). If there were no improvisation, we could mark the musical form as AABA, but because the performers never repeat phrase A in exactly the same way, a more careful marking is A1 A2 B A3. The recording fades in at the end of A3; then we hear four complete choruses of the tune before it fades out at the beginning of phrase A2. As the recording ends, the homophonic texture fractures into a polyphonic interplay of independent melodies. I have set the rhythm within a meter of four quarter-note beats. The melody accentuates beats 1 and 3. Beats 2 and 4 play off beats 1 and 3, giving the music a sense of lift.

CD 1/1

Postal workers canceling stamps at the University of Ghana post office (2:59). The whistled tune is the hymn "Bompata," by the Ghanaian composer W. J. Akyeampong (b. 1900). Field recording by James Koetting. Legon, Ghana, 1975.

Percussion

It is hard to reconstruct exactly who played what on the recording; only by slowing the tape speed could I "get inside" the percussion texture. Guided by timbre and rhythm, I hear three percussive "voices":

Transcription 3-1
Postal workers' melody.

Note: $\frac{4}{}$ means four quarter notes per measure without implication of stress patterns.

- A high-pitched, loud, dry sound (A) plays an ostinato (repeated phrase) on the upbeat of counts 2, 3, and 4. This part (the scissors) shapes musical time, giving a distinctive rhythmic character to the tune and other percussive voices.

- The middle voice in the ensemble (B) may be the sound of moving the letters into position, augmented with tapping on the table just for fun. This part is probably a composite of separate actions by several people. With much less silence than the other two parts, this part increases the density of the music's texture. The workers occasionally break the bubbling flow, allowing brief moments of silence that greatly enhance the music's rhythmic design.

Transcription 3-2
Postal workers' percussion "voices."
(In this chapter, I refer to the musical "parts" that I hear on sound recordings as "voices.")

- The lowest-pitched, resonant bass sound (C) plays occasional fills. This must be inking the stamp. Often it responds to the tune like an accompaniment, but at other times its interjections seem disconnected to the tune's progress. The prominent rhythmic figure shown in Transcription 3-2 answers the scissors' part in call-and-response.

Each layer in the texture has a different rhythmic character. Through a clever balance of action and silence, the players generate a forward motion in musical time while remaining within a repeating circle of percussion.

This example gives us a feeling for African music in general. The next example affords a more detailed look at a type of music with profound connections to the history of a specific African ethnic group, the Ewe people.

Agbekor: Music and Dance of the Ewe People

Drawing on my field research in West Africa during the 1970s, we shall now consider a type of singing and drumming called *Agbekor* (pronounced ah-*gbeh*-kaw). As we shall hear on CD 1, Tracks 15 and 16, Agbekor's music features a percussion ensemble and a chorus of singers. A complex lead drumming part rides on a rich polyrhythmic texture established by an ensemble of bells, rattles, and drums of different sizes. Songs are clear examples of call-and-response. *Agbekor* is a creation of Ewe-speaking people (pronounced *eh*-way) who live on the Atlantic coast of western Africa in the nation-states of Ghana and Togo.

The Ewe People
History

Triumph over adversity is an important theme in Ewe oral history. Until they came to their present territory, the Ewe people had lived precariously as a minority within kingdoms of more populous and powerful peoples such as the Yoruba and the Fon. One prominent story in their oral traditions recounts their exodus in the late 1600s from Agokoli, the tyrannical king of Notsie, a walled city-state located in what is now southern Togo. Intimidating Agokoli's warriors with fierce drumming, the Ewes escaped under cover of darkness. Moving toward the southwest, they founded many settlements along a large lagoon near the mouth of the Volta River. At last Wenya, their elderly leader, declared that he was too tired to continue. Thus, this Ewe group became known as the *Anlo* (pronounced *ahng-law*), which means "cramped." Other families of Ewe-speakers settled nearby along the coast and in the upland hills.

In these new lands, the Ewe communities grew and multiplied. Eventually the small Ewe settlements expanded into territorial divisions whose inhabitants could all trace male ancestors to the original villages. Family heads or distinguished war leaders became chiefs. Despite bonds of common culture and history, each division zealously cherished its independence. The Ewe people have never supported a hierarchical concentration of power within a large state (compare them with the Mande and Dagbamba kingdoms, discussed later in this chapter).

Ever since those early days, the important unit of Ewe social life has been the extended family. Members of a lineage—that is, people who can trace their genealogy to a common ancestor—share rights and obligations. Lineage elders hold positions of secular and sacred authority. The ever-present spirits of lineage ancestors help their offspring, especially if the living perform the necessary customary rituals. The eighteenth and nineteenth centuries saw the Ewes in frequent military conflict with neighboring ethnic groups, with European traders, and even among themselves. The Anlo-Ewe gained a fearsome reputation as warriors.

Religious Philosophy

An Ewe scholar has commented on the sacred worldview of his people:

> A traveler in Anlo is struck by the predominating, all-pervasive influence of religion in the intimate life of the family and community. . . . The sea, the lagoon, the river, streams, animals, birds and reptiles as well as the earth with its natural and artificial protuberances are worshipped as divine or as the abode of divinities. (Fiawo 1959:35, in Locke 1978:32)

The Ewe supreme being, Mawu, is remote from the affairs of humanity. Other divinities, such as Se (pronounced seh), interact with things in this world. Se embodies God's attributes of law, order, and harmony; Se is the maker and keeper of human souls; Se is destiny. Many Ewes believe that before a spirit enters the fetus, it tells Se how its life on earth will be and how its body will die. If you ask Ewe musicians the source of their talent, they will most likely identify the ancestor whose spirit they have inherited. Ask why they are so involved in music making, and they will say it is their destiny.

Ancestral spirits are an important force in the lives of Ewe people.

> The Ewe believe that part of a person's soul lives on in the spirit world after his [or her] death and must be cared for by the living. This care is essential, for the ancestors can either provide for and guard the living or punish them. . . . The doctrine of reincarnation, whereby some ancestors are reborn into their earthly kin-groups, is also given credence. The dead are believed to live somewhere in the world of spirits, *Tsiefe,* from where they watch their living descendants in the earthly world, *Kodzogbe.* They are believed to possess supernatural powers of one sort or another, coupled with a kindly interest in their descendants as well as the ability to do harm if the latter neglect them. (Nukunya 1969:27, in Locke 1978:35)

Funerals are significant social institutions, because without ritual action by the living a soul cannot become an ancestral spirit. A funeral is an affirmation of life, a cause for celebration because another ancestor can now watch over the living. Because spirits of ancestors love music and dance, funeral memorial services feature drumming, singing, and dancing. Full of the passions aroused by death, funerals have replaced war as an appropriate occasion for war drumming such as *Agbekor.*

Knowledge of Ewe history and culture helps explain the great energy found in performance pieces like *Agbekor*. Vital energy, life force, strength—these lie at the heart of the Ewe outlook:

> In the traditional . . . Anlo society where the natural resources are relatively meager, where the inexplicable natural environment poses a threat to life and where the people are flanked by warlike tribes and neighbors, we find the clue to their philosophy of life: it is aimed at life. (Fiawo 1959:41, in Locke 1978:36)

Agbekor: History and Contemporary Performance

Legends of Origin

I conducted these interviews with the assistance of a language specialist, Bernard Akpeleasi, who subsequently translated the spoken Ewe into written English.

During my field research, I interviewed elders about how *Agbekor* began. Many people said it was inspired by hunters' observations of monkeys in the forest. According to some elders, the monkeys changed into human form, played drums, and danced; others say that the monkeys kept their animal form as they beat with sticks and danced. Significantly, hunters, like warriors, had access to esoteric power.

> In the olden days hunters were the repository of knowledge given to men by God. Hunters had special herbs. . . . Having used such herbs, the hunter could meet and talk with leopards and other animals which eat human beings. . . . As for Agbekor, it was in such a way that they saw it and brought it home. But having seen such a thing, they could not reveal it to others just like that. Hunters have certain customs during which they drum, beat the double bell, and perform such activities that are connected with the worship of things we believe. It was during such a traditional hunting custom that they exhibited the monkey's dance. Spectators who went to the performance decided to found it as a proper dance. There were hunters among them because once they had revealed the dance in the hunting customary performance they could later repeat it again publicly. But if a hunter saw something and came home to reveal it, he would surely become insane. That was how Agbekor became known as a dance of the monkeys. (Kwaku Denu, quoted in Locke 1978:38–39)

Although many Ewes consider them legend rather than history, stories like this signify the high respect accorded to *Agbekor*. Hunters were spiritually forceful leaders, and the forest was the zone of dangerously potent supernatural forces. We feel this power in a performance of *Agbekor*.

Agbekor as War Drumming

The original occasion for a performance of *Agbekor* was war. Elders explained that their ancestors performed it before combat, as a means to attain the required frame of mind, or after battle, as a means of communicating what had happened.

> They would play the introductory part before they were about to go to war. When the warriors heard the rhythms, they would be completely filled

with bravery. They would not think that they might be going, never to return, for their minds were filled only with thoughts of fighting. (Elders of the Agbogbome Agbekor Society, quoted in Locke 1978:44)

Yes, it is a war dance. It is a dance that was played when they returned from an expedition. They would exhibit the things that happened during the war, especially the death of an elder or a chief. (Alfred Awunyo, quoted in Locke 1978:43)

If they were fighting, brave acts were done. When they were relaxing after the battle, they would play the drums and during the dance a warrior could display what he had done during the battle for the others to see. (Kpogo Ladzekpo, quoted in Locke 1978:43)

The Meaning of the Name *Agbekor*

I asked whether the name *agbekor* has meaning. One elder told me this:

I can say it signifies enjoying life: we make ourselves happy in life. The suffering that our elders underwent was brought out in the dance, and it could be that when they became settled, they gave the dance this name, which shows that the dance expresses the enjoyment of life. (Kwaku Denu, quoted in Locke 1978:47)

Another elder told me that when people played *Agbekor* during times of war, they called it *atamuga* (pronounced ah-*tam*-gah), which means "the great oath." Before going to battle, warriors would gather with their war leaders at shrines that housed spiritually powerful objects. They would swear on a sacred sword an oath to their ancestors to obey their leaders' commands and fight bravely for their community. When the Anlo no longer went to war, the name changed to *Agbekor* (Kpogo Ladzekpo, quoted in Locke 1978:45–46).

The word *Agbekor* is a compound of two short words: *agbe* ("life") and *kor* ("clear"). The professional performer Midao Gideon Foli Alorwoyie translates *Agbekor* as "clear life": The battle is over, the danger is past, and our lives are now in the clear (Locke 1978:47). Many people add the prefix *atsia* (plural *atsiawo*), calling the piece *atsiagbekor* (pronounced ah-chah-*gbeh*-kaw). The word *atsia* has two meanings: (1) stylish self-display, looking good, or bluffing and (2) a preset figure of music and dance. As presented shortly, the form of the lead drumming and the dance consists of a sequence of *atsiawo*.

Learning

In Ewe music-culture, most music and dance is learned through enculturation. *Agbekor*, on the other hand, requires special training. The eminent African ethnomusicologist J. H. K. Nketia describes learning through slow absorption without formal teaching:

The very organization of traditional music in social life enables the individual to acquire his musical knowledge in slow stages, to widen his experience of the music of his culture through the social groups into which he is progressively incorporated and the activities in which he takes part. . . . The young have to rely largely on their imitative ability and on correction by others when this is volunteered. They must rely on their own eyes, ears and memory. They must acquire their own technique of learning. (Nketia 1964:4)

Gideon Alorwoyie explains how one learns from the performance of an expert:

All you have to do is know when he is going to play. . . . You have to go and pay attention to what you hear . . . to how the drums are coordinated and to the drum language, to what the responses are to the calls, and so on. You have to use your common sense right there to make sure that you get the patterns clear. Up to today, if you want to be a drummer, you go to the place where people are playing and then pay attention and listen. That's it. (Davis 1994:27)

Because of its complexity *Agbekor* is hard to learn in this informal way. Members of an *Agbekor* group practice in a secluded area for up to a year before they appear in public. Instruction entails demonstration and emulation. With adept dancers in front, the whole group performs together. No one breaks it down and analyzes it. People learn sequences of movement and music not through exercises but in a simulated performance context. (Compare this with the teaching of *karnataka sangeeta,* described in Chapter 6.)

This style of learning depends on gifted students who can learn long rhythmic compositions merely by listening to them several times. For certain people, drumming comes as easily and naturally as spoken language. Ewes know that drumming talent often comes from one's ancestors. A precocious youngster may be the reincarnation of an ancestor who was a renowned musician. One village drummer told me of a special drummer's ritual:

My father was a drummer and he taught me. It was when he was old and could no longer play that he gave me the curved sticks. A ceremony has to be performed before the curved sticks are handed over to you. . . . If the custom is not done the drum language will escape your mind. (Dogbevi Abaglo, quoted in Locke 1978:53)

Gideon Alorwoyie explains the effects of this ritual:

Once the custom has been made, you can't sleep soundly. The rhythms you want to learn will come into your head while you sleep. . . . The ceremony protects the person in many ways. It protects your hands when you play and protects you from the evil intentions of other people who may envy you. . . . Whenever you see a master drummer in Africa, I'm telling you, he has got to have some sort of backbone. (Locke 1978:54–55)

Performing Organizations

Times have changed since Ewe hunters created *Agbekor.* Britain, Germany, and France administered Ewe territory during a brief colonial period (1880s to 1950s); now the Ewe people live in the nation-states of Ghana and Togo. Today, relatively few villages have preserved their heritage of *Agbekor.* But the tradition vigorously continues within drum and dance societies of sev-

Figure 3-1
The Anya Agbekor Society
(with the author) in performance.

Godwin Agbeli

eral types: mutual aid organizations, school and civic youth groups, and theatrical performing companies. Throughout Africa, voluntary mutual aid societies are an important type of performing group (Ladzekpo 1971). *Agbekor* groups of this kind are formal organizations with a group identity, institutionalized procedures, recognized leaders, and so forth. Many members are poor and cannot afford funeral expenses. People solve this financial problem by pooling resources. When a member dies, individuals contribute a small amount so the group can give a lump sum of cash to the family. The society's performance of music and dance makes the funeral grand.

In the mid-1970s I studied *Agbekor* with members of this type of cooperative society, the Anya Agbekor Society of Accra (see Figure 3-1). One of their leaders recounted how the group came into existence:

> The first Anya Agbekor group in Accra was formed by our elder brothers and uncles. They all scattered in the mid-sixties and that group died away. We, the younger ones, decided to revive it in 1970. Three or four people sat down and said, "How can we let this thing just go away? Agbekor originated in our place, among our family, so it is not good to let it go." We felt that it was something we had to do to remember the old family members. We formed the group to help ourselves. (Evans Amenumey, quoted in Locke 1978:63)

I also studied with school groups trained by my teacher Godwin Agbeli. In colonial times, missionaries whipped students for attending traditional performance events. These days, most Ewes value their traditional repertory of music and dance as a cultural resource. Since Ghana achieved statehood in 1957, the national government has held competitions for amateur cultural groups from the country's many ethnic regions. Young people often join groups because rehearsals and performances provide social opportunities. Like many African nations, Ghana sponsors professional performing-arts troupes. With its spectacular, crowd-pleasing music and dance, *Agbekor* is a staple of their repertory.

A Performance

On Sunday, March 6, 1977, in a crowded working-class section of Accra, the Anya Society performed in honor of the late chief patron of the group. The evening before, the group had held a wake during which they drummed *Kpegisu,* another prestigious war drumming of the Ewe (Locke 1992). Early Sunday morning they played *Agbekor* briefly to announce the afternoon's performance. Had the event occurred in Anyako, the group would have made a procession through the ward. People went home to rest and returned to the open lot near the patron's family house by 3:30 in the afternoon for the main event.

The performance area was arranged like a rectangle within a circle. Ten drummers sat at one end, fifteen dancers formed three columns facing the drummers, ten singers stood in a semicircle behind the dancers, and about three hundred onlookers encircled the entire performance area. All drummers and most dancers were male. Most singers were female; several younger women danced with the men. Group elders, bereaved family members, and invited dignitaries sat behind the drummers. With the account book laid out on a table, the group's secretary accepted the members' contributions.

The action began with an introductory section called *adzo* (pronounced ah-*dzo*), that is, short sections. Dancers sang songs in free rhythm. After the *adzo,* the main section, *vutsotsoe* (pronounced voo-*tsaw*-tso-eh), that is, fast drumming, started. The first sequence of figures honored the ancestors. Following this ritually charged passage, the dancers performed approximately ten more *atsiawo.* The lead drummer spontaneously selected these "styles" from the many drum and dance sequences known to the group. The singers were also busy. Their song leader raised up each song; the chorus received it and answered. One song was repeated five to ten times before another was begun.

After about twenty minutes the *adzokpi* (pronounced ah-*dzoh*-kpee) section of the performance began. Group members came forward in pairs or small groups to dance in front of the lead drummer. The dance movement differed for men and women. As in genres of Ewe social dancing, friends invited each other to move into the center of the dance space. When everyone had their fill of this more individualistic display, the lead drummer returned to the group styles. Soon, he signaled for a break in the action by playing the special ending figure.

During the break, the group's leaders went to the center of the dance area to pour a libation. Calling on the ancestors to drink, elders ceremonially poured water and liquor onto the earth. An elder explained later:

Perhaps because the word *atsia* means "stylishness," many English-speaking Ewe musicians refer to the preformed drum and dance compositions as "styles."

We pour libation to call upon the deceased members of the dance [group] to send us their blessings [so we can] play the dance the same way we did when they were alive. How the Christians call Jesus, call God, though Jesus is dead—they do not see him and yet they call him—it is in the same manner that we call upon the members of the dance [group] who are no more so that their blessings come down upon us during the dancing. (Kpogo Ladzekpo, quoted in Locke 1978:82–83)

The performance resumed with *vulolo* (pronounced voo-*law*-law), that is, slow drumming, the processional section of *Agbekor.* After about fifteen minutes, they went straight to *vutsotsoe,* the up-tempo section, and then *adzokpi,* the "solos" section. After a brief rest they did another sequence of group figures at slow and fast pace, followed by individual display.

At the peak of the final *adzokpi* section elders, patrons, and invited guests came out onto the dance area. While they danced, singers and dancers knelt on one knee as a mark of respect. After dancing back and forth in front of the drummers, they returned to their position on the benches in back of the drummers.

By 6:00, with the equatorial sun falling quickly, the performance had ended. As the group members contentedly carried the equipment back to the Anya house, the audience dispersed, talking excitedly about the performance.

Although a performance of *Agbekor* follows a definite pattern, it is not rigidly formalized. A. M. Jones, a pioneering scholar of African music, has commented on the elasticity of African musical performance: "Within the prescribed limits of custom, no one quite knows what is going to happen: It depends quite a lot on the inspiration of the leading performers. These men [and women] are not making music which is crystallized on a music score. They are moved by the spirit of the occasion" (Jones 1959:108).

CD 1/15

Agbekor (5:35). Traditional music of the Ewe people. Field recording by David Locke. Anlo-Afiadenyigba, Ghana, 1976.

Music of the Percussion Ensemble

We now turn to music of the percussion ensemble for the slow-paced section of *Agbekor* (see Transcription 3-12). Instruments in the *Agbekor* ensemble include a double bell, a gourd rattle, and four single-headed drums (see Figure 3-2). Listen to CD 1, Track 16, to hear the bell by itself, followed by each instrument with the bell (*axatse, kaganu, kidi, kloboto,* and *totodzi),* and finally the polyrhythm of all the parts.

One by one the phrases are not too difficult, but playing them in an ensemble is surprisingly hard. The challenge is to hear them within a polyphonic texture that seems to change depending on one's point of musical reference. The reward in learning to play these parts is an experience of African musical time.

CD 1/16

Demonstration: *Agbekor* (3:54). Performed by David Locke.

I have decided not to present the music of the lead drum here. Not only is the material quite complicated, but I believe it best if students approach lead drumming only after a significant period of study, preferably with an Ewe teacher.

The Bell

"Listen to the bell"—that is the continual advice of Ewe teachers. Every act of drumming, singing, and dancing is timed in accordance with the recurring musical phrase played on an iron bell or gong called *gankogui* (pronounced gahng-*koh*-gu-ee). On first impression, the part may seem

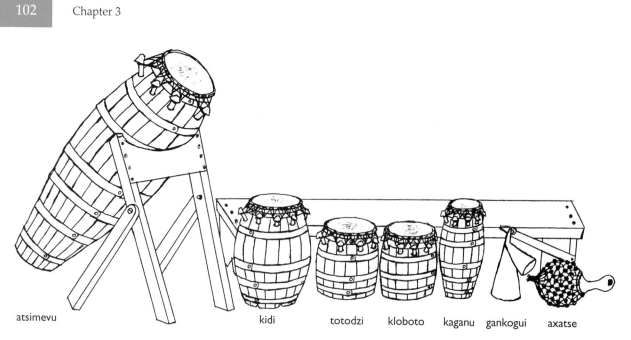

Figure 3-2
Agkebor ensemble.
(Drawing by Emmanuel Agbeli)

simple, but when set in the rhythmic context of Ewe drumming, it becomes a musical force of great potency. Repetition is key. As the phrase repeats over and over, participants join together in a circling, spiraling world of time.

Transcription 3-3
Gankogui (bell) phrase.

Seven strokes with a wooden stick on the bell make one pass through the phrase. Transcription 3-3 represents the bell part as a sequence of long and short notes. As the part repeats in polyrhythmic context, the musical ear groups the bell tones into a variety of patterns. Although the sonic phenomena never change, the part appears different. We experience an aural illusion.

Despite the chameleonlike nature of the bell part, two phrase shapes matter more than the others (Transcription 3-4).

Transcription 3-4
Two shapes of the bell phrase.

The note marked with the asterisk may be struck on the lower pitched of the *gankogui*'s two bells, a helpful landmark if one becomes rhythmically disoriented. For clarity, I have numbered the bell tones.

Tempo, Pulsation, and Time-Feels

Although many contrasting rhythmic phrases occur simultaneously in the percussion ensemble, competent Ewe musicians unerringly maintain a steady tempo. Rather than confusing players, musical relations among parts help them maintain a consistent time flow.

The time-feel (meter) most significant to Ewe performers is the "four-feel." Together with the explicit bell phrase, these four beats provide a constant, implicit foundation for musical perception. Each is a ternary beat, meaning that each has three quicker units within it. When my students first learn a dance step, a drum part, or a song melody, I advise them to lock into the bell phrase and the four-feel beats. Interestingly, this type of groove—often marked by a $\frac{12}{8}$ time signature—is widespread in African-American music (see Chapter 4).

Godwin Agbeli uses an Ewe children's game to teach the polyrhythm of bell and the four-feel beats.

In this chapter I use an unconventional version of time signatures. A number in the numerator shows the number of beats per measure, and a musical note in the denominator shows the time-value of these beats. All beats in the measure have equal "weight" or metric stress.

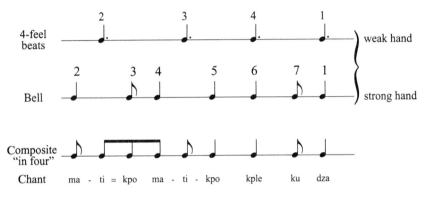

Transcription 3-5
The chant "Matikpo matikpo kple ku dza" with bell and four-feel beats.

The chant "Matikpo matikpo kple ku dza" means "I will jump, I will jump [to the sound of] 'kple ku dza'"; children leap upward as they say "kple" and land with a hand clap on "dza." Practice the bell and four-beat combination by striking your thighs with open palms. When this is flowing easily, bring out the contrast between the parts by changing the weak hand to a fist.

To an Ewe musician, these four-feel beats automatically imply a "six-feel" (six quarter notes, or $\frac{6}{4}$ meter).

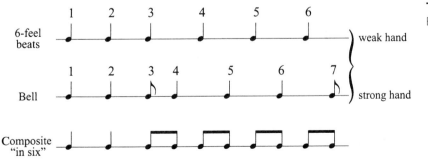

Transcription 3-6
Bell and six-feel beats.

The four- and six-feels are inseparable; they construct musical reality in two ways at once. Using both hands as shown in Transcription 3-6, try playing the bell phrase and the six-feel. The bell part feels different. This is the power of 3:2. After mastering the bell and four-feel hand pattern, add a foot tap on the six-feel. Now you have more fully entered the rhythmic world of Ewe music.

How does this analytic perspective relate to an Ewe point of view? How do they hear it? These questions are hard to answer. First, we cannot assume that there is just one pervasive Ewe perspective. Second, until recently Ewe musicians had no reason to think about musical structure in terms suited to intercultural education of the kind attempted in this book. After many years of research, performance, and teaching, I believe that my approach here accurately conveys the perspective of my Ewe teachers (see Locke 1982). However, the discovery of ethnographic truth is not my only intent. I also ask practical questions: Does this approach help one hear the music with insight? Does it help people play? Students must answer this question for themselves. I hope the answer is yes!

The *axatse* (pronounced ah-*ha*-tseh) is a dried gourd about the size of a cantaloupe covered with a net strung with seeds. In some *Agbekor* groups its role is to sound out the four-feel beats. In another frequently heard phrase, downward strokes on the player's thigh match the *gankogui* while upward strokes against the palm fill in between bell tones. The longer duration of the tone that matches bell stroke 1 gives definition to the shape of the bell phrase; it suggests to the musical ear that the bell phrase begins on stroke 2 and ends on stroke 1.

Transcription 3-7
Axatse phrase.

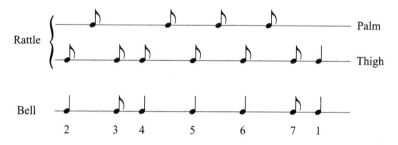

As the only instrument played by many people at once, the *axatse* "section" provides a loud, indefinite-pitched sound vital to the ensemble's energy.

The high pitch and dry timbre of the slender *kaganu* (pronounced kah-gahng) drum cuts through the more mellow, midrange sounds of the other drums. The *kaganu* part articulates offbeats, that is, moments between the four-feel beats.

Transcription 3-8
Kaganu phrase.

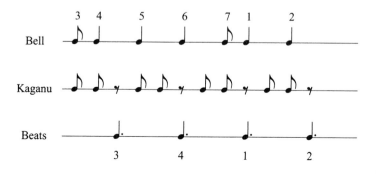

Although not every *Agbekor* group uses the same phrase (Locke 1983:23–27), a good one for newcomers to learn marks the second and third pulses within each four-feel beat. Many Ewe teachers advise students to focus on the synchrony between *kaganu* and bell tones 3 and 4; remember—listen to the bell! The late Freeman Donkor, one of my first teachers of Ewe music, said that the rhythm of *kaganu* brings out the flavor of the other parts, like salt in a stew.

The *gankogui, axatse,* and *kaganu* parts create a distinctive quality of musical temporal experience (Locke 1988). The long and short tones in the bell phrase sculpt time into asymmetrical proportions. Symmetrical units also are important: the duration of the bell phrase is a literal measure of time; the tones of *axatse* and *kaganu* mark that measure into four equal ternary units. All four beats are strong, but the moments when bell and beat fall together—beats 4 and 1, bell tones 6 and 1—are specially marked in musical awareness; beat 3 is distinctive because it marks the midpoint in the bell phrase. These stable qualities of musical time provide the solid rhythmic foundation for the shifting offbeats found in the songs and lead drumming.

In descending order of relative pitch, the three other drums in the ensemble are *kidi, kloboto,* and *totodzi* (pronounced *kee*-dee, *kloh*-boh-toh, and toh-toh-*dzee*). Each drum adds its own phrase to *Agbekor*'s unique polyphony. There are two ways of striking a drum skin. In bounce strokes the stick bounces off the drum skin, producing an open ringing sound; in press strokes the stick presses into the drum skin, producing a closed muted sound. Bounces contribute the most to the group's music; presses keep each player in a groove. The parts discussed as follows are widespread, but some *Agbekor* groups use slightly different versions.

- In the *kidi* part, three bounces and three presses move at the twelve-unit pulsation rate; the phrase occurs twice within the span of one bell phrase (see Transcription 3-9). Polyrhythmic relationships to the time parts help in learning the *kidi*: (a) in each group of bounces and presses the third stroke is on a beat, (b) bell tones 5 and 6 match open *kidi* tones, and (c) *kidi* closely coincides with *kaganu.*

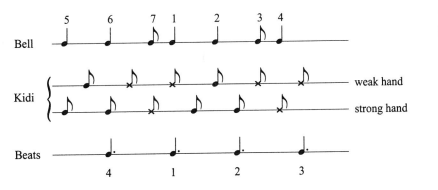

- The *kloboto* phrase has the same duration as the bell phrase (see Transcription 3-10). As if inspired by bell tones 7–1, the part's main idea is a brief bounce-press, offbeat-onbeat figure. *Kloboto's* insistent accentuation of offbeat moments can reorient a listener into perceiving them as onbeats. This type of implied beat shift (displacement) adds to the multidimensional quality of the music. For example, a person concentrating on *kloboto* may hear the second stroke in each pair of *kaganu* tones to be on the beat. Competent Ewe musicians, however, never lose orientation—they always know the *kloboto* presses are right on the four-feel time.

Transcription 3-10
Kloboto phrase.

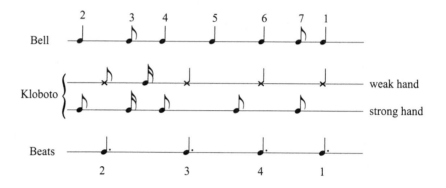

- The *totodzi* part begins and ends with the *kloboto* (see Transcription 3-11). Its two bounce strokes match bell tones 2 and 3, its three press strokes match four-feel beats 3, 4, and 1. Notice the impact of sound quality and body movement on rhythmic shape: The phrase is felt as two strong-hand bounces followed by three weak-hand presses, not according to a three-then-two timing structure.

Transcription 3-11
Totodzi phrase.

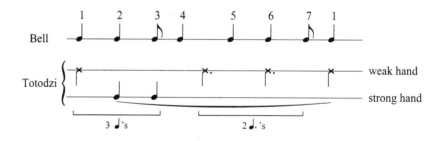

To get into the drumming, begin by hearing each phrase "in four" and in duet with the bell. Then, stay "in four" but hear ever-larger combinations with other parts. Next, switch to the six-feel. The point is to explore the potency of these phrases, not to create new ones. Stretch your way of hearing, rather than what you are playing. Strive for a cool focus on ensemble relationships, not a hot individual display (Thompson 1973).

Drum Language

As happens in the instrumental music of many African peoples, Ewe drum phrases often have vernacular texts. Usually only drummers know the texts. Even Ewe speakers cannot understand drum language just by hearing the music—they must be told. Secrecy makes restricted information valuable and powerful. In many parts of Africa "speech must be controlled and contained if silence is to exercise its powers of truth, authenticity, seriousness and healing" (Miller 1990:95).

During my field research, I asked many experts whether they knew drum language for *Agbekor*. Saying he learned them from elders in his hometown of Afiadenyigba, Gideon Alorwoyie shared the following with me. *Agbekor*'s themes of courage and service are apparent.

Transcription 3-12
Agbekor drum language.

His word-for-word and free translations appear beneath the Ewe texts.

Ewe Text and Translation of *Agbekor* Drum Language

Totodzi   *Dzogbe dzi dzi dzi.*
         battlefield/on/on/on
         We will be on the battlefield.

Kloboto   *Gbe dzi ko mado mado mado.*
         Battlefield/on/only/I will sleep/I will sleep/I will sleep
         I will die on the battlefield.

Kidi   *Kpo afe godzi.*
         Look/home/side-on.
         Look back at home.

Kaganu   *Miava yi afia.*
         We will come/go/will show
         We are going to show our bravery.

Songs
Texts

Agbekor songs engage the subject of war. Many songs celebrate the invincibility of Ewe warriors; others urge courage and loyalty; some reflect on death and express grief. Songs memorialize heroes but do not provide detailed historical information. Unlike the freshly composed songs found in contemporary idioms of Ewe traditional music, *Agbekor* songs come from the past. A song's affective power derives, in part, from its association with the ancestors.

Structural Features

In performance, a song leader and a singing group share the text and melody. As illustrated in the songs presented shortly, this call-and-response idea supports a variety of subtly different musical forms. The tonal system of *Agbekor* songs has evolved entirely in response to the human singing voice, without being influenced by musical instruments. An ethnomusicologist can identify scales, but in comparison to tuning in South Indian music-culture, for example, an Ewe singers' intonation seems aimed at pitch areas rather than precise pitch points. Melodic motion usually conforms to the rise and fall of speech tones, but Ewe speakers easily understand song lyrics even if the melodic contour contradicts the tonal pattern of the spoken language. Songs add another layer to the rhythm of *Agbekor.* Not surprisingly, a song's polyrhythmic duet with the bell phrase is all-important.

On CD 1, Track 15, we hear excerpts from my recording of a performance by an *Agbekor* group from the town of Anlo-Afiadenyigba on August 14, 1976. There are three slow-paced songs, one song in free rhythm, and one fast-paced song, which will be discussed in turn.

Slow-Paced Songs

Song 1 announces that people should prepare for the arrival of the *Agbekor* procession. It has a rounded ABA musical form: ‖: A¹ A² :‖ B B A². In the A section, the group repeats the leader's text but with a different tune. In the B section, the melodic phrases are shorter, the rhythm of call-and-response more percussive. The song ends with leader and group joining to sing the group's first response.

CD 1/15

Agbekor (5:35). Traditional music of the Ewe people. Field recording by David Locke. Anlo-Afiadenyigba, Ghana, 1976.

  a. Three slow-paced songs (0:00–2:52)

  b. One song in free rhythm (3:02–4:20)

  c. One fast-paced song (4:27–5:35)

Text, Song 1

Leader:	‖:	*Emiawo miegbona 'feawo me.*	
		Afegametowo/viwo, midzra nuawo do.	A¹
Group:		repeat lines 1 and 2 :‖	A²
Leader:	‖:	*Oo!*	
Group:		*Midzra nuawo do.* :‖	B
All:		repeat lines 1 and 2	A²
Leader:	‖:	We are coming into the homesteads.	
		People/Children of the noble homes, get the things ready.	
Group:		Repeat lines 1 and 2 :‖	
Leader:		Oh!	
Group:		Get the things ready.	

The song's rhythm moves in the three-then-two groove. I hear the song's final pitch as its tonal center (here set on E). The intonation of the

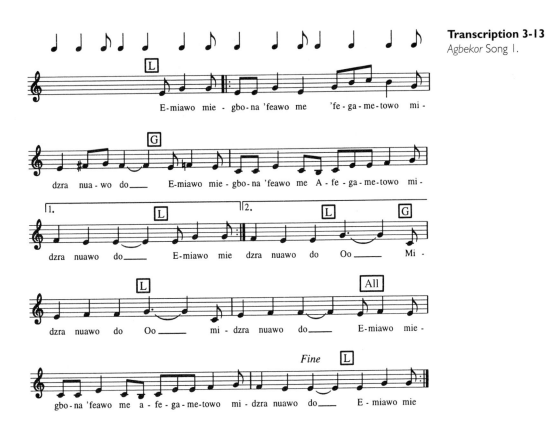

Transcription 3-13
Agbekor Song 1.

second scale degree is variable—sometimes natural, sometimes flat, often somewhere in between. When the song's transcribed pitches are ordered into a scale, we see five pitches with two half steps—1 ♭2 or ♯2 ♭3 5 ♭6. (Compare with the *pélog* scale in Chapter 7.)

Song 2, set at sunrise on the day of battle, urges Manyo and his warriors to "be cunning." Leader and group divide the text: the leader identifies the actors and the action, then the group evokes the scene. Unlike the rounded form of song 1, this song has a linear AB musical form: A[1] B[1] A[2] B[2].

Leader:	*Agbekoviawo, midze aye.*	A[1]	**Text, Song 2**
Group:	*Ada do ee,*	B[1]	
	Kpo nedze ga nu.		
	Ada do!		
Leader:	*Manyo hawo, midze aye ee*	A[2]	
Group:	Repeat lines 2–4	B[2]	
Leader:	*Agbekor* group, be cunning.		
Group:	The day has come.		
	Beat the double bell.		
	The day has come.		
Leader:	Manyo's group, be cunning.		
Group:	Repeat lines 2–4.		

Transcription 3-14
Agbekor Song 2.

'Gbe-ko-viawo   mi-dze   'ye   A - da do ee ____   kpo ne-dze

ga   nu   a-da   do   Ma-nyo hawo   mi-dze   'ye   A - da do   ee   kpo ne-dze

Fine L

ga   nu   a-da   do   'Gbe-ko-viawo   mi-dze

This song has five pitches with no half steps (see Transcription 3-14). As I hear it, the melody moves between two tonal centers: the phrases in A1 B1 strongly cadence on A; A2 shifts the tonal center to G; B2 begins there, but then it ends back on A. Form, melody, and tonality combine in creating a circular musical effect.

Song 3 expresses an important sentiment in *Agbekor* songs: celebrating the singers' power and denigrating the opponent (see Transcription 3-15). Here, the enemy is a "hornless dog," that is, an impotent person, and "we" are incomparably great. Ewe composers often make this point by means of rhetorical questions: "Who can trace the footprints of an ant?" that is, Who can defeat us? "Can the pigeon scratch where the fowl scratches?" that is, Can the enemy fight as strongly as we can? "Can a bird cry like the sea?" that is, How can the enemy compare to us? In these playful self-assertions and witty put-downs, we see a parallel with the genres of African-American expressive culture called "signifying" (Gates 1988; see Chapter 4 for examples).

Text, Song 3

Leader:	‖:	*Avu matodzo,*	A¹
		Dewoe lawuma?	
Group:		Repeat lines 1 and 2 :‖	A²
Leader:	‖:	*Dewoe?*	B¹
Group:		*Dewoe lawuma?* :‖	B²
All:		*Avu matodzo*	A²
		Dewoe lawuma?	
Leader:		A hornless dog.	
		Are there any greater than we?	
Group:		Repeat lines 1 and 2.	
Leader:		Any?	
Group:		Greater than we	
All:		Repeat lines 1 and 2	

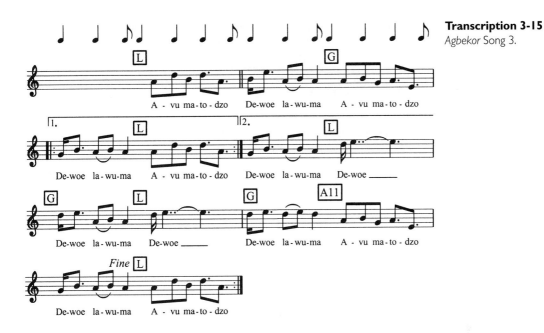

Transcription 3-15
Agbekor Song 3.

Adzo Songs

Rhythmically free songs make up the *adzo* section here. They have longer texts than do songs from the slow- and fast-paced portions of an *Agbekor* performance. Like songs 1 and 3, song 4 begins with two sections of leader-group alternation but has a noticeably longer third section sung by the whole group. The issues raised in song 4 are not new to us; this song, however, does make a factual historical reference to Avusu Kpo, an enemy war leader.

CD 1/15

Agbekor (5:35). Traditional music of the Ewe people. Field recording by David Locke. Anlo-Afiadenyigba, Ghana, 1976.
   b. One song in free rhythm (3:02–4:20)

Leader:	‖:	'Gbekoviwo, xe de ado ahoyo gbe,	A
		Be tsawoyo?	
Group:		Xe ke lado gbe,	B
		Gavi tsawoyo? :‖	
Leader:		Tu nedi!	C¹
Group:		Miahee de alada me.	D
Leader:		Hewo nu,	C²
Group:		Miahee de alada me.	D
All:		Be la bada fo soshi	E
		Ko de alada me.	
		Tu la kaka,	
		Mietsoe da de agboawo dzi	
		Xe de mado ahoyo gbe ee?	
		Avusu Kpowoe mado lo na xe	
		Be xe nedo dika na alado me.	
		Tsawoyo	
		Repeat lines 3 and 4	B
Leader:	‖:	Members of the *Agbekor* group, can a bird cry like the sea, "Tsawoyo?"	

Text, Song 4

Group:	Which bird can cry like the sea, "Gavi Tsawoyo?" :‖
Leader:	Fire the gun!
Group:	We will turn it aside!
Leader:	The tips of knives,
Group:	We will brush them aside!
All:	A wild animal has found a horsetail switch
	And put it at his side.
	The gun broke,
	We put it on the barricade.
	Can a bird cry like the sea?
	Avusu Kpo and his people cannot talk in proverbs to the bird.
	[unknown]
	"Tsawoyo."
	Repeat lines 3 and 4

CD 1/15

Agbekor (5:35). Traditional music of the Ewe people. Field recording by David Locke. Anlo-Afiadenyigba, Ghana, 1976.

    c. One fast-paced song (4:27–5:35)

Text, Song 5

Fast-Paced Songs

Like many songs from the fast-paced section, song 5 celebrates heroic passion. For example, another song says simply, "Sweet, to put on the war belt is very sweet." Song 5 opens with the vivid image of a confrontation between two war gods *(So)*. The Fon from Dahomey and the Anlo are about to fight; the beautiful warriors are preparing; will they have the courage to enter the fray?

Leader:	‖:	*So kpli So, ne ava va gbedzia*	A
		Tsyo miado.	
Group:		*Woyawoya*	B
		Ava va gbedzia,	
		Tsyo miado. :‖	
Leader:		*Oo,*	C
Group:		*Fowo do gbea,*	C
		Miayia?	
		Anlowo do gbe.	
Leader:		*Oo,*	D
Group:		*Anawo do gbea*	
		Tsyo miado.	
All:		Repeat lines 3–5	B
Leader:	‖:	So and So—if war breaks out on the battlefield	
		We will have to dress gorgeously.	
Group:		"Woyowoya"	
		War breaks out on the battlefield.	
		We have to dress gorgeously. :‖	
Leader:		Oh,	

Group:	The Fon are out on the battlefield, Should we go? The Anlo are out on the battlefield.
Leader:	Oh,
Group:	The cowards are out on the battlefield. Should we go? The Anlo are out on the battlefield. Repeat lines 3–5.

As we have seen *Agbekor* is a group effort. Music and dance help cement social feeling among members of an *Agbekor* society. Others types of African music depend more on the virtuosity and special knowledge of individuals. We turn now to an example of such a solo tradition. Information for the next section of the chapter draws primarily on the research of the ethnomusicologist Roderic Knight.

On CD 1, Track 17, we hear the artistry of Mariatu Kuyateh (vocal), her husband, Kekuta Suso (stringed instrument), and Seni Jobateh (speech and percussion) as they perform the piece "Lambango." You may be drawn toward Kuyateh's wordy solo song and Suso's virtuosity on the *kora* (a twenty-one-string bridge-harp). These experts in speech, song, and the playing of instruments are often called *griots* (pronounced *gree*-oh). Not only musicians, they are counselors to royalty, entertainers for the public, and guardians of history (see Figure 3-3).

Mande Jaliya:
"Lambango"

CD I/17

"Lambango" (3:02). Mande song. Mariatu Kuyateh. Performed by Mariatu Kuyateh, Kekuta Suso, and Seni Jobateh. Field recording by Roderic Knight. The Gambia, 1970.

Roderic Knight

Figure 3-3
Mariatu Kuyateh and Kekuta Suso (with *kora*). Boraba, Gambia, 1970.

The performers, who call themselves *jalolu* (singular *jali*), are professional "sound artisans" of the Mande ethnic tradition (see Charry 2000). *Jaliya,* that is, what *jalolu* do, has played many important roles in Mande civilization since the thirteenth century, when Sunjata Keita founded the empire of Mali. At its apogee (fourteenth to sixteenth centuries), Mali exerted authority over a vast territory of river and grassland stretching west from the Upper Niger to the Atlantic coast. Age-old patterns of Mande culture remain influential today.

Historical and Social Background
Cultural Crossroads

Distinct civilizations meet in the West African savanna south of the desert and north of the forest—Sudanic African, Tuareg, Berber, Arab, European. The routes of intercultural communication run between north and south as well as east and west. For Arabic speakers on trading caravans between the Mediterranean and the Sudan (*Bilad es Sudan,* "Land of the Blacks"), the Sahara was a sand sea. The semiarid Sahel was its southern "coast." East–west travel followed rivers such as the Gambia, the Senegal, and most importantly the Niger, whose seasonal floods fostered an agricultural base for empire.

Mali

A succession of great states arose in this broad cultural crossroads: first Ghana, then Mali, Songhai, Kanem-Bornu, Hausa, Mossi, and others. Mali was fabulously wealthy. It was a centralized, hierarchically organized empire with distinct social classes. Islamic libraries and universities of world renown flourished in great cosmopolitan cities. A class of literati (writing in Arabic) operated the empire's systems of commerce and law.

The duty of Mande *jalolu* was to serve this array of wealthy patrons.

> The jali held the only records of genealogy and history and was the only one who knew and could perform the music called for on important occasions. The people who most often employed the services of these people were in a position to provide ample recompense in the form of lodging, cattle, clothing and other manifestations of wealth. For the jali . . . this meant that he was virtually assured of permanent patronage. . . . As one jali has put it, "The jali was king." (Knight 1984:62)

Learning helped determine one's status in such cities as Timbuktu. Some intellectuals became praise singers (*muddah*) who received alms for lauding the Prophet Muhammad (Saad 1983:86). Such refined professionals included erudite *jalolu.* In the Islamic Sudan, the formal exchange of praise for wealth remains a respected institution. In this music-culture, gifts to a *jali* are not commercial payments for products sold but rather are respectful offerings that mark the interdependence of praiser and praised.

Although the political leaders were nominally Muslim, the bulk of the population kept faith with pre-Islamic religion. Some Mande peoples still

retain a mythic consciousness that links natural landmarks to the primor-
dial, creative feats of superhuman ancestors (Dieterlen 1957, in Skinner
1973). In addition to serving their elite patrons, the *jalolu* transmit these
ancient, secret mysteries to every member of society (Laye 1983).

After 1600, the history of these Sudanic empires is a story of fracture
and gradual decline. Forces of change included internal rebellion, invasion
by a Moroccan expeditionary force (1591), the Atlantic slave trade (1700s),
Islamic jihads (1800s), and finally British and French colonialism (1900s).
All the while, in songs like "Lambango," the Mande bards told legends of
the empire's founder, Sunjata Keita, and news of more recent heroes.

Kingdoms Along the Gambia

At the western edge of the Mande heartland, many small kingdoms formed
along the Gambia River. Modeled on the much larger empires of the Upper Niger, each state had its hierarchy of royals, courtiers, warriors, state
officials, merchants, clerics, and so on. Prospering through trade with
Europe—notably, slaves for manufactured goods—the elite were remarkably cosmopolitan.

> French traders in the eighteenth century reported that the *mansas* of
> Niumi [kings of a state on the north bank of the Gambia] lived in Euro-
> pean-style houses and dressed in elaborate costumes. . . . [One] mansa's
> daughter, who was said to read and write French, Portuguese and English,
> had established herself as the chief intermediary between the traders and
> her father. At one time married to a Portuguese, she lived in a large square
> European house and held soirees for the commercial community in a style
> that boasted fine table linen and other imported luxuries. (Quinn 1972:41)

A distinctive music-culture of *jali* with *kora* developed in these kingdoms
along the Gambia.

Music-Culture
Social Organization

Where do the *jalolu* fit within the Mande system of social rank and its associated roles? Slavery existed in this African society; even today, descendants
of the freeborn *(horon)* are distinguished from persons of slave descent
(jong), especially in the matter of marriage. Among the freeborn, *nyamalo*—
craft specialists including *jalolu*—occupy a separate niche from *sula*—non-
specialists, including royals, Islamic literates, merchants, and farmers—who
are a *jali*'s prospective patrons. Among *nyamalo,* boys inherit their fathers'
craft as a lifelong profession; young women marry within their fathers'
occupational group (see Knight 1984:60–66).

Duties to Patrons

In former times when kings were rich, *jali* and patron shared a mutually
beneficial relationship. Playmates as children, they retained their intimacy
as adults.

Griots woke the king each morning by singing his praises outside his quarters, they accompanied him wherever he traveled, singing and playing behind him and especially when he met another king, they were in attendance singing their patron's praises. From time to time a court griot would entertain the king and members of his court by reciting accounts of the careers of some of the king's forebears, perhaps of some deeds of the king himself. . . . The whole narration glorified the king, often bathing him in the reflected glory of his mighty ancestors. . . . [The griot] would take real pride in [this] history and would want to present it in the best possible light, for he would surely feel able to share in the glory of his patron's family. (Innes 1976:5)

Before our era, the *jali* received the wholehearted respect merited by a learned artist with significant duties in the affairs of state. A *jali*'s performance bridged time and space, bringing the historical and mythic past into the lives of the living.

When the jali sings the name of a past hero, he views what he is doing as waking him up, bringing him back to life *(Mb'a wulindila)*. . . . If in the end the listener can say of the music, *Wo le dunta n na* (It has entered me), then the desired effect will have been achieved" (Knight 1984:73).

This music-culture changed after The Gambia became a British protectorate in 1894. Since the wealth of the royals was much reduced, their patronage alone could not sustain a *jali*. Thus today, *jalolu* must serve a broader clientele by freelancing at social occasions such as weddings and naming ceremonies where people value their knowledge and artistry. Yet even in our cash-oriented, dislocated world, where an African royal may hold a menial job in Europe, the *jalolu* retain warm relations with their patrons and provide a vital link to profound dimensions of Mande culture.

Transmission

A *jali* learns the craft of playing a musical instrument through a formal apprenticeship with a single master. During adolescence and young adulthood, fathers send their sons to a relative who enforces a strict training regimen. Some *jalolu* specialize in the *kora,* others play xylophone *(balo)* or a plucked, long-neck lute *(konting, ngoni,* or guitar). Young women, whose primary duty is to sing, participate in a more informal apprenticeship. While they serve their elders, young *jalolu* gradually learn an impressive body of knowledge. *Jalolu* keep elaborate genealogies and stories of their patrons' forebears. More than dry objective historical accounts, their performances entail rousing artistry designed to elicit the respect and gratitude of an audience.

The Jali's Knowledge

A key element in *jaliya* is speech *(kuma).* Narratives in the Gambian tradition refer to two historical periods: (1) the times of Sunjata and the formation of Mali (1200s) and (2) the times of the last *mansas* (1800s). The stories are told in the vernacular with few poetic devices; the *jali* enlivens the characters by recreating their words. Songs contain wise sayings about people and situations that are always relevant to the living. Here are some examples (Knight 1984:78–80):

Islamic fatalism:	"Before God created life, he created death."
Moral judgments:	"The talkative kings are plentiful, but men of great deeds are few."
	"Misery is hard on a woman, shame is hard on a man."
Advice:	"The world is ever-changing. If someone doesn't know your past, don't tell him your present affairs."
Observations:	"Life is nothing without conversation."
On wealth:	"Wealth is not a tonic for life; wealth is to save you from disgrace."
	"The wealthy inherit the wealth."
On *jaliya:*	"For the person who puts one hundred in my hand, I will give him a hundred-worth praise with my mouth."
	"The great carrier of loads has put me on his back—the elephant never tires of carrying his trunk."

Elements of Performance
Kora

The *kora* is an indigenous African instrument with a unique array of parts (Figure 3-4). Scholars of musical instruments (organologists) classify the instrument as a bridge harp, a variety of spike harp. Spike harps have a long neck that passes entirely through the resonator, usually a large skin-covered half-calabash. The bridge harp variety, of which the kora is the best example, has a high bridge with notches on the sides through which the strings pass; the harp designation refers to the plane of the strings,

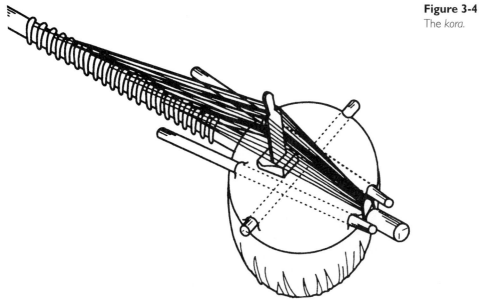

Figure 3-4
The *kora.*

perpendicular to the soundboard (see Charry 1994, 2000; DeVale 1989; Knight 1971, 1972).

The *kora* has left and right sides, just like the human body. Plucking in left-right alternation, the player takes full advantage of this bilateral symmetry. Sometimes a flat metal rattle attached to the bridge enhances the flavor of the rhythm and timbre. As in "Lambango," pieces may call for *konkon*, an ostinato (repeated phrase) rapped on the resonator. By adjusting the tuning rings along its neck, the *jali* tunes his *kora*'s twenty-one strings in patterns of seven pitches per octave. Just as the tonality of each Javanese *gamelan* is a unique variant of a general standard, the intervals between pitches on a kora are not precisely reckoned against an invariant abstract standard. "Lambango" is in the *sauta* tuning (see Figure 3-5).

Figure 3-5
Bridge of the *kora*, with strings shown as pitches in *sauta* tuning.
(Drawing by Roderick Knight)

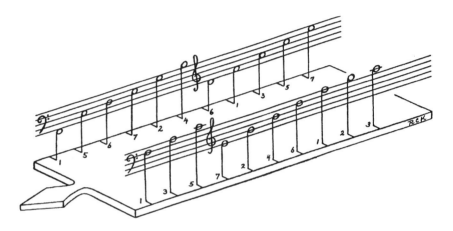

As in most music-cultures, Mande musicians metaphorically link musical pitch to physical space through the words like *high-low* and *ascend-descend*. English speakers and Mande speakers, however, use these terms in opposite ways (Charry 2000:325). For instance, *kora* players call the bass strings "high," the treble strings "low." This is because the longer, thicker strings are physically above the shorter, thinner strings when a *jali* holds the instrument. An ascending passage in Western terms "goes down" for the *kora* player.

During performance, when the emphasis is on text, the *kora* player accompanies the singer with *kumbengo*, an instrumental ostinato. Played over and over with subtle variation, the *kumbengo* establishes the tonal and metric framework of a piece. Virtuosic instrumental passages *(birimintingo)* provide interludes between vocal sections. On CD 1, Track 17, Suso accompanies Kuyateh by playing *kumbengo* with occasional *birimintingo*-like passages. Unlike full-fledged *birimintingo* that forcefully suspend the *kumbengo*'s framework, these fills always remain within its time span.

During apprenticeship, lessons focus on the *kumbengo*. Talented youngsters pick up *birimintingo* riffs as they listen to their master's playing. Interestingly, a master does not teach tuning until an apprentice is ready to leave. "Giving him an actual lesson on how to tune the instrument is regarded as the final key to his independence. This lesson is therefore withheld from him until his master feels he is fully qualified to embark on his own career" (Knight 1984:77).

Verbal Art

The "Lambango" recording shows that singers can mix several styles of verbal presentation in one performance. At different points in a performance *jalolu* may tell stories in everyday speech, sing tunefully, or declaim highly formulaic praises, proverbs, and references to specific heroes in narrative songs. The preferred timbral quality, a forceful chest resonance sung with a tensed throat, evokes the strength of the Mande heroes in sound itself.

The vocalist works with two building blocks of form: *donkilo,* a tune with several phrases of text, and *sataro,* an open-ended, extemporaneous passage of spoken or chanted text. After a section of *sataro,* a singer may return to the *donkilo,* or give way for an instrumental break. In her performance of "Lambango," Kuyateh begins by ever so briefly singing the tuneful *donkilo;* the rest of the performance is *sataro.* As Jobateh taps the *konkong* part, he interjects comments and praises with stylized speech.

Women *(jali musolu)* set the standard for all singers. As one *jali* told Roderic Knight:

> A *ngara* [superior singer] is a woman who is not afraid of crowds, not afraid of anything, except God. She can stand before a crowd with all eyes upon her and not become confused *(kijo fara).* She can shout *(feteng),* literally "split" the air with her voice, but do it with feeling *(wasu)* and sentiment *(balafa),* so that people will sympathize with her. She sticks to her forte *(taburango)* in performing, never jumbling the words together *(faranfansandi)* so that they are unintelligible, but choosing words which contain the essences of her message *(sigirango),* words which all listeners will agree are true *(sahata).* (Nyulo Jebateh, quoted in Knight 1984:74)

A Hearing of "Lambango"

I have never studied *jaliya* with experts. The following section is an interpretation of "Lambango" based on my careful listening to the sound recording. I urge you to apply this type of close hearing to all the sound recordings in *Worlds of Music.*

The repeating phrases of the *kora* and *konkong* establish the tonal and rhythmic context for the song. The slowly moving knocks in the *konkong* part mark three moments within a cycle of eight beats: 5 6 7 8 1 2 3 4. During beats 5–1 the texture sounds multilayered and polyrhythmic; during beats 1–5, however, we hear only the *kora's* treble voice.

CD 1/17

"Lambango" (3:02). Mande song. Mariatu Kuyateh. Performed by Mariatu Kuyateh, Kekuta Suso, and Seni Jobateh. Field recording by Roderic Knight. The Gambia, 1970.

Song

Kuyateh's song works within the restrained melodic range of a fifth or sixth. Her pitches conform to the tuning system of the *kora,* and her melody helps establish the tonal center of the piece. A Western analyst could describe the contour of her melodies as terraced descent with some undulation. She phrases the rhythms freely, giving the impression that her voice floats elusively over the tightly interlocked instrumental parts. The text comes in a rapid explosion of syllables; occasionally, however, she sings several pitches to one syllable of text (melisma). Like members of an African-American church (see Chapter 4), Jobateh responds to Kuyateh's "sermon" with affirmation and elaboration.

Text

This rendition of "Lambango" celebrates three twentieth-century Gambian leaders: Musa Molo (lines 1–10), Dembo Dansa (lines 11–21), and Jewuru Kurubali (lines 22–23). The text cites places where significant events in their lives occurred, praises their generosity, and honors them through recitation of stylized praise lyrics (*jamundiro*). The text is not a continuous narrative but rather a series of praises and a commemoration of events. The *kora* player Alhaji Papa Susso and the ethnomusicologist Roderic Knight have provided the following transcription and translation.

Text and Translation, "Lambango"

1 [spoken]
Nte Kekuta Suso, ning Seni Jobate, ning Mariatu Kuyate. Ntelu be rekotola jang bi.
I am Kekuta Suso, with Seni Jobateh and Mariatu Kuyateh. We are recording here today.

2 [sung]
Ye, mba jaja, Jaba Sirimang ning Jaba Tarawari. Fulo ning kelo be mang kanyang.
[*Jamundiro* for Musa Molo.] The Fulas and war are not one and the same.

Jamundiro—Stylized praise lyrics for Musa Molo, a king of the Fula people, neighbors to the Mande.

3 [spoken]
Bande banna. Fulo Sirimang jang.
Wealthy Fula. Sirimang, the Fula here.

4 [sung]
Wo Bala. Jigi-o Bala banta, Nya-naani Musa.
Oh, Bala. Bala is gone, Four-eyed Musa.

Bala is a nickname for Musa. "Four-eyed" means "all-seeing."

5 [sung]
Aniya na Bala. Parumba kumbengo diyata Bala la, Nya-naani Musa.
Aniya's Bala. The events at Parumba went in Bala's favor, Four-eyed Musa.

"Went in Bala's favor"—Literally, "were sweet for Bala."

6 [spoken]
Bala Mafaro. Surabali janjungo diyata a la.
Bala the Great. The campaign at Surabali was successful for him.

Parumba and Surabali were strongholds of the Soninke people, a Mande subgroup; the text alludes to battle between Fula and Soninke.

7 [sung]
Aniya la Bala. Surabali kumbengo diyata Bala la, Nya-naani Musa.
Aniya's Bala. The events at Surabali were sweet for Bala, Four-eyed Musa.

8 [sung]

Bala mfa Musa me do go jameng to (?) Bala mfa Musa aning bulu si simba (?)
Bala mfa Musa aning ke domoda (?). Jigo-o Bala, Bala sumayata.
[*Jamundiro.*] Bala has grown cold [is dead].

Jamundiro—Praise to the effect that Bala was a man who did not enter a battle if he knew he might die in it.

9 [spoken]

A fele laring Keserekunda. A ning malo mang ta Yomali Kiyama.
He is buried in Keserekunda. He went without shame to the next world.

10 [sung]

Wo ka mansaya ke, duniya; wolu bee, i jamano banta.
Those people made kingship in this world; all of them, their days are gone.

11 [sung]

Wo ka mansaya di, Kibili-o Demba; E, Yasin Baro la Demba sumayata.
Those people gave us kingship, Kibili-o Demba; Eh, Yasin Barrow's Demba has grown cold.

12 [spoken]

Salimata Bunja Fara. Demba Damudu aning Demba Tegelema (?). Wo fanang be Kanjelebeti.
[*Jamundiro* for Demba Danso.] He too lies at Kanjelebeti.

13 [sung]

Kibili-o Demba. Bu Majila na Demba sumayata (?). Demba . . . Kanjelebeti.
Kibili-o Demba. Yasin Baro la Demba sumayata.
[*Jamundiro* for Demba.] Demba has died and lies at Kanjelebeti. Yasin Barrow's Demba has grown cold.

14 [spoken]

Wo fanang mu ninsi dimba le ti. A ka a dingolu balundi, aning wandi dingolu balundi. Salimata Bunja Fara. Wo le mu Dembo Danso ti.
He was like a mother cow. He could feed his own young and those of others too. Salimata Bunja Fara. That was Dembo Danso.

15 [sung]

Wo lungolu bee mang di. Lungolu bee mang di mogo fanang na lungolu bee mang di (?).
Every day is not a holiday (?).

16 [sung]

Nte Musa fele lota Dembo da la lung do la. A ko, "Mansa jong si kemo di n na?" Dembo kamfata.
I saw Musa standing at Dembo's door one day. He said, "What king can give me a hundred?" This made Dembo angry.

To be asked for only a hundred was demeaning to Dembo, famous for his largesse in giving cows or slaves.

17 [sung]

Nying ne mang na keme di . . . Musa Fili. Konte la Demba mang tumbung ke (?).
Did he not give a hundred to Musa Fili? Konte's Demba did not make ruins of the village (?).

18 [sung]

Keme ni mansolu banta; jali mara mansolu dogoyata.

The hundred-giving kings are gone; the *jali*-patron kings are few.

19 [sung]

Ntelu keta konoba ti. M be yaarana; sita yoro te n na. I salam aleka.

We *[jalis]* have become like vultures. We are soaring; we have no place to sit down. My peace be upon you.

"Sit down"—that is, searching for patrons.

20 [spoken]

Salimata Bunja Fara, Dembo Damudu aning Dembo Tegelema (?). A ye Kosemari ke, a ye Jakaling ke.

[Jamundiro for Dembo Danso]. He did well for the villages of Kosemari and Jakaling.

21 [sung]

Siba-o, wolu bee tambirinna ko (?). Sarakata Bunja Fara, Bunja Mamadi.

Siba-o, those are all in the past. [*Jamundiro* for Bunja, an associate of Dembo and son of Mamadi.]

22 [sung]

Praise for Sunjata Keita.

Ko, ni i be na 'waye' folo la, i sa folo Ma Biraima Konate. Yamaru jang, siba-o.

Say, when you begin your "waye" [singing], you should begin with praise for Ma Biraima Konateh.

23 [sung]

Sibo banta. I salam aleka.

The great one is gone. Peace be upon you.

A Drummer of Dagbon

Musicians have had important functions in the political affairs of many African traditional states. We turn now to the life story of one such person.

On CD 1, Track 18, we hear singing and drumming of the Dagbamba people (also known as Dagomba) from the southern savanna of western Africa (Ghana). I recorded the music in 1984. The performers are *lunsi* (pronounced *loon*-see; singular *luna,* pronounced *loong*-ah), members of a hereditary clan of drummers. Like a Mande *jali,* a *luna* fulfills many vital duties in the life of the Dagbamba—verbal artist, genealogist, counselor to royalty, cultural expert, entertainer. The *lunsi* tradition developed in Dagbon, the hierarchical, centralized kingdom of the Dagbamba (Chernoff 1979; Djedje 1978; Locke 1990).

The Drums

Lunsi play two kinds of drums—*gungon* (pronounced goong-*gawng*) and *luna* (see Figure 3-6). For both types, a shoulder strap holds the drum in position to receive strokes from a curved wooden stick. The *gungon* is a cylindrical, carved drum with a snare on each of its two heads. The cedarwood of a *luna* is carved into an hourglass shape. By squeezing the leather cords strung between its two drumheads, a player can change the tension of the drum skins, which changes the pitch of the drum tones. In the hands

Figure 3-6
Lunsi in performance.

Patsy Marshall

of an expert, the drum's sound closely imitates Dagbanli, the spoken language of the Dagbamba. *Lunsi* "talk" and "sing" on their instruments. These musicians are storytellers, chroniclers of the history of their people and their nation.

A Praise Name Dance

"Nag Biegu" (pronounced *nah*-oh bee-*ah*-oo) is one of the many Praise Name Dances *(salima)* of Dagbon. Its title means "ferocious wild bull," referring to an enemy leader whom Naa Abudu defeated in a dramatic man-to-man fight. This *salima* praises Naa Abudu, a king of Dagbon in the late 1800s who is remembered for his courage and firm leadership. Scoffing at the challenge of a war leader from a neighboring nation, Naa Abudu said, "I am dangerous wild bull. Kill me if you can." As they dance to the drumming, people recall the bravery of the king.

The music has a verse-chorus form. In the verse, the vocalist and leading *luna* drummers praise Naa Abudu and allude to events of his chieftaincy; the answering *lunsi* and two *gungon* drummers punctuate the verses with booming, single strokes. The drummed chorus phrase works like a "hook" in a pop song, that is, a catchy, memorable phrase.

CD 1/18

"Nag Biegu" (Ferocious Wild Bull")
(2:08). Traditional Praise Name
Dance song of Dagbon. Performed by
lunsi drummers of the Dagbamba
people. Field recording by David
Locke. Ghana, 1984.

Transcription 3-16
"Nag Biegu" chorus phrases and verse
answer. (The rhythm in measures 5–7 is
a standard, if simpler, version of the
more exciting phrases heard on the
recording.)

The Dagbanli text and an English translation are as follows:

Text, "Nag Biegu"

Dagbanli	English
Nag Biegu la to to to,	It is Nag Biegu
Nag Biegu la to to to,	It is Nag Biegu
Nag Biegu la to—n nyeo!	It is Nag Biegu—that's him
Nag Biegu la to,	It is Nag Biegu
Nag Biegu la to,	It is Nag Biegu
Nag Biegu la to—kumo!	It is Nag Biegu—kill him!

Life Story: Abubakari Lunna

I have tape-recorded many interviews with my teacher from Dagbon, Abubakari Lunna. When I met Mr. Lunna in 1975, he was working as a professional with the Ghana Folkloric Company, a government-sponsored performing arts company based in Accra, the capital of Ghana. In 1988 he retired from government service and returned to northern Ghana, where he served his father, Lun-Naa Wombie, until Mr. Wombie's death. Presently, Mr. Lunna supports his large family as a drummer, farmer, and teacher. The following excerpt of his life story focuses on his teachers.

Figures 3-7 and 3-8
(*left*) Studio portrait of Abubakari as a young man.
(*right*) Studio portrait of Lun-Naa Wombie, Abubakari's father.

"My Education in Drumming"

My father's grandfather's name is Abubakari. It is Abubakari who gave birth to Azima and Alidu; Azima was the father of [my teacher] Ngolba and Alidu was father of Wombie, my father. Their old grandfather's name is the one I am carrying, Abubakari. My father never called me "son" until he died; he always called me "grandfather." I acted like their grandfather; we always played like grandson and grandfather.

When I was a young child, my father was not in Dagbon. My father was working as a security guard in the South at Bibiani, the gold town. I was living with one of my father's teachers, his uncle Lun-Naa Neindoo, the drum chief at Woriboggo, a village near Tolon. When I was six or seven, my mother's father, Tali-Naa Alaasani [a chief of Tolon], took me to his senior brother, a chief of Woriboggo at that time. I was going to be his "shared child." In my drumming tradition, when you give your daughter in marriage and luckily she brings forth children, the husband has to give one to the mother's family. So, I was living in the chief's house.

I was with my mother's uncle for four or five years when he enrolled me in school. They took four of us to Tolon, my mother's home. I lived with my mother's father. We started going to the school. Luckily, in several weeks' time my father came from the South. He called my name, but his uncle told him, "Sorry. The boy's grandfather came and took him to be with the chiefs. Now he is in school." My father said, "What?! Is there any teacher above me? I am also a teacher. How can a teacher give his child to another teacher for training in a different language?" Early in the morning, he walked to Tolon. He held my hand. I was happy because my father had come to take me [see Figure 3-8].

My father spent one month. When he went to the South, he took me with him. Unfortunately, at Bibiani my father didn't have time to teach me. One year when my father came back to Dagbon for the Damba Festival [an annual celebration of the birth of The Holy Prophet Muhammed], he told my grandfather, Lun-Naa Neindoo, "If I keep Abubakari at Bibiani, it will be bad. I want to leave him at home. I don't want him to be a southern boy."

I began learning our drumming talks and the singing. Lun-Naa Neindoo started me with *Dakoli Nye Bii Ba,* the beginning of drumming [that is, the first repertory learned by young *lunsi*]: "God is the Creator. He can create a tree, He can create grass, He can create a person." You drum all before you say, "A Creator, God, created our grandfather, Bizung [the first *luna*]." The elders have given *Dakoli Nye Bii Ba* to the young ones so that they can practice in the markets. When they know that you are improving, they start you with drumming stories and singing stories. On every market day we, the young drummers, came together and drummed by ourselves.

When the Woriboggo chief made my father *Sampahi-Naa,* the drum chief second to the *Lun-Naa* [the highest rank of drum chief], he could not go back to Bibiani. My father said, "Now, I am going to work with you on our drumming history talks." He began with the story of Yendi [seat of the paramount chieftaincy of Dagbon]: how Dagbon started, how we traveled from Nigeria and came to Dagbon, how we became drummers, how it happened that our grandfather Bizung made himself a drummer. If he gave me a story today, tomorrow I did it correctly.

There are significant differences of ecology, history, and culture between what Abubakari calls "the North" and "the South."

While his father comes from a long line of drummers, Abubakari's mother comes from a royal family.

Just as the royals of Dagbon have an elaborate hierarchy of chieftaincies, so the *lunsi* have a pyramidlike system of titled positions of authority.

I was with my father for a long time, more than five years. My father was hard. I faced difficulty with my father because of his way of teaching. My father would not beat the drum for you. He would sing and you had to do the same thing on *luna.* If you couldn't do it, he would continue until you got it before adding another.

[Later] . . . my father sent me to my teaching-father, Ngolba. He had a good voice, a good hand—every part of drumming, he had it. He had the knowledge, too, and people liked him. When he was drumming, he would make people laugh. People would hire him: "We are having a funeral on this day. Come and help us." I traveled with him, carrying his *luna.* Because of his drumming, Ngolba never sat at home; every day we went for drumming. That was how people got to know me. Any time I was walking, people started calling, "Ngolba, small Ngolba." And with my sweet hand and my quick memory, everyone liked me.

Already I knew something in drumming, so for him to continue with me was not hard. I only had to listen to his story and follow him. When we went to a place and he told stories, I tried to keep it in my mind. When we were resting that night, I asked him, "Oh, my uncle, I heard your talk today. Can you tell me more about it?" There, he would start telling me something. That is how I continued by education with Mba Ngolba. I was very young to be drumming the deep history rhythms with a sweet hand.

My father called Ngolba and advised him, "I am not feeling happy about all the traveling you and Abubakari are doing. Drummers are bad. Somebody might try to spoil your lives. Find something to protect yourself. And protect Abubakari too." Father Ngolba—I can never forget him. Sometimes, when I was sitting at home, he would call me to get something to drink. I couldn't ask him, "Father, what is this?" In Dagbon, you can't ask him—you have to drink it. My Mba Ngolba did it for me several times.

Another reason why I liked my teacher, my Father Ngolba, is that despite his quick temper, he didn't get angry with me. He loved me. He didn't take even one of his ideas and hide it from me. Even if I asked him about something common that many drummers know, the thing left—he didn't hide it. He would tell me, "I have reserved something. If you bring all your knowledge out in public, some people with quick learning can just collect it."

I respected Ngolba like my father. During farming time I got up early in the morning and went straight to the farm. When he came, he met me there already. If it was not farming time, I would go to his door, kneel down, and say good morning to him. I would stay there, not saying anything until at last he would ask me, "Do you want to go some place?" Only then could I go. Teachers can give you laws like your own father. That is our Dagbamba respect to teachers.

Father Ngolba died in the South. When an old drummer dies, we put a *luna* and a drumstick in the grave. The man who was with Ngolba when he died told me, "Your father said, 'Only bury me with this drumstick—don't add my *luna* to bury me. Give my *luna* to Abubakari.'" I said thank you for that. We finished the funeral back in Dagbon. The second brother to Ngolba spoke to all their family, "Ngolba told me that if it happens he dies, Abubakari should carry on with his duties. He should take his whole inheritance. And Ngolba had nothing other than his *luna.*" I have his *luna;* it is in my room now.

"Mba" means "father"; for a *luna* drummer, your teacher becomes your teaching-father.

According to Dagbamba etiquette, children never question the orders of their father.

Figure 3-9
Abubakari holding the frame of Mba Ngolba's *luna.*

David Locke

Shona Mbira Music

The recording of "Nhemamusasa" (CD 1, Track 19) features another uniquely African type of musical instrument. It is known outside Africa as "thumb piano"; speakers of the Shona language call it *mbira* (pronounced mmm-*bee*-rah). The "kaleidophonic" sound of its music (Tracey 1970:12) provides us with another insight into the musical potential of 3:2 rhythmic structures. Further, the *mbira* tradition shows another way African music can transform a group of separate individuals into a participatory polyphonic community. Information for this section draws primarily on the research of the ethnomusicologist Paul Berliner (1993).

Cultural Context
History

The Shona, who live in high plateau country between the Zambezi and Limpopo Rivers, are among the sixty million Bantu-speaking people who predominate in central and southern Africa. Since about 800 C.E., kingdoms of the Shona and neighboring peoples have ruled large territories; stone fortresses such as the Great Zimbabwe number among Africa's most impressive architectural achievements. These kingdoms participated in a lively Indian Ocean commerce with seafaring powers such as the Arabs, Persians, and Indians (Mallows 1967:97–115). The Portuguese arrived about 1500. Eventually, the large-scale Shona states faded under pressure from other African groups, notably the more militaristic Ndebele in the 1800s. The Shona became a more decentralized, agricultural people.

At the turn of the twentieth century English-speaking settlers took over the land and imposed their culture and economy on the local Africans. The colonial period in what was then called Rhodesia was brief, but it radically affected most local institutions. As in neighboring South Africa, a systematic policy of land grabbing left Africans materially impoverished. Racist settlers scorned African culture; many local people came to doubt the ways of their ancestors. For two decades after the independence of other contemporary African nation-states in the 1950s and 1960s, white Rhodesians maintained their dominance. Finally, a war of liberation (1966–1979) culminated in majority rule and the birth of the nation-state Zimbabwe in 1980.

Music played a part in the struggle. Popular and traditional songs with hidden meanings helped galvanize mass opinion; spirit mediums were leaders in the war against white privilege (Frye 1976; Lan 1985). After decades of denigration by some Africans who had lost faith in traditional culture, the *mbira* became a positive symbol of cultural identity.

Shona Spirits

From the perspective inherited from the Shona ancestors, four classes of spirits (literally *mweya* or breath) affect the world: spirits of chiefs *(mhondoro)*, family members *(mudzimu)*, nonrelatives or animals *(mashave)*, and witches *(muroyi)* (Lan 1985:31–43). Although invisible, ancestral spirits nonetheless have sensory experience, feel emotions, and take action to help and advise their beloved descendants. *Mbira* music helps connect the living with their ancestors.

Humans and spirits communicate by means of possession trances. In possession, a spirit enters the body of a living person, temporarily supplanting his or her spirit. Once embodied in its medium, an ancestral spirit can advise his or her living relatives, telling them things they have done wrong and how to protect themselves and ensure good fortune. Similarly, a *mhondoro* spirit may advise a gathering of several family groups regarding matters that affect the entire community, such as the coming of rain. Possessions occur at *mapira* (singular *bira*), all-night, family-based, communal rituals. *Mbira* music and dancing are significant elements in these events (Berliner 1993:186–206; Zantinger n.d.).

The Mbira
Construction

Mbiras of many different styles of construction occur throughout Africa and its diaspora. Most *mbiras* have four features of construction: (1) a set of long, thin keys made of metal or plant material, (2) a soundboard with a bridge that holds the keys, (3) a resonator to shape and amplify the sound of the plucked keys, and (4) jingles that buzz rhythmically when the keys are plucked. Like the *kora*, the instrument matches the bilateral symmetry of the human body; that is, left-side keys are for the left thumb, right-side keys are for the right thumb and index finger. The longer, bass keys lie toward the center of the soundboard; the shorter, treble keys toward its edges (Berliner 1993:8–18).

On our recording of "Nhemamusasa" we hear an instrument that is frequently used at spirit possession ceremonies: the *mbira dzavadzimu*, literally "*mbira* of the ancestors" (pronounced mmm-*bee*-rah dzah-vah-*dzee*-moo). Figure 3-10 shows a characteristic layout of its keys and one tuning arrangement.

In performance, musicians place the *mbira* within a large gourd resonator *(deze)* that brings out the instrument's full tone; when playing for personal pleasure or during learning-teaching sessions, the resonator may not be needed (see Figure 3-11).

Bottle cap rattles or snail shells attached to the soundboard and resonator provide the important buzzing ingredient to the music. Performances usually include hand clapping, singing, and a driving rhythm played on a pair of gourd rattles called *hosho*.

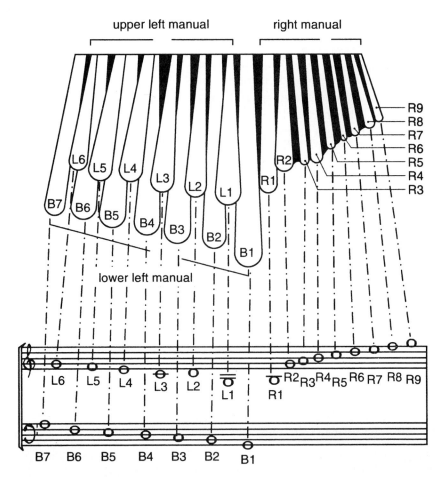

Figure 3-10

A tuning plan for the *mbira dzavadzimu.*

Figure 3-11
Mbira players.

Paul Berliner

Tuning *(Chuning)*

Shona musicians refer to the tonal qualities of an *mbira*'s sound with the English word *tuning* or the modified term *chuning*. Artists use *chuning* to refer not only to interval configurations but also to qualities of tone, sound projection, pitch level, and overtones (Berliner 1993:54–72). The *mbira dzavadzimu* is tuned to a seven-pitch scale over a range of three octaves; interval size varies among different chunings. Musicians debate the affective quality of different chunings and symbolically link the *mbira* keys with features of culture such as family relationships, emotional or physical responses to music, and animal imagery.

The Player and the Instrument

In performance, the instrument faces toward the player. Repeatedly plucking the keys in prescribed patterns, musicians establish cycles of harmony, melody, rhythm, and counterpoint. Each key on the *mbira* emits a fundamental pitch and a cluster of overtones; the resonator shapes, reinforces, prolongs, and amplifies this complex tone. The buzzing bottle caps not only provide rhythm to the music's texture but also add to the instrument's array of tuned and untuned sounds. Tones overlap. The *mbira*'s sound surrounds the player. In this music, the whole is far more than the sum of the parts (Berliner 1993:127–35).

   Creative, participatory listening is an essential aspect of this music-culture. Performer and audience must hear coherent melodies in the *mbira*'s numerous tones. Many pieces exploit the creative potential of 3:2 relationships; often one hand is "in three or six" while the other is "in two or four." Hand-clapping phrases provide a good way to join in the performance and experience this polymetric feeling (see Transcription 3-17).

Transcription 3-17
Hand-clapping phrases for *mbira* music.

For players immersed in the process, the *mbira* takes on a life of its own. Here is how Dumisani Maraire, one of the first teachers of Shona music to non-Africans, explains it:

> When a mbira player plays his instrument . . . he is . . . conversing with a friend. He teaches his friend what to do, and his friend teaches him what to do. To begin with, the mbira player gives the basic pattern to the mbira; he plays it, and the mbira helps him produce the sound. He goes over and over playing the same pattern, happy now that his fingers and the mbira keys are together. So he stops thinking about what to play, and starts to listen to the mbira very carefully. (Maraire 1971:5–6)

"Nhemamusasa"

According to the Shona, ancestral spirits love to hear their favorite *mbira* pieces. Musical performance is an offering that calls them near, thus making possession more likely. Because of its important social use, this repertoire remains stable over many generations. Pieces for *mbira dzavadzimu*, most of which have been played for centuries, are substantial musical works with many fundamental patterns, variations, styles of improvisation, and so forth. These pieces have two interlocking parts: *kushaura*, the main part, and *kutsinhira*, the interwoven second part. Since each part is polyphonic in its own right, the interaction of parts creates a wonderfully multi-layered sound. The vocal music, which has three distinct styles—*mahonyera* (vocables), *kudeketera* (poetry), and *huro* (yodeling)—adds depth to the musical texture and richness to the meanings expressed in performance. In our discussion here, we only scratch the surface of the *kushaura* part of one piece.

On CD 1, Track 19, we hear "Nhemamusasa" (pronounced *neh*-mah-moo-*sah*-sah), revered by the Shona as one of their oldest and most important pieces. It was played for Chaminuka, a powerful spirit who protects the

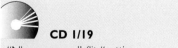

CD 1/19

"Nhemamusasa" (lit. "cutting branches for shelter"), *kushaura* section (2:39). Traditional Shona. Field recording by Paul Berliner. Zimbabwe, 1971.

entire Shona nation. The song title literally means "cutting branches for shelter." One of Berliner's teachers reports that "'Nhemamusasa' is a song for war. When we [the Shona] were marching to war to stop soldiers coming to kill us, we would cut branches and make a place [tent shelter] called a *musasa*" (John Kunaka, quoted in Berliner 1993:42). In 1991 Erica Kundizora Azim, an experienced American student of *mbira,* heard a contemporary interpretation of the song's meaning from a female Shona friend:

Text, "Nhemamusasa"

Homeless people sit in their shantytowns with nothing to do.
No work.
Trouble is coming.

Evidently the piece evokes profound feelings. For the Shona, sentiments evoked by pieces such as "Nhemamusasa" make them effective for use in rituals of spirit possession. Even for those of us without inside knowledge of Shona cultural history, the musical surface of "Nhemamusasa" sparks powerful feelings.

Rhythm

Tapping out a four-stroke plucking pattern—right index, left thumb, right thumb, left thumb—provides insight into a Shona *mbira* player's experience of the *kushaura* part of "Nhemamusasa." When the pattern repeats over and over, any of the four actions may be taken as the first one. Within this circular structure that has no beginning or end, melodies arise from the *mbira* as players apply the plucking pattern to the appropriate keys.

Each melodic phrase requires three repetitions of the four-pulse pattern; four of these twelve-pulse phrases make one pass through "Nhemamusasa's" principal musical unit. From the perspective of playing technique, the pulse structure can be expressed in the equation $(3 \times 4) \times 4 = 48$. Given the right-left alternation in the plucking pattern, we can also interpret the pulse structure as $(6 \times 2) \times 4 = 48$. The music's most fundamental time-feel does not derive from playing technique, however. Instead, players feel a steady flow of ternary beats, that is, three pulses per beat. Within each twelve-pulse melodic phrase, the three explicit four-pulse plucking units are felt in terms of four implicit three-pulse beats. From the perspective of the player's inner feeling, the pulse structure is $(4 \times 3) \times 4 = 48$. Transcription 3-18 shows the several ways one twelve-pulse phrase can be felt: *x*-shaped note heads are beamed together in groups of three to show the player's basic four-feel; different placements of crossing time-feels "in three" and "in six" are suggested by brackets above and beneath the staff.

The flow of ternary beats is emphasized audibly by the *hosho* and the *kutsinhira mbira* parts. In our recording, the coexistence of the two different pulse structures generates a powerful musical effect. The example highlights the interaction of *kushaura* and *kutsinhira:* It begins with the *kushaura* part by itself, then the *kutsinhira* joins and the whole ensemble swings into action. I hear the music "in three" at the start and then find myself reoriented to the four-feel when the other parts enter.

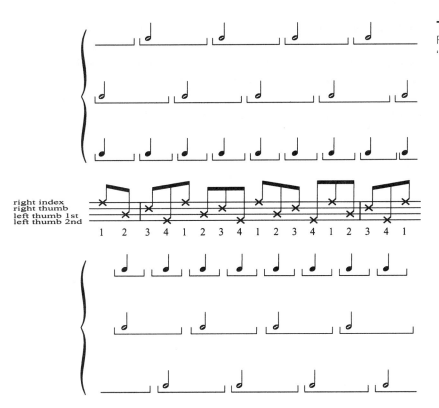

Transcription 3-18

Plucking pattern for the *kushaura* part of "Nhemamusasa."

Melody

Table 3-1 illustrates how a polyphonic texture is generated within this rhythmic and tonal environment. First, consider melodies closely connected to the movements of a player's fingers. Over the course of a forty-eight-pulse cycle, the plucking pattern generates five pitch rows, one each from keys plucked by (1) right index, (2) first left-thumb stroke, (3) right thumb, (4) second left-thumb stroke, and (5) right index and right thumb as a pair. Read Table 3-1 from left to right to get the pitch sequence of each row; read rows 1–4 from top to bottom, left to right to get the pitches in the sequence of four-unit plucking patterns. For example, in the first sequence, (1) the right index plays c′, (2) the first left thumb stroke plays c, (3) the right thumb plays g and (4) the second left thumb stroke plays C.

Table 3-1

Pitch sequence in "Nhemamusasa."

	1 2 3 4	1 2 3 4	1 2 3 4	1 2 3 4	1 2 3 4	1 2 3 4	1 2 3 4	1 2 3 4	1 2 3 4	1 2 3 4	1 2 3 4	1 2 3 4
1)	c′	c′	b	c′	c′	b	c′	c′	c′	d′	d′	c′
2)	c	e	d	c	e	e	c	f	e	d	f	e
3)	g	g	g	g	g	a	g	a	a	a	a	a
4)	C	e	d	C	e	e	C	f	e	d	f	e
5)	c′ g	c′ g	b g	c′ g	c′ g	b a	c′ g	c′ a	c′ a	d′ a	d′ a	c′ a

Without rhythm these pitch rows are musically incomplete. When set in a polymetric context, melodies emerge. The plucking pattern suggests melodies "in three" and "in six," but the inner feeling guides the ear to melodies "in four." By creatively combining these time-feels in their musical imaginations, experienced Shona listeners hear many interweaving melodies. For example, the tied eighth-notes in Transcription 3-19 visually emphasize the four-feel; three-feel and six-feel conceptions emerge by isolating the notes played by each finger.

Transcription 3-19

The *kushaura* melody in "Nhemamusasa."

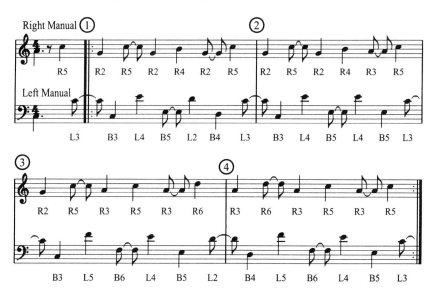

Many melodies emerge from the crossover between hands. Transcription 3-20 shows one such "inherent" melody (see Kubik 1962).

Transcription 3-20

An inherent melody in "Nhemamusasa."

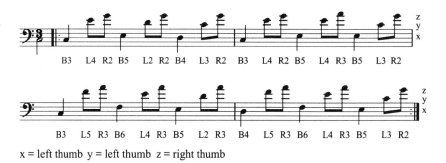

x = left thumb y = left thumb z = right thumb

The right thumb "voice" functions like a drone (first on g, then on a) in relation to the steady movement of the two left-thumb "voices." Because of their proximity in pitch, the ear hears the tones sounded by the first left thumb and the right thumb as cohesive rhythmic figures that articulate the upbeats of a three-feel unit ($\frac{3}{2}$ time) marked off by the second left-thumb stroke—3 4 1 3 4 2 3 4 3. The multiple possibilities of beginnings and endings are evident in the pattern of octave leaps in the left thumb: Does the lower pitch anticipate the higher? Does the higher note echo the bass?

Thomas Mapfumo and Chimurenga Music

This section on Shona music-culture closes with an example of what might be termed modern traditional music: "Nyarai" by Thomas Mapfumo and Blacks Unlimited on CD 1, Track 20. Mapfumo has dubbed this style *chimurenga* music. With its pop band instrumentation and studio production, the music sounds new, but Mapfumo and his audience hear its links to *mbira* music (Bender 1991:163; Eyre 1991:51). Mapfumo and his guitarist, Jonah Sithole, intentionally model their arrangements on traditional music (Eyre 1988:87–88). Like some types of *mbira* music, "Nyarai" is recreational music for dance parties that also comments on topical issues.

Chimurenga music helps us realize that centuries-old traditions need not be obsolete or nostalgic (Waterman 1990). The word *chimurenga* ("struggle") refers both to the war against the white regime in Rhodesia and to a style of music that rallied popular support for the cause (Bender 1991:160–65; Eyre 1991; Manuel 1988:104–6). In the 1970s the music became popular among Africans despite white censorship of song lyrics and an outright ban on artists and recordings. Just as African slaves in the Americas encoded their own meanings in the texts of African-American spirituals, African freedom-fighting songwriters used allusion to make their points. The baffled censors knew a song was subversive only when it was on everyone's lips, but by then the word was out.

Thomas Mapfumo remembers the development of the *chimurenga* music in the following interview with the music journalist Banning Eyre (square brackets mark Eyre's comments, curly braces mark mine):

> I grew up in the communal lands, which used to be called reserves, for the African people. . . . I grew up with my grandparents who were very much into traditional music. Each time there was an mbira gathering, there were elder people singing, some drumming, some clapping. I used to join them. In the country, there were no radios, no TVs. . . .
>
> {Later Mapfumo lived with his parents in the city and joined bands doing rock and roll covers.}
>
> I was into a lot of things . . . even heavy metal. There were rock band contests held in Salisbury {now Harare} . . . . Some South African bands would cross the Limpopo [River] into Rhodesia to compete. There were a lot of black bands playing rock 'n' roll music, and we were one of them. But not even one black band ever won a contest. And I asked myself: "What are we supposed to be if this isn't our music? If they [the whites] claim it to be their music, then we have to look for our own music." As a people who had actually lost our culture, it was very difficult to get it back. . . .
>
> {After several years of singing with different bands that toured the beer halls of Rhodesia in the early 1970s, Mapfumo began writing more serious lyrics.}
>
> One afternoon, we came up with a nice tune opposing Mr. Ian Smith [the final prime minister of white-minority-ruled Rhodesia]. . . . This tune was called "Pa Muromo Chete," which means "It Is Just Mere Talk." Mr. Smith had said he would not want to see a black government in his life-

time, even in a thousand years. So we said it was just talk. We were going to fight for our freedom. This record sold like hot cakes because the people had got the message. Straight away, I composed another instant hit called "Pfumvu Pa Ruzheva," which means "Trouble in the Communal Lands." People were being killed by soldiers. They were running away from their homes, going to Mozambique and coming to live in town like squatters. Some people used to cry when they listened to the lyrics of this record. The message was very strong. . . .

The papers were writing about us. . . . Everyone wanted to talk to us about our music, and the government was very surprised, because they had never heard of a black band being so popular among their own people. They started asking questions. . . .

{In 1979 Mapfumo was detained by the police. After liberation, the popularity of the *chimurenga* style declined, but in the late 1980s he regained local popularity with songs that criticized corruption.}

We were not for any particular party. . . . We were for the people. And we still do that in our music. If you are a president and you mistreat your people, we will still sing bad about you. Never mind if you are black or white or yellow. . . .

{His lyrics still make social comment.}

Today, Zimbabwe is free. . . . So we are focusing our music worldwide. . . . We have been in a lot of world cities. We have seen people sleeping in the streets and governments don't look after these people. That is what our music is there for today. We will never stop singing about the struggle. (Eyre 1991)

CD 1/20

"Nyarai" ("Be Ashamed"), excerpt (2:29). Thomas Mapfumo. Performed by Thomas Mapfumo and Blacks Unlimited. *Thomas Mapfumo: The Chimurenga Singles, 1976–1980*. Gramma Records Zimbabwe. Shanachie CD 43066.

"Nyarai" ("Be Ashamed") was recorded after the government headed by Robert Mugabe came to power in Zimbabwe. Our recording is an excerpt from the longer recorded version. Its traditional stylistic features include musical form based on an eight-beat melodic/harmonic cycle (I–IV–I–V), polyphonic interplay of melodies on two guitars and bass, collective improvisation, occasional climaxes using higher register, and insistent articulation by percussionists of the onbeats and selected offbeats. The lyrics celebrate victory and chide people who are unreconciled to change. The song is a praise poem for the warriors, their leaders, their families, and their supporters.

Text, "Nyarai"

We are celebrating the birth of Zimbabwe
Mothers are proud of Zimbabwe
Fathers are proud of Zimbabwe
We boys are proud of Zimbabwe
Girls are proud of Zimbabwe

Congratulations comrades
And congratulations to all the others
Who fought the *Chimurenga* war
To liberate Zimbabwe
All our ancestral spirits give thanks
The whole nation gives thanks

Congratulations to Mr. Mugabe
And many others
Who fought the liberation war
They liberated Zimbabwe
All ancestral spirits adore the liberators
Congratulations Mr. Machel
And many others who fought the *Chimurenga* war
They liberated Zimbabwe
But there are some reactionaries
Who don't like to be ruled by others
What sort of people are you?
Why are you not ashamed, when you have been defeated
Be ashamed
Be ashamed
Be ashamed
When you have been defeated
Get out
When you have been defeated

Who do you want fight with?
Isn't the war over?
What is left to be done in Zimbabwe?
Mr. Mugabe has won
He has brought peace
Congratulations to the *povo* [black liberation soldiers]
You fought in the *Chimurenga* war
You liberated Zimbabwe

Text translation, "Nyarai" by Thomas Mapfumo courtesy of the Information Office, Zimbabwe High Commission, London.

Our final example of African music-culture differs dramatically from the traditions of the Ewe, Mande, Dagbamba, and Shona. It brings us full circle to the communal, inclusive spirit of African music so clearly present in the music of the Ghanaian postal workers. Information for this section relies on the field research of Michelle Kisliuk (Kisliuk 1991, 1998).

On CD 1, Track 21, we hear the singing, hand clapping, and drumming of the BaAka people (pronounced *bah*-ka). The immense, ancient, thickly canopied tropical forest exerts a powerful influence on life in central Africa. The BaAka are one of several distinct ethnic groups who share certain physical, historical, cultural, and social features as well as adaptations to the natural world (Turnbull 1983). Here I shall refer to these groups collectively as Forest People. Because of their physical size, non-Africans have called the Forest People "Pygmies." It is an ethnocentric label; their size is a benefit in the forest and plays a minor role in the way they are viewed by their larger African neighbors.

The BaAka People Singing: "Makala"

For millennia the Forest People existed in ecological balance with their environment. Sheltered in dome-shaped huts of saplings and leaves, they lived with kin and friends in small, loose-knit groups. Because these hunting bands needed only portable material possessions, they could easily shift their encampments every few months according to the availability of food. They obtained a healthy diet through cooperative hunting and gathering, allowing them ample time for expressive, emotionally satisfying activities such as all-night sings. The social system was informal and flexible: men and women had roughly equal power and obligations, consensus decisions were negotiated by argument, children were treated gently. Individuals were not coerced by formal laws, distant leaders, or threatening deities. The forest was God, and people were children of the forest (Turnbull 1961:74).

At this point you may be wondering why the preceding paragraph was written in the past tense. During the colonial and postcolonial eras, external forces have confronted the Forest People to a degree unprecedented in their history. They now live within nation-states forged in violent anticolonial wars; multinational timber and mining companies are at work in the forest; scholars and adventurers visit some of them regularly. In short, the Forest People now face great changes.

Earlier I mentioned the Western ethnocentric view of the Forest People. Throughout history, other peoples have drawn on this culture in various ways. Let us now look at three images that reflect the conflicting roles that the Forest People play in the world's imagination.

Three Images of the Forest People
Primal Eden

For thousands of years, members of the world's imperial civilizations have found renewal in the music of the Forest People. In 2300 B.C.E. an Egyptian pharaoh wrote to a nobleman of Aswan who had journeyed south to the Upper Nile:

> Come northward to the court immediately; thou shalt bring this dwarf with thee, which thou bringest living, prosperous and healthy from the land of the spirits, for the dances of the god, to rejoice and (gladden) the heart of the king of Upper and Lower Egypt, Neferkere, who lives forever. (Breasted 1906, in Davidson 1991:55)

Today, aided by books and recordings, the Forest People continue to exert a pull on the world's imagination. In particular, the beautiful life of the BaMbuti recounted in Colin Turnbull's *The Forest People* has entranced many. Recordings by Simha Arom have introduced listeners to the intricacy of BaAka vocal polyphony (Arom 1987). For many people, this music-culture evokes cherished values—peace, naturalness, humor, community. In the music of the Forest People we want to hear an innocence lost to our complex, polluted, violent world.

Primitive Savage

Paired with this image of primal utopia is the notion of primitive savagery. According to this view, Pygmies represent an early stage of cultural evolution, a primitive way of life associated with the Stone Age. By definition primitives do not know the achievements of "high" civilization—science, mathematics, engineering, philosophy; they have no electricity, no industry, no nations, no armies, no books. If this is the stuff of civilization, then like other native peoples in remote locations on earth, the Forest People must be "primitive."

But calling a human group "primitive" establishes a dangerous inequality. It can justify genocide; enslavement; servitude; colonialism; underdevelopment; land grabbing for lumbering, mining, agriculture, and tourism; and reculturization through evangelism, schooling, wage labor, and military service. From this imperialist perspective, cultures that differ from the "modern" way must change or be eradicated.

Unique Culture in a Global Village

Instead, we can characterize the Forest People with concepts that are less emotionally charged. They are nonliterate and nonindustrial, with a relatively unspecialized division of labor and a cashless barter/subsistence economy; theirs is a homogeneous society with small-scale, decentralized social institutions, egalitarian interpersonal social relations, and relative gender equality. Their God is everywhere in this world, and they exist within the web of nature.

Forest life is not an idyllic paradise, however. Hunters sometimes share meat from the day's hunt only after other members of their group complain about its unfair distribution. People suffer with disease, hunger, violence, and anxiety. For the past four hundred years they have shared the forest with Bantu and Sudanic agriculturalist villagers; more recently, they have adjusted to international forces. Compared to one's own culture, the Forest People may seem better in some ways, worse in others. Undoubtedly, their culture is unique.

The next section presents a detailed description of a BaAka song. This will set the stage for seeing how the music-culture of the Forest People functions as a resource in their adaptation to change.

"Makala," a Mabo Song

Setting

The performance-studies scholar and ethnomusicologist Michelle Kisliuk recorded "Makala" (pronounced *mah*-kah-lah) in December 1988 in the Central African Republic. The setting was a performance event, or *eboka*, of *Mabo* (pronounced *mah*-boh), a type of music and dance associated with net hunting (see Figure 3-12). Hunting not only provides food but is a key cultural institution as well. At this performance, novices (*babemou*) and their

Figure 3-12
BaAka in perfomance.

Michelle Kisliuk

entourage from one group had walked to a neighboring camp to receive hunting medicine and related dance instruction from experts *(ginda)*. Over the course of two days, performers presented *Mabo* for this ritual purpose as well as for the pleasure of learning new songs and dance flourishes. At times a small-scale affair involving only the *Mabo* specialists and their students, the *eboka* sometimes swelled into a much larger social dance attended by a crowd of BaAka and villagers. Kisliuk recorded this song on the evening of the first day (Kisliuk 1998: 98ff.).

Form and Texture

An *eboka* of *Mabo* consists of sections of singing, drumming, and dancing. Each song has a theme, that is, a text and tune. By simultaneously impro-vising melodic variations, singers create a rich polyphony. After five to fif-teen minutes of play with one song, they begin another. From time to time, the *eboka* is "spiced up" with an *esime,* a section of rhythmically intensified drumming, dancing, and percussive shouts (Kisliuk 1998:40–41).

Timbre

Men and women of all ages sing "Makala." Using both chest and head voices, they obtain a great variety of tone colors that range from tense/raspy to relaxed/breathy. One striking feature, yodeling, involves quick shifts between head and chest voices. Musical instruments include drums and hand claps. Two different drum parts are played on the drum skins that cover the ends of carved, cone-shaped logs. Often, Forest People enrich the percussion by rapping with wooden sticks on the drum's body and striking together metal cutlass blades; Transcription 3-21 visualizes some of their favorite polyrhythmic combinations. Forest People also make music with instruments such as flutes, trumpets, and harps, but not in *Mabo.*

CD 1/21

"Makala" (name of unknown person) (2:20). Traditional BaAka song. Field recording by Michelle Kisliuk. Central African Republic, 1988.

"Ngbòlù"

	1	2	3	4	5	6	7	8	9	10	11	12	13	14	15	16	17	18	19	20	21	22	23	24
Wooden Sticks		I			I			I			I			I			I			I			I	
Drum 2	▲		▲		▲				▲		▲		▲		▲		▲					▲		▲
Bell	*		*		*		*	*		*		*		*		*		*	*		*		*	

"Mò.kóndi"

	1	2	3	4	5	6	7	8	9	10	11	12	13	14	15	16	17	18	19	20	21	22	23	24
Drum 2	●			●		●	●			●	●			●			●		●	●		●	●	
Sticks	I		I			I		I			I			I			I		I			I		
Drum 1	▲			▲	▲			▲	▲	▲		▲			▲	▲			▲	▲	▲			
Bell	*		*	*		*		*		*		*		*		*	*		*		*		*	

"Yómbè"

	1	2	3	4	5	6	7	8	9	10	11	12	13	14	15	16	17	18	19	20	21	22	23	24
Drum 2	●			●			●			●			●			●			●			●		
Sticks		I			I			I			I			I			I			I			I	
Drum 1		▲		▲	▲	▲		▲			▲			▲		▲	▲	▲	▲			▲		
Bell	*		*		*		*		*	*		*		*		*		*		*		*	*	

"Mò.nzòli"

	1	2	3	4	5	6	7	8	9	10	11	12	13	14	15	16	17	18	19	20	21	22	23	24
Drum 2	●	●			●	●			●	●			●	●			●	●			●	●		
Sticks			I			I			I			I			I			I			I			
Drum 1	▲			▲		▲			▲		▲			▲		▲			▲			▲		
Bell	*	*		*		*		*		*		*	*		*		*		*		*		*	

"Mò.mbénzélé"

	1	2	3	4	5	6	7	8	9	10	11	12	13	14	15	16	17	18	19	20	21	22	23	24
Drum 2	●	●			●	●			●	●			●	●			●	●			●	●		
Sticks			I			I		I			I			I			I			I			I	
Drum 1	▲	▲	▲	▲	▲			▲			▲			▲			▲			▲			▲	
Bell	*		*		*		*		*	*		*		*		*		*		*		*		

Transcription 3-21

Charted BaAka polyrhythms. (Arom 1991:305. Used with permission.)

Theme

Transcription 3-22a shows the main melody of "Makala" (adapted from Kisliuk 1991:219; see Kisliuk 1998:98). Because many different parts occur simultaneously, just listening to the recording does not easily reveal the song's melodic theme. Kisliuk learned the theme when hearing it sung in isolation from other parts by a young woman walking along a path. Singers often do not raise the theme until they have established a richly interwoven polyphony; even then, they are free to improvise on its melodic features.

ee ya ee ya Ma - ka - la eh   ee ya na le le oh __ ho ho

Transcription 3-22a

Isolated melodic theme of "Makala."

Transcription 3-22b

Excerpt of a version of the theme (first stave) and variation (second stave) of "Makala."

Makala's theme establishes several important musical features of "Makala." The song's musical form relies on the continuous reiteration of the eight-beat phrase. The melody's intervals may be written with four pitches, given here as D, C, B♭, G. Shaped into two four-beat motives, the tune oscillates between movement and repose: The B♭ on beat four moves toward a cadence at beat eight on C. The tune's rhythm moves toward the cadences on beats four and eight.

As in Native-American songs, singers mostly use vocables (see Chapter 2). The sparse text of "Makala" is typically cryptic (Kisliuk 1998:99).

Text, "Makala"

moto monyongo	beautiful person
Makala	name of an unknown deceased person from the Congo, where *Mabo* originated
na lele, oh	I cry [implying a funeral setting in this song]

Turnbull reports that songs of the BaMbuti often mean "We are children of the Forest" or "The Forest is good." In troubled times they sing a longer text: "There is darkness all around us; but if darkness *is,* and the darkness is of the forest, then the darkness must be good" (Turnbull 1961:93).

Polyphony

The polyphonic texture of this choral music is complex (see Transcription 3-23). Like a well-made multitrack rock and roll recording, the layered parts in "Makala" sound fresh with each listening. Forest People use many different qualities of multipart song. I hear musical processes that can be labeled as heterophony, drone/ostinato, layering, counterpoint, and accompaniment. Happily, reality confounds neat analysis; there are no absolute distinctions among these polyphonic devices.

CD I/21

"Makala" (name of unknown person) (2:20). Traditional BaAka song. Field recording by Michelle Kisliuk. Central African Republic, 1988.

Music-Culture as an Adaptive Resource

Restoring Balance

The active force of music-making contributes to the Forest People's enduring yet ever-changing way of life. The BaMbuti encode the practical, moral effect of song in their words for conflict and peace: *akami,* noise, and *ekimi,* silence or ordered sound (Turnbull 1983:50–51). Troubles arise when

Transcription 3-23
Polyphony in "Makala."

Heterophony: many simultaneous versions of a tune.

Drone/ostinato: reiteration of a rhythmic pattern on very few pitches.

Layering: parts with distinct polyphonic functions arranged according to pitch range (tessitura).

Low-pitched parts outline the tonal movement of the theme.

Middle-pitched melodies introduce two new tonalities and other contrapuntal rhythmic features.

(continues)

Transcription 3-23
(continued)

High-pitched yodeling (*diyenge* singular, *mayenge* plural) adds new counterthemes and more heterophony.

Counterpoint: distinctive countermelodies, often in the yodeling parts.

Accompaniment: two drum parts and hand clapping (adapted from Kisliuk 1991:219).

synergy among people and symbiosis with the forest is disrupted. Communal singing "wakes the forest," whose benevolent presence silences the *akami* forces (Turnbull 1961:92). With yodels echoing off the trees, the forest physically becomes one of the musicians.

Enacting Values and Creating Self

Improvised, open-ended polyphony embodies egalitarian cultural values such as cooperation, negotiation, argument, and personal autonomy. By making social relations tangible, performance helps individuals develop identity within a group. Kisliuk gives a firsthand report of her participation:

> My senses tingled; I was finally inside the singing and dancing circle. The song was "Makala," and singing it came more easily to me while I danced. As I moved around the circle, the voices of different people stood out at moments, affecting my own singing and my choices of variations. I could feel fully the intermeshing of sound and motion, and move with it as it transformed, folding in upon itself. This was different from listening or singing on the sidelines because, while moving with the circle, I became an active part of the aural kaleidoscope. I was part of the changing design inside the scope, instead of looking at it and projecting in. (Kisliuk 1998:101)

Autonomy Within Community

Most members of a BaAka community acquire music-making skills as they grow up (enculturation). During times of crisis, the group needs the musical participation of every member. For example, in a memorable scene from *The Forest People,* even when others in the hunting group insult and ostracize a man for setting his hunting net in front of the others', he joins the all-night singing and is forgiven (Turnbull 1961:94–108).

Although collective participation in performance is highly valued, individuals may stand out. Kisliuk writes that the community knows the composers of individual songs and originators of whole repertories like *mabo.* Explicit teacher-student transmission does take place between the old and young of one group and among members of groups from different regions. Turnbull wrote of an acclaimed singer/dancer who seems particularly emotional and prone to time/space transformation during performances: "He was no longer Amabosu; he had some other personality totally different, and distant" (Turnbull 1961:89). BaAka repertory has a varied history and a dynamic future. Music connects the people to their past, while helping them negotiate their present.

Contrary to the images of chaos and despair conveyed by international mass media, we have encountered African music-cultures of stability, resourcefulness, and self-respect. Abubakari Lunna's life story reveals the rigor of an African musician's education. The erudition, commitment, suffering, and love are profound. Although he says good drumming is

Conclusion as Discussion

"sweet," clearly it is not frivolous or just fun. Like the music of Frank Mitchell, we could call it "deep" (see Chapter 2). We have seen that many Africans value the achievements of their ancestors. The Ewe rigorously study *Agbekor* and recreate it with passionate respect in performance. Innovative *chimurenga* music draws its inspiration from classics of Shona repertory. Mande songs link wisdom of the elders to problems of today.

African music-cultures are strongly humanistic. The human body inspires the construction and playing technique of musical instruments like the *mbira* and *kora.* The spontaneous performances of postal workers and the ritual ceremonies of Forest People point out an important feature of many African music-cultures: Music serves society. As we have experienced, many kinds of African music foster group participation.

Although I encourage African-style musicking, musicians who cross cultural borders need sensitivity to limits and contradictions. To me, nothing approaches the power of time-honored repertory performed in context by born-in-the-tradition culture bearers. The history of an African musical heritage like Mande *jaliya* casts a humbling light onto recent idioms. When non-Africans play African music, especially those of us with white skin, the legacy of slavery and colonialism affects how an audience receives the performance. Thomas Mapfumo, who as a young rock and roller faced discrimination, now competes in the commercial marketplace with international bands that cover African pop songs. How many enthusiasts for African music love its aesthetic surface but regard spirit possession as superstition?

Music is a joyful yet rigorous discipline. The hard work of musical analysis yields important benefits. By making clear the sophistication of African musical traditions, analysis promotes an attitude of respect. Analysis helps us understand the inner structure of music; it provides an ear map for appreciative listening and informed performance. This chapter has emphasized notation examples with rhythms based on 3:2. As we have seen, this profound and elemental timing ratio animates many African traditions.

Analysis of musical structure raises big questions that resist simple answers: Can thought be nonverbal? What approach to music yields relevant data and significant explanation? By treating music as an object, does analysis wrongly alienate music from its authentic cultural setting? How can people know each other? Each chapter in this book benefits from this type of questioning. We seek to know how people understand themselves, but we must acknowledge the impact of our own perspective. Not only does an active involvement in expressive culture provide a wonderful way to learn about other people, but music can change a person's own life as well. From this perspective, ethnomusicology helps create new and original music-cultures.

Inquiry into music-cultures need not be a passive act of cultural tourism. On the contrary, a cross-cultural encounter can be an active process of self development. When we seek knowledge of African music-cultures, we can also reevaluate our own. As we try our hands at African music, we encounter fresh sonic styles and experience alternative models of social action. Just as African cultures are not static, each student's personal world of music is a work in progress.

References

Amoaku, W. Komla. 1985. "Toward a Definition of Traditional African Music: A Look at the Ewe of Ghana." In *More Than Drumming,* edited by Irene Jackson, 31–40. Westport, Conn.: Greenwood Press.

Appiah, Anthony. 1992. *In My Father's House.* Cambridge, Mass.: Harvard Univ. Press.

Arom, Simha. 1987. *Centrafrique: Anthologie de la Musique des Pygmees Aka.* Ocora CD559012 13.

———. 1991. *African Polyphony and Polyrhythm.* Cambridge, England: Cambridge Univ. Press.

Asante, Molefi. 1987. *The Afrocentric Idea.* Philadelphia: Temple Univ. Press.

Bebey, Francis. 1975. *African Music: A People's Art.* Translated by Josephine Bennet. New York: Lawrence Hill.

Bender, Wolfgang. 1991. *Sweet Mother: Modern African Music.* Chicago: Univ. of Chicago Press.

Berliner, Paul. 1993. *The Soul of Mbira.* Rev. ed. Berkeley: Univ. of California Press.

Bohannan, Paul, and Phillip Curtin. 1995. *Africa and Africans.* 4th ed. Prospect Heights, Ill.: Waveland Press.

Breasted, J. H. 1906. *Ancient Records of Egypt.* Chicago: Univ. of Chicago Press.

Charry, Eric. 1994. "West African Harps." *Journal of the American Musical Instrument Society* 20:325–27.

———. 2000. *Mande Music: Traditional and Modern Music of the Maninka and Mandinka of Western Africa.* Chicago: University of Chicago Press.

Chernoff, John. 1979. *African Rhythm and African Sensibility.* Chicago: Univ. of Chicago Press.

Davidson, Basil. 1991. *African Civilization Revisited: From Antiquity to Modern Times.* Trenton, N.J.: Africa Word Press.

Davis, Art. 1994. "Midawo Gideon Foli Alorwoyie: The Life and Music of a West African Drummer." M.A. thesis, Univ. of Illinois–Urbana-Champaign.

DeVale, Sue Carole. 1989. "African Harps: Construction, Decoration, and Sound." In *Sounding Forms: African Musical Instruments,* edited by Marie-Therese Brincard, 53–61. New York: American Federation of Arts.

Dieterlen, Germaine. 1957. "The Mande Creation Myth." In *Peoples and Cultures of Africa,* edited by Eliot Skinner. Garden City, N.Y.: Doubleday.

Djedje, Jacqueline. 1978. "The One-String Fiddle in West Africa." Ph.D. diss., Univ. of California–Los Angeles.

Eyre, Banning. 1988. "New Sounds from Africa." *Guitar Player,* October, pp. 80–88.

———. 1991. "On the Road with Thomas Mapfumo." *The Beat* 10(6): 48–53, 78.

Fiawo, D. K. 1959. "The Influence of the Contemporary Social Changes on the Magico-Religious Concepts and Organization of the Southern Ewe-Speaking People of Ghana." Ph.D. diss., Univ. of Edinburgh.

Frye, Peter. 1976. *Spirits of Protest.* Cambridge, England: Cambridge Univ. Press.

Gates, Henry Louis. 1988. *Signifying Monkey: A Theory of African American Literary Criticism.* New York: Oxford Univ. Press.

Innes, Gordon. 1976. *Kaabu and Fuladu: Historical Narratives of the Gambian Mandinka.* London: School of Oriental and African Studies, Univ. of London.

Jackson, Bruce. 1972. *Wake up Dead Man: Afro-American Worksongs from Texas Prisons.* Cambridge, Mass.: Harvard Univ. Press.

Jackson, Irene, ed. 1985. *More Than Drumming.* Westport, Conn.: Greenwood Press.

Jones, A. M. 1959. *Studies in African Music.* London: Oxford Univ. Press.

Kisliuk, Michelle. 1991. "Confronting the Quintessential: Singing, Dancing, and Everyday Life Among the Biaka Pygmies (Central African Republic)." Ph.D. diss., New York Univ.

———. 1998. *"Seize the Dance!": BaAka Music Life and the Ethnography of Performance.* New York: Oxford University Press.

Knight, Roderic. 1971. "Towards a Notation and Tablature for the Kora." *African Music* 5(1): 23–36.

———. 1972. "Kora Manding: Mandinka Music of the Gambia." Sound recording and booklet. Tucson, Ariz.: Pachart Ethnodisc er 12102.

———. 1984. "Music in Africa: The Manding Contexts." In Gerard Behague, ed., *Performance Practice.* Westport, Conn.: Greenwood Press.

Koetting, James. 1992. "Africa/Ghana." In *Worlds of Music.* 2nd ed. New York: Schirmer Books.

Kubik, Gerhard. 1962. "The Phenomenon of Inherent Rhythms in East and Central African Instrumental Music." *African Music* 3(1): 33–42.

Ladzekpo, Kobla. 1971. "The Social Mechanics of Good Music: A Description of Dance Clubs Among the Anlo Ewe-Speaking People of Ghana." *African Music* 3(1): 33–42.

Lan, David. 1985. *Guns and Rain.* Berkeley: Univ. of California Press.

Laye, Camara. 1983. *The Guardian of the Word.* Translated by James Kirby. New York: Vintage Books.

Locke, David. 1978. "The Music of Atsiagbekor." Ph.D. diss., Wesleyan Univ., Middletown, Conn.

———. 1982. "Principles of Offbeat Timing and Cross-Rhythm in Southern Eʋe Dance Drumming." *Ethnomusicology* 26(2): 217–46.

———. 1983. "Atsiagbekor: The Polyrhythmic Texture." *Sonus* 4(1): 16–38.

———. 1988. *Drum Gahu.* Tempe, Ariz.: White Cliffs Media.

———. 1990. *Drum Damba.* Tempe, Ariz.: White Cliffs Media.

———. 1992. *Kpegisu: A War Drum of the Ewe.* Tempe, Ariz.: White Cliffs Media.

Mallows, A. J. 1967. *An Introduction to the History of Central Africa.* London: Oxford Univ. Press.

Manuel, Peter. 1988. *Popular Musics of the Non-Western World.* London: Oxford Univ. Press.

Maraire, Dumisani. 1971. *The Mbira Music of Rhodesia.* Booklet and record. Seattle: Univ. of Washington Press.

Miller, Christopher. 1990. *Theories of Africans.* Chicago: Univ. of Chicago Press.

Mphahlele, Ezekiel. 1962. *The African Image.* London: Faber and Faber.

Nketia, J. H. Kwabena. 1964. *Continuity of Traditional Instruction.* Legon, Ghana: Institute of African Studies.

Nukunya, G. K. 1969. *Kinship and Marriage Among the Anlo Ewe.* London: Athlone Press.

Quinn, Charlotte. 1972. *Mandingo Kingdoms of the Senegambia.* Evanston, Ill.: Northwestern Univ. Press.

Saad, Elias. 1983. *Social History of Timbuktu: The Role of Muslim Scholars and Notables.* Cambridge, England: Cambridge Univ. Press.

Senghor, Leopold Sedar. 1967. *The Foundations of "Africanite" or "Negritude" and "Arabite."* Translated by Mercer Cook. Paris: Presence Africaine.

Skinner, Eliot, ed. 1973. *Peoples and Cultures of Africa.* Garden City, N.Y.: Doubleday.

Thompson, Robert F. 1973. "An Aesthetic of the Cool." *African Arts* 7(1): 40–43, 64–67, 89.

Tracey, Andrew. 1970. *How to Play the Mbira (Dza Vadzimu).* Roodepoort, Transvaal: International Library of African Music.

Turnbull, Colin. 1961. *The Forest People.* New York: Simon & Schuster.

———. 1983. *The Mbuti Pygmies: Change and Adaptation.* New York: Holt, Rinehart, & Winston.

Waterman, Christopher. 1990. "Our Tradition Is a Modern Tradition." *Ethnomusicology* 34(3): 367–80.

Zantinger, Gei. n.d. "Mbira: Mbira dza Vadzimu: Religion at the Family Level." Film. Available from Univ. Museum, Univ. of Pennsylvania.

Additional Reading

Brincard, Marie-Therese, ed. 1989. *Sounding Forms: African Musical Instruments.* New York: American Federation of Arts.

Nketia, J. H. Kwabena. 1974. *The Music of Africa.* New York: Norton.

Additional Listening

Berliner, Paul. 1995. *Zimbabwe: The Soul of Mbira.* Nonesuch Explorer Series 9 72054-2.

Chernoff, John. 1990. *Master Drummers of Dagbon.* Vol. 2. Rounder CD 5406.

Knight, Roderic. 1991. 1972. *Mandinka Kora.* Ocora 70.

Locke, David. n.d. *Drum Gahu: Good-Time Drumming from the Ewe People of Ghana and Togo.* White Cliffs Media WCM 9494.

Lunna, Abubakari. 1996. *Drum Damba featuring Abubakari Lunna, a Master Drummer of Dagbon.* White Cliffs Media WCM 9508.

Mapfumo, Thomas. 1989. *Thomas Mapfumo: The Chimurenga Singles, 1976–1980.* Shanachie SH 43066.

CHAPTER

4

North America/Black America

Jeff Todd Titon

M usic of work, music of worship, music of play: The traditional music of African-American people in the United States has a rich and glorious heritage. Neither African nor European, it is fully a black-American music, forged in America by Africans and their descendants, changing through the centuries to give voice to changes in their ideas of themselves. Through all the changes, the music has retained its black-American identity, with a core of ecstasy and improvisation that transforms the regularity of everyday life into the freedom of expressive artistry. Spirituals, the blues, jazz—to Europeans, these unusual sounds are considered America's greatest (some would say her only) contribution to the international musical world.

Of course, modern black music does not sound unusual to North Americans, and that is because for many years the black style has been so pervasive. Locate a CD reissue of some popular music from the first decade or two of the twentieth century. This music will sound stilted, square, extravagantly dramatic, unnatural, and jerky—not because of the recording process, but because of the influence of grand opera singing and marching band instrumental styles of the period. But in the 1920s, aptly called the Jazz Age, Bessie Smith and other African-American jazz and blues singers revolutionized the craft of singing popular music. Their approach lay close to the rhythm and tone of ordinary talk, and this natural way of singing caught on. Blues, gospel, jazz, swing, bop, rhythm and blues, rock and roll, funk, soul music, Motown, Muscle Shoals, disco, rap, hip-hop: The currents of African American music in the twentieth century transformed popular music in North America—then Europe—and eventually throughout the world.

The easiest way to get acquainted with a music-culture in the United States is to survey its popular music on the radio. Most North American cities have one or two radio stations programming African-American music. Listen for a couple of weeks; you will hear mostly contemporary

Music of Worship

151

black music, with occasional side trips into older forms and styles. But on Sundays the standard fare is recorded religious music, along with remote broadcasts of worship services from black churches in the city and surrounding suburbs. These live church broadcasts showcase a broad spectrum of black religious music: modern gospel quartets, powerful massed choirs, and soloists whose vocal acrobatics far exceed those of their counterparts in nonreligious music. Some of these broadcasts include congregational singing: camp-meeting choruses, particularly among Pentecostals, and hymns, particularly among Baptists.

Listen now to a hymn sung by a black Baptist congregation in Detroit. It is the first verse of the familiar Christian hymn "Amazing Grace," but the performance style is unfamiliar to most people outside the black church. A deacon leads the hymn. Because the microphone was placed next to him during the recording, his voice is heard above the rest. He opens the hymn by singing the first line by himself: "Amazing grace how sweet it sound." The congregation then joins him, and very slowly they repeat the words, sliding the melody around each syllable of the text. Next, the deacon sings the second line by himself: "That saved a wretch like me"; then the congregation joins him to repeat it, slowly and melismatically (that is, with three or more notes per syllable of text). The same procedure finishes the verse.

That one verse is all there is to the performance. The singers do not use hymnbooks; they have memorized the basic tune and the words. Notice that the congregation, singing with the deacon, do not all come in at the same time; some lag behind the others a fraction, singing as they feel it. Not everyone sings exactly the same tune, either. Some ornament the basic tones with more in-between or melismatic tones than others do. The singers improvise their ornamentation as they go along. It is a beautiful and quite intricate performance; try singing along. Probably you will find it difficult. The transcription (4-1) of one way of singing the first two lines may be helpful, but after listening many times you may be able to sing it even without reading the transcription; after all, the people in the congregation learned it by ear.

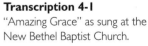

CD 1/22

Amazing Grace (2:36). Traditional. Performed by deacon and congregation of the New Bethel Baptist Church. Field recording by Jeff Todd Titon. Detroit, Michigan, 1977.

Transcription 4-1
"Amazing Grace" as sung at the New Bethel Baptist Church.

(continues)

Notation in this chapter employs an arrow above a note head to indicate a pitch slightly higher (or lower) than notated but insufficiently high or low to be notated by the neighboring chromatic step. A solid line between successive note heads indicates a vocal glide. Time value of grace notes should be subtracted from the previous note. An *x* on a staff space or line indicates the approximate pitch of an unstable, half-spoken syllable. A fermata above a note head indicates a pitch held slightly longer than notated; an inverted fermata indicates a pitch held slightly shorter than notated. This additional notation is an attempt to make the Western staff-scale notation system more responsive to world music styles.

Recorded and transcribed by Jeff Todd Titon, Detroit, Michigan, June, 1978.

Next, look at the lyrics to "Amazing Grace."

Text, "Amazing Grace," Verse 1

Deacon (solo)

Amazing grace how sweet it sound
That saved a wretch like me
I once was lost but now am found
Was blind but now I see.

Deacon and Congregation Together

Amazing grace how sweet it sound
That saved a wretch like me
I once was lost but now am found
Was blind but now I see.

This way of organizing the singing in church, in which a leader sings a line and then repeats it with the congregation, is called *lining out.* Lining out psalms and, later, hymns was a standard practice in colonial America. Black slaves and freedmen worshipped with whites and picked up the practice from their example. The influence then became mutual. Today lining out remains in a great many black Baptist churches throughout the United States. (Among white churches it survives chiefly among Old Regular Baptists in the coal-mining country of the southern Appalachian mountains.)

This version of "Amazing Grace" has many characteristics typical of African-American music in the United States. The words are sung in English, and they fall into stanzas as most English folk songs do. But the style of the performance is black African. *Movement:* The singers sway freely to the music, dancing it with their bodies. *Social organization* of the singing group: As we saw in Chapter 3, the leader-chorus, call-and-response is the predominant African group vocal organization. *Timbre:* The singing tone quality alternates between buttery smooth and raspy coarse. *Pitch* is variable around the third, fifth, and seventh degrees of the scale. The tune is playful—ebbing and eddying like the ocean tide.

We can understand these attributes of traditional African-American music more clearly if we contrast this version of "Amazing Grace" with a British-American version of the same hymn, from a church in northwestern Virginia (CD 1, Track 23). The white song leader stands erect like the soldier of the cross he is, chest out, eyes front, unmoving save for his hand,

CD 1/23

Amazing Grace (2:52). Traditional. Performed by the congregation of the Fellowship Independent Baptist Church, led by Rev. John Sherfey. Field recording by Jeff Todd Titon. Stanley, Virginia, 1977.

which marks the regular and clearly audible beat. Leader and congregation sing together instead of in call-and-response alternation. The choral texture is polyphonic instead of heterophonic. Transcription 4-2 of the first two lines compares his singing with the tune as it is printed in the church hymnbook (Transcription 4-3).

Transcription 4-2

"Amazing Grace" as sung at the Fellowship Independent Baptist Church. The transcription follows the melody as sung by the song leader. For comparison, the lower staff shows the melody as written in the church hymnal. (See also Transcription 4-3.)

Recorded and transcribed by Jeff Todd Titon. Stanley, Virginia, August 1977.

The song leader's tone quality is unvaryingly coarse, giving an impression of energetic seriousness rather than playful ecstasy. His tune is stately, measured, and decorated. His slight variations are deliberate, and they differ slightly from one another in each of the four verses that make up the

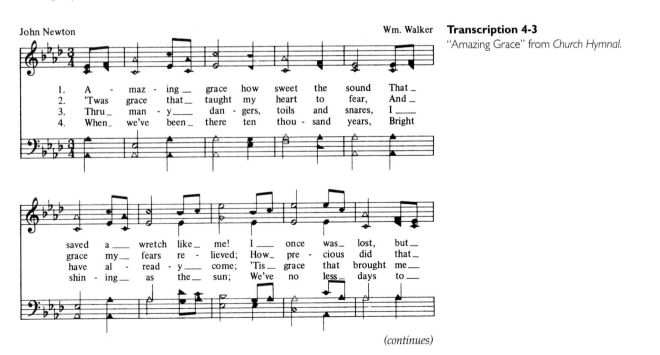

Transcription 4-3

"Amazing Grace" from *Church Hymnal.*

(continues)

Transcription 4-3
(continued)

now   I'm   found,   Was __ blind,   but __ now   I   see.
grace   ap - pear,   The __ hour   I __ first   be - lieved.
safe   thus   far,   And __ grace   will __ lead   me   home.
sing   God's   praise,   Than __ when   we __ first   be - gun.

Tennessee Music and Printing Co., Cleveland, Tennessee, 1951.

performance. But they are restrained in comparison to the melodic decoration sung by the black deacon. A few more hearings of this British-American example reveal subtleties such as the upward catch on the release of certain tones, as, for instance, at the end of the word *grace* in the first line. Try imitating each version of this well-known song; both are much admired examples of their kind. Your efforts to sing will increase your understanding of the musical styles as well as your pleasure in the musical experience.

A radio survey of black music reveals a vital church music culture. Suppose we enter the black church where I recorded the first song and observe it firsthand (Figure 4-1). It is a Baptist church with a large sanctuary, seating perhaps fifteen hundred on this warm Sunday morning. The men are dressed in blue or black vested suits, with black socks and shoes. A few of the younger men are conspicuous in tan, baby-blue, or burgundy suits with matching shoes. The women wear dark suits or dresses, and many have on fashionable hats; all of them wear stockings and dress shoes. Choir members wear green robes over their formal attire. To keep a breeze, they swing cardboard fans supplied by the funeral homes that have printed their advertisements on them.

When we hear "Amazing Grace," we have come to the deacons' devotional, an early part of the worship service consisting of old-time congrega-

Figure 4-1
A young deacon chants an improvised prayer. The microphone connects with the church's public address system. Detroit, Michigan, 1978.

Jeff Todd Titon

tional hymn singing, scripture reading, and a chanted prayer offered by a deacon while the rest hum and moan a wordless hymn in the background. The praying deacon improvises his chanted prayer—the words and tune—which begins as speech and then gradually turns to a chant with a definite tonal center, moving at the close in a regular meter; the congregation punctuates the deacon's phrases with shouts of "Yes," "Now," and so forth, which are intoned on the tonal center (C in the transcription). This, of course, is another example of call-and-response. Transcription 4-4 shows the closing section of chanted prayer. The congregation's response (Yes!) is in parentheses; the transcription follows the melody (lines 3–10 in the text) as chanted by the deacon, who improvises the words and tune as the spirit moves him.

Transcription 4-4
Lines 3–10 from chanted prayer by deacon and congregation at the Little Rock Baptist Church.

Recorded and transcribed by Jeff Todd Titon. Detroit, Michigan, October 1977.

Text, Closing Section of Chanted Prayer

O Lord. (Congregation: *Yes!*)
Have mercy today, Father. *(Yes!)*
You know where we at. *(Yes!)*
You know our hearts. *(Yes!)*
5 You know our hearts' desire. *(Yes!)*
Please Jesus! *(Yes!)*
Please Jesus! *(Yes!)*
Go with us today. *(Yes!)*
I know you know me. *(Yes!)*
10 You know all about me. *(Yes!)*
Now Lord. *(Now Lord!)*
Now Jesus. *(Now!)*
When we can't pray no more *(Yes!)*
over here. *(Yes!)*
(Spoken): Give us a home somewhere in thy kingdom.

The deacons lead the devotional from the altar area, and after the devotional is through, the activity shifts to the pulpit, where announcements are made, offerings are taken up, and responsive reading is led. Interspersed are modern gospel songs, sung by soloists and the high-spirited youth choir, accompanied by piano and organ. The preacher begins his spontaneous sermon in a speaking voice, but after about fifteen minutes he shifts into a musical chant (Transcription 4-5), all the while improvising and carrying on his message.

Text, Sermon

Nicodemus was a ruler.
He was a
rich man.
You know everybody loves money.
5   Everybody loves to look, be looked upon.
Everybody loves to be called somebody.
Ah I imagine Nicodemus was ah in that category.
And ah he heard about God.
I don't know where he heard about him back but he heard of
10   something about God
What he was doing.
And ah
he
made it up in his
15   mind
that he was going to see God.
And ahh he made
an appointment with him.
And ahh the Scripture says that it was at night.
20   It's all right
in the midnight
to make appointment with him.
It's all right
to make appointment with him
25   if it is at noon day.
You should make appointment with him.
I made appointment with him one day
and ahh
I told him my situation.
30   Oh Lord.
And everything went all right.
Mmm
hallelujah.
And Nicodemus said,
35   he said, "I know
that no man can do these things
except God be with him."

You know God says
in the
40 Scripture here,
he say you can do all things.
"You can do all things in my name
if you'll vow in me
and I'll abide in you."
45 You should get in Christ.
You should get in touch with God.
Learn a little more about him.
And when you've found Christ
just wrap around him and
50 and everything will be all right.

Transcription by Jeff Todd Titon. Minneapolis, Minnesota, August 1968.

Our excerpt comes from the chanted portion of a sermon by Rev. George Trawick, Pastor of St. Mark's Baptist Church, Minneapolis, Minnesota, which I recorded in August of 1968. Transcription 4-5 (lines 20–25) follows the melody as chanted by the preacher, who improvises the words and tune as the Spirit moves him rather than reading from a printed text.

Transcription 4-5
Lines 20–25 from chanted portion of sermon delivered by Rev. George Trawick. In reading the words, pause about one-half second at the end of each measured line.

Recorded and transcribed by Jeff Todd Titon. St. Mark's Baptist Church, Minneapolis, Minnesota, August 1968.

This change from speech to chant (the chant is sometimes called "whooping") is accompanied by a change from a playful timbre that alternates between clear and coarse and between light and buzzy, to a rather continuously hoarse timbre. As they did for the praying deacon, the congregation responds to the preacher's phrases with shouts of "Well," "Yes," and so forth, on the tonal center. Sometimes the preacher fits his chant into a regular meter for brief periods, lasting from perhaps ten seconds to a minute. But more often the chanted phrases are irregular. Still, compared with phrases in ordinary conversation, they are relatively uniform and, when punctuated by the congregation, they give the impression of regularity.

Figure 4-2
Reverend C. L. Franklin, pastor, chanting ("whooping") as he delivers the sermon's climax. New Bethel Baptist Church, Detroit, Michigan, 1978.

Jeff Todd Titon

The Reverend C. L. Franklin of Detroit spoke to me of the rhythm of his chanted preaching: "It's not something I can beat my foot to. But I can *feel* it. It's in me." It is also in the members of the congregation who sway back and forth with each phrase. Rev. Franklin's sermons were extraordinarily popular—he toured the nation to preach in the 1950s and 1960s, often with his daughter, Aretha. Recordings of his sermons can often be found in the gospel bins in record stores in black communities.

Eventually the sermon closes and an invitational song follows, led by a soloist from the choir (Figure 4-3). Three or four people heed the invitation and come forward to join the church. A final offering is taken up, the preacher gives the benediction, and the choir comes down from the choir stand, locks arms in the altar area facing the pulpit, and joins the congregation in singing "Amen."

Altogether, song and chant have taken up at least half the running time of the worship service: the old-style singing of the deacons' devotional, the traditional chant of the prayer and sermon, and the modern gospel songs. The music is literally moving; it activates the Holy Spirit, which sends some people into shouts of ecstasy, swoons, shakes, holy dance, and trance (Figure 4-4). If they get so carried away that they are in danger of fainting or injuring themselves, they are restrained by their neighbors until members of the nurses' guild can reach them and administer aid. In this setting, music is an extremely powerful activity—and the church is prepared for its effects.

Much of the music of black Christian worship in the United States is traditional. We have seen that the lining-out tradition dates from colonial America, and many of the hymns sung have the same vintage. The Negro spiritual developed later, born of the camp-meeting revivals in the late eighteenth and early nineteenth centuries. The delivery style of these chanted prayers and sermons is at least as old as the early nineteenth

Figure 4-3
Soloist and choir of the Temple of Faith.
Detroit, Michigan, 1978.

Figure 4-4
Religious music quickens the Holy Spirit
and sends a woman into trance. Detroit,
Michigan, 1977.

century, and probably older, though of course the deacons and preachers
improvise the content. Today they can be heard in their most traditional
form as the "choruses"—one verse repeated several times—in Pentecostal
services, while in black Baptist and Methodist services they are featured
in carefully arranged, multiversed versions sung by trained choirs in a tradition that hearkens back to the Fisk Jubilee Singers of the late nineteenth
century:

Transcription 4-6

"Swing Low, Sweet Chariot."

G. D. Pike, *The [Fisk] Jubilee Singers* (Boston: Lee and Shephard, 1873), 166.

Music of Work

A work song, as the name suggests, is a song workers sing to help them carry on. It takes their minds off the monotonous and tiring bending, swinging, hauling, driving, carrying, chopping, poling, loading, digging, pulling, cutting, breaking, and lifting (Figure 4-5). A work song also paces the work. If the job requires teamwork, work song rhythms coordinate the movements of the workers (Figure 4-6).

Work songs were widely reported among black slaves in the West Indies in the eighteenth century and in the United States in the nineteenth. Most scholars believe black work songs must have been present in the

Figure 4-5
Farmer plowing a field in Tupelo, Mississippi, 1936.

Walker Evans. Courtesy of the Library of Congress.

American colonies, even though the documentary evidence is thin. While African-American work songs may have been influenced by British work songs (sea chanteys and the like), the widespread, ancient, and continuing African work song tradition is the most probable source.

Work music is hard to find in the United States today. Where people once sang, machines now whine. But in an earlier period, African-Americans sang work songs as they farmed and as they built the canals, railroads, and highways that became the transportation networks of the growing nation. This daily music helped make the African-American sound what it was then and what it is now. In his autobiography *My Bondage and My Freedom* (1855), ex-slave Frederick Douglass wrote,

> Slaves are generally expected to sing as well as to work. A silent slave is not liked by masters or overseers. "Make a noise," "make a noise" and "bear a hand," are the words constantly addressed to the slaves when there is silence amongst them. This may account for the almost constant singing heard in the southern states.

After Emancipation, the singing continued whenever black people were engaged in heavy work: clearing and grading the land, laying railroad track, loading barges and poling them along the rivers, building levees against river flooding, felling trees. And the inevitable farm work: digging ditches, cutting timber, building fences, plowing, planting, chopping out weeds, and reaping and loading the harvest.

The words and tunes of these work songs fit the nature of the work. People working by themselves or at their own pace in a group sang slow songs without a pronounced beat; the singer hummed tunes or fit in words as desired, passing the time. For example, as a farm boy Leonard "Baby Doo" Caston learned to sing field hollers by copying the practice of older farmhands (CD 1, Track 24):

CD 1/24

Field Holler (0:43). Traditional solo work song. Performed by Leonard "Baby Doo" Caston. Field recording by Jeff Todd Titon. Minneapolis, Minnesota, 1971. (Background noise from the apartment is audible.)

Figure 4-6
Workers lining track. Alabama, 1956.

Frederic Ramsey, Jr.

Transcription 4-7
Field holler as sung by Leonard "Baby Doo" Caston.

Recorded and transcribed by Jeff Todd Titon. Minneapolis, Minnesota, May 1971. (Titon 1974a)

Text, Other Stanzas to Field Holler

1. I'm going up the country, baby, and I can't take you.
   There's nothing up the country that a monkey woman can do.

2. Hey—captain don't you know my name?
   I'm the same old fellow who stole your watch and chain.

3. I'm going away, baby, to wear you off my mind.
   You keep me worried and bothered all the time.

Not surprisingly, the words of these songs show that the singers wanted to be elsewhere, away from work. In group labor that required teamwork and a steady pace, people sang songs with a pronounced beat, which coordinated their movements. About forty years ago a rowing work song, "Michael, Row the Boat Ashore," was recorded by a group of white singers who had probably never come any closer to the work than crewing on the Connecticut River, but their version became a best-selling record on the popular music charts. The song was first reported in the 1867 collection *Slave Songs in the United States* (Transcription 4-8). The words to work songs are open-ended; that is, the song leader can improvise new lines ("Michael, row the boat ashore" or "O you mind your boastin' talk") and repeat old ones until his stock is exhausted and his voice gives out, while

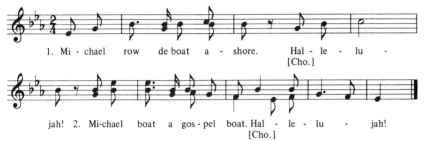

Transcription 4-8
Lines 1–2 from "Michael, Row the Boat Ashore."

Slave Songs of the United States, compiled by William Francis Allen, Charles Pickard Ware, and Lucy McKim Garrison (New York: A. Simpson & Co., 1867), 23–24.

the rest of the workers merely sing the responsorial burden ("Hallelujah!") after each line, in a call-and-response pattern.

Text, "Michael, Row the Boat Ashore"

3. I wonder where my mudder deh (there). *(Hallelujah!)*
4. See my mudder on de rock gwine home.
5. On de rock gwine home in Jesus' name.
6. Michael boat a music boat
7. Gabriel blow de trumpet horn.
8. O you mind your boastin' talk.
9. Boastin' talk will sink your soul.
10. Brudder, lend a helpin' hand.
11. Sister, help for trim dat boat.
12. Jordan stream is wide and deep.
13. Jesus stand on t' oder side.
14. I wonder if my maussa deh.
15. My fader gone to unknown land.
16. O de Lord he plant his garden deh.
17. He raise de fruit for you to eat.
18. He dat eat shall neber die.
19. When de riber overflow
20. O poor sinner, how you land?
21. Riber run and darkness comin'.
22. Sinner row to save your soul.

What makes a good song leader? What is the purpose of work songs? Collecting work songs in 1947 inside the Mississippi State Penitentiary at

Parchman, Alan Lomax asked these questions of the African-American inmates whose singing he recorded:

LOMAX: Do you think it makes work easier when you sing?

INMATE: Yessir.

LOMAX: Do you think you can do more or do you think you can slack off when you sing?

INMATE: Nosir, what makes it go so better—when you're singing, you forget, you see, and the time just pass on 'way; but if you get your mind devoted on one something, it look like it will be hard for you to make it, see—make a day—the day be longer, look like. . . . So to keep his mind from being devoted on just one thing, why, he'll just practically take up singing, see. . . .

LOMAX: What's the most important thing about a good leader . . . does he have a real good voice or a strong voice or what?

INMATE: Well . . . now it wouldn't just exactly make any difference about the dependability of his voice or nothing like that, boss; but it would, it take the man with the most experience to my under-standing to make the best leader in anything. You see, if you'd bring a brand new man here, if he had a voice where he would sing just like Peter could preach, and he didn't know what to sing about, well, he wouldn't do no good, see, but here's a fel-low, he, maybe he ain't got no voice for singing, but he's been cooperating with the peoples so long and been on the job so long till he know just exactly how it should go, and if he can just mostly talk it, why, and you understand how to work, well it would go good with you—it don't make any difference about the voice. . . .

LOMAX: You mean he has to know the timing?

INMATE: Yessir . . . that's what it takes, the time, that's all it is. You can just whistle and, if you know the time and can stay in time with the axes, you can whistle and do, cut just as good as you can if you were singing . . . but you have to be done experienced.

(Lomax 1976. © Alan Lomax. Used by permission.)

The aesthetic standards of the African-American work song call for a good sense of the beat and the ability to time it to the work at hand. A sweet-sounding voice that is always in tune may be desirable in other situations, but it is not important in the group work song tradition.

In some southern prisons black inmates sang work songs. For example, the song "Rosie" (CD 2, Track 1, Transcription 4-9) was used to regulate the axe blows when the workers were felling large trees. Sometimes as many as ten men circled the tree and chopped, five pulling their axes out just before the other five all struck at once. Axes were swinging through the air at all times, back and forth; the work was dangerous and the timing was crucial. Without work songs, the white and Latino inmates chopped two to a tree.

CD 2/1

"Rosie" (2:50). Traditional work song. Performed by prisoners at Mississippi State Penitentiary. Field recording by Alan Lomax. Parchman, Mississippi, 1947.

M. K.   **Transcription 4-9**

"Rosie." Worksong sung by inmates of Mississippi State Penitentiary, Parchman, Mississippi, 1947.

(continues)

Transcription 4-9
(continued)

Collected by Alan Lomax; transcribed by Mieczyslaw Kolinski. From Courlander 1963.
Reprinted courtesy of Columbia University Press.

With work songs, the black inmates chopped four, six, eight, or ten to a tree. The work went faster and better, and the singing group felt pride and solidarity in its accomplishment.

In the words of Bruce Jackson, an experienced collector of prison work songs,

> The songs [may] change the nature of the work by putting the work into the worker's framework rather than the guards'. By incorporating the work with their song, by, in effect, co-opting something they are forced to do anyway, they make it *theirs* in a way it otherwise is not. (1972:30).

In African-American music, whether of work or worship, calls answered by responses emblematize the social nature of this music. This is not a predictable and predetermined music. Improvisations in lyrics and melodies, as well as changes in timbre, show the high value African Americans place on innovation, creativity, and play.

Music of Play

As we have seen, the performance of religious songs and work songs in the black tradition includes elements of play. For example, churchgoers admire the beautiful performance of a verbally adept preacher as he plays with the resources of language and gesture, and they clap their approval as a solo singer sustains a climactic pitch or goes through intricately improvised melodic variations with great feeling. Work songs introduce a playful, distancing attitude toward the labor at hand. Like call-and-response, this sort of play with pitch, timbre, and rhythm is a marker of African and of African-American music.

Although religious songs and work songs contain elements of play, their main purpose is worship and work. In contrast, music of play serves mainly as entertainment, performed mainly for pleasure even when its effect is also educational, cathartic, or ecstatic.

Imagine that we walk through the black neighborhood outside the church after the service we "attended" earlier in the chapter. We find ourselves surrounded by the music of play. Children skip rope on the side streets, chanting jump rope rhymes and taunts at one another. Teens walk down the street listening to CD players. Deep bass tones boom out through powerful car stereos that throb with the latest hip-hop hits. Jukeboxes can be heard in the bars and barbecue joints that line both sides of the main street. When night falls, some of the bars have live entertainment—a local band that plays the blues, and in a fancy nightspot a nationally known jazz combo. Downtown in the city auditorium a nationally known artist is scheduled, while in the public gardens a concert of classical music offers the premiere performance of an electronic composition by a black composer who teaches at the city university.

Blues

Clearly, the music of play in black America offers a dizzying array of forms. The rest of this chapter focuses on just one African-American music of play: blues. The blues is a music familiar to many, but its very familiarity presents problems. Chief among them is the misconception that blues, because it is so popular throughout North America, is primarily a musical form ("the twelve-bar blues") and a musical resource, a component of the musical air that we all breathe, isolated from any particularities of time and place. In truth, blues is tied intimately to African-American experience and cannot be understood without reference to its historical development within African-American culture. A second area of confusion arises over the relationship between blues and jazz. Is blues a part of jazz? Did blues flow into the river of jazz? Blues can be understood as a feeling—"the blues"—and as a specific musical form. Jazz, which engenders complex and varied feelings, is best thought of as a technique, as a *way* of forming. Jazz musicians applied their technique to the blues form, but blues did not lose its identity.

Muddy Waters (Figure 4-7), Howlin' Wolf (Figure 4-17), B. B. King, Albert Collins, John Lee Hooker (Figure 4-20), and Buddy Guy, who rose to national prominence as blues singers, came from a vital tradition. For decades the blues music-culture—with its singers, country juke joints, barrelhouses, city rent parties, street singing, bar scenes, nightclubs, lounges, recordings, and record industry—was a significant part of the black music-culture in the United States. In the 1960s, when desegregation and the Civil Rights Movement changed African-American social and economic conditions, blues faded in popularity among African Americans while it gained a large and appreciative white audience. Nowadays the blues music-culture incorporates white as well as black musicians, and its audience is worldwide.

Figure 4-7
Muddy Waters (McKinley Morganfield),
studio portrait. Chicago, Illinois, early
1950s.

Blues and the Truth

The best entry into the blues is through the words of the songs. It is hard to talk at length about words in songs, and harder still to talk about music. As Charles Seeger, one of the founders of the Society of Ethnomusicology, reminds us, it would be more logical to "music" about music than to talk about it (Seeger 1977:16). And in the blues music-culture, when the setting is informal, that is just what happens when one singer responds to another by singing verses of his or her own. Another common response to blues is dancing. Dancers and listeners as a rule have no interest in an articulate body of blues criticism. Speaking of oral literature as a whole, Dennis Tedlock points up the paradox with gentle irony:

> Members of primary oral cultures generally limit themselves to brief remarks about performances when they say anything at all, and such remarks are quickly forgotten. There is no such thing as an oral performance of the great critical discourse of the past. (Tedlock 1977:516)

The most common response to blues music is a feeling in the gut, dancing to the beat, nodding assent, a vocalized "that's right, you got it, that's the truth"—not unlike the black Christian's response to a sermon or a gospel song. A good, "deep" blues song leaves you feeling that you have heard the truth in a way that leaves little more to be said.

Yet much *can* be said about the words to blues songs. Because the words pass from one singer to another as a coin goes from hand to hand, they become finely honed and proverbial in their expression: economical, truthful. Response to the words of the songs can be talked about in words. Moreover, blues lyrics have a legitimate claim to be considered as serious literature. As the literary critics Cleanth Brooks, R. W. B. Lewis, and Robert Penn Warren have written,

> In the world of music the recognition of blues as art is well established. But waiving their value as musical art, we may assert that they represent a body of poetic art unique and powerful. . . . No body of folk poetry in America—except, perhaps, the black spirituals—can touch it, and much of the poetry recognized as "literature," white or black, seems tepid beside it. (Brooks, Lewis, and Warren 1973:II, 2759)

We begin by taking an extended look at a single blues performance (CD 2, Track 2), "Poor Boy Blues," by the Lazy Bill Lucas Blues Band (Figure 4-8). Bill Lucas is the vocalist; he accompanies himself on electric guitar,

CD 2/2

"Poor Boy Blues" (3:16). Performed by Lazy Bill Lucas Trio. Field recording by Jeff Todd Titon. Minneapolis, Minnesota, 1970.

Jeff Todd Titon

Figure 4-8
Lazy Bill Lucas. Minneapolis, Minnesota, 1968.

and he is joined by two other musicians, one on acoustic guitar and the other on drums. Listen to the recording now, paying particular attention to the lyrics.

Text, "Poor Boy Blues"

1. I'm just a poor boy; people, I can't even write my name.
   I'm just a poor boy; people, I can't even write my name.
   Every letter in the alphabet to me they look the same.
2. Mother died when I was a baby; father I never seen.
   Mother died when I was a baby; father I never seen.
   When I think how dumb I am, you know it makes me want to scream.
3. Ever since I was the age around eleven or twelve,
   Ever since I was the age around eleven or twelve,
   I just been a poor boy; ain't caught nothing but hell.
4. When I was a child Santa Claus never left one toy.
   When I was a child Santa Claus never left one toy.
   If you have any mercy, please have mercy on poor boy.

Response to the Lyrics of "Poor Boy Blues"

I did not choose "Poor Boy Blues" because the words were outstanding; they are typical. For me, some of it is good, some not; some of it works, some does not. "I'm just a poor boy; people, I can't even write my name" produces an automatic response of sympathy for the poor boy, but it is not a very deep response. I am sorry for the poor boy's illiteracy, but, heck, everyone has problems. When the line repeats I am anxious to hear how the stanza will close. "Every letter in the alphabet to me they look the same" brings to my mind's eye a picture of a strange alphabet in which all letters look alike or, rather, in which the differences in their shape have no meaning. The image is clear, it works, and it involves me. This poor boy may be illiterate, but he is perceptive. And not only does the image itself succeed, but the delay of the most important word in the line, *same,* until the end, and the impact of its rhyme with *name,* convinces me I am hearing the truth. Blues singer Eddie "Son" House (Figure 4-9) told me about how he put his blues stanzas together: "I had enough sense to try to make 'em, rhyme 'em so they'd have *hits* to 'em with a meaning, some sense to 'em, you know" (Titon 1994:47). The inevitable rightness of the rhyme—you expect it and it rewards you—hits harder than an unrhymed close, particularly because the end rhyme always falls, in blues, on an accented syllable.

I do not respond to "Mother died when I was a baby"; I resist a statement that sounds sentimental. This is not because I think of myself as some kind of tough guy, but because I want the sentiment to be earned. I much prefer the statement at the close of the line: "father I never seen." The effect is in the contrast between the mother who died and the father who might as well be dead. In the image of the father who has never been seen is the mystery of not knowing one's parents. It is not just missing love; for all we know the poor boy was raised by loving relatives. But a child takes after

Jeff Todd Titon

Figure 4-9
Eddie "Son" House. Minneapolis,
Minnesota, 1971.

parents, inherits the biology, so to speak; without knowing your parents
you do not fully know yourself. That is the real terror of the poor boy's life.
"When I think how dumb I am, you know it makes me want to scream" is
a cliché; the rhyme is forced. Okay, scream. Nor do I respond to the third
stanza when I hear it; but when I think about it, it seems curious that the
poor boy says he began to catch hell from age eleven or twelve. I guess that
he was catching it all along but did not fully realize it until then. That is a
nice point, but a little too subtle to register during a performance. I would
have to sing it several times myself to appreciate that aspect of it.

The final stanza takes great risk with sentimentality, calling up Christmas memories, but it succeeds by a matter-of-fact tone: "When I was a
child Santa Claus never left one toy" dispels the scene's stickiness. Santa
Claus never left a toy for anyone, but a child who believes in Santa can
enjoy an innocent world where presents reward good little boys and girls. If
he could not believe in Santa, I wonder if he ever had any part of the innocent happiness people seem to need early, and in large doses, if they are
going to live creative lives. Or it could have been the other way around:
He believed in Santa, but Santa, never bringing him a toy, simply did not
believe in him.

The song now leads up to it final line, a plea for mercy. "You" are addressed directly: If you have any mercy, show it to the poor boy. Will you? If you heard this from a blind street singer, would you put some coins in his cup? Would you be more likely to show mercy to the poor boy than to someone down on his luck who just walks up and asks for spare change? The song will strike some people as sentimental, calling up an easy emotion that is just as quickly forgotten as it is evoked. T. S. Eliot, in a widely influential argument, said that in a work of literature any powerful emotion must have an "objective correlative"; that is, the work itself must demonstrate that there is good reason for the emotion (Eliot [1920] 1964). Has "Poor Boy Blues" given you good reason for mercy? Have you been told the truth, or were you played for a sucker?

Autobiography and the Blues

We have been considering the words in a broad, English-speaking context. Considering the effect of "Poor Boy Blues" on a generalized listener can take us only so far. What do the words mean to someone in the blues music-culture? What do they mean to Lazy Bill Lucas? Does the "I" in the "Poor Boy Blues" represent Lucas? What, in short, is the relationship between the song and the singer?

More than any other subject, the correspondence between the words to blues songs and the lives of the singers has fascinated people who write about the blues. The blues singer's image as wandering minstrel, blind bard, and untutored genius is idealized, but, according to Samuel Charters, "There is no more romantic figure in popular music than the bluesman, with everything the term involves. And it isn't a false romanticism" (1977:112). The result is that most books on blues are organized biographically. Some writers have gone so far as to derive the facts of an otherwise obscure blues singer's life and personality from the lyrics of his or her recorded songs. On the other hand, published life stories of blues singers in their own words are rare (see, for example, Brunoghe 1964; Titon 1974a). If we read these first-person life stories properly, we can understand them as far more reliable expressions of the blues singer's own personality than song lyrics are, because the lyrics are often borrowed from tradition. Nonetheless, most people assume that the lyrics of a blues song do speak for the singer. Paul Oliver wrote, for example, "One of the characteristics of the blues is that it is highly personalized—blues singers nearly always sing about themselves" (Oliver 1974:30). If that is true, then "Poor Boy Blues" should be a reflection of the life and thoughts of Lazy Bill Lucas.

I was a close friend of Bill Lucas's for six years, playing guitar in his blues band for two of them. During the course of our friendship I tape-recorded his recollections of his life, edited and excerpted for publication first in *Blues Unlimited* (Titon 1969), a British blues research journal, and later in the accompanying notes to his first American LP (Titon 1974b). Let us look, then, at parts of Lucas's life history and see if "Poor Boy Blues" speaks for him.

The Life History of Bill Lucas, Blues Singer

I was born in Wynne, Arkansas, on May 29, 1918. I never heard my mother say the exact *time* I was born: she was so upset at the time I guess she wouldn't remember. I have two sisters and three brothers; I was third from my baby sister, the third youngest.

Ever since I can remember, I had trouble with my eyesight. Doctors tell me it's the nerves. I can see shapes, I can tell colors, and I know light and dark, but it's hard to focus, and no glasses can help me. An operation might cure it, but there's a chance it could leave me completely blind, and I don't want to take that gamble.

My father was a farmer out in the country from Wynne. He was a sharecropper, farming on the halvers. In 1922 we moved to Short Bend, Arkansas, but my father wanted to get where there were better living conditions. A lot of his neighbors and friends had come up to Missouri and told him how good it was up there.

About every two or three years we moved from one farm to another. Some places you had good crops, according to the kind of land you had. Some places we had real sandy land, and that wasn't good; but in the places that were swampy, that black land, that was good. You know when you're sharecropping cotton and corn you look for the best location and the best living conditions. And you could move; you didn't have a lease on the place.

So my family moved to Advance, Missouri, in 1924. We moved by night but that doesn't mean we had to slip away. They loaded all our stuff in a wagon and we caught the ten o'clock train. That was my first train ride; I loved the train then. Advance was about twenty-five miles west of the river; it wasn't on the highway, just on the railroad. It was a little town of five hundred; it consisted of two grocery stores and a post office which doubled over into a saloon. We never did go to town much except on Saturdays. In the summertime we'd go in about every week to carry our vegetables to sell in a wagon: watermelons and cabbage and stuff.

My father wanted to own his own farm, but that was impossible. That was a dream. He didn't have enough money to buy it and there weren't any loans like there are nowadays. We owned cattle, we owned pigs. We had about thirteen milk cows, and we had leghorn chickens that gave us bushels of eggs. We were better off than our neighbors because we would sometimes swap our eggs for something we didn't have. We were blessed with eggs and chickens and milk. We were blessed. I tried to, but I never did learn how to milk. I wasn't too much use on the farm. I did a lot of babysitting but not too much else.

There weren't many guitars around, but in 1930 my daddy got me a guitar. I remember so well, just like it was yesterday, he traded a pig for it. Money was scarce down there; we didn't have any money. The boy wanted $7 for it. We didn't have money but we had plenty of pigs. Our neighbors had some boys that played guitar, but they never did take pains and show me how to do it. I would just watch 'em and listen. I learned from sounds. And after they were gone, then I would try to make the guitar sound like I heard them make it sound. It was easier to play single notes than chords. Right now till today I don't use but two fingers to play guitar; I don't play guitar like other people. I wanted the guitar because I liked the noise and it sounded pretty.

Halvers: A sharecropping arrangement in which the landlord supplied the tenant with a shack, tools, seed, work animals, feed, fuel wood, and half the fertilizer in exchange for half the tenant's crop and labor.

After I got it and come progressing on it, a tune or two here or there, my dad and mama both decided that would be a good way for me to make my living. I knew all the time I wanted to make a career out of it, but after I came progressing on it, well they wanted me to make a career out of it too. But they said I had to be old enough and big enough to take care of it, not to be breaking strings and busting it all up.

My father got me a piano in 1932 for a Christmas present. That was the happiest Christmas I ever had. He didn't trade pigs for that; he paid money for it. Got it at our neighborhood drugstore. It was an upright. It had been a player piano but all the guts had been taken out of it. Well, at the time I knew how to play organ, one of those pump organs; I had played a pump organ we had at home that came about the same time as the guitar. A woman, she was moving, she was breaking up housekeeping, and she gave us the organ. It had two pedals on it and you'd do like riding a bicycle. So it didn't take me long to learn how to bang out a few tunes on the piano.

I didn't know what chords I was making. We got a little scale book that would go behind the keyboard of the piano and tell you all the chords. It was a beginner's book, in big letters. I could see that. You know, a beginner's book *is* in big letters. And I wanted to learn music, but after I got that far, well, the rest of the music books were so small that I couldn't see the print. And that's why I didn't learn to read music.

I did learn to read the alphabet at home. My parents taught me, and so did the other kids. I used to go to school, but it was just to be with the other kids, and sometimes the kids would teach me. I was just apt; I could pick things up. I had a lot of mother-wit.

So I bumped around on the piano until 1936, when we left the country and came to Cape Girardeau, Missouri. I had to leave my piano; we didn't have room for it. I almost cried. That was when I started playing the guitar on street corners. My dad had day work; that was the idea of him moving to the city, trying to better his living conditions. I forget what he went to work as: I think he worked in a coal yard. We stayed at my sister's house; one of my oldest sisters was married. But we had to go back to Commerce, Missouri. My dad couldn't make it in Cape Girardeau so we went to Commerce. I don't know what he thought he was going to do there because that was a little hick town, wasn't but about three hundred in population there. He didn't farm there; I vaguely can remember what we did now.

At that time I didn't know too much about blues. We had a radio station down there but they all played big band stuff and country and western music. But we didn't call it country and western music back then; we called it hillbilly music. Well, hillbilly music was popular there and so I played hillbilly music on the guitar and sang songs like "She'll Be Coming 'round the Mountain" and "It Ain't Gonna Rain No More" and "Wabash Cannonball." The only time I heard any blues was when we'd go to restaurants where a jukebox was and they'd have blues records. And my daddy had a windup phonograph, and we had a few blues records at home by Peetie Wheatstraw and Scrapper Blackwell and Curtis Jones—the old pieces, you know. So I learned a little bit about blues pieces off the records I'd hear around home. I heard Bessie Smith and Daddy Stovepipe and Blind Lemon Jefferson.

At that time I didn't have any knowledge of music. I liked any of it. I even liked those hillbilly songs. And when I heard the blues I liked the blues, but I just liked the music, period. And when I played out on street corners, I'd be playing for white folks mostly, and that was the music they seemed to like better, the hillbilly music. So I played it because I'd been listening to it all the time on the radio and so it wasn't very hard for me to play. The blues didn't *strike* me until I heard Big Bill Broonzy; that's when I wanted to play blues guitar like him.

We lost our mother in 1939. We buried her in Commerce, and we left Commerce after she died. My dad, he went to St. Louis in 1940, still trying to find better living conditions. Later that year he brought me to St. Louis, and that's where I met Big Joe Williams. At that time he wasn't playing in bars or taverns; he was just playing on the street. So he let me join him, and I counted it an honor to be playing with Big Joe Williams because I had heard his blues records while I was still down South. And so we played blues in the street.

But I didn't stay in St. Louis long. My dad and I came to Chicago the day after New Year's in 1941. Sonny Boy Williamson was the first musician I met with up there. I met him over on Maxwell Street, where they had all their merchandise out on the street, and you could buy anything you wanted on a Sunday, just like you could on a Monday. They had groceries, clothes, hardware, appliances, right out on the street, where people could come to look for bargains. That was a good place to play until the cops made us cut it out. I played a lot with Sonny Boy. Little suburban places around Chicago like Battle Creek, and South Bend. We were playing one-nighters in taverns and parties. Sonny Boy would book himself, and I went around with him. There wasn't much money in it; Sonny Boy paid my expenses and a place to stay with his friends. He was known all up around there. He played with me when he couldn't get nobody else. I didn't have a name at the time. But I had sense enough to play in time and change chords when he changed; it wasn't but three changes anyhow. We didn't play nothing but the funky blues. He just needed somebody to keep time, back him up on guitar.

Big Bill Broonzy was my idol for guitar, and I'd go sit in on his shows. He'd let me play on the stand between times; I'd play his same songs. Bill knew I couldn't do it as well as he did, so he wasn't mad. In fact he appreciated me for liking his style. I also liked T-Bone Walker, but he made so many chord changes! I was unfortunate to learn changes; I never did know but three changes on the guitar.

I used to play with Little Walter on the street, too, in the black section, where they wanted the blues. I quit playing that hillbilly music when I left St. Louis. In St. Louis I was getting on the blues right smart after I met up with Big Joe Williams. But white folks in Chicago or here in Minneapolis don't like hillbilly music. They tell you right away. "What you think I am? A hillbilly?"

I started in my professional career in 1946 when I joined the union. We all joined the union together, me and Willie Mabon and Earl Dranes, two guitars and a piano. We took our first job in 1946 on December 20, in the Tuxedo Lounge, 3119 Indiana, in Chicago. They paid union scale, but scale wasn't much then. The leader didn't get but twelve dollars a night, the sidemen ten dollars. We worked from 9 P.M. until 4 A.M. It was a real

Sonny Boy Williamson: Harmonica player John Lee Williamson (d. 1948).

"I didn't have a name": He means that the name Bill Lucas was unknown to the blues audiences.

Little Walter: Walter Jacobs, the most imitated blues harmonica player after World War II.

nice club. These after-hours clubs always had good crowds because after two o'clock everybody would come in. We had a two-week engagement there, and I thought it was real good money. But then we were kicked back out on the street.

Little Walter and I used to play along with Johnny Young at a place called the Purple Cat—1947. That's where he gave me the name "lazy" at. We'd been there so long Little Walter thought I should go up and turn on the amps, but I never did go up and do that thing, so that's why he started calling me "lazy" Bill, and the name stuck.

In 1948 I started in playing with Homesick James, and sometimes also with Little Hudson. I started out Little Hudson on playing. When I first met him in Chicago around 1945 or 1946 he wasn't playing. Of course he had a guitar, but he wasn't *doing* nothing. I started him and encouraged him and so he'd come and sit in with me and Sonny Boy or me and Willie Mabon or whoever I'd be playing with. He just started like that. And when he got good he was respected. He had a right smart amount of prestige about him, Hudson did. I switched to playing piano in 1950 because they had more guitar players than piano players. But of course I'd been playing piano all along—just not professionally, that's all. Little Hudson needed a piano player for his Red Devils trio. Our first job was at a place called the Plantation, on Thirty-first Street, on the south side of Chicago.

I don't know where he got the idea of the name from, but the drummer had a red devil with pitchforks on the head of his bass drum. And he played in church, too! Would you believe they had to cover up the head of the drum with newspapers? He'd cover the devil up when he'd go to church.

I had a trio, Lazy Bill and the Blue Rhythm, for about three or four months in 1954 [Figure 4-10]. We were supposed to do four records a year

Figure 4-10
Lazy Bill and His Blue Rhythm, studio photo. Chicago, Illinois, 1954. From left to right: Lazy Bill Lucas, James Bannister, "Miss Hi-Fi," and Jo Jo Williams.

for Chance, but Art Sheridan went out of business and we never heard about it again. We did one record [see CD 2, Track 3].

Well, I didn't keep my group together long. You know it's kind of hard on a small musician to keep a group together in Chicago very long because they run out of work, and when they don't get work to do, they get with other guys. And there were so many musicians in Chicago that some of 'em were underbidding one another. They'd take a job what I was getting twelve dollars for, they'd take it for eight dollars.

I was doing anything, working with anybody, just so I could make a dime. On a record session, any engagement at all. For a while I was working with a disc jockey on a radio station. He was broadcasting from a dry cleaners and he wanted live music on his broadcast. I did it for the publicity; I didn't get any money for that. Work got so far apart. Every time I'd run out of an engagement, it would be a long time before another one came through. And so Mojo and Jo Jo, they had come up here to Minneapolis. They had been working at the Key Club, and they decided they needed a piano player. I wasn't doing anything in Chicago; I was glad to come up here. I had no idea I was going to stay up here, but I ended up here with a houseful of furniture.

Jo Jo: George "Mojo" Buford, harmonica player, and Joseph "Jo Jo" Williams, bass player.

©1974 by William Lucas and Jeff Todd Titon. A fuller version accompanies Titon 1974b.

Lazy Bill Lucas and "Poor Boy Blues"

Bill Lucas's account of his life ends in Minneapolis in 1964. The following year I began my graduate studies at the University of Minnesota and met him at a university concert. By that time he had two audiences: the black people on the North Side of the city who still liked the blues, and the white people in the university community. The 1960s was the period of the first so-called blues revival (Groom 1971), during which thousands of blues records from the past four decades were reissued on LPs, dozens of older singers believed dead were "rediscovered" and recorded, and hundreds of younger singers, Bill Lucas among them, found new audiences at university concerts and coffeehouses and festivals. The revival, which attracted a predominantly young, white audience, peaked in the great 1969 and 1970 Ann Arbor (Michigan) Blues Festivals, where the best of three generations of blues singers and blues bands performed for people who had traveled thousands of miles to pitch their tents and attend these three-day events. Bill Lucas was one of the featured performers at the 1970 festival. For his performance he received four hundred dollars plus expenses, the most money he ever made for a single job in his musical career.

In the 1960s and 1970s Bill Lucas could not support himself from his musical earnings. A monthly check (roughly a hundred times the minimum hourly wage) from government welfare for the blind supplemented his income in Minneapolis. Most of Minneapolis's black community preferred soul and disco music to blues, while others liked jazz or classical music. Nor was there sufficient work in front of the university folk music audience for Bill. He sang in clubs, in bars, and at concerts, but the work was unsteady. When I was in his band (1969–1971), our most dependable job was a six-month engagement for two nights each week in the "Grotto Room" of a pizza restaurant close to the university. Classified by the musicians' union as a low-level operation, it paid the minimum union scale for an evening's work from 9:00 P.M. to 1:00 A.M.: $23 for Bill, $18 for sidemen. On December 11, 1982, Bill Lucas died. A benefit concert to pay his funeral expenses raised nearly two thousand dollars.

His life history not only gives facts about his life but also expresses an attitude toward it. We can compare both with the words of "Poor Boy Blues" to see whether the song speaks personally for Bill Lucas. Some of the facts of the poor boy's life correspond, but others do not. I asked him whether the line about all the letters in the alphabet looking the same held any special meaning for him, and he said it did. Unless letters or numbers were printed very large and thick, he could not make them out. On the other hand, unlike the poor boy in the song who never saw his father, Lucas and his father were very close. Moreover, his experiences of Christmas were happy, and one year he received a piano. What about the attitudes expressed in the song and in the life history? Neither show self-pity. Bill did not have an illustrious career as a blues singer; he scuffled during hard times and took almost any job that was available. Yet he was proud of his accomplishments. "I just sing the funky blues," he said, "and people either like it or they don't."

"Poor Boy Blues" cannot therefore be understood to speak directly for Bill Lucas's personal experience, but it does speak generally for it, as it speaks for tens of thousands of people who have been forced by circumstances into hard times. Thus, in their broad cultural reach, the words of blues songs tell the truth.

Learning the Blues

One question that bears on the relation between Lazy Bill Lucas and "Poor Boy Blues" is the authorship of the song. In fact, Lucas did not compose it; it was put together by St. Louis Jimmy Oden and recorded by him in 1942. Lucas learned the song from the record. Learning someone else's song does not, of course, rule out the possibility that the song speaks for the new singer, for he or she may be attracted to it precisely because the lyrics suit his or her experiences and feelings.

In the African-American music-culture almost all blues singers learn songs by imitation, whether in person or from records. There is no such thing as formal lessons. In his life history, Lucas tells how he listened to neighbors play guitar and how he tried to make it sound like they did. After he developed a rudimentary playing technique, he could fit accompaniments behind new songs that he learned from others or made up himself.

Unquestionably the best way to come to know a song is to make it your own by performing it. Listen once again to "Poor Boy Blues" and concentrate now on the instrumental accompaniment. The guitarists and drummer keep a triple rhythm behind Lucas's singing. When Lucas pauses, the guitar responds with a sequence of single-note triplets.

CD 2/2

"Poor Boy Blues" (3:16). Performed by Lazy Bill Lucas Trio.

Transcription 4-10
Rhythmic outline, "Poor Boy Blues."

Transcribed by Jeff Todd Titon.

This triplet rhythm is a common way of dividing the beat in slow blues songs. When accented monotonously, as in many rock and roll tunes from the 1950s, it becomes a cliché. Music students familiar with dotted rhythms (from marches and the like) should resist the temptation to hear this as a dotted rhythm. Recordings of white musicians before World War II attempting to play blues and jazz very often do not flow or "swing" because the musicians are locked into dotted rhythms.

Poor Boy Blues

Lazy Bill Lucas

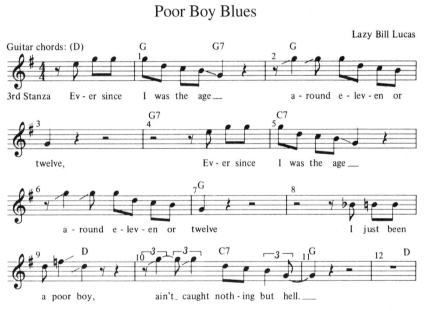

Transcription 4-11
"Poor Boy Blues," stanza 3, as sung by Lazy Bill Lucas.

Recorded and transcribed by Jeff Todd Titon. Minneapolis, Minnesota, May 1970.

Next listen to the rhythm of Lucas's vocal, and try to feel both rhythms, vocal and accompaniment, at the same time. You might find this attempt difficult. The reason is that Lucas very seldom sings squarely on the beat. Transcription 4-11 of his melody is an oversimplification for the sake of readability, but even here we see a great deal of syncopation, in delayed entrances or anticipations of the beat. Lucas is not having a hard time *finding* the beat; on the contrary, he deliberately avoids it.

The musical brilliance of "Poor Boy Blues" rests on the difference between vocal and instrumental rhythms. Accents contrast; at times each part has its own meter. While the accompanying instruments stay in triple meter, Lucas sings in alternating duple and triple. In other words, passages of two-against-three polymeter (especially apparent at the outset of measures 1, 5, and 9 in Transcription 4-11) alternate with passages of three-against-three single meter. I have written 4-11 in $\frac{4}{4}$ to bring out the contrast. One feels that Lucas initiates each vocal phrase in triple meter, then quickly shifts to duple, hurrying his phrasing in imitation of speech rhythm.

In Chapter 3 we saw that two-against-three polymeter characterizes black African music. Here we see a deep connection between African and African-American music: rhythmic complexity and polymeter. But our example from the blues does not reflect continuous polymeter, as in Africa. Rather, blues music (and jazz, and reggae) *shifts* into and out of polymeter, playfully teasing the boundary. When these shifts occur rapidly, the boundary between single meter and polymeter breaks down. The result is a new sense of time: the graceful forward propulsion we hear as "swing" that makes us feel like moving our whole body in response.

To sing "Poor Boy Blues" as Lucas does, begin by simply *saying* the words (page 172) to get a feel for the speech rhythms. If you read music, use Transcription 4-11 as a guide, but always follow the recording. Listen to the way he slides up to the high G in measures 2, 6, and 10, indicated on the transcription by a solid line just before the note heads. Then hear how he releases "poor" (measure 9) and slides directly afterward into "boy." This sliding and gliding is another type of musical "play," this time with the pitch, not the beat. Finally, listen to him attack the word "twelve" (measures 3 and 7) just ahead of the bar rather than as written.

The Blues Scale

Lucas sings "Poor Boy Blues" in a musical scale I have called the blues scale (Titon 1971).

Transcription 4-12
The blues scale (key of G for convenience).

 This scale typifies blues, jazz, spirituals, gospel tunes, and other black-American music. An original African-American invention, the blues scale also is the most important scale in rock music. It differs significantly from the usual Western diatonic major and minor scales, and it does not correspond to any of the medieval European church modes. The blues scale's special features are the flatted seventh and the presence of *both* the major and minor third. (Another special feature, seemingly a later development, is the flatted fifth.) A typical use of this double third, sometimes called "blue note" by jazz writers, is shown in measure 8 of Transcription 4-11: Lucas enters on the minor third and proceeds directly to the major third. This is yet another example of "playing" with the pitch in black-American music.

If you are a guitarist, you can easily play along with the record by following Transcription 4-11 and reading the chord diagrams in Figure 4-11.

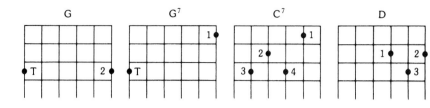

Figure 4-11
Guitar chord positions for "Poor Boy Blues."

Lucas plays "Poor Boy Blues" in the key of G. With the exception of his G and G7 chords, he employs standard first-position fingering. He prefers the dominant to the dominant seventh (here D instead of D7) on guitar, but the opposite when he plays piano. He makes most of his single-note runs in the first position, but sometimes he moves up the guitar neck on the first two strings to play the highest notes. If you pick out the accompaniment from the record by ear, you will be learning blues guitar in one of the traditional, time-honored ways.

Lucas accompanies himself on piano in another rendition of "Poor Boy Blues," on *Lazy Bill Lucas*, Philo LP 1007.

Composing the Blues

Besides learning blues songs from other singers and from records, blues singers make up their own songs. Sometimes they think a song out in advance; sometimes they improvise it during performance. Often a performance embodies both planning and improvisation. The blues song's first composition unit is the line. If you sing the blues most of your life, blues lines will run through your mind like proverbs, which many indeed are: for instance, "You never miss your water till your well runs dry." A male singer might rhyme it with a line like, "Never miss your woman till she say good-bye." (A female singer's rhyme: "Never miss your good man till he say good-bye.") The singer has just composed his stanza:

> You never miss your water till your well runs dry,
>
> No, you never miss your water till your well runs dry,
>
> I never missed my baby till she said good-bye.

A blues singer rarely "composes" self-consciously. Instead, lines and stanzas seem to "just come," sometimes in a rush but more often one at a time and widely spaced. The blues singer Booker White called the songs he made up "sky songs": "I have an imaginary mind to do things like that. Didn't have nary a word written down. I just reached up and got 'em" (Evans 1971:253). Another blues singer, Robert Pete Williams, described how his songs came to him:

> The atmosphere, the wind blowing carries music along. I don't know if it affects you or not, but it's a sounding that's in the air, you see? And I don't know where it comes from—it could come from the airplanes, or the moaning of automobiles, but anyhow it leaves an air current in the air, you see? That gets in the wind, makes a sounding, you know? And that sounding works up to be a blues. (Wilson 1966:21)

Statements such as these show the universal aspect of the blues and present the singer as an interpreter of the natural world. The sounding airplane, and the moaning automobile trace a human pattern in the surrounding atmosphere that only the gifted interpreter, the translator, the blues singer can hear. When the singer turns it into a song for all to hear, the universal truth is apparent.

If the blues singer plans the stanzas in advance, he or she memorizes them, sometimes writing them down. As we have seen, the stanzas may or may not speak directly for the personal experience of the singer. St. Louis Jimmy, the author of "Poor Boy Blues," said this about another of his songs, "Goin' Down Slow":

> My blues came mostly from women. . . . "Goin' Down Slow" started from a girl, in St. Louis—it wasn't me—I've never been sick a day in my life, but I seen her in the condition she was in—pregnant, tryin' to lose a kid, see. And she looked like she was goin' down slow. And I made that remark to my sister and it came in my mind and I started to writin' it. . . . I looked at other people's troubles and I writes from that, and I writes from my own troubles. (Oliver 1965:101–2)

Songs that blues singers memorize usually stick to one idea or event. A memorized song, Lucas's "Poor Boy Blues" has four stanzas on the circumstances leading to the poor boy's cry for mercy. In contrast, the words in an improvised song seldom show the unity of time, circumstances, or feeling evident in a memorized song. After all, unless you have had lots of practice, it is hard enough to improvise rhymed stanzas, let alone keep to a single subject (compare McLeod and Herndon 1981:59 on improvised Maltese song duels). So an improvising singer usually throws in some memorized, traditional stanzas along with stanzas he or she puts together on the spot.

A Blues Song in the Making

Today a few blues songs are improvised in performance, but most are memorized beforehand. This memorization is a later trend in the history of the blues and results from the impact of commercial blues records (they began in the 1920s) on singers born after about 1910. Singers who wanted to make records studied them and got the idea that a song ought to last about three minutes (the length of a 78-rpm record) and stick to one theme—as most recorded blues songs did. So they composed and memorized their songs, and they memorized other singers' songs. Of course, they could not avoid learning traditional stanzas and building a mental storehouse of them, but more and more they sang from memory instead of improvising. Today the influence of records is overpowering, so singers seldom change lyrics when learning other people's songs and, like rock bands trying to "cover" hit records, they copy the instruments, too. In short, most blues singers today think a blues song should have a fixed, not variable, text.

In 1954 Art Sheridan, the owner of Chicago-based Chance Records, asked Lazy Bill Lucas to make a record. During the early 1950s Lucas had

CD 2/3

"She Got Me Walkin'" (3:01). William "Lazy Bill" Lucas. Performed by Lazy Bill and His Blue Rhythm: Lazy Bill Lucas, piano and vocal; Louis Myers, guitar; Elga Edmonds, drums. Words and music by William Lucas. Chance 10" 78-rpm record. Chicago, Illinois, 1954.

played piano as a sideman on several of Homesick James Williamson's recordings, and he was a member of The Blues Rockers, a group with the minor recording hits "Calling All Cows" and "Johnny Mae." For his own session as leader, Lucas was billed as "Lazy Bill and His Blue Rhythm." He chose an original song, "She Got Me Walkin'" (CD 2, Track 3). Lucas composed the lyrics in advance and memorized them for the recording session.

Text, "She Got Me Walkin'"

1. My baby got me walkin' all up and down the street (2 times)
   She left me for another man 'cause she wanted to be free.

    2. My baby told me one day,
      And I laughed and thought it was a joke;   } **Quatrain**
      She said I'm going to leave you,
      You don't move me no more.

She got me walkin' all up and down the street;   } **Refrain**
She left me for another man 'cause she wanted to be free.

    3. I don't want to see Snook,
      Not even Homesick James;
      The way my baby left me,
      I really believe he's to blame.

She got me walkin' all up and down the street;
She left me for another man 'cause she wanted to be free.

Words and music by William Lucas. Used by permission.

The first thing you may notice in "She Got Me Walkin'" is that the stanza form differs from that of "Poor Boy Blues." In that song Bill Lucas sang a line, then more or less repeated it, and closed the stanza with a rhyming punch line. Most blues stanzas fall into this three-line pattern, particularly traditional stanzas. But some, like stanzas 2 and 3 of "She Got Me Walkin'," fall into a different line pattern consisting of a quatrain (four lines rhymed abcb) and a rhymed two-line refrain that follows to close out each stanza. You can easily hear the contrast between the three-line stanza and the quatrain-refrain stanza. The quatrain fits in four short bursts into the first four measures (bars) of the twelve-bar blues, while the refrain fits into the last eight bars. The quatrain-refrain pattern became popular after World War II. It usually offers vignettes in the quatrain to prove the truth of the repeated refrain. Because any stanza form is by nature preset, it acts as a mold into which the improvising singer pours his or her words. Of course just *any* words will not do, because the refrain has to repeat, lines must rhyme, and the whole thing has to make sense.

Lucas told me that he thought getting the names of some of his musician friends into "She Got Me Walkin'" would make the song more popular. The uninitiated listener would find the nicknames a little mysterious and might be intrigued. "Snook" was the harmonica player Snooky Pryor. James Williamson had recorded under the name "Homesick James" and was well-known to the people who frequented the Chicago bars and clubs

Figure 4-12
Lazy Bill Lucas in his apartment.
Minneapolis, Minnesota, 1971.

Jeff Todd Titon

to hear blues. When I asked Lucas whether the lyrics were based on a true story, he replied "More or less." The "she" of the song turns out to be none other than Johnny Mae, whom Bill had sung about for The Blues Rockers a few months earlier. Johnny Mae was Homesick James' girlfriend.

As Lucas's lyrics show, during the years following World War II blues musicians in Chicago formed a social as well as a musical community. They kept each other company, played on each other's recordings, substituted for one another at various club dates, and both competed with and supported one another in the music business and social world. These relationships persisted for years. For example, Muddy Waters and Howlin' Wolf were rivals. Even as late as 1970, at the Ann Arbor Blues Festival, this rivalry was evident. Waters was scheduled to come onstage after Wolf's set, but Wolf prolonged the set well beyond the agreed-upon ending time in a bid to steal time from Waters.

The life histories and social ties of blues singers have clearly influenced their music. Our discussion to this point has focused on the lives and songs of blues musicians. The next sections provide a close look at an instrument associated with the early blues. Following the blues tradition of learning by doing, we shall begin by learning how to build a one-stringed diddly-bow (see Figure 1-9, p. 29).

How to Make and Play
a One-Stringed Diddly-Bow

The musical bow, a single string stretched on a frame of some kind, like a hunting bow, is a widespread tribal musical instrument. Related to it is the one-stringed diddly-bow, a traditional African-American instrument. Many blues singers who grew up on Southern farms recall it as their first musical instrument (CD 2, Track 4).

Despite its simple construction and playing technique, the diddly-bow produces a very satisfactory blues sound. It is easy to build and learn to play it even if you have never built an instrument before. Figure 4-13 provides a list of building materials and a construction diagram for a portable diddly-bow, smaller and handier than the traditional instrument that was affixed to the wall of a barn. You can get free wood from the scrap pile of a sawmill or lumberyard. For a few dollars, any musical instrument store should be able to supply you with a single guitar machine head, some hard plastic material for the bridge and nut, and a steel string. Try to get a banjo string with a "loop end" that will fit easily over the wooden screw at the bridge end of the instrument.

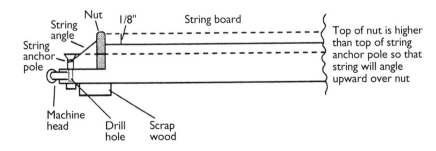

Figure 4-13
How to make a portable, one-stringed diddly-bow.

Saw a notch for the nut near one end of the piece of wood, then cut the wood back to the end. Glue a piece of scrap wood to the bottom of the cutaway. Drill a hole for the string anchor pole and attach the machine head to the scrap wood bottom. Make sure that the top of the string anchor pole is lower than the top of the nut (Figure 4-14).

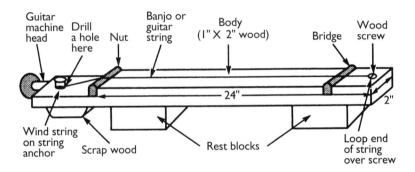

Figure 4-14
Close-up of nut end of diddly-bow.

Glue the nut flush against the notch so that the top of the nut is about 1/8 inch higher than the string board. Saw a notch for the bridge near the other end of the string board, and glue in the bridge so that it is about

1/4 inch higher than the string board. Insert a small wooden screw between the bridge and the short end of the string board, leaving about 1/16 inch clearance between the board and the head of the screw to fit the string loop on. Glue two pieces of scrap wood underneath the string board to serve as a table rest. Attach the loop end of the banjo string over the wooden screw, then push the other end through the machine head anchor pole, taking up most of the slack. Knot the string around the anchor pole and turn the machine head knob, tightening the string until, when you pluck it, it produces the same pitch as the tonic (here, the lowest and most frequently played tone) on One-String Sam's accompaniment for "I Need $100" (CD 2, Track 4). Check the pitch against the recording.

Play your diddly-bow by plucking the string near the bridge with the thumb of one hand while sliding a smooth device such as a bottleneck, lipstick case, piece of copper tubing, pipe tool, or closed pocket knife atop the string with the other hand. For the moment, concentrate on the hand that does the plucking, and leave the sliding hand out of it entirely. Now hold the diddly-bow with the heel of your plucking hand falling just between the wooden screw and the bridge; slight pressure will prevent the instrument from moving on the table. Turn your hand counterclockwise and make a half-fist with your fingers loosely tucked so that your thumb is parallel to the string and can pluck the string comfortably in a motion away from your body.

One-String Sam accompanied himself on a small, portable diddly-bow as he sang "I Need $100" in Detroit in the 1950s (CD 2, Track 4). I could not make out the lyrics of stanza 2 with much confidence.

CD 2/4

"I Need $100" (2:59). Performed by One-String Sam, c. 1956. Detroit, Michigan. Reissued on *Detroit Blues: The Early 1950s*. Blues Classics LP, BC-12.

Text, "I Need $100"

1. You know I talked with mother this morning,
   mother talked with the judge.
   I could hear her, eavesdropping, you know I
   understood their words.
   She said, "I need $100. You know I—.
   You know I need $100 just to go my baby's bond."
2. You know me and my little girl got up this morning.
   She said she wanted to freeze to death.
   Told her in the icebox to look in, baby I
   freeze my ice myself.
   I just need $100. I say I need—.
   You know I need $100 just to go my baby's bond.
3. You know I left your mother standing, baby,
   In her doorway crying.
   Come begging and pleading don't
   mistreat your little girl of mine.
   I said, "Mother-in-law I need $100. All I need's—.
   All I need $100 just to go my baby's bond."
4. You know my houselady come telling about
   want to talk for an hour,

want to go to the Red Cross people you know
want a sack of Red Cross flour.
I told her all I need's $100. All I need's—.
Baby if I had $100, I could go and go my baby's bond.

The rhythm that One-String Sam uses in "I Need $100" is the same triplet rhythm that Bill Lucas used in "Poor Boy Blues": CHUNG, k'CHUNG, k'CHUNG, k'CHUNG, and so on:

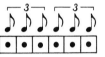

The simplicity of the instrument allows us to invent a diddly-bow notation that shows how to play "I Need $100" or any other song. In the diddly-bow notation each triplet beat will be marked with a box:

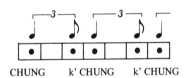

Transcription 4-13
Diddly-bow notation

The basic rhythm for "I Need $100" comes out like this:

CHUNG   k' CHUNG   k' CHUNG

Transcription 4-14
Basic rhythm, "I Need $100."

With your thumb plucking away from your body, play the diddly-bow in that rhythm for a while until it is comfortable. If your hand gets cramped, stop and shake it out. Keep it loose; move the whole thumb as a unit, not just the upper part above the knuckle. Come back to playing it every so often, and by the end of a day it will have become second nature.

That is about all there is to the right-hand part (or left-hand part, if you are left-handed) of "I Need $100." The other hand's part is even simpler; in fact, most of the time it does nothing at all while you pluck the tonic as you have just been practicing. At other times it slides a bottleneck or other smooth device along the top of the string to make the whining, zinging sounds you hear on the record.

Traditionally, the diddly-bow is played with a bottleneck slide. Any hard object that can be held easily in your hand will serve, but glass makes the best sound. Find a bottle with a cylindrical neck (Figure 4-15). You can find a glass cutter at a hardware store or a specialty shop. Glass cutters give a sure, neat cut; but be careful not to cut yourself. Alternatively, use a glass medicine bottle whole, without cutting off the neck. Finally, bottlenecks have become so popular in the past few years that it is now possible to buy them in stores that sell guitars.

Figure 4-15

Choosing the right bottle.

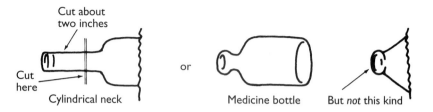

Hold the bottleneck comfortably in your hand so you can rest it and slide it gently but firmly up and down the string of the diddly-bow from the nut to the area where your other hand plucks the string. If you press too hard, the string will touch the fingerboard and the sound of the plucked string will be muffled. Gentle pressure gives a clear, ringing tone.

Practice sliding the glass on the diddly-bow. Make certain you have a good grip on the bottleneck so you can take it off the string when playing the tonic and can put it on the string at various locations. Pluck the string as you slide.

Figure 4-16

Marking intervals on the diddly-bow.

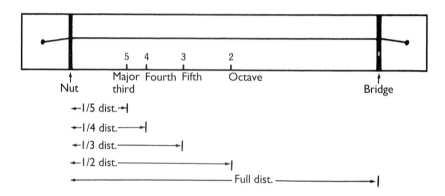

Now, find the various simple pitch intervals with the slide on the string (Figure 4-16). The octave will be sounded when the slide is about halfway between the nut and the bridge. With a pen or pencil, mark this point on the string board with the number 2 (for one-half the distance to the bridge). The perfect fifth will be sounded when the slide is one-third of the distance between the nut and bridge. Mark this point on the string board with a 3. The perfect fourth will be sounded when the slide is one-fourth the distance between the nut and bridge. Mark this point on the string board with a 4. The major third will be sounded when the slide is one-fifth the distance between the nut and bridge. Mark this point with a 5. These will be your reference points for the intervals used in "I Need $100," and of course they will come in handy when you want to play other songs.

The marks you have just made on your string board will easily be incorporated in our diddly-bow notation to indicate where to place the slide. A dot inside the notation box indicates that the slide is off the string; this is the tonic. A number inside a notation box tells you where to place the slide as you pluck the string with the other hand. Try this:

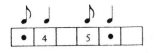

Transcription 4-15
Four-tone sequence on the diddly-bow.

This four-tone sequence is one of Sam's typical moves in "I Need $100." He plucks the tonic for a count of one triplet, then puts on the slide at 4, plucks the string, and holds the tone for a count of two triplets. Next he moves the slide on the string back to 5—actually, slightly to the nut side of 5, because he uses a neutral rather than a major interval of a third—and plucks the string for a count of one triplet. Finally, he takes the slide off and plucks the tonic for a count of two triplets. Listen to the recording and pick out the spots where he plays this sequence.

When you have mastered this four-tone sequence, you will be well on your way to Sam's accompaniment for "I Need $100." Transcription 4-16 offers box notation for the accompaniment Sam uses in the first stanza. The wavy lines after 3 and 2 indicate a vibrato, which Sam makes by wiggling the slide back and forth quickly on the string in the general area of the string board mark. Now turn on the recording and play along with One-String Sam.

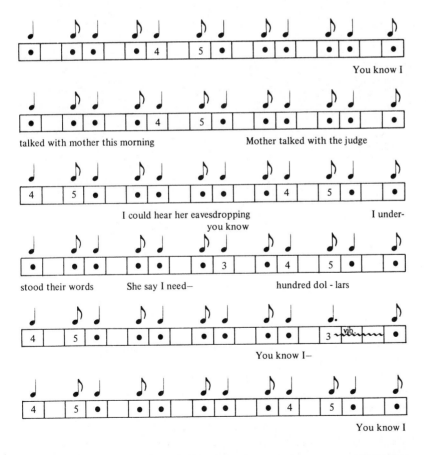

Transcription 4-16
Diddly-bow accompaniment for "I Need $100," as played by One-String Sam on CD 2, Track 4.

(continues)

Transcription 4-16
(continued)

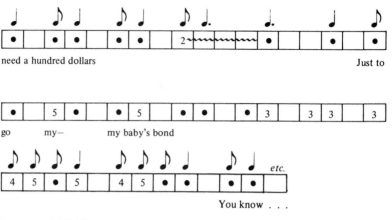

need a hundred dollars   Just to

go   my—   my baby's bond

etc.

You know . . .

Transcribed by Jeff Todd Titon.

Social Context and the Meaning of the Blues

Blues is best understood as both a musical form and a feeling. The blues songs we have taken a close look at, "Poor Boy Blues," "She Got Me Walkin'," and "I Need $100," are typical and can bring us toward a structural definition of blues as a song form. Textually, blues songs consist of a series of rhymed three-line or quatrain-refrain stanzas, each sung to more or less the same tune. Blues tunes usually consist of twelve-measure (bar) strophes, and they employ a special scale, the blues scale (Transcription 4-12). They are rhythmically complex, employing syncopation and, at times, differing rhythms between singing and instruments. Many other attributes of blues songs—melodic shape, for instance, or the typical raspy timbre—lie beyond the scope of an introduction but may be followed up elsewhere (see Titon 1994).

Although the feelingful aspects of blues are embodied in such musical aspects as the singer's delivery and in the way the musicians "play around" with the blues scale and rhythmic syncopation, the most direct expression of blues feeling comes from the lyrics. Most blues lyrics are about lovers, and they fall into a pattern arising from black-American life. The blues grew and developed when most African-Americans lived as sharecroppers on Southern cotton farms, from late in the nineteenth century until just before World War II, when farm mechanization began to displace the black workers, and factory work at high wages in the Northern cities attracted them. Down home, young men and women did not marry early; they were needed on the farm. If a young woman became pregnant, she had her baby and brought the child into the household with her parents. She did not lose status in the community, and later she often married the father of her child. When a woman did marry young, her partner usually was middle-aged and needed a woman to work and care for his children from a prior marriage. It was good to have plenty of children; when they came of age to work, more hands could go into the cotton and corn fields. Adoption was common; when families broke up, children were farmed out among relatives.

Sociologists and anthropologists, some of them black (such as Charles Johnson), studied this sharecropping culture in the 1920s and 1930s. Interested in patterns of love, marriage, and divorce, the fieldworkers found that partners separated because one could not live with the other's laziness, violence, or adultery. These reasons added up to "mistreatment," the very word they used. A woman was reported as saying her current lover was "nice all right, but I ain't thinking about marrying. Soon as you marry a man he starts mistreating you, and I ain't going to be mistreated no more" (Johnson [1934] 1966:83). Blues songs reflected these attitudes; mistreatment was the most common subject. Once the subject was established, people began to expect mistreatment as the appropriate subject for blues songs, and although many blues were composed about other subjects, the majority had (and still have) to do with lovers and mistreatment. After World War II the sharecropping culture was less important; the action now took place in the cities where most black people had gone: Atlanta, New York, Washington, Detroit, Memphis, St. Louis, Chicago, Dallas, Houston, Los Angeles, Oakland. But black family patterns persisted among the lower classes in the urban ghettos, and so did the blues.

Blues lyrics about mistreatment fall into a pattern. The singer casts himself or herself in the role of mistreated victim, introduces an antagonist

Figure 4-17
Howlin' Wolf (Chester Burnett).
Ann Arbor Blues Festival, Ann Arbor,
Michigan, 1969.

Jeff Todd Titon

(usually a mistreating lover), provides incidents that detail the circumstances of the mistreatment, and draws up a bill of indictment. Then, with the listener's tacit approval, the victim becomes the judge, and the drama turns on the verdict: Will he or she accept the mistreatment, try to reform the mistreater, or leave? Resigned acceptance and attempted reform resolve a minority of blues songs. Most often the victim, declaring independence, steps out of the victim's role with an ironic parting shot and leaves. "Dog Me Around," as sung by Howlin' Wolf (Figure 4-17), is typical in this regard.

Text, "Dog Me Around"

1. How many more years have I got to let you dog me around?
   How many more years have I got to let you dog me around?
   I'd just as soon rather be dead, sleeping way down in the ground.
2. If I treat you right you wouldn't believe what I've said.
   If I treat you right you wouldn't believe what I've said.
   You think I'm halfway crazy; you think I ought to let you have your way.
3. I'm going upstairs, I'm going to bring back down my clothes.
   I'm going upstairs, I'm going to bring back down my clothes.
   If anybody asks about me, just tell 'em I walked outdoors.

"Dog Me Around," by Howlin' Wolf (Chester Burnett). Copyright ©1974, Modern Music Publishing Co., Inc. Used by permission.

In stanza 1 the singer complains of mistreatment, saying his lover treats him like a dog. We learn in stanza 2 that the singer may also be guilty; "If I treat you right" implies mistreatment on both sides of the relationship. (Stanza 2 could be interpreted as dialogue spoken by the singer's mistreating lover, but without an obvious clue like "She said," point of view seldom shifts in blues lyrics.) The singer resolves the drama in stanza 3 when he declares that he will leave his lover. "Just tell 'em I walked outdoors" is an understatement that shows how little the affair means to him.

Blues music helps lovers understand each other. Because the themes are traditional and shared by the community, blues songs also give listeners community approval for separation in response to mistreatment. The listener who recognizes his or her situation in the lyrics of a blues song receives a nice definition of that situation and a possible response to it. At a Saturday night party, or at home alone, a mistreated lover finds consolation in the blues (Figure 4-18).

Of course, mistreatment is not the only theme in blues lyrics. They portray virtually all kinds of relationships among partners. For example, in "Kokomo Blues" (CD 2, Track 5) Fred McDowell sings the following:

CD 2/5

"Kokomo Blues" (2:40). Fred McDowell. Performed by Fred McDowell, vocal and guitar; Jeff Todd Titon, guitar; Mitchell Genova, drums. Field recording by Michael Justen. Minneapolis, Minnesota, July 1970.

Text, "Kokomo Blues"

1.   Well kokomo me baby,
      kokomo me right,
      kokomo your daddy,
      he'll be back tomorrow night.

Figure 4-18
Dancing at a juke joint. Alabama, 1957.

Frederic Ramsey, Jr.

> Crying, I, Baby don't you want to go.
> Down to that eleven light city, sweet old Kokomo.

2. Well, kokomo me baby,
    kokomo me twice,
    kokomo your daddy,
    I'll be back tomorrow night,
    Crying, I, Honey don't you want to go.
    Down to that eleven light city, sweet old Kokomo.

3. Well, one and one is two;
    three and more makes six;
    Keep messin' around, baby,
    gonna get somebody's trick.
    Crying, I, Baby don't you want to go.
    Down to that eleven light city, sweet old Kokomo.

"Kokomo Blues" by Fred McDowell, © 1996 Tradition Music (BMI), administered by BUG. All rights reserved. Used by permission.

McDowell (Figure 4-19) was notable for his rural Mississippi juke-joint guitar style. In contrast to the solo flights of the lead guitar in a typical urban blues or rock band, McDowell's guitar playing is based on short, repeated melodic phrases whose infectious rhythms are wonderfully suited to dancing. While listening to "Kokomo Blues" you may find it hard to keep still. These short repeated phrases, or riffs, put the musicians and dancers into a rhythmic groove. This rhythmic technique can be found in all genres of African American music, including jazz, gospel, soul, disco, and hip-hop.

Figure 4-19
Fred McDowell. Minneapolis, Minnesota,
1970.

Jeff Todd Titon

The Blues Yesterday

In this chapter we have approached blues as an African-American music.
And that is historically true: African-Americans invented blues music. But
many non-African-American readers of this book already know something
about blues, because blues today extends well beyond the boundaries of
the African-American music-culture. Today more people recognize the
name of the British blues singer-guitarist Eric Clapton than the names
Muddy Waters and Howlin' Wolf. About thirty-five years ago blues entered
mainstream U.S. culture, and in our mass-mediated global village today
blues is an attractive commodity. You can hear blues played in Prague, Dar
es Salaam, and Tokyo by citizens of Czechoslovakia, Tanzania, and Japan.
Nowadays blues is regarded as a universal phenomenon, accessible to all.
The folklorist Alan Lomax believes that blacks were the first Americans to
feel the alienation characteristic of the twentieth century, and that blues is
the quintessential expression of that alienation.

It is true that African-Americans invented blues, and it is also true that
early on people outside the black communities were attracted to it. The
white folklorist Howard Odum, for example, collected blues songs in the
South prior to 1910. The African-American composer W. C. Handy popularized blues in the 1910s with songs such as "St. Louis Blues," but white

singers such as Sophie Tucker recorded blues songs before African-American singers were permitted to do so. African-American blues queens such as Bessie Smith made blues the most popular African-American music in the 1920s, and it attracted a small white audience as well as a large black one. The 1920s also brought the first recordings of downhome blues: Blind Blake, the greatest ragtime guitarist; Charley Patton, a songster regarded as the father of Mississippi Delta blues; and a host of others brought the music out of the local juke joints and house parties and onto recordings that were circulated back into the black communities. Jimmie Rodgers, the first star of country music, whose brief career lasted from 1927 through 1933, sang many blues songs, particularly his "blue yodels." Rodgers, a white Mississippian, learned many of his songs and much of his relaxed singing style from black railroad men. Blues has been an important component within country music ever since. African-American rhythms, jazz instrumental breaks, and the blues scale were critical in the formation of bluegrass, which ironically is usually regarded as an Anglo-American musical tradition (see Cantwell 1984). Further, the banjo—the quintessential bluegrass instrument—is derived from an African instrument.

Blues has always been a popular form within jazz and remains so today, often regarded there as a "roots" music. In the 1930s and 1940s blues "shouters" such as Jimmy Rushing with Count Basie's orchestra bridged the line between blues and jazz. African-American rhythm and blues of the 1940s followed in the tradition of these blues shouters, such as Wynonie Harris, Tiny Bradshaw, and Joe Turner, along with crooners such as Charles Brown. In the meantime an urban blues sound arose featuring singers with small bands led by electric guitar. Aaron "T-Bone" Walker invented it in the 1940s, Riley "B. B." (Blues Boy) King made it immensely popular in the 1950s, and a host of imitators, black and later white, followed. Rock and roll in the 1950s began as a white cover of black rhythm and blues, but by the early 1960s black Americans competed well in that arena, and singers like Ray Charles and Motown groups like Diana Ross and the Supremes became immensely popular. Ray Charles's biggest hit, "What'd I Say," was a blues song; blues such as "Maybelline" were among Chuck Berry's best-selling recordings; it even became possible for downhome singers such as Jimmy Reed, whose "Big Boss Man" climbed high on the pop charts, to cross over into the white music charts.

Blues was crucial in British rock during the 1960s. Groups such as The Rolling Stones (whose name came from one of Muddy Waters's songs, and whose early albums featured covers of Chicago blues) participated in the British blues revival. Dozens of British blues bands could be found in such cities as London and Liverpool, and talented instrumentalists such as John Mayall and Eric Clapton arose from this ferment in the 1960s. An American blues revival in the same decade gave the white musicians Paul Butterfield and Charlie Musselwhite a start, and a new phenomenon appeared: bands whose personnel included a mixture of black and white musicians. Muddy Waters, for example, featured the white harmonica player Paul Oscher and in the 1970s had a white guitarist, Bob Margolin, in his band. Lazy Bill

Lucas, the leader of the band I played in during the 1960s, led an integrated band. At the 1970 Ann Arbor Blues Festival, Luther Allison and Johnny Winter sang and played a set together (Figure 1-3).

Since the late 1960s many white-American rock bands have covered black blues hits from the 1950s and 1960s. The screaming guitar lines of heavy metal music are an interpretation (some would say a misinterpretation) of the blues lead-guitar styles of B. B. King, Albert King, Freddy King, Elmore James, and others. Most rock fans do not realize the debt that rock owes to blues and the African-American community. But in the 1960s most of black America saw blues as old-fashioned. Outside of strongholds in the Mississippi Delta and Chicago, blues accounted for a small proportion of jukebox records and received little radio airplay. Black intellectuals dismissed blues as a music of resignation, unfit for the contemporary climate of civil rights and black power. Soul music was much more attractive. Yet during this same decade many blues singers revived their careers, finding a new audience. The blues revival of the 1960s brought commercially recorded blues music and black musicians before a largely white public in North America and Europe. Buddy Guy and John Lee Hooker, popular today, were active but overshadowed in the 1960s revival (see Figure 4-20).

Magic Sam, B. B. King, Muddy Waters, and Howlin' Wolf represented variety in the modern electric blues sound, while singers who had made recordings before World War II performed acoustically on the folk music

Figure 4-20
John Lee Hooker and admirer. Ann Arbor Blues Festival, Ann Arbor, Michigan, 1970.

Jeff Todd Titon

circuit, sounding much as they had decades ago: Roosevelt Sykes, Mississippi John Hurt, Son House, Skip James, John Lee Hooker, Lightnin' Hopkins, Big Joe Williams, and Booker White, to name a few. Few blues singer-guitarists were more highly sought after during the 1960s blues revival than Johnny Shines (Figure 4-21), a man with roots in the Mississippi Delta and a direct connection to the legendary bluesman Robert Johnson.

Johnny Shines

Johnny Shines (1915–1992) was born in Frazier, near Memphis, Tennessee. As a teenager he liked to listen to blues records by Charley Patton and Blind Lemon Jefferson; in 1932 he heard Howlin' Wolf in person and bought his first guitar.

> I was sitting and watching Wolf every night—that is every night I could get where he was—all night long, too. Finally one night everything just fell in place and I started playing. I had no lessons or nothing, nobody taught me anything. Even the whole time later when I ran around with Robert [Johnson], he never took the time to show me nothing. I just picked up things as I went along.

Shines traveled and played blues with Johnson from about 1935 to 1937. Years later, after Johnson's tragic death, Shines moved to Chicago where he made a few outstanding recordings of his own. Never able to support himself full-time as a musician, he did construction work and quit the

Jeff Todd Titon

Figure 4-21
Johnny Shines at the Smithsonian Institution's Festival of American Folklife, 1991.

music business altogether in the 1950s, but like so many other blues singers he was "rediscovered" and found a new audience among young, white blues aficionados during the 1960s blues revival.

Like Robert Johnson, Shines had a light, tense voice and often pitched his songs at the top of his vocal range, going into falsetto at times. Shines ornamented his vocal melodies more than most blues singers did. His guitar playing, whether acoustic or electric, owed a debt to Johnson and to the early Chicago blues guitarists, but he never developed the solo lead guitar technique of a T-Bone Walker or B. B. King.

The subjects of Shines's lyrics were more varied than those of most singers. Here is his version of a blues that he told me he learned from a relative: "From Dark Till Dawn" (CD 2, Track 6).

(Spoken:) This is a very old song. This is a song that my mother's cousin used to sing when I was a little bitty—well, it don't have to be that old though, do it!— I just thought. I was just a little fellow, you know. I used to stand in the field and listen to her sing this song, you know. And I thought it sounded so pretty, and I didn't forget it.

1. "Won't you tell me, mama, how you want your rollin' done?
   Won't you tell me, mama, how you want your rollin' done?
   I'm gonna please you mama, if I have to roll from dusk to dawn."
2. I'm gonna build me a mansion out on some old lonesome hill,
   I'm gonna build me a mansion out on some old lonesome hill,
   Where if one woman don't like it, there'll be a hundred and five that will.
3. Well, I was born in Tennessee, down on a cotton farm.
   I'm my daddy's own child; I am his only son.
   Well, he taught me how to love; and I swear that is a job well done.

"From Dark Till Dawn," words and music by John Shines, © Uncle Doris Music, ASCAP. Used by permission.

Although mistreatment is the subject of most blues lyrics, others boast of the singer's talents as a lover. Songs like Muddy Waters's "Hoochie-Coochie Man" are filled with bravado, and at first glance "From Dark Till Dawn" seems to fall into the same category. But if you think about the lyrics more carefully, you realize that the point of the first stanza is not so much that the singer is a capable lover, but that he is sensitive enough to want to please his lover, even if it takes all night. Further, the second stanza admits the possibility that he might not be pleasing to all women. The third, on the other hand, is a boast; yet it is the boast of someone standing in a line of tradition, crediting his father, who showed him what it meant to love a woman. In this context "love" becomes more than simply "rolling from dusk till dawn."

Of the blues musicians I met during the 1960s blues revival, Shines was the most thoughtful, both on stage and off. At the Wisconsin Delta Blues Festival, where I recorded him singing "From Dark Till Dawn" in 1970, he told me he was resentful that more blues fans were interested in

CD 2/6

"From Dark Till Dawn" (3:29). John Ned "Johnny" Shines. Performed by Johnny Shines, vocal and guitar. Field recording by Jeff Todd Titon. Beloit, Wisconsin, March 1970. (Background noise from the audience is audible.)

Text, "From Dark Till Dawn"

what he could tell them about the legendary Robert Johnson than in Shines's own compositions and performance. Irony was his way of dealing with that situation. He would not always tell interviewers the right answers to their questions. Performing was difficult for him; it required great effort.

He invited me to visit him at his home in Alabama, and when I did so a few months later, he was a much happier man. He showed me portions of the autobiography he was writing; he spoke with conviction about racism in the record industry; he listened patiently while I played some pieces on my guitar for him, and he gave me some good suggestions. A year before his death in 1992, I spent a week with him at the Smithsonian Folklife Festival, where he was a featured artist. In the last years of his life he used his music to help educate people (black people in particular) about black history. He found it unsettling that white America had adopted blues music as its own. The Festival was a good vehicle for him because in this museum setting he could present his ideas on how African Americans must look to black music as a primary resource in order to understand black history in a racist society.

Blues has its share of heroes and heroines who died too young. John Lee (Sonny Boy) Williamson, stabbed to death in Chicago in 1947, was an outstanding singer and blues harmonica player. Robert Johnson, poisoned in his twenties by his girlfriend's jealous husband, would have changed the course of blues history had he lived. As it was, although he had only two recording sessions, his impact on post–World War II Chicago blues was immense.

Magic Sam

We turn now to the music of another Mississippi-born, blues singer-guitarist who died before his time: Magic Sam (Sam Maghett, 1937–1969). His first instrument was the diddly-bow. As a young teenager he moved to Chicago with his family. His club and record career began in the 1950s when he was still a teenager. After a stint in the armed services, he re-turned to the clubs on the West Side of Chicago, where his generation of musicians was moving Chicago blues toward soul—the music of James Brown, Otis Redding, Aretha Franklin—the most popular African-American music of the 1960s. Magic Sam recorded three albums for Del-mark in Chicago, where he had made a reputation for his soaring vocals and flashy guitar playing. But those who had heard him in the clubs said these studio albums failed to capture the brilliance of his live performances.

Magic Sam's luck changed abruptly at the 1969 Ann Arbor Blues Festi-val in Michigan. B. B. King, Howlin' Wolf, Muddy Waters, Albert King, John Lee Hooker, Freddy King, James Cotton, Big Mama Thornton, Otis Rush, T-Bone Walker, Lightnin' Hopkins—virtually all the major contemporary blues artists performed at this three-day affair. Roosevelt Sykes, Big Joe Williams, Sleepy John Estes, and Son House represented an older genera-tion whose careers had begun before World War II. Luther Allison, Jimmy Dawkins, and Magic Sam were among those representing the future. It was a huge cutting contest, as each artist tried to outdo the others. Writing about this event, the blues critic John Fishel concluded, "If one set [stood] out as surpassing all others in excitement and virtuosity, it [was] Magic Sam's" (Fishel 1981).

It was Sunday afternoon, August 3, the last day of the festival, about 3 o'clock—not prime time. Casual in the extreme, Sam arrived a half-hour late. He had to borrow a drummer from another band. Yet somehow in the performance they came together at the highest heat. It was all the more remarkable because of the sparse instrumentation: guitar, bass, and drums. Yet Magic Sam was no ordinary guitarist. On "You Don't Love Me," recorded at the festival from the audience (CD 2, Track 7), Sam played his guitar as both a lead and rhythm instrument, catching a riff that both hearkened back to the deepest blues of the Mississippi Delta and pointed forward to the grooves of the future. Above it all Sam's voice carried effortlessly to the audience of ten thousand, who picked up the groove and, as if lifted to their feet by some unseen force, danced for the remaining twenty minutes of his set.

Dick Shurman presented Magic Sam as a postmodern master:

> His music had roots in the boogie he loved and in the tension and challenge created by the distraction of a noisy, bustling bar. He was able, *par excellence,* to turn the response of the audience into a foil and a force in the music. Partly because of his reliance on whatever equipment was available (like amps without reverb units and borrowed guitars) and partly because of the loose circumstances and the long nights (usually playing until 4 A.M.), Magic Sam was a world apart from the studio's time limits, structures, and formulas. (1981)

Sam's career took off immediately after Ann Arbor. In the next month he toured the European blues clubs, a sure sign that he had arrived. But on December 1, 1969, he died of a heart attack. He was 32 years old.

The Blues Today

For an example of contemporary blues we turn to a masterpiece by an older singer, Otis Rush. "Ain't Enough Comin' In" (CD 2, Track 8) was voted the outstanding blues recording of the year 1994 by the readers of *Living Blues* magazine. Although four years later Rush recorded another excellent album (*Any Place I'm Going,* House of Blues 51415 1343 2PR, 1998), "Ain't Enough Comin' In," which Rush wrote and arranged, is as outstanding a performance of contemporary urban blues as can be heard today. The song starts with an authoritative drumbeat, and immediately the electric bass sets a heavy rhythmic riff that repeats until the end of the song, changing pitch when the chords change. In its rhythmic constancy the bass provides something akin to the bell pattern in *Agbekor* (see Chapter 3) that anchors the entire performance. The drummer plays simply but forcefully and unerringly, marking the beat 1–2–3–4, with the accent on 3. A rock drummer would be busier than this—and a lot less relentless. The electric bass is louder than the drums, which is characteristic of black popular music since the 1970s.

CD 2/7

"You Don't Love Me" (3:35). Willie Cobbs. Performed by Magic Sam (Sam Maghett), vocal and guitar; Sam Lay, drums; unknown bass player. Field Recording by Jeff Todd Titon. Ann Arbor, Michigan, 1969.

CD 2/8

"Ain't Enough Comin' In" (5:53). Otis Rush. Performed by Otis Rush on *Otis Rush: Ain't Enough Comin' In.* Mercury CD 314518769-2. 1994.

1. Oh, I ain't got enough comin' in to take care of what's got to go out.
   It ain't enough love or money comin' in, baby, to take care of what's got
   to go out.
   Like a bird I got my wing clipped, my friends; I've got to start all over
   again.

2. If the sun ever shine on me again,
   Oh lord if the sun ever shine on me again.
   Like a bird I got my wing clipped, my friends; I've got to start all over
   again.

3. Now when it's all over and said and done, money talks and the fool gets
   none;
   The tough get tough and the tough get goin'; come on baby let me hold
   you in my arms.

4. It ain't enough comin' in to take care of what's got to go out.
   Ain't enough love or money comin' in, baby, to take care of what's got
   to go out.
   My friends, I got my wing clipped; I've got to start all over again.

5. When it's all over and said and done, money talks and the fool gets none;
   The tough get tough and the tough get goin'; come on baby let me hold
   you in my arms.

6. Ain't enough comin' in to take care of what's got to go out.
   It ain't enough love or money comin' in to take care of what's got to go
   out.
   Like a bird I got my wing clipped, my friends; I've got to start all over
   again.

7. If you don't put nothin' in you can't get nothin' out;
   You don't put nothin' in, baby, you can't get nothin' out;
   Like a bird I got my wing clipped, my friends; I've got to start all over
   again.

Words and Music by Otis Rush, © 1994 Otis Rush Music, administered by BUG. Used by permission.

Listeners who can recognize the difference between major and minor chords will realize that this is a minor blues, built on the minor i-iv-v chords instead of the major ones. The first chorus is instrumental. Rush plays the electric guitar lead above a riffing rhythm section that includes a trumpet and saxophone as well as an organ. The direct, spare playing here sets a somber mood for his powerful vocals that follow. The song features a bridge section ("Now when it's all over . . .") that departs from the usual twelve-bar blues pattern, but you will recognize that otherwise (except for the minor key) the song has a typical blues structure. After the vocals Rush takes the tune twice through with a guitar solo, and this is followed by two choruses in which a saxophone leads, taking some of Rush's ideas and developing them. The bridge returns, followed by two more verses, and Rush takes it out with one more instrumental chorus. Hear how the sound of the guitar vibrates at the beginning of the last chorus. This is a tremolo, and Rush is known for getting this effect by pushing his fingers from side to side on the strings (a hand tremolo) rather than using the tremolo bar attached to the electric guitar.

Rush's vocal style is striking. Like many blues singers he hoarsens his voice at times to show great emotion, but he also makes his voice tremble at times, an effect that mirrors his guitar tremolo (and vice versa). Blues writers have called Rush's voice "tortured" with a "frightening intensity" and a "harrowing poetic terror" (Rowe 1979:176) and "tense and oppressive" (Herzhaft 1992:300). There is no denying that Rush has a full, powerful voice. Its vehemence and falling melodic curve may remind you of the Navajo Yeibichai singers (Chapter 2).

Rush's lyrics are clever and subtle. In the beginning of his career he relied on the professional songwriter Willie Dixon, but after his first hit songs he decided that he could "write one better than that" (Forte 1991:159). When I hear the first line, I think "ain't enough comin' in" refers to money; but in the second line Rush lets me know that I should think of the parallel between love and money: The singer feels that he's giving too much and not getting enough of either in return.

Who is Otis Rush? Is he the latest singer-guitarist to capitalize on the blues revival of the 1990s? Not at all: Otis Rush has been a blues legend since the 1950s, well-known to musicians and serious blues aficionados if not to the general listening public. Stevie Ray Vaughn named his band Double Trouble in honor of Rush's finest song from that decade. Led Zeppelin covered Rush's "I Can't Quit You Baby," with guitarist Jimmy Page lifting Rush's instrumental break note-for-note (Forte 1991:156). Rush's guitar playing turned Eric Clapton into a disciple. When Rush met Clapton in England in 1986 he called Clapton a "great guitar player" and modestly went on, "Everybody plays like somebody. It's good to know that somebody's listening. To me, I'm just a guitar player. I'm not trying to influence nobody, I'm just trying to play, and play well. And hopefully I can sell some records" (Forte 1991:161).

Otis Rush was born in Philadelphia, Mississippi, in 1934 and began playing at age ten. Left-handed, he plays the guitar upside-down, with the bass strings closer to the ground; this accounts for some of his special sound (see Figure 4-22). For example, to "bend" a note on the treble strings, Rush pulls the string down, whereas a right-handed guitarist must push the string up (harder to do). Like Bill Lucas, he first sang country music, not blues. It was not until the late 1940s, when he came to Chicago and began visiting the blues clubs, that he decided to sing and play the blues.

Although B. B. King, T-Bone Walker, and Magic Sam were among the musicians who influenced him most strongly, Rush developed his own version of modern blues guitar. His style is subtle, spare, cool—the instrumental equivalent of caressing a lover. There is nothing egotistical about it, no showing off. His use of silence is brilliant. "Well, I can play fast stuff, but I try to take my time and make you feel what I'm doin'," he told Jas Obrecht.

Figure 4-22
Otis Rush performing at the Ann Arbor
Blues Festival, Ann Arbor, Michigan,
1969. Note that he plays left-handed.

Jeff Todd Titon

"You can play a bunch of notes so fast, but then you turn around, and
somebody out there listening says, 'What did he play?' Sound good, but
can't remember nothin'. Take your time and *play*. Measure it out enough
where they got time to hear what you're doing" (2000:243). Like a fine aged
wine at its peak, at its best his music has great presence, neither under-
stated nor flashy: substantial, direct, powerful, and commanding respect.

Rush takes risks onstage and in recordings. Often he would rather try
something new than stick with the same old thing. "I can make that guitar
say what you sayin' right now," Rush told Obrecht. "I can say The Lord's
Prayer on my guitar and you'll say, 'That's every word of it.' Just like you
talkin' there? I can make my guitar say just what you said. . . . I can sing
with my guitar, just like I sing with my voice" (2000:243). Rush's guitar isn't
merely imitating his vocals. It replies to them and extends them, in another
example of the African call-and-response aesthetic. The album from which
"Ain't Enough Comin' In" is taken represented a long overdue turning
point in Rush's career. He is, today, one of the very best of the older generation of blues singer-guitarists, a generation whose music was formed prior
to the blues revival of the 1960s.

A Few Final Words

Throughout this book, the music-cultures that the authors have chosen are by and large the product of particular regions and communities made of people who share such things as a common language and heritage. But this is not the only kind of music-culture. Mass-mediated popular music, presented outside community settings in concerts, recordings, radio, and television, forms communities of listeners and would-be performers who may otherwise have little in common. As we have seen, until the 1960s the blues music-culture was based in African-American communities; today it embraces people from all over the world. Blues is but one of many local and regional musics that have become immensely popular outside their area of origin: reggae is another. Today world music is presented from the concert stage in many cities in North America and Europe. What kind of music-culture do the connoisseurs of world music represent?

Consider what happens once a musical genre has been popularized by the mass media, written about, studied, defined: Some of that interpretive activity is carried back to performers, and now people expect the music to conform to those definitions. Record producers, promoters, writers, and lately scholars, few of them raised in African-American communities, are partly responsible for codifying the rules of the blues genre. How, once standardized, can blues music change and grow, yet still remain blues? Must singers stay with the old forms, changing only their contents—new wine in old bottles; new lyrics, new instrumentation, in old settings? Must festival promoters choose blues singers on the basis of how well they conform to the genre? Should a folklore police enforce the rules?

Now, in the twenty-first century, we are in the midst of a new blues revival as older African Americans honor blues as roots music and new generations (black and white) discover the music for the first time. Acoustic blues has also made a comeback among African-American performers. In the 1960s blues revival, the only notable young African-American acoustic blues guitarist was Taj Mahal. Today young African-American singers such as Keb' Mo', Corey Harris, and Alvin Youngblood Hart are carving out successful careers as acoustic blues singer-guitarists.

Today's most active blues music-culture is in Chicago, a city with a history of great hospitality to the blues. Dozens of blues clubs may also be found in such cities as Houston; St. Louis; Memphis; Clarksdale, Mississippi; Oakland–San Francisco; and Detroit. Well-known blues singers such as B. B. King and Buddy Guy tour nationally and, sponsored by the U.S. Department of State, as goodwill ambassadors abroad.

Not long ago I was at a club in Chicago and heard a woman blues singer with a very powerful voice, backed by a four-piece band. It turned out she had studied voice in preparation for the opera, then decided she would have a better career singing blues. Do these historical, economic, and audience changes mean we should abandon our music-culture models (Chapter 1) in the face of real-world complications? No, but we need to keep in mind that it is a *model,* an ideal. Music-cultures respond to economic, artistic, and interpretive pressures from without as well as within;

music-cultures are not isolated entities. Their histories reveal that response to these pressures; "catching" or defining a music at any given time comes at the expense of the long view.

References

Brooks, Cleanth, R. W. B. Lewis, and Robert Penn Warren. 1973. *American Literature: The Makers and the Making.* 2 vols. New York: St. Martin's Press.

Brunoghe, Yannick, ed. 1964. *Big Bill Blues.* New York: Oak.

Cantwell, Robert. 1984. *Bluegrass Breakdown.* Urbana: Univ. of Illinois Press.

Charters, Samuel. 1977. *The Legacy of the Blues.* New York: Da Capo.

Courlander, Harold. 1963. *Negro Folk Music U.S.A.* New York: Columbia Univ. Press.

Eliot, T. S. [1920] 1964. "Hamlet and His Problems." In *The Sacred Wood.* Reprint, New York: Barnes & Noble.

Evans, David. 1971. "Booker White." In *Nothing But the Blues,* edited by Mike Leadbitter. London: Hanover Books.

Fishel, John. 1981. "Magic Sam and the Ann Arbor Blues Festival." Liner notes to *Magic Sam Live.* Delmark DL-645/646.

Forte, Dan. 1991. "Otis Rush." In *Blues Guitar,* edited by Jas Obrecht, pp. 156–62. San Francisco: GPI Books.

Groom, Bob. 1971. *The Blues Revival.* London: Studio Vista.

Herzhaft, Gerard. 1992. *Encyclopedia of the Blues.* Fayetteville: Univ. of Arkansas Press.

Jackson, Bruce. 1972. *Wake up Dead Man: Afro-American Worksongs from Texas State Prisons.* Cambridge, Mass.: Harvard Univ. Press.

Johnson, Charles S. [1934] 1966. *Shadow of the Plantation.* Reprint, Chicago: Univ. of Chicago Press.

Lomax, Alan. 1976. Brochure notes to *Negro Prison Songs from the Mississippi State Penitentiary.* Reissue of Tradition LP 1020 (see "Additional Listening"). Vogue Records VJD 515.

Lucas, William ("Lazy Bill"). 1974. *Lazy Bill Lucas.* Philo LP 1007.

McLeod, Norma, and Marcia Herndon. 1981. *Music as Culture.* 2nd ed. Darby, Pa.: Norwood Editions.

Obrecht, Jas. 2000. "Otis Rush." In *Rollin' and Tumblin': The Postwar Blues Guitarists,* edited by Jas Obrecht. San Francisco: Miller Freeman.

Oliver, Paul. 1965. *Conversation with the Blues.* London: Cassell.

———.1974. *The Story of the Blues.* Reprint, Radnor, Pa.: Chilton Books.

Rowe, Mike. 1979. *Chicago Breakdown.* New York: Da Capo.

Seeger, Charles. 1977. *Studies in Musicology, 1935–1975.* Berkeley: Univ. of California Press.

Shurman, Dick. 1981. "Magic Sam: An Overview." Liner notes to *Magic Sam Live.* Delmark DL-645/646.

Tedlock, Dennis. 1977. "Toward an Oral Poetics." *New Literary History* 8.

Titon, Jeff Todd. 1969. "Calling All Cows." *Blues Unlimited,* nos. 60–63.

———. 1971. "Ethnomusicology of Downhome Blues Phonograph Records, 1926–1930." Ph.D. diss., Univ. of Minnesota.

———. 1994. *Early Downhome Blues: A Musical and Cultural Analysis.* 2nd ed. Chapel Hill: Univ. of North Carolina Press.

————, ed. 1974a. *From Blues to Pop: The Autobiography of Leonard "Baby Doo" Caston.* Los Angeles: John Edwards Memorial Foundation.

————. 1974b. *Early Downhome Blues: A Musical and Cultural Analysis.* Urbana: Univ. of Illinois Press.

Wilson, Al. 1966. "Robert Pete Williams: His Life and Music." *Little Sandy Review* 2, no. 1.

Additional Reading

Albertson, Chris. 1972. *Bessie.* New York: Stein and Day. Biography of Bessie Smith.

David, Angela Y. 1998. *Blues Legacies and Black Feminism.* New York: Vintage Books.

Evans, David. 1982. *Big Road Blues.* Berkeley: Univ. of California Press.

Fahey, John. 1970. *Charley Patton.* London: Studio Vista. The life and music of an important Mississippi blues singer.

Ferris, William. 1978. *Blues from the Delta.* New York: Doubleday.

Finn, Julio. 1992. *The Bluesman.* New York: Interlink.

Floyd, Samuel A. 1995. *The Power of Black Music.* New York: Oxford Univ. Press.

Franz, Steve. 1996. "The Life and Music of Magic Sam." *Living Blues,* no. 125, pp. 33–44.

George, Nelson. 1988. *The Death of Rhythm and Blues.* New York: Dutton.

Grissom, Mary Allen. 1969 [1930]. *The Negro Sings a New Heaven.* Reprint, New York: Dover Books.

Jones, LeRoi. 1963. *Blues People.* New York: Morrow.

Keil, Charles. 1966. *Urban Blues.* Chicago: Univ. of Chicago Press.

King, B. B., with Dave Ritz. 1996. *Blues All Around Me: The Autobiography of B. B. King.* New York: Avon.

Leib, Sandra. 1981. *Mother of the Blues.* Amherst: Univ. of Massachusetts Press. A good book about Ma Rainey.

Oster, Harry. 1969. *Living Country Blues.* Hatboro, Pa.: Folklore Associates.

Palmer, Robert. 1981. *Deep Blues.* New York: Viking Press.

Ramsey, Frederic, Jr. 1960. *Been Here and Gone.* New Brunswick, N.J.: Rutgers Univ. Press. Interesting account of folk music.

Shaw, Arnold. 1978. *Honkers and Shouters.* New York: Collier Books. A good book about rhythm and blues.

Titon, Jeff Todd. 1990. *Downhome Blues Lyrics.* 2nd ed. Urbana: Univ. of Illinois Press. Anthology of post-WWII lyrics.

Tooze, Sandra B. 1997. Muddy Waters: The Mojo Man. Toronto: ECW Press.

Tracy, Steven, ed. 1999. *Write Me a Few of Your Lines: A Blues Reader.* Amherst: Univ. of Massachusetts Press.

Williams, Melvin D. 1974. *Community in a Black Pentecostal Church.* Pittsburgh, Pa.: Univ. of Pittsburgh Press.

Additional Listening

B. B. King Live at the Regal. ABCS509.

Bessie Smith: The World's Greatest Blues Singer. Columbia GP33.

Blues in the Mississippi Night. Rykodisc RCD 90155.

The Essential Gospel Sampler. Columbia CK 51763.

Let's Get Loose: Folk and Popular Blues Styles. New World NW 290.

Negro Blues and Hollers. Library of Congress AFS L59.

Negro Church Music. Atlantic SD-1351.

Negro Prison Songs. Tradition 1920.

Negro Religious Songs and Services. Library of Congress AFS L10.

One-String Blues. Takoma B 1023.

Religious Music: Congregational and Ceremonial. Library of Congress LBC 1.

Robert Johnson: The Complete Recordings. Columbia C2K 46222.

Roots 'n' Blues: The Retrospective. Columbia C4K 47911.

Roots of the Blues. New World NW 252.

Viewing

The Blues Accordin' to Lightnin' Hopkins. 1979. VHS videotape, 31 min. Color. Directed by Les Blank. El Cerrito, CA: Flower Films.

Bukka White and Son House. 1991. VHS videotape, 60 min. Black and white. Yazoo Video. Riveting performances of Mississippi Delta blues.

Otis Rush: Mastering Chicago Blues Guitar. n.d. (c. 1993). VHS videotape, 90 min. Color. Pound Ridge, N.Y.: Hot Licks Productions. Instruction and some footage of Rush's fine playing.

A Singing Stream. 1987. VHS videotape, 57 min. Color. Directed by Tom Davenport. Delaplane, Va.: Davenport Films. African-American religious music.

Wild Women Don't Have the Blues. 1989. VHS videotape, 58 min. Color. Directed by Christine Dall. San Francisco: California Newsreel. A documentary on women blues singers.

Bosnia and Central/Southeastern Europe: Music and Musicians in Transition

Mark Slobin

*T*his chapter will concentrate on how change has come to local musics, using as a case study a corner of southeast Europe: Bosnia (see map) and two nearby countries. We start with the period just after World War II, beginning around 1950—a time when great change came to the region: Communist rule, which lasted through 1990, replaced a group of slowly modernizing, largely rural societies with ambitious totalitarian governments that pushed industrialization and urbanization.

Regardless of these forces, old ways continued into new times, as we hear in a song recorded in the early 1950s about the rain, a universal theme for song making. Listen to "Paparudele" (CD 2, Track 9), sung here by Gypsy children in the countryside of Romania, east of Bosnia. This song may remind some students of the traditional American song "Rain, Rain, Go Away"; songs about nature can be found around the world.

CD 2/9

"Paparudele" ("Come, little rain") (0:27). Performed by Gypsy children in Găşteşti village, Romania. World Library of Folk and Primitive Music 17: Romania. Rounder 11661-1759-2.

Text, Romanian Drought Song, "Paparudele"

Paparuda, ruda (come, little rain, come!), come out and water us with your full buckets over the whole crowd. When you come with the hose, let it flow like water; when you come with the plough, let it run like butter; when you come with the sieve, let it be a barn-full. Give me the keys, old woman, that I may open the doors and let the rain come down. Come, little rain, come!

Text, American Children's Song, "Rain, Rain, Go Away"

Rain, rain, go away, little (name of singer) wants to play.
Rain, rain, go away! Come again some other day.

The two rain songs share similarities: the type of singer (children) and the subject (a force of nature), but many sharp differences place them in contrast. The American song is a straightforward command chanted by a child who cannot go out and play. The words mean just what they say, and no special costume or equipment is necessary to perform the song. In addition, the text is sung solo and even includes the child's name. Though addressed to the rain, it is meant for the singer. There is no social context for the tune: It does not speak for a group. No special meaning attaches to the rain other than that it gets in the way of fun.

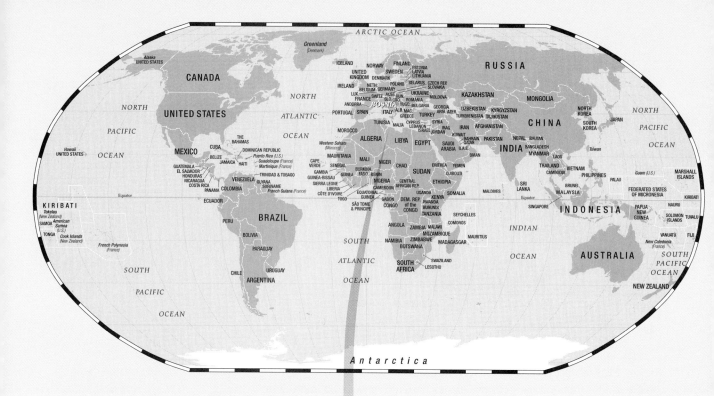

ARCTIC OCEAN

Greenland
(Denmark)

ICELAND NORWAY FINLAND
UNITED SWEDEN
KINGDOM DENMARK ESTONIA
LATVIA
LITHUANIA

RUSSIA

CANADA

IRELAND NETH. POLAND BELARUS CZECH REP.
BELGIUM GERMANY SLOVAKIA
LUX. SWITZ. AUST. UKRAINE KAZAKHSTAN
FRANCE HUN. MOLDOVA
BOSNIA ROMANIA
ANDORRA SLO. CRO. YUGO. GEORGIA
PORTUGAL SPAIN ITALY ALB. MAC. BULGARIA ARM. AZER. UZBEKISTAN KYRGYZSTAN

MONGOLIA

NORTH
KOREA

NORTH
ATLANTIC

OCEAN

NORTH
PACIFIC

OCEAN

UNITED STATES

GREECE TURKEY
TUNISIA SYRIA IRAQ IRAN AFGHANISTAN
MALTA CYPRUS LEBANON TURKMENISTAN TAJIKISTAN
ISRAEL JORDAN

CHINA

SOUTH
KOREA JAPAN

NORTH
PACIFIC

OCEAN

Hawaii
UNITED STATES

MEXICO

THE
BAHAMAS
CUBA
DOMINICAN REPUBLIC
Puerto Rico (U.S.)
JAMAICA HAITI Guadeloupe (France)
Martinique (France)

MOROCCO

ALGERIA LIBYA EGYPT SAUDI
ARABIA BAHRAIN PAKISTAN
QATAR NEPAL BHUTAN
U.A.E. INDIA BANGLADESH
OMAN MYANMAR

LAOS

Taiwan

Guam (U.S.)

MARSHALL
ISLANDS

GUATEMALA
EL SALVADOR
HONDURAS
NICARAGUA
COSTA RICA
PANAMA

BELIZE

MAURITANIA MALI NIGER CHAD SUDAN
CAPE SENEGAL
VERDE GAMBIA BURKINA ERITREA YEMEN
GUINEA-BISSAU GUINEA FASO BENIN NIGERIA CENTRAL ETHIOPIA
SIERRA LEONE CÔTE D'IVOIRE AFRICAN REP.
LIBERIA TOGO DJIBOUTI
SOMALIA

THAILAND VIETNAM
CAMBODIA PHILIPPINES

BRUNEI
MALAYSIA

PALAU

FEDERATED STATES
OF MICRONESIA

KIRIBATI

VENEZUELA
GUYANA
COLOMBIA SURINAME
French Guiana (France)

SÃO TOME
& PRINCIPE GABON CONGO DEM. REP.
of the
CONGO UGANDA KENYA
RWANDA
BURUNDI
TANZANIA

SRI
LANKA

MALDIVES

SINGAPORE

INDONESIA

PAPUA
NEW
GUINEA

NAURU

Equator

ECUADOR

EQUATORIAL
GUINEA

Equator

TUVALU

KIRIBATI
Tokelau
(New Zealand)
SAMOA American
Samoa
(U.S.)
TONGA

PERU

BRAZIL

BOLIVIA

ANGOLA ZAMBIA MALAWI
MOZAMBIQUE
ZIMBABWE
NAMIBIA BOTSWANA MADAGASCAR

SEYCHELLES

COMOROS

MAURITIUS

INDIAN

OCEAN

SOLOMON
ISLANDS

AUSTRALIA

VANUATU
New Caledonia
(France)

FIJI

SOUTH
PACIFIC

OCEAN

Cook Islands
(New Zealand)

French Polynesia
(France)

PARAGUAY

SOUTH

ATLANTIC

OCEAN

SWAZILAND

SOUTH
AFRICA LESOTHO

CHILE URUGUAY

SOUTH

PACIFIC

OCEAN

ARGENTINA

NEW ZEALAND

Antarctica

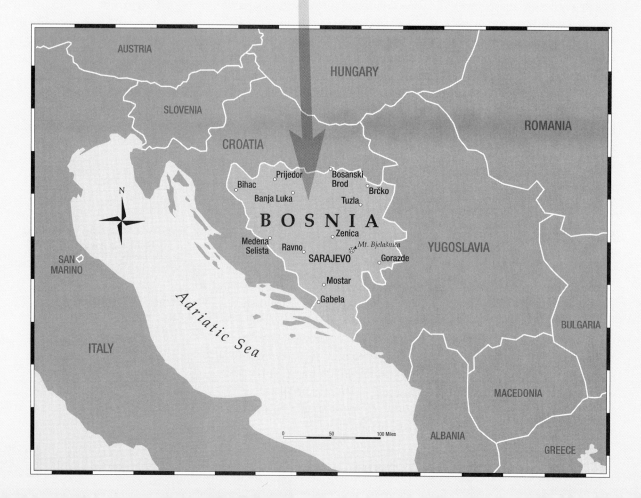

AUSTRIA

HUNGARY

SLOVENIA

ROMANIA

CROATIA

N

Prijedor Bosanski
Bihac Brod
Brčko
Banja Luka Tuzla

BOSNIA

Zenica

YUGOSLAVIA

SAN
MARINO

Medena
Selista Ravno Mt. Bjelašnica
SARAJEVO Gorazde

Mostar

Adriatic Sea

Gabela

BULGARIA

ITALY

MACEDONIA

0   50   100 Miles

ALBANIA

GREECE

The words to the Romanian song differ drastically. They seek the rain's bounty instead of better weather for playtime. From rain, the text shifts to the image of the plow and butter, calling on the fertility of the earth and the beasts. Instead of denying the course of the seasons, the song impatiently begs nature to continue the cycle of the seasons, from winter to spring—it seeks to continue, rather than stop, action. The song rings with particular urgency because it is sung during times of drought, which threatens crops and therefore the villagers' subsistence. In short, the group performance emphasizes a social context for the song.

In the performance of the Romanian song, no detail seems accidental. The children wear skirts made from flowers that are symbols of spring, and they carry sieves, survival of a rain symbol of the ancient Greek gods. The children themselves, and even the villagers, are probably unaware of the remarkable durability of these symbols over the centuries. The presence of children might stand for the rising generation, associated with the forces of growth (versus decline and death). Growth seems invoked when the adults sprinkle the singing, dancing children with water. The "old woman" who controls the keys to the rain is probably related to the effigy of a hag carried and burned by children in other parts of the region as part of a spring ritual: She stands for winter and must die. Thus a local village musical performance is connected to a network of regional beliefs and musical performances.

The children are *Roma* ("Gypsies"), members of an ethnic group often treated throughout the region as outcasts from mainstream society yet respected for their music-making talents. The song taps into a subtle sense of status along with basic human values, while the entire performance of "Paparudele" also belongs to the realm of magic and ritual, with the children acting as ambassadors to the forces of nature. What seems to be "simple" turns out to be a complicated cultural package involving props, social organization, deeply held beliefs, and a specific melodic-textual structure crafted for a particular social moment: the time of drought.

What about the musical differences between the two rain songs? The American song needs no special rehearsing, because there is just one melody line and only two notes. Try singing the Romanian song. First, divide your group into two parts: one chants the unchanging *hai ploitsa, hai!* line while the others have words (do it on a syllable like "la"). The singers with words also have different notes to think about: six here, as opposed to only two in the American song. As should be clear from this entire book, music from a technologically simpler environment is not necessarily less complicated musically—in fact, the opposite is often true.

The rain song and its evocation of community come from a world of traditional music. That world has always been turbulent; peasants in eastern Europe, as everywhere in agriculturally based societies, have always been subject to epidemics, natural disasters, invasions, tyrants, and greedy landlords who controlled their economic fate. There was never a timeless, culturally unified zone of unchanging tales and songs. Most people knew at least two languages or dialects, and many were also highly mobile, traveling from place to place or continent to continent for work and trade. Music traveled freely along mountain paths and highways. In the twentieth century the slow spread of electrical and electronic media—record player, radio, then cassette and television—meant that people anywhere could be swayed by the seductive rhythms of the tango, the hot sound of jazz, or the hard beat of rock. Yet family, local, and national pride and memory ensured continuity. Along with every new layer of music making, older material such as the rain song was handed down, creating a multilayered musical world. Even today, old-style peasant songs play their part in shaping identity, or what is now often called "heritage." They coexist with rock, rap, and the latest outside influence.

This chapter focuses on a corner of the world that has undergone extreme change. There was once a multiethnic, federated nation-state called Yugoslavia that disintegrated violently in the early 1990s into its component parts, most of which became new states. Whole regions exchanged or expelled populations in a process that involved extreme brutality, leaving thousands dead and millions homeless and leading to war crimes trials. In 1999 American and European forces under NATO bombed one region, Serbia, as part of a human rights intervention, then occupied the area called Kosovo. The situation in the region remains tense and difficult as of 2001. So it is not surprising that along with a selection of stable traditional and contemporary musical styles, this chapter cites three kinds of musical change: (1) dramatic and destructive transformation due to political upheaval, (2) aesthetic and commercial shifts of style, and (3) personal reshaping by musicians who have moved away from their homeland to the United States. This chapter concentrates on one country—Bosnia—with a comparative look at Bulgaria.

Bosnia: From Tradition to Destruction

We shall start high in the mountains near the city of Sarajevo, in Bosnia. From 1945 until 1991 Bosnia and nearby Herzegovina formed one of six republics of Yugoslavia (which means "land of the south Slavs"). Sarajevo had grown dramatically after World War II into a city of a half million as peasants from mountain and lowlands villages, as well as from smaller towns and cities, flocked to the new, emerging industries of that ancient town. The city's hosting of the 1984 Olympic Games marked a high point in its development as a world-class metropolis. Sadly, the regional war that followed the dissolution of Yugoslavia caused great loss of life and culture in the Sarajevo area, beginning in 1992. In response to this historic disjuncture, this chapter presents the local music culture as it existed in 1990, followed by a partial update of the situation as of 2001.

The chapter will introduce the villagers of the highlands first, then introduce the people in the lowlands and cities. We shall focus on the Muslim population, people who have always spoken the same Slavic language as their neighbors but who were converted to Islam during the 425-year occupation of the area by the Turkish-led Ottoman Empire (1463–1878).

Music in a Muslim Highlander Village

Mount Bjelašnica (pronounced Bee-el-osh-nitsa), "the White Mountain," stands as a snow-covered island in the Dinaric mountain range in an area where the mild Mediterranean climate confronts the cold continental weather to the east. Winters are long and harsh, and the soil is not good for farming. Much of the local highlanders' traditional work involves keeping large flocks of sheep. Women do a lot of the livestock herding and milking, and they have started to take cheese, milk, and butter to market. In recent years men have supplemented the family income by working in industrial jobs in nearby towns and cities. As is common in such isolated environments, a small group of villages shares a cultural core, and people give themselves a local name, here *planinstaci/planinke* (masculine/feminine), from the word *planina,* mountain. As one local woman has said, "Everything is almost the same in all fourteen villages." The villagers have a variety of names for other people, groups near and far that they find unlike themselves.

Electricity reached this far-off plateau only in 1976. Its main musical impact was to make a much greater variety of music available. This import from the outside world was matched in recent years by an outflow of male villagers to work not just in nearby towns but as far away as Austria and Germany as part of a huge labor migration from the southern to the more prosperous northern regions of Europe. Many returning emigrants built modern houses with all the electronic conveniences, creating a new local social group: urbanized villagers.

As a result, the highlanders' music making offers a good example of musical layering. The older village song styles, which we shall survey first, are extremely localized. The secular songs do not even contain much Islamic content, which was more fully developed in cities. The main local

Figure 5-1
Older styles. Planinica, 1967.

William G. Lockwood

song genres differ only somewhat from those of neighboring ethnic and religious groups, implying a strong shared regional taste that is at the heart of what we usually call folk music. The three types of local song everyone knows are all polyphonic—that is, they consist of different parts simultaneously sung by a small group of singers rather than by one person singing alone or by everybody singing the same tune (unison). Voices do the work of communication in the fields and in the village square, so there are few musical instruments up on Mt. Bjelašnica. The outflow of workers to the cities and the fact that boys no longer do the herding has meant that people have largely forgotten their old handmade instruments, such as shepherd's flutes. For special occasions—fairs, festivals—songs and some electric instruments are joined with voices as accompaniment to dance. Despite all the change and the forgetting of many earlier forms of folklore, such as epic singing about local heroes, for Bosnian Muslims "folksong is perhaps the most viable verbal form of folklore . . . today" (Lockwood 1983:28)

One of the best times to catch a lively song and dance scene is a *mevlud* festival. A *mevlud* is a local version of a widespread ceremony based partly on reading a sacred text that centers on the birth of the Prophet Muhammad. These celebrations can take place at many different times in private to mark personal occasions, but they also are held as large public occasions every weekend in August, when city workers are on vacation and can come home from as far away as Germany to have a good time in their native village. The *mevlud* has three parts: a religious ceremony, a fair, and an evening gathering. Village girls put on elaborate outfits, while young women who have moved to the city dress in a more urban style. Trucks arriving at the scene of the host village are covered with singing celebrants, with one truck trying to outdo another in song.

During the fair, hundreds of people gather on a meadow, with various groups of singers and musicians competing for space and attention. This is a moment of courtship, when young men and women size each other up, sing about each other, and present themselves the way they want to be understood: rural or urban, available or unavailable, bashful or bold. Girls stick with the singing group they have grown up with, but men move around from group to group. Intergroup competition lends an edge to the singing, and everyone evaluates one another's performances. Body posture, song texts, and attitude differ considerably, as we shall hear. Women tend to sing in a well-rehearsed, tight manner meant to show that they have thought things through, are organized, and work hard, characteristics valued in a wife. The songs are complicated, multipart creations that depend on thorough knowledge of and long experience with the songs. A leader sets the pace. Only unmarried women sing, so they use the opportunity to enjoy their art during their peak singing years as well as to affirm sisterhood and to display themselves to the whole community, including parents, potential in-laws, and prospective husbands. Songs may praise women's solidarity as well as tease men or comment on the beauties and virtues of highlander life.

Throughout Bosnia and Herzegovina, a popular form of song among several ethnic groups is called *ganga*. *Ganga* singers meet at an early age and continue singing together for decades, fine-tuning their sensitivity to each other's sound and skills (see Figure 5-2). Should a woman from a nearby village marry into another village, it might be hard for her to find singing partners even if her style is quite close to the local way of singing. Her new singing companions will immediately notice even the slightest shade of difference in the nuances of local *ganga*. This highly valued form of singing sounds strange to outsiders, even to others in nearby regions, let alone western European or American listeners. This perception is due mostly to the insistence on very close intervals, which "grate" on the unaccustomed ear, and the uncompromising intensity of the delivery. The musical structure reflects the social organization of the group: A respected leader sets the tone, literally, and the other singers, usually two, contribute an accompanying pattern called "cutting," "chopping," or "sobbing" that is vocally and emotionally powerful, as you can hear on CD 2, Track 10.

The pauses in the men's *ganga* are quite long. During these pauses, they do not look like they are about to sing, as they puff on cigarettes and look nonchalant, but then they break into coordinated song. A solo voice dominates in the first phrase (A); for the second and third (B, C), the group splits into parts that get extremely close and then break into an exuberant rise at the end. As the two lines get closer, the intensity of the effect of blended voices increases as the resonance produces "beats," sharp patterns of acoustic interaction, that are increased by the vocal techniques of the singers.

CD 2/10

"Sisters, Hold on to Your Chastity" (0:40). Traditional women's *ganga* song of the Muslim highlands. Performed by Azra Bandić, Mevla Luckin, and Emsija Tatarović. Field recording by Mirjana Laušević. Umoljani village, Bosnia, 1990.

CD 2/11

"What Lifts the Heart of a Rascal?" (1:24). Traditional men's *ganga* song of the Muslim highlands. Performed by Safet Elezovic, Muhamed Elezovic, Zejnil Maslesa. Field recording by Mirjana Laušević. Gornji Lukomir village, Bosnia, 1990.

Mirjana Laušević

Figure 5-2

The singers of CD 2, Track 10, the highlander women's *ganga* song. From left to right, Azra Bandić, Mevla Luckin, and Emsija Tatarović, near the village of Umoljani, 1989. Compare with Figure 5-8, taken after the war in 2000.

Transcription 5-1 gives a schematic version of the two *ganga* songs on the accompanying recordings.

Transcription 5-1a
Schematic of women's *ganga* song.

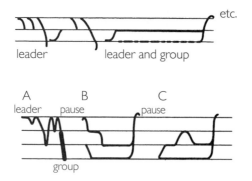

Transcription 5-1b
Schematic of men's *ganga* song.

To experience *ganga* properly, you need to sing it or listen to friends' songs. Singers are quite aware of the acoustic quality they are producing. They perceive their powerful voices not just physically, but sensually as well. They look forward to the extra resonance that emerges from singing pitches very closely together, enjoying the "cutting edge" of the vibrations. This means that *ganga* is difficult to record. When the Bosnian ethnomusicologist Ankica Petrović took a group of women into the recording studio, the sound engineers tried to put a microphone on each singer separately to "clarify" the sound as individual tracks, but the women refused. They were used to performing their songs in a tight semicircle, touching shoulders, so they could listen properly to each other and create the right mood. This technique confused the engineers, but not the women. They told the technicians exactly where to place the microphone for the best sound quality.

Ankica Petrović has delved deeply into many sides of the singers' aesthetic, their feelings and thoughts about their music. She finds a direct correlation between musical features and this aesthetic (Petrović 1977:335):

> The melodic range and intervals in this polyphonic singing reflect mutual human relationships within the framework of small interacting communities, while the importance of individual personality is emphasized by individual improvisation. At the end of the ganga, when songs finish on two different tones a major second apart, it is as if different individuals are given the same rights in the community.

When *ganga* is sung right, it has a powerful effect on its performers and listeners (1977:331):

> Good performances can move them to tears and shudders, but with a sense of happiness; and they arouse feelings of love and sexual passion among younger people, as well as strong feelings of regional identity among both young and old alike.

Let us look at the text of the women's song. In this lyric a "tear" is something precious you do not easily let fall. "Take" here means marry. The song is a warning to girls: Do not let yourself be seduced by kisses, because an aggressive young man is probably not the reliable suitor you are looking for.

Sisters, hold on to your chastity like a tear;
The one who kisses you will not take you.

Text, "Sisters, Hold on to Your Chastity"

A typical male song takes quite a different angle on boy-girl relationships. Young men use the word *baraba* in most songs to describe themselves, which can be translated as "rascal," "rogue," or "hellraiser."

What lifts the heart of a rascal?
A liter of wine and a fine girl.

Text, "What Lifts the Heart of a Rascal?"

Their way of singing is relaxed, self-confident, and boastful. Manhood is the main topic of their songs. However, both men and women also sing songs that praise singing itself as a foremost means of expression.

Men's text:
Since we have not sung, brother
The village is unhappy.

***Ganga* Texts on the Topic of Singing**

Women's texts:
I will sing out of spite for my sorrow
So it won't conquer me when it tortures me.
Oh God, what would happen if there were no singing?
What would my heart do with all its burden?

One can compare men's and women's texts to get a sense of the different takes on similar themes, in a way that imitates a sort of gender duel. In fact, this occurs in a kind of singing that is traditional in other villages of Bosnia.

		***Ganga* Texts on Gender Relations**

Men's: Enjoy your girlhood, girl, while you are at your mother's.
          Once you're with me, you won't enjoy it.

Women's: I didn't know, I didn't believe
          That the fawn [boyfriend] is dearer than Mom.

Men's: Come, come you dark one, it won't be in vain.
          Let a rascal kiss you just once.

Women's: If I knew, dear, that I'd be yours
          You wouldn't be able to count my kisses.

Men's: Little one, I love your bowlegs
          More than a crate of Sarajevo beer.

Women's: My dear, your buddy got the better of you:
          Instead of you, I love him.

Men's: Love me or love me not, little one,
          My hand has caressed you.

Women's: You can love whomever you want now,
          You loved me once as well.

This relationship between singing and gender, both performed and closely watched by everyone, can be found around the whole region. For nearby Albanians, Jane Sugarman proposes the following (1989:209):

> Singing, rather than merely reflecting notions of gender, also shapes those notions in return. Singing provides Prespare [the villagers she lived with] with a means of tangibly living out their strongly contrasting notions of femininity and masculinity. Through singing they are temporarily able to mold their individual selves into the form of a cultural ideal . . . or they may use their singing to suggest its revision. . . . [Young adults] will experiment increasingly with ways of conveying through song new views of themselves as women and men.

Common to both sexes is a strong sense of place, embodied in many song texts that praise one's own village and ridicule others. But men and women convey different senses of self in songs and dances. By and large, the highlander male repertoire is outwardly oriented and frank, the women's more intimate, poetic, and metaphoric; like men, however, women can choose how they dress and present themselves in dance. Mobility and outside musical styles have had their impact on how the sexes regard each other, or at least what ideal of femininity women might choose, urban or rural. Young women express this choice visibly in selecting a dance style. The village girls want to express their strength and energy through dancing. They lift their legs high and stamp their feet. Those who want to display their urban manners dance closer to the ground, with smaller steps. Those who have lived in the town and cities away from the

Figure 5-3
Older styles: A woman sings a song to attract bees into their hive. Planinica, 1967.

William G. Lockwood

highlands can choose to identify themselves as more sophisticated, with less stress on their wood-carrying, sheep-herding, and cow-milking skills, underscoring the urban-rural divide that has run through the local scene ever since increased mobility allowed for more lifestyle choices. As one *ganga* text says, "All honor to the mountain, but I want to go to the valley / Let everyone go where she wants," or, as a girl from the village of Potoci sings: "I wouldn't get married in Potoci; I would rather poison myself," referring to her strong wish to move to the lowlands, to the larger towns and cities of Bosnia. It is to these lowlands urban settings that we now turn.

Music of Rural and Urban Lowlands Muslims

There are many other forms of singing, as well as more instrumental music, in the lowlands than the highlands. The most typical instrument of the region is the *šargija* (*shar*-ghee-ya), which came originally from the east from what were Turkish-controlled regions in the old days. This instrument became part of Bosnian life, played by Muslims and neighboring Serbs and Croats alike. The šargija is a plucked, stringed instrument; over the years the number of strings has slowly increased. As happens in many folk music settings, people in recent decades have wanted their instruments to produce more sound, projecting more loudness and richness; eventually, instrument types become electrified and amplified as radio, recordings, and outside influences have offered people new ideals of what music "should" sound like.

In the recording (CD 2, Track 12) the šargija, which once had four strings, now has six (some have seven) and more frets, to allow for more notes to be played; the tuning is g´-g´-g´-c-f´-g´´, where the bass string, c, is surrounded by three drones on g´ and a lower and higher melody string. The text praises the instrument itself.

CD 2/12

"*O šargija*" (1:06). Traditional Muslim lowlands song with *šargija* lute. Performed by Škiba and friends. Field recording by Mirjana Laušević. Bosnia, 1990.

O šargija, made of poplar wood
May the one who builds you never get sick.

Text, "O šargija"

This song combines several musical threads that weave in and out of other examples. Two men sing together, but not mechanically: there is a lot of give and take in the way they jointly produce the words, as well as in each man's voice quality and approach to the rhythm and phrasing of the words. This is an example of what ethnomusicologists call *heterophony:* They are doing the "same" thing, but in an individual way, an approach just noted for both men and women's *ganga* singing.

Another aspect of local musical thinking lies in the sense of rhythm. Notice that you can tap your foot or snap your fingers to some sections of the song but not to others. This elastic sense of time is common to many musical styles of southeastern Europe and nearby areas of the eastern Mediterranean. Yet another interesting quality of this song is the way the šargija part involves not just one line but multiple voices, closely positioned, that might remind one of *ganga* singing, even including the very close intervals. Further, each instrumental section is different—again, a flexible approach to detail pervades performance.

All of these aspects of the song add up to an aesthetic, a perspective on how musical units should be put together, that forms the basis of a local and regional sound. In other words, a way of thinking, not just performing, lies behind traditional music making. As the folksinger Todora Varamezov of Bulgaria told the ethnomusicologist Timothy Rice, "Folk songs you can ornament and change as you want. If you change it, then you sing from the heart. It's not like you have learned it lifelessly, as if it's an obligation. Different people sing it different ways." At the same time, there is a limit to variation: "If singers altered the melody too much, they could count on hearing about it from the 'aunts' and 'grannies' who were watching and listening" (Rice 1994:110). "Tradition," then, means that both individual variation and collective responsibility coexist in each performance in this type of music making, where people stand face-to-face and ear-to-ear and pay close attention. In music coming from pop recording studios or government-sponsored composers' desks, as we shall see later, the musical aesthetic and the social contract about music are tightly intertwined.

One of the important types of songs associated with the Bosnian Muslim population is the *sevdalinka.* The root-word, *sevda,* comes from Turkish and implies love in terms of passion, and also sadness. Originally, *sevdalinkas* were adaptations of tunes of *ilahija* sacred songs. *Sevdalinkas* can have many different singing and accompaniment styles and topics. When village girls began hearing *sevdalinkas* on the radio and trying to sing them, this represented an early shift away from rural forms like *ganga* before more modern forms, such as pop and rock, became available (Lockwood 1983:35).

Our example (CD 2, Track 13), sung by an older man, Himzo Polovina, is about a wedding rather than referring to the more common *sevdalinka* theme of romantic love. As in all *sevdalinkas,* symbols and metaphors, rather than straightforward commentary, make the point. To refer to the wedding is to touch on a key memory of village life. As a researcher from nearby Hungary puts it:

> Weddings rank foremost among popular customs: they are a veritable accumulation of ceremonies continuing mythical, religious-ritual, legal, economic, musical, and mimic elements. In some places they became almost festive plays with their chief and supporting characters, supernumeraries, fixed scene, time, music, dances, and audience. (CMPH 1956:689)

Among Bosnian Muslims, weddings can go on for an entire week (see Figure 5-4) and include a great deal of music characterized by gender and generations, much like festival music. But the setting for the wedding song heard here differs dramatically from the traditional village scene. Recorded in an urban radio studio, it comes through a radio speaker, not from the lively, charged space of a rural wedding, and is sung and played by professionals, not amateur village musicians. The accompaniment for the recording is a *tamburitza* orchestra. This type of ensemble dates back to about the

William G. Lockwood

Figure 5-4
Dancing at a village wedding. Planinica, 1967.

1840s, when people in various European countries (notably Italy and Russia) were organizing orchestral ensembles out of older stringed folk instruments. Then, as now, folk music offered a romantic connection to a preindustrial past imagined to be gentler than the modern world. At the same time, organizers of such groups have always insisted on precise, almost mechanized performance, an aesthetic deeply opposed to the more informal village way of music making.

It is not accidental that this new aesthetic arose with urbanization and the onset of a regimented work force in urban industrial contexts. As time went on, these folk orchestras also became connected to national pride and local identity. In the period of cultural control by the Communist Party, national identity and artistic expression were both tightly organized by the state. This approach was tried out first in the former Soviet Union, the world's largest multiethnic country for nearly seventy-five years (1917–1991) and the first nation-state to have a system based completely on socialist principles. A complex bureaucracy made of many organizations controlled culture, and all media—print and electronic, news and entertainment—were run by the government, with no private enterprise allowed.

This state-managed cultural system spread to several eastern European countries when they were under direct influence of Soviet power as implemented by local regimes (1945–1990 or so). This "east bloc" included Poland, Czechoslovakia (now the Czech Republic and Slovakia), Hungary, Romania, and Bulgaria. Bosnia was part of Yugoslavia, whose leader, Tito, had broken away from Soviet control in 1948 but who maintained a comparable system of government led by the Communist Party. The state decided what could or could not be published, listened to, or supported. As we shall see, the Yugoslav system was freer than that of its neighbors, producing some maverick musical results, but the radio orchestra that accompanies this *sevdalinka* aims at an official rather than an informal or folk sound.

CD 2/13

"Trepetljika trepetala" ("That which trembles"), excerpt (1:17). Lowlands *sevdalinka* song with *tamburitza* orchestra. Himzo Polovina. Live radio performance. Sarajevo, Yugoslavia, 1986.

This work has been tightly arranged for voice and folk orchestra. This type of orchestration offers a good example of managed traditionalism. You can hear the careful professionalism of "official culture" in the precisely orchestrated instruments and the somewhat reined-in voice of the singer. In fact, the directors of this ensemble prided themselves on working out the "sloppiness" of folk musicians (interview with Mirjana Laušević, 1994). This attitude combines the precommunist, bourgeois love for "updating" folk music with the socialist approach to "disciplining" national culture.

In the lyrics of the *sevdalinka* song, the figure of the golden thread from heaven that enwraps the bride, groom, and wedding party is an old image, a stock figure that appears in many songs.

Text, "Trepetljika trepetala"

That which trembles is full of pearls.
These white castles of ours [homes] are full of joy
All the kinfolk are in the castle.
The mother is celebrating the wedding of the son.
Everybody is happy, but the mother most of all.
They brought her the [flower name]-smelling maiden
The golden thread stretched from the clear sky
And wrapped around the groom's fez [a type of Muslim hat]
From the fez, it stretched around the bride's veil.

Words and music by Himzo Polovina. © Himzo Polovina. Used by permission of Edmir Polovina.

The emigration of eastern Europeans spread the idea of folk ensembles like the *tamburitza* orchestra to such places as the United States, where the idea took hold. For example, a Pittsburgh-based folk song and dance ensemble called the Tamburitzans was founded in 1936 (see Forry 1978) and continues to charm audiences in the United States and beyond. Their promotional literature characterizes the group as "a spirited troupe" that has "captivated audiences throughout the Americas, the former Soviet Union and Europe with its joyful performances. . . . Wearing colorful native folk costumes, the Tammies offer a trip into some of the most fascinating parts of the Balkans and other lands with their lively village dances and vibrant songs" (World Music Institute brochure, 1994). The words *colorful, native, folk,* and *vibrant* coupled with *village, fascinating,* and *Balkans* evoke a concert experience that will be comfortably exotic, historic, ethnographic, yet also familiar (note the Americanized nickname, "the Tammies") and, above all, highly professional.

The same New York concert series that included the Tammies in 1994 also featured the first American tour of an old folk-based troupe from Slovakia (in eastern Europe) that promised "dazzling folkdances, music and songs of a country which lies in the heart of Europe . . . highlighted by breathtaking acrobatic dances expressing the poetry, lyricism and passion of the Slovak people, their history and culture." Note the connection between the adjectives stressing showmanship—*dazzling, acrobatic*—and those underscoring soulfulness: *poetry, lyricism, passion.* This approach to marketing goes back to the original purposes of professional "folk" ensembles: the projection of a local sensibility and history culled from peasant sources into an arena of modern theatrical performance by nonpeasants who "clean up" and "perfect" the expressive culture of ordinary villagers. This impulse began in intellectual circles over a hundred years ago, flourished under the state patronage of communist regimes, and continues in emigration and in postcommunist life as an expression of identity and as a vehicle for cross-cultural presentation and arts marketing. The idea has spread around the world, from the postcolonial national dance troupes of African countries to the folk ensemble of aboriginal peoples of Taiwan.

At the same time, the particular styles of music presented in this chapter have made a significant, long-term impact on amateur song-and-dance practices in the United States (as well as western Europe), where for about fifty years the cultural landscape in college towns and cities across the country has featured informal "Balkan" groups. Something about the infectious dance rhythms and soulful singing of the region cuts across many social and geographic boundaries.

Popular Music Styles: "Newly Composed Folk Music" and Rock

One of the bureaucratically-defined styles of music that emerged in Yugoslavia's last decades (1960s–1980s) was called "newly composed folk music." Ordinarily we think of folk music as something handed down from generation to generation. But with millions of Yugoslav villagers moving to big cities beginning in the 1950s, the whole lifestyle of a large percentage of the population soon became "newly composed" (see Figure 5-5). Similar seismic shifts of populations and musical styles took place in many countries of the world near the middle of the twentieth century. In the United States, for example, masses of black and white southerners moved to the big cities of the north during the 1930s and 1940s, creating the urban blues (see Chapter 4) and parallel styles such as honky-tonk country music. In Peru, Mexico, India, and elsewhere, music based loosely on elements drawn from earlier rural styles but "juiced up" in the city became the norm for a majority of the world's people, and Yugoslavia was no exception.

The difference in eastern Europe was that the state, rather than a group of local entrepeneurs, monitored this development. Although the government allowed some star performers to develop, it maintained control of record-pressing plants, the airwaves, and the types of taxation placed on different kinds of music. For a long time in Yugoslavia, musics considered useful to social engineering were not taxed, while those considered distracting or vulgar were taxed to show disapproval and to help subsidize the "right" kinds of music. Nevertheless, "newly composed folk music" took

Figure 5-5
Villagers from Planinica moving to the town of Bugojno, 1967.

William G. Lockwood

over the consciousness of most Yugoslavs, who identified with the combination of folk sounds with big-city topics, voices, and instrumentation.

One example of newly composed folk music, "Mani zemlju koja Bosnu nema," comes from the work of Lepa Brena, the stage name of a young Bosnian Muslim woman from the city of Brčko. This fiery young singer hit the top of the pop charts early in Yugoslavia, also starring in music-video-like films. A distinctive feature of the Yugoslav music-culture was the fact that the bureaucracy and Communist Party were perfectly willing to allow such stardom, even with its money-making potential, to flourish within a socialist state. Lepa Brena's combination of seductiveness and local pride made her a major star.

Text, Excerpt from "Mani zemlju koja Bosnu nema" by Lepa Brena

Stanza: I've been in eternal Rome, I've seen the Greek sea,
          But there's no better place than my Brčko.
Chorus: Don't bother with a country that doesn't have Bosnia
          Or with a man who dozes when next to a woman.

Here, the highlands that started our survey stand unmistakably for the heart of Bosnian life. This is very like the nostalgic appeal in U.S. country music to "the old mountain home." The pairing of sexual love with love of homeland is common in pop musics throughout the world, the erotic often serving as a metaphor (in literature, music, or film) for nationalism but also a way of selling songs.

Though newly composed folk music was an urban form of expression, it did not cover all the possibilities of city sounds in former Yugoslavia, nor does it in the same region today. At first a direct imitation of British and American groups, genres, and styles, rock slowly became domesticated in all the European countries, finding its niche in the welter of local musics. In Bosnia, as elsewhere, it was largely educated, middle-class youth that took up this world style. In the socialist system, the children of bureaucrats, managers, and arts professionals had a higher status and a different outlook than did the children of former peasants. Many rock songs spoke to the concerns of rock worldwide—urban alienation, the generation gap, problems of love—but these had a more political edge in a controlling system such as communism.

By 1992, neither the older folk styles nor the socialist collectivist spirit nor the commercialized erotic localism of Lepa Brena could speak to Bosnia's condition. As part of the dissolution of Yugoslavia and the declaration of new nation-states, Bosnia became a battleground as soon as it declared its sovereignty. Not only did its neighbors Serbia and Croatia engage their forces, but the multiethnic Bosnian population of Serbs, Croats, and Muslims split into warring camps and coalitions as well. Through the end of 1995, thousands were killed, millions became refugees, and vast stretches of town and countryside were devastated by fierce fighting. The villages on Mt. Bjelašnica described earlier were destroyed by Bosnian Serbs as was 85 percent of Lepa Brena and Mensur Hatić's town, Brčko (discussed later). Sarajevo, the capital of Bosnia, remained under Bosnian Serb siege for three years. This was a particularly bitter turn of fate, because most people knew the city as a place of relative harmony, where ethnic and religious distinctions had seemed to dissolve into a congenial cosmopolitan culture between 1945 and 1990.

Music has also become a battleground. Pop and rock stars have emigrated or have taken sides in the conflict, causing reorientation of their audience. Lepa Brena, for example, chose to become a star for the Serbian side. Songs, genres, and bands that were once national became identified with various warring factions, who all turned to music videos to promote their cause. As some of the national dust began to settle around 2000, the music scene in each successor state began both to diverge from one another and to draw on wider sources ranging across southeastern Europe, including Turkey.

Such scenes have occurred elsewhere in the world, causing severe dislocation and disjuncture. The musical life of such war-torn countries as Afghanistan and the former Soviet lands of Armenia, Georgia, and Tajikistan have been changed irrevocably. Even in more peaceful places, economic need and incentives have caused a huge world labor force to move from home, a phenomenon for which the bureaucratic-sounding term *deterritorialization* has been coined. Uprooted from familiar surroundings, often traumatized by memory, these world wanderers always find music to be a lifeline connecting them to their past and to their loved ones far away. So it seems fitting to include in our short survey two musicians who are not living in Bosnia but come from it, in this case carrying Bosnian traditions to the United States, with each musician doing so in very different circumstances: Mensur Hatić and Flory Jagoda.

Mensur Hatić: Versatile Musical Traveler

Mensur Hatić (pronounced *ha*-titch) was born in Bijelijna, halfway between the Bosnian towns of Brčko and Tuzla, in 1961 and grew up in Brčko, the predominantly Muslim city celebrated in the song by Lepa Brena, his compatriot. Musical from an early age, he was exposed to a variety of musics, taking advantage of both a network of public classical music school opportunities particularly stressed in socialist countries and of the local ethnic and popular styles. His father, an accomplished singer-accordionist who knew a great many *sevdalinkas,* taught them to Mensur and encouraged him on the accordion. After high school, the army, and a year of college, he began to play professionally, touring and making commercial recordings. Owing to Yugoslavia's location and the presence of many Yugoslav workers abroad, he and his band could leave on Friday, play in Germany, and be back home on Monday.

Mensur's life through 1990 was richly layered in musical experience and travel. As a versatile musician, he quickly adapted himself to a continental network of Yugoslav touring groups and audiences, catering to the hundreds of thousands of expatriates scattered around western Europe. He enhanced his earning power by apprenticing in instrument building and repairing in major factories in Italy and Germany and by certifying himself as a music teacher in his hometown. With a secure base in Brčko, where he built himself a house complete with elaborate stereo system, Mensur was both traditionalist and postmodernist, deeply Bosnian but

Figure 5-6

Mensur Hatić (accordion) and Youri Younakov (clarinet) of Ivo Papzov's band Trakiya, playing at the Balkan Music and Dance Workshop, sponsored by the East European Folklife Center, at Camp Ramblewood, Maryland, 1994. The Balkan music scholar Carol Silverman is at center.

Mirjana Laušević

internationalist as well, looking for the chance to use his skills to gain a foothold in a dynamic but insecure local economy and intercultural atmosphere. While other musicians in exile have failed to find a foothold, lost outside the atmosphere of their particular audience, Mensur's flexibility has served him well.

Just before the onset of war in former Yugoslavia, Mensur left for the United States, apparently anticipating and avoiding the conflagration that would engulf his town and country. He now lives in St. Louis, where he has started a small music school where he teaches classical and ethnic accordion, and he plays for clubs, Bosnian celebrations, and multicultural events at sites such as the Missouri Historical Society.

Listen to a piece that Mensur wrote himself (CD 2, Track 14), inspired by living near a train station. He takes the sound of the train and improvises on it quite originally. This sort of piece is, as Mensur says, a kind of universal language; wherever trains have played an important part in people's lives, musicians have written train pieces.

The piece has four distinct components:

1. A slowly accelerating theme at the beginning
   (A in Transcription 5-2)
2. Train-whistle sounds
3. A repeated, insistent short melody (B)
4. A one-time improvised tune over steady bass (C)

These combine in the pattern ABCBA, with the train-whistle interjections providing an overall framework. The speeding-up of A at the beginning is matched by a slowing-down reprise of A at the end to make the whole piece cyclical.

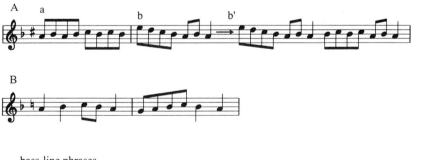

CD 2/14

"Zadnja Stanica Brčko" ("Last Stop Brčko") (3:33). Written and performed by Mensur Hatić. Field recording by Mark Slobin. Detroit, Michigan, 1994.

Transcription 5-2
Components of "Last Stop Brčko" by Mensur Hatić. Transcription by Mark Slobin.

In terms of style, two of Mensur's approaches are worth noting. One is the melodic structure of A. As you can see, it is actually made up of two segments we can call a and b. Mensur plays ab, but then b itself repeats in its own extended form, b'. This freely expanding sense of melody is part of the improvisational aesthetic of folk music. The second place this can be heard is in the accompaniment to B and C sections (bass-line phrases in

Transcription 5-2), played on the accordion buttons (the melody being played on the keys). Using the basic interval of a fourth (transcribed here as the notes E and A), Mensur creates a steady bass line that moves against the melody, again in a free, shifting pattern of small melodic units.

Flory Jagoda: Keeper of the Sephardic Jewish Tradition of Bosnia

Before World War II (pre-1940), the twelve thousand Jews of Sarajevo made up about 10 percent of the city's population and acted as lively, long-term contributors to the local culture and music. Tunes were shared by Jews, Muslims, Croats, and Serbs, each community adapting melodies to their own ritual or social needs. The Bosnian Jews were mostly of Sephardic background. This means their ancestors were part of a wave of immigration from Spain after 1492, when the Christian rulers who reconquered Spain from the Muslims forcibly exiled the Jews and Muslims. The Jews, who had developed a long, collaborative cultural relationship with the Muslims, fled to Muslim-controlled areas of southeastern Europe, the eastern Mediterranean, and northern Africa. These Spanish Jews, or

Figure 5-7
Flory Jagoda, a Bosnian Sephardic Jewish singer who lives in the United States.

Courtesy Flory Jagoda.

Sephardim, had strong traditions of poetry and song dating back to the Middle Ages that they took with them to their new homes. Learning local languages, they also kept on speaking their own vernacular, a Spanish-based language called Ladino, or Judeo-Spanish.

During World War II, the Bosnian Jews suffered the fate of some six million Jews across Europe: being deported to death camps by Nazi occupiers. Less than a thousand survived. This small postwar remnant maintained its culture in the nearly half-million strong population of the newly swollen Sarajevo. During the early stages of the Yugoslav war of the 1990s, the Jews, who were onlookers to the conflict, helped as mediators. But by the mid-1990s, very few Jews were left in Bosnia to carry on their centuries-old traditions; most having emigrated to Israel, the United States, or elsewhere.

Flory Jagoda was born in Sarajevo in 1923 to a Sephardic family— Altarac—known for its singers and musicians. She escaped from the region during World War II and emigrated to the United States, where she eventually became the sole survivor of her family. By escaping her community's destruction, she has managed to preserve the heritage of her childhood. She also enhances her tradition by making her own arrangements of folk materials, performing with other family members in an ensemble that has recorded and toured widely. Here is what Flory Jagoda says about her childhood and what she learned from her *nona,* her grandmother:

> In my Nona's kitchen there was a drawer that was magic to us children. It contained sheets upon sheets of paper written in Hebrew script which we could not decipher, but those words, when sung by my Nona, we understood. These Ladino songs had been learned from her mother, and her mother before her, and so on for generations. . . . I am trying . . . to again open my Nona's drawer and pass on a taste of the talent and way of life which produced the Altarac family, that it might live on, both in the songs I remember and in my own musical memories of that now-disappeared time. (Jagoda 1991)

For Flory Jagoda, then, music provides cultural continuity. When she escaped from the German occupation, she took her accordion with her, but she had to leave her grandmother's book of songs behind. Now she says that "those songs my Nona sang and the accordion that saved my life were the only things I brought with me to America, the only things that were left from my childhood" (interview by M. Laušević, 1992). Individual musicians, such as Mensur Hatić, can choose to keep their ears open for new sounds to assimilate for both economic viability and the sheer pleasure of learning. Whole communities, such as the Sephardic Jews of Sarajevo, can also select and accommodate new musics because of a sense of survival, because they have lived in many environments, or because they enjoy the sheer aesthetic satisfaction by singing and playing across the full range of surrounding musical resources.

The song selected here from Flory Jagoda's ample storehouse (CD 2, Track 15) is about Sarajevo—specifically, about the men of the family, who can hardly wait for the end of the Sabbath so they can go out and party.

CD 2/15

"Klaro del dija" ("Break of Day") (1:52). Traditional Sephardic Jewish song of Bosnia. Performed by Flory Jagoda, vocal and guitar, with Howard Bass and The Hesperus. Field recording by Abby Sternberg, Institute of Musical Traditions Concert. Silver Spring, Maryland, 2000.

She sings with her family group, who provide guitar and vocal backup, thereby contributing to the transmission of their great-grandmother's songbook. The course of such transmission is often complex. For example, in the late 1980s Flory Jagoda returned to Sarajevo to give a concert. Some of her songs were later played on the local television station, probably the first time Jewish songs were publicly aired. These songs were greeted enthusiastically by the remaining Jewish community, which had lost its tradition through the radical disjuncture of war and postwar cultural assimilation. So through the American channel of Jagoda's visit, this Sephardic music went back into circulation after a fifty-year absence. The year 2000 saw the premiere of a fine documentary film on Flory Jagoda's life, *The Key from Spain.* The title comes from the tradition among Sephardic families of keeping the key to their ancestral houses in Spain during the centuries of diaspora.

Text, Traditional, "Klaro del dija"

The roosters are starting to crow;
It's time to get up.
Let's not wait; the sun and the day
Start up the happy crowd.
From *havdala* to the Šadrvan
When the girls dance and sing.
Until tomorrow, at dawn,
The crowd disperses.

Havdala is the Jewish ceremony that marks the transition from the Sabbath to the weekday world, on Saturday at sunset. The Šadrvan was a well-known Sarajevo cafe in the old days, located near the Jewish neighborhood.

Between them, Mensur Hatić and Flory Jagoda represent two common but contrasting versions of musical diaspora—music of a population that feels far from home. Both have felt disjuncture and cultural loss through warfare. For the Sephardic Jews the loss is total, as Sarajevo will likely never have a significant Jewish population. Flory Jagoda's adaptation to these conditions has been to embark on a personal quest for both the preservation and arrangement of music as a monument to a bygone culture and for her own sense of continuity. Feeling the effect of a recent war, the much younger Hatić finds that flexibility and resourcefulness are key to economic survival in the music business while he keeps a watchful eye on events back home to determine where his future lies. Both musicians use music as a lifeline in turbulent cultural waters, an impulse shared by countless millions of deterritorialized and migrant peoples at the beginning of the twenty-first century.

Update: Bosnia, 2001

As of 2001, Bosnia is still occupied by international forces and divided into three substates of Serbs, Croats, and Muslims. Musical life has survived, revived, and transformed in many ways. Here we focus on just two musical sites visited earlier in this chapter: the highlander villages and the Sarajevo rock scene.

Village Life

After all but two of the highland villages described earlier were burned down in 1992, many villagers fled to the Sarajevo suburbs or found themselves as refugees in west Europe, Australia, Canada, or the United States. Suddenly they had to lead very different lifestyles. After the Dayton peace agreement, many refugees returned. International military forces have built new, wider roads to the villages. Religious organizations have rebuilt mosques, and some humanitarian organizations have helped rebuild houses, which have neither the charm nor the usefulness of traditional mountain homes (see Figure 5-9). Villages that used to bulge with the people, livestock, haystacks, and manure piles remain almost empty, as few villagers have returned.

August is again the prime time for *mevlud* festivities; many villagers now arrive not in trucks but in personal vehicles with foreign license plates. The fairs are smaller: Many young men were killed on the front lines, and many returned refugees distance themselves from their old lifestyle, which they view as primitive and uncomfortable. However, good *ganga* singing survives.

Ten years later, in 2000, the three girls you heard on CD 2, Track 10, were still singing together (compare Figures 5-2 and 5-8). Because of the war they were not yet married, although shortly after the recording they did in fact all marry highlander men. Now listen to two selections that show both continuity and change in their singing. The recording on CD 2, Track 16, is the same song they sang on CD 2, Track 10, with its old-time text about girls' modest status. While they are singing a young man (now a husband of one of the singers) stops by to listen, embarrassing the singer. This close interaction of singing men and women reflects the new social context, as opposed to the more careful segregation of the past.

CD 2/16

"Sisters, Hold on to Your Chastity" (1:06). As sung in 2000 by the same singers on CD 2, Track 10. Field recording by Mirjana Laušević. Umoljani village, Bosnia, 2000.

CD 2/17

"What Do You Love the Best, Little Devil?" (1:02). Contemporary women's *ganga* song. Performed by Azra Bandić, Mevla Luckin, and Emsija Tatarović. Field recording by Mirjana Laušević. Umoljani village, Bosnia, 2000.

Figure 5-8

The singers of CD 2, Track 10, as they looked in 2000: From left to right, Azra Bandić, Mevla Luckin, and Emsija Tatarović. Compare with Figure 5-2, taken eleven years earlier.

Mirjana Laušević

Although it retains the traditional *ganga* style, the 2000 recording starts with a surprisingly different text that underscores this moment of changed attitudes.

Text, Opening Lines of "What Do You Love the Best, Little Devil?"

What do you love the best, little devil?
To cheat on guys is the dearest thing to me.

Figures 5-9 and 5-10 show the old village and the newly reconstructed village. In the modernized houses, young teenagers are well attuned to local and global popular music. When one singer played an old recording

Figure 5-9
The village of Umoljani in 1989 before it was destroyed.

Mirjana Laušević

Figure 5-10
The village of Umoljani in 2000 after it was rebuilt.

Mirjana Laušević

of *mevlud* singing, his children stopped listening to a German pop music cable channel, then fell on the floor laughing, telling their father to stop embarrassing them. Yet the old forms continue.

The Pop Music Scene

As mentioned earlier, the war of the 1990s caused the national Yugoslav pop music scene to fragment into national worlds (Croatian, Serbian, Bosnian). Familiar elements were recycled and reinterpreted. With the coming of an uneasy peace and replacement of the wartime leadership, new musical configurations are emerging. Here we present one example, of a current star, Dino Merlin, who is helping to recreate a Bosnian mainstream sound that almost vanished because of the destruction of the musicians and the recording infrastructure. Merlin freely acknowledges his debt to the 1980s band Bijelo Dugme and sustains some of their sound. He says,

> I think that for all these fifteen years, I've been atypical in relation to ex-Yugoslav bands because—I myself don't know for what reason; perhaps an irrational one, or some love reason, and love is always so close to the irrational—I have always sung about Bosnia. (Interview with Ljerka Vidić Rasmussen, 1999)

Through his popular appeal and crafted songwriting, Merlin is one of the musicians who are well received not just in Bosnia, but also in Croatia, Slovenia, and even Serbia.

Listen to CD 2, Track 18, to hear one of his recent songs. It was performed live at a 1998 concert where 50,000 Sarajevans jammed the center of town and sang along. "Jel' Sarajevo gdje je nekad bilo" features expressive Mediterranean instrumentals on clarinet and sax and a nostalgic text about a city that survived almost total destruction, but not without scars. Merlin's lyrics are folklike, drawing power from the old stock of images in lines such as "leaves are turning yellow," or "has my old mother recovered."

CD 2/18

"Jel' Sarajevo gdje je nekad bilo" ("Is Sarajevo Still Where It Was?") (4:19). Dino Merlin. *Dino Merlin Live*. In Takt Records. Sarajevo, Bosnia, 1998.

Text, "Jel' Sarajevo gdje je nekad bilo"

1. Sometimes at night I hear you walking
   At times it feels like an old mother's steps.
   Everything dear to the heart is far away;
   Only pain understands those in love.
   Leaves are turning yellow, and I'm silent.
   The heart senses that you are not mine.

2. Is Sarajevo where it used to be
   Or is just what my heart feels?
   Has anything changed?
   Has the water of the Miljacka [river] dried up?
   Has my old mother recovered?
   Has my beloved left me?

Words and music by Dino Merlin. Used by permission of the artist.

Bulgaria: Another Approach to Musical Change

Yugoslavia's path to dissolution and destruction offers one kind of story about the change in eastern European music since 1990. Nearby countries that have not suffered from violent transition reveal some of the same trends but in the light of a more peaceful cultural evolution. Here is an example from Bulgaria, which will amplify the Bosnian situation just outlined and extend it geographically.

In Bulgaria the state-ensemble approach to creating official culture that we heard on CD 2, Track 13, has an extraordinary history. Throughout the 1960s and 1970s, classically trained composers working for the government transformed village songs into elaborate arrangements featuring careful harmony and a "clean" sound. In the late 1980s, groups representing this kind of official music, sung and played by state radio troupes, toured western Europe and the United States and were acclaimed by Western pop stars, selling many recordings under a heading invented by French promoters: "the mysteries of Bulgarian voices." Meanwhile, that particular form of official music was rapidly losing its validity and popularity back in Bulgaria as part of the slow social, political, and cultural transition from the isolated, communist era into an age of democracy and individual enterprise. The vanguard of musical change included the clarinetist Ivo Papazov and his band Trakiya, who transformed what was called *svatbarska muzika*, "wedding music," into a technologically and musically sophisticated blend of local and global styles.

Born in 1952, Papazov founded his band in 1974. Because he has a mixed ethnic background, Turkish and *Rom* (Gypsy), he represents a minority voice that has been an important factor in local music making for generations. In fact, his name was originally Ibrahim Hapazov, much less Bulgarian than it is now. The commentary on the song that started this chapter, the children's rain song from nearby Romania, mentioned that *Rom* played a special part as musicians in traditional eastern European culture. The Turkish side of Papazov's background is also socially significant. Like Bosnia, Bulgaria was ruled by the Turkish Ottoman Empire for over 400 years, until the late nineteenth century. This background at first made Papazov a problematic figure for the then-communist Bulgarian government, which tried to assert a homogenized "Bulgarian" ethnicity and viewed any recognition of ethnic difference as a potentially punishable offense. Music is hardly an "innocent" fact of culture and, as in the case of Ivo Papazov and in most of the modern world, often serves as the leading edge of identity conflicts and attempts at administrative control.

Papazov's approach was to take traditional sounds from weddings and other celebrations and galvanize them through electronic amplification and backup instruments (such as electric bass) and by adding blues, jazz, and rock riffs as part of long, exuberant sets performed for huge crowds. He brought with him a strong background in improvisation from Turkish and *Rom* tradition. Often standing in direct opposition to official music making, Papazov and other *svatbarska muzika* bandleaders became so popular that the government had to take account of them, finally offering some grudging approval at about the time the old system fell and left the political and economic field open to those who, like Papazov, were ready for new openings.

He began to make recordings for sale in the West and to tour in Europe and America, articulating a philosophy of musical blending based on a tradition that found a receptive market as "world music" began to filter into the local bins at music stores in the Western world. As the ethnomusicologist Donna Buchanan says,

> He views his folk jazz fusion style as a medium through which to improvise freely—a technique he learned by listening to recordings of Charlie Parker and Benny Goodman. Perhaps most telling is his comment that, "I can eat the same dish twenty times, but I can't play one and the same thing twice," which captures clearly the essentiality of improvisation to wedding music. (In press)

Another *svatbarska muzika* star, Teodosi Spasov, says that "improvisation is the means through which [the musician] achieves the free flight of his artistic fantasy. Improvisation is that which separates the free artistic souls from the whole terrestrial globe" (Buchanan in press).

Papazov goes so far as to call his music *balkanski dzhaz*, "Balkan jazz" (*the Balkans* being the general term for southeastern Europe), but his sights are set beyond his region as well, as Buchanan points out:

> He is struggling to create a musical style that supersedes his local senses of identity as a member of the ethnic Turkish and Rom subculture within Bulgaria, as a citizen of the Bulgarian nation, and as a representative of the Balkans. His stylistic aspirations bridge these affiliations with western musical idioms, creating an emblematic musical pastiche positioned squarely in the political economy of transnational popular culture. (1996:28)

Ivo Papazov and his band Trakiya recorded *Hristianova kopanitsa* (CD 2, Track 19) in 1991. It is based on a local dance-tune style of western Bulgaria. In her notes to this piece, Carol Silverman writes that "fast, asymmetric rhythms are characteristic of Bulgarian music; this example is, however, almost too fast to dance to!" (Silverman 1991). The rhythm here is a rather complicated pattern familiar to Bulgarian listeners and dancers: short-short-long-short-short ($2 + 2 + 3 + 2 + 2$ counted out). The piece consists of both solo and group play, with plenty of lively bass and drum rhythm backup; all of this reflects the classic jazz Papazov was listening to. Jazz is another style of modern music that took standard tunes meant for dancing and kept increasing the level of virtuosity until it became hard to dance to and changed into a concert format. Indeed, some of Papazov's fans have complained that Trakiya's music is not "old-timey" enough for them. The Bulgarian band's approach might also be compared with bluegrass, a post–World War II genre from the upper South in the United States that drew attention with its alternation of dazzling star solos on fiddles, banjos, and mandolins.

Hristianova kopanitsa starts with the basic folk tune, sparklingly played two times through. Notice that the melodic material is similar to Mensur

CD 2/19

Hristianova kopanitsa (dance) (3:26) Ivo Papazov. Performed by Ivo Papazov and Trakiya. *Balkanology*. Rykodisc CD HNBC 1363. Bulgaria, 1991.

Hatić's train piece, both emphasizing the distance (an augmented second) between the second and third notes of the scale (Transcription 5-2, A). This tonal material is common to a large area of southeastern Europe among many ethnic groups but not found much to the north and west. After the opening statements of the tune, freely improvised solos follow on saxophone, accordion, and clarinet before the band comes back together to reprise the tune to end the piece. Notice how the drum set, from U. S. tradition, and the electric bass, a newcomer replacing older folk instruments, get freer and freer in their backup play as the piece progresses. Overall, this performance draws on notions of form familiar to local listeners, but also reminds one of the basic outline of the bebop jazz piece: statement of theme (the "head"), solos, return at end to theme.

Even so, a traditional rhythmic framework forms the bedrock beneath the solos, just as older village sounds provide the basic melodic patterning—scale, style of ornamentation of a basic tune. Adding electric bass and jazz drum set to a clarinet-and-accordion sound is a more recent trend: The Papazov style is an eloquent, sometimes witty, and always brilliant fusion of the traditional and the current, the Bulgarian and the imported.

The word *prestidigitation,* which usually refers to the way a magician's hand "is quicker than the eye," literally means "fast fingers." Despite the novelty of Papazov's approach to modern musical magic, the concepts of patterned ornamentation and quickness of hand and mind are basic to more traditional Bulgarian styles as well. In marveling at the older *gaida* (Bulgarian bagpipe) styles that are part of the sound memory inherent in Papazov's work, Timothy Rice talks about "the mystery of ornamentation." Describing his attempts to learn the *gaida,* Rice writes,

> If the structural principles of gaida music are relatively straightforward, its rich ornamentation—and musicians' ability to play at enormous speeds—still seemed magical. . . . My preexisting Western concepts handled the rudiments of Bulgarian melody and rhythm adequately, but the manner of playing remained a mystery. (1994:77).

Rice goes on to describe at length his conquest of digital subtleties through immersion in experience:

> Perhaps the most profound discovery was that I learned to fuse my concepts of melody and ornamentation into a single concept expressed most vividly in the hands, not in musical notation—precisely the kind of integration I imagine young Bulgarian boys achieved when they learned this tradition. (1994:77)

Other pieces of Papazov's work are even more pronounced in their borrowings from rock, blues, and jazz, adapted to local southeastern European/Turkish materials and approaches. Papazov's music has already become "classic," and there are many new waves of tradition-based musical change on the way in Bulgaria now that the musical free market is open for business and competition. Many of them have *Rom* influence. Recently, researchers have coined the term *ottopop* to describe the way musical influences are bouncing back and forth within the old Ottoman cultural zone.

Another nearby country, Hungary, has had a very different way of coming to terms with the folk music past. For some thirty years, young musicians from Budapest, the capital, have been finding old peasant musicians and learning from them. Then they recreated the music to suite more contemporary taste. In the process, the singer Marta Sebestyen became well-known internationally, with her latest album dubbing her "world music star." In an interview, Sebestyen talks about how she learned to sing so well in a tradition she did not grow up with:

> Everybody's asking me, "Where the hell did you learn this style?" I was born with a sensibility, the ability of catching sounds and melodies. At the same time, with many visits and trips to Transylvania we added more, in experience, to learn the style. My maestros, my masters, were the old ladies and old men of the village. I was singing with these people, just sitting with them, eating with them, just holding their hands and going to church together, and that means a lot. If you try to learn these songs from notebooks, you'll never learn it. Something is missing—that is the real emotion, which you can only experience when you are there. (Ronay 1991)

Sebestyen also points to an overlap in sensibility that allows people like herself to take an older national tradition and keep it fresh:

> When they [the villagers] were singing, besides the collective pain, they were singing about their own pain, so it's very personal, which comes through the music. When I sing, I can also tell about my own problems in the song, and that's wonderful, and that's what makes these songs very up to date. (Ronay 1991)

Summary

Although musical traditions everywhere face constant change, eastern Europe offers a striking recent example of major transition. This chapter centered on Bosnia, part of the country of Bosnia and Herzegovina that was once part of a country called Yugoslavia, which collapsed violently around 1990 amid widespread destruction.

In Bosnia we started with a seemingly isolated mountain village with a Muslim population. There, old song styles accompanied a herding economy, but the music-culture had already been augmented by men and women bringing back new sounds after going out to nearby cities to work. Some men even went to other parts of Europe for jobs but returned for hometown festivals where a variety of musics were displayed.

We followed Bosnian music through its participation in a national commercialized popular music style, "newly-composed folk music" and also noted its appearance in government-sponsored "official culture" ensembles. Since the time the musical examples you heard here were recorded, Bosnian music has undergone significant change because of the destructive interethnic war that began in 1992. For example, war songs connected to music videos, some rap-based, became very popular, while local folk traditions like those of the Mt. Bjelašnica highlanders we surveyed have been largely curtailed. Meanwhile, newer pop stars such as Dino Merlin speak to the situation of Sarajevo, which looks back to its prosperous, multicultural past and forward, cautiously, to a more stable future as part of a revamped and revived Bosnia.

To round out the discussion, we briefly visited nearby Bulgaria, which shifted without bloodshed from a communist system to a capitalist-based democratic system. In nearby Hungary there is a slightly different slant, based on the pioneering collection of work of urban musicians going to the countryside, then adapting the music of old folk players to modern ears, and only then moving into "world music" experimentation.

Although all these issues of musical change are globally relevant, they are particularly poignant in the case of the dramatic shift of social, economic, and political orientation in our target area of central and southeastern Europe.

References*

Buchanan, Donna. 1996. "Wedding Music, Social Identity, and the Bulgarian Political Transition." In *Retuning Culture: Music and Change in Eastern Europe,* edited by M. Slobin. Durham, N.C.: Duke Univ. Press.

CMPH (Corpus Musicae Popularis Hungaricae). 1956. Vol. III/B *Lakodalom,* edited by L. Kiss. Budapest: Hungarian Academy of Sciences.

Forry, Mark. 1978. "Becar Music in the Serbian Community of Los Angeles: Evolution and Transformation." In *Selected Reports in Ethnomusicology* 3, no. 1, edited by J. Porter. Los Angeles: University of California.

Jagoda, Flory. 1991. Liner notes to *Kantikas di mi nona.* Global Village C139.

Lockwood, Yvonne. 1983. *Text and Context: Folksong in a Bosnian Muslim Village.* Columbus, Ohio: Slavica Publishers.

Petrović, Ankica. 1977. Ganga: A Form of Traditional Rural Singing in Yugoslavia. Ph.D. dissertation, Queen's University, Belfast.

Rice, Timothy. 1994. *May It Fill Your Soul: Experiencing Bulgarian Music.* Chicago: University of Chicago Press.

Ronay, Esther. 1991. *Beyond the Forest.* Film.

Silverman, Carol. 1991. Liner notes to Ivo Papazov, *Balkanology*. Rykodisc CD HNBC 1363.

Sugarman, Jane. 1989. "The Nightingale and the Partridge: Singing and Gender Among Prespa Albanians." *Ethnomusicology* 33:191–215.

Additional Reading

"Europe" *The Garland Encyclopedia of World Music.* Vol. 8, edited by T. Rice, J. Porter, and C. Goertzen. New York: Garland. Excellent short articles on the musics of all the European countries.

Kligman, Gail. 1981. *Caluş: Symbolic Transformation in Rumanian Ritual.* Chicago: Univ. of Chicago Press.

---

*This chapter is the result of the significant assistance, for which I am most grateful, from two former students, Mirjana Laušević (highlander village) and Ljerka Vidić Rasmussen (urban popular music), and their original mentor, Ankica Petrović, the doyenne of Bosnian music studies. The section on Bulgaria benefited greatly from the insights of Carol Silverman.

———. 1988. *The Wedding of the Dead.* Chicago: Univ. of Chicago Press. Both Kligman titles provide good examples of work on southeastern European peasant ritual.

Lockwood, William G. 1975. *European Moslems: Economy and Ethnicity in Western Bosnia.* New York: Academic Press. Ethnography of Bosnian Muslims.

Petrović, Ankica. 1977. Ganga: A Form of Traditional Rural Singing in Yugoslavia. Ph.D. diss., Queen's University, Belfast. The genre of ganga.

Slobin, Mark. 1996. *Retuning Culture: Music and Change in Eastern Europe.* Durham, N.C.: Duke University Press. Anthology on central and eastern Europe that provides a survey of questions raised here by numerous authors, some cited in this chapter.

Sugarman, Jane. 1997. *Engendering Song: Singing and Subjectivity at Prespa Albanian Weddings.* Chicago: University of Chicago Press. An excellent study of issues of gender and Albanian traditions.

Additional Listening

Since the onset of war in the 1990s, it is difficult to keep track of shifting ownership of record labels and availability of locally produced albums for most of former Yugoslavia. Of the performers featured in this chapter, Flory Jagoda has three albums on the Global Village label; Mensur Hatić has a self-produced CD, *Zadnja Stanica Brčko* (available from hatic@aol.com), with an updated version of "Last Stop Brčko." Rounder recordings is serially publishing the entire Alan Lomax catalog, including the groundbreaking "World Library of Folk and Primitive Music" series of the early 1950s from which "Paparudele," used in this chapter, comes. *Volume 5: Yugoslavia* (Rounder 11661-1745-2), an excellent introduction to the old folk music, has updated liner notes by Ankica Petrović and Rajna Klaser, and the Bulgaria album is forthcoming. Another important album, issued at the height of the Bosnia war as a tribute to folk music, is *Echoes from an Endangered World* (Smithsonian Folkways CD SF 40407).

Marta Sebestyen and her band Muzsikás are always available in world music selections of record stores, with classic albums such as *Blues for Transylvania* (Hannibal HNCD 1350) or the recent compilation *Marta Sebestyen: Star of World Music* (Hungaroton 37979).

India/South India

David B. Reck

pproaching the vibrant city of Chennai in southern India from the air, we would notice, first of all, the rich blue-green of the Bay of Bengal spreading out to the horizon in the southeast. Along the coastline, parallel to the broad white ribbon of sand and moving inland, stretch broad avenues and huge whitewashed government buildings designed by the British, who named their provincial capital "Madras." But it had always been called, simply, *chennai*—"the city"—in Tamil, the language of the region and state of Tamilnadu. The climate, similar to that of coastal Central America, is described jokingly by local guidebooks as having three seasons: "the hot, the hotter, and the hottest!" In truth, November through January—the season of music festivals—can be quite pleasant with a sea breeze in the evenings and the temperatures dipping into the seventies at night.

Figure 6-1
Mount Road, one of the busiest commercial streets in Madras.

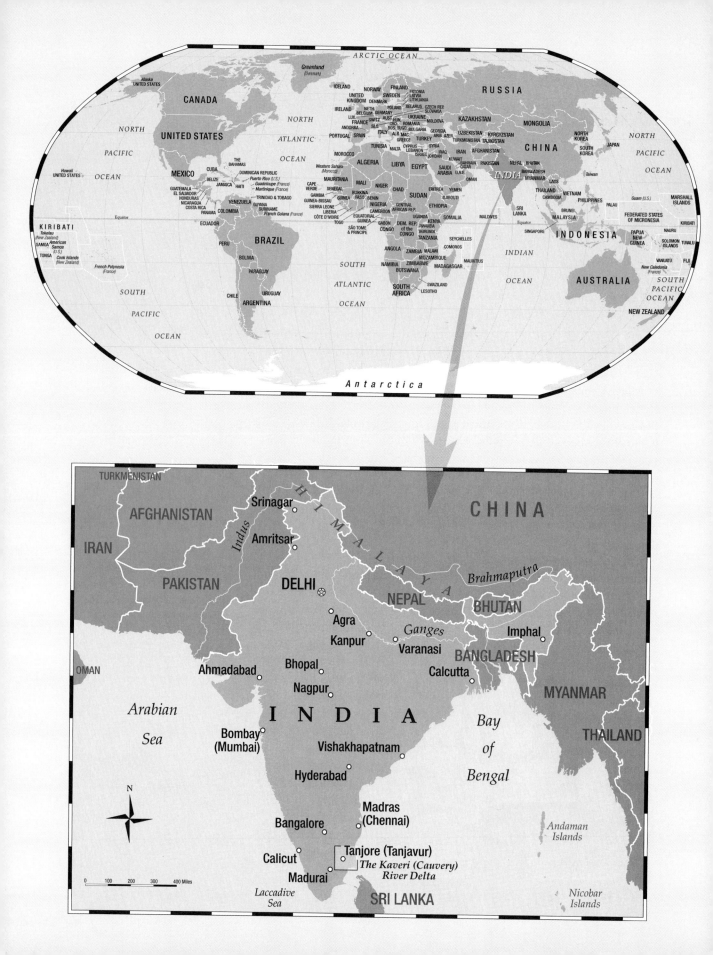

Figure 6-2
A poster advertises *Thillana Mohanambal*, a popular Tamil movie adapted from a famous novel about the romance and marriage of a dancer and a musician.

In the old days Chennai was a leisurely and genteel city. Most houses and buildings were one and two stories, with only the temple *gopurams*, the ornately carved towers, projecting up overhead. Coconut palms, banyan, neem, jacaranda, *ashok*, and other trees shaded houses and streets, while an array of tropical plants filled every yard and garden. Classical Indian music and *bhajans*, religious songs, echoed from radios, temples, and outdoor concert halls. The day might begin early at 5:30 or 6:00, but the town shuts down at 10:00 each night to the smell of incense and flowering jasmine and the songs of nightingales.

In Chennai today, with an estimated population of between seven and eight million, modern glass and concrete buildings—apartment high-rises, hotels, shopping centers, and corporate headquarters—increasingly jut upward from the sea of green foliage. The streets are clogged with the seemingly chaotic traffic of cars, buses, trucks, vans, auto rickshaws, motorcycles, mopeds, and pedestrians moving in a cacophony of horns and motors beneath a carbon monoxide haze. There is even an appropriately named Hotel Traffic Jam.

Overhead each day dozens of Indian and international flights approach the busy airport. Twenty local television stations vie with international channels such as the BBC, ESPN, Nickelodeon, MTV, or Hong Kong's Star Channel, as sari-clad models posing as homemakers plug instant soup, shampoo, or dishwashing detergent. The South-Indian movie industry, centered in Chennai, is thriving. Each film is filled with high drama, intrigue, action-packed fight scenes, sexy dances, pathos, and—most importantly—pop songs created by world-class lyricists, composers, and arrangers. The pop songs blaring from every tea stall and boom box combine traditional Indian instruments and voices with electric guitars and state-of-the-art synthesizers as Indian *raga* scales fuse with rock and roll chord progressions and backup harmonies.

In popular culture the movie stars are the kings and queens of contemporary Indian society, their every activity, casual remark, or love affair dutifully chronicled by hundreds of film magazines in a dozen languages. Painted images of actors and actresses strut in two- and three-story cutouts that dominate the facades of palatial movie theaters. They gleam from the posters plastered on every bare wall and vie with the blinking glitter of neon advertisements at every major intersection.

Shop windows display refrigerators, air conditioners, TV sets, VCRs, automobiles, kitchen appliances, furniture, shoes, and ready-made clothing. Modern hospitals with some of the best doctors in world and the latest technology of modern medicine are spread throughout the city. Massive factories and mills produce fabric, steel, automobiles and trucks, polymers, motorcycles, electronic goods, and railway locomotives. Computers and software are everywhere, as here and throughout the world India establishes itself as the place where excellent technical schools train a generation of whiz kids whose expertise and innovation feed the global high-tech industry.

In the flash and color and familiarity of the modern world it is easy to forget that South Asia—India, Pakistan, Bangladesh, Nepal, Sri Lanka and several smaller countries—is home to one of the world's most ancient civilizations.

Its continuous history goes back thousands of years, beyond three centuries of British colonialism, past the great forts and tombs of the Moguls (around 1400–1800 C.E.), through the courts of countless kingdoms and illustrious emperors such as the Buddhist Asoka (third century B.C.E.), past the ruins of the ancient well-planned Indus Valley cities of Mohenjo-Daro and Harappa (roughly 2500–1700 B.C.E.), disappearing into prehistoric collective myth and legend preserved in oral traditions. The basic philosophies and beliefs of Hinduism still flourish; the gods are alive and well, venerated in temples, homes, and religious festivals. (About a tenth of the population is Moslem.) Caste still plays a role in politics and in marriage and household customs. Marriage ceremonies are big events celebrated with ancient rites lasting for hours.

Down the block from the air-conditioned supermarket, the video store, or the modern pharmacy we can still find the crowded shops of the bazaar: spices and grains piled high in pyramids in wicker baskets, exotic perfumes in dozens of colors and fragrances, finely woven rugs, and exquisite hand-loomed silks and cotton fabrics spread out like a rainbow. In towns and villages the skilled craftsmen for which India is famous follow the trades of their forefathers: carving in stone or sandalwood, weaving, making intricate jewelry, hammering out fine metalwork in brass or copper, painting, engraving, or making musical instruments. In homes and restaurants a seemingly infinite variety of traditional deliciously spiced dishes in regional styles continue to make South Asia a paradise of fine cooking. Somehow, magically, the ancient traditions persist in a radically changing world, the new and old, the traditional and the innovative, thriving in a unique coexistence.

Everywhere, jarring juxtapositions confront the visitor. A farmer in a loin cloth plows behind bullocks in a field next to an airport runway as a Boeing 747 roars by. A mud and thatch hut sits in the shadow of a luxury high-rise apartment. A nuclear power station, its machinery garlanded with flowers, is dedicated at an hour set by astrologers with four-thousand year old Hindu chants. A traditional classical music performance takes place around the corner from a trendy coffee shop blasting out the latest American rock and roll or Indian hits.

Jawaharlal Nehru, independent India's first prime minister, liked to describe his culture as a palimpsest, a manuscript parchment written on again and again in which everything written before is never fully erased. Everything written before is somehow still there, visible and readable, buried or blurred perhaps, but never fully replaced or forgotten. The new is constantly added on, but the old, the traditional continues. The multi-faceted and complex nature of Indian civilization is one characteristic that makes it so rich in comparison with the increasingly monolithic nature of much of rest of the modern world.

History, Culture, Politics

The Environment of Indian Musics

The facts about India are staggering. Its almost one billion people—one of every five people on earth—live in an area about a third the size of the United States (from the Mississippi River to the eastern seaboard). The country hosts fifteen major languages, almost as many alphabets, and dozens of regional dialects. Its continuous history, as noted earlier, stretches back five thousand years and beyond, making the history of relatively new countries such as the United States or Canada seem like mere blips on the cosmic screen.

Owing perhaps to its geography—a triangular peninsula cut off from neighboring lands by jungles, deserts, and the towering Himalaya Mountains—South Asia has developed forms of culture and lifeways distinctly its own. Even so, its size and the variety of its terrain and people account for great regional differences.

The largest such difference is between the Hindi-related language groups of the North and the Dravidian-speaking peoples of the South, a division that is paralleled in the two main styles of Indian classical music: the northern Hindusthani style and the southern Carnatic tradition.

Numerous influences have come into India over the centuries. The earliest resulted from the migration of Aryan people from central Asia beginning in the third millennium B.C.E. whose language related to those of Europe in the Indo-European language family. (Thus the English words for *father* and *mother* can be traced back to both Latin [*pater* and *mater*] and Sanskrit [*pitr* and *matr*].)

Perhaps the most important later influences came from Islamic conquests beginning in the twelfth century C.E. and peaking with the great Mogul emperors of the sixteenth and seventeenth centuries. Persian and Arabic architects, painters, poets, and musicians migrated into the subcontinent to be influenced, in turn, by indigenous styles of the arts. The resulting synthesis of Indian aesthetics with Islamic imports from western Asia can be seen in the ethereal beauty of the Taj Mahal or heard in the soaring improvisations of *sitar* and *tabla.*

In making India "the crown jewel of the empire," the English colonists brought railways, democratic systems of government, bureaucracy, universities, and European instruments such as the violin, harmonium, and clarinet, which talented local musicians readily adapted to Indian music, although then they did not adopt European musical styles. European influences continue today. Globalization and instant communication allow Indian musicians to become familiar with Bach, Vivaldi, Beethoven, the Beatles, or the latest rap stars; Charlie Parker, Elvis, or Mahalia Jackson. The saxophone, electric guitar, mandolin, and electronic keyboard have all been adopted to Indian styles and accepted and enjoyed.

You can see that, again and again, foreign cultural ideas and technology have migrated into India over the centuries. Once in the subcontinent, they have been absorbed, assimilated, digested, played with, and combined with indigenous cultural elements, emerging eventually in a new and undeniably Indian synthesis. For example, the India *raga* system of complex scales, intonations, and phrases is uniquely Indian while still clearly related to the classical musical systems of Iran, Turkey, the Arabian peninsula, and North Africa. The complex *sitar* and *tabla,* distinctly adapted to the specific intricacies of Indian music, have "country cousins" in the *setar* of Afghanistan and the *tabala* of Morocco.

The arts, along with the sciences and religious and philosophical thought, have always been highly valued in South Asia, and they have flourished from the earliest times. The palaces, temples, forts, monuments, cities, and tombs built by great kings and dynasties remain among the wonders of world architecture. Indian sculpture in stone, wood, and bronze and Indian painting (such as book-sized miniatures or the ancient murals at Ajanta and Ellora) rank among the greatest masterpieces of world art. Indian artisans to this day support an export trade of fine handicrafts admired worldwide. Traditional literature is dominated by the two Sanskrit epics—the *Ramayana* and the *Mahabharata*—written from oral sources sometime between 400 B.C.E. and 400 C.E. In Carnatic music many song texts refer to events in these epics. India has produced thousands of major authors, poets, and playwrights ranging from the court poet Kalidasa (who lived in the fourth and fifth centuries) to contemporary authors such as Salman Rushdie or R. K. Narayan, both of whom write in English. In the late twentieth century a host of extraordinary filmmakers have appeared. Perhaps the best known is Satyajit Ray, whose works from *The Apu Trilogy* to *Charulata* (described by some scholars as "the perfect film") have gained him recognition as one of a handful of masters of contemporary cinema. His film *The Music Room* is the story of an impoverished maharaja's love for music.

Indian civilization has also seen great religious development—and religion and the arts, especially music and dance, have always been inseparable. The four *vedas* (believed to have crystallized as early as 1200 B.C.E.) and the later *Upanishads* (or "Forest Books") contain religious and abstract philosophical thought that has fascinated Western thinkers such as Emerson and Thoreau and scientists such as Robert Oppenheimer. The *Puranas* (first century to the present) are filled with the myths of the gods and goddesses of popular Hinduism. These stories and adventures occur as themes not only in sermons and storytelling but also in music and dance, in popular movies and television serials—even in comic books. The ancient physical and mental discipline of yoga is now practiced all over the world. And in recent times, saintly men such as Mahatma Gandhi (1869–1948) have preached the nonviolence combined with social activism adapted by Martin Luther King, Jr., in the U.S. Civil Rights Movement and many others in confronting the injustices of the world.

Unfortunately, when one reads about India in American or European newspapers it is usually not about the region's remarkable history and cultural accomplishments but rather about some disaster or another. True, the problems of modern South Asia are immense. A virtual state of war exists between India and Pakistan; both are nuclear powers. Successive governments have attacked but not completely solved problems of overpopulation, terrorism, poverty, corruption, intolerance, and an agriculture dependent upon unpredictable monsoon rains. Yet the political system, however chaotic it may appear to an outsider, is based on British parliamentary rule. India is the earth's largest democracy, and its elections are run far more efficiently and accurately than those in the United States. Rapid change is occurring in the face of the apparent inertia of age-old traditions. A growing and prosperous middle-class exhibits world-class competence and brilliance, particularly in the sciences, technology, and business—and in the arts. In the palimpsest that is South Asia, we find a constant interplay between the ancient and the modern. The old, the traditional, seems able to persist through all the changes of time and history. This coexistence of the old and the new is part of the amazement and fascination of India—and perhaps also its greatest strength.

Many Musics

If we were to stroll through one of the residential neighborhoods of Chennai, we might come into contact with many types of music. In a typical day in the morning, first of all, come the vendors each pushing a cart of his wares—the vegetable man or woman, the pots and pans salesman, the waste newspaper collector, the coconut man (who will climb your tree for a fee), the ice cream guy, the sweets and candy vendors, and so on. Like different types of birds, each has a distinctive (and musical) call recognized by the alert ears of local homemakers. As the day wears on a mendicant may appear playing a small gong or the sacred conch shell trumpet (*shanku*) and chanting a sacred song. Once in a great while a snake charmer may walk the street with a python draped around his shoulders as he whines snake charming scales on the *punji*—a kind of miniature bagpipe of gourd and

Figure 6-3
An itinerant snake charmer, R. Vedan, plays the *punji*, an instrument traditionally associated with the charming of snakes—in this case, a python.

reeds. Or a wandering hereditary minstrel may go door to door singing her songs for an offering of rice and a few coins. Clearly we have entered the realm of folk music.

In the afternoon on TV, over the radio, or blasting from the neighborhood music cassette shop we would hear mostly Indian popular music, also called "cine songs" because almost all popular music originates in hit movies in Hindi, Tamil, or other regional languages. Virtually all movies have songs that periodically interrupt the plot with MTV-like visuals in exotic settings or elaborate song-and-dance production numbers. The actors and actresses always lip-sync the words, which are actually sung by "playback singers," the true stars and superstars of India's pop music scene.

Cine music is to some ears a curious and sometimes bizarre blend of East and West. Choppy and hyperactive melodies often in "oriental" scales are belted out by nasal singers over Latin rhythms and an eclectic accompaniment that may include drum set, keyboards, guitars, strings, xylophones, bongos, *sitar*, *tabla*, or bamboo flute. It is an anything goes, "if it sounds good use it " approach to music; the "anything" today might include harmony and counterpoint, rap and synthesizers. Although the lyrics, like those of pop music everywhere in the world, tend to focus on the eternal emotions and complications of love and romance, they are often religious, deeply philosophical, or comical.

Listen to "Engal Kalyanam" ("Our Wedding") on CD 2, Track 20. This song takes a light-hearted look at the commotion and excitement of an

CD 2/20

"Engal Kalyanam" ("Our Wedding"), cinema song (3:25). Music by M. S. Viswanathan, lyrics by Vali. Performed by P. Susheela, T. M. Soundararajan, P. B. Sreenivos, and L. R. Eswari. From *Hits from Tamil Films*, Vol. 6. EMI Odeon (India) EAECS 5519. LP. Calcutta, India, 1969.

Figure 6-4
C. P. Saraswathi, a wandering minstrel, accompanies herself on the *kudam*. A member of a household offers her rice in exchange for her song.

Indian wedding, with the ever-present relatives and the joyful feelings of the happy couple:

Text, "Engal Kalyanam"

Our wedding is a "confusion wedding"!
Sons-in-law put up the money,
And the father-in-law puts up the canopy to receive the gifts.[1]

Morning is the wedding, and evening is the wedding night!
Enliven! A love marriage![2]
Tomorrow at the altar we'll exchange garlands, won't we?
And won't the drums play with the pipes?[3]

The lovers' tale is performed in the eyes.
It's a great struggle—to perform in the eyes!
A colorful chariot is running beside me;[4]
Heaven is coming to us!

Mother-in-law puts on eye makeup,
While the sons-in-law stare at her mirror;
The [wedding] procession winds along the street with firecrackers,
While everyone gives their blessings.

[1] The canopy (*pandal*) under which the ceremony takes place is of bamboo and palm leaves.
[2] Brides and grooms are traditionally chosen by parents for their children, so a "love marriage," in which a boy and girl fall in love and then get their respective parents to agree to their wedding, is very special, and unusual—except in movies.
[3] The double-reed pipe (*nagasvaram*) and the *tavil* drum play for all South-Indian ritual occasions such as in temples, in religious processions, and at marriages (see Figure 6-2).
[4] That is, the groom is like a heroic god riding in a chariot.

Figure 6-5
The traditional wedding of a young
couple is laced with ancient ritual and
music. Note the garlanded images of
Hindu deities on the wall.

Shall we have ten to sixteen children?
Shall the trimness of our [youthful] bodies be lost?
You claimed you hated men,
Yet you gave me desire!
If I am like Kama, the god of love,
You are the reason!

Your [blushing] cheeks invite me;
Your thoughts ask for me, I can tell!
Your eyes—are like bright lightning . . .
What are the pleasures we haven't experienced?

The bride's father had prayed to the god of Tirupati
That the marriage might be performed there,
So the bride and groom might have auspicious lives.[5]

The Sons-in-law better come home now
And give a send-off to the bride's father,
So that he can take up *sanyasin!*[6]

Free translation from the Tamil by S. B. Rajeswari (1989).

[5] Tirupati is the site of the hilltop temple to Lord Venkateswara and the most popular
shrine in South India.
[6] That is, now that the bride's father has managed all the complications of getting his
daughter married off, his sons can take over the worries of the household, and he can
retire to a forest hermitage to pursue the meditative life of a recluse detached from
the world.

Although the style of "Our Wedding" is somewhat out of date—it is a "golden oldie"—one might notice certain strong characteristics that mark this song as unmistakably Indian: the frenetic pace of the claphammer rhythms; the nasal timbre in the voices; the language of the lyrics—Tamil—and their cultural references and context; a strong bass line but no real harmonic progressions; the quick, sudden shifts in musical texture (like the quick cutting of images in the film that originally accompanied the song); the variety of musical instruments; and the use of sound effects—you may have noticed the "Woody Woodpecker theme" borrowed from Hollywood cartoons!

More recent songs may show greater and more sophisticated use of Western elements and orchestration, a more lyrical, crooning use of the human voice, and extraordinarily beautiful melodies. In fact, the timbres, forms, and instrumentation of Indian pop music continue to evolve in extremely varied and creative ways, especially when compared with the relatively static makeup of Western ensembles such as rock bands, jazz bands, symphony orchestras or the rigid industry-controlled formulas for most American pop songs. The more one listens to Indian pop music, the more one can appreciate its unique qualities, enjoy the beauty of its lyrics and themes, and gain a better understanding of why this is the favorite music of almost a billion people, old and young, rich and poor, educated and uneducated. Perhaps someday the great contemporary Indian songwriters (called "music directors") such as A. R. Rahman and Ilaiyaraja will gain the recognition that they deserve on the world scene.

Religious music is another important category of music in India. Among the dozens of other devotional traditions of South Asia—folk, pop, or classical; Hindu, Moslem, or Christian—is that of the *bhajan*.

A *bhajan* is a song, devotional in nature and relatively simple technically, that is sung primarily as an offering to God. *Bhajans* might be sung by a soloist with a backup of violins, flutes, harmonium, and drums (or any combination thereof), with additional rhythmic support coming from small ringing bell-cymbals, clackers, or even hand claps. Or *bhajans* might be sung in a congregational call-and-response manner with a leader singing out verses or improvising, while the group responds with either a repetition or a refrain.

As suggested earlier, the ensemble of *chinna melam* ("small band") consisting of two or more *nagasvaram* double-reed pipes, *tavil* drums, and *sruti*-box drone is associated with temple worship, religious processions, weddings, and auspicious occasions of all kinds, such as the opening of a music festival or a new store. But the music that the *nagasvaram* plays is largely that of South-Indian classical music, which itself includes song texts almost entirely religious in nature.

Listen to "Devi Niye Tunai," a classical song composed by the twentieth-century composer, Papanasan Sivan (CD 2, Track 21). The singer is Shobha Vasudevan, a recent graduate in music from the University of Madras. The *mridangam* accompanist is David P. Nelson, a disciple of the distinguished drummer T. Ranganathan, of Wesleyan University. The song

CD 2/21

"Devi Niye Tunai" ("O Devi! with Fish-Shaped Eyes") (4:37), by Papanasan Sivan. Performed by Shobha Vasudevan, vocal, and David P. Nelson, *mridangam*. Recorded for author by recording engineer Owen Muir. Amherst, Massachusetts, January, 2001.

text (in Tamil language) praises the Devi Meenakshi, a beautiful goddess with fish eyes (always open) or fish-shaped eyes, who is worshiped in the great temple in the southern city of Madurai (Figure 6-6).

Text, "Devi Niye Tunai"

chorus or refrain

raised notes

(Pallavi:) devi neeye tunai ten madurai vaazh meena lochani
(Anupallavi:) devaati devan sundaresan cittam kavar bhuvana sundari–amba
(Repeat pallavi)
(Charanam:) malayadhvajan maadavame kaancana maalai pudalvi mahaaraagjni alaimahal kalaimahal pani keervaani amudanaya iniya muttamizh valartta
(Repeat pallavi)
(Pallavi:) O Devi! with fish-shaped eyes, One who dwells in the south, in Madurai, protect me.[1]
(Anupallavi:) You are the one great beauty in the world who has captured the heart of the Lord of Lords, Sundaresa.[2]
(Charanam:) O, the One born out of the penance of the Lord of the [Himalaya] Mountains, Daughter of the mountains, great in wisdom, O Devi, [even] the daughter of waves and the daughter of the arts bow in respect to you.[3]

Free translation from the Tamil by Shobha Vasudevan.

[1] *Devi* means "goddess." The English *diva* derives from this word.
[2] Sundaresa is the great god Shiva whose marriage to Meenakshi is celebrated in a festival every year.
[3] "The daughter of waves" is Lakshmi, the goddess of wealth; "the daughter of the arts" is Saraswati, goddess of music and learning.

Notice that each phrase of the song undergoes one or more melodic variations, and that the *kriti* (literally, "composition") falls into three sections—the *pallavi* ("sprouting"), the *anupallavi* ("after the sprouting"), and the *charanam* ("the foot, verse") with the phrase from the first section repeated after each of the other two like a refrain. This is the form (with infinite variations) followed by almost all songs in South-India's classical music.

Figure 6-6
Meenakshi Temple, Madurai, India.

David Reck

sa   ri   ga   ma   pa   da   ni   sa

Keeravani raga's scale—if one removes the intensive ornamentation—is similar to the Western harmonic minor scale. The composer/poet has cleverly worked the name of the *raga* into the song text in the last line of the *charanam.*

The *tala* is *Adi tala,* the most common of the South-Indian time cycles. It has eight beats subdivided 4 + 2 + 2, and is counted in the following way:

Adi tala: 4 + 2 + 2 = 8 beats

  1   2   3   4   /5   6   /7   8 //

Clap ⌣ Clap   Clap

  Finger Count*   Wave   Wave

*2nd beat = little finger and thumb.
 3rd beat = ring finger and thumb.
 4th beat = middle finger and thumb.

Hand claps articulate the accents of the *tala* with the strongest accent on the first beat, and weaker accents on beat 5 and beat 7.

Karnataka Sangeeta, the Classical Music of South India

The classical music of South India is called *karnataka sangeeta,** or in English simply Carnatic music. It is named after the Carnatic plateau, which dominates the middle of the inland south. The roots of this music lie in the distant past, in the courts and palaces of rajas and maharajas, in the great kingdoms of the Cholas, the Cheras, and the Pallavas, and in the stately temple complexes built between the twelfth and seventeenth centuries—such as those at Madurai, Chidambaram, Rameswaram, and Tanjore—which are among the wonders of world architecture (see Figure 6-6).

Carnatic music shares many of its early theoretical sources with the north. The *Natya Sastra* by Bharata, an extensive and detailed treatise on theater, dance, and music dates from between the second century B.C.E. and the fifth century C.E. Through the centuries many more important scholarly books on music have been written in Sanskrit and regional languages, perhaps the most noteworthy being the medieval *Sangeeta Ratnakara* (c. 1210–1247) by the scholar, Sarangadeva.

Sculpture in the ancient temples and palaces as well as murals and miniature paintings give us vivid visual images of the instruments, orchestras, dance styles, and the where and how of musical performance through several thousand years. Although the stone and paper images are silent, they bear a striking resemblance to what is seen in performance today. In

Karnataka sangeeta is pronounced kawr-*naw*-tuh-kuh sawn-gee-tuh ("gee" with a hard "g" as in "get"); Carnatic is pronounced kawr-*naw*-tik.

addition, many written descriptions of musical performance appear in the epics, the *Mahabharata* and *Ramayana*, as well as in stories and religious and mythological works. But the actual sound and practice of India's classical music traditions in the past has been lost, that is, up to the twentieth century, before the advent of sound recording, movies, and television.

Any oral tradition, such as that of Indian classical music, lives primarily in the hands, voices, memory, and creative imagination of individual human beings. In this tradition, the music can never be frozen in time, either by being written down (in words or notation) or by being preserved as a visual entity (as can a painting or photograph). The music, in a sense, lives uniquely in each performance, in the unique rendition of a song on a particular day, at a particular hour, and in the ephemeral spontaneity and creativity of improvisation. Today videos and CDs can preserve a particular performance, but whether this fixity, this documentation, will change the essentially oral nature of Indian music and the liquid way musicians approach their tradition remains to be seen.

From around the thirteenth century, scholars began to notice a difference between the classical Hindusthani style of the north and the Carnatic style of the south. Both use the idea of the *raga* (melodic mode) and *tala* (metric cycle), but the specifics of the *ragas* and *talas* vary. In general the northern style and its instruments—such as the *sitar* and *tabla*—have been more greatly influenced by Persian and other elements of pan-Islamic culture. In Hindusthani music expansive improvisations move gradually (over an hour or more) from near immobility to sections of great speed and virtuosity. In contrast, the Carnatic music of the more conservative Hindu south is built around an immense repertoire of precomposed devotional songs. The musical texture in the south is more busy and active, notes are incessantly ornamented, and improvisations fall within fixed sections.

Carnatic music began to stabilize in the sixteenth century with Purandara Dasa (1484–1564), who composed both songs and the basic exercises still used by students today. In the "golden age" of the late eighteenth and nineteenth centuries, composers created thousands of exquisite songs, and the performance style common today began to stabilize. Three great saint-composer-poets dominate this period: Syama Sastry (1762–1827), Tyagaraja (1767–1847), and Muttusvamy Dikshitar (1776–1836).

Figure 6-7

Three great saint-composers as seen in contemporary prints (left to right): Muttusvamy Dikshitar, Tyagaraja, and Syama Sastry.

A clever proverb describes the music of each. Dikshitar's songs are like a coconut: The "hard shell" of his intellectual structures and scholarly words must be broken to get to the sweetness inside. Sastry's music is like a banana: The fruit is not so difficult to get to, but one must still peel off the bitter "skin" of difficult rhythm before enjoying the flavor. But Tyagaraja's songs are like grapes or mangoes: The "sweet fruit" of both poetry and music are immediately accessible. It is no wonder, then, that Tyagaraja's songs dominate the repertoire, cherished by musicians and audiences alike.

The Sound World

India's classical music is marked by strong and unmistakable characteristics, an environment of sound that—like the spices of curries or the brilliantly colored silk saris worn by South-Asian women—signals at once which place on the planet this music is from. Let us imagine attending a performance of this music. First, we notice the incessant, unchanging sound of a drone of several pitches, often with a nasal buzz created acoustically through the generation of a rich mixture of overtones. Against this unchanging background a single melody, perhaps echoed by another voice or instrument, begins to develop. The melody differs greatly from those of Western classical or popular music: Its lines tend to be sinuous, complex, asymmetrical, and marked by subtle bends and slides and intense ornamentation. The notes of its scale may also zigzag through intervals unfamiliar to Western ears, in tones flatter or sharper than those of the piano keyboard. A "note"—called a *svara*—in Carnatic music is quite different from the fixed, stable note in Western music. A *svara* can be a tiny constellation of ornamented pitches. Further, movement from one *svara* to the next may be in a sliding, gliding movement rather than in the stepwise movement between Western notes (see Figure 6-8).

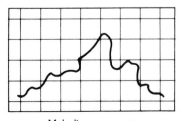

A "note" in Indian music

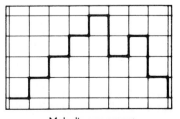

A note on the piano

Figure 6-8
Notes and melodic movement in Indian music, compared with piano.

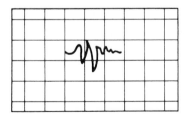

Melodic movement
in Indian music

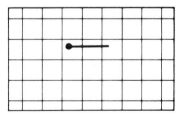

Melodic movement
on the piano

We then notice that improvisation plays a key role in performance in Indian music. The musician is inventing music on the spot, although certain key phrases recur again and again.

An interesting timbre or tone color strikes us. This sound world distinctly prefers nasal timbre, whether in the human voice or in musical instruments (CD 3, Track 1). Even adopted European instruments such as the clarinet or violin are played in a manner to increase their "nasalness."

Music paper or notation is nowhere to be seen: The performers are clearly working by ear in an oral tradition. There is no conductor, but each performer has a comfortable and well-defined role to play.

When the drum comes in, we are immediately struck by the energy and complexity of the drummer's rhythms, played with the fingers and hands. The drum is carefully tuned to the tonal center heard on the drone. We can sense a strong beat, but the metrical units seem to be much longer and more complicated than those of the $\frac{2}{4}$, $\frac{3}{4}$, and $\frac{4}{4}$ units that dominate Western musical thought.

As the performance progresses—each segment may go on for twenty minutes or even an hour—careful listening might reveal the presence of a song with its recurring phrases, themes, and variations, and if the melodic soloist is a singer we can hear syllables of a song text interspersed in the melody. Those of us who understand Indian languages (or have a helpful aficionado sitting nearby to explain), will soon learn that the song texts are usually religious—devotional or philosophical—though beautiful love lyrics also are found.

In the hands of the drummer rhythmic improvisation utilizing complex patterns and strokes also seems to play a role, as well as remarkable interplay between the percussionist and the melodic soloist. Once in a concert there will be a drum solo with rhythms so complicated that we find it hard at times to hear the cycles, or even the beat, until everything comes together at the end.

Concerts usually begin between 5:30 to 6:30 in the evening except at music festival time in December through January, when they take place almost continuously from around 8:30 in the morning until as late as midnight. Programs are sponsored by *sabhas,* cultural clubs that bring to their members and the general public music, dance, plays, lectures, and even an occasional movie. The large and prestigious *sabhas* have their own buildings, often large shedlike structures with overhead fans and open sides to catch the evening breeze. Other *sabhas* may use an auditorium, lecture hall, or temple. The audience may sit in rattan chairs or, more traditionally, on large striped rugs or mats spread on the floor. The musicians sit on a raised platform or stage, and they are sure to have cronies or fellow musicians sitting in close proximity in front to offer reactions and encouragement through stylized motions like head wobbling or a throwing out of the hands palm upward, enthusiastic verbal comments, or tongue-clicking (which means not "Oh, oh!" as in U.S. culture but "Wonderful! Marvelous! Fantastic!").

A Carnatic music concert is built on a series of segments, each based on a song. Many of the songs will be preceded or followed by some of the forms of improvisation described later.

Figure 6-9
A vocal music ensemble. The singer is B. Rajam Iyer; the violinist is M. S. Gopalakrishnan. The string *tambura* provides a drone, as does a *sruti*-box, which is partially obscured behind the singer. M. A. Easwaran plays the *mridangam.*

Concerts are relaxed and informal compared with classical music concerts in the West. Members of the audience may count time with their hands, periodically exchange comments with friends, or occasionally get up in the middle of a concert to buy snacks or a soft drink at the refreshment stand. Usually there are no printed programs. Mature musicians may not even fully plan their program in advance, and a knowledgeable audience is familiar with the repertoire of songs, *ragas* (melodic modes), and *talas* (time cycles). A concert today lasts between two and three hours without an intermission, although in the recent past concerts could go on for three and a half hours or longer.

The Ensemble: Musical Texture

Most concerts feature a vocalist (or vocal duet), and the singer(s) may be accompanied by another singer (usually a disciple), a violin, and the *mridangam* drum—sometimes with one or more percussionists playing the *ghatam* (large clay pot), the *kanjira* (Indian tambourine), or (rarely today) the *morsang* (Jew's harp). Solo instrumental or duet concerts might feature the violin, adapted from Europe but played in an Indian fashion, the *venu* (bamboo flute), the plucked stringed *veena,* or other instruments adapted from the West such as the saxophone, electric guitar, or mandolin. The background drone is provided by the four-stringed *tambura* or the small reed organ *sruti petti* ("*sruti*-box"); both these drone instruments have battery operated electronic equivalents today that are easy to tune and carry around. The double-reed *nagasvaram* with its usual accompanying drum, the *tavil,* also appears frequently in concerts (see Figure 6-2).

Before we go further, a note on women and music is in order. Women have always played an important role in Indian music. Two of the greatest saint/composers—the medieval Rajasthani princess Mirabai and in the

drone cycles thru all 4 strings over & over

south, Andal—were women. In the contemporary scene many of the most prominent musicians are women, particularly as singers but also on instruments such as the violin, *veena,* and flute. On the other hand, women do not generally play single- or double-reed instruments such as the *nagasvaram* or the clarinet, nor do they commonly play percussion instruments.

We saw earlier that in a concert each musician and instrument has a role to play. These roles, which create the musical texture, might be described as functional layers: the background drone, the melody, and the rhythm/percussion.

Figure 6-10
Layers of the musical texture with added instruments.

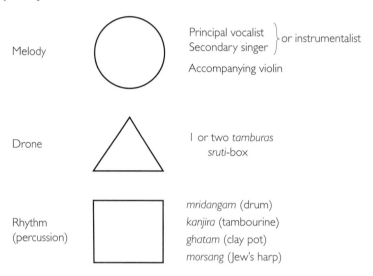

Within each layer there may be one or more musicians. The principle melodic soloist dominates the ensemble. (In a duet there would be two "principles.") A backup musician may support the principle melodic soloist: A vocalist, for example, might be supported by a student who would sing along on the songs.

The next important role is the melodic accompanist. In South India today this is usually a violinist, partly because the violin is always used to accompany a vocalist. The melodic accompanist plays three important roles: He or she must (1) play along on all the songs (following the notes of the soloist instantaneously); (2) echo and support the soloist's improvised phrases in the *alapana* (which frequently precedes the song), adding a short *alapana* of his or her own; and (3) alternate with the soloist in the *kalpana svara* improvisations, which bring the performance to a climax. In certain situations and ensembles with an instrumental melodic soloist, a second instrument of the same type might provide the melodic accompaniment: a second *nagasvaram* behind the solo *nagasvaram,* a second *veena* behind the *veena* soloist, and so on.

The drone, or *sruti,* layer usually includes one or more specialized instruments. The *tambura* is a four-stringed plucked instrument tuned to the tonal center and fifth. Its buzzing timbre is created by inserting a small length of thread under each playing string on the flat but slightly rounded top of the bridge. By placing the thread at exactly the right node a rich blend of overtones is picked up on each string—it is this sound which is perhaps the most recognizable "Indian" sound of all. The tuned reed *sruti*-box can also be used. Played with a bellows, it gives a continuous reed-organ-like sound. Today both the *tambura* and the *sruti*-box have electronic counterparts: small synthesizers that can duplicate the sound of either instrument. Plugged in or running on batteries, they can be tuned to any pitch; unlike their counterparts, they eliminate the need for an additional musician to play them.

Finally, there is the bedrock of the ensemble, the percussion. The double-headed barrel-shaped *mridangam* drum is the principle accompanying percussion instrument in Carnatic music. Tuned to the tonal center of the melodic soloist and played with the palms and fingers of both hands, it is capable of producing up to fifteen distinct sounds on its multilayered drumheads. It is often the only accompanying rhythm instrument. When other percussion instruments are added in this functioning layer, their players must follow the signals of the *mridangam* player regarding when to play together or singly, or when to sit out. The other percussion instruments used in classical music performance (listed in the order of importance and frequency of use) are the *ghatam,* a large clay pot with a ringing, metallic sound; the *kanjira,* a tambourine with a snakeskin head and jangles made of coins; and the *morsang,* a Jew's harp that plays the same rhythms as the other percussion instruments.

In our performance (CD 3, Track 1) note that there are only two performers. Ranganayaki Rajagopalan plays the *veena* (the melodic layer and the drone) and Raja Rao plays the *mridangam* (the rhythmic layer). An electronic *sruti*-box plugged into the wall supplies a drone background.

Now that we have looked at the makeup of a South-Indian ensemble, we shall explore two concepts that are central to an understanding of India's classical music. These are *raga,* the melodic system, and *tala,* the time cycles and the rhythmic system. (*Raga* and *tala* are pronounced *raw*-guh and *taw*-luh.)

Raga: The Melodic System

The ancient texts define a *raga* as "that which colors the mind." In fact, in Sanskrit the primary meaning of the word is "coloring, dying, tingeing." This connection with generating feelings and emotions in human beings—with "coloring" the mind and the heart—is important because a *raga* really has no equivalent in the West. It is a kind of mystical expressive entity with a musical personality all its own. This "musical personality" is, in part, technical—a collection of notes, a scale, intonation, ornaments, resting or pillar tones, and so on. Most of all it includes a portfolio of characteristic musical gestures and phrases—bits and pieces of melody—that give it a distinct and recognizable identity. Each *raga* has its rules about the way a musician may move from one note to another and about *gamakas*—particular ways of ornamenting certain notes with slides and oscillations—but these are by no means fixed. Although some of the facts about a particular *raga* and how it is to be played or sung can be verbalized or written down, the concept of *gamaka* is too much a part of the oral tradition and therefore too elusive to be understood only in terms of facts. One gets to know a *raga* gradually by hearing master musicians play it and by performing it oneself over many months and years. It is said that getting to know a *raga* is like getting to know a close friend: One learns to recognize the face, the expressions, the way of walking, tone of voice, clothes style, and eventually the inner personality with all its quirks and delights.

Traditional texts associate particular *ragas* with certain human emotions (ranging from sorrow to love), colors, animals, deities, a season of the year, a time of day (late at night or early morning, for example), or with certain magical properties (causing rain, calming the mind, creating warmth, and so forth). Some *ragas* are said to be auspicious; others dark and complex and mysterious; and still others happy and simple. Although South-Indian musicians do not focus much with these associations, they are aware of the expressive force of *ragas* and their capability to touch deep emotions in the human heart.

Each *raga* is built from a complex combination of technical elements that combine to give it a musical personality. The notes of a *raga* move against the blank screen of the drone, the *sruti,* and that the pitches of a *raga,* even when highly ornamented, constantly move in flux—in dissonance and consonance—against this unchanging background of tonal center and perfect fifth.

Figure 6-11

A *raga* painting depicting Raga Vasanta (Spring). Here the God Krishna, renowned for his flute playing, and his female accompanists celebrate the joys of Spring.

In Carnatic music all *ragas* relate to a *melakarta,* a basic "parent" or "generative" scale. There are seven notes in each *melakarta* scale—*sa, ri, ga, ma, pa, da, ni.* In the following chart the Western note C, following Indian custom, has been arbitrarily chosen as being the tonal center *sa.* Note that in Carnatic music the principle musician may choose whatever note is comfortable for the tonal center. Shobha Vasudevan (CD 2, Track 21) sings at a tonal center of G, while Ranganayaki Rajagopalan (CD 3, Track 1) usually tunes her *veena* to E♭ or E.

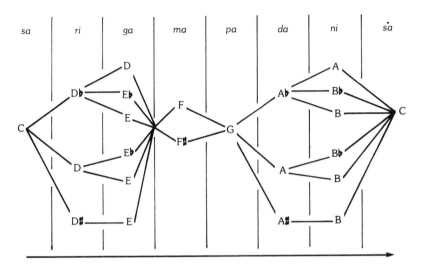

Figure 6-12
Melakarta system showing *raga* scales.

We can see (following the lines from left to right) that for the tonal center and the fifth (*sa* and *pa,* the notes of the drone) there is only one possibility. For the fourth (*ma*) there are two possibilities: the perfect fourth from the tonic (shown as F) and the raised fourth (shown as F♯).

Each of the other notes of the seven-note scale—the second (*ri*), the third (*ga*), the sixth (*da*), and the seventh (*ni*)—occurs in three varieties. When we follow the appropriate tracks for each, we find there are seventy-two tracks and therefore seventy-two basic parent scales in the system. These scales, if all the other elements that form a *raga* are added to them, are known as *melakarta ragas.*

But the system does not end here. Dozens of other *ragas* may derive from each *melakarta* in one or more of the following ways. (Notice that the notes in a *raga* may differ when the basic melodic movement ascends and when it descends.)

1. Omit one or more of the "parent's" notes in either ascent or descent or both (for example, making a scale pentatonic or with six tones).
2. Make the basic scale zigzag in ascent or descent, or both.
3. Add an occasional "visiting note," an "accidental," not in the "parent" *melakarta* scale.
4. Characterize a *raga* through flattening or sharpening tones, special *gamaka* ornamentation, or melodic phrases.

There are thus hundreds of *ragas* in common use—and potentially many more. Some *ragas* are popular, while others are rare; some are "major," others are "minor"; some are deep and complicated, others are "light." Some are old, but others are newly invented. Some have been in the Carnatic music tradition for centuries, while others have traveled down from North India. As one begins to listen seriously and in depth to Carnatic music on CDs or in concerts, one discovers that the seemingly infinite variety of *ragas* and the expressive use musicians make of them, shaping them into beautiful melodic compositions or spinning them out in improvisation, are the heart and soul of India's classical music.

Tala: The Time Cycle

Tala, the organization of time in music, is part of a conceptual spectrum in Indian thought that moves from a fraction of a second—as the ancient texts picturesquely put it: the time it takes a pin to puncture a lotus petal—to the great *yugas*, or "ages," each of which spans millions of years. The musician regards time initially as a beat, or regular pulse. On the microscopic level each beat may be divided and subdivided into faster units: 2s, 4s, 8s, 16s, and so on, but also into 3s, 5s, 7s, and 9s. On the larger level beats are grouped into regularly recurring metric cycles. These cycles are called *talas*. In theoretical texts there are hundreds of *talas*, but in Carnatic music today only the following five *talas* are found in common practice:

Figure 6-13
Counting *talas*.

Adi tala (fast or slow tempo): 4 + 2 + 2 = 8 beats

```
    1  .  2  .  3  .  4  .  /5 .  6  .  /7 .  8  .  //
      (&)  (&)  (&)  (&)    (&)  (&)    (&)  (&)

  Clap  ─────────────────Clap        Clap
          Finger count        Wave        Wave
```

Rupaka tala: 1 + 2 = 3 beats

```
    1   /2   3   //
  Clap Clap
           Wave
```

(Khanda) Chapu Tala: 2 + 3 = 5 beats

```
    1   2   /3   4   5   //
  Clap  *  Clap Clap  *
  *space (i.e., nothing)
```

Misra Chapu tala: 3 + 2 + 2 = 7 beats

```
    1   2   3   /4   5   /6   7   //
  Clap Clap  *  Clap  *  Clap  *
```

Triputa tala: 3 + 2 + 2 = 7 beats

 1   2   3   /4   5   /6   7   //

Clap ⌣ Clap   Clap

   Finger count* Wave   Wave

2nd beat = little finger and thumb.
3rd beat = ring finger and thumb.

The *tala* cycles obviously differ from the common time signatures in Western music in that the accents occur in uneven groupings (4 + 2 + 2, 3 + 2 + 2, 1 + 2, and so on). These groupings are marked by hand claps. In a concert performance of Carnatic music, the beginning of the counting of *tala* marks the beginning of a composition; it is also at this point at which the *mridangam* drum enters. (Only in the tradition of the *nagasvaram* does the drummer also play in nonmetrical sections.)

The Drummer's Art

In performance the *mridangam* player and other percussionists play in an improvisatory style based on hundreds of rhythmic patterns and drum strokes that they have learned, invented, absorbed, and stored in their brains and hands. In the heat and speed of performance the percussionist may use precomposed patterns, arranging them like a master of collage in predictable or unpredictable groupings. Or he may create entirely new patterns spontaneously, but within the limits and grammar of his rhythmic language.

The drummer's art centers on about fifteen drum strokes—distinctive individual tones produced on different parts of the drumhead by different finger combinations or parts of the hands. These strokes, individually and as part of rhythmic patterns, can be expressed in *sollukattus,* spoken syllables that duplicate both drum strokes and rhythmic patterns. Some patterns with *sollukattu* drawn from elementary lessons are given in Transcription 6-2.

The drummer's art is complex. At first he must accompany songs, the *kritis,* and other compositions of the Carnatic music tradition. He must know each song, picking up the flow and feeling, shaping his accompaniment to the internal rhythm of the song.

The drummer emerges from the background during long-held notes in the melody, or at cadences, marking endings with a formulaic threefold repetition called a *mora.* When the melodic soloist is improvising within the *tala* cycles, the alert drummer is quick to recognize and respond to patterns, to echo them, or to ornament them rhythmically. The South-Indian percussionist, however, does not merely "play off the top of his head." Through years of training, study and listening, his brain in a sense has been programmed with hundreds of rhythmic building blocks, formulas, and possibilities for larger combinations. He is also calculating constantly, like a master mathematician, how his formulas and patterns of asymmetrical lengths will fit into the *tala* cycles to come out right at the end.

But the drummer does much, much more than merely manipulate pieces of an invisible rhythmic jigsaw puzzle. He creates within a system. In the process he may compose variations, superimpose startling juxtapositions, flow from simple and easy timekeeping to mind-boggling com-

Transcription 6-2

Map of South Indian drummer's art.

LEVEL I:

Basic drumstrokes and sound on the *mridangam*—2 or 3 for the left hand, about 14 for the right hand and fingers.

ta - di - tom - nam - etc.

LEVEL 2:

Tiny cell-like rhythmic patterns, such as:

connected with various stroke arrangements:

ta - ki-ta	ta - ka - di - mi	ta - lan - gu
di - ki-ta	ki - ta - ta - ka	
tom - ki-ta	na - ka - tan - gu	
nam - ki-ta		
	etc.	

LEVEL 3:

Brief rhythmic patterns of several (or more) beats built from combinations of rhythmic cells, like:

na-ka-tan-gu   ki - ta - ta - ka

or:

din - ta-din - ta-ta-din - ta - ta-din - ta - ki -ta

LEVEL 4:

Longer strings of rhythmic pattern combinations, and *moras* (3-times-repeated ending formula) like:

di - tan - ki-ta   na-ka-tan-gu   ki-ta-ta-ka   tom- -

tan-gu   ki-ta-ta-ka   tom- -

tan-gu   ki-ta-ta-ka   tom-   **(x 3)**

(The above *mora* pattern repeated three times fits 25 beats, 3 cycles of *adi tala* (4 + 2 + 2 = 8 × 3) plus a resolution beat. If done right, the final "*tom*" should come on the downbeat of the next *tala*, i.e., on the 25th beat.)

plicated patterns, stop for meaningful pauses, and start again. He may work with the melodic soloist or work cleverly against him or her, always thinking, always calculating.

At one point in the concert after the main piece played by the soloist, the drummer—and his associates, if any—will play a *tani avartanam,* a rhythmic solo. For those interested in rhythm this is the high point of the concert.

Although we have only touched the surface of the drummer's art, we can begin to appreciate a system as complicated as any on earth, a counterbalance to the melodic beauties of the *raga* system. As an old Sanskrit verse says: *Sruti marta laya pita.* "Melody is the mother, rhythm is the father."

A Carnatic Music Performance

A concert in South India is marked by a string of compositions, each in a *raga* and *tala,* optionally extended by the forms of improvisation to be described shortly. Each section of a concert will thus have a composition, usually a *kriti* as its centerpiece. (An exception is the mostly improvised form called *ragam, tanam, pallavi,* which has a single line of melody as its centerpiece.) Listen to the performance on CD 3, Track 1, played on the multistringed plucked *veena* by Ranganayaki Rajagopalan accompanied by Raja Rao on the *mridangam.* The performance begins with two improvised sections—*alapana* and *tanam*—for *veena* alone. *Alapana* and *tanam* always precede a *kriti* and introduce the listener to the *raga,* the melodic mode, in which the *kriti* is set. The beginning of the *kriti* "Sarasiruha" in Natai *raga, Adi tala,* is marked by the entrance of the drum. A lively improvised *kalpana svara* section for *veena* with drum accompaniment follows, with a brief drum solo, the *tani avartanam,* at the end. Before examining the performance itself in greater detail, however, we must meet the musicians.

Figure 6-14
The performers of "Sarasiruha" (CD 3, Track 1), Raja Rao, *mridangan* (left) and Ranganayaki Rajagopalan, *veena.*

David Reck

Ranganayaki Rajagopalan, who is now about seventy years old, was in 1936 a very unruly child. Her parents had "loaned her out" to a childless uncle and his wife in the prosperous southern town of Karaikudi. The uncle was a friend of a great *veena* virtuoso, Karaikudi Sambasiva Iyer, who lived in the town supported by merchant patrons the rajas, the kings, of the south.

As the story goes, one day Ranganayaki's uncle appeared with his four-year-old niece at the great musician's house. As the elders were talking about music, to illustrate a point Sambasiva sang a tone. To his surprise the young girl, playing nearby, sang the same tone. Sambasiva sang another note. The child duplicated that note. Then he tapped a short rhythm with two rocks; without effort she duplicated the rhythm precisely. Recognizing the child's rare talent, the great musician took in the four-year-old Ranganayaki as a member of his household, into a traditional musical apprenticeship known as the *gurukula* system.

The discipline was extremely rigorous, with lessons beginning at 6:00 in the morning and continuing throughout each day, as the master teacher taught her and the other youngsters living in his household. Mistakes or laziness were met with strokes from a bamboo rod, but effort and accomplishments were rewarded with kind words. Rajagopalan describes her life during that period as "not a normal childhood. I had no friends or anything. It was *asura sadhakam* (devil's practice)" (Personal communication, 2000). But her musical genius gradually developed. By age twelve she was regularly accompanying her *guru* on the concert stage and giving solo recitals as well. The close relationship continued after her marriage at the age of fifteen and until her *guru*'s death in 1958.

Over the years Rajagopalan has enjoyed a distinguished career. Reviews have characterized her as "a musician's musician," one who is "dedicated to her tradition and unmoved by playing to the crowd," and "one of the great veena virtuosi of the twentieth century." With her phenomenal memory she is considered to be a rare repository of the compositions of her tradition, while her skills at improvisation "reflect a creative genius rarely heard today." She has toured Europe and the United States twice. She is regularly featured in National Broadcasts of All India Radio. In 2000 she received the National Award for Music from the Sangeet Natak Akademi, presented by the president of India. Speaking of the tradition of which she is the greatest living exponent, she says: "Words cannot describe it. One can only feel it while listening to it. It is just like *saying* that sugar is sweet. You can only really understand the sweetness by tasting it" (Personal communication, 2000).

Srimushnam V. Raja Rao is one of the great contemporary performers on the *mridangam.* Also known as "a musician's musician," he has accompanied many of the leading singers and instrumentalists of Carnatic music both in India and abroad. He particularly takes pride in his ability to accompany the soft tones of the *veena* with a light but precise touch of fingers and hands on the drumheads. He accompanied Rajagopalan on her first European tour.

Rajagopalan's instrument, the *veena*, has three drone strings and four playing strings. The chromatically placed brass frets are set in black wax, which is scalloped to allow room for the fingers to bend the strings in ornamentation. A set of complex fingerings, slides, and pulled multipitched ornaments (*gamakas*) enable the musician to interpret the character of each *raga* and its subtle intonation.

Rao's instrument, the *mridangam,* has a barrel-shaped body carved from jackwood. Both of its heads are made from multiple layers of leather, the outer layers cut with a circular hole in the middle. The lower (untuned) left-hand head has a blob of damp wheat paste applied to its center to give it a booming sound. The center of the right-hand head (which is tuned) has a hard metallic black spot made of many polished layers of rice paste and other ingredients. The use of the fingers as miniature drumsticks allows the drummer to play passages of incredible speed and virtuosity.

We shall now look at the five sections of "Sarasiruha." Timings corresponding to the CD selection appear in the margin at the start of each discussion, as follows.

CD 3/1

"Sarasiruha" (22:32). *Kriti* in Natai *raga, Adi tala,* by Pulaiyur Doraismy Ayyar. Performed by Ranganayaki Rajagopalan, *veena*; Raja Rao, *mridangam.* Recorded for author by recording engineer Rahul K. Raveendran. Chennai, India, 2001.

Alapana

0:00–3:15

The first section of the performance (CD 3, Track 1) is an *alapana,* a free-flowing exposition and exploration of the *raga,* its facets and phrases, its *gamaka* ornamentation, its pushes and pulls of intonation, as well as its mood and character. An *alapana* is nonmetrical, that is, it has no regular beat or recurring *tala* cycles. Instead, its phrases evolve in flowing proselike "breath rhythms," phrases that eventually come to rest on important pillar tones, or resting notes.

An *alapana* has a general plan set both by the tradition as a whole and by the improvisational habits of the musician. In general, the phrases of an *alapana* begin slowly and gradually increase in speed and complexity as they move higher and higher in the range of the voice or instrument. After a peak there is a descent back to the lower register with an ending on the tonal center *(sa).* The voice or melodic instruments perform *alapanas* against the drone background.

The *raga* of the *alapana* is derived from that of the *kriti,* the composition, which it precedes. In our performance the *raga* is *Natai,* an ancient and powerful *raga* associated with the great god Shiva in the form of Nataraja ("the Lord of Dance"). The dance of Shiva is said to shake the universe with its power and fury. The basic scale of Natai is as follows:

Transcription 6-3
Scale, *Natai raga.*

The most noteworthy characteristic of this *raga* is the shake or oscillation on the second note of the scale, *ri* (D♯ in our notation) as it descends downward to the tonal center *(sa)*. This note and its proximity to *ga* (E in our notation) gives it a sound startlingly similar to the major/minor third found in the African-American tradition of blues. If you listen carefully or hum along with the performance, eventually you will begin to recognize the series of musical phrases and gestures that give *Natai raga* its character, its "musical personality."

Tanam

3:20–8:15

Tanam is a highly rhythmic exposition of the *raga*. It is usually played or sung only once in a concert and takes place after the *alapana* and before the *kriti*. On the *veena* the musician plucks the playing and drone strings in asymmetrical improvised patterns while simultaneously working through the various notes and phrases of the *raga*. Although there are no *tala* cycles (or drum) in *tanam,* there is a strong sense of beat—but the illusory "beats" constantly change and shift. Just as in *alapana* the overall shape of a *tanam* follows the range of the instrument (or voice) from low to high in graduated steps and back down again. The Karaikudi school is famous for its *tanam*, especially when played in a *raga malika* ("garland of *ragas*") in the *panca ghana ragas* ("the five rocklike *ragas*"). *Natai raga* is the first of the *ragas* played in this set.

Kriti "Sarasiruha"

8:25–15:45

All compositions in Carnatic music are songs, melodies with words. In performance one or more musicians sing and/or play the songs against a drone with an improvised rhythmic accompaniment by the percussionist(s). The composer of a song is usually also a poet who writes his or her own lyrics (though the poetry may be in free verse). Although the song text sometimes centers on love, it usually focuses on religious themes. The thousands of songs of the tradition have been passed down from generation to generation like jewels on a string. Because they are not precisely notated but, rather, taught and learned orally, songs do not have definitive versions. As a song is passed down from *guru* to disciple on its journey in time from the composer to the present, many variant versions appear. Yet the composition remains recognizably itself—the main turns of phrase and the song text remain despite the variations in detail.

The *kriti* (composition) is the major song form of Carnatic music performance. (The word *kriti* is linguistically related to the same pre-Greek root as the English word *creation*.) Almost every major composer in the tradition has written in this form. A brief *kriti* might be as short as five or six minutes; a long *kriti* in slow tempo could last for fifteen minutes or more. The *kriti* is amazingly flexible in its structure. Although it generally comprises the three sections described earlier —the *pallavi, anupallavi,* and *charanam*—it may be contracted or expanded in an almost infinite number of ways. The most common way a composer can expand a *kriti* is to create a series of *sangatis* (variations) on one or more of its phrases. As they spin out over repetitions

Figure 6-15
Saraswati, Goddess of Music.
Drawing by Navarana.

of the initial phrase's song text, the *sangatis* grow increasingly complex and virtuosic. Many of the phrases in "Sarasiruha" have *sangatis*.

"Sarasiruha" is a *kriti* by the nineteenth-century composer Pulaiyur Doraismy Ayyar. It is addressed to the goddess of music and learning, Saraswati (see Figure 6-15). A free translation of its text follows:

Text, "Sarasiruha"

(Pallavi:)   O Mother who loves the lotus seat,
Ever delighting in the music of *veena*,
Ever joyful, and ever merciful to me.

(Anupallavi:)   Save me who have taken refuge in you!
O You with feet as tender as sprouts,
You charm the hearts of poets.
You dwell in the lotus.
You of the jeweled bracelets.

(Charanam:)   Lotus-eyed Mother who is gracious to the lowly who seek
your mercy,
Mother with a face as lovely as the autumn moon,
Pure Lady! O Saraswati, chaste, ever fond of learning.
Lady with breasts like ceremonial vessels,
Complete Being, who holds a book in her hand which bestows
all dominion.

_____

Free translation by Indira Peterson.

Although the words of the song are not audible in an instrumental performance, the musicians and knowledgeable members of the audience know the song text well. The importance of this knowledge can be seen in the performance of "Sarasiruha": At the place in the *charanam* where the name of the goddess Saraswati appears in the song text (14:33–15:10), the musical phrase is repeated over and over again, as if an invocation, before Ranganayaki moves forward to the completion of the *kriti*.

Kalpana Svaras

15:46–18:05

Kalpana literally means "imagined," and *svaras* are the "notes" of the scale of the *raga* being performed. *Kalpana svaras,* the section of improvised "imagined notes," occurs as an improvised "interruption" either in the latter part of the *kriti* rendition or after the *kriti* has been completed. Identifying this section in a vocal performance is easy, because the performer sings the names of the notes of the *raga* scale—*sa, ri, ga, ma, pa, da, ni*—instead of a verbal song text. In an instrumental performance, the musicians articulate or pluck each note.

The *kalpana svaras* always returns to a phrase from the *kriti,* a familiar island in a sea of improvisation. This phrase, its beginning note, and the place where it begins in the *tala* cycle are important, because ultimately each turn of the *kalpana svaras* will lead back to it. Indeed it is called the *idam,* the "place." In Ranganayaki's performance the *idam* is the opening phrase of the *kriti*:

Transcription 6-4

Idam of *Kalpana svaras* in the performance of "Sarasiruha." This is the first phrase of the *kriti*. The song text is not heard in instrumental performances.

At first the improvised *svaras* will be short, perhaps only filling the last part of one *tala* cycle before returning to the phrase of the *idam.* As time goes on the *svara* improvisations will grow in length and complexity, extending through more and more cycles of the *tala* as the performer's imagination runs free. A final extended improvisation will bring the *kalpana svara* section to a climax before its return to the *idam* and the song.

The Drum Solo: Tani Avartanam

18:06–22:20

After what is called the "main item"—either the *kriti* with the most extended improvisations or the form called *ragam-tanam-pallavi*—the *mridangam* player (and other percussionists, if any) come to the foreground with an extended solo. In a full concert this solo will extend for ten to fifteen minutes or more. In our performance, Raja Rao's solo is concise. As noted earlier, the drum solo gives the percussionist the chance to display the full range of his skills and rhythmic imagination. In each section of the solo the drummer will explore a certain range of patterns and architectural ideas. Finally the solo will end on an extended *korvai,* a cadential pattern repeated three times. This pattern leads back to an entrance of the *idam* from the *kriti* by the melodic soloist and the conclusion of the performance.

One form of improvisation not used in our performance, *niraval,* is a set of improvisations based on a phrase from the *kriti* and its song text. Always preceding the *kalpana svara* section, this form of improvisation is particularly beautiful in a vocal concert, as the repeating words of a phrase of the song are covered in an expanding web of melismatic notes and ornamental phrases.

On another occasion, at another performance, the musician might decide—using the same *kriti* as a centerpiece—to shape the performance in a different way. The *kriti* might be performed alone, for example, after a perfunctory *alapana* of a few phrases. Or the *tanam* and drum solo might be omitted. While the shape of the *kriti* will remain basically the same, the nature of the improvisations might vary as the musician draws on the procedures, ideas, and performance habits stored in his or her memory and on the interpretation of a particular *raga* on a particular day. This fluidity of performance sparked by the creative instincts of the South-Indian musician is one of the delights of the Carnatic music tradition.

As noted earlier, India's culture has long assimilated outside influences and made them its own. The presence of the violin, the saxophone, the guitar, and the mandolin in Carnatic music, and the all-inclusive nature of South-India's cine and pop music industry are obvious examples. As the globalization of music through television, movies, CDs, and cassettes continues, mutual influences between India and the West are bound to increase. For example, since the 1970s South-Indian musicians have seen the connections between jazz improvisation and India's classical music traditions. From that awareness the genre known as *fusian* was born, an interface between East and West that continues to excite a younger generation of musicians and listeners. The violinists L. Shankar and L. Subramanian have worked extensively with American and European jazz and rock musicians over the past twenty years, as has the extraordinary *tabla* player Zakir Hussain.

In the late twentieth and early twenty-first centuries an increasing number of South Asians have been working, studying, and living abroad. Cohesive communities of transplanted Indians, many trained in music, now appear in almost every major city or university town on earth. The children of first-generation immigrants often find themselves in a bicultural world where the "Indianness" of their home and family must be balanced

Indian Music and the West

against the pervasive dominance of the mainstream culture of their adopted country. Cultural clubs and temples support the study and presentation of concerts of classical Indian music and dance. Various Indo-pop styles, such as "bhangra" in Great Britain or "tassa-beat soca" in Trinidad, have also evolved. Here the drones, scales, and sometimes the instruments and languages of Indian music fuse with the beat and electric sound of mainstream rock and pop styles.

Indian music has infiltrated the West since the late 1950s. The *sitar* virtuoso Ravi Shankar was a seminal figure. Having spent years in Paris as a boy with the dance troupe of his brother, Uday Shankar, he has been able to move with ease in the elite worlds of Western classical and pop music. By the late 1960s his concerts with the master *tabla* virtuoso Alla Rakha at venues as varied as the Edinburgh Music Festival and the Monterey Pop Festival eventually gave him superstar status in Europe and the United States, as well as in India.

Over the years Shankar has released many collaborative recordings. These include the *West Meets East* dialogues with famous Western musicians—among them the classical violinist Yehudi Menuhin, the flute virtuoso Jean-Pierre Rampal, the jazz musician Paul Horn, and the minimalist composer Philip Glass. In the album *East Greets East* (1978) he performed with traditional Japanese musicians. His *Shankar Family and Friends,* an early 1970s recording made in San Francisco with several dozen Indian and Western musicians (including one listed enigmatically as "Harris Georgeson") includes some fascinating music.

In the mid-1960s Shankar acquired the most illustrious of his students, George Harrison of the Beatles. Harrison's interest in Indian classical music and religious philosophy resulted in a series of finely crafted Indian-based songs ranging from "Love Me Do" to "The Inner Light" (recorded in Bombay) and the post-Beatles "My Sweet Lord." Many of John Lennon's songs of the mid-sixties also had Indian influences, although, as in the beautiful song "Rain," the synthesis is often more opaque. In the musical texture of "Tomorrow Never Knows," Lennon included drones, exotic riffs, and Indian instruments floating in a complex hallucinogenic collage of backward tapes and sound effects (described by one critic as "a herd of elephants gone mad!"). All of this backs the otherworldly dream state of the lyrics themselves inspired by the *Tibetan Book of the Dead* as interpreted by the LSD guru Timothy Leary.

In "Love Me Do," from the Beatles 1966 album *Revolver,* the *sitar* begins with a brief introduction of the notes of a *raga*-like scale in unmeasured time—a hint of an *alapana.* A background drone of *tambura* and bass guitar continues throughout. The *tabla* drumbeat enters, establishing a driving metrical pulse of *tala*-like cycles. Harrison's vocal line is sung in flat tones and ends with a descending melisma of distinct Indian vocal sound. In the second section of the song the repetitive riffs alternating between *sitar* and voice reflect the "question and answer" interplay of Indian musicians in performance. Then there is an instrumental break with the *sitar* and *tabla* improvising first in cycles of seven beats, then in five, and finally in three, all of which leads to a final rendition of chorus and verse. A fast instrumental postlude corresponds to the ending climactic sections of a North-Indian performance. All of this in a three-minute song!

Indo-pop music has continued to flourish in Great Britain, where large immigrant communities from the former colonies continue to generate new genres and sounds. The singer and composer Sheila Chandra, born in 1965, has treated diverse influences from East and West with intelligence and sensitivity. A former child television star, in the 1980s she joined with Steve Coe and Martin Smith to form an innovative East/West fusion band, Monsoon. In her more recent work, such as the albums *Silk* (1991) and *Weaving My Ancestor's Voices* (1992), Chandra has focused on the unique qualities of her voice—often set against electronic and acoustic drones— and explored the synthesis of world vocal traditions from the British Isles, Spain, North Africa, and India.

As Indian classical and popular musicians continue to absorb the varied musics of the world around them, and as world musical traditions continue to be instantaneously accessible, perhaps the ancient traditions of classical Indian music north and south, Hindusthani and Carnatic, will continue to find echoes, reflections, interpretations, and responses in the music of the West.

References

The Beatles. 1966. *Revolver.* Parlophone CDP 7 464412. CD.

Chandra, Sheila. 1991. *Silk.* Shanachie 64035. CD.

———. 1992. *Weaving My Ancestor's Voices.* Caroline CAROL 2322-2. CD.

Shankar, Ravi. 1978. *East Greets East.* Deutsche Grammophon 2531-381.

———. n.d. *West Meets East* (with Yehudi Menuhin) I–III. Angel S-36418, S-36026, SQ-37200.

Additional Reading and Viewing

Basham, A. L. 1959. *The Wonder That Was India.* New York: Grove Press.

Brown, Robert E. 1971. "India's Music." In *Readings in Ethnomusicology,* edited by David P. McAllester, 192–329. New York: Johnson Reprint.

Edwardes, Michael. 1970. *A History of India.* New York: Universal Library.

Kumar, Kanthimathi, and Jean Stackhouse. 1988. *Classical Music of South India: Karnatic Tradition in Western Notation.* Stuyvesant, N.Y.: Pendragon Press. Beginning lessons and simple songs with free translations of song texts.

Lanmoy, Richard. 1971. *The Speaking Tree: A Study of Indian Culture and Society.* New York: Oxford Univ. Press.

Mohan, Anuradha. 1994. "Ilaiyaraja: Composer as Phenomenon in Tamil Film Culture." M.A. thesis, Wesleyan Univ.

Nelson, David. 1989. *Madras Music Videos.* Available from D. Nelson, 340 Westhampton Road, Northampton, MA 01060. Videotapes of concert performances of South-Indian music.

Reck, David. 1983. "A Musician's Toolkit: A Study of Five Performances by Thiru-gokarnam Ramachandra Iyer." Ph.D. diss., Wesleyan Univ.

———. 1985. "Beatles Orientalis: Influences from Asia in a Popular Song Tradi-tion." *Asian Music* 16(1): 83–149.

Sambamoorthy, P. 1963. *South Indian Music.* Book 4. Madras: Indian Music Publish-ing House.

———. 1964. *South Indian Music.* Book 3. Madras: Indian Music Publishing House.

Shankar, Ravi. 1968. *My Music, My Life.* New York: Simon & Schuster.

Wade, Bonnie. 1988. *Music of India: The Classical Traditions.* Riverdale, Md.: Riverdale.

Additional Listening

Annotated Web Site

The following Web site http://www.medieval.org/music/world/carnatic/cblsup.html has an annotated list of CDs, each with commentary, plus relevant information on South-Indian (Carnatic) music, composers, performers, and music styles. In particu-lar, you might want to look for the following CDs.

An Anthology of South Indian Classical Music. Ocora 5900001/2/3/4. 4 CDs.

Gopinath, Kadri. *A Tribute to Adolphe Sax.* Oriental 230/231. [saxophone]

Iyer, Semmangudi Srinivasa. *The Doyen of Carnatic Music.* Oriental 140. [vocal]

Jayaraman, Lalgudi J. *Violin Virtuoso: Lalgudi J. Jayaraman.* Oriental AAMS-125.

Krishnan, T. N. *The Vibrant Violin of "Sangita Kalanidhi."* Oriental 140.

Mahalingam, T. R. ("Mali"). *Divine Sounds of the Bamboo Flute.* Oriental 183/184. 2 CDs.

Moulana, Sheik Chinna. *Nadhasvaram.* Wergo SM-1507. [nagasvaram]

Music for Bharata Natyam. Oriental 176. [South-Indian dance music]

Narayanaswamy, K. V. *Guru Padam.* Koel 063. [vocal]

Padmanabhan, Rajeswari. *Surabi.* SonicSoul Acoustics. [veena; no number; released in 1998].

Ramani, N. *Lotus Signatures.* MOW CDT-141. [flute]

Ranganayaki Rajagopalan. Makar 029. [veena]

Sankaran, Trichy. The Language of Rhythm. MOW 150. [mridangam]

Subbulakshmi, M. S. *M. S. Subbulakshmi: Live at Carnegie Hall.* EMI India 147808/809. 2 CDs. [vocal]

——— . *M. S. Subbulakshmi: Radio Recitals.* EMI India CDNF 147764/65. 2 CDs. [vocal]

Viswanathan, T. *Classical Flute of South India.* JVC VIGG-5453.

Other Recordings

Ilaiyaraja. n.d. *How to Name It.* Oriental Records ORI/AAMS CD-115. CD.

McLaughlin, John. n.d. *Best of Mahavishnu.* Columbia PCT-36394.

———. n.d. *Shakti.* Columbia Jazz Contemporary Masters CK-46868. CD.

Shankar, Ravi. 1971. *Concerto for Sitar and Orchestra.* Angel SPD 36806.

———. n.d. *Ragamala: Concerto for Sitar and Orchestra No. 2.* Angel DS 37935.

Major Sources for Recordings

Music of the World (MOW label). P.O. Box 3620, Chapel Hill, N.C. 27515; (888) 264-6689; http://www.rootsworld.com/rw/motw/indexx2.html

Oriental Records. P.O. Box 387, Williston Park, N.Y. 11596; http://www.orientalrecords.com

Raag Music. Los Angeles, Calif.; (310) 479-5225; http://www.webcom.com/raag/ca-v-art.html

SonicSoul Acoustics. 15183 Dane Lane, Portland, Oreg. 97229; (503) 531-0270; kartha1@aol.com

CHAPTER

 7

Asia/Music of Indonesia

R. Anderson Sutton

Indonesia is a country of astounding cultural diversity, nowhere more evident than in the stunning variety of musical and related performing arts found throughout its several thousand populated islands. Known formerly as the Dutch East Indies, Indonesia is one of many modern nations whose boundaries were formed during the centuries of European colonial domination, placing peoples with contrasting languages, arts, systems of belief, and conceptions of the world under a single rule. The adoption of a national language in the early twentieth century was a crucial step in building the unity necessary to win a revolution against the Dutch (1945–1949). Today, a pan-Indonesian popular culture has been contributing to an increased sense of national unity, particularly among the younger generation. Nevertheless, recent strife between ethnic groups, which dominated international headlines about Indonesia at the turn of the millennium, has challenged this sense of unity. Indeed, though we can identify some general cultural traits, including musical ones, shared by many peoples of Indonesia, to speak of an "Indonesian" culture or style of music is problematic. Regional diversity is still very much in evidence.

Most Indonesians' first language is not the national language (Indonesian) but one of the more than two hundred separate languages found throughout this vast archipelago. Further, although many are familiar with the sounds of Indonesian pop music and such Western stars as Britney Spears and NSync, they also know their own regional musical traditions. In Indonesia many kinds of music exist side-by-side in a complex pluralism that reflects both the diversity of the native population and the receptiveness of that population to centuries of outside influences. Indonesia is, then, a country that truly is home to worlds of music.

What first impression might this country give you? You would probably arrive in the nation's capital, Jakarta, a teaming metropolis of more than nine million people—some very wealthy, most rather poor. Jakarta is near the western end of the north coast of Java, Indonesia's most heavily populated (but not largest) island. (See the map on the next page.) The mix of Indonesia's many cultures among themselves and with that of the West is

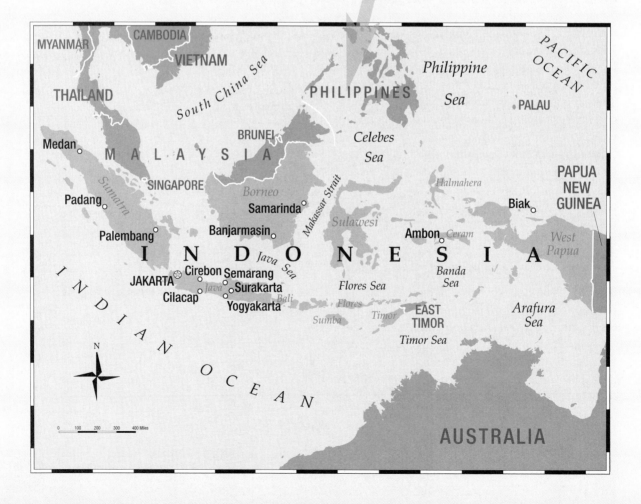

nowhere more fully realized than in this special city. Many kinds of music are heard here. Western-style nightclubs and discos do a lively business until the early hours of the morning. Javanese *gamelan* (percussion ensemble) music accompanies nightly performances of *wayang orang* theatre (an elaborate type of dance-drama from central Java). You might also run across Jakarta's own *gambang-kromong* (small percussion ensemble) and perhaps a troupe from Bali, Sumatra, or any of the many other islands performing at the national arts center Taman Ismael Marzuki or the Indonesian cultural park Taman Mini. As you begin to find your way around the city by taxi, bus, or three-wheeled *bajaj,* you may develop a taste for highly seasoned food. You will certainly get a sense of Indonesia's many cultures by roaming this complex city. Much of what you encounter, however, has a strong presence in the various regions in which it is rooted.

Java is an island about the size of New York State (just less than 50,000 square miles). With over 100 million people, Java is one of the most densely populated regions in the world. (Indonesia's total population is about 210 million.) Most of the central and eastern two thirds of the island is inhabited by Indonesia's largest ethnic group, the Javanese, roughly 75 million people who share a language and other cultural traits, including music, though some local differences persist. In the western third of the island live the Sundanese, whose language and arts are distinct from those of the Javanese. Despite its dense population, Java remains mostly a farming society, with wet-rice agriculture as the predominant source of livelihood. Although most Javanese profess to be Muslim, only a minority follow orthodox practice. Many adhere to a blend of Islam with Hinduism and Buddhism (introduced into Java over one thousand years ago) and with what most scholars believe to be an even earlier layer of belief in benevolent and mischievous spirits and in ancestor veneration. The worldview that embraces these many layers of belief is often referred to as *kejawèn*—literally, "Javanese," or "Javaneseness," a term that indicates its importance in Javanese self-conception. Since the mid-1980s, however, Javanese have increasingly embraced a less syncretic Islam.

Central Java

From Jakarta a twelve-hour ride on bus or train through shimmering wet-rice fields, set in the plains between gracefully sloping volcanic mountains, leads to Yogyakarta (often abbreviated to "Yogya" and pronounced "Jogja"). Yogya is one of two court cities in the cultural heartland of Central Java. The other, about forty miles to the northeast, is Surakarta (usually called "Solo"). Most Javanese point to these two cities as the cultural centers where traditional *gamelan* music and related performing arts have flourished in their most elaborate and refined forms. These courtly developments are contrasted with the rougher styles associated with the villages and outlying districts.

Yogya is a sprawling city with a population of about 450,000. It has several multistory malls and hotels but few other buildings taller than two stories. Away from the several major streets lined with stores flashing neon signs and blaring popular music, Yogya is in many ways like a dense collection of villages. Yet at its center is one of Java's two main royal courts, the official home of the tenth sultan (His Highness Hamengku Buwana X). Unlike any Western palace or court, this is a complex of small buildings and open pavilions appropriate for the tropical climate. It was not designed merely for comfort, however. Endowed with mystical significance as an earthly symbol of the macrocosmos (the ordered universe), the court is oriented to the cardinal directions. The ruler, whose residence is located at the very center of the court, is imbued with divine powers, as were the Hindu-Javanese kings many centuries ago.

In many of these pavilions are kept the court *gamelan* ensembles. Some date back many centuries and perform only for rare ritual occasions, while others have been built or augmented more recently and are used more frequently. Like other treasured heirlooms belonging to the court, most of these groups are believed to contain special powers and are shown respect and given offerings. Also kept in the palace are numerous sets of finely carved and painted *wayang kulit* (puppets made of water buffalo hide) used in all-night performances of highly sophisticated and entertaining shadow plays. Classical Javanese dance, with *gamelan* accompaniment, is rehearsed regularly and performed for special palace functions.

Though the court is still regarded as a cultural center, it is far less active now than it was prior to World War II (during which the Japanese occupied Indonesia). Much activity in the traditional Javanese arts takes place outside the court, sponsored by private individuals and by such modern institutions as the national radio station and public schools and colleges. In the rural villages, which long served as a source and inspiration for the more refined courtly arts, a variety of musical and related performing arts continue to play a vital role in Javanese life.

Gamelan

The word *gamelan* refers to a set of instruments unified by their tuning and often by their decorative carving and painting. Most *gamelans* consist of several kinds of metal slab instruments (similar in some ways to the Western vibraphone) and tuned knobbed gongs. The word *gong* is one of the few English words derived from Indonesian languages. (Two others are *ketchup* and *amok*.) In English, *gong* may refer to any variety of percussion instrument whose sound-producing vibrations are concentrated in the center of the instrument, rather than the edge, like a bell. In Javanese it refers specifically to the larger hanging knobbed gongs (see Figure 7-1) in *gamelan* ensembles and is part of a family of words relating to largeness, greatness, and grandeur—*agung* ("great," "kingly"), *ageng* ("large"), and *gunung* ("mountain"). In addition to gongs and other metal instruments, a *gamelan* ensemble normally has at least one drum and may have other kinds of instruments: winds, strings, and wooden percussion instruments (xylophones).

Some ancient ceremonial *gamelans* have only a few knobbed gongs and one or two drums. The kind of *gamelan* most often used in central Java

Arthur Durkee, EarthVisions Photographics

Figure 7-1
The *gamelan* Kyai Kanyut Mèsem ("Tempted to Smile") in the Mangkunegaran palace, Surakarta, Central Java. In foreground: *gong ageng* and *gong siyem*.

today is a large set, comprising instruments ranging from deep booming gongs three feet in diameter to high-pitched gong-chimes and slab instruments, with three drums, several bamboo flutes, zithers, xylophones, and a two-stringed fiddle.

Instruments in the present-day *gamelan* are tuned to one of two scale systems: *sléndro,* a five-tone system made up of nearly equidistant intervals, normally notated with the numerals 1, 2, 3, 5, and 6 (no 4); and *pélog,* a seven-tone system made up of large and small intervals, normally notated 1, 2, 3, 4, 5, 6, and 7. Some *gamelan* are entirely *sléndro,* others entirely *pélog,* but many are actually double ensembles, combining a full set of instruments for each system. A Western piano can replicate neither of these scale systems. Transcription 7-1 shows the Western major scale, consisting of "whole tone" and "half tone" intervals (that is, eight adjacent white keys on the piano, starting with C as "do"), in comparison with sample intervals for one instance of *sléndro* and one of *pélog* (these are not entirely standardized, as I shall explain below).

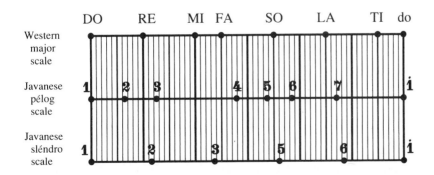

Transcription 7-1
Western scale and representative *pélog* and *sléndro* scales.

Based on measurements of *gamelan* Mardiswara (Surjodiningrat, Sudarjana, and Susanto 1972:51–53).

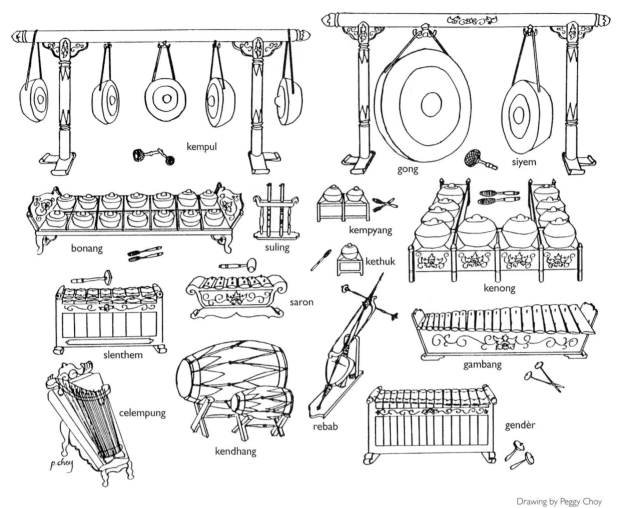

Figure 7-2
Central Javanese *gamelan* instruments.

Drawing by Peggy Choy

The instrumentation of a full *sléndro-pélog gamelan* varies slightly, but it usually includes all or most of the instruments given in the following list. Most of these are illustrated in Figure 7-2.

Knobbed Gong Instruments

gong ageng	Largest of the hanging gongs, suspended vertically from a wooden frame; one or two in each *gamelan;* often simply called *gong;* played with a round, padded beater
siyem	Middle-sized hanging gong; usually from one to four in each *gamelan*
kempul	Smallest hanging gong; from two to ten per gamelan; played with a round, padded beater
kenong	Largest of the kettle gongs, resting horizontally in a wooden frame; from two to twelve per *gamelan;* played with a padded stick beater

kethuk	Small kettle gong; one for each scale system; played with a padded stick beater
kempyang	Set of two small kettle gongs, for *pélog;* played with padded stick beater
bonang barung	Set of ten, twelve, or fourteen kettle gongs resting horizontally in two parallel rows in a wooden frame; one set for each scale system; often simply called *bonang;* played with two padded stick beaters
bonang panerus	Smaller member of the *bonang* family; same as *bonang barung* but tuned an octave higher; one for each scale system

Metal Keyed Instruments

saron demung	Largest member of the *saron* (single-octave metallophone) family; six or seven thick metal keys resting over a trough resonator; usually one or two for each scale system; often simply called *demung;* played with a wooden mallet
saron barung	Like *saron demung* but an octave higher; usually from two to four for each scale system; often simply called *saron*
saron peking	Like *saron barung* but an octave higher; often simply called *peking*
gendèr slenthem	Six or seven thin metal keys suspended by strings over cylindrical resonators made of bamboo or metal; one for each scale system; often simply called *slenthem;* played with a padded disc beater
gendèr barung	Thirteen or fourteen thin metal keys, suspended over cylindrical resonators; one for *sléndro,* two for *pélog bem* (with tones 1, 2, 3, 5, and 6 in each octave) and *barang* (with tones 2, 3, 5, 6, and 7 in each octave); often simply called *gendèr;* played with two padded disc beaters
gendèr panerus	Like *gendèr barung* but an octave higher

Other Melodic Instruments

gambang	Seventeen to twenty-three wooden keys resting over a trough resonator; one for *sléndro;* one or two for *pélog;* if two, like *gendèr barung* and *gendèr panerus;* if only one, exchange keys enable player to arrange instrument for *bem* (with scale 1, 2, 3, 5, and 6 in each octave) or for *barang* (with 2, 3, 5, 6, and 7); played with two padded disc beaters
celempung	Zither, usually supported at about a thirty-degree angle by four legs, with twenty to twenty-six strings arranged in ten to thirteen "double courses" (as on a

	twelve-string guitar); one for *sléndro,* one or two for *pélog* (cf. *gambang*); plucked with thumbnails
siter	Smaller zither, resting on floor or in horizontal frame, with from ten to twenty-six strings in single or double courses, one for *sléndro,* one or two for *pélog* (cf. *gambang* and *celempung*); plucked with thumbnails
suling	End-blown bamboo flute; one for *sléndro,* one or two for *pélog*
rebab	Two-stringed fiddle; one or two per *gamelan*

Drums

kendhang gendhing	Largest of the hand drums; two leather heads, laced onto a barrel-shaped shell; one per *gamelan*
kendhang ciblon	Middle-sized hand drum; like *kendhang gendhing;* often simply called *ciblon*
kendhang ketipung	Smallest hand drum; often simply called *ketipung*
bedhug	Large stick-beaten drum; two leather heads, tacked onto a cylindrical shell; one per *gamelan*

There is no standard arrangement of these instruments in the performance space except that they are almost always placed at right angles to one another, reflecting the Javanese concern with the cardinal directions (see Figure 7-3). Generally the larger gong instruments are in the back, with the *saron* family immediately in front of them, *bonang* family and *bedhug* drum to the sides, other melodic instruments in front, and *kendhang* drums in the center. The placement of the instruments reflects

Figure 7-3

Gamelan musicians in the Kraton Kasunanan (royal palace) in Surakarta, Central Java. In foreground: *bonang* (left), *slenthem* (right). Notice that the musicians sit at right angles to each other.

Arthur Durkee, EarthVisions Photographics

their relative loudness and their function in the performance of pieces, to be discussed shortly.

The *gamelan* instruments are normally complemented by singers: a small male chorus (*gérong*) and female soloists (*pesindhèn*). Java also supports a highly developed tradition of unaccompanied vocal music, which serves as a major vehicle for Javanese poetry. Although Javanese have recorded their sung poetry in several writing systems for over a thousand years, these are normally sung rather than read silently or aloud. Even important letters between members of the nobility were, until the twentieth century, composed as poetry and delivered as song. Although the postal system has eliminated this practice, vocal music, whether with *gamelan* or unaccompanied, enjoys great popularity in Java today.

The relation between vocal and instrumental orientations in *gamelan* music is reflected in the two major groupings of instruments in the present-day Javanese *gamelan:* "loud-playing" and "soft-playing." Historical evidence suggests that these two groupings were once separate ensembles and were combined as recently as the sixteenth or early seventeenth century. Associated with festivals, processions, and other noisy outdoor events, loud-playing ensembles were strictly instrumental. Soft-playing ensembles were intended for more intimate gatherings, often indoor, and involved singing. Even today performance style distinguishes these two groupings. In loud-playing style, only the drums and louder metal instruments are used (see left-hand column of list). In soft-playing style, these instruments, or most of them, are played softly, and the voices and instruments listed in the column on the right are featured.

"Loud-Playing" Instruments	"Soft-Playing" Instruments
gong ageng	*gendèr barung*
siyem	*gendèr panerus*
kempul	*gambang*
kenong	*celempung*
kethuk	*siter*
kempyang	*suling*
bonang family	*rebab*
saron family	
slenthem	
kendhang family	
bedhug	

Gamelan Construction

Bronze is the preferred metal for *gamelan* manufacture, owing both to its durability and to its rich, sweet sound quality. Brass and iron are also used, especially in rural areas. They are considerably cheaper than bronze and easier to tune but less sonorous. Bronze *gamelan* instruments are not cast; they are forged in a long and difficult process. Though the metal worker in many societies occupies a low status, in Java he has traditionally been held in high regard. Forging bronze instruments not only requires great skill but retains a mystical significance. Working with metals, transforming molten copper and tin (the metals that make bronze alloy) into sound-producing instruments, is believed to make one especially vulnerable to dangerous forces in the spirit world. For this reason the smiths make ritual preparation and may actually assume mythical identities during the forging process. The chief smith is ritually transformed into Panji, a powerful Javanese mythical hero, and the smith's assistants to Panji's family and servants (see Becker 1988; Kunst 1973:138).

The largest gongs may require a full month of labor and a truckload of coal for the forge that heats the metal. Only after appropriate meditation, prayer, fasting, and preparation of offerings does a smith undertake to make a large gong. The molten bronze is pounded, reheated, pounded, reheated, and gradually shaped into a large knobbed gong that may measure three feet or more in diameter. A false hit at any stage can crack the gong, and the process must begin all over.

Gamelan Identity

A *gamelan,* particularly a bronze set with one or two fine large gongs, is often held in great respect, given a proper name, and given offerings on Thursday evenings (the beginning of the Muslim holy day). Though *gamelan* makers have recently begun to duplicate precise tuning and decorative designs, each *gamelan* is usually a unique set, whose instruments would both look and sound out of place in another ensemble. Formerly it was forbidden even to attempt to copy the tuning and design of palace *gamelan* instruments, as these were reserved for the ruler and were directly associated with his power.

The variability in tuning from one *gamelan* to another is certainly not the result of a casual sense of pitch among Javanese musicians and *gamelan* makers. On the contrary, great care is taken in the making and in the occasional retuning of *gamelan* sets to arrive at a pleasing tuning—one that is seen to fit the particular physical condition of the instruments and the tastes of the individual owner. For example, I spent one month with a tuner, his two assistants, and an expert musician as they gradually reached consensus on an agreeable tuning, and then altered the tuning of the many bronze gong and metal slab instruments through a long process of hammering and filing—all by hand. Bronze has the curious property of changing tuning—rather markedly during the first few years after forging and more subtly over the next twenty to thirty years, until it is finally "settled." It might seem that the lack of a standard tuning would be cause for musical chaos, but the actual latitude is rather small.

Gamelan Performance Contexts

Despite the changes wrought by modern institutions in the contexts of music making and the ways music is understood, Javanese music is more closely interrelated with other performing arts and more intimately bound to other aspects of life than are the arts in the West. Concerts of *gamelan* music, with an audience sitting quietly and paying close attention to the music, have only recently appeared and serve mostly to present new, experimental works. In contrast, presentations of the more traditional *gamelan* music are best understood as social events that involve *gamelan* music. They usually commemorate a day of ritual importance, such as a birth, circumcision, or wedding. Normally a family sponsors such an event and invites neighbors and relatives, with others welcome to look on and listen (Figure 7-4). The invited guests are served food and are expected to socialize freely throughout the duration of the event. No one expects the guests to be quiet during the performance of pieces or to pay rapt attention to them the way an audience does at a Western concert. Rather, the music, carefully played though it may be, is seen to contribute to the festiveness of the larger social event, helping to make it *ramé* (lively, busy in a positive way). Connoisseurs among the guests will ask for a favorite piece and may pay close attention to the way the ensemble or a particular singer or instrumentalist performs, but not to the exclusion of friendly interaction with the hosts and other guests. Although the music is intended to entertain those present (without dance or drama), it also serves a ritual function, helping to maintain balance at important transitional points in the life of a person or community.

More often, *gamelan* music is performed as accompaniment for dance or theater—a refined female ensemble dance (*srimpi* or *bedhaya;* see Figures 7-5, 7-6), a flirtatious female solo dance, a vigorous, martial lance

Arthur Durkee, EarthVisions Photographics

Figure 7-4
Musicians playing the *gamelan* Kyai Kanyut Mèsem. Mangkunegaran palace, Surakarta, Central Java. In foreground: *Sarons, kempul,* and gongs on left; *saron peking* and *bonangs* on right.

Figure 7-5
Dancers at Pujokusuman in Yogyakarta perform a *srimpi*, female court dance.

Peggy Choy

dance, or an evening of drama based on Javanese legendary history, for example. A list of traditional genres currently performed in Central Java with *gamelan* accompaniment would be long. Some are presented primarily in commercial settings, with an audience buying tickets. Others most often involve a ceremony.

The genre held in the highest esteem by most Javanese, and nearly always reserved for ceremony, is the shadow puppet theatre (*wayang kulit*, see Figure 7-7), which dates back no fewer than 1,000 years. Beginning with an overture played on the *gamelan* during the early evening, shadow puppet performances normally last until dawn. With a screen stretched before him (almost all Javanese puppeteers are male), a lamp overhead, and puppets to both sides, one master puppeteer (*dhalang*) operates all the puppets, performs all the narration and dialogue, sings mood songs, and directs the musicians for about eight hours with no intermission.

Although the musicians do not play constantly throughout the evening, they must constantly remain ready to respond to a signal from the puppeteer. He leads the musicians and accents the action of the drama through a variety of percussion patterns he plays by hitting the wooden puppet chest to his left and the clanging metal plates suspended from the rim of the chest. If he is holding puppets in both hands, he uses his foot to sound these signals. He must be highly skilled as a manipulator, director, singer, and storyteller.

The puppeteer delivers not a fixed play written by a known playwright but rather his own rendition of a basic story—usually closely related to ver-

Figure 7-6
Dancers at the Pakualaman palace in Yogyakarta perform a *bedhaya*, female court dance, here with innovative costumes.

Arthur Durkee, EarthVisions Photographics

sions performed by other puppeteers, but never exactly the same. It might be a well-known episode from the *Ramayana* or *Mahabharata*, epics of Indian origin that have been adapted and transformed in many parts of Southeast Asia and have been known in Java for one thousand years.

During a shadow puppet performance, the *gamelan* plays music drawn from a large repertory of pieces, none specific to a single play and many of which are played in other contexts as well. A good musician knows many hundreds of pieces, but like the shadow plays, the pieces are generally not totally fixed. Many regional and individual variants exist for some pieces. More importantly, the very conception of what constitutes a "*gamelan* piece" or "*gamelan* composition" (in Javanese: *gendhing*) differs from the Western notion of musical pieces, particularly within the Western "classical" tradition.

Gamelan Music: A Javanese Gendhing in Performance

We can best begin to understand what a Javanese *gendhing* is by considering one in some detail—how it is conceived and how it is realized in performance. Listen to *Bubaran* "Kembang Pacar" (CD 3, Track 2). This is from a tape I made in a recording session in Yogya with some of the most highly regarded senior musicians associated with the court. It was played on a bronze *gamelan* at the house of one of Yogya's best known dancers and choreographers, R. M. Soedarsono, who founded the National Dance Academy (ASTI) in Yogya and recently retired from serving as Rector of the Indonesian Institute for the Arts (ISI). Note that it is an example of loud-playing style throughout, in the *pélog* scale system, with small and large

Javanese normally refer to *gendhing* by their formal structure, in this case *bubaran* (meaning sixteen beats per *gongan*, four *kenong* beats per *gongan*), the name of a particular melody, here, "Kembang Pacar" (a kind of red flower), the scale system (*pélog*), and the modal category (*pathet nem*).

CD 3/2

Bubaran "Kembang Pacar" ("Red Flower"), *pélog pathet nem* (3:04). Central Javanese *gamelan* music in loud-playing style, performed by musicians affiliated with the royal palace in Yogyakarta. Field recording by R. Anderson Sutton. Yogyakarta, Java, Indonesia, 1980.

intervals. It uses the tones 1, 2, 3, 5, and 6, with an occasional 4, but no 7. What about its structure? How does this piece—or, more precisely, this performance of this piece—organize the sounds it employs?

Unless they are connected directly to a previous piece in a medley sequence, Javanese *gendhing* begin with a solo introduction, played on one instrument or sung by a solo singer. Here a short introduction *(buka)* is played on the *bonang* by the well-known teacher and musician Pak Sastra-pustaka (1913–1991). During the latter portion, this *bonang* is joined by the two drums *kendhang gendhing* and *ketipung,* played (as is customary) by one drummer—in this case, the court musician Pak Kawindro. The drummer in a Javanese *gamelan* acts as a conductor, controlling the tempo and the dynamics (the relative levels of loudness and softness). He (or she) need not be visible to other musicians, since the "conducting" is accomplished purely through aural signals. The drummer does not stand in front of the ensemble but sits unobtrusively in the middle of it.

Although we discussed the choice of *Bubaran* "Kembang Pacar" at this recording session, experienced musicians recognize the identity of the *gendhing* from the introduction and do not need to be told what piece is about to be performed. The *bonang* player (or other musician providing an introduction) may simply play the introduction to an appropriate piece and expect the other musicians to follow. At the end of the introduction, most of the rest of the ensemble joins in, the large gong sounds, and the main body of the *gendhing* begins.

The structure of this main body is based on principles of balanced, binary (duple) subdivision and of cyclic repetition. The basic time and melodic unit in *gendhing* is the *gongan,* a phrase marked off by the sound of either the largest gong *(gong ageng)* or the slightly smaller gong *siyem.* For most *gendhing* these phrases are of regular length as measured in beats of the *balungan,* the melodic part usually played on the *slenthem* and the *saron* family—almost always some factor of two: 8 beats, 16 beats, 32 beats, 64 beats, 128 beats, 256 beats. (In the genre of pieces that serve as the staple for accompanying dramatic action, as we shall see later, *gongan* are of irregular length, and the regular unit is marked instead by the smaller *gong kempul.)* A *gongan* is subdivided into two or four shorter phrases by the *kenong,* and these are further subdivided by *kempul, kethuk,* and in some lengthier pieces *kempyang.*

These structural principles result in a pattern of interlocking percussion that repeats until an aural signal from the drummer or one of the lead melodic instruments (*bonang* in loud-playing style, *rebab* in soft-playing) directs the performers to end or to proceed to a different piece. Whereas in Western music composers must provide explicit directions for performers to repeat a section (usually by means of notated repeat signs), in Javanese *gamelan* performance repetition is assumed.

As we speak of "phrases" in describing music, borrowing the term from the realm of language, Javanese also liken the *gongan* to a sentence and conceive of the subdividing parts as "punctuation." For *Bubaran* "Kembang

Pacar," after the gong stroke at the end of the introduction, the pattern of gong punctuation shown in Transcription 7-2 is repeated throughout.

Transcription 7-2
Interlocking punctuation pattern.

```
                    .   .   .   .   .   .   .   .
t = kethuk          t w t N t P t N t P t N t P t N
N = kenong                                        G
P = kempul
G = gong or siyem
w = rest
. = one beat in balungan melody
```

The time distribution of these punctuating beats is even, but the degree of stress or weight is not (even though no beat is played louder than any other on any single instrument). Javanese listeners feel the following progression of stress levels, based on the levels of subdivision.

Transcription 7-3
Stress levels in punctuation pattern.

```
SUBDIVISIONS
full gongan:                                          G
1st level:          N           N           N        N
2nd level:      w       P           P           P
3rd level: t      t       t       t       t       t       t

         wk  md  wk  str wk  md  wk  str wk  md  wk  str wk  md  wk  xstr

beat no. 1   2   3   4   5   6   7   8   9   10  11  12  13  14  15  16


         (wk = weak; md = medium; str = strong; xstr = very strong)
```

The strongest beat is the one coinciding with the largest and deepest sounding phrase marker, the gong (G), and with the *kenong* (N)—at the end of the phrase. Javanese would count this as one, *two*, three, *four*, and so on, with the strongest beat being the sixteenth. This is the only beat where two punctuating gong instruments coincide. This "coincidence" releases the rhythmic tension that has built up through the course of the *gongan,* giving a sense of repose.

Although in the West we may dismiss events as "mere coincidence," in Java the simultaneous occurrence of several events, the alignment of days of the week and dates (like our Friday the 13th), can be profoundly meaningful. It is not uncommon to determine a suitable day for a wedding, or for moving house, based on the coincidence of a certain day in the seven-day week with a certain day in the Javanese five-day market week, and this in turn within a certain Javanese month (in the lunar calendar, rather than the solar calendar used in the West). The simultaneous occurrence of what to Westerners would seem to be unrelated (and therefore meaningless) events—such as the sounding of a certain bird while a person is carrying out a particular activity—can be interpreted in Java as an important omen.

This deep-seated view of the workings of the natural world is reflected in the structure of *gamelan* music, where coincidence is central to the coherence of the music. The sounding of the gong with the *kenong* marks the musical instant of greatest weight and is the only point at which a *gendhing* may end. Other, lesser points of coincidence also carry weight. If we consider the piece in terms of the *balungan* melody, the next strongest stress comes at the coincidence of the *balungan* with the *kenong* strokes. And in pieces with longer *gongan* (for example, 32, 64, or 128 beats), many of the *saron* beats do not coincide with any punctuating gong, making each *kenong* stroke and even each *kethuk* stroke an instance of stress and temporary repose.

The ethnomusicologist Judith Becker and her former student Stanley Hoffman have found it useful to represent the cyclic structure of *gendhing* by mapping patterns onto a circle, relating the flow of musical time to the recurring course traced by the hands of a clock. The pattern used in *Bubaran* "Kembang Pacar," then, can be notated as shown in Transcription 7-4.

Transcription 7-4

Punctuation pattern of *Bubaran* "Kembang Pacar" represented as a circle.

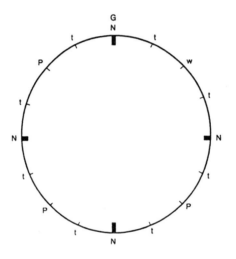

Becker has argued convincingly that the cyclic structure of Javanese *gendhing* reflects the persistence of Hindu-Buddhist conceptions of time introduced to Java during the first millennium C.E. and not wholly eliminated by the subsequent adoption of Islam. (For an elaboration of this theory, see Hoffman 1978, Becker 1979, and especially Becker 1981.)

In the performance of many pieces today, the players of most of the punctuating instruments have a choice of pitch. Their choice is normally determined by the *balungan* melody tone played simultaneously or the one about to be emphasized in the following phrase. However, when performing in loud-playing style musicians sometimes use a single pitch throughout; this reflects the practice of earlier times, when only one *kempul* and one or two *kenong* were made for each *gamelan.* Here the musicians opt for this older practice; they use *kempul* tone 6 throughout and a special *kenong* tuned to tone 5 in the octave below the other *kenong.* The *kethuk,* as is customary in Yogya, is tuned to tone 2. The gong player chooses to sound the *gong ageng* for only the first and last gong strokes; otherwise he plays the smaller *gong siyem,* tuned to tone 2.

Let us now consider the *balungan* melody of this piece (CD 3, Track 2) performed on the *saron* and *slenthem* and notated as follows:

```
                                                                      G
                                                                   ___N
Introduction        (on bonang):   5 3 5 .   2 3 5 6   2 4 5 4   2 15555


                                                                      G
Main Body
punctuation (same each gongan):    t w t N   t P t N   t P t N   t P t N
                       1st gongan: 3 6 3 5   3 6 3 5   3 6 3 5   6 5 3 2
                       2nd gongan: 6 5 3 2   6 5 3 2   6 5 3 2   5 3 5 6
                       3rd gongan: 2 1 2 6   2 1 2 6   2 1 2 6   3 5 3 2
                       4th gongan: 5 3 5 .   2 3 5 6   2 4 5 4   2 1 6 5
```

The system used here and elsewhere in this chapter is the cipher notation system now widely used throughout central and eastern Java. Dots in place of numerals indicate the sustaining of the previous tone. Dots below numerals indicate the lower octave and dots above indicate the higher octave. An extra space or two is often given after groups of four beats as a means of marking a "measure"—though in Java the stress is on the *last* beat, not the first. Today many Javanese musicians refer to notation to learn or to recall particular pieces, but they do not generally read from notation in performance. Further, the notation usually includes only the *balungan* melody and introduction; the parts played on other instruments are recreated in relation to the *balungan* melody and are open to some degree of personal interpretation.

The piece consists of four *gongan* (each, of course, with the same *bubaran* structure), played one after the other. Each of the first three begins with a measure that is played three times in succession and ends on the same tone as the previous gong tone. This kind of regularity enhances the balanced symmetry provided by the punctuation structure. The fourth *gongan,* which stands out with its one sustained note (fourth beat) and lack of internal repetition, is melodically quite similar to the introduction and leads right back into the first *gongan.*

To help you distinguish the sounds of the different layers of punctuation and melody in this piece, listen to a rendition performed by students in the Javanese *gamelan* performance ensemble at the University of Wisconsin–Madison, in which you will first hear just the *balungan* melody, then the other parts added one by one (CD 3, Track 3). Note that, because *gamelan* tuning is not standardized, the exact pitches of the *pélog* tones in the *gamelan* you hear in Track 3 of CD 3 differ noticeably from those of the *gamelan* in Track 2 of CD 3. Neither is considered "out of tune"; they are merely different.

The four-*gongan* melody of *Bubaran* "Kembang Pacar" is first played alone, with no punctuation, drum, or elaboration. As the four-*gongan* melody (or "statement") repeats, one layer of punctuation, drum pattern, or elaboration is added with each *gongan.* There are four full statements in this selection.

Statement 1
    4th *gongan:*   *Gong ageng* enters at the end of the first full statement of the melody (that is, at the end of the 4th *gongan*)

Transcription 7-5
Introduction and *balungan* melody in the Javanese cipher notation system.

CD 3/3
Demonstration: *Bubaran* "Kembang Pacar," *pélog pathet nem* (3:55). *Balungan* melody alone, followed by addition of other instruments one by one. Performed by University of Wisconsin-Madison Javanese *gamelan* ensemble, directed by R. Anderson Sutton. Recorded at the University of Wisconsin–Madison, December 2000.

Listening, *Bubaran* "Kembang Pacar"— CD 3, Track 3

Statement 2

1st *gongan:*	*Kenong* enters on every fourth beat.
2nd *gongan:*	*Kempul* enters, playing on the 6th, 10th, and 14th beats.
3rd *gongan:*	*Kethuk* enters, playing on every other beat (1st, 3rd, 5th, and so forth).
4th *gongan:*	*Kendhang gendhing* and *ketipung* enter.

Statement 3

1st *gongan:*	*Peking* (highest *saron*, doubling the *balungan*) enters.
2nd *gongan:*	*Bonang barung* (middle *bonang*, elaborating the *balungan*) enters.
3rd *gongan:*	*Bonang panerus* (highest *bonang*, doubling the *bonang barung*) enters.

Once all the instruments have entered, the ensemble finishes out the third full statement of the four-*gongan* piece and continues through a fourth, slowing to end.

The main body can be repeated as many times as the drummer desires or as is appropriate to the context in which it is performed. Pieces in *bubaran* form are normally played at the end of performances (*bubar* means to disperse). The guests or audience are expected to leave during the playing of the piece; thus the number of repetitions may depend on the length of time it takes those in attendance to get up to leave.

Having explored the structure of this piece as performed, let us focus our attention on the part played by the drummer, using the smallest and largest drums in combination. Throughout the piece he plays a pattern generic to the *bubaran* form. That is, the drumming for any of the forty or so other pieces in this form would be the same: a particular introductory pattern, several variant patterns for the main body, and a special contrasting pattern that is reserved only for the final *gongan* and that, together with the slowing of tempo, signals the ending. The patterns comprise a series of drum strokes. Each stroke has a name that imitates the actual drum sound: *tak, dung,* and *dang*—T, d, and D.

Transcription 7-6

Bubaran drum patterns—a generic vocabulary of drum strokes, each with an onomatopoetic name that imitates the actual drum sound (*tak, dung,* and *dang*—T, d, and D).

T—*Tak* is a short, crisp sound produced by slapping the smaller head of the *ketipung* with the palm.

d—*Dung* is a high, resonant sound produced by one or two fingers striking the larger head of the *ketipung*.

D—*Dang* is a deep sound produced by hitting the larger head of the *kendhang gendhing*, often in combination with *tak* on the *ketipung*.

```
Introduction:                                                         N/G
     5    3    5    .    2    3    5    6    2    4    5    4    2   1 5 5 5  5
                                               T    T    d    D    T   d   d    .


Main Body:
              t    w    t    N    t    P    t    N    t    P    t    N    t    P    t   N/G
  (e.g.)      3    6    3    5    3    6    3    5    3    6    3    5    6    5    3    2
  A:          d    d    d D  .    d    d    d D  .    d    d    d D  .   d D d D    d D  .
                                                     (played in 1st, 2nd, & 4th gongan)


              2    1    2    6    2    1    2    6    2    1    2    6    3    5    3    2
  B:         T d D  .  T d D  .  T d D  .  T d D  .  T d D  .  T d D  .  d D d D    d D  .
                                                     (played in 3rd gongan)


              5    3    5    .    2    3    5    6    2    4    5    4    2    1    6    5
  Ending:    T d  d   d    D   T d d D T d D    d D T d T d T  D d    D   d d  .
                                                     (played in 4th gongan, last time)
```

It is the drummer who first begins to play faster, thereby signaling the ensemble to speed up at the end of the second time through the large cycle of four *gongan.* As a warning that he or she intends to end, the drummer alters the last few strokes in the penultimate *gongan* (in this case from dDdD dD. to dDdD TdD). This way the other musicians all know to slacken the tempo, though the precise rate is determined by the drummer. The playing of the ending pattern through the last *gongan* confirms his or her intentions.

We have seen how the punctuating gong parts and the drumming fit with the *balungan* in *Bubaran* "Kembang Pacar." We can now turn to the elaborating melodic instruments—here the middle-range *bonang (barung)* and higher-range *bonang (panerus)*—which normally play at a faster rate, subdividing the *balungan* part and providing variations based on the *balungan* melody. In pieces with *balungan* played at slower tempos, the highest-range *saron (peking)* also provides a limited degree of melodic elaboration, but in Yogyanese court style it is sometimes omitted (as it is here).

It was mentioned earlier that the only part normally notated is the *balungan.* Other melodic parts are derived through processes generally understood by practicing musicians. Ideally all musicians can play all the parts. In reality, this is true only in the best professional groups; however, most musicians have at least a passive knowledge of the workings of all the instruments and know how to respond to various signals and nuances.

The two *bonang* here perform in a style called "walking," usually alternating left and right hands in sounding combinations of tones derived from the *balungan.* Transcription 7-7 shows the *bonang barung* part as it is played the first time through the four *gongan.* The arrangement of kettle gongs on the instrument is given in the upper portion of the transcription; the lower portion shows the actual *bonang* playing in relation to the *balungan.*

```
                    4̇   6̇   5̇   3̇   2̇   1̇   7̇
Kettles on bonang:
                    1    7    2    3    5    6    4
```

Transcription 7-7
Cipher notation for the *bonang barung* part as played the first time through the four *gongan*—"walking" style.

```
Bonang Playing in Bubaran Kembang Pacar:

balungan:   3   6   3   5   3   6   3   5   3   6   3   5   6   5   3   2
bonang:     3 6 3 6 3 5 3 5   3 6 3 6 3 5 3 5   3 6 3 6 3 5 3 5   6 5 3 5 6 . 6 .
                                                                            2   2

balungan:   6   5   3   2   6   5   3   2   6   5   3   2   5   3   5   6
bonang:     6 5 3 5 6 . 6 .   6 5 3 5 6 . 6 .   6 5 3 5 6 . 6 .   5 3 5 3 6 6̇ 6 .
                    2   2             2   2             2   2                   6

balungan:   2   1   2   6   2   1   2   6   2   1   2   6   3   5   3   2
bonang:     2̇ i 2̇ i 5 6 i 6   2̇ i 2̇ i 5 6 i 6   2̇ i 2̇ i 6 6 6 .   3 3̇ 3 . 2 2̇ 2 .
                                                              6         3         2

balungan:   5   3   5   .   2   3   5   6   2   4   5   4   2   1   6   5
bonang:     5̇ 3 5̇ 3 5 5 5̇ .   2̇ 3 2̇ 3 5 6 5 6   2̇ 4 2̇ 4 5 4 5 4   2̇ i 2̇ i 6 5 3 5
                          5
```

In subsequent repetitions the *bonang barung* part is similar but not identical. The variations reflect the sensibilities of the player, who both adjusts to tempo changes and alters his or her patterns purely for the aesthetic enjoyment of variation. The *bonang* player has not learned a particular *bonang* part or set of variations, note for note, for this one piece. Rather, the player has thoroughly internalized a vocabulary of patterns known by tradition to fit with certain phrases of *balungan*. What the player usually will have learned about the particular piece, other than its *balungan*, is the octave register in which to play variations (for example, 3 6 3 6 rather than 3̇ 6̇ 3̇ 6̇).

The *bonang panerus* plays similar sorts of variations of the *balungan* melody but at twice the rate of the *bonang barung*. Transcription 7-8 gives *balungan, bonang barung,* and *bonang panerus* parts for the first *gongan*. The arrangement of kettles is identical to that of *bonang barung*, with each tuned an octave higher than the corresponding *bonang barung* kettle.

Transcription 7-8
Bonang barung and *panerus* parts for *Bubaran* "Kembang Pacar," first *gongan*.

```
balungan:    3   6   3   5   3   6   3   5   3   6   3   5   6   5   3   2

bon. bar.:  3 6 3 6 3 5 3 5  3 6 3 6 3 5 3 5  3 6 3 6 3 5 3 5  6 5 3 5 6 . 6 .
                                                                      2   2

bon. pnr.: 363.3636353.3535 363.3636353.3535 363.3636353.3535 656.6535626.626.
```

You can see in this transcription how the two *bonang* vary by repetition: 3 6 in the *balungan* becomes 3 6 3 6 in the *bonang barung* part and 363.3636 in the *bonang panerus* part—all heard simultaneously. The players do not mechanically repeat this pattern throughout, however; they can substitute alternate tones (such as 6 5 3 5 instead of 6 5 6 5) and make other choices. In any case we can see why the Javanese refer to the *saron* and *slenthem* melody as *balungan*. The term literally means "outline" or "skeleton," and the *balungan* provides just that for the elaborating instruments (and for voices in soft-playing style). The degree to which the *saron* and *slenthem* part actually sounds like an outline depends on its tempo and the resulting levels at which the elaborating instruments subdivide it.

Irama Level

In the performances of *Bubaran* "Kembang Pacar" (CD 3, Tracks 2 and 3), the *bonang barung* plays at twice the density of the *balungan*, subdividing it by two. This ratio defines one of five possible levels of *balungan* subdivision known as *irama* levels. If the tempo had slowed sufficiently (as we shall see in the next piece), the *bonang barung* would have doubled its ratio with the *balungan*, subdividing each beat by four. Ward Keeler aptly likens the process to a car shifting gears, in this case downshifting as it goes up a steep grade (Keeler 1987:225). To maintain its relationship with the *bonang barung*, the *bonang panerus* would double as well, resulting in an eight-to-one ratio with the *balungan*. At the slowest *balungan* tempo, the *bonang barung* would have a ratio of sixteen beats to one *balungan* beat; and the *bonang panerus*, along with several of the soft instruments, would play a full thirty-two beats for each *balungan* beat!

Performing Your Own Gamelan Music

To get the feeling of *gamelan* ensemble performance, all you need is a group of seven or eight people. You can either use available percussion instruments, such as Orff instruments, or simply use your voices. Start by assigning each punctuating instrument to one person. The gong player can simply say "gong" (in a low, booming voice), the *kempul* player "pul" (middle voice), the *kenong* player "nong" (long and high), and the *kethuk* player "tuk" (short and low). Another can be assigned to play the drum pattern (saying the syllables given in the Transcription 7-6 patterns). Then the remaining performers can divide among themselves the *balungan* melody and, if they are inclined, some *bonang* elaboration. With a larger group, people can double up on all instruments except the drum.

First try the piece we have listened to, because the tune is familiar. The "drummer" should control the tempo and play the ending pattern, slowing down, to end. Try different versions, with different numbers of repetitions. You can end at any gong tone; it does not have to be at the end of the fourth *gongan.* Then try the piece given in Transcription 7-9, called *Bubaran* "Udan Mas" (literally, "Golden Rain"). You can hear it on the 33⅓ rpm recording *Javanese Court Gamelan from the Pura Paku Alaman* (Nonesuch H-72044). The gong punctuation is the same as in *Bubaran* "Kembang Pacar," but the melody is different.

```
Introduction:                                                      N/G
                   7   7   7   5   6   7   2̇   2̇   7   6   5   6   7   6   5
                                                T   T   d   D   T   d   d

Main Body:
             t   w   t   N   t   P   t   N   t   P   t   N   t   P   t   N/G
(balungan:)  6   5   3   2   6   5   3   2   3   3   2   3   6   5   3   2

(bonang:) 6 5 6 5 2 . 2 .  6 5 6 5 2 . 2 .  3 3 3 . 3 3 . .  6 5 6 5 2 . 2 .

(balungan:)  7   5   6   7   5   6   7   2   2   7   6   5   6   7   6   5

(bonang:) 7 5 7 5 6 7 6 7  5 6 5 6 7 2̇ 7 2̇  2̇ 7 2̇ 7 6 5 6 5  6 7 6 7 5 5 5 .
```

Transcription 7-9
Bubaran "Udan Mas," *pélog pathet barang.*

Approximate equivalents in Western pitches for **pélog** scale:

(1 = D), 2 = E, 3 = F, (4 = Ab), 5 = A, 6 = Bb, 7 = C (1 and 4 not used here)

The sequence is as follows: introduction, first *gongan* twice, second *gongan* twice, first *gongan* twice, second *gongan* twice, and so on, until your drummer signals an ending. Try to learn it well enough not to need the notation so that, like a Javanese musician, you will be using your ears rather than your eyes.

A Javanese Gendhing in Soft-Playing Style

Listen to the next recording, *Ladrang* "Wilujeng," *pélog pathet barang* (CD 3, Track 4). *Wilujeng* literally means "safe" or "secure." It is often performed at the beginning of ceremonies or rituals to ensure the safety of not only the community involved but also the ceremony or the performance itself. The recording was made at the house of my teacher Suhardi, who lived just outside of Yogya and directed the professional *gamelan* musicians at the Yogya branch of the national radio station, Radio Republik Indonesia (R.R.I.). Some of the performers were professional musicians (at R.R.I. and elsewhere); others were Suhardi's neighbors who gathered at his house for regular weekly rehearsals on his *gamelan*.

The instruments, which filled much of his modest house when they were spread out for playing, are mostly iron and brass. Perhaps you noticed the contrast in sound quality as the metal percussion instruments first entered. For soft-playing style, however, the quality of singing and the various soft-sounding instruments matters the most, rendering the contrast between bronze and other metals far less significant than it is in loud-playing style. For this reason some Javanese say that the soft-playing music is more a music of the common people (who cannot afford large bronze ensembles) and the loud-playing music more a music of the court and nobility.

Pathet

Like *Bubaran* "Kembang Pacar," *Ladrang* "Wilujeng," *pélog pathet barang* uses the *pélog* scale system, but it is classified as *pathet barang*. Javanese generally identify three *pathet* in each of the two scale systems, ordered in relation to the progression in which they are featured in the all-night shadow puppet performances:

	Sléndro pathet	*Pélog pathet*
about 9:00 P.M.–midnight	*nem*	*lima*
about midnight–3:00 A.M.	*sanga*	*nem*
about 3:00 A.M.–6:00 A.M.	*manyura*	*barang*

In actual shadow puppetry today, the first phase may start before 9:00 P.M. and last until well after midnight. The second often begins as late as 2:00 A.M. and the third as late as 4:30. Several schemes are given for music performed outside of the shadow puppet context, but current practice indicates little relation between time of day and *pathet*. Instead, pieces in *sléndro pathet nem* or *pélog pathet lima*, which are usually calm and subdued, tend to be played relatively early in a performance, regardless of the time of day.

Much effort has been spent in defining *pathet* with reference to the melodies of *gamelan* pieces, particularly the *balungan*. The famous Dutch ethnomusicologist Jaap Kunst noted that certain phrase finals were more common in one *pathet* than another, especially for pieces played primarily in *sléndro* (Kunst 1973). Mantle Hood, one of Kunst's students and a major force in establishing ethnomusicology in the United States, devoted an entire book to the subject, concluding that *pathet* can be distinguished by different cadential patterns in the *balungan* part and the avoidance of certain tones (Hood 1954).

With a larger body of data than was available to Hood, Judith Becker found *pathet* to be "based upon three interlocking factors: (1) melodic pattern, formula, or contour, (2) the pitch level of that pattern and (3) the position of the pattern within the formal structure of a piece" (Becker 1980:81). In *sléndro,* for instance, a measure with the contour of three conjunct steps downward can occur in any *pathet.* Measures beginning on tone 5 and descending to 1 (5 3 2 1) are relatively common in both *sléndro pathet manyura* and *sléndro pathet sanga,* but in *manyura* they normally do not end in a strong position (for example, with a gong stroke), whereas in *sanga* they often do. Measures with the same descending contour, but beginning on tone 6 and descending to 2 (6 5 3 2) are common in both *pathet manyura* and *pathet nem,* but those ending in gong position are more likely to be *pathet nem.*

Javanese often speak of register or pitch level in relation to *pathet,* likening it in some ways to Western concepts of key. Indeed many *gendhing* are played in several *pathet,* just as Western popular tunes are often transposed from one key to another. The relationship to key is most apparent not in the single-octave *balungan* melody but in the parts played on instruments with wider ranges and in the singing. Instrumentalists and singers learn a vocabulary of melodic patterns, which they can readily transpose up or down—and even between scale systems. For example, the pattern one uses to arrive at tone 6 in *sléndro pathet manyura* can be realized one tone lower, with the same physical processes, to end on 5 in *sléndro pathet sanga.* In fact, most Javanese say that *pathet sanga* is simply *pathet manyura* down one tone. But *sléndro pathet nem,* said to be the lowest of the three *sléndro pathet,* is often described by musicians as consisting of an ambiguous mix of phrases from the other two *sléndro pathet,* as is the case in our third example (discussed later).

Pélog pathet are understood slightly differently. *Pathet barang* is easily distinguished by the presence of tone 7 and the avoidance of tone 1. Differentiating *pathet lima* from *pathet nem* presents greater problems, since both avoid tone 7, employ the other six *pélog* tones, and do not seem to be simply one or more tones above or below the other. Javanese musicians often disagree over which of these two is the correct *pathet* category for a given piece. Perception of a piece's mood, which is determined by other factors besides melodic contour and register, may also contribute. The calmer pieces would be classified as *lima* and livelier ones as *nem.*

The point here is not to try to present a thorough survey of the many ideas about the concept of *pathet.* Rather, I hope you have learned that *pathet* is somewhat more complicated than its Western counterpart, "mode." The word *pathet* literally means "limit" and is related to other Javanese words for stopping or delimiting. In many ways it indicates something about the limitations of the piece in question—the tones that will be played or emphasized in the *balungan* melody, the pitch level of the other parts, the mood, and (especially for shadow puppetry accompaniment) the time of day or night at which it is appropriately played. Although the association with mood and time of day suggest comparison with Indian *raga* (see Chapter 6), *pathet* is actually a very different concept. *Ragas* are differentiated from one another by details of interval structure and ornament, as well as contour, but not by register. Hundreds of *ragas* are known, thousands theoretically possible. Indian musicians do not, however, transpose pieces from one *raga* to another, because the *raga* is essential to the aesthetic impact of the piece. *Pathet* is a far more general concept. Only a few *pathet* are identified for each of the two scale systems, and transposition from one *pathet* to another occurs with some frequency.

A Close Examination of Ladrang "Wilujeng"

Ladrang "Wilujeng" differs from *Bubaran* "Kembang Pacar" (CD 3, Track 2), in many ways. It is in soft-playing style, with voices and the various soft-sounding instruments featured. The introduction is played on the *rebab* (fiddle), with the subtle slides and nuances one could not produce on a fixed-pitch instrument such as the *bonang.* The pattern of punctuation (*ladrang*) is nearly the same as in the previous piece, but it is expanded to fit with *gongan* phrases of thirty-two beats rather than sixteen. The players of the *kempul* and *kenong* do not limit themselves to one tone, but instead use a variety of tones, matching or anticipating important tones in the melody.

Instrumental Playing in *Ladrang* "Wilujeng"

Ladrang "Wilujeng"is often performed in *sléndro pathet manyura* as well as *pélog pathet barang* simply by transferring the melodic patterns from one system to the other. Transcription 7-10 presents the introduction, the *balungan,* and the gong punctuation (with pitch choices for *kempul* and *kenong*).

CD 3/4

Ladrang "Wilujeng" ("safe, secure"), *pélog pathet barang* (8:47). Central Javanese *gamelan* music in "soft-playing" style. Performed by musicians of Ngudya Wirama *gamelan* group under the direction of Ki Suhardi. Field recording by René Lysloff. Yogyakarta, Java, Indonesia, 1980.

Transcription 7-10

Ladrang "Wilujeng," *pélog pathet barang.* For each section (A and B) the gong punctuation is shown on the first line (letters and numerals) and the *balungan* on the second.

```
                                                              _____N/G
Introduction:               7 3 2  6 72. 3  7 7 3 2  7 67276

A: (umpak section)

     t   w   t N3  t  P6  t  N5  t  P3  t  N6  t  P3* t  N6/G
    2 7 2 3  2 7 5 6  3 3 . .   6 5 3 2  5 6 5 3  2 7 5 6  2 7 2 3  2 7 5 6
                                                   *(if going to ngelik, P6)

B: (ngelik section)
     t   w   t N6  t  P7  t  N6  t  P6  t  N7  t  P6  t  N6/G
    . . 6 .  7 5 7 6  3 5 6 7  6 5 3 2  6 6 . .   7 5 7 6  . 7 3 2  . 7 5 6
```

This piece is considerably more challenging to follow than *Bubaran* "Kembang Pacar." It slows and changes *irama* level in the third measure (3 3 . . .), settling by the end of the first *gongan* to a tempo of about 36 *balungan* beats per minute. The first section (A) is played twice, then the second (B) once, then first twice again, the second again, and so on, ending in the first: A A B A A B A A B A. For the final two *gongan,* the tempo first speeds up (but with no change in *irama* level) to about forty-two beats per minute and then slows gradually to the final gong. A solo female singer (*pesindhèn*) sings for most of the first two *gongan.* At the beginning of the first B and from then on, all the singers join in unison. Further, the *balungan* part is no longer played explicitly. Instead the *balungan* instruments play simple variations based on the *balungan.*

As you listen to the recording (CD 3, Track 4), pay attention to the timings on your CD player's display or use a stop watch. Elapsed time is given for the end of each *gongan* and for other significant events.

0:00	Beginning of introduction, on *rebab*
0:07	Gong at end of introduction, ensemble enters
0:18	Change of *irama* level
0:49	Gong at end of first A
1:41	Singers enter in unison
1:42	Gong at end of second A
2:36	Gong at end of first B
3:30	Gong at end of third A
4:24	Gong at end of fourth A
5:17	Gong at end of second B
6:11	Gong at end of fifth A
6:44	Drummer signals acceleration in tempo
7:01	Gong at end of sixth A
7:46	Gong at end of third B
8:11	Drummer signals gradual slackening in tempo
8:41	Final gong at end of seventh A

Timed Listening to *Ladrang* "Wilujeng," *pélog pathet barang*

The drummer, with the same two drums used in the previous example *(kendhang gendhing* and *ketipung)*, plays standardized patterns specific to *ladrang* formal structure: a *ladrang* introduction, a *ladrang* slowing-down pattern (in the first *gongan*), standard patterns for most of the rest of the performance (with a standard variation each time the B section is played), and finally an ending pattern during the final *gongan*. In accord with the soft-playing style, the drumming is softer and sparser than in loud-playing style. Transcription 7-11 presents the standard pattern used, with minimal variation, throughout all the A sections but the final one.

```
2   7   2   3   2   7   5   6   3   3   .   .   6   5   3   2
. . . . . . . d   d . d D . . . . . d . d .dDd.Dd . . . d D . d D

5   6   5   3   2   7   5   6   2   7   2   3   2   7   5   6G
d D . d .dD . T d d d D d .dD d .dD dD.dD.dD.dD . . . d .dD d D
```

Transcription 7-11
Drum pattern, *Ladrang* "Wilujeng," *irama dadi.*

Other instrumentalists play variations of the *balungan* melody, producing such a complex heterophony that some scholars identify *gamelan* music as polyphonic, noting the stratification of layers: parts moving at a wide variety of tempi—some at a much faster rate or higher density than others. Generally the smaller, higher pitched instruments play at the faster rates and the larger, deeper ones at the slower rates. One can get a sense of this stratification by considering the frequency with which the gong is struck, comparing it with *kenong* (here four times per gong), then *balungan* (here eight beats per *kenong*), and then the subdividing parts (middle *bonang* and highest *saron* four times per *balungan* beat; highest *bonang* and many of the soft-playing instruments eight times per *balungan* beat). Thus, the instruments playing at the fastest rate, mostly those of higher pitch, actually play 256 beats for every one beat of the gong!

I mentioned earlier that in this example the *balungan* is varied even on the instruments that usually sound it explicitly. After the first two *gongan,* where the *balungan* is played normally, the *saron* play simple variations, adding neighboring tones, while the *slenthem* lags by a quarter beat, all of which contributes to a dreamy blurring that allows the vocal melody to assume prominence.

The combination resulting from the interlocking of *slenthem* and *saron* here is identical to what the much higher-pitched *saron peking* plays, duplicating and anticipating the *balungan* tones in a manner that also resembles closely the "walking" style of *bonang* playing. This means of varying the *balungan* characterizes *peking* playing generally; it is not limited to the few cases where the *balungan* is only implied.

Transcription 7-12

Saron peking passage, *Ladrang* "Wilujeng."

```
(balungan:    3   5   6   7P   6   5   3   2N)

saron peking:  3355335566776677 6655665533223322
```

Throughout *Ladrang* "Wilujeng" the *bonangs* play in walking style, mixed with occasional reiteration of single tones or octave combinations, as found in the first example, *Bubaran* "Kembang Pacar." The lengthier time interval between *balungan* beats here, however, provides an opportunity for greater melodic and rhythmic independence from the *balungan* melody. For example, the following phrase is played (with occasional variation) on the *bonang barung* with the *balungan* 2 7 5 6.

Transcription 7-13

Bonang barung passage, *Ladrang* "Wilujeng."

```
balungan:          2       7       5       6N

bonang barung:   2̇ 7 7̄5̄5 5 7 . . 5 7 7̄5̄. 6 7 . 6
```

The various soft-playing instruments provide more elaborate variations that are more independent of the *balungan* part and often inspired by phrases in the vocal parts. Because they blend together in the thick texture of soft-playing style, distinguising all the soft instruments is difficult. As an example, consider the *gambang* (xylophone), which plays mostly "in octaves"—the right hand usually sounding the same tone as the left, but one octave higher. The excerpt is from the middle of the A section, fourth statement (4:05 to 4:20 on CD 3, Track 4).

Transcription 7-14

Gambang passage, *Ladrang* "Wilujeng."

```
balungan:                 5             6             5             3P

r.h.    2̇ 3 2̇ 3 5 5 3 5 5 3 5 3 5 3 5 6 2̈̇ 7 6 5 3 5̇ 2 7 6 6 6 2̇ 2̇ 7 2̇ 3

l.h.    2 3 2 3 5 2 3 5 2 3 5 3 2 3 5 6 2̇ 7 6 5 3 5 2 7̣ 6̣ 7̣ 6̣ 2 6̣ 7̣ 2 3


balungan:                 2             7             5             6

r.h.    3̇ 5 6 7 6 2̈̇ 7 6 5 6 3 2̇ 7 3 2̇ 7 7 2̇ 7 2̇ 7 6 5 3 3 5 3 5 6 6 5 6

l.h.    3 5 6 7 6 2̣ 7 6 5 6 3 2 7̣ 3 2 7̣ 2 7̣ 2 7 6 5̣ 3 3 5 3 5 6̣ 3 5 6
```

In other statements of this passage, the *gambang* part is similar, but not identical. Good players draw from a rather large vocabulary of patterns and vary the repeated passages in performance with a degree of individual flexibility, though not with the range of spontaneity associated with improvisation in jazz or Indian music. The *gambang* player, like the other *gamelan* musicians whose part is not completely fixed, operates with a system of constraints (not quite "rules" or "laws"). At the end of a measure, the *gambang* and *balungan* tones almost always coincide; at the midpoint (second beat), they usually do; on other beats they often do not, even though the *gambang* sounds eight (or in some cases as many as thirty-two) times as many tones as the *balungan.*

Singing in *Ladrang* "Wilujeng"

Solo singing with *gamelan* is also based on notions of flexibility and constraint. During the first two *gongan* one of the female vocalists sings florid vocal phrases that weave in and out of the *balungan* part. Although her part employs a much freer rhythm than the steady pulsation of most of the instruments (for example, the *gambang* discussed earlier), her melody is also constructed from phrases that usually end on the same tone as the *balungan* phrase, even though in current practice she often reaches that tone a beat or two later than most of the other instruments. Although her phrases resemble those of other singers, in some small ways they are her individual patterns. The vocal text used by the solo singer (difficult to determine in this recording) is not specific to the piece; it is one of many in a well-known verse form fitted to the structure of this *ladrang* and to many pieces in this and other forms.

In contrast to the soloist, the chorus sings a precomposed melody. The text, although agreed upon before performance, is again a generic one, used in many *gamelan* pieces and having no connection with the meaning of the title of this piece. To a great degree, Javanese melodies and texts lead independent lives. For example, one may sing a single melody with a variety of texts or sing a single text in a variety of *gamelan* pieces; such choices depend on the wishes of the performers or sometimes (but rarely) the requirements of a particular dramatic scene.

The choral text presents many riddles in which the meaning of seemingly unrelated phrases in the first part suggests the meaning or sound of words or phrases in the second part. The Javanese greatly enjoy this kind of literary indirection, which we can see as an aesthetic expression of the high value placed on subtlety and indirection in daily life. To understand the connections, one must know traditional Javanese culture rather well: history, legends, nature, foods, place-names (in both the real and the mythological worlds), and the Javanese shadow puppet tradition with its many hundred characters. Javanese poetry is difficult to render in English. The Javanese is given first, with word-by-word translation second (with some double meanings), followed by a freer translation.

Text, *Ladrang* "Wilujeng," *pélog pathet barang*

1. *Manis rengga, satriya ing Lésanpura*
   sweet decoration (colorful sweet snack), knight of/in Lésanpura
   > Beautifully adorned, the knight from Lésanpura. [a kingdom
   >   in the *Mahabharata*]
   Setyanana yèn laliya marang sira
   Be loyal if forget to you
   > You should be loyal, even if you forget yourself.

2. *Tirta maya, supaya anyar kinarya*
   Water pure, so that quickly be made
   > Beautiful clear water, let it be done quickly.
   Ning ing driya, tan na ngalih amung sira
   purity/emptiness of/in heart, not exist move only you
   > With the purifying of my heart, there is nothing that moves, only you.

3. *Kala reta, satriya ngungkuli jaya*
   Time red (centipede), knight surpass glory/victory
   > At dawn, the knight proves exceptional in his glory.
   Sun mbang-embang hamisésa jroning pura
   I hope/yearn for have power within domain/palace
   > I yearn to exercise power here in this domain.

Some of the riddles here are obscure even to most Javanese. An explanation of two of them should give you an idea of how they work. In the first line of stanza 1, the words *satriya ing Lésanpura* (a knight in the kingdom of Lésanpura) suggest the sound of the first word of the second line *setyanana,* as the shadow puppet character named Setyaki is a well-known knight who came from Lésanpura. *Kala reta,* in the first line of the third stanza, suggests not the sound but one meaning of the root particle in the compound *mbang-embang* in the second line. Though the two-word expression *kala reta* can mean "centipede," the two words translate individually as "time" *(kala)* and "red" *(reta). Bang,* the root of *mbang-embang,* is another word for red, and *bang-bang wétan* (literally "red-red east") is a Javanese expression for dawn. In this example, as is common in pieces where male and female singers join to sing, the text is interspersed with extra words and syllables whose meaning may be obscure (underlined in Transcription 7-15), and portions of the text may be repeated. These characteristics strongly suggest the relatively greater importance of what we would call the "musical" elements (pitch and rhythm) over the words, with the word meaning often obscured and the words serving primarily as vehicles for beautiful melody. Transcription 7-15 shows the scheme for the first stanza (with *balungan* and gong punctuation given above the vocal line).

The second stanza operates the same way, with repetition of the last four syllables at the end of one A section and repetition of the first four syllables of the second line in the next A. Only the final stanza (here the third, but this could have gone on for many more stanzas) ends after one B and one A and thus does not reach the *"Adèn, adèn"* interjections and the repetition of the first four syllables we would expect in the next A if the performance did not end where it does.

Chorus enters at end of second <u>umpak</u> (1:45 on stopwatch):   6 6N/G
                                                                    <u>Andhé</u>

<u>ngelik</u>:

```
      .    .   6    .   7   5   7  6N   3   5   6  7P   6   5   3  2N
     -------------7----2---  2-376--------  2-327-----675----6532
                    é         ba- bo        Ma- nis     reng-    ga

      6    6   .   .P   7   5   7  6N   .   7   3  2P   .   7   5  6N/G
     ---------  6-535----6-722----3276----- 567-  5-632----- 723--223276
                sa- tri-  ya    ing              Lé- san-      pu- ra,
```

<u>umpak</u>:
```
      2    7   2    3   2   7   5  6N   3   3   .  .P   6   5   3  2N
     ---------       2--3232--76--53-----  3-566-----5675----6532
                     Ba-bo ba- bo          Se- tya-   na-      na

      5    6   5   3P   2   7   5  6N   2   7   2  3P   2   7   5  6N/G
     --------  6-753--2-2-2---232-376-------  2--33------722----3276
               yèn laliya marang si-ra        ma- rang   si-     ra
```

<u>umpak</u>:
```
      2    7   2    3   2   7   5  6N   3   3   .  .P   6   5   3  2N
     ---------       2--3232--76--53-----  3-566-----5675----6532
                     A- dèn a- dèn           Se- tya-   na-      na

      5    6   5   3P   2   7   5  6N   2   7   2  3P   2   7   5  6N/G
     (no vocal, until end of line, where next verse begins):    6 6
                                                               An-dhé
```

Biography of Ki Nartosabdho—A Gamelan Musician, Composer, and Puppeteer

So far we have focused mostly on musical sound and its structure. But what of the people who are most drawn to this music—the musicians themselves? Javanese and foreign scholars alike have often mentioned the close interrelationship among the arts in Java. In fact, the status of "musician" does not preclude one from dancing or performing puppetry. Many of the better performers in one art are quite competent in several others. In the following pages a consummate artist, one famous as a *gamelan* musician, composer of new pieces, and shadow puppeteer, speaks for himself.

The biography provided here is based on an interview my wife and I conducted with the late Ki Nartosabdho in 1979. (His music is discussed at length in Becker 1980.) We began by asking him how he became a shadow puppeteer. He proceeded to tell us the story of his life from early childhood memories, with just a few questions from us, which I have chosen to omit here.

Since I sat at my school desk in second grade, I had a knack for the arts. Which ones? Painting. Children's paintings, but even so, with cubist style, realism, expressionism, and my own creations: for instance, a lamb being chased by a tiger, things like that. Now, they really did not give lessons in those kinds of painting for children my age, but I made every effort to see duplications of pictures made by other painters at that time. After beginning to learn to paint, I began to learn classical style dance. I'd dance the role of a monkey, an ogre, and so forth. We actually learned a lot about classical dance—not everything, but a good deal. At that time I lived in my small village, in the Klatèn area [between Yogya and Solo]—called Wedhi. I was born in Wedhi on August 25, 1925. There, when I was twelve years old and in third grade, we had a teacher who gave dance lessons. He was from Solo. We studied so hard that we were able to put on quite an impressive show. It was really rare for village children to have the opportunity to study with a "classical" dance teacher from Solo.

After dance, I began to learn Western music—violin, guitar, cello, and *keroncong*. [The *keroncong* is a small chordophone, like an ukulele, played in the Western-influenced Indonesian genre of the same name. The violin, guitar, and cello he studied were for this same genre, and not for "classical" Western music]. By village standards I did just fine, but not by city standards. After that, I studied *gamelan* music. All these interests took their toll—requiring one to spend time, emotions, and especially money. Especially for musical instruments, what was I to use to purchase one? A guitar in 1937 cost six gulden—Dutch money—or we would say six *rupiah* [Indonesian currency]. I was the eighth of my brothers and sisters; I was the youngest. And I was born into a family that was poor—lacking in possessions, in work, and especially in education. So it is clear that, no matter how much I wanted something, I could not continue my education without any income. My father died just after I began second grade, and my mother, a widow, was already old. So I earned money by making masks—yes, masks in order to be able to continue school. And I managed to finish fifth grade. And I used to have Dutch language classes after school, but they cost 1.25 gulden each month, so I only took Dutch for two months. They threw me out—because I couldn't pay!

Now, rather than hang aimlessly about the house, when I was a teenager, I took off, without even asking my mother's permission. Where in the world would I go, I didn't know. Like a bird in flight, not knowing where I might perch. It was as if I needed some time to suffer. —Excuse me, I don't usually come out with all this about myself, but today I am.— Anyway, like a bird in flight, no idea where I should perch. I might even be called a *gelandangan* [homeless street person]. If not a *gelandangan,* then an outcast, or a forgotten soul.

I felt that the perch I should take was only to join and follow performing groups: both *kethoprak* [musical drama, with stories from Javanese legendary history] and *wayang orang* [musical dance-drama, based on the same Indian epics as shadow puppetry]. First I joined a *kethoprak* group, working as an actor and as a *gamelan* musician. But what I got for it was very minimal—both artistically and financially. And what was more, the coming of the Japanese reinforced my feeling that I had to keep drifting. A life of wandering about, and in tattered clothing. There were lots of clothes then that no human being should have to wear [burlap bags, etc., as the Japanese took much of the cloth during their occupation], but like it or not, circumstances required it. In Javanese there is a the saying: *nuting jaman kalakoné* ["following the times is the way to act"—or, "go with the flow"]. There are lots of sayings and stories that still have mystical content in Indonesia, still plenty. And you should know, even though in your country there is so much great technology, in Indonesia traditional and mystical matters still persist, and are even gaining in strength.

So, I played with about ten *kethoprak* groups: only one month, then move, three months and move, at the longest, only four or five months, then move. It is called *lècèkan*—not taking care of oneself. Then one day I was playing drum for a *kethoprak* group named Sri Wandowo, playing in Klatèn. This was in 1945, just before the Proclamation of Independence [August 17]. There was a manager, the manager of the Ngesthi Pandhawa *wayang orang* troupe, who happened to be eating at a little eating stall behind the *kethoprak* stage where I was playing. As he ate, he heard my drumming and it made an impression. After going home—from eating frogs' legs—he called three of his troupe members and asked them to find out who it was playing *kendhang* for the *kethoprak*. After that, in brief, I left Sri Wandowo and joined Ngesthi Pandhawa. And what startled the other members was that I was the only member who was nervy enough to play drum at his first appearance. I had lots of experience drumming, but what I knew needed "upgrading."

Now, this guy named Narto [Nartosabdho] was a man without up-grading. Three quarters of the Ngesthi Pandhawa members scorned me, ridiculed me, and seemed disgusted by my behavior. A new member already nervy enough to direct and play drum? Now, in the old days, Ngesthi Pandhawa was just an ordinary *wayang orang* troupe, with lots of free time in its schedule. Well, I took steps for "evolution"—not "revolution," but "evolution." Where was our "evolution"? On the stage of Ngesthi Pand-hawa, both in the *gamelan* music and in the dance, and in the new pieces I composed—I should say "we" composed. These were very popular with the public, with the audience. From village tunes to new tunes unknown in Java, such as waltz-time. [Several other composers have also experimented with *gamelan* music in triple meter, including the Yogyanese Hardjosoe-broto. It is not clear who can rightfully claim to have done it first.] The piece was *Sang Lelana* ("The Wanderer"). Also there was *Aku Ngimpi* ("I Dream") and *Sampur Ijo* ("The Green Scarf"), even for dance!

And [the vocal parts] for these waltz pieces could be duet or trio: one, two, or three voices [singing different melodies]. When we tried these out at Ngesthi Pandhawa, there were people who predicted that I would go crazy. My response was that we are all human. God gives us cattle, not beefsteak. Once we are given cattle by God, we have the right to trans-form it into something that is appropriate and useful, in accordance with our taste. All the better if we can bring in rhythms (meters) from outside Indonesia, as long as we don't change or destroy the original and authen-tic Indonesian rhythms. For example [Nartosabdho taps—on the "x"s in this transcription—and hums],

```
   x     x     x     x     x     x     x     x     x
Gong . . 3 5 7 6 6 . 5 3 6 5 5 . 3 2 7 2 . . 5 6 5 3N

     . . 7 2 6 7 7 . 3 2 7 2P
```

Transcription 7-16
Ki Nartosabdho's demonstration of *gamelan* with triple meter.

Yes, three-four. Now in the old days this didn't exist. And even now, when it does, it causes hassles for all the instruments played with two hands—drum, *gendèr*, *gambang*—hassles, but it turns out it is possible. At first [they played] only the simplest of patterns; now it is enjoyed by many listeners: experts [players] and those who only wish to listen. Now obviously I faced some defiance, lots of criticism that I was destroying [tradition]. I was called "destroyer." But I didn't take it just as criticism, but rather as a whip—to push me to find a way. Indeed the criticism was justified. So maybe not only in my country, but in yours too, if there is something startling and seemingly irrational suddenly applied [in the arts], it gives rise to much protest and criticism, right? So maybe the life of mankind everywhere is the same. What differs is just their appearance, their language, their traditions, but life is the same, right?

As it turned out I did okay. My manager gave me something: not money, but a name. Before, I had been Sunarto, now Nartosabdho [from *sabda*—see later]. I gratefully accepted this honor, though not without careful consideration of its justification. In Indonesia often a name is taken from one's profession. For example, Pak Harja Swara (*swara* = "voice," "sound") works as a vocalist, *gérong*. Then Harjana Pawaka. *Harjana* means "safe" (cf. *wilujeng*), and *pawaka* means "fire"; he was on the fire brigade, someone who puts out fires. Wignya Pangrawit: *wignya* means "skilled," and *pangrawit* "a *gamelan* player"; so he was someone skilled at playing *gamelan*. Then Nyata Carita: *nyata* is "clear," "evident," and *carita* is "story"; he was a puppeteer who was accomplished, skilled in storytelling. And I was given the addition *sabda*. *Sabda* is "the speech of a holyman." But here I was a composer and drummer at Ngesthi Pandhawa, specializing in *gamelan* music. It did not seem possible that I would utter such speech. I taught singing and *gamelan*. So I wondered how my profession might fit with this name *sabda*.

[In *wayang orang*, one person sits with the musicians and acts as a "*dhalang*"—not operating puppets, but providing narration and singing the mood songs known as *sulukan*. We learned from interviewing other members of the Ngesthi Pandhawa troupe that one night when the usual *dhalang* was unable to perform, Nartosabdho took over and, to the amazement of the audience, showed himself to have a fine voice, facility with the somewhat archaic *dhalang's* language, and a thorough knowledge of the story. This preceded his debut as a *wayang kulit dhalang*/puppeteer.]

Well, on April 28, 1958 I earned the title "*dhalang*" [here, puppeteer for *wayang kulit*, not *wayang orang*] in Jakarta, at R.R.I. People heard that I was learning to do shadow puppetry, and in January 1958 I was called by the broadcast director, Pak Atmaka—he's still alive. Would I do a broadcast? [Javanese shadow puppetry, though it uses beautifully carved and painted puppets, is often broadcast over the radio. The audience follows the story by recognizing the particular vocal quality given to each character by the puppeteer, and they also enjoy the music.] I replied that I would not be willing right away. The broadcast would be heard all over Indonesia, maybe even outside the country. This was before all the private radio stations, so broadcasts from the central studio could be heard clearly [at great distances]. I agreed to perform in a few months, in April. What shape should my puppetry performance take, how classical, how innovative? Could I match the quality of my accomplishments in *gamelan* music? How to proceed, it is always a puzzle. There was a woman, a singer (*pesindhèn*) who made a promise: if I could perform shadow puppetry all night, she would give me a kiss. A kiss of respect, right, not an erotic kiss, not a "porno" kiss!

Sometime after coming home to Semarang from performing in Jakarta, I had a guest. His name was Sri Handaya Kusuma, and he came on behalf of the Medical Faculty in Yogya. He wanted a performance around Christmas time. [Though few Javanese are Christian, Christmas is a holiday, and schools are normally on a short break beginning shortly before Christmas and lasting until after the New Year.] I was asked to perform a "classic" story. Now requests began to come in one after the other: Jakarta, Yogya, Surbaya, Solo. Yes, I was earning money, but more importantly I was also earning my name. Nowadays I perform once or twice a week, but have more requests than that. I have even played at the presidential palace in Jakarta for Pak Harto [former President Suharto] four times.

How did I learn? I am what you would call an "autodidact." I read and so forth, but it also took looking at a lot of shadow puppetry performances. I would watch all the puppeteers I could, not only the older ones, but also the younger. And each performance, by whatever puppeteer, offered something new that I could and should incorporate in my own performance.

What about musicians? When I first played in Jakarta, it was the R.R.I. musicians who accompanied me. Elsewhere, I would take a few of those closest to me, my *gendèr* player, Pak Slamet, who came from Yogya and still plays at R.R.I. Semarang. And my drummer was the late Pak Wirya. Since 1969 I have had my own group, Condhong Raos, mostly younger musicians, under thirty-five years of age.

In the early 1970s I began to make cassettes, first of my new *gamelan* pieces, then of full-length shadow puppet performances. There were some discs produced by Lokananta [the National Recording Company] in the 1960s, too. My first set of *wayang* cassettes was the story "Gatutkaca Sungging," recorded in 1974, if I remember correctly. Not so long ago. I don't really have a favorite story—how can you say one is better than another? If someone wants to hire a puppeteer and asks for "Parta Krama," ["Parta, i.e. Arjuna, gets married"] for example, no puppeteer should say he doesn't like that story. That wouldn't be very good!

What changes do I foresee in the next five or ten years? It may be possible to predict changes in technology, but not in culture, not in the arts. Some people think *wayang kulit* should be given in Indonesian language. To me, if a change adds to the beauty of the art, then it can be accepted. If not, then it cannot be. In Javanese there are many ways to say "eat," or "sleep" [He goes on to give examples. Different honorific levels of vocabulary permeate Javanese but are almost entirely absent from Indonesian. Nartosabdho implies, without stating explicitly, that he finds *wayang* more beautiful in Javanese and would like to keep it that way.] I have taken *gamelan* music from various areas of Java, even Sunda and Bali, and used them in the *gara-gara* [a comic interlude occurring at the beginning of the *pathet sanga* section, c. 1:00 A.M.]. Not only have I studied these different songs, but I have even taken liberties with them. But other aspects of my puppetry have not been influenced by other regional styles. My style is basically Solonese. Who can predict if it will change, or how it will change?

Figure 7-7
Puppeteer Ki Gondo Darman performing *wayang kulit* at the ASKI Performing Arts Academy in Surakarta.

Arthur Durkee, EarthVisions Photographics

The preceding few pages have presented my English translation of much of what Ki Nartosabdho told my wife and me when we visited him in his modest home in Semarang. Though he was still giving one or two strenuous all-night *wayang* performances per week, he was already suffering from a kidney disease. In late 1985 Ki Nartosabdho died and left a legacy of hundreds of new *gamelan* vocal pieces, hundreds of musical recordings, and close to one hundred recordings of all-night *wayang* performances. His group Condhong Raos still performs music, but at present no one stands out as such a clear "superstar" within the world of traditional Javanese performing arts—a world that, until the era of mass media, really knew no "star system" at all.

Gamelan Music and Shadow Puppetry

Now that we have had a glimpse of a man deeply involved in both *gamelan* music and shadow puppetry, it is fitting to consider some of the music most closely associated with shadow puppet performance. Both the pieces we have studied so far are seldom played for dance or dramatic accompaniment. The musical staples of the shadow puppet repertory are pieces with dense *kenong* and *kempul* playing and *gongan* of varying length—pieces that generate a level of excitement, partly because of the dense gong punctuation. Each *pathet* includes at least three of these staple pieces: relatively calm, somewhat excited, and very excited. The gong punctuation is densest in the very excited pieces and least present in the calmest pieces. The puppeteer determines which piece is to be played; he must be just as thoroughly at home with the *gamelan* music as he is with the many hundreds of characters and stories that comprise this tradition.

We are going to listen to two versions of one of these pieces, the Yogyanese *Playon* "Lasem," *sléndro pathet nem* (CD 3, Tracks 5 and 6), which exemplifies the "somewhat excited" category. Depending on the mood the puppeteer wishes to establish, the piece can be played in loud-playing or in soft-playing style, or switched at any point. (The calmest of the three is usually in soft-playing style; and the most excited is always performed in loud-playing style.) Also, the length of the piece can be radically tailored to suit the needs of the dramatic moment. Sometimes it may go on, through repetition of a central section, for five or ten minutes. During the course of the all-night performance at which I recorded these examples, the puppeteer (Ki Suparman) signaled this piece to be played eighteen times—all, of course, within the *pathet nem* section of the night, which lasted from about 9:00 P.M. to about 1:30 A.M.

Transcription 7-17 gives *balungan* notation for the entire piece, as well as the *gong ageng* or *siyem* sound at the end of each line, as written. The *kenong* plays on every *balungan* beat, the *kempul* every second beat (except where the gong sounds), and the *kethuk* between the beats.

```
Introductory portion:      (signal....)  5          Length of Gongan
                   6 5   6 5 6 5   2 3 5 6               10 beats
               1 6 5 6   2 3 5 3   2 1 2 1               12 beats
               2 1 2 1   6 5 3 5   2 3 5 6               12 beats
               1 6 5 6   5 3 2 3   1 2 3 2**             12 beats

Repeated portion:
    [: 5 6 5 3   5 6 5 3   6 5 2 6   5 2 3 5*           16 beats
                           3 2 3 2   6 5 2 3             8 beats
       5 3 5 3   5 2 3 5   1 6 5 3   2 1 3 2            16 beats
                           6 6 1 2   3 5 6 5             8 beats
               2 1 2 1   2 1 3 2   5 6 1 6              12 beats
                           3 2 5 3   6 5 3 2 :]         8 beats
   Endings:
   *  from gong tone 5 (first rendition):   2 1   3 2 1 6
   ** from gong tone 2 (second rendition):  5 3   2 1 2 6
```

- -

```
Punctuation Pattern for playon/srepegan form:

   kempul & gong:      P  (repeat x ?)    G      e.g.:  P   P   P   P   G
   kenong & kethuk:  tNtN  (repeat x ?)  tNtN          tNtNtNtNtNtNtNtNtN
   balungan:          . .   (etc.)        . .           6 5 6 5 6 5 2 3 5 6
```

Transcription 7-17
Balungan notation for *Playon* "Lasem,"
sléndro pathet nem.

Notice that here the frequency of "coincidence" between gong punctuators is very high: every second beat! To Javanese, this makes for exciting music, appropriate for scenes charged with emotion, even for fights. Quick rapping on the puppet chest signals the musicians to play. The drummer, playing the middle-sized drum (*ciblon*), and sometimes the *kenong* player as well, enter just before the rest of the ensemble.

The first rendition we shall hear takes a little over a minute, only beginning to repeat when the puppeteer signals the playing of a special ending phrase. All the musicians must know one or two of these ending phrases for each gong tone and be ready to tag the appropriate one onto any *gongan* if the signal comes. This first rendition begins in soft-playing style but speeds and gets loud by the end of the first *gongan*, then proceeds through the entire melody, begins to repeat the main section, and ends, on signal, after the first *gongan*.

CD 3/5

Playon "Lasem," *sléndro pathet nem*, Rendition 1 (1:20). Central Javanese *gamelan* music for shadow puppetry. Performed by *gamelan* group under the direction of Ki Suparman. Field recording by R. Anderson Sutton. Yogyakarta, Java, Indonesia, 1974.

CD 3/6

Playon "Lasem," sléndro pathet nem,
Rendition 2 (0:33). Central Javanese
gamelan music for shadow puppetry.
Performed by *gamelan* group under
the direction of Ki Suparman. Field
recording by R. Anderson Sutton.
Yogyakarta, Java, Indonesia, 1974.

In the second rendition (CD 3, Track 6), entirely in loud-playing style, the musicians never even reach the "main" section. To add variety to this rendition, played quite late during the *pathet nem* section (c. 12:30 A.M.), the *saron* players play variant phrases for some of the passages notated earlier, although the *slenthem* player holds to the previous version.

Even without such change, we can see that this one piece has the potential for a great variety of renditions, through changes in tempo, instrumentation, and ending points. This is the essence of shadow puppet music—a very well known piece, played over and over, but uniquely tailored each time to fit precisely with the dramatic intentions of the puppeteer and kept fresh by the inventiveness of the instrumentalists and singers who constantly add subtle variations.

Bali

Just east of Java, separated from it by a narrow strait, lies the island of Bali. The unique culture and spectacular natural beauty of this island have fascinated scholars, artists, and tourists from around the world. In Bali almost everyone takes part in some artistic activity: music, dance, carving, painting. Although the Balinese demonstrate abilities that often strike the Westerner as spectacular, they maintain that such activities are a normal part of life. The exquisite masked dancer by night may well be a rice farmer by day, and the player of lightning-fast interlocking musical passages who accompanies him may manage a small eating stall.

Most of the several million people inhabiting this small island adhere not to Islam, Indonesia's majority religion, but to a blend of Hinduism and Buddhism resembling that which flourished in Java prior to the spread of Islam (fifteenth to sixteenth century C.E.). In this the Balinese and Javanese share elements of a common cultural heritage. As in Java, we find percussion ensembles known as *gamelan* (or *gambelan*), with metal slab instruments and knobbed gong instruments that look and sound quite similar to those of the Javanese *gamelan*. Some of the names are the same (*gendèr, gong, gambang, saron, suling, rebab*) or similar (*kempur, kemong*). Most ensembles employ some version of the *pélog* scale system (some with all seven tones, others with five or six). The accompaniment for Balinese shadow puppetry (as in Java, called *wayang kulit*) employs the *sléndro* scale system, although the instruments used consist only of a quartet of *gendèrs* (augmented by a few other instruments for *Ramayana* stories). Many Balinese pieces employ gong punctuating patterns similar in principle to those of Java. The Balinese play *gamelan* for ritual observances, as in Java, though usually at temple festivals, or in procession to or from them, rather than at someone's residence.

Nevertheless, certain characteristics clearly distinguish the musics of these two neighboring cultures. For example, the Balinese maintain a variety of ensembles, each with its distinct instrumentation and associated with certain occasions and functions. There is no single large ensemble that one can simply call "the Balinese *gamelan*." However, the style of music one hears performed on most ensembles in Bali shares several characteristics:

(1) strictly instrumental, (2) characterized by changes in tempo and loudness (often abrupt), and (3) requiring a dazzling technical mastery by many of the musicians, who play fast interlocking rhythms, often comprising asymmetrical groupings of two or three very fast beats. People often comment that Balinese music is exciting and dynamic in comparison to other Indonesian musics, exploiting contrasts in the manner of Western art music.

They may also comment on the shimmery quality of the many varieties of bronze ensembles. This quality is obtained by tuning instruments in pairs, with one instrument intentionally tuned slightly higher in pitch than its partner. When sounded together, they produce very fast vibrations. In the West, piano tuners rely on these same vibrations, called "beats," to "temper" the tuning, although on a piano it is intervals that are made intentionally "out of tune" rather than identical strings sounding the same tone. Of course, the intentionally "out-of-tune" pairs of metallophones are perceived to be "in tune" (that is, "culturally correct") in Bali, just as the piano is in Western culture.

The most popular ensemble in Bali today is the *gamelan gong kebyar,* which developed during the early twentieth century along with the virtuosic dance it often accompanies (also called *kebyar*—literally, "flash," "dazzle"). *Kebyar* music is indeed "flashy," requiring not only great virtuosity of the players, but also a consummate sense of ensemble—the ability of many to play as one.

Listen to "Kosalia Arini" (CD 3, Track 7), a piece composed by the prolific Balinese composer and skilled drummer Wayan Beratha in 1969 for a *gamelan* festival. This piece demonstrates features typical of *gamelan gong kebyar,* many of which contrast markedly with Javanese *gamelan* music and with older styles of Balinese music. These include episodic structure—the piece is clearly divided into sections with contrasting instrumentation,

CD 3/7

"Kosalia Arini" (10:48), by Wayan Beratha. *Gamelan gong kebyar.* Performed by STSI (Sekolah Tinggi Seni Indonesia) *gamelan* musicians, directed by Nyoman Windha and Pande Gde Mustika. Recorded by Michael Tenzer and Ketut Gde Asnawa, with Yong Sagita. STSI campus, Denpasar, Bali, August, 1998.

Figure 7-8
The *gamelan gong kebyar* of Bali.

Wayne Vitali

rhythm, and texture. Portions of the piece involve cyclic repetition, but the overall design is neither cyclic nor rigidly binary as we saw in Javanese *gamelan* pieces.

Michael Tenzer, a U.S. scholar, composer, and performer of Balinese *gamelan gong kebyar,* has provided a detailed analysis of this piece (Tenzer 2000:367, 381–83), from which the following much briefer commentary derives. Most basic are the contrasts between what Tenzer calls "stable" (cyclic) and "active" (noncyclic) sections.

The overall piece proceeds through four main sections. As you listen, notice the changes (often abrupt) in tempo, instrumentation, dynamics (soft and loud), and register (high pitch or low pitch). Each section is identified not only by characteristic rhythm and texture but also by tonal center.

Timed Listening to "Kosalia Arini" Tonal Center C♯	0:00–2:20	First section features "asymmetrically phrased fragments," mostly with the metal-keyed instruments (various registers of *gendèr* instruments), juxtaposing interlocking *(kotekan)* and noninterlocking fragments, with occasional loud and flashy full ensemble fragments *(kebyar* interruptions).
Tonal Center D	2:21–2:40	A flute solo with low *gendèr.*
	2:41–2:54	Other *gendèrs* enter and mark the transition to the next section.
	2:55–4:45	A cyclic section, consisting of 4-beat phrases, with interlocking throughout.
	4:46–4:47	A full-ensemble *kebyar* interruption.
	4:48–4:58	A short passage featuring the small kettle-gong chime *(reyong).*
	4:59–5:18	A second cyclic section that begins with drum variations.
Tonal Center E	5:19–7:27	Section proceeds with alternately featured *gendèr* and *reyong.* Stops abruptly, with no gong.
	7:28–7:39	Another transitional passage, on *gendèr* instruments.
Back to Tonal Center C♯	7:40–10:45	Third cyclic section, now with eight-beat phrases, ending with a twelve-beat coda.

Though repetitive in some sections, the whole piece is much more like a fantasia or an exuberant study in contrasts (especially in dynamics and in rhythm) than even the most dramatic renditions of Javanese pieces.

North Sumatra

Going from Bali or Java to North Sumatra involves a considerable distance, both culturally and geographically. Although influenced to some degree by Indian culture during the first millennium C.E., the Batak people, the main inhabitants of the province of North Sumatra, have largely converted to Protestant Christianity or to Islam. The Christian Bataks sing hymns at their Sunday church services with an exuberance and an accuracy of pitch that would put most Western congregations—and even many choirs—to shame. More importantly, many indigenous musical genres still thrive among the Batak, and many of these are central to rituals only marginally related to Christianity or Islam, if at all. Just as the majority of Javanese Muslims partake in rituals involving *gamelan* music and Hindu-based shadow puppetry, so the Batak Christians adhere in varying degrees to beliefs and ritual practices that were prevalent prior to the coming of Christianity.

The most celebrated Batak ensembles are the varieties of percussion and wind ensembles known as *gondang* or *gordang*, which usually include a set of tuned drums that are counterparts to the kettle-gong chimes *(bonang* or *trompong)*. These can be heard on several fine recordings available commercially (see end of chapter). Our brief encounter with music in North Sumatra is from a ritual observance I attended among the Karo Batak, who live in the highlands west of Medan and north of the large and beautiful Lake Toba.

A woman in the town of Kabanjahe was planning to open a beauty parlor in part of her house and wished to have the space ritually purified and to secure blessing for her new business by seeking harmony with the spirit world. This she hoped to accomplish by sponsoring and participating in a ceremony involving music and dance and during which she would contact her immediate ancestors through the help of a spirit medium. Members of her family gathered, along with sympathetic neighbors (but not some of the more orthodox Christians, who were not so sympathetic) and even a few foreign visitors, including myself. To my surprise I was urged to take photographs and record the event.

The ceremony lasted for nearly five hours, with several long sections of continuous music. Family members and some neighbors joined the woman

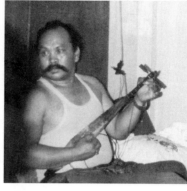

Figure 7-9
Tukang Ginting plays the Karo Batak *kulcapi.* Kabanjabe, North Sumatra.

R. Anderson Sutton

R. Anderson Sutton

Figure 7-10
Members of Tukang Ginting's *gendang keteng-keteng* group, playing the bamboo tube zither *(keteng-keteng).* Kabanjabe, North Sumatra.

in a traditional line dance. The spirit medium sang incantations, sometimes while dancing. He spoke gently to the woman and sometimes loudly to the spirits. With some difficulty the woman eventually went into trance, and the evening was deemed a success.

The musical group engaged for the evening was a small ensemble performing *gendang keteng-keteng,* a form of traditional Batak music employing a small two-stringed, boat-shaped lute *(kulcapi),* two bamboo tube zithers *(keteng-keteng)* and a porcelain bowl *(mangkuk).* On each of the tube zithers, thin strips had been cut and stretched, forming taut filaments. A small bamboo disk was attached to one filament on each. These remarkable instruments create a kind of interlocking percussive filagree. In addition, when the filaments with the disks are struck, they vibrate over a hole cut in the bamboo to produce a deep, vibrato sound remarkably like a small gong. The ensemble played continually for many hours, with the spirit medium singing part of the time. Melody, filling in, gong punctuation—here were the essential elements, it seemed, for music making not only throughout much of Indonesia but much of Southeast Asia as well.

The few excerpts I provide on the recording (CD 3, Track 8) cannot give a real sense of the long ritual, but they offer an introduction to musical sounds that contrast with the *gamelan* ensembles we have heard and yet bear a distant likeness to them. The first excerpt is from the early part of the ceremony. The *kulcapi* player, Tukang Ginting, provides what is basically a repeating, cyclic melody that he varies. The "clickety" sounds are the two percussionists playing the bamboo *keteng-keteng* instruments, filling in the texture to give constant "busy" sound, which seems to characterize much music throughout Indonesia. What is especially remarkable, in light of the other music we have heard, is how the porcelain bowl and the gong sounds relate. The gong sound occurs at regular intervals, as one so often finds in Java and Bali. It is subdivided by the porcelain bowl sound, which coincides with the gong sound and at the midpoint between them like a *kenong* subdividing and coinciding with a gong in Java.

The second excerpt is from a climactic moment in the evening when the woman first thought she was going into trance. (She did not succeed at this point but did an hour or so later.) The players increase the musical intensity by compressing the time interval between gong beats; the tempo speeds up and then doubles during this excerpt. The porcelain bowl consistently subdivides the time between gong beats, even in the very fast portion, resembling structurally the *wayang kulit* music of Java (like the *playon* we studied earlier).

With its gong punctuation, coincidence, cyclic melody, binary rhythms, and fast-moving and dense percussion playing, this music seems clearly a relative of the *gamelan* music we heard earlier. Although this discussion has stressed the similarities, realize that these are only *structural* similarities, easy to identify from a theoretical perspective. The differences are so profound that the Batak and Javanese care little for each other's music. To the Javanese, clacking bamboo is no substitute for the varied drum strokes of the *kendhang,* the interlocking melodies of the *bonang,* or the heterophonic

CD 3/8

Gendang keteng-keteng, two excerpts (1:58). Traditional Batak music. Performed by ensemble led by Tukang Ginting on *kulcapi.* Field recording by R. Anderson Sutton. Karo Batak highlands of North Sumatra, 1979.

wanderings of the various soft-playing ensemble instruments in the Javanese *gamelan*. To the Batak, the thick-textured and often mighty sound of a full Javanese *gamelan* cannot attain the personal intimacy of the small *kulcapi* ensemble nor the spontaneity of the *kulcapi* player that we have just heard.

Perhaps these few examples of traditional music from several regions of Indonesia will help you begin to gain an understanding of the national motto *Bhinneka Tunggal Ika*—an Old Javanese phrase meaning "Unity in Diversity." In the arts we indeed find great variety, but underlying elements shared by these arts attest to the appropriateness of the motto. As we turn to examples of recent popular music, we find another layer of Indonesia's musical diversity—one that many Indonesians experience and that is especially meaningful to younger Indonesians from many regions.

Indonesian Popular Music

Most of the music Indonesians would identify as "popular" is, like most popular music anywhere in the world, characterized by the use of at least some Western instruments and Western harmony (see Hatch 1989). Essentially a commercial genre, it is disseminated through the mass media and performed by recognized stars. Unfortunately, space does not allow us to explore the interesting history of Western-influenced music in Indonesia, which has primarily been in the popular vein. We shall, however, consider three superstar individuals or groups that represent each of three contrasting styles within the "pop" music world in Indonesia.

Rhoma Irama, Dangdut

The first contemporary style is called *dangdut,* in imitation of the sound formerly made on hand drums and more recently on trap set and electric guitar. The musician known during the 1970s and 1980s as the "king of *dangdut*" was Rhoma Irama. Born in 1947 in West Java, he learned to play electric guitar and showed greater interest in music than in the formal schooling his mother struggled to afford. In his late teens he dropped out of school and joined the underground music movement, heavily influenced by Western rock (and banned by then-president Sukarno).

Irama soon became disenchanted with rock. By his own account, he then consciously set out to create a sound that would satisfy the craving of Indonesian youth for a "modern" musical style but that would also sound clearly Indonesian (or at least "Eastern") in contrast to Western rock (Frederick 1982:109). He turned to a Western-influenced genre, *orkès melayu* music, whose origins are traced to the urban areas of North and West Sumatra. This genre incorporated influences from the soundtracks of the many Indian films that have long enjoyed wide popularity in Indonesia (see Chapter 6). Even with its quasi-Western harmonic basis, this music was clearly Eastern, characterized by highly ornamented singing and flute playing.

Rhoma Irama set out to make a commercial mark, and he succeeded spectacularly. Like most pop stars he has sung about love, but he has also presented forthrightly his own ideas about his country and, perhaps most persistently, about his religion. He was one of the first Indonesian popular artists to make the pilgrimage to Mecca, and has used both his music and his films to spread his Islamic message. One of his first hits (1977) was a piece about greed, entitled "Rupiah" (the national currency). It was banned by government officials who thought it "debased the national currency" (Frederick 1982:117). Another early song, also banned, was "Hak Azasi" ("Basic Rights"), which described human rights—including freedom of religion and freedom of speech.

Listen to "Begadang II" (CD 3, Track 9), which was the most popular song of 1978 and established Irama as a star. The song bears the same title as the hit film for which it served as the theme song. *Begadang* is a Jakarta term for staying up all or most of the night, usually to socialize with friends. This song provides a typical example of the *dangdut* musical sound as Irama developed it.

CD 3/9

"Begadang II" ("Staying up All Night") (3:33), by Rhoma Irama. Popular *dangdut* music. Performed by Rhoma Irama and his Soneta Group. *Begadang II.* Yukawi Indomusic. 1978.

Text, "Begadang II"

1. *Apa artinya malam minggu* What good is Saturday night
   Bagi orang yang tidak mampu? For those who are not well-to-do?
   Mau ke pesta tak beruang; Want to go to a party, but have no money;

   Akhirnya nongkrong di pinggir jalan. Wind up squatting by the side of the road.

2. *Begadang, marilah kita begadang,* Stay up, let's stay up,
   Begadang sambil berdendang; Stay up and sing;
   Walaupun kita tidak punya uang Even though we don't have money
   Kita juga bisa senang. We can still have fun.

3. *Bagi mereka yang punya uang* Those who have money
   Berdansa-dansi di nite club; Dance at night clubs;
   Bagi kita yang tak punya uang Those of us who have no money
   Cukup berjoget disini. Just dance here [by the road].

4. *Bagi mereka yang punya uang* Those who have money
   Makan-makan di restoran; Always eat in nice restaurants;
   Bagi kita yang tak punya uang Those of us who have no money
   Makannya di warung kopi. Just eat at makeshift roadside stalls.

"Begadang II" by Rhoma Irama. Used by permission.

The text shows Irama's clear orientation toward lower-class youth. Like most of his music, it appeals to the youthful urge to dance and often accompanies popular social dancing akin to rock or disco dancing in the West.

Twenty-two years after this hit, Irama was still producing cassettes, although he no longer dominated the market. He has also starred in several films in which—to the chagrin of more conservative Indonesian Moslems—he proselytizes for Islam through his loud, electric *dangdut* music. Unlikely as it may seem, then, Rhoma Irama gained his fame as an Islamic rock star and enjoyed enormous commercial success. His passion for communicating his vision of a more perfect society, holding closely to the teachings of Islam, led him into the realm of politics. In 1982 he endorsed the Islamic opposition party and played at a rally in Jakarta that erupted in violence shortly before the elections took place. Yet by the early 1990s he had, most likely with some reluctance, joined the incumbent political party and even played at functions of the very body that represented the clearest threat to Islamic political power in Indonesia: the army.

Responses to Globalization

From Irama's *dangdut,* we now turn to two recent examples of popular music (one released in 2000, the other in 1998). The forces of globalization have intensified since the 1980s, inundating the Indonesian marketplace with the commercial cultural products of the West, including various forms of American pop, rock, and jazz. Our final two musical examples represent different responses to this process. The first, by a group called Krakatau (named after the famous volcanic island lying just west of Java), involves a careful synthesis of Sundanese (that is, West Javanese) *gamelan* and fusion jazz. The second, by a rock group known as Ahmad Band, represents a full embrace of Western alternative and heavy metal styles, with a strong element of political and social protest in the lyrics.

Krakatau, Sundanese *Gamelan,* and Fusion Jazz

Krakatau (Figure 7-11) was founded in the late 1980s by Dwiki Dharmawan, a jazz keyboardist whose skill in imitating the styles of Joe Zawinul (Weather Report) and Chick Corea won him an award from the Yamaha Music Company of Japan in 1985. The early recordings of Krakatau present original fusion jazz tunes with complex harmonies and rhythms. They include jazz songs, some in English, sung by a female Javanese-Sundanese singer, Trie Utami, who offers polished and sophisticated imitations of African-American jazz vocal styles. Yet beginning around 1993 and 1994, members of the group, particularly Dharmawan and Utami, grew tired of merely imitating the music they admired from the West. Because the core members had all spent much of their youth in West Java (Sunda), they decided to incorporate Sundanese musical elements into their music, adding local experts on *saron, bonang, rebab,* and *kendang.* In short, they set out to create a hybrid variety of music, mixing Western and indigenous Indonesian musical instruments and elements.

Experiments in such combinations have been taking place in Indonesia for centuries. Special challenges are posed by the fact that many Indonesian instruments and songs use tunings and scales, such as *sléndro* and

Figure 7-11
Krakatau in performance.

pélog, that are not compatible with Western ones (take a look back at Figure 7-2). In the nineteenth century, brass band instruments were played with *pélog gamelan* instruments in the courts of Central Java, representing a symbolic fusion of Javanese and Dutch power. In the early twentieth century, Javanese composers began to write pieces combining Javanese singing with Western instruments.

In the 1990s, Indonesia saw a sudden growth in experimental combinations of pop/rock instruments and indigenous Indonesian ones. The musician often acknowledged as the inspiration for this trend is Guruh Sukarno Putra, who produced a landmark album (commercial cassette, *Guruh Gipsy*) in 1976 involving piano, synthesizers, and rock instruments playing along with Balinese *gendèrs* and drums and incorporating Central Javanese vocal styles and West Javanese scales and melodies. Guruh is the youngest living son of the founding father of the Republic of Indonesia, President Sukarno. His music has sometimes been referred to as *pop berat* (literally "heavy pop"; see Hatch 1989), a music more varied and challenging to listen to than the easy rhythms of *dangdut.* But where Guruh drew on various regional Indonesian styles, the members of Krakatau have attempted to focus on their own region, Sunda.

In 1994 they released *Mystical Mist,* in which some pieces sounded more like jazz fusion and others more Sundanese. In their most recent release, *Magical Match,* the blend is more even throughout. One of the ingenious ideas they have employed is the tuning of their Western instruments to the scales of Sundanese traditional music. Dwiki programmed in a complex alteration of pitches for his keyboard and worked out special fingerings so that when he strikes certain combinations of black and white keys on his keyboard, he can produce the tones of *sléndro, pélog,* or other scales typical of Sundanese traditional music. The bass player uses an electric bass with no frets (the horizontal metal strips found on guitars that facilitate production of the Western scale). With skillful placement of his fingers, he can play bass patterns in *sléndro* and other non-Western scales. On this album Trie Utami sings not like a jazz singer but with the distinctive timbre of a Sundanese female singer *(pesindhèn)*. The example on our recording, however, is purely instrumental, illustrating most clearly the skill of the musicians in creating a piece that tries to be not just Sundanese and not just Western but a "magical match" of the two.

Listen to "Shufflendang-Shufflending" (CD 3, Track 10). The title mixes the English word *shuffle* (a type of African-American ecstatic song/dance combination performed in worship, also known as "ring-shout") and the Sundanese words for drum *(kendang)* and *gamelan* musical piece *(gendhing)*. Krakatau is joined by Zainal Arifin, Adhe Rudiana (who teaches traditional music at the Indonesian College of Performing Arts in Bandung, West Java), and recent graduates Yoyon Darsono, Elfik Zulfiqar, and Tudi Rahayu.

CD 3/10

"Shufflendang-Shufflending" (4:11). Ethno-jazz fusion, Sundanese. Performed by Krakatau: Dwiki Dharmawan, keyboard; Pra Budidharma, fretless bass; Budhy Haryono, Western drum set ("traps"); joined by Yoyon Darsono, *rebab* and flute; Adhe Rudiana, *kendang;* Elfik Zulfiqar and Tudi Rahayu, *saron;* Zainal Arifin, *bonang. Magical Match.* Kita Music. 2000.

Timed Listening, "Shufflendang-Shufflending"

0:00	Piece begins with a repeated figure (ostinato) on Western instruments in fusion jazz style.
0:15	Hints of a *pélog* scale.
0:42	Abruptly, *sarons* play in *sléndro.*
0:51	*Sarons* play in *pélog.*
1:00	*Sarons* return to *sléndro.*
1:10	A switch to *rebab* in *pélog.*
1:37	Back to jazz and the rotation continues, although not in exact repetition.
3:52	Sundanese drumming shortly before fadeout.

While it is possible to enjoy the sounds and the rhythm without knowing their origins, the meaning this music has for Krakatau members and for their fans in Indonesia is its ability to "Sundanize" jazz or pop music and to "jazz" or "modernize" Sundanese music at the same time. Its ambiguity provides a bridge between the seemingly incompatible worlds of local Indonesian/traditional culture and Western/modern culture. Dharmawan and other members of the group, whom I got to know in August 2000, did not have a clear sense of what to call their music. We talked about "new age," "world music," and "ethno-pop." They clearly hope that this music will reach beyond Indonesia to attract listeners from around the world, not only to their own music but also to the rich treasury of Indonesia's traditional music.

The Ahmad Band: Indonesian Rock Music

Let us turn now to an example of alternative rock, performed by the Ahmad Band on *Ideologi Sikap Otak,* released in 1998 just as Indonesia was undergoing extraordinary political upheaval, with student demonstrations and confrontations that led to the resignation of Indonesia's authoritarian president, Suharto, in May of that year. The Ahmad Band is named for its founding songwriter, Dhani Ahmad Manaf (Figure 7-12), one of the core members of Dewa 19, an enormously popular (and more mainstream) group, whose many singles and albums have topped the Indonesian charts since the mid-1990s. Several other musicians joined Dhani (as he is known) to form the Ahmad Band: Andra Ramadhan (guitarist for Dewa 19), Bimo (drum), Bongky (bass), and Pay (guitar). Dhani invited me to his studio several times, and we talked at great length about music. It was clear from the start that he had almost no interest in indigenous Indonesian "traditional" music of any kind. He said it was hard enough to write and produce good rock songs, let alone try to mix in traditional instruments or other stylistic elements. Some of his music, especially the music he composes and performs with the popular Dewa 19, presents the usual pop themes of love and youth. Dhani also has strong political convictions, however, which he has expressed musically with his alternative group, Ahmad Band.

Listen to "Distorsi" (CD 3, Track 11), an alternative rock protest song about hypocrisy and corruption.

CD 3/11

"Distorsi" ("Distortion") (5:19). Dhani Ahmad Manaf. Indonesian rock music performed by Ahmad Band: Dhani, vocal; Andra Ramadhan, guitar; Bimo, drum; Bongky, bass; Pay, guitar. *Ideologi Sikap Otak.* Aquarius P 9173. 1998.

Text, "Distorsi"

Maunya selalu memberantas kemiskinan	They always want to combat poverty,
tapi ada yang selalu kuras uang rakyat	but there's always someone who drains off (siphons) the people's money.
ada yang sok aksi buka mulut protas protes	There are show-offs who open their mouths in protest,
tapi sayang mulutnya selalu beraroma alkohol	but it's a shame their mouths always smell of alcohol.

Figure 7-12

"Dhani" (Dhani Ahmad Manaf) in performance with the Ahmad Band.

yang muda mabuk, yang tua korup	The youth are drunk, the elders corrupt,
mabuk terus, korup terus	continually drunk, continually corrupt.
jayalah negeri ini,	Great is this country,
jayalah negeri ini.	great is this country.
maunya selalu menegakkan keadilan	They always want to strengthen justice,
tapi masih saja ada sisa hukum rimba	but there is still the residue of the law of the jungle,
setiap hari mabuk	every day drunk,
ngoceh soal politik	babbling about politics,
setiap hari korup	every day corrupt,
ngoceh soal krisis ekonomi	babbling about the economic crisis.
perut kekenyangan bahas soal kelaparan	Those with full stomachs discuss hunger.
kapitalis sejati malah ngomongin	True capitalists even talk about
soal keadilan sosial	social justice,
selalu monopoli!	always monopoly!
ngoceh soal pemerataan	babble about even distribution,
setiap hari tucau	every day shooting up [narcotics],
ngomel soal kebobrokan.	grumbling about collapse.

"Distorsi" by Dhani Ahmad Manaf. Used by permission.

The song does not mention specific names (Suharto, for example, or his cabinet ministers, or his rich business cronies). To do so would have risked immediate and severe measures—not only censorship but imprisonment. Instead, like other protest music in Indonesia, this song makes bitter complaints without pointing a finger. However, Indonesian listeners understand and are moved to action by this and other protest songs, just as much as they are by impassioned speeches at political rallies.

These three examples of popular music from Indonesia offer some important contrasts in style and message. The contrasts among them can begin to give you an idea of the complexity of Indonesia's popular music— still mostly unexplored by research scholars. Despite his recent political shift, Rhoma Irama is a strong Muslim. His roots are humble and he speaks to the disenfranchised masses. Krakatau's public image is secular and at once regional (Sundanese *gamelan*) and international (jazz fusion). Both Irama and Krakatau perform music that has developed from a blend of disparate musical elements. Ahmad Band, in contrast, strives consciously to create within the stylistic norms of Western alternative rock, producing confrontational music. Where Irama's *dangdut* music has consistently and consciously been molded by mass taste and has found popularity throughout the entire nation, the others appeal to a narrower market: sophisticated urbanites (especially Sundanese and Javanese) for Krakatau and disaffected urban youth for Ahmad Band.

All three have aspired to use their music to do more than entertain. Though with different approaches, both Irama and Ahmad Band offer a social message to their listeners and followers. Krakatau provides a bridge between local tradition and international modernity. Each carves out a social place for its music and maintains a separate artistic style as a result. Despite the upheaval and frequent unrest in parts of Indonesia today, this country still prides itself on its people's ability to tolerate diversity and coexist. These three popular examples offer a glimpse of that diversity and show us that it applies not only to traditional regional culture but also to popular music disseminated nationally.

References

Becker, Judith. 1979. "Time and Tune in Java." In *The Imagination of Reality: Essays in Southeast Asian Coherence Systems,* edited by A. L. Becker and Aram A. Yengoyan, 197–210. Norwood, N.J.: Ablex.

———. 1980. *Traditional Music in Modern Java: Gamelan in a Changing Society*. Honolulu: University of Hawaii Press.

———. 1981. "Hindu-Buddhist Time in Javanese Gamelan Music." In *The Study of Time, 4,* edited by J. F. Fraser. New York: Springer-Verlag.

———. 1988. "Earth, Fire, *Sakti,* and the Javanese Gamelan." *Ethnomusicology* 32(3): 385–91.

Frederick, William. 1982. "Rhoma Irama and the Dangdut Style: Aspects of Contemporary Indonesian Popular Culture." *Indonesia* 34:103–30.

Hatch, Martin. 1989. "Popular Music in Indonesia (1983)." In *World Music, Politics and Social Change,* edited by Simon Frith. Manchester, England: Manchester University Press.

Hoffman, Stanley B. 1978. "Epistemology and Music: a Javanese Example." *Ethnomusicology* 22(1): 69–88.

Hood, Mantle. 1954. *The Nuclear Theme as a Determinant of Patet in Javanese Music.* Groningen, The Netherlands: J. B. Wolters.

Keeler, Ward. 1987. *Javanese Shadows, Javanese Selves.* Princeton, N.J.: Princeton Univ. Press.

Kunst, Jaap. 1973. *Music in Java: Its History, Its Theory, and Its Technique.* Edited by Ernst Heins. 3rd ed. 2 vols. The Hague: Martinus Nijhoff.

Surjodiningrat, Wasisto, P. J. Sudarjana, and Adhi Susanto. 1972. *Tone Measurements of Outstanding Javanese Gamelans in Jogjakarta and Surakarta.* Yogyakarta: Gadjah Mada University Press.

Tenzer, Michael. 2000. *Gamelan Gong Kebyar: The Art of Twentieth-Century Balinese Music.* Chicago: University of Chicago Press.

Additional Reading

On Music

Bakan, Michael B. 1999. *Music of Death and New Creation: Experiences in the World of Balinese Gamelan Beleganjur.* Chicago: University of Chicago Press.

Becker, Judith, and Alan Feinstein, eds. 1984, 1987, 1988. *Karawitan: Source Readings In Javanese Gamelan and Vocal Music.* 3 vols. Ann Arbor: University of Michigan Center for South and Southeast Asian Studies.

Herbst, Edward. 1997. *Voices in Bali: Energies and Perceptions in Vocal Music and Dance Theater.* Hanover, N.H.: University Press of New England, Wesleyan University Press.

Hood, Mantle, and Hardja Susilo. 1967. *Music of the Venerable Dark Cloud: Introduction, Commentary, and Analysis.* Los Angeles: University of California Press.

Kartomi, Margaret. 1980. "Musical Strata in Java, Bali, and Sumatra." In *Musics of Many Cultures,* edited by Elizabeth May, 111–33. Berkeley: University of California Press.

Lindsay, Jennifer. 1992. *Javanese Gamelan: Traditional Orchestra of Indonesia.* 2nd ed. New York: Oxford University Press.

Manuel, Peter. 1988. *Popular Musics of the Non-Western World: An Introductory Survey.* New York: Oxford University Press. (See especially pp. 205–20.)

McPhee, Colin. 1966. *Music in Bali.* New Haven, Conn.: Yale University Press.

Simon, Artur. 1984. "Functional Changes in Batak Traditional Music and Its Role in Modern Indonesian Society." *Asian Music* 15(2): 58–66.

Sumarsam. 1995. *Gamelan: Cultural Interaction and Musical Development in Central Java.* Chicago: University of Chicago Press.

Sutton, R. Anderson. 1987. "Identity and Individuality in an Ensemble Tradition: The Female Vocalist in Java." In *Women and Music in Cross-Cultural Perspective,* edited by Ellen Koskoff, 113–30. Westport, Conn.: Greenwood Press. Reprint, Urbana: Univ. of Illinois Press, 1989.

———. 1993. *Variation in Central Javanese Gamelan Music.* DeKalb, Ill.: Center for Southeast Asian Studies, Northern Illinois University.

Tenzer, Michael. 1991. *Balinese Music.* Berkeley, Calif.: Periplus.

Vetter, Roger. 1981. "Flexibility in the Performance Practice of Central Javanese Music." *Ethnomusicology* 25(2): 199–214.

On Indonesia

Anderson, Benedict R. O'G. 1965. *Mythology and the Tolerance of the Javanese.* Ithaca, N.Y.: Cornell Modern Indonesia Project.

Becker, A. L. 1979. "Text Building, Epistemology, and Aesthetics in Javanese Shadow Theater." In *The Imagination of Reality: Essays in Southeast Asian Coherence Systems,* edited by A. L. Becker and Aram A. Yengoyan, 211–43. Norwood, N.J.:Ablex.

Geertz, Clifford. 1960. *The Religion of Java.* New York: Free Press.

Holt, Claire. 1967. *Art in Indonesia: Continuities and Change.* Ithaca, N.Y.: Cornell Univ. Press.

Ricklefs, Merle C. 1993. *A History of Modern Indonesia since c. 1300.* 2nd ed. Stanford, Calif.: Stanford Univ. Press.

Additional Listening

Java (including West Java and Jakarta)

Bedhaya Duradasih, Court Music of Kraton Surakarta II. King Record, World Music Library, KICC 5193.

Betawi and Sundanese Music of the North Coast of Java: Topeng Betawi, Tanjidor, Ajeng. Music of Indonesia, 5. Smithsonian Folkways SFW CD 40421.

Chamber Music of Central Java. King Record, World Music Library, KICC 5152.

Court Music of Kraton Surakarta. King Record, World Music Library, KICC 5151.

The Gamelan of Cirebon. King Record, World Music Library KICC 5130.

Indonesian Popular Music: Kroncong, Dangdut, & Langgam Jawa. Music of Indonesia, 2. Smithsonian Folkways SF 40056.

Java: Langen Mandra Wanara, Opéra de Danuredjo VII. Ocora CD C559014/15.

Java: Palais Royal de Yogyakarta. Volume 4: La musique de concert. Ocora (Radio France) C 560087.

Javanese Court Gamelan. Elektra/Nonesuch Explorer Series 972044-2.

Klenengan Session of Solonese Gamelan I. King Record, World Music Library, KICC 5185.

Langendriyan, Music of Mangkunegaran Solo II. King Record, World Music Library, KICC 5194.

Music from the Outskirts of Jakarta: Gambang Kromong. Music of Indonesia, 3. Smithsonian Folkways SF 40057.

The Music of K. R. T. Wasitodiningrat. CMP Records CD 3007.

Music of Mangkunegaran Solo I. King Record, World Music Library, KICC 5184.

Shadow Music of Java. Rounder CD 5060.

Songs Before Dawn: Gandrung Banyuwangi. Music of Indonesia, 1. Smithsonian Folkways SF 40055.

The Sultan's Pleasure, Javanese Gamelan and Vocal Music from the Palace of Yogyakarta. Music of the World CDT-116.

Bali

Bali: Court Music and Banjar Music (Musique de cour et musique de banjar). Réédition Auvidis, Unesco collection, Musiques et musicians D 8059.

Bali: Gamelan and Kecak. Elektra Nonesuch Explorer Series CD 979204-4.

Bali: Les Grands Gong Kebyar des Anneés Soixante. Ocora, Harmonia Mundi, C 560057–C 560058 (2 CDs).

Gamelan Gong Gede of Batur Temple. World Music Library, King Records KICC 5153.

Gamelan Gong Kebyar, Bali. Elektra Nonesuch CD 79280-2.

The Gamelan Music of Bali. World Music Library, King Records KICC 5126.

Gamelan Semar Pegulingan "Gunung Jati," Br. Teges Kanginan. World Music Library, King Records KICC 5180.

Gender Wayang of Sukawati Village. World Music Library, King Records KICC 5156.

Golden Rain: Gong Kebyar of Gunung Sari, Bali. Elektra Nonesuch CD 79219-2.

Kecak Ganda Sari. *Kecak from Bali.* Bridge BCD 9019.

Music in Bali. World Music Library, King Records KICC 5127.

Music of the Gamelan Gong Kebyar, Bali. Vital Records 401-2 (2 discs).

Other Indonesian Islands

Batak of North Sumatra. New Albion Records NA 046 CD.

Gongs and Vocal Music from Sumatra. Music of Indonesia, 12. Smithsonian Folkways SFW C 40428.

Indonesian Guitars. Music of Indonesia, 20. Smithsonian Folkways SFW CD 40447.

Kalimantan: Dayak Ritual and Festival Music. Music of Indonesia, 17. Smithsonian Folkways SFW C 40444.

Kalimantan Strings. Music of Indonesia, 13. Smithsonian Folkways SFW CD 40429.

Lombok, Kalimantan, Banyumas: Little-known Forms of Gamelan and Wayang. Music of Indonesia, 14. Smithsonian Folkways SFW CD 40441.

Melayu Music of Sumatra and the Riau Islands. Music of Indonesia, 11. Smithsonian Folkways SFW CD 40427.

Music from the Forests of Riau and Mentawai. Music of Indonesia, 7. Smithsonian Folkways SFW CD 40423.

Music from the Southeast: Sumbawa, Sumba, Timor. Music of Indonesia, 16. Smithsonian Folkways SFW CD 40443.

Music of Biak, Irian Jaya. Music of Indonesia, 10. Smithsonian Folkways SFW CD 40426.

Music of Madura. Ode Record Company CD ODE 1381.

Music of Maluku: Halmahera, Buru, Kei. Music of Indonesia, 19. Smithsonian Folkways SFW CD 40446.

Music of Nias and North Sumatra: Hoho, Gendang Karo, Gondang Toba. Smithsonian Folkways SF CD 40429.

Night Music of West Sumatra. Music of Indonesia, 6. Smithsonian Folkways SFW CD 40422.

Sulawesi: Festivals, Funerals, and Work. Music of Indonesia, 18. Smithsonian Folkways SF CD 40445.

Sulawesi Strings. Music of Indonesia, 15. Smithsonian Folkways SFW CD 40442.

Vocal and Instrumental Music from East and Central Flores. Music of Indonesia, 8. Smithsonian Folkways SFW CD 40424.

Vocal Music from Central and West Flores. Music of Indonesia, 9. Smithsonian Folkways SFW CD 40425.

Viewing

Karya: Video Portraits of Four Indonesian Composers. 1992. Videocassette. Produced and Directed by Jody Diamond. Distributed by American Gamelan Institute, Box 5036, Hanover, NH 03755. Balinese, Javanese, and Batak composers talk about their recent work.

The JVC Video Anthology of World Music and Dance. 1990. Thirty videocassettes plus guide. Edited by Fujii Tomoaki, with assistant editors Omori Yasuhiro and Sakurai Tetsuo, in collaboration with the National Museum of Ethnology (Osaka). Produced by Ichikawa Katsumori. Directed by Nakagawa Kunihiko and Ichihashi Yuji. Victor Company of Japan, Ltd., in collaboration with Smithsonian Folkways Recordings. Distributed by Rounder Records, Cambridge, Mass. 02140.

• Volume 9 contains footage of Javanese shadow puppetry (poor quality), along with studio footage of Balinese *kecak* ("monkey chant") and Sundanese music (recorded in Japan).

• Volume 10 contains a variety of Balinese examples, recorded in Bali, mostly employing a *gamelan semar pegulingan* (even for contexts in which this ensemble is not appropriate).

Bali

Bali Beyond the Postcard. 1991. Videorecording and 16mm. Produced and directed by Nancy Dine, Peggy Stern, and David Dawkins. Distributed by Filmakers Library, 124 East 40th Street, New York, NY 10016; and by "Outside in July," 59 Barrow Street, New York, NY 10014. Gamelan and dance in four generations of a Balinese family.

Compressed Version of a "Gambuh" (Dance Drama) in Batuan. 1981. 16 mm. Produced by T. Seebass and G. van der Weijden. Distributed by Institut für den Wissenschaftlichen Film, Göttingen, Germany. Performance of *gambuh,* "classical" Balinese dance drama.

Releasing the Spirits: A Village Cremation in Bali. 1991 [1981]. Videocassette. Directed by Patsy Asch, Linda Connor, et al. Distributed by Documentary Educational Resources, Watertown, Mass. Cremation rituals in a central Balinese village.

Shadowmaster. 1980. Videocassette and 16 mm. Directed by Larry Reed. Distributed by Larry Reed Productions, 18 Chattanooga Street, San Francisco, Calif. 94114. Fiction film about the social and artistic life of a shadow puppeteer in Bali.

Java

Bird of Passage. 1986. 16 mm. Directed by Fons Grasveld. Distributed by Netherlands Film Institute, Postbus 515, 1200 AM Hilversum, The Netherlands. Javanese traditions in Java, Suriname, and the Netherlands.

The Dancer and the Dance. (1990?). Videocassette and 16 mm. Produced by Felicia Hughes-Freeland. Distributed by Film Officer, Royal Anthropological Institute, 50 Fitzroy Street, London, England W1P 5HS. Javanese court dance in its current social context.

Traditional Dances of Indonesia, Dances of Jogjakarta, Central Java: Langen Mandra Wanara. 1990. Videocassette from 16mm film made in 1975. Directed and produced by William Heick. Distributed by University of California Extension Media Center, 2176 Shattuck Ave., Berkeley, Calif. 94704. Dance-opera presenting episode from the *Ramayana.*

Traditional Dances of Indonesia, Dances of Surakarta, Central Java: Srimpi Anglir Mendung. 1990. Videocassette from 16mm film made in 1975. Directed and produced by William Heick. Distributed by University of California Extension Media Center, 2176 Shattuck Ave., Berkeley, Calif. 94704. Refined female court dance. (Ten additional videorecordings from the same distributor present additional dances from Java, Bali, and West Sumatra.)

North Sumatra

Karo-Batak (Indonesien, Nordsumatra)—Gendang-Musik "mari-mari" und "patam-patam." 1994. 16 mm. Directed by Artur Simon. Distributed by Institut für den Wissenschaftlichen Film, Göttingen, Germany. Ceremonial music performed by *gendang keteng-keteng* ensemble.

Karo-Batak (Indonesien, Nordsumatra)—Tänze anlässlich einer Haarwaschzeremonie in Kuta Mbelin. 1994. 16 mm. Directed by Franz Simon and Artur Simon. Distributed by Institut für den Wissenschaftlichen Film, Göttingen, Germany. Dances associated with the hair-washing ceremony of Kuta Mbelin, North Sumatra. (Fourteen additional films from the same distributor cover performing arts of Karo and other Batak groups in North Sumatra and of Kayan-Dayak groups in West Kalimantan [Borneo].)

CHAPTER

 8

East Asia/Japan

Linda Fujie

resent-day Japan impresses the first-time visitor as an intense, fascinating, and sometimes confusing combination of old and new, of Eastern and Western and things beyond categorization. Strolling through the Ginza area of Tokyo, for example, you find many colorful remnants of an earlier age sprinkled among the gigantic department stores and elegant boutiques, and always there is the ubiquitous McDonald's (pronounced ma-ku-do-nar-u-do-su). Tiny noodle shops and old stores selling kimono material or fine china carry the atmosphere of a past era. Looming over a central boulevard, in the midst of modern office buildings, is the Kabuki-za, a large, impressive theater built in the traditional style.

As the visitor begins to sense from the streets of Japan's capital, many aspects of Japanese life today—from architecture to social attitudes to music—are an intriguing mix of the traditional and the foreign. Japan has absorbed cultural influences from outside her borders for centuries, many of which originate in other parts of Asia. The writing system comes from China, and one of the major religions, Buddhism, is from India, through Korea and China. Connections with Chinese and Korean music and musical instruments are a fundamental part of the history of traditional music in Japan. In the late nineteenth and twentieth centuries, European and American ideas and objects have also had a major impact on Japanese culture.

Although cultural borrowing has clearly been important in Japanese history, the stereotype of the Japanese as "mere imitators" must also be laid aside. The Japanese have developed a unique culture, both through their own creativity and by imaginatively adapting foreign elements into their own culture. Throughout history, geographical and political circumstances have isolated Japan to the extent that such independent creativity and adaptation were necessary. A group of islands separated from the Asian continent by an often treacherous sea, Japan set itself apart for several centuries. This isolation reached its height in the Tokugawa, or Edo, period (1600–1867), when Japan's borders were mostly closed to the outside

In this chapter, "traditional music" in relation to Japan will refer to those musical genres developed mainly in pre-Meiji Japan—that is, before 1868 and the beginning of a period of strong Western influence on Japanese music.

331

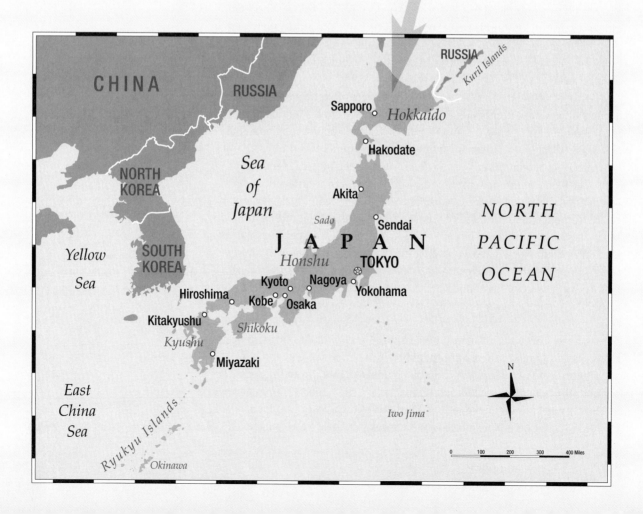

world. Many customs and ideas that Westerners consider "traditionally Japanese" were developed during this period. Most traditional music presented in this chapter, for instance, dates from the Tokugawa period, though its roots may go back farther.

On the whole, Japan's culture combines a deep respect for tradition with creativity and flexibility. Many layers of culture, musical and otherwise, exist side by side, different yet harmonious. One sign of this diversity lies in the music the Japanese listen to today.

In concert halls, theaters, clubs, and bars, Japanese looking for entertainment find all kinds of live musical performances: Japanese traditional music, Western classical music, rock, jazz, punk, country and western, and music from around the world. In addition, television, radio, tapes, and compact discs provide recorded music of every imaginable type.

The kinds of music Japanese most enjoy listening to and performing usually vary by the age of the listener. Japanese children learn to play the recorder and sing European, American, and Japanese folk songs in their schools; many also take private lessons on a Western musical instrument. Children learn and sing theme songs from television shows and commercials, and these sometimes become hit records. As teenagers, many Japanese listen to the latest hits from the West as well as to Japanese popular music. Teenagers know a great deal about the latest developments in sound technology and spend more on music—recordings and equipment—than does any other segment of the population. Among young adults, tastes tend toward the mellower popular music genres, such as contemporary folk and so-called golden oldies, or Western classical music or traditional folk songs. At this stage in life, singing with the *karaoke* (ka-ra-oh-kay) machine can become an important form of musical entertainment. Middle-aged adults like to listen to older Japanese and Western popular songs, Western classical music, and Japanese folk songs. Along with older people, the middle-aged are most likely to enjoy traditional Japanese music, which they hear on television and at live performances.

Given the high quality of audio and video equipment available in contemporary Japan, it is not surprising that people use the mass media for most of their music listening. About one in four Japanese listens to music solely through television sets (NHK 1982:38). Each week, Japanese public and private television stations broadcast a dozen or more music-variety shows. Many of these feature popular music, but some offer performances of *kabuki* theater, Western opera, or symphonies. Young people in particular listen to music on cassette tape players, compact discs, and the radio (NHK 1982:47). Japanese also listen to many live performances featuring both Japanese and foreign performers. On the whole, however, Japanese listening resembles that in many other highly industrialized countries: the people listen more to recorded music than to live performances, and they are not always fully attentive to it. Music is heard in the background of everyday

Listening Habits of Contemporary Japanese

This information is based on the results of a 1981 comprehensive survey of Japanese musical tastes (NHK 1982:68–77).

life, whether it is Muzak in a coffee shop or music coming from a radio or television set kept on while people go about their normal activities.

In the past hundred years, the Japanese have become more involved with new music, devoting less time to traditional music. Since the Meiji period (1868–1911) Western music has been influential, and the education system has officially encouraged its spread. Despite the overwhelming influence of music from outside Japan, however, traditional music remains viable. The *kabuki* and *bunraku* theaters in the larger cities are still well attended, as are concerts of traditional instrumental and vocal music. Teachers of instruments such as the *shakuhachi* and the *shamisen* still find many interested pupils of all ages, and televised instruction for such instruments in recent years has helped bolster their popularity. Perhaps the large amount of Western influence has helped young people appreciate the different beauty of Japanese music and its special relationship to Japanese history and culture.

General Characteristics of Japanese Traditional Music

To begin to understand traditional Japanese music, you will find it helpful to examine its general characteristics. There are exceptions to these generalizations, but they should be used as a point of reference for the musical examples that follow.

Pitch and Scales

Like Western music, Japanese music divides the octave into twelve tones. The Japanese tonal system is based on the Chinese system, which in turn developed in a way similar to that of the Pythagorian system of the West. These notes, when put in pitch sequence, represent an untempered chromatic scale of twelve semitones. While equal temperament has strongly influenced contemporary performers, the exact intervals between notes still differ in traditional music according to genre, school, the piece performed, and the individual performer (Koizumi 1974:73). No single set of pitches is used by all musicians. For example, the mode system used in *gagaku* (orchestra music derived from T'ang China) differs from that used in music for the *koto* (a thirteen-stringed zither). The *gagaku* modal system is linked to Chinese systems, whereas the *koto* system developed several centuries later in Japan.

Considering this diversity in scale systems, it is not surprising that music historians have developed a wide range of theories to describe them. According to one of the traditional theories, much Japanese music (excluding older genres such as *gagaku* and Buddhist chanting) is based on two pentatonic scales, either with or without semitones. The scale used frequently in music for the *koto* and the *shamisen* (a three-stringed lute) is called the *in* scale and contains semitones (for example, D, E♭, G, A, B♭). The *yo* scale, without semitones (D, E, G, A, B), is often heard in folk songs and early popular songs such as "Nonki-bushi" (CD 4, Track 5). Transcription 8-1 shows the two scales with their auxiliary notes in parentheses.

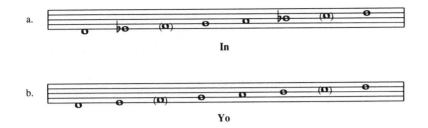

a.

In

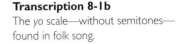

Transcription 8-1a
The *in* scale—with semitones—found in *koto* and *shamisen* music.

b.

Yo

Transcription 8-1b
The *yo* scale—without semitones—found in folk song.

A more recent theory holds that the traditional concept of the pentatonic scale (such as the *in* and *yo* scales) does not adequately explain what is found in the music itself. Instead, it is more useful to interpret Japanese music on the basis of "nuclear tones," located a fourth apart, and the main notes that appear between them (Koizumi 1974:76). Actually, the pitches thus produced are the same in the genres of music just mentioned: the *miyako-bushi* scale applies to *koto* and *shamisen* music, and the *minyō* scale is found in folk song.

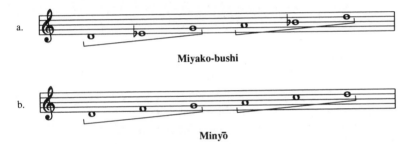

a.

Miyako-bushi

Transcription 8-2a
The *miyako-bushi* scale—*koto* and *shamisen* music.

b.

Minyō

Transcription 8-2b
The *minyō* scale—folk song.

What is new in this theory is the emphasis on fourths. In fact, much melodic movement tends to emphasize this interval (for example, the use of *miyako-bushi* nuclear tones in "Hakusen no," CD 4, Track 2).

Timbre

The Japanese aesthetic sense favors the use of a broad range of sounds and tone qualities in music. In particular, "unpitched" sounds are commonly heard in the middle of instrumental melodies. When we hear a sound wave with a stable frequency, it is easy for us to distinguish pitch. But if the frequency varies too quickly, we do not hear a pitch. A cymbal, for example, is unpitched compared with an oboe. In Japanese music, examples of unpitched sound include the breathy sound made on the *shakuhachi* bamboo flute and the hard twang produced when the plectrum strikes the *shamisen* lute. Just as Japanese poetry is full of appreciation for unpitched sounds of nature such as water flowing or trees whispering in the wind, Japanese music recreates such sounds for the enjoyment of their listeners. (An example of this characteristic can be heard in "Tsuru no sugomori" CD 4, Track 1).

Melody and Harmony

The diversity of Japanese melodies makes generalization difficult. For example, the melodies of folk songs differ greatly in rhythm, pitch, and structure from those of *shakuhachi* music. Japanese melodies often contain short motifs that are repeated, in part or in their entirety, throughout a piece. (See, for example, "Hakusen no," CD 4, Track 2, in which segments of phrases are repeated and varied.) In the theater, quoting melodic patterns from other contexts is a favorite device to inform the audience of the thoughts of a character or to foreshadow an upcoming event. Complete repetition of phrases sometimes occurs at the beginning and end of a piece, such as in the *shamisen* accompaniment to "Hakusen no," thereby lending an air of finality to the conclusion.

In the *shakuhachi* piece "Tsuru no sugomori" (CD 4, Track 1), the pitch movement in the melody strikes the non-Japanese listener as extremely slow; in fact, the dynamic and timbre changes, rather than rapid changes in pitch, give the melody its life. In contrast to this, much vocal music contains elaborate vocal ornamentation, as heard in the recordings of "Hakusen no" (CD 4, Track 2) and "Nikata-bushi" (CD 4, Track 3).

The interval of the fourth often appears in the melodic material of Buddhist chanting and in instrumental music such as *koto* and *shamisen* music—even larger leaps occur often in the latter case. In vocal music, both syllabic and melismatic treatment of text can be found, but narrative styles such as the music of the puppet theater described later tend toward syllabic text setting, which emphasizes the words.

Only Western-influenced Japanese music uses Western harmony; traditional music is dominated by a monophonic or heterophonic sound. Most common when two or more instruments (or voice and instrument) play together is a heterophonic texture, in which both or all parts play basically the same melody but in slightly different versions.

Rhythm

One distinctive characteristic of Japanese music lies in the flexibility of pulse in many pieces. We sense a pulse in music when we hear notes that are dynamically accented. In Western music, pulses almost always occur at regular time intervals (forming "beats") and are arranged most commonly in groups of two, three, four, or six (creating a "meter"). Music can also have irregular intervals between the pulses, however, and this is sometimes called "beatless" or "flexible" or "free" rhythm. Those accustomed to Western music may have difficulty at first listening to music that lacks a steady beat, because it seems "hard to follow" without the firm rhythmic structure they expect. But this music conveys a powerful expression of feeling because of its freedom and flexibility. Such beatless rhythm is found in many kinds of Japanese music, from folk song to music of the *shakuhachi* (CD 4, Tracks 1–3).

When there is a sense of beat in Japanese music, those beats usually occur in groups of two, four, or eight. Triple meter is rare, though it occurs in some folk and children's songs. Even when a steady beat is present, there can be a sense of flexibility to it, as in the festival music example presented later.

Japanese music uses a wide variety of tempos, from very slow to very fast. Often, in music associated with the theater, the tempo accelerates as excitement and drama build in the play. A typical musical form called *jo-ha-kyū*, described later, is outlined through changes in tempo.

Tempos are not determined by metronome but are learned through imitation and trial and error. As in a Western classical music ensemble, when a Japanese ensemble sits down together to rehearse, it is not uncommon for one member to say, "That was a bit too fast last time, don't you think?" or "Why did we slow down at that point?" Through negotiation and trial and error, they settle into a tempo and changes in that tempo that most members find acceptable. Experienced solo performers tend to play the same piece at almost the same tempo each time, though performances of the same work by different performers sometimes show a surprising tempo variance. This variation can be linked to difference in stylistic school or to personal interpretation.

Musical Form

The most common musical form in Japanese music is called *jo-ha-kyū*. It is based mainly on rhythmic rather than melodic changes. Found in music for the *gagaku* orchestra, this form profoundly affected *nō* theater as well as other instrumental and vocal genres.

Jo means "introduction" and is the slow beginning section: *ha* is literally "breaking apart," and here the tempo builds; finally, *kyū*, or "rushing," finds the tempo reaching its peak, then slowing before the piece ends. As a loose form, this tripartite structure applies in some cases to entire pieces as well as to sections of those pieces and individual phrases, as in the "Roku-dan" piece described later.

To summarize, the three characteristics of traditional Japanese music that most exemplify its uniqueness and beauty are (1) variety of timbres, including unpitched sounds; (2) heterophonic treatment of voices in an ensemble; and (3) flexibility of pulse found in both solo and ensemble music. These elements occur in most of the traditional music described in this chapter.

In the following sections, we shall examine several different kinds of Japanese music that illustrate the colorful diversity of musical life in Japan today. The history of each instrument or musical genre provides a fascinating look into the rich, vibrant life of traditional Japanese cities and villages during the times of the *samurai,* wandering Buddhist priests, and *geisha*. The first four types developed largely during the Tokugawa period:

- The *shakuhachi* flute is linked to the social turbulence of early Tokugawa times, as well as to Zen philosophy and aesthetics. A *shakuhachi* piece provides an example of free rhythm, one of the most important characteristics of Japanese music.

- Also during the Tokugawa period, merchants took up the *koto* zither and made it one of the most commonly played instruments. The example of *koto* music displays the *dan* form of musical structure as well as the *jo-ha-kyū* principle.

- The *geisha* and a female composer of the late Tokugawa period contributed greatly to the development of the short *kouta* songs. These songs, sung to the accompaniment of the *shamisen*, exemplify heterophonic texture in Japanese music.

- A description of the *bunraku* puppet theater and its music, *gidayū-bushi*, illustrates the strong connection of music with the theater and describes teaching methods old and new.

These kinds of music are generally labeled "art" or "classical" music. Compared with "folk" music, art music has stricter guild systems, more regulation over skill level, and more professionalism. The terms *art* and *folk* are imported from the West, however, and the dividing line between the two categories has become blurred today as folk musicians become more professionalized and form their own guild systems.

Next, we shall look at two kinds of music termed "folk": folk song from northern Japan and instrumental festival music from Tokyo. Although both of these date from the Tokugawa period or earlier, they will be described in their contemporary contexts to show how traditional music is faring in modern-day Japan. Musically, the folk song example shows the use of microtones and the intricate ornamentation that characterize folk music from the northern region; the festival music example illustrates ensemble practice. Finally, we shall explore present-day Japanese popular music, which shows musical features of both East and West, and the world of *karaoke* singing, which offers a unique mix of live singing and technology.

The Shakuhachi (Bamboo Flute)

Considering its range of tones—from soft and ethereal to rough and violent—the *shakuhachi* appears surprisingly simple in construction. This flute is made of a length of bamboo from the bottom part of a bamboo stalk, including part of the root. The name *shakuhachi* derives from the length of the standard instrument. *Shaku* signifies a traditional unit of measure (equivalent to about 30 centimeters) and *hachi* stands for 8, together meaning 1.8 *shaku*, or about 54 centimeters. (Players use other lengths as well, sometimes to match the range of the other ensemble instruments.) The standard *shakuhachi* has four holes in the front of the instrument and one in the back for the thumb of the left hand.

The *shakuhachi*'s construction determines its versatility in pitch and tone production. Held vertically, the flute has a mouthpiece at the top that is cut obliquely on the side away from the player. By partially covering the finger holes and changing the angle of the lips to the mouthpiece, a player can produce a wide variety of pitches and tone qualities. Not only does the *shakuhachi* easily produce microtones, but it also generates tones ranging from "pure" (with few overtones) to quite breathy, sounding almost like white noise. Many Western-influenced contemporary compositions have been written for the *shakuhachi* because of its versatility in pitch and tone quality.

Solo *shakuhachi* performance flourished during the Tokugawa period (1600–1867), a golden age in Japanese cultural life. During this time of peace, the *shōgun* living in Tokyo ruled over a united country, while the Kyoto emperor held only nominal power. After centuries of violent struggles between different factions of aristocrats and military leaders, Japan welcomed peace and prospered under it.

But long-lasting peace meant trouble for members of the *samurai* class. *Samurai* warriors enjoyed high status during the years of fighting, but afterward many *samurai* of lower rank were released from their duties, becoming *rōnin*, or "masterless *samurai*." The Tokugawa regime found it expedient to uphold the social class system established in earlier times: At the top were *samurai*, followed by farmers, craftsmen, and finally merchants. By issuing edicts designed to set up boundaries between these classes, the government tried to prevent movement between them. For this reason, even though they had no means of support, *rōnin* were not allowed to change their class status as *samurai*, though some managed to do so. Some became teachers or writers, others became farmers, and still others became hired bodyguards for rich merchants. The image of the proud, swaggering, brave *samurai*, as projected in movies, is largely based on the *rōnin* of the Tokugawa period, who were actually unemployed *samurai*.

The term *rōnin* has been given a new meaning by the Japanese. High school graduates who fail college entrance examinations and must wait until the following year (or years) to pass the exams are also called *rōnin*.

Another option for the *rōnin* was to take religious orders and beg on the streets and highways of Japan. In fact, people in Tokugawa society considered it more honorable to beg than to "lower" oneself by becoming a merchant or farmer. One group of *rōnin* who took religious orders were called *komusō*. *Komusō* (literally, "emptiness monks") were Buddhist priests who wandered the countryside, playing the *shakuhachi* and begging. The standard *komusō* costume included a large, basket-shaped hat made of cane, through which the wearer could see but not be seen. It was rumored that the *komusō* were government spies, taking advantage of their right to travel throughout the country wearing a costume that shielded their identity (Blasdel 1988:103–7).

These *samurai*-turned-priests made their mark on the *shakuhachi* repertoire. The *honkyoku*, or main solo repertoire for the instrument, derives from the pieces played by the *komusō*. All of these pieces, the most spiritual and meditative of the present-day *shakuhachi* repertoire, have a free rhythm; that is, they lack a regular beat.

Komusō were organized into the Fuke sect of Buddhism, which propagated a Zen basis for *shakuhachi* playing. Zen Buddhism, a philosophy that has spread throughout much of Asia and the world in various forms, is based on the idea that the pursuit of truth does not require the intellect. We can search to know *about* things, but we do not really *know* them. To know them, we must throw away our notions of scientific investigation and logical reasoning and instead rely on a heightened awareness and intuition about life.

Various means for reaching that state of heightened awareness of enlightenment (*satori* in Japanese) have been proposed. These include

Figure 8-1
Kawase Junsuke playing the *shakuhachi*.

Linda Fujie

pondering *kōan*, or paradoxical riddles (the most famous is "What is the sound of one hand clapping?") and the practice of *zazen*, sitting in silent meditation. In the Fuke sect, playing the *shakuhachi* was also regarded as a means for reaching enlightenment. For this reason, the *shakuhachi* was not called a musical instrument by its performers but a *hōki*, or "spiritual tool." The spiritual approach to the playing of the instrument is called *suizen*, or "blowing Zen."

According to *suizen*, the goal of *shakuhachi* coincides with the goal of Zen: to reach enlightenment, proceeding into unlimited "knowing." How this is done is not formulated precisely (as it cannot be, from the Zen perspective), but one common notion is called *ichōon jōbutsu*, or "enlightenment in a single note." According to this theory, one could reach enlightenment suddenly when blowing a single tone.

Breathing is crucial in *shakuhachi* playing and its connection with Zen. The exhaling of breath is heard in the dynamic level and tone quality of a pitch; at the same time, it carries the possibility of instant spiritual enlightenment. Thus, each moment of "performance," whether the intake of breath or its slow release, whether the subtle, delicate shading of a tone or the explosion of air through the instrument, can be interpreted in the context of a larger spiritual life.

The breathing pattern is important in learning to play the *shakuhachi.* Each phrase takes one full breath, with dramatic shifts in dynamic level according to how quickly the air is expelled. The typical phrase in *shakuhachi honkyoku* music follows the natural breathing pattern, the sound growing fainter toward the end of the phrase as the air in the lungs runs out. When this dynamic pattern is broken by a gradual or sudden increase in volume, it makes a pronounced impression on the listener.

The performer of the *shakuhachi* piece on CD 4, Track 1, is Kawase Junsuke, one of the best-known *shakuhachi* musicians in Japan and the head of a stylistic school of playing (see Figure 8-1). On the CD his sister, Kawase Hakuse, joins him by playing the *shamisen;* she is also an active performer, particularly in the *kabuki* theater.

"Tsuru no sugomori" ("Nesting Cranes") is part of the *honkyoku* (solo) repertory of the Kinko style of performance. The music describes a winter scene during which cranes make their nests. The fast trills on the *shakuhachi* imitate the bird's fluttering wings. "Tsuru no sugomori" is performed in one of the most famous *kabuki* plays, *Kanadehon chushingura,* or *Treasury of Local Retainers,* during a scene when parting lovers suddenly notice the scene outdoors.

The first time you listen to this piece, just sit back and relax, appreciating the overall mood. For later listening, Transcription 8-3 shows the general outline of the piece in Western notation. (The version recorded here is performed in the *kabuki* theater and therefore accompanied by *shamisen,* but this part is not notated in the transcription.) Because Western notation does not convey uneven rhythms well, the transcription offers only approximate time values. Phrases—defined by points at which a breath is taken by the musician—are numbered for reference.

CD 4/1

"Tusuru no sugomori" ("Nesting Cranes") (3:41). Performed by Kawase Junsuke, *shakuhachi* (flute), and Kawase Hakuse, *shamisen* (lute). Field recording by Linda Fujie. Tokyo, Japan, 1989.

Japanese names are given in the Japanese order: family name followed by given name.

Transcription 8-3

"Tsuru no sugomori." (All transcriptions in this chapter by Linda Fujie.)

(continues)

Transcription 8-3
(continued)

, = breath taken   ↑↓ = pitch goes up/down by quarter tone

After listening to this piece a few times, you may sense that certain phrases are repeated; in fact, this short piece has many melodic repetitions. For example, phrase 1 is heard again (with some modifications) in phrases 6, 9, 17, and 24. Phrases 1–5 are repeated in phrases 9–13, and most of the other phrases are variations on previous melodic material. The changes in pitch and dynamics create a clear climax.

One of the most obvious characteristics of this piece is the constant change in dynamics within one phrase. Almost every phrase increases or decreases in volume; in many cases the musician increases the volume during one long note and decreases it during the next. Musicians must learn and practice this careful breath control for years to prevent running out of breath and to maintain constant control over tone quality.

A knowledge of some of the techniques used to play *shakuhachi* will help explain how some of the tones in this performance are produced. Sometimes the player flattens or sharpens a pitch by changing the angle of the lips to the mouthpiece. This is called *meri* when the pitch is lowered, producing a soft tone, and *kari* when the pitch is raised. (Occasionally the pitch is lowered and again raised, as at the end of phrase 22.)

The musician also changes pitch through finger techniques, depending on the effect desired. A finger can slowly open or close a hole, it can quickly tap a hole (creating an accent), or cover only a portion of a hole. These techniques are necessary because tonguing is not used to separate notes in *shakuhachi* playing.

Different techniques of breathed released into the flute also create interesting effects such as *muraiki,* an explosion of breath into the instrument. In addition, *shakuhachi* players use flutter tonguing, finger tremolos, and vibrato—all of which can be heard in the first few phrases of "Tsuru no sugomori." One common technique of producing vibrato is to shake the head, either from side to side or up and down, while blowing into the instrument.

This piece shows at least two of the three basic characteristics of Japanese music listed earlier: a variety of timbres within one piece and a flexibility of pulse. Some notes have a thin sound, while others have rich, full tone. Some notes sound "purer" to our ears, and others are breathier. The *shakuhachi* player expresses the music through such changes in timbre. With the exception perhaps of contemporary music, this variety of tone quality is rarely found within a single piece written for a Western wind instrument. In terms of Japanese musical aesthetics, however, the texture and expression of the piece depends in part on this contrast of timbres.

The lack of a regular pulse means that learning a piece requires a good ear and an excellent sense of timing on the part of the student. Most forms of musical notation convey the durations of notes easily if the music has a steady pulse. But without such a pulse, the original time values are difficult to communicate in a written score. Perhaps this is one reason that musical notation never developed into an important teaching tool in most forms of traditional Japanese music. Because Japanese musicians could not rely on scores to teach them the rhythm of a piece, they used them more as a device to help them remember how the piece should sound. First, of course, performers must acquire this memory by listening to their teacher (and perhaps other students) many times.

The idea of *ma* (literally "space" or "interval") is linked to both rhythm and the Zen background of *shakuhachi* playing. *Ma* refers to the overall timing of a piece—not just the pauses and rests but also the relationship between sound and silence on which all music is fundamentally based. It embraces the idea that sound enhances silence and silence enhances sound. This emphasis on silence conforms with Zen ideas concerning the importance of emptiness and space. The player who is aware of *ma* begins his or her notes with an instinctive care for the length and quality of the silences before and after. This concept applies particularly to music with a beatless rhythm, because the sounds and silences fall at irregular points and the player is more active in creating those moments.

Performers often link the concept of *ma* to the quality of a musical performance. Musicians speak of "good *ma*" or "bad *ma*," referring to the quality of the sounds and silences and their proportion to one another. When this proportion is deemed appropriate—a subjective judgment that comes only from years of experience—then the performance has been successful.

Although the Fuke sect priests have long disappeared from the roads of Japan, many players keep the *shakuhachi* tradition alive today, both in Japan and abroad. Because of the instrument's versatility of pitch and timbre, composers and performers like to use it in various contemporary genres, such as jazz, fusion, and New Age music. At the same time, the meditative, spiritual nature of the *honkyoku* is continually reaffirmed through performances given by several active *shakuhachi* masters, such as Yamaguchi Gorō, Aoki Reibo, and others.

The Koto (Zither)

The graceful music of the *koto* is familiar to many foreigners, because it has become well known outside Japan through concerts, records, and tapes. Whether played as a solo instrument or in an ensemble, with a vocal part or without one, the *koto* has for several centuries been one of the most popular traditional instruments of Japan.

The contemporary *koto* is a long (about 1.8 meters), wooden instrument with thirteen stings, traditionally silk but now also nylon. Bridges (called *ji*) hold the strings above the surface of the instrument, one for each string. These bridges are movable, so the player can set them at different places along the string, depending on the desired tuning.

Like the prototype of the *shakuhachi,* the ancestor of the *koto* came to Japan from China during the early centuries of cultural exchange, after which the instrument gradually acquired its present form. After several centuries of use by an elite few, the *koto* gradually spread in popularity to different segments of Japanese society during the Tokugawa period. At this time changes in teaching and in the *koto* repertoire stimulated many men and women to learn it (Malm 1959:169). Growing numbers were merchants, the class that officially held the lowest status but was gaining rapidly in wealth and influence. By the beginning of the Meiji period in 1868, the *koto* could be found in many private homes as well as in teahouses and theaters, and skilled *koto* performance had become a sign of good breeding for young women. Most of the *sōkyoku* (or *koto* music) pieces performed today were written during the Tokugawa period, when new schools and styles of playing arose. At this time the *koto* was used in ensembles with the *shamisen* and later the *kokyū* or *shakuhachi*, combinations that brought an important form of chamber music into Japanese life.

One of the most famous *koto* pieces is entitled "Rokudan," or "Six Sections." It is typical of the *danmono* type of instrumental pieces, consisting of several "steps," or sections, known as *dan.* Each *dan* contains 104 beats and is repeated several times, with great variation. A short introduction of four to eight beats (four beats in the case of "Rokudan") begins the piece, and each *dan* follows the last without a break. In listening to this stately piece, you will hear in the beginning four beats of "introduction" a long note of two beats followed by a descending note a fourth away, and then an interval of a fifth.

Several recordings of "Rokudan" are available on CDs and tapes. One performance can be found on the CD *Sō,* volume 6 of the series "Japanese Traditional Music," which is listed under "Additional Listening" at the end of this chapter. A transcription of this piece appears in Adriaansz 1973:66–93.

Transcription 8-4
Introductory figure in "Rokudan."

This figure is easy to hear throughout the piece. The following beat of silence represents the first beat of the material repeated in each *dan.*

Six *dan,* each 104 beats long, follow. The *danmono,* however, is anything but a simple theme-and-variation form, because the sections are difficult to tell apart. Even after listening to the piece several times, one might not be able to tell where a new *dan* begins, because the melody of each *dan* is made up of short figures that are generally difficult to distinguish. The second and third *dan* are perhaps recognizable as related to the first, for they are relatively close to the melodic content of the first *dan;* after that the similarity in thematic material becomes less clear. Some basic melodic figures are heard again, but in a different part of the *dan,* or in a different range or rhythmic pattern.

Rather than trying to distinguish each section, then, it makes more sense to listen for the repetition of the short melodic figures as well as larger overall patterns. Some of the brief melodic-rhythmic patterns that recur include a descending dotted figure and octave leaps. As for larger patterns, the *jo-ha-kyū* structure mentioned near the beginning of this chapter may be applied to the piece as a whole. The first two *dan* make up the *jo,* or introductory section; the second two *dan* find the tempo increasing, as in a *ha* section; and the tempo reaches its height in the final two *dan,* or the *kyū* section. The tempo slows down only toward the end, in the last twenty-two beats or so, ending in a long glissando. This form is also followed in individual *dan,* in which one can sense a gradual building of tension.

A careful listener can hear a variety of timbres and interesting tonal effects. Sometimes the pick of one finger sliding down the string creates a pitchless sound; sometimes glissandos brush the strings. There may be changes in pitch that sound like a sliding from one note to the next and back again. This occurs when the left hand changes the pressure on the string as the right hand plucks it. Such delicate shifting of pitch and tone color give *koto* music a special beauty.

The Kouta (Short Song) and Shamisen (Lute)

Another of the well-loved Japanese traditional instruments is the *shamisen,* a three-stringed, long-necked lute (see Figure 8-2). In contrast to the *shakuhachi,* which has associations with austere spirituality and meditation, the *shamisen* is often used to convey an outpouring of emotion and drama. For this reason it is considered an excellent instrument for the theater, expressing highly dramatic situations in the *bunraku* puppet theater to great effect. It is also used in another major theatrical form, *kabuki,* and sometimes to accompany folk song, as in CD 4, Track 3. In a more intimate setting, the *shamisen* also accompanies short, evocative songs called *kouta* (literally, "short song").

The present-day *shamisen* is a descendent of a long line of related instruments stretching back to the *sanshin* of Okinawa, the *san-hsien* of China, and perhaps farther back to the Middle East or Central Asia. The Okinawan *sanshin* is covered with snakeskin, but on the Japanese mainland

Theories that the Chinese *san-hsien* derived from Egyptian or Persian sources are summarized in Kikkawa 1981:157–58.

Figure 8-2

Geisha performing at a party. The woman on the right holds a *shamisen.*

Linda Fujie

the instrument is traditionally covered with cat skin, or sometimes dog skin. (As these are now expensive, however, plastic is commonly found on *shamisen* used for practice.) There are different kinds of *shamisen,* varying in shape, weight, material, and overall size; the type used depends on the musical genre played. The instrument that accompanies *kouta* songs, for example, is smaller and lighter than the one used in *bunraku* puppet theater.

The body of the *shamisen* is made of a wooden box that is roughly square and covered on both sides with skin or plastic. A long piece of wood, forming the unfretted neck, is inserted into this box. Pegs at the top of the neck hold the three strings, each string of a different thickness. In some kinds of music, a large plectrum is used for striking and plucking the instrument. Sometimes in *kouta,* however, the bare fingers or fingernails pluck the strings, producing a lighter, less percussive, sound.

A rather unusual sound in the *shamisen* confirms the importance of unpitched sounds in Japanese music. This is a special buzz or hum called *sawari* (literally, "touch"), which is purposefully added to the instrument when it is made. The lowest string does not rest on the upper bridge but resonates against a special cavity made near the top of the instrument's neck. This string sets a noise in motion, to which the other strings can contribute in sympathetic vibration. The result is a pitchless buzzing sound that is essential to the tonal flavor of the *shamisen.* Whereas instruments used in Western classical music are constructed to avoid such buzzing noises, Japanese instrument makers intentionally build these timbres into their instruments. Buzzing is also deliberately built into many African instruments (see Chapter 3).

The *kouta* is a song form that evokes many images and allusions in a short time, generally, one to three minutes. *Kouta* as we know it today dates from the mid-nineteenth century, although the same name was used to describe another kind of song in earlier centuries (Kurada 1982:894–95).

The development of the present-day *kouta* is closely linked to the participation of women in Japanese traditional music. One of the earliest composers of *kouta* was O-Yo (1840–1901). The daughter of the head master of *kiyomoto* (a style of *shamisen* music used in *kabuki*), O-Yo was an excellent musician. As a woman, she was not allowed to take over her father's position after his death; instead she married a man who then inherited his title. But O-Yo took up most of his duties.

Because only men appeared on the *kabuki* stage, O-Yo was not allowed to play the *shamisen* there. She nevertheless performed at private parties in teahouses and restaurants. For such private gatherings she probably composed *kouta* such as "Saru wa uki," thought to be the first *kouta* ever composed (Kikkawa 1981:350). Although women were banned from participating in many of the elite forms of music performance in Japan, they played a key role in teaching that music to generations of male performers. O-Yo herself was an important transmitter of the *kiyomoto* tradition of her father, teaching it to many people from all parts of Japan.

O-Yo's musical world and her involvement with both an older form of music *(kiyomoto)* and a new form *(kouta)* can best be understood in the context of the *iemoto* guild system. This system, active also in O-Yo's time, exerts a powerful influence on the traditional arts—music, dance, flower arranging, the tea ceremony, and many other artistic areas. The guild is the transmitter of knowledge and the legitimizer of teachers and performers in each art form.

In music, several different guilds may be involved with one type of music (for example, music for the *shakuhachi* or for the *nō* theater), but each guild will have its own slightly different performance style and repertoire. For example, one who wishes to become a *shakuhachi* performer must decide which style he or she wants to learn, then become affiliated with the guild that follows that style. Often this affiliation lasts as long as the individual performs on the *shakuhachi.*

Guilds not only transmit knowledge but also control quality. Each guild sets the standards for teachers and pupils. If an individual works diligently, he or she may receive a license to teach and an artistic name from the guild. The *iemoto* system thus provides a structure through which the arts have been taught, performed, and preserved for hundreds of years in Japan.

The hierarchy of this *iemoto* system is rigid, bearing some similarity to the familial-paternalistic social structures found throughout Japanese society. Traditionally, the leader of each school inherits that position and strictly regulates rights to perform or teach. In theory, this system controls the "correct" transmission of musical information; in reality, it also allows some leaders to exploit their helpless students. A greedy leader, for instance, might demand large amounts of money for the licenses required to be recognized as a qualified performer and teacher of his school, and the student would have no choice but to pay.

On the other hand, the number of scrupulous *iemoto* leaders and teachers far outweighs the number of exploitative ones; most teachers provide a great deal of support and encouragement to their students. Overall, the *iemoto* system has contributed positively to maintaining the artistic level in traditional Japanese music. Its strict regulation of performance standards has preserved musical traditions that could otherwise have changed drastically or even died out through the years.

According to the rules of this system, new composition in many genres of music was discouraged or even forbidden. This conservatism reflects a reverence for tradition in the arts that still prevails among Japanese musicians today. Many believe that the "classic" body of music has been handed down with painstaking precision for decades or centuries through the toil of countless musicians. The composition of a new piece of music by an individual was for years considered "arrogant self-expression." If a new piece were composed and proved to have merit, it had to be ascribed to the leader of the guild, who in turn might attribute it to an earlier *iemoto* leader. This reluctance to accept new compositions meant that if they were written, they often had no official recognition. For this reason, when someone like O-Yo composed new music, it was in a new genre such as *kouta.* Because there was no *iemoto* associated yet with that kind of music, the restrictions that would otherwise apply toward composition did not exist.

Today we can still see this restriction on new composition to some degree among the forms of traditional music. Although new pieces are now written for traditional instruments in Japan, they are often created outside of the traditional genres, such as in a mixture of *kabuki* music and rock known as *"kabuki* rock." Otherwise, as a rule, only high-ranking members of an *iemoto* create new compositions in a traditional mode.

By the end of the Tokugawa period, the *kouta* was linked to the *geisha* of the city of Edo (which became known as Tokyo in 1868) and the life of the teahouses. For many people today, the lively, intense world of Edo during the Tokugawa period epitomizes the Japanese spirit. Although the official Japanese capital was Kyoto, where the emperor resided, Edo was the actual seat of government where the *shōgun* held state in his castle. It was also the most populous city in Japan as well as one of the largest in the world. The influx of people from all over the country, crowded into tenements and wildly pursuing wealth, pleasure, or both, spurred the coining of the phrase *"Edo wa tenka no hakidamari"* ("Edo is the nation's rubbish heap").

The streets teemed with *chōnin,* townspeople who were members of either the merchant or the artisan classes. With the expansion of the economy during the peaceful Tokugawa period, some *chōnin* became wealthy and powerful. They patronized the theaters, teahouses, and brothels, making their increasingly sophisticated mark on the aesthetics of the drama, music, and dance of the period: a sense of style that combines wit, sensuousness, and restraint. The Edo pursuit of momentary pleasure represents the epitome of the *ukiyo,* or "floating world."

The *kouta,* as sung by the *geisha* of such licensed quarters as the Yoshiwara area of Edo, reflects their world of beauty and style. The songs' lyrics often convey romantic or erotic themes, but such references are subtle. Puns, double entendres, and poetic devices appear frequently in *kouta* lyrics, and sometimes even a Japanese will miss their suggestive undertones.

Though declining in numbers, *geisha* are still trained in Japan to entertain at such occasions. The traditional musical instrument of the *geisha* is the *shamisen,* which is used often to accompany vocal music such as the *kouta.* Our recording was made by a *geisha* in the 1960s who lived near the former Yoshiwara quarter of Tokyo.

In "Hakusen no" ("A White Fan"), our *kouta* example on CD 4, Track 2, both the image of a white fan and the beauty of nature metaphorically represent romantic commitment. This particular song shows little of the whimsical side of *kouta*; it is considered suitable for wedding banquets or private parties. At the wedding banquet, this song would be sung to the honored couple.

The vocal melody contains several thematic phrases that repeat in slightly varied forms. The letters next to the text that follows show one way of interpreting these phrases. Repeating letters indicate phrases that are repeated exactly or nearly exactly, while letters in parentheses signify more modified repetitions. For example, the seven different phrases marked "B" have in common long, repeated notes followed by a descending interval, highly ornamented, of a third to a sixth, or some part of this combination.

CD 4/2

"Hakusen no" ("A White Fan") (3:23). Performed by Shitaya Kotsuru for Nippon Columbia WK-170

Text, "Hakusen no"

A	*Hakusen no*	A white fan
B	*sue hirogari no*	spreading out
C	*sue kakete*	lasting forever
B	*kataki chigiri no*	the firm pledges
(A)	*gin kaname*	like the silver node of the fan
(B)	*kagayaku kage ni*	shimmering in shadows
D	*matsu ga e no*	the boughs of pine trees
E	*ha-iro mo masaru*	the splendid leafy color of
(B)	*fukamidori*	a deep green
E	*tachiyoru niwa no*	the clearness of the pond
(E)	*ike sumite*	in the garden approached
(B)	*nami kaze tatanu*	undisturbed by waves of wind,
C	*mizu no omo*	the surface of the water
B	*urayamashii de*	What an enviable life,
(B)	*wa nai ka na.*	don't you think?

Traditional Japanese poetry arranges lines according to their syllabic content, favoring lines with five and seven syllables. The text of "Hakusen no" contains alternating lines of five and seven syllables. (Extended vowels and the letter *n* at the end of a syllable count as separate syllables.)

A poetic device known as *kakekotoba,* or "pivot word," is found in the sixth line: the word *kagayaku* ("shimmering") can be interpreted as referring to both the silver node of the fan (the pin holding the fan together at the bottom) and the pine tree boughs "shimmering" in the shadows. Such pivot words are often found in Japanese poetry and are made possible by the flexibility of Japanese grammar.

Several auspicious symbols appear in the text. The pine tree has a special beauty and longevity for the Japanese. A clear pond, "undisturbed by waves or wind," also presents a peaceful, auspicious image of the future life of a couple. The words *sue hirogari* literally refer to the unfolding of a fan but can also mean to enjoy increasing prosperity as time goes on.

As in the *shakuhachi* example, the difficulties of conveying uneven time values in Western notation are apparent in Transcription 8-5, "Hakusen no." The vocal part has been inserted rhythmically in relation to the steady beat of the *shamisen,* which is the easiest part to follow.

Transcription 8-5

Vocal and *shamisen* parts, "Hakusen no."

(continues)

This transcription shows only the vocal and *shamisen* parts. In the recording, we also hear an accompanying ensemble made up of the *kotsuzumi* and *otsuzumi* drums and the *nōkan* flute. These instruments, typical of the *nō* theater, were added to the commercial recording of this song; *geisha* also sing "Hakusen no" with the *shamisen* alone. Another sound not transcribed above are the calls known as *kakegoe*, which help to cue the ensemble as well as add to the atmosphere of the song.

Earlier in this chapter a heterophonic relationship between two or more parts was defined as typical of Japanese ensemble music. Such a heterophony characterizes the voice and *shamisen* in "Hakusen no." Rather than sounding simultaneously on the same beat, the two parts tend to weave in and out; sometimes the voice precedes the *shamisen* in presenting the melody and sometimes the *shamisen* plays the notes first. The result of this constant staggering and shifting is a duet in which both voice and instrument share and enhance the melody. An example of this heterophony can be found in the third line, as the *shamisen* anticipates several of the sung notes. Listening carefully to the entire song, try to find other such examples. Are there also times when the voice anticipates what the *shamisen* will play?

One of the most interesting aspects of the vocal part is the flexibility of beat, which contrasts to the even beat of the *shamisen.* See, for example, how the rhythm of the vocal and *shamisen* parts fit together in the line beginning "*tachiyoru . . .*"; just as the listener thinks a predictable pattern has been established, the rhythm shifts. For centuries the sophistication of this kind of rhythmic contrast has appealed to the Japanese ear. Together, melodic and rhythmic variety in Japanese ensemble music create a complex, often exciting musical texture.

The *shamisen* part opens and closes the song with the same rhythmically emphasized theme, and it occasionally plays a short solo phrase between lines of text. Sometimes, small motifs are repeated; one that occurs several times is shown in Transcription 8-6, here:

Transcription 8-6

Motif in *shamisen* part, "Hakusen no."

This and other similar motifs in the *shamisen* part stress the notes D and G. The scale used in "Hakusen no" is the *in* scale (shown in Transcription 8-1a), based on D. However, there are constant shifts to the same scale based on G, which is closely related to the D scale. A prominent difference between the two scales is that G scale has an A♭, whereas the D scale contains an A natural. Another scale shift takes place in the line "*kagayaku . . . ,*" which stresses the notes G, D♭, and C, denoting a temporary change to the C-based *in* scale. Such rapid changes from one scale to another are common in Japanese music even in short songs such as *kouta*.

Hearing this song, the listener is drawn into the refined yet playful atmosphere of the Tokugawa teahouses. Now we shall turn to a more dramatic atmosphere, the highly charged puppet theater.

Gidayū-bushi (Music of the Puppet Theater)

During the Tokugawa period, theater was one of the most popular forms of entertainment among the townspeople. While *nō* was a favored pastime of the elite, attendance at *kabuki* and *bunraku* (puppet theater) was restricted to members of the artisan and merchant classes (Ernst 1956:10). This restriction did not prevent members of the higher *samurai* class from sneaking into the theaters, sometimes wearing large hats or scarves over their heads to hide their identity.

Music is important in *kabuki* and *bunraku* theater, both as a background to the actions onstage and as an essential element of the play itself. In *bunraku*, for example, two musicians—a narrator-singer and a *shamisen* player—tell the story, speak and sing for the puppets, and provide scenes with background music.

Japanese puppet theater uses elaborately costumed, large-sized dolls that are almost brought to life by skilled puppeteers and musicians. The *bunraku* plays include some of the most beautifully written works of Japanese drama, expressing intense emotions that appealed to the tastes of the Tokugawa townspeople. The skillfully manipulated dolls, realistic scenery, and emotion-packed music help create a passionately dramatic scene that often reduces audiences to tears (Figure 8-3).

A tough *samurai*.

A more refined *samurai*.

Figure 8-3
Bunraku doll heads.
Credit: Linda Fujie

A plain young girl of the merchant class.

The elegant head of a young beauty.

Important puppets require three manipulators: one for the head and right hand, one for the left hand, and one for the feet. Apprentice manipulators normally require several years of training on the feet, and then several more years on the left hand before they become chief manipulators who are allowed to manipulate the head and right hand. These manipulators wear black, with hoods over their heads, so as to "disappear" into the background.

To the right of the main stage is a smaller stage on which the narrator-singer (*tayū*) and *shamisen* player sit. At the beginning of the performance, or in the middle of a play when a change in musical personnel is needed, the wall of the smaller stage rotates to reveal the musicians on the other side. (For some scenes, more than one *tayū* or *shamisen* player may be needed, and these make their entrance from the wings of the stage in a less dramatic way.) Before beginning the play, the *tayū*, who is sitting on

Well-known manipulators can appear with their faces exposed, and even wear festive costumes, but the emotional content of the scene ultimately dictates the costumes of manipulators. In solemn scenes, for example, all manipulators will normally appear hooded and in black.

Figure 8-4
Music of *bunraku.* On the left, the
shamisen player, and the right, the *tayū*
(narrator).

the floor, lifts the text from the lacquered lectern on which it rests and
bows with it—a sign of respect and a prayer for a good performance
(see Figure 8-4).

Together, the narrator and the *shamisen* player try to fill the puppets
with life, expressing emotion that is sometimes blatant and exaggerated,
sometimes subtle and subdued. As one *tayū* has stated:

> The whole point of *bunraku* is to portray human emotions and situations
> in life so that people's hearts are moved, so that they feel something spe-
> cial about the particular aspect of life the play deals with, whether loyalty,
> sacrifice, one of the many forms of love, or a dilemma one encounters in
> life. (Adachi 1985:65)

Working toward this goal, neither *tayū* nor *shamisen* player is regarded
as more important than the other; instead, they form a closely cooperating
team. Sensing each other's feelings (as well as those of the audience), the
two make subtle adjustments in their singing and playing in order to convey emotion through the dolls as effectively as possible. One narrator
working in Osaka (the traditional capital of *bunraku*) told me:

> When I play with a *shamisen* player that I've known and performed with
> for many years, we are so accustomed to sensing each other's moods and
> feelings from performing onstage that I can tell as soon as we sit down
> together whether or not he's had a fight with his wife that morning!

The *tayū* is referred to as male here,
but there have been female narrators
as well, particularly from the mid-
nineteenth to the early twentieth
century. Today, female amateur *tayū*
perform in some small theaters
throughout the country (Motegi
1988:206–20).

To a listener unfamiliar with *bunraku,* the energetic narration of the
tayū can sound startlingly exaggerated. Indeed, it seems amazing that one
man can have the stamina to shout, growl, and sing out for such a long
time, filling the hall with his large voice. Developing this kind of stamina
takes years of training, and sore throats are not uncommon among those in
this profession. One narrator describes his training this way:

> No matter how big the theater, we never use a microphone; all is pro-
> duced from our bodies alone. You must practice producing the voice from
> your lower abdomen. When we become narrators, we're told, "Make your
> voice come from your *hara* (lower abdomen)!" And we wonder how that

is possible. We learn abdominal breathing, a breathing movement in your stomach. You take in big breaths and let out just enough. You must feel in every part of your body that the voice accompanying the breath is there. But before you understand how the voice can come out of the abdomen, you really have to suffer a lot. (Personal communication with Toyotake Sakitayu, April 26, 1986.)

Some *tayū* even use a small bag of sand, inserted inside the kimono near the stomach, which they use as a kind of leverage for their hands and stomach muscles to obtain the air they need.

Traditional training of the *tayū* and *shamisen* player was more strict in the past than at present. Until the early part of the twentieth century, the apprentice narrator or *shamisen* player normally moved into his teacher's home at the age of six or seven. After years of helping with household chores, he was permitted to help his master prepare for performances and then, finally, to receive lessons himself. In the meantime, before beginning his own lessons, the apprentice had already listened to thousands of hours of lessons and performances of those around him, absorbing much about the music. In actual lessons, he needed to learn to imitate what he heard quickly, because new material might be presented only once or twice before he was expected to have memorized it. The *shamisen* player Tsuruzawa Juzō, born in 1899, described his training in the following way:

> Nowadays people ask about the hardships of my early training. At the time I didn't think a thing about it. Life was that way then and young people were used to discipline, punishment, and grueling training. . . . My teacher would play a passage, maybe fifteen minutes long, just once. I was expected to play along with him. Next I was made to play the passage solo. My teacher would sit there scowling at me, scolding, sometimes hitting me in the face. Knowing the punishment that lay in store, I learned quickly to listen very, very carefully, straining every fiber in my body to absorb everything I possibly could with eyes, ears and mind.
>
> In those days, our whole life was Bunraku. We had no movies, no coffee shops, no radios, no popular music to distract us. . . . Our heads were full of Bunraku and only Bunraku. (Adachi 1985:79)

After World War II, however, this teaching process changed dramatically. The *bunraku* theater went through difficult times after 1945, partly because of a decline in the wealth of its former sponsors and partly from an overall decrease of interest in the traditional arts. As professional *bunraku* performers found it more difficult to make a living, new trainees declined in number. Even those who were willing to study for a career with such an uncertain future were often discouraged by the rigorous training involved. To counter these trends, new teaching methods were developed to ensure that *bunraku* music, *gidayū-bushi,* would be passed on to future generations. These methods rely on relatively short training hours; one can finish the *tayū* training course of the National Theater in two years, for example. New features of this training course include the use of standardized instructional methods, scores, and tape recorders to record lessons and performances. Although these methods do produce an adequate narrator or *shamisen*

The National Theater of Japan is a government-sponsored institution that contains facilities for the presentation of traditional theater, dance, and music, as well as for the training of future artists.

player in a short amount of time, the resulting uniformity of performance and interpretation is deplored by older musicians:

> They [the performers trained by the new methods] make no distinction in their playing between scenes with different settings. Even the same melody should have different emotional tones, depending on the context. It all comes from practicing with tapes, without giving any thought to the meaning of the text. They master the form but cannot express the content. With tapes you can practice in your sleep. (Motegi 1984:105)

In short, the modern methods used to transmit *bunraku* music allow students to learn faster and with less pain. But the new training produces a different quality of performer.

All of the musical genres described in this chapter so far are closely tied to the social life of the Tokugawa period, from which several common threads emerge. For one, we see how the four-tiered class system shaped and defined various aspects of musical life. Many musical and art forms were limited, even by official decree, to a specific class: the *shakuhachi* to the *rōnin* priests, or the *kabuki* and *bunraku* to the merchant class. Social change during the Tokugawa period also reflected changes in music and class, as formerly elite instruments such as the *koto* spread to the lower merchant class.

The next two kinds of music that we shall examine, folk song and festival music, have traditionally belonged to the farming class or the poorer merchants in the cities. But people from many levels of society, in Tokugawa times as now, know these musics. Folk and festival music are still found in many everyday locations: in the streets, in the fields, and at social occasions of both the city and countryside.

Minyō (Folk Song)

In preindustrial Japan people sang folk songs, or *minyō*, while they planted the rice in spring, threw their fishnets into the sea, wove cloth, and pounded grain. Folk songs accompanied many daily activities, serving to relieve boredom, to provide a steady beat for some activity, to encourage a group working at some task, to provide individual expression, and so forth.

While the everyday uses of folk song have not entirely disappeared from Japan, fewer contemporary Japanese are finding them relevant to their lives. Seventy-six percent of the Japanese population lives in cities, where everyday activities involve riding crowded trains and sitting at desks all day rather than planting rice and weaving cloth (Sōri-fu 1982:22). Still, based on a 1982 survey of musical preferences, folk song, or *minyō*, is one of the most popular forms of music in Japan today (NHK 1982:68).

The continuing popularity of folk songs is tied to their identification with the countryside and a sometimes romanticized vision of rural life on the part of city dwellers. Folk songs evoke a past thought to be simpler and more natural, and this appeals to many Japanese today. The same is true in many parts of the modern industrialized world, but the uses of folk song today, and the institutions that surround its presentation and preservation, contrast in interesting ways as they reflect the particular music-cultures in which they are found (see, for example, folk song in Chapter 5).

In addition to an association with rural life, many Japanese folk songs connect with a specific region of the country. This is the case in "Nikata-bushi," CD 4, Track 3, from the region of Akita, in northwestern Japan. With the growth of industry in the years after World War II, many Japanese left the rural areas to find work in the cities. Today people from a particular region—or their descendants—gather in many of these urban areas and sing folk songs as reminders of the villages from which they came.

Despite increasing geographic mobility and cultural homogenization, the Japanese identification of people and songs with their original home areas is still very strong. For example, a Tokyo laborer whose family roots are in the northern prefecture of Akita will be expected to enliven a festive gathering with an Akita folk song. (Hughes 1981:30)

Furusato, or the concept of a home community, maintains a strong emotional grip on today's urban dwellers—even those who left home several decades earlier. The folk song, with its associations and allusions to a particular region, expresses their nostalgia for a faraway place. Thus, nostalgia not only for a different time but also for a different place underlies their popularity.

Finally, perhaps because *minyō* were traditionally sung by ordinary people instead of trained professionals, the Japanese still find them easy to learn and appreciate—for the Japanese not only listen to folk songs but usually learn to sing a few as well, either from family and friends or in elementary school. Often they sing them at parties, when they are called on to sing a favorite song. Real enthusiasts take lessons with a good singer and attend folk song clubs or other gatherings where they can perform in front of other enthusiasts. Amateur folk song contests have become a regular feature on Japanese television, presenting folksingers from around the country. In these contests, singers give their renditions of folk songs, which are then evaluated by a board of "experts," who might tell the singer that his or her vibrato is too broad or hand gestures too dramatic for that particular song.

Folk song preservation societies have sprung up around the country (Groemer 1994). These societies are formed by amateurs who aim to "preserve" a particular local song and a style of performing that song. The activities of these clubs help foster pride and a sense of identity among the dwellers of a village or a neighborhood within a city (Hughes 1981, 1990–1991).

Because of televised *minyō* and the changing tastes of the public, folk song performance has become more professional and standardized in recent years. For example, *kobushi,* the sometimes complex vocal ornamentation of a melodic line, is frequently used to separate the good performers from the bad. One critic of this trend claims,

> There is a tendency to think that the most excellent kind of folk song is that sung by a person with a good voice who can produce interesting kinds of vocal ornamentation. But if folk song is valued only for interesting

Figure 8-5
Folksinger of Akita. On the right is Asano Sanae, who sings "Nikata-bushi" (CD 4, Track 3). A fellow apprentice, Asano Yoshie, stands on the left. Folklife Festival of the Smithsonian Institution, Washington, D.C., 1986.

Linda Fujie

CD 4/3

"Nikata-bushi" ("Song of Nikata") (5:08). Performed by Asano Sanae, vocal; Asano Umewaka, *shamisen* (lute). Field recording by Karl Signell. Washington, D.C., 1986.

ornamentation, it becomes nothing more than a "popular song." (Asano 1966:211)

The critic noted, however, that national tastes and ways of thinking have changed so much since 1945 that perhaps there is no way to avoid change in folk singing.

Training to sing folk song at a professional level demands years of study. In recent years, folk song has developed its own *iemoto*-like system, modeled after the system found in traditional art music. For example, Asano Sanae (see Figure 8-5), the singer of "Nikata-bushi" (CD 4, Track 3), has been a pupil of the *shamisen* player Asano Umewaka for several years. In the manner of the *iemoto* system, she received her artistic name from him, including her teacher's last name. As a teenager, she moved from Osaka to Akita to become his apprentice, and she now participates regularly in concerts and competitions. Her teacher, in his seventies at the time of this recording, grew up in the Akita area and spent most of his life as a farmer, while slowly gaining a local and then a national reputation as a fine player of the Tsugaru *shamisen*, a type of *shamisen* used for virtuoso accompaniment of folk song. His former students live throughout Japan and teach his style of *shamisen* playing and singing.

According to Asano Sanae, Asano Umewaka (Figure 8-6) can be hard taskmaster, but he teaches his pupils with great care. She underwent a kind of apprenticeship, helping with household chores and her teacher's performances while receiving lessons. Therefore, she experienced the same everyday exposure and learning from repetition as had the *gidayū-bushi* apprentices of earlier time.

Listening to "Nikata-bushi," we hear first the sound of the *shamisen* but with a stronger tone than we heard in the *kouta* example. This *shamisen* is indeed different in construction, with a larger body, longer neck, and

Linda Fujie

Figure 8-6
Asano Umewaka before singing Akita folk songs at the Folklife Festival of the Smithsonian Institution, Washington, D.C., 1986.

thicker skin. The first notes sound on the open strings, allowing the player to tune his instrument before beginning the piece. (You can hear the pitch change slightly as the player adjusts the strings.) The same "tuning" occurs later, in the instrumental interlude between verses.

The song text is composed of two stanzas, each set in the syllabic pattern typical of folk song, 7–7–7–5.

Text, "Nikata-bushi"

1. *Nikata tera-machi*   The temple town Nikata
   no hana baasama   a woman selling flowers
   hana mo urazu ni   she doesn't sell them
   abura uru.   but enjoys them herself instead.

2. *Takai o-yama no*   On a high mountain
   goten no sakura   a cherry blossom tree at a mansion
   eda wa nana eda   has seven branches
   yae ni saku.   and blossoms abundantly.

The text of each stanza is set to almost identical music, even down to the ornamentation used. Similarly, the patterns heard in the *shamisen* part between the two stanzas almost repeat the patterns played in the introduction.

As in the *kouta* example, the instrument plays a more or less steady pulse while the voice has a flexible rhythm. Look, for example, at the long notes and ornamentation in the vocal part, as seen in Transcription 8-7, which shows the beginning of the second stanza. A time line underneath the notation marks the regular beats of the *shamisen* part, so that the vocal part can be seen in relation to a steady unit of time.

This transcription was made at half speed, in order to catch the different pitches that normally hit our ears at a rapid pace. Pitches that are

Transcription 8-7

"Nikata-bushi."

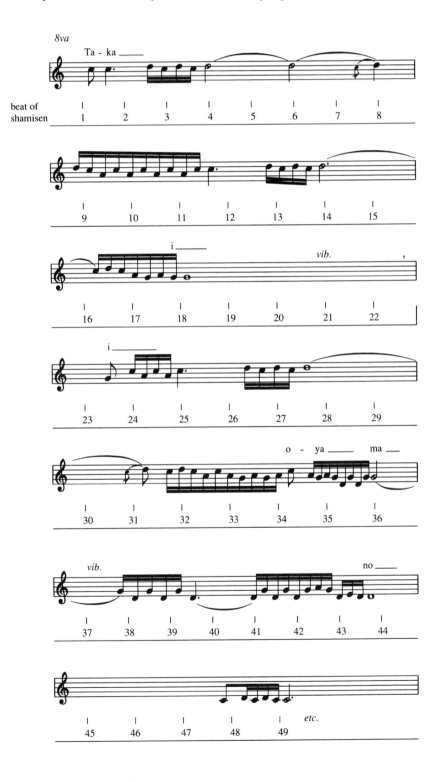

discernible at that speed are notated; vibrato within a range of less than a semitone is simply marked *"vib."* Looking at the different methods of ornamenting notes, we find many instances of rapid fluctuations between the note just voiced and a new note, before the new note is sounded and held. We also find several instances (for example, during the word *o-yama*) when a trill is performed between two notes that are as far apart as a perfect fourth. This technique of ornamenting the line requires great vocal control.

The perfect fourth and perfect fifth are important intervals in many Japanese folk songs. In the transcribed section, for example, the longest notes are D″, G′ and D′, the pivotal notes throughout the song. Both the *yo* scale and *minyō* tetrachords can be discerned here. Just before the voice enters with each verse, the *shamisen* player makes an exclamation that sounds like "huh!" This is another example of *kakegoe,* as first heard in the *kouta* selection.

Asano Sanae's elderly teacher might be considered a "true," old-fashioned folksinger and *shamisen* player in this Tsugaru style, having learned it from childhood in his native area. On the other hand, his student has studied purposefully to become a professional folksinger. Her performance reflects this training in many ways, as in her ornamentation, precision, clarity of voice, and general presentation. Her singing of *minyō* interests us, however, because Japanese increasingly value these qualities today in a *minyō* singer.

Matsuri-bayashi (Festival Music)

Strolling down the street, visitors to Japan may be lucky enough to run into a boisterous crowd celebrating a *matsuri,* or Shinto festival. As people spill over from the sidewalks into the streets, a parade marches by with people dressed up in *kimonos,* some riding in floats or carrying huge portable shrines. In the heart of all the activity is a Shinto shrine, with the distinctive red *torii* gate, where scores of vendors sell steaming noodles and old-fashioned toys, or offer chances to win a goldfish. In the background, the music of the festival, *matsuri-bayashi,* adds life and gaiety to the scene as the sounds of a graceful bamboo flute and booming drums fill the air (Figure 8-7).

Even in Tokyo, the capital and largest city of Japan, Shinto festivals are still held within the business districts and small neighborhoods scattered across the city. Every corner of the city—even in the most expensive commercial districts—has a Shinto shrine that serves as the tutelary or guardian shrine for that area. By offering prayers and festivities to the god-spirit, or *kami,* housed in the shrine, the residents receive the spirit's blessings for the year.

Although there is no legal or official relationship between a Shinto shrine and its neighborhood, many residents still feel it is important to help sponsor and participate in the traditional festival each year. They form committees and raise money to buy costumes, repair the parade floats, and so on. Older neighborhoods with a stable population usually maintain the festival because of tradition—the residents have enjoyed their neighborhood *matsuri* for several generations. In Japanese cities, the neighborhood

Figure 8-7
A Tokyo festival. The grounds of the Shinto shrine are covered with the booths of food and game vendors.

Linda Fujie

has been traditionally an important social unit—neighbors all knew one another and helped each other when needed, through both formal neighborhood associations and informal ties.

Since the end of World War II, however, there has been a dramatic rise in the mobility of the population as well as an increase in the white-collar sector. Neighbors tend to know each other less and share fewer professional ties. As a result, urban neighborhood social ties have become more fragile. Thus, some neighborhoods with a high turnover of population are also finding the traditional *matsuri* a good way to encourage a feeling of neighborhood friendliness.

With the high cost of living in Tokyo, families with roots in that city are moving in greater numbers to the suburbs. But there still remain some people who have lived in Tokyo for several generations. For example, the Ueno family are teachers and performers of festival music who live in the heart of *shitamachi,* or the "downtown" area (see later discussion and CD 4, Track 4). This is the older commercial area, long since passed up in large-scale development projects, where narrow streets are still lined with small, two-story wooden houses. Tokyo has some of the highest land prices in the world, and most houses seem to take up an unbelievably small amount of land. They are built so that their sliding front door comes right up to the sidewalk, leaving no land left unused. To provide some greenery in their surroundings, many residents put out pots of flowers and small trees on the sidewalk. Because the walls of the house are so thin, one can often hear, just walking by, all that goes on within—the television blaring, arguments between children, dishes being washed, and so on. Some of the buildings have small shops on the first floor, above which the shopkeepers and their families live. The women go shopping for groceries at the neighborhood stores, though they also sometimes shop at the big department stores outside their neighborhood. If there are no bath facilities in the house, the whole family bathes in the neighborhood public bathhouse. Bringing soap and plastic bucket with them, they spend time there each day chatting with friends. This close proximity and everyday contact with neighbors brings about a spirit of cooperation and solidarity rarely seen in the suburbs of Tokyo.

When it is time to hold a festival at the small neighborhood shrine, much of the neighborhood becomes involved. The festival is usually held over two or three days. On a stage on the shrine grounds, a musical group—the *matsuri-bayashi*—plays throughout the day as a musical offering to the *kami* spirit. At some shrines, mimed skits and dances are also performed to musical accompaniment.

The main event of the festival is a parade that winds through the neighborhood streets. Its principal element is the *mikoshi,* a portable shrine that temporarily holds the *kami.* The *kami*'s ride through the neighborhood blesses the area for the coming year. The shrine is elaborately decorated in gold and black lacquer and sometimes weighs as much as two tons (making it less "portable" than the translation of the term suggests). From fifty to more than one hundred men (and lately women, too) hoist it on their shoulders and, tossing it up and down, carry it through the streets for several hours. Shouting repeatedly *"was-shoi"* or some such exclamation to coordinate their movements, the *mikoshi* bearers, dressed in traditional cotton jackets and pants, make a colorful sight. Along the parade route, spectators cheer them on. During this often rowdy parade, several festival music groups play at different locations: Some remain at the permanent shrine, some perform on platforms along the parade route, and others play on floats in the parade (Figure 8-8).

Linda Fujie

Figure 8-8

Matsuri-bayashi of Tokyo in performance at Columbia University, New York, 1983. The two *shimedaiko* drums are on the right, the *ōdaiko* on the left.

Ensemble and Technique

Five musicians play the music of the *matsuri-bayashi* of Tokyo. Two play the shallow double-headed drums called *shimedaiko* (or, more commonly in Tokyo, *shirabe*); one plays the *ōdaiko,* a deep-barreled drum; one the *shinobue,* a transverse bamboo flute; and one the *yosuke,* a handheld gong. In other parts of Japan, different instruments are used for festival music, but these almost always include flutes and drums.

A close musical relationship is crucial to the performance of *matsuri-bayashi.* Each of the musicians, while specializing on one instrument, must learn them all to become proficient. Only then can each one listen to the others' parts and know exactly where every player is in the piece. This degree of familiarity is important because the different instruments often "bend" the rhythm slightly by either holding back or speeding up their tempi. The gong player must keep an absolutely steady beat, though not sounding all the possible beats. After treating the constant beat so flexibly throughout most of the piece, all the instruments should meet exactly together at the end of each phrase. When well done, this simultaneous finish is regarded as the sign of a truly skillful ensemble. But if a member of the ensemble gets "lost" while playing with the beat in this way, the result can be disastrous. Only the best ensembles, with years of experience performing together, can carry off this rhythmic game properly.

The example of *matsuri-bayashi* heard on CD 4, Track 4, is called "Yatai" and is the opening and closing section of a longer piece called "Kiri-bayashi" by the Ueno group. (The *yatai* is the wagon used to carry the *matsuri-bayashi* musicians in the festival parade.) The highly ornamented flute melody leads in and out of each section, while the vigorous drum patterns resound at increasing tempi. The main part of this section, after a short introduction, consists of seven repeated phrases (sometimes with variations thrown in), which accelerate with each repetition. At the end of one of these cycles the flute signals for the group to enter a final "coda" section.

In "Yatai," the first drum that enters is a *shirabe;* it sets the tempo for the entire piece. The flute enters with its introductory phrase, joined soon after by the two *shirabe* drums; finishing this section is a two-beat stroke by the large *ōdaiko* drum.

Even in this piece, with a heavy regular beat provided by the *shirabe* drums, the flute part and the deeper *ōdaiko* can vary the tempo just a little in order to make the rhythm more interesting. The flute's heavy ornamentation masks some of this rushing and holding back, but still the player is expected to meet the others at the end of each phrase.

This is the first piece taught to a new pupil in *matsuri-bayashi* by the Ueno family of downtown Tokyo: rapid repetition occurs, student copies teacher. Comparing their typical *matsuri-bayashi* lessons to the lessons in *gidayū-bushi,* we see some similarities to the past but without the pressure of the old days. A lesson with Ueno Mitsuyuki and his son Mitsumasa might proceed as follows.

CD 4/4

"Yatai" ("The Festival Wagon"), excerpt from *Kiri-bayashi* (1:18). Performed by Ueno Shachu. Field recording by Linda Fujie. Tokyo, Japan, 1981.

Although the elder Ueno passed away in 1983, the present tense is used here to refer to his life and work.

The student slides open the front door and calls out, "Good evening." On being invited to enter, the student immediately removes his shoes and takes a big step up to the level of the first floor of the house. There, on the *tatami* mats, the student bows to Ueno-*sensei* (*sensei* means teacher) and his family, who are all seated in an inner room. The lesson takes place in the room entered by the front door, and because musical instruments and household items are stacked along the walls, the sitting space is only about two by two meters. The family is still eating dinner and talking loudly to each other over the sound from the television set.

The teacher likes to chat with students before beginning a lesson. He might talk about his experiences in Tokyo during the war, or the latest *kabuki* performance he attended, or a recent argument with a neighbor. Then, after more students have arrived, either he or his son begins the lesson. In place of a real drum they use an old tire because of the neighbor's complaints about late-night practice sessions. This tire is placed in the middle of the tiny front room. Students and teacher sit on their knees around it, sticks in hand. The teacher begins to teach a new phrase of a piece by hitting the tire in mirror image of the way the performer normally plays, so that the students looking at him can easily learn the correct hand movements.

While striking the "drum" (the *shirabe,* or small drum, part is normally taught first), the teacher also calls out syllables to help the students remember the rhythm of the phrase they are playing. When there is no drum part, he hums or sings the flute melody and inserts some of the *ōdaiko* beats as well by hitting the side of the tire with one of his sticks. All parts are taught through a type of *solmization* (the syllables that stand for pitch or rhythm). Most genres of traditional Japanese music have their own solmization systems.

In *matsuri-bayashi,* the solmization of the *shirabe* part in the main section of "Yatai" is shown in Transcription 8-8. You can reproduce this rhythmic pattern by tapping a flat surface with your fingers. Begin each phrase with the right hand and do not use the same hand for two consecutive beats, except at the beginning of a new phrase (which should start with the right hand again). Comparing this solmization (which is sometimes called *shōka* in Japanese) to the Western notation shown, we can see that "ten" equals two half-beats, "tsu" equals a half-beat rest, and "ke" equals a half-beat following a half-beat rest. (No syllables are spoken on the last beat of the phrase, though a rest of one beat occurs there.)

Transcription 8-8
Drum rhythm and syllables that represent each beat; *shirabe* part in the main section of "Yatai" (*matsuri-bayashi*).

Students write down these syllables to help them remember the rhythmic patterns of the drums, and a similar system helps them to memorize the flute melody. However, merely hearing the syllables, without hearing them performed, gives only a vague notion of how they are to be played. The "score" that results is at best a memory device to help the student recall what was taught. As we have seen, Japanese music characteristically lacks a detailed notation system. The teacher is critical to a student's mastering any musical form. Without teachers who are willing to convey a great deal of their musical knowledge, students would be helpless, for scores do not give them access to real musical knowledge.

A good relationship with a knowledgeable teacher is also essential if a student wants to learn any *hikyoku,* or secret pieces. Found in many genres of traditional music, including *matsuri-bayashi,* the secret repertoire consists of rarely performed pieces handed down only to the most trusted of pupils. In the style of festival music taught by the Ueno family, the son said that secret pieces are not technically difficult but are valued mainly because of their exclusivity. In the past, this knowledge was so guarded that some *hikyoku* have disappeared because teachers have died before finding pupils worthy of learning their secrets.

The lives of Ueno Mitsuyuki and his son vividly exemplify the traditional and contemporary backgrounds of those who love Tokyo festivals and festival music. *Matsuri-bayashi* is traditionally performed by amateurs such as the Uenos, while *kagura,* the mimed plays based on Shinto themes, is carried out by professional actors and musicians. According to the father, performing *matsuri-bayashi* strictly as an amateur is important because it makes the music a pious act of offering entertainment to the gods, not a "performance" or "show" (see Figure 8-9). Therefore, he performs only at the festivals themselves. The son, however, while preferring to play at festivals, also plays occasionally with some of the professional *kagura* musicians who have learned how to play *matsuri-bayashi.* These musicians are frequently hired to provide a musically festive atmosphere at secular occasions such as wedding receptions and department store openings.

For both father and son, however, *matsuri-bayashi* remains secondary to their main profession, which is *chōkin,* or metal carving. This intricate art uses silver and gold to create jewelry (such as pins and ornaments for the *kimono*), sword guards, Japanese pipe holders, and small, elegant statues of Buddha. A combination of engraving and inlay, this technique requires years of training and great patience.

Biography of Ueno Mitsuyuki

The life of Ueno Mitsuyuki epitomizes the spirit of the Edo *matsuri-bayashi.* Born in 1900 in the old downtown area of Tokyo, Ueno proudly tells of his family's long history in Edo. They came to Edo at the beginning of the Tokugawa era (in the early seventeenth century) from Aichi Prefecture. His grandfather was of the *samurai* class, which was dissolved with the class system during the Meiji period. In the 1880s Ueno's father learned metal carving and *matsuri-bayashi.* Ueno's mother, as the daughter of the priest of an important shrine in the area, was active throughout her life in their own neighborhood festival.

At age fourteen, Ueno began to study metal carving seriously, dropping for a time all other hobbies and interests. After he had finished his metal-carving training with his father, Ueno studied *matsuri-bayashi* with his uncle, a talented musician. Ueno says,

> In the old days, the teacher told the students they were stupid and played poorly and maybe even hit them, but without explaining exactly what was wrong. In this way, I learned both *matsuri-bayashi* and metal carving—the technique became a part of my bones. But these days, people want to be told exactly what is wrong so that they can learn the art quickly and start making money from it.

He learned *matsuri-bayashi* easily and soon became well-known for his flute-playing style.

Too old to be accepted in the military during World War II, Ueno became active in the neighborhood association, which organized drills and fought fires in his area. He recalls the many times U.S. planes dropped bombs on Tokyo, which quickly set the closely packed wooden houses on fire, leaving thousands homeless within minutes. But he also blames the military leaders of Japan for dragging their country into such a bloody war and laments the loss of life on all sides.

When he was thirty-six, relatively late in life, Ueno married a woman from his own neighborhood in Tokyo. His son Mitsumasa was born in 1953. By then already in his fifties, Ueno was determined to teach the boy the skills he knew as early as possible. Knowing how long it would take to learn the intricate arts of metal carving and *matsuri-bayashi,* Ueno feared that he would not have enough time to teach everything he knew to his son. He began teaching Mitsumasa the drum part of *matsuri-bayashi* when the boy was three, and metal carving when he was seven. Lessons were conducted every day for one hour after school. By the time he was fifteen, Mitsumasa had become proficient enough in both arts to satisfy his father that his skills had been faithfully transmitted to the next generation.

Ueno told me that he was never bored. Every day he rises after only four or five hours of sleep and, no matter what the weather, strolls to the various shrines in his neighborhood at 4:00 A.M. to offer prayers. He then begins his workday upstairs in his workshop, together with his son. Sitting side by side, they work almost every day of the week. Father and son stop for a meal at midday; in the early evening, with the disappearance of daylight, they finish their day's work. (Because the work is so intricate, working by daylight is much easier than by artificial light.) Around 7:00 P.M. three days a week, the first pupils arrive and the music lessons begin. As there is a great deal of chatting and serving of tea, the lessons sometimes go on until 10:00 or 11:00 P.M.

The father exhibits a characteristic typical of the *Edokko,* or "child of Edo"—a nonchalant attitude toward money. For instance, he refuses to sell favorite pieces of his metal carving. Also, he readily turns down

Figure 8-9
Ueno Mitsuyuki playing *matsuri-bayashi.*

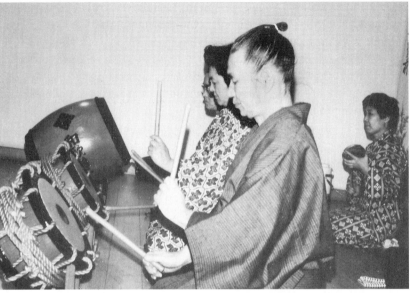

Linda Fujie

commissions for work, even when in need of it, if making the requested object does not appeal to him. As Ueno put it, "If you had the choice between gold and silver or paper (money), which would you prefer? And we're not talking about just plain gold and silver, but something you've created out of them which is unique in the world." Then he gave a self-deprecatory laugh and said, "Do you believe there are such innocent people left in the world as myself?" By the same token, the Uenos accept only a small amount of money for the music lessons they give. The father once confided that they would rather give the lessons free but found that people did not take them seriously without paying.

In spite of their relative poverty and busy lives, the Uenos still find the materials and the time to create with their own hands many of the items needed for the annual neighborhood festival. These include masks and costumes for the mimed plays in which they participate, as well as the drawing of designs to be dyed on to the material of the musicians' *kimonos.*

Ueno feels that his profession of metal carving and his hobby of *matsuri-bayashi* have one important quality in common. This is the feeling, as a practitioner, that one is never "finished" or has reached a point of perfection. As he said, "This is what makes life interesting: That which you want to do is never in a state of perfection, so you always have to strive to do better. That's why I enjoy metal carving and why I enjoy *matsuri-bayashi.*"

As for the son, Mitsumasa, from the earliest moment he can remember, his father reiterated the importance of his learning both metal carving and *matsuri-bayashi* as soon as possible. In the beginning, Mitsumasa says, he was actually not very interested in carving, but his father said, "Just give it a try." And so, he says, "I've been giving it a try for over twenty-five years now!"

Now the son is proud of carrying on the work of his father, both the metal carving and the festival music. Mitsumasa is one of the few young practitioners of metal carving, and he has already won many prizes for his work. As for *matsuri-bayashi,* he says, "I've got that music in my blood now, so as long as I'm around, I want to be playing it." As was the case with his father, the son's flute playing has become well admired, and professional musical troupes seek his services.

Today, both folk song and festival music are becoming professionalized and standardized. Folk song in particular seems to be adopting the standards of the "art" genres such as *shakuhachi* and *koto* music, with their *iemoto* systems, rankings, and artistic names. As for *matsuri-bayashi,* the younger Ueno and many other Tokyo *matsuri-bayashi* players feel the lure of professional troupes, aware of the income and prestige they could attain as members of such companies. As musicians join *iemoto* and professional organizations, the pressure to conform to certain performance standards increases.

Popular Music

In the past, the traditional Japanese music genres had been conveyed from performer to audience without electronic media for many centuries. At a single performance the audience of these genres was relatively small, and success depended on establishing rapport with that audience. Today, music performances regularly appear on radio, television, and other media. Millions of people unseen to the musicians may hear a single recorded performance.

In addition to changing the ways traditional music is played and perceived, mass media and technology have also stimulated the growth of a new kind of music in Japan, which we shall call "popular music." Since 1907, when the first commercial music recording was released in Japan, the composition, performance, and appreciation of music has changed dramatically. Music recorded specifically for commercial release in Japan, with the aim of appealing to the mass audience, exhibits several characteristics:

1. Performance within a set time limit (generally three to five minutes)
2. A focus on themes that appeal to a broad public (though regional or specialty audiences are also sometimes targeted)
3. Stanza form and a steady beat, making the music more accessible to the Japanese who have become more accustomed to Western music
4. Performers' attempts in live performance to reproduce the recorded version of the music so as to fulfill audience expectations
5. Dramatic rise and fall in popularity over time

This "Top 40" mentality was novel to the Japanese; in their previous experience it was common for many kinds of music dating from different eras in Japanese history to survive side by side as vital elements of the country's musical life. Now, through the association of songs with a specific point in time, generations have begun to identify with "their" songs, with the result that music can be used as an age marker.

Through the mass media, music performed by "others" (particularly professionals) became more available to more people than ever before.

Popular music is defined here as music primarily created for and transmitted by the various mass media. Although some genres of so-called popular song that flourished among the masses in pre-Meiji Japan have exerted an impact on the popular music of today, only those genres particularly linked to contemporary popular genres are discussed here.

Today, scarcely a home in Japan does not have a radio, television set, or stereo, and many have all three. As people listen to the same recordings and to the same performance of a song, they are united by a common musical experience; they also develop certain expectations as to what music should sound like.

Of course, a similar process has occurred worldwide as popular music has penetrated all corners of the globe. In Japan, the spread of music through records, tapes, and compact discs has advanced rapidly. In fact, since the mid-1970s, their combined sales have exceeded "those of all other capitalist nations, except the USA" (Mitsui 1984:107). Furthermore, the Japanese have far more opportunities to hear American and European popular music than Western listeners generally have to hear non-Western popular music. One industry survey shows that since 1970 about two-fifths of all popular music recordings produced in Japan were recorded by foreign musicians, most of whom were American or European (Mitsui 1984:107).

Historical Background

The types of popular music found today in Japan developed as the modern Japanese state emerged. Interestingly, in a country known in the past for its high degree of cultural homogeneity, the present-day music scene has become exceedingly diverse. The rise of this heterogeneous music-culture and specifically "Japanese" popular music can be traced to the latter half of the nineteenth century. At this time, wide-ranging reforms were introduced to Japanese society to enable the country to deal with Western powers. The traditional class system was abolished, and the authority of the Tokugawa regime was replaced by a government headed by the Emperor Meiji. He left Kyoto and set up a new capital in Edo, which was renamed "Tokyo," or Eastern Capital. This government introduced a constitutional monarchy and made many structural changes in the society to allow a mercantile and industrial economy to flourish.

After their long era of isolation, the Japanese felt it necessary to "modernize" life around them, which for a while meant adopting Western models. Leaders rapidly installed a system of compulsory education and decided, from reading about the Dutch and French school systems, that Japan also needed compulsory singing in its schools. In the late 1870s Izawa Shuji, a Japanese school principal who had studied in Massachusetts, and Luther Whiting Mason, an American who was the director of music for the Boston primary schools, developed a plan for music instruction in Japanese public schools.

In the following years *shōka* songs were introduced to teach songs that blended Japanese and Western elements. The newly composed songs used melodies based on a traditional Japanese scale within the structure of a stanza form and a regular meter. Other songs introduced in the schools contained Western melodies such as "Auld Lang Syne" and "Swanee River" set with Japanese texts. Through both *shōka* and Western songs, the Japanese masses were introduced to Western musical structure, scale, and rhythm.

In the last decades of the nineteenth century, different opinions emerged over Japan's future direction. One faction claimed that Japan should work toward a democracy similar to that of the United States. Others, however, supported a strong monarchy and political power for the small group of advisers around the emperor. These people believed that the emperor should stand as the symbol of the nation and its long history and spirit; he would lead the Japanese to a new era of world leadership.

In the end, those who supported the monarchy gained political supremacy, and their spiritual descendants eventually led Japan to political and military expansion and World War II. But during the Meiji period these arguments were far from settled, and the public became highly involved in them. In the 1880s, when the People's Rights Movement urged further democratization through the establishment of a parliament, a new kind of song called *enka* evolved to express the goals of the movement. The words of one such song, "Oppekepe," written in 1887, show how political the early *enka* were. Actually, the words to this song are not so much "sung" to a melody as recited like a rhythmic chant.

Text, "Oppekepe"

I'd like to make those who dislike "rights and happiness" [for the people] drink the water of freedom. Those in their fancy Western hairdos and hats, who dress in stylish garb, their outward appearance may be fine but their political thinking is inadequate; they don't understand the truth of the land. We should sow the seeds of freedom in their hearts.

Author's translation.

The very title of "Dynamite Song," popular from 1886 to 1888, indicates its incendiary purpose. Its first stanza reads as follows:

Text, "Dynamite Song"

Yamato [meaning "Japanese"] spirit is polished with rain
From the tears of the advocates of People's Rights.
Promote the national interest and the people's happiness
Foster the National Resources
Because if this is not done—
Dynamite! Bang!

(Malm 1971:278)

These deeply political *enka* songs were transformed through the decades to become sentimental songs full of nostalgia and longing; but their early influence on the development of Japanese popular song as a whole is unmistakable.

The *enka* song called "Nonki-bushi" ("Song of the Lazy Man") was composed in 1918 and was an early "hit" (CD 4, Track 5). Its composer was Soeda Azembo, one of the most famous of the early Japanese popular music composers. Soeda began his career as an *enka* singer, but by the early twentieth century the *enka* had already changed dramatically in character,

CD 4/5
"Nonki-bushi" ("Song of the Lazy Man") (2:37). *Enka* song. Music by Soeda Azembo, lyrics by Ishida Ichimatsu. Performed by Ishida Ichimatsu for Nippon Columbia SP-ban fukugen.

as you will realize from listening to this selection. The lyrics exemplify a typical "silly" song that was popular in the vaudeville halls of the day and reappeared many times over the years in Japan (see text that follows).

The singer of this original recording, Ishida Ichimatsu, also wrote the lyrics to this song. Born in 1902, Ishida was studying law in Tokyo when he met Soeda through a musical club. He then began his career in songwriting and singing, producing many 78-rpm hit records. In the post–World War II years, Ishida entered politics and was reelected several times to the National Diet before his death in 1956.

Text, "Nonki-bushi"

1. *Nonki no tōsan*
   o-uma no keiko
   o-uma ga hashirihajimete
   tomaranai.
   Kodomo wa omoshirosō ni
   Tōsan, doko e yuku.
   Doko e yukun da ka
   o-uma ni kiito kure
   He he nonki da ne.

   The lazy man
   rides a horse
   and it begins to run
   and won't stop.
   A child enjoys this, asking,
   "Hey, where are you going?"
   "If you want to know where I'm
   going, better ask the horse!"
   Ha, ha, how lazy!

2. *Nonki na tōsan no*
   bōya ga hadaka de
   kaachan ga kimono o
   kiyo to shikattemo
   bōya wa iya da to itte
   kimono o kinai
   . . . Choito Tōsan, bōya ga
   hada de komarimasu wa yo.
   Nanda nanda bōya kaze o hiitara
   doo surun da
   dete kita tōsan ga maruhade
   He he nonki da ne.

   The lazy man—
   his son was naked
   and the mother scolded him
   to put on his kimono.
   The boy said he wouldn't
   put on his kimono.
   "Hey, Father, our son is naked—
   do something!"
   "What's this! Son, what will
   you do if you catch a cold?"
   said the father, coming out stark naked.
   Ha ha, how lazy!

3. *Nonki na tōsan*
   O-mawari-san ni natta kedo
   Saaberu ga jama ni natte
   arukenai
   ichido koronde mata mata
   korobi
   Sakki okinakereba yokatta
   mono ni to sa
   he he nonki da ne.

   The lazy man
   became a policeman but
   his saber got in the way
   and he couldn't walk.
   He fell once, then again
   and again.
   "It would've been better if
   I hadn't gotten up again!"
   Ha ha, how lazy!"

4. *Nonki na tōsan*
   teppo katsuide
   haruka kanata o naganureba
   tsugai no hato poppo ga
   narande tomatteru.
   Aida o neratte uttara

   The lazy man
   carries his rifle
   looking at a far-off tree branch
   a pair of pigeons are
   sitting together.
   "If I aim for the middle, I

dotchika ataru daro.	should hit one, I guess!
he he nonki da ne.	Ha, ha, how lazy!

5. *Nonki na tōsan*   The lazy man
   koe hariagete   shouted to the others,
   mina kite miro taihen da   "Everyone, come and see—
   hayaku kite miro   come quickly and see
   mattaku taihen da   it's incredible!
   are miro suita densha ga   Look there—an empty train
   tōtteiru   is going by!"
   he he nonki da ne.   Ha, ha, how lazy!

Comparing this song to the earlier examples of Japanese vocal music found in this chapter, we find some astonishing differences: a steady beat in the melody, the repetition of stanzas, a new quality of the voice, and the narration of small stories in each stanza. The effects of Western popular music here are obvious. On the Japanese vaudeville stage, the repetitive structure allowed the performer to add new stanzas—perhaps pertaining to timely political issues, or making fun of someone in the audience—as he desired.

One aspect of Japanese vocal music remains, however, as a vestige of the rich tradition of ornamentation. Listen to CD 4, Track 5, and follow Transcription 8-9 for the quick ornaments placed over some notes in the

Transcription 8-9
First stanza, "Nonki-bushi."

first verse. The following stanzas also have these ornaments. To this day, recreating these ornaments is considered essential in the performance of *enka,* even among amateurs. A short introduction is played by a violin based on the melody of the last phrase, "He he, nonki da ne" ("Ha ha, how lazy"). This same phrase appears briefly between each stanza and at the conclusion of the song. Otherwise, the violin follows the vocal line with only slight embellishments.

When "Nonki-bushi" was written, the practice of harmonizing *enka* with chords had not yet replaced the single string instrument—first *shamisen,* then the violin, in later years the guitar—in supporting and occasionally embellishing the melodic line.

In the 1990s the *enka* still has many fans, but it has undergone several transformations since the days of "Nonki-bushi." In the years after World War II, *enka* became a highly sentimental song genre that most commonly evoked images of *sake* bars, with the ubiquitous red lantern hanging outside, port towns (the site of many sad farewells), and foggy or rainy, lonely evenings.

One might imagine that the older generation would be most likely to appreciate such nostalgic expressions of sadness. Indeed, for many younger people who grew up with rock music, *enka* sounds too old-fashioned and sentimental for their taste. By the mid-1970s the audiences for *enka* were growing older, and the genre did not seem to hold much appeal for younger listeners. But then a new phenomenon called *karaoke* appeared on the scene, reinvigorating the *enka* and bringing it to a new, younger audience.

Karaoke

Karaoke (ka-ra-oh-kay) means "empty orchestra" and designates the technological development that allowed anyone with the proper equipment to sing their favorite songs to a full orchestral accompaniment. A typical setup includes a tape machine, which plays a prerecorded cassette tape of the musical accompaniment to a favorite song, and one or two microphones for amplifying the voice as the amateur sings the melody.

Enka were, and continue to be, the songs of choice for most *karaoke* users. Although other kinds of music found on *karaoke* tapes include Japanese folk and contemporary "pop" songs, as well as Western popular songs, the majority are some kind of *enka.* A *karaoke* singer may either sing the lyrics of these songs from memory or consult a book containing the lyrics to hundreds of songs.

A large variety of *karaoke* machines are produced in Japan, ranging in price from about $200 to $5,000 and averaging about $2,000. The difference in price is determined by the machine's features. The more expensive models are used in restaurants, bars, wedding halls, and banquet rooms. At these places, customers or guests sing songs of their choice from a wide selection available on tape, singing either alone or in pairs. Models priced in the middle range are often installed in smaller bars as well as touring buses and trains so that Japanese traveling in groups can sing to each other on long trips. The inexpensive models are designed for home use, so that users can practice for these "public" performances. There are even battery-powered models for outdoor use.

Sales of *karaoke* machines indicate how widespread its popularity has become. In 1978, 100,000 sets were sold, but within five years, this figure had jumped to 1,100,000 sets, resulting in $625 million in sales. A report in *Time* magazine noted that this is more than was spent that year in the United States on gas ranges ("Closet Carusos" 1983:47).

The *karaoke* technology made available to the consumer was developed to support and enhance his or her voice as much as possible. One can adjust the volume of the vocal part in relation to the instrumental background and even switch on an echo device when desired (to add a kind of "singing-in-the-shower" effect). Some equipment is digitized, permitting singers to change the key of the original accompaniment tape to one in their own register. Even the musical accompaniment is designed to be helpful to the singer: The orchestra stays in the background to avoid stealing the show from the singer, but one instrument reinforces the melodic line, in case the singer becomes lost.

This equipment has reinforced the traditional Japanese custom of group singing. Japanese feel that singing helps to establish a relaxed atmosphere and feeling of closeness with others. Social groups—based on professional, school, familial, or community relationships—matter greatly in Japanese life, and the Japanese put much effort into harmonious relationships within these groups. For example, to improve relations among company employees, management organizes special activities such as group tours to spas and drinking parties. On these occasions, *karaoke* is used to break down the social barriers created by the company hierarchy. For this purpose, mere conversation, even when mixed with drinking, does not suffice, because it is based on knowledge and wit. But *karaoke* is a different kind of socializing, and the most sentimental, nostalgic ideas can be expressed—and are even encouraged—when sung through the *karaoke* machine.

Karaoke singing also reinforces group harmony through the expectation that each member of a group will participate by singing in front of the group. Even if someone feels embarrassed and wants to refuse, he or she usually gives in and sings at least one song in order to maintain the spirit of group harmony. In recent years, *karaoke* has become popular around the world; one can find "*karaoke* bars" in South America, Europe, and the United States, for example. However, public *karaoke* singing in these continents does not influence and control group social dynamics to the same degree as in Japan and other Asian countries.

Karaoke technology also works as an outlet for stress. For instance, the echo feature gives singers a sense of removal from their everyday identity. One Japanese living in America stated, "It's great to hear your own voice, resounding throughout the room. You feel all your tension disappear." Some businessmen in Japan enjoy going to *karaoke* bars after work just for that purpose: to relieve the accumulated stress from a day of work by belting down a few drinks and belting out a few songs. One survey shows that *karaoke* is most popular among male, white-collar workers between the ages of twenty and forty-nine; the same survey also found that, within any age group, those who enjoyed *karaoke* the most were "those who like to sing" and "those who like to drink" (NHK 1982:24–25).

Even Japanese businessmen living abroad find *karaoke* bars in which they can spend their after-hours time. In New York City, for example, where a large population of Japanese businessmen work, some twenty or more *karaoke* bars had sprung up by the mid-1980s, and a fierce competition had broken out among them to install the latest technological developments. One such development is the laser disc video machine, which shows a series of scenes to accompany each song. Besides the added visual stimulation, this apparatus also allows the singers to look up at the screen and at their listeners, rather than having their heads buried in the lyric book.

Although the content of *karaoke* differs from that of traditional music, there is an interesting similarity in the way *enka* songs (as sung over *karaoke* machines) and traditional music are learned. Both involve aural skills—listening very carefully to an "original" version (of the recording in the case of *enka,* and of the teacher in traditional music) and imitating it as skillfully as possible. These days, some notation can also be involved. Real *karaoke* enthusiasts may even study with a teacher for pointers or technique. For the most part, though, singers become familiar with the melody and interpretation of a song after listening to a recorded professional version many times.

At the top level of performance, *karaoke* performances are expected to produce more than exact imitations of another's performance. For example, more expensive models of *karaoke* machines can automatically score a performer on a scale of 1 to 100. One enthusiast told me that in his experience "exact" reproduction of a song in its original interpretation might bring you a score of 98 or 99, but not 100. For the highest score, one needs an element of "personal expressiveness" as well as complete mastery of the original version. In the traditional music genres described earlier, we have seen this same standardization of music performance among the lower-ranking performers, with expectations for personal creativity at the master level.

By the same token, master performers of *gidayū-bushi* music, festival music, and so forth need to go beyond imitating their teachers. For most, however, simply meeting the criteria of imitation—as promoted at most levels of the *iemoto* system—is a lifelong task. Few performers reach the stage where personal interpretation is acceptable, and even then it can be controversial.

Karaoke's impact on the musical life of the typical Japanese should not be underestimated. The use of these machines by people of all ages has widened the average person's song repertoire. The musical generation gap, prompted by the growth of popular music, has narrowed somewhat as a result of *karaoke* activity. Within one social group, members of different generations hear and learn songs from one another's repertories. Singing together encourages this intergenerational learning process.

The music industry has had good reason to be pleased with *karaoke*'s popularity. This technology not only provides a new avenue for merchandizing recorded music (the *karaoke* tapes) but in some cases stimulates sales of the original version of a popular song—when people like a song sung by someone at a bar, they sometimes purchase the record themselves in order to learn it.

Enka's popularity has spread to younger age groups because of social *karaoke* singing. At the same time, *enka* composers have adapted their songs to the tastes of the younger generation. Background accompaniment ranges from the earlier simple guitar accompaniment to sophisticated orchestral arrangements and heavier, rock-type beats. "Upbeat" *enka* have been issued, with fast tempi and optimistic lyrics, though these are still in the minority. Finally, vocal ornamentation, so emphasized in earlier *enka,* is toned down in the newer versions because the youth are more accustomed to hearing Western-style vocalization.

"Naite Nagasaki," or "Crying Nagasaki," the *enka* song on CD 4, Track 6, is typical of the more old-fashioned variety of *enka* meant for a middle-aged audience. Recorded in 1988 by a *geisha,* the mournfully romantic theme of the song, its orchestral background, and its vocal style appeal to people who visit a bar with a *karaoke* machine after a long day at work and want to indulge in a little emotionalism. The text describes a woman alone in her room as she contemplates the departure of her lover.

CD 4/6

"Naite Nagasaki" ("Crying Nagasaki") (3:35). Performed by Kanda Fuku-maru for Nippon Columbia AH-210.

Text, "Naite Nagasaki"

1. *Saka no mukō ni*   On the other side of the hill
   yogisha ga mieru   I can see the night train.
   Anata noseteku   Taking you away,
   nobori no ressha   the northbound train.
   Okuritai kedo   I want to send you off
   okureba tsurai   but if I do it will be painful.
   Heya no mado kara   From the window of my room
   te o furu watashi   I wave good-bye to you.
   Naite naite naite   Crying, crying, crying,
   Nagasaki   Nagasaki,
   Ame ni narisō, ne.   It looks like rain, doesn't it?

2. *Wakarenakereba*   That you were someone
   naranaihito to   with whom I'd have to part—
   shitte inagara   although I knew this,
   moyashita inochi   a burning fate,
   sugaritsukitai   wanting to cling to you,
   Maruyamadōri   along the Maruyamadōri [street name]
   jitto koraete   with steady endurance,
   aruita watashi   I walked:
   Naite naite naite   Crying, crying, crying
   Nagasaki   Nagasaki.
   Ame ni narisō, ne.   It looks like rain, doesn't it?

3. *Minato yokaze*   The night wind from the port
   fukikomu kabe ni   blows against the wall
   furete setsunai   making flutter
   anata no heyagi   your robe hanging there.
   nigai o-sake o   I drown myself
   abiteru watashi   in bitter *sake.*
   Naite naite naite   Crying, crying, crying
   Nagasaki.   Nagasaki.
   Ame ni narisō, ne.   It looks like rain, doesn't it?

Several images here are common to many *enka* songs. The setting of the port town of Nagasaki conjures up romantic associations and particularly the sadness of lovers parting. The scenes of drowning oneself in *sake,* crying in the windy night, and—on top of all that—rain are also found in hundreds of other *enka* songs. For such themes, the Japanese prefer to use a natural minor scale, sometimes with the sharped seventh added. At times, the melody also emphasizes the sad mood, for example in the setting of the words "Naite, naite," as though the singer were sobbing.

The form of the song is also typical of *enka,* as we have already seen in "Nonki-bushi"—a simple strophe with a refrain. It opens and closes with instrumental sections, which also recur between strophes. As soon as the voice enters, the background accompaniment becomes minimal, consisting mainly of a bass guitar playing a bass line and other orchestral and electronic instruments filling in the harmony. This accompaniment begins to expand toward the end of the stanza as the vocal part reaches the climax at "Naite, naite . . ." (Transcription 8-10).

Transcription 8-10

First stanza, "Naite Nagasaki."

(continues)

Harmonically, *enka* tend to use a conservative progression of chords, like most Western popular music. There is a brief modulation to the relative major (on the last "Nagasaki"), but otherwise the main movement is between the tonic, subdominant, and dominant of A minor.

Compared with "Nonki-bushi," "Naite Nagasaki" contains far more complicated orchestration, the use of background singers, and other elements indicating Western popular music influence. However, the occasional use of vocal ornamentation reflects Japanese taste in vocal quality. Examples can be found in the slight tremolo heard in the voice in the line *"nobori no ressha,"* the occasional use of vibrato before the end of a stanza, and the final ornamented fall from the B to the A at the end of the transcribed stanza.

The large Japanese music industry produces many other kinds of popular music in addition to *enka.* Some are strongly influenced by Western genres; some show connections to Japanese musical traditions. The term *kayōkyoku* describes Japanese popular song as a whole, and particularly the songs, including *enka,* that mix Western and Japanese musical elements. This combination is usually a blend of Japanese melodies made from pentatonic scales with Western harmonic progressions and metrical organization. Since the mid-1970s, however, many of the contemporary songs have been written in Western scales, especially major modes, conforming to the imported music listened to by Japanese youth.

The following labels identifying different kinds of Japanese popular music are quite confusing (as they can be in Western popular music as well) because they are so often inconsistently applied. Here we look at the most common of these labels: *gunka,* folk song, new music, and pops.

Gunka

Literally "military songs," *gunka* were first composed and gained popularity during the Russo-Japanese War of 1904–1905. More songs were composed in succeeding military engagements. People in their seventies now strongly associate such songs with their youth during World War II and therefore are still extremely fond of them. Influenced by military music of the West, these songs are written in stanza form, often with trumpet and other brass instruments in the instrumental accompaniment. Not all are enthusiastic about fighting and war. Some songs were written from the point of view of a lonely mother waiting for her soldier-son to come home, or of a soldier on the front who has just lost his best friend in battle.

Folk Song

Fōku songu can apply to either Western "new" folk songs, as sung by musicians such as Joan Baez and Bob Dylan, or to the Japanese songs written mainly in the 1960s and 1970s that were influenced by such music. Japanese folksingers of this period typically wrote the words and music of the songs they sang. This practice differed from the separation of songwriter, lyricist, and singer that had formerly predominated in Japanese popular music. Musically, these songs scarcely differ from their Western counterparts; the lyrics, however, are sung in Japanese and often refer to social or political issues that are specifically Japanese.

New Music

Also written phonetically to imitate the English words *(nyū myūshiku)*, this term developed in the late 1970s to designate a music that had grown out of the "folk song" style. Represented at first by singer-songwriters such as Yoshida Tokurō and Minami Kōsetsu, "new music" songs generally convey an introverted, personal point of view that appeals to today's young people. In this type of song, the melody, usually written in the natural minor scale and in short phrases, is given more importance than the presence of a strong beat.

Pops

Appearing from the late 1970s and aimed at a teenage audience, music of this kind is ordinarily sung by teenagers themselves, some as young as fourteen. These singers, mostly female, are discovered by production companies that send talent scouts all over the country. On locating a promising candidate, the company decides on the appropriate image for the singer, trains her to sing in a certain way, and choreographs her performances. Television is an important medium for these teenage performers, as a new singer can gain instant fame with an appearance on one of the numerous musical variety shows. Performing in costumes that accentuate an image of youth and innocence, dozens of these singers rise and fall in the Japanese music business each year, while a few lucky ones manage to maintain long-term careers.

These songs usually sound Western in arrangement and melody and, to add a touch of sophistication and exoticism, often include a few words of English in the lyrics. Typically, English words or phrases are alternated with Japanese lines, but the English may not be strictly idiomatic.

In addition to *gunka, fōku songu,* new music, and pops, Japanese enjoy easy listening, rock, punk, and many other kinds of popular music, mostly based on Western models but sometimes deviating from those models in interesting ways. In addition, popular music and musicians from other parts of Asia have gained popularity since the early 1990s. This trend can be linked to the rising number of Asian immigrant workers and to the increase in travel by Japanese to Taiwan and Southeast Asia.

Final Words

We have reviewed a small sample of the wide variety of music heard in Japan today. This sample contains many examples of the mixture of native with foreign elements in the evolution of new musical forms. The *shakuhachi* was developed from an instrument of Chinese origin that entered Japan around the eighth century. The Zen philosophy that underlay the instrument's use in meditation also originated in China. The prototype of the *shamisen,* used to play *kouta* and music of the puppet theater and to accompany traditional folk song, can be traced to Okinawa, China, and beyond. Most of the instruments of the festival music ensemble also originated in China and underwent adaptation in Japan. Finally, popular music as a whole is based on Western form, rhythmic and harmonic structure, and instrumental accompaniment; only the melodic component and the lyric content in some cases reflect Japanese traditions.

Of course, one can question the concept itself of "tradition" or the "traditional culture" of a nation or people, especially in terms of "purity" of origin. What culture group in the world has not borrowed cultural elements from another, with the roots of that borrowing going so far back that few think of the idea or custom as "borrowed"?

We find, in examining the Japanese music-culture, the expression of some aspects of the varied Japanese character. For instance, popular nonsense songs like "Nonki-bushi" (CD 4, Track 5) find their roots in a certain outlandish sense of humor that the Japanese sometimes indulge in. (Anyone who has watched Japanese television for any length of time, particularly game shows, can attest to this.) On a more sober note, the idea of emptying one's soul and reaching a state of selflessness as preparation for the performance of both *shakuhachi* and the music of the *bunraku* theater reflects the strong underlying influence of Zen thought in Japanese culture. This influence touches many other areas of Japanese daily life, not only in mental preparation for a future task but also in the stress on self-control and self-discipline. Finally, the indulgence in pathos and extreme emotional anguish, as expressed in *enka* songs as well as in the music of the puppet theater, reveals another side of the Japanese character. Listening to Japanese music and learning about its connections to past and present society, we become aware of the richness of Japanese life.

References

Adachi, Barbara. 1985. *Backstage at Bunraku: A Behind-the-Scenes Look at Japan's Traditional Puppet Theater.* New York: Weatherhill.

Adriaansz, Willem. 1973. *The Kumiuta and Danmono Traditions of Japanese Koto Music.* Berkeley: Univ. of California Press.

Asano Kenji. 1966. "Nihon no minyō" (Folk Song of Japan). Tokyo: Iwanami Shinsho.

Blasdel, Christopher Yohmei. 1988. *The Shakuhachi: A Manual for Learning.* Tokyo: Ongaku no Tomo Sha.

"Closet Carusos: Japan Reinvents the Singalong." 1983. *Time,* February 28, p. 47.

Ernst, Earle. 1956. *The Kabuki Theatre.* Honolulu: Univ. Press of Hawaii.

Groemer, Gerald. 1994. "Fifteen Years of Folk Song Collection in Japan: Reports and Recordings of the 'Emergency Folk Song Survey.'" *Asian Folklore Studies* 53(2): 199–225.

Hughes, David. 1981. "Japanese Folk Song Preservation Societies: Their History and Nature." In *International Symposium on the Conservation and Restoration of Cultural Property,* edited by the Organizing Committee of ISCRCP. Tokyo: Tokyo National Research Institute of Cultural Properties.

———. 1990–1991. "Japanese 'New Folk Songs,' Old and New." *Asian Music* 22(1): 1–49.

Kikkawa Eishi. 1981. *Nihon ongaku no rekishi* (The History of Japanese Music). Osaka: Sōgensha.

Koizumi Fumio. 1974. *Nihon no ongaku* (Japanese Music). Tokyo: National Theater of Japan.

Kurada Yoshihiro. 1982. "Kouta." In *Ongaku daijiten* (Encyclopedia Musica), edited by Shitanaka Kunihiko. Tokyo: Heibonsha.

Malm, William. 1959. *Japanese Music and Musical Instruments.* Rutland, Vt.: Charles E. Tuttle.

———. 1971. *Modern Music of Meiji Japan.* In *Tradition and Modernization in Japanese Culture,* edited by Donald H. Shirley. Princeton, N.J.: Princeton Univ. Press.

Mitsui Toru. 1984. "Japan in Japan: Notes on an Aspect of the Popular Music Record Industry in Japan." *Popular Music* 3:107–20.

Motegi Kiyoko. 1984. "Aural Learning in *Gidayu-bushi*: Music of the Japanese Puppet Theatre." *Yearbook for Traditional Music* 16:97–107.

———. 1988. *Bunraku: Koe to oto to hibiki* (Bunraku: Voice and Sound and Reverberation). Tokyo: Ongaku no Tomo Sha.

NHK Hōsō Seron Chōsajo, eds. 1982. *Gendaijin to ongaku* (Contemporary People and Music). Tokyo: Nippon Hōsō Shuppan Kyōkai.

Sōri-fu (Prime Minister's Office). 1982. *Population of Japan: 1980 Population Census of Japan.* Tokyo: Statistics Bureau.

Additional Reading

Brandon, J., W. Malm, and D. Shively. 1978. *Studies in Kabuki: Its Acting, Music and Historical Context.* Honolulu: Univ. Press of Hawaii.

Crihfield, Liza. 1979. *Kouta: "Little Songs" of the Geisha World.* Rutland, Vt.: Charles E. Tuttle.

Dalby, Liza Crihfield. 1983. *Geisha.* Berkeley: Univ. of California Press.

Fujie, Linda. 1986. "The Process of Oral Transmission in Japanese Performing Arts: The Teaching of *Matsuri-bayashi* in Tokyo." In *The Oral and the Literate in Music,* edited by Yoshihiko Tokumaru and Osamu Yamaguti. Tokyo: Academia Music.

Gestle, C. Andrew, Kiyoshi Inobe, and William P. Malm. 1990. *Theater as Music: The Bunraku Play "Mt. Imo and Mt. Se": An Exemplary Tale of Womanly Virtue.* Michigan Monograph Series in Japanese Studies, 4. Ann Arbor: Center for Japanese Studies, Univ. of Michigan. (With 2 sound cassettes.)

Gutzwiller, Andreas, and Gerald Bennett. 1991. "The World of a Single Sound: Basic Structure of the Music of the Japanese Flute Shakuhachi." *Musica Asiatica* 6:36–59

———. 1992. "Polyphony in Japanese Music: Rokudan for Example." *Chime* 5:50–57.

Hughes, David. 1990–1991. "Japanese 'New Folk Songs,' Old and New." *Asian Music* 22(1): 1–49.

Keene, Donald. 1990. *No and Bunraku: Two Forms of Japanese Theater.* New York: Columbia Univ. Press.

Kishibe Shigeo. 1984. *The Traditional Music of Japan.* Tokyo: Ongaku no Tomo Sha.

Okada Maki. 1991. "Musical Characteristics of *Enka.*" *Popular Music* 10(3): 283–303.

Additional Listening

Japan: Ainu Songs. Unesco Collection/Auvidis CD D8047.

Japon: Kinshi Tsuruta. Satsuma Biwa. Ocora CD HM83.

Japon: Musique du Nô. Shakkyo (Pont en pierres). CD Ocora HM65.

Japon: Shômyô. Buddhist Liturgical Chant, Tendai Sect. Ocora CD HM80.

Kagura. Japanese Shinto Ritual Music. Hungaroton HCD CD 18193.

The Music of Japan, IV—Buddhist Music. Unesco Collection/Musicaphon LP BM30-L2015.

Music of the Bunraku Theatre. JVC World Sounds CD VICG-5356.

Yoshitsune: Songs of Medieval Hero Accompanied by the Biwa. BMG Victor LP CR10080-81.

Collections

"Nihon no dentô ongaku" [Japanese Traditional Music]. CD Series. King Record Co. (2-12-13 Ottowa, Bunkyo-ku, Tokyo 112).

Vol. 1. *Gagaku.* KICH 2001.

Vol. 2: *Nôgaku.* KICH 2002.

Vol. 3: *Kabuki.* KICH 2003.

Vol. 4: *Biwa.* KICH 2004.

Vol. 5: *Shakuhachi.* KICH 2005.

Vol. 6: *Sô.* KICH 2006.

Vol. 7: *Sankyoku.* KICH 2007.

Vol. 8: *Shamisen I.* KICH 2008.

Vol. 9: *Shamisen II.* KICH 2009.

Vol. 10: *Percussion.* KICH 2010.

"Music of Japanese People." CD Series. King Record Co. (2-12-13 Ottowa, Bunkyo-ku, Tokyo 112).

Vol. 1: *Harmony of Japanese Music.* KICH 2021.

Vol. 2: *Japanese Dance Music.* KICH 2022.

Vol. 3: *Japanese Work Songs.* KICH 2023.

Vol. 4: *Jam Session of Tsugaru-Shamisen.* KICH 2024.

Vol. 5: *Music of Okinawa.* KICH 2025.

Vol. 6: *Music of Yaeyama and Miyako.* KICH 2026.

Vol. 7: *Music of Amami.* KICH 2027.

Vol. 8: *Music of Japanese Festivals.* KICH 2028.

Vol. 9: *Soundscape of Japan.* KICH 2029.

Vol. 10: *A Collection of Unique Musical Instruments.* KICH 2030.

Viewing

A Shamanic Medium of Tagaru. 1994. Video, 92 min. Color. Directed by Yashuhiro Omori. Osaka, Japan: National Museum of Ethnology (distributor).

Shinto Festival Music. 1994. Video, 29.5 min. Color. Produced by Eugene Enrico and David Smeal. Norman, Okla.: Center for Music Television (distributor).

Nagauta: The Heart of Kabuki Music. 1994. Video, 30 min. Color. Produced by Eugene Enrico and David Smeal. Norman, Okla.: Center for Music Television (distributor).

Video Collections

The following video series are devoted to various forms of Japanese music, dance and theater and distributed by Multicultural Media, Ltd., Barre, Vt.; (802) 223-1294.

A Video and Sound Anthology of Japanese Classical Performing Arts, vols. 1–25. Video cassettes with books. Produced by Victor Company of Japan, Ltd.

The Video and Sound Anthology of Japanese Traditional and Folk Arts, vols. 1–14. Video cassettes with books. Produced by Victor Company of Japan, Ltd.

CHAPTER

9

Latin America/Ecuador

John M. Schechter

*L*atin America is a kaleidoscope of cultural and ecological patterns, producing a myriad of distinctive regional lifeways. It comprises a continent and a half with more than twenty different countries in which Spanish, Portuguese, French, and dozens of Native-American languages in hundreds of dialects are spoken. It is at once the majestic, beautiful Andes mountains, the endless emptiness of the Peruvian-Chilean desert, and the lush rain forests of the huge Amazonian basin. Native-American cultures that were not eradicated by European diseases have in many cases retained certain distinctive languages, belief systems, dress, musical forms, and music rituals. Most Latin American cultures, though, share a common heritage of Spanish or Portuguese colonialism and American and European cultural influences. For instance, several ports in Colombia and Brazil served as major colonial centers for the importation of black slaves; Latin America remains a rich repository of African and African-American music-cultural traditions, including rituals, musical forms and practices, and types of musical instruments.

In Latin American culture, mixture is the norm, not the exception. When you walk through the countryside of Ecuador, for example, you hear a Spanish dialect borrowing many words from Quichua, the regional Native-American language. The local Quichua dialect, conversely, uses many Spanish words. South of Ecuador, in the high mountain regions of Peru, the harp is considered an indigenous instrument, although European missionaries and others in fact brought it to Peru. In rural areas of Atlantic coastal Colombia, musicians sing songs in Spanish, using Spanish literary forms, but these are accompanied by African-style drums and rhythms and by Amerindian flutes and rattles. In northern highland Ecuador, African-Ecuadorians perform the *bomba,* a type of song that features African-American rhythms, Quichua Indian melodic and harmonic features, and Spanish language—with sometimes one or two Quichua words. Overall, it is hard to maintain strict cultural divisions because the intermingling of

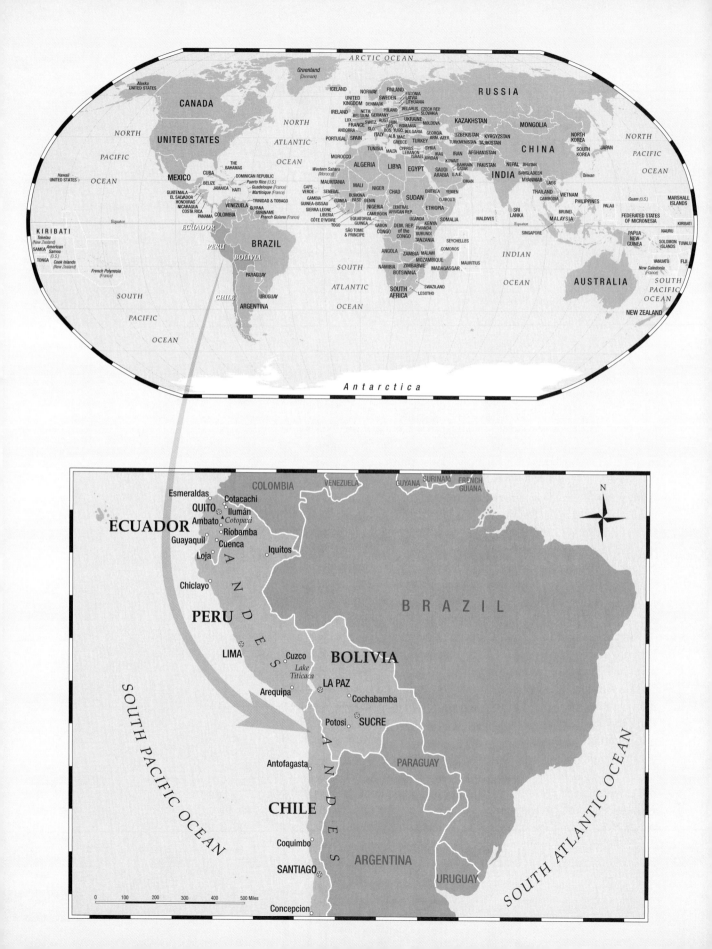

Iberian (Spanish and Portuguese), African, and Native-American strains is so profound in the Latin American experience.

When you first think of Latin American music, you might hear in your mind's ear the vibrancy of the rhythms in salsa. There is an enormous variety of beaten and shaken rhythm instruments, such as claves, bongos, congas, and maracas, both in salsa and throughout Latin America. In distinctive sizes and shapes, the guitar figures prominently in Latin American folk music. In Peru and Bolivia, for example, a type of guitar called the *charango* may have as its body the shell of an armadillo. There are other types of Latin American music with which you might also be familiar, including bossa nova, calypso, and tango.

Listen to "Pajarillo" (CD 4, Track 7). What is most impressive about it? Is it the very fast tempo, with the basic quarter-note beat going beyond the top marking (208) on the metronome? Or is it the way the guitarist (here playing a *cuatro*, in Venezuela a small, four-string guitar) strums his chords not only with remarkable speed and agility but also in an apparently fixed rhythmic pattern? The variety of percussion of the salsa band is now concentrated in a single instrument, the maracas, resounding with machinelike precision. The singer skillfully delivers his text ("Ah, fly, fly, little bird; Take wing, if you want to fly away . . .") in a free, declamatory style, but he uses mostly pitches that fall within the two principal chords in the piece, D minor (tonic) and A major (dominant).

This is an example of the *joropo*, the national dance of Venezuela, heard here in a 1968 recording. There are several standard types of *joropo* ensembles; the one we just heard—*cuatro,* maracas, and harp—is but one. To understand the apparently fixed rhythm, we can use an onomatopoeic device taught to *cuatro* players in Venezuela to try to capture the character and rhythmic feel of *joropo.* The *cuatro* strumming pattern is vocalized as shown in Transcription 9-1.

The Venezuelan Joropo

 CD 4/7

"Pajarillo" ("Little Bird") (2:31). *Joropo* of Venezuela. Recorded by Isabel Aretz, Luis Felipe Ramón y Rivera, and Álvaro Fernaud. Song 5 "Golpe (Joropo)." Barinas State, 1968. *Música Folklórica de Venezuela.* Disques Ocora OCR 78/Ocora Radio France. LP. Distribution Harmonia Mundi.

↓ = Down-strum	‖: CU - RRU - **CHA** - CU - CU - **CHA** :‖,
↑ = Up-strum	↓ ↓ ↓ ↑ ↓ ↓ ↓ ↑
corresponding to the rhythm:	‖: ♪ ♪ ♪ ♪ ♪ ♪ ♪ :‖

Transcription 9-1
Cuatro strumming pattern.

Rolling your *r*'s on *rru,* say, "Cu-rru-*cha*-cu-cu-*cha*" as fast as you can, repeatedly, along with the "Pajarillo" recording, and you will find yourself in synch with the *cuatro*'s rhythmic strumming. You will find yourself chasing after—and with luck, beginning to catch—Venezuelan *joropo.*

The harp's function is related but somewhat different. Here outlining a three-quarter meter in Transcription 9-2, sometimes with closely related rhythmic forms, the harp provides not only rhythmic but melodic and ultimately harmonic underpinning, with patterns such as those shown in Transcription 9-3.

Transcription 9-2
Rhythmic pattern played by harp.

Transcription 9-3
Melodic and harmonic patterns played by the harp in the Venezuelan *joropo* "Pajarillo."

and

(i)   (iv)   (V)

After establishing these basic patterns, however, the harpist improvises on their melodic contours and syncopates their rhythms to contribute to the unique motoric sound of *joropo*. The harp is vital in Venezuelan *joropo*; it has been essential in Latin American music for hundreds of years and it remains so today, as this chapter will later demonstrate.

Chilean Nueva Canción

CD 4/8

"El lazo" ("The Lasso") (3:53). Chile. Composed and performed by Víctor Jara. n.d. *Víctor Jara: Desde Lonquén hasta siempre.* Monitor Music of the World, vol. 4. Monitor Records MFS 810.

Víctor Jara

Although the guitar is played in ensembles, by itself it accompanies solo folk song throughout Latin America. As in the Venezuelan *joropo*, the instrument typically provides a characteristic regional rhythm. Moving from north to south on the South American continent—from Venezuela to Chile—we listen to "El lazo," a powerful folk song composed (c. 1964) and performed on guitar by a great figure in Chilean modern music, Víctor Jara (CD 4, Track 8).

The regional rhythm in Transcription 9-4 is not the driving "Cu-rru-*cha*-cu-cu-*cha*" of the Venezuelan *joropo* but a variant of the *cueca*, a Chilean folk dance. This pattern can be felt in either $\frac{3}{4}$ or $\frac{6}{8}$ time.

Transcription 9-4
Cueca rhythmic pattern in "El lazo."

A speechlike section, identical at the beginning and end of the song, frames the piece. The thought is somber: "When the sun bent low" . . . "on a dark ranch" . . . "on a humble ranch"; and the picture stark: an old man at sunset, on a poor ranch, in Lonquén, Víctor Jara's childhood village. The melody is similarly stark and hesitant, in the minor key, and chantlike. Try singing the first three lines to get the feeling of the mood Jara is setting. Like the song itself, the "spoken" section, or recitative, is framed, beginning and ending with the same text couplet, set to the same melody.

Text, "El lazo" ("The Lasso")

Cuando el sol se inclinaba lo encontré,
en un rancho sombrío de Lonquén.

When the sun was setting I found him,
in a gloomy hut in Lonquén.

En un rancho de pobre lo encontré,
cuando el sol se inclinaba en Lonquén.

In a poverty stricken hut I found him,
when the sun was setting in Lonquén.

Transcription 9-5
"El lazo."

1. *Sus manos siendo tan viejas*
   eran fuertes para trenzar,
   eran rudas y eran tiernas
   con el cuero del animal.

   His hands, although so old,
   were strong in their plaiting.
   They were rough and they were tender
   with the animal skin.

2. *El lazo como serpiente*
   se enroscaba en el nogal
   y en cada lazo la huella
   de su vida y de su pan.

   The plaited lasso, like a snake,
   curled around the walnut tree
   and in every mesh was woven
   his life and his bread.

3. *Cuanto tiempo hay en sus manos*

   y en su apagado mirar
   y nadie ha dicho—está bueno
   ya no debes trabajar.

   How much time is contained in his hands
   and in his patient gaze
   and nobody has said: "That's enough,
   you should not work anymore."

Las sombras vienen laceando
la última luz del día.
El viejo trenza unos versos pa'
maniatar la alegría.

The shadows fell interlacing
the last light of the day.
The old man weaves some verses
to capture some gaiety.

4. *Sus lazos han recorrido*
   sur y norte, cerro y mar,
   pero el viejo la distancia
   nunca la supo explicar.

   His lassos have traveled
   south and north, coast and mountain,
   but the old man never learned
   what distance really means.

5. *Su vida deja en los lazos*
   aferrados al nogal.
   Después llegará la muerte
   y también lo laceará.

   He leaves his life in plaited leather
   knotted to the walnut tree.
   Soon death will come
   and that too will be plaited in.

6. *Qué importa si el lazo es firme*
   y dura la eternidad,
   laceando por algún campo
   el viejo descansará.

   What does it matter if the lasso is firm
   and lasts for eternity.
   Intertwined with some country place
   the old man at last will rest.

Cuando el sol se inclinaba lo encontré,
en un rancho sombrío de Lonquén.

When the sun was setting I found him,
in a gloomy hut in Lonquén.

En un rancho de pobre lo encontré,
cuando el sol se inclinaba en Lonquén.

In a poverty stricken hut I found him,
when the sun was setting in Lonquén.

With the stage set, Jara spins the details, through stanzas 1 through 6, and through the midsong recitative, which is as halting as the opening one although different musically. The tale concerns an aged man, portrayed with hands old yet strong, rough yet tender, plaiting whips and lassos. In the Latin American countryside, one often comes upon older men and women plaiting animal hide for whips, or cactus or wool fiber for rope, sandal tops, bags, or blanket ends. A good example can be seen in the film *Juan Félix Sánchez* (1982), written and directed by Calogero Salvo, which focuses on the craft of a Venezuelan Andean weaver and his wife. This type of work requires great skill and enormous patience. Jara's admiration for the craftsperson's talent and patience is undisguised. The man of Lonquén is known far and wide for his whips, and their creation is his very life.

Listening to "El lazo," we become aware of the constant *musical* "plaiting" as well, as Jara weaves a variety of arpeggiations into a cohesive musical fabric. We feel the musical shuttle moving nearly continuously, through the stanzas and the middle recitative. The music acts as a metaphor for rope plaiting, with the musical gesture evoking the plaiting gesture.

Jara further interweaves the music with the metaphors and similes in the text. The plaited lasso, like a snake, is curled around the walnut tree, the shadows tie together the final daylight, and the old man himself braids verses to bind up joy. We also admire the man of Lonquén because his work is *firme*—it endures. Jara exalts the skill and dedication of the plaiter of Lonquén and, by association, of Chilean rural craftspeople in general. This musician-poet expresses humble admiration for rural artists in other songs, too, such as his "Angelita Huenumán," (1964), in which he sings the praises of a Mapuche Indian woman (Jara's mother, Amanda, was of Mapuche ancestry) who dedicates her life to making beautiful blankets. Once again, focus on the hands.

Why does Jara glorify the creative genius of rural Chileans? The answer lies partly with Jara himself, a man of Lonquén, in rural Chile; it also lies partly with his place in the modern song movement—*Nueva Canción* or "New Song"—of Chile and, sometimes with different names, of all Latin America.

Nueva Canción is a song movement through which people stand up for their own culture—for themselves as a people—in the face of oppression by a totalitarian government or in the face of cultural imperialism from abroad, notably the United States and Europe. It developed first in the southern cone of South America—Argentina, Chile, and Uruguay—during the 1950s and 1960s, and it has since spread throughout Latin America. As we know from our own history, the 1960s in particular witnessed violent upheavals. Latin America echoed the assassinations and urban violence in the United States: Nearly every country in South America, as well as Cuba and the Dominican Republic in the Caribbean, saw revolution, massacre, underground warfare, or other forms of violent social and political confrontation at that time.

In Argentina, the Perón regime saw the country prosper, bringing rural dwellers, many of indigenous ancestry, to the city of Buenos Aires with their own musical heritages. In addition, Argentine radio stations were instructed to program substantial amounts of national music. Thus, where the tango had dominated popular music until the mid-1950s, a new Argentine music began to be created in the late 1950s and early 1960s, by such groups as Los Chalchaleros, Los Fronterizos, and notably, by the guitarist-composer-singer Atahualpa Yupanqui. A careful researcher into Argentine musical folklore, Atahualpa Yupanqui combined a remarkable guitar technique with evocative melody and poetry to create a truly new music. The metaphoric thrust of Jara's "El lazo" appears prominently, for example, in Yupanqui's poignant "Camino del indio," in which the composer depicts a rural path as the window through which we see the sufferings of the Indian of the *campo,* or countryside. Yupanqui and other Argentine artist-pioneers sought to create songs with profound musical and textual meaning, rooted in their country's rural folklore, and instilled with the goal of renewal, of reinvigoration (Carrasco Pirard 1982:605–6).

Violeta Parra

The breath of renewal spread to Uruguay and to Chile, where Violeta Parra was a fundamental moving force in the development of *la Nueva Canción Chilena*. A multifaceted artist—musician, poet, painter, tapestry embroiderer, sculptor, potter—Violeta Parra immersed herself in the folklore of Chile, initially in her home region of Chillán in southern Chile, then in Santiago Province, and ultimately throughout the length of the country. Her enormous collecting efforts significantly helped make Chilean folksongs legitimate and known on the national level. In 1964 she set up a cultural center in La Reina, on the outskirts of Santiago, where she coached musicians. Both here and at the Peña de los Parra—a coffeehouse focusing on folklore, run by Isabel and Ángel, her two oldest children—the *Nueva Canción* movement took shape in the 1960s. Many of its pioneering artists had done their own fieldwork, traveling widely through the Chilean countryside to hear and document principally rural traditions in music and music-related customs. Thus, the *Nueva Canción* musicians sought to reproduce authentic, traditional styles (such as Jara's *cueca* variant, in "El lazo") and to use traditional instruments (such as Violeta Parra's preference for the *charango*) to express their views on contemporary events and issues. The 1969 Primer Festival de la Nueva Canción Chilena, sponsored by the Universidad Católica in Santiago, gave the now recognizable movement a name (Morris 1986:119–20).

Like Jara's "El lazo," Violeta Parra's own songs may draw on natural contexts. For example, "Rin [a Chilean rhythm] del angelito" (1964–1965) depicts the joyous atmosphere of a Chilean wake for a dead child. This subject also drew Víctor Jara to compose a song ("Despedimiento del angelito" ["Farewell of the Little Angel"]); we shall look more closely at a child's wake later in this chapter. On the other hand, Parra's music may be highly satirical, as in her composition "¿Qué dirá el Santo Padre?" ("What will the pope say?"), written around 1957.

Partial Text, from "¿Qué dirá el Santo Padre?"

Miren cómo nos hablan de libertad	Look how they speak to us of liberty
Cuando de ella nos privan en realidad.	When really they deprive us of it.
Miren cómo pregonan tranquilidad	Look how they proclaim peace
Cuando nos atormenta la autoridad.	When the authorities torment us.
Chorus	
¿Qué dirá el Santo Padre que vive en Roma	What will the pope, who lives in Rome, say
Que le están degollando sus palomas?	To the fact that they are beheading his doves?
Miren cómo nos hablan del paraíso	Look how they speak to us of Paradise
Cuando nos llueven penas como granizo.	When afflictions rain down on us like hail.

The Chilean writer Fernando Alegría comments that Parra first cries out here against injustice, then appeals to the pope to make a statement on these conditions—yet he remains silent throughout the song. Like the majority of Latin Americans, most Chileans are Roman Catholics; the Catholic Church has frequently been in the forefront of the struggle for human rights in Latin America. Violeta Parra's plea ultimately brought a response from the Vatican: In April 1987 Pope John Paul II visited Chile, spoke out against conditions of oppression, and met with indigenous peoples, encouraging them to sustain their cultural values (Levy 1988).

Finally, though by no means have we exhausted the full range of song types produced by this great artist, Violeta Parra also has composed love poetry. In the highly moving "Gracias a la vida," ironically written just before her 1967 suicide, the artist thanks life for having given her the eyes, ears, words, feet, heart, laughter, and weeping through which she might perceive and approach the man she loves.

The Front Lines of Social Change

Nueva Canción artists seek to reinvoke and revalidate traditional lifeways of forgotten but valued individuals and peoples. These musicians also express their social consciousness, speaking out in a clear voice against conditions of oppression and advocating social change. For example, Víctor Jara's "Preguntas por Puerto Montt" (1969), notably devoid of metaphor and speaking in a direct and accusatory tone, is a stream-of-consciousness monologue decrying a March 6, 1969, government-sanctioned attack on unarmed peasant families in this Chilean port city. In the 1970 Chilean presidential campaign, Quilapayún, an important *Nueva Canción* ensemble formed in the mid-1960s, accompanied speakers for Salvador Allende's broad-based Popular Unity party, which had brought together workers, peasants, and students into a mass movement. A musical example of this remarkable spirit of unity is Jara's "Plegaria a un labrador" ("Public Prayer to a Worker"), which was composed for the first Festival of Chilean Song in 1969. Modeled on the Lord's Prayer, this impassioned call for worker solidarity begins with the line "Stand up and look at your hands."

Partial Text, from "La plegaria a un labrador"

Levántate y mírate las manos,	Stand up and look at your hands,
Para crecer, estréchala a tu hermano,	Take your brother's hand, so you can grow,
Juntos iremos unidos en la sangre,	We'll go together, united by blood,
Hoy es el tiempo que puede ser mañana.	The future can begin today.
Líbranos de aquel que nos domina en la miseria,	Deliver us from the master who keeps us in misery,
Tráenos tu reino de justicia e igualdad . . .	Thy kingdom of justice and equality, come . . .
Hágase por fin tu voluntad aquí en la tierra,	Thy will be done, at last, here on earth,
Danos tu fuerza y tu valor al combatir. . . .	Give us the strength and the courage to struggle. . . .

In 1973 the elected Marxist government of President Allende was overthrown in a bloody coup. Allende and some 2,800 others lost their lives, hundreds disappeared, and thousands were jailed. On September 18, 1973, a young man ushered Joan Jara into the Santiago city morgue, where she found the body of her husband, Víctor Jara, "his chest riddled with holes and a gaping wound in his abdomen. His hands seemed to be hanging from his arms at a strange angle as though his wrists were broken" (Jara 1984:243). The singer who had cried out in word and song on behalf of "him who died without knowing why his chest was riddled, fighting for the right to have a place to live" ("Preguntas por Puerto Montt"), the singer whose songs had so often lauded eloquently the hands of his people (in "El lazo," "Angelita Huenumán," and "Plegaria a un labrador"), had met his fate—in a stroke of terrifying irony—with his own chest riddled with holes, his own hands made lifeless.

Numerous *Nueva Canción* musicians were imprisoned or remained in exile, but to gain support for human rights in Chile they continued to spread the message of *Nueva Canción* in performances abroad. Within Chile, the movement went underground and was transformed into *Canto Nuevo.*

After the overthrow of Allende, the music of *Nueva Canción* was prohibited on the airwaves and removed from stores and destroyed. Certain prominent folkloric instruments associated with *Nueva Canción,* such as the *charango,* were also prohibited (Morris 1986:123). In this repressive political and cultural atmosphere, the metaphoric character we have seen in the songs of Atahualpa Yupanqui, Víctor Jara, and Violeta Parra became exaggerated and intensified, in order to express thoughts that would have been censored if stated directly. For example, in "El joven titiritero" ("The Young Puppeteer") by Eduardo Peralta, a puppeteer's departure and hoped-for return served as a metaphor for exile and renewed hope.

The status of *Canto Nuevo* was precarious. The government issued permission to perform a concert, but then abruptly revoked permission; radio programs featuring its music were established, then eliminated; Jara cassettes were at one moment confiscated, sold openly in stores the next. With subsequent changes in political conditions, banished musicians were permitted to return to Chile. For instance, the group Inti Illimani returned from Italy in 1988, after fifteen years in exile.

In February 1994 Inti Illimani performed at the University of California at Berkeley. This concert showed how much the ensemble had evolved since a group of Santiago university students had created it in 1967. In addition to the familiar *Nueva Canción* panpipes, *charango,* and *kena* (Andean vertical notched flute), the seven-member aggregate now incorporated instruments not native to Chile or to the Andes: hammered dulcimer and soprano saxophone. The ensemble's multi-instrumentalists now performed sophisticated, tailored arrangements, featuring contemporary, highly coloristic harmonizations of traditional Andean and Caribbean genres. To these points, Inti Illimani musicians have remarked that the ensemble's extended years in exile—half their total years of existence—have led them to more universal creative roots (González 1989:272–73). The group's repertoire in this highly polished performance was remarkably variegated, showcasing the breadth of Latin American (if elaborately disguised) forms: hocketing panpipes (see the discussion of Bolivian *k'antu* later in this chapter), Peruvian *wayno,* Venezuelan *joropo,* Chilean *cueca,* Ecuadorian *sanjuán* (discussed later in this chapter), "traditional" *Nueva Canción* (Jara's "El aparecido" [1967], made famous in an Inti Illimani arrangement), Cuban *son,* and Mexican *ranchera.* Inti Illimani toured the United States in fall 1995, performing in Nebraska, Michigan, Wisconsin, Missouri, Illinois, and Washington D.C.

New Song lives on as an international movement. It has traditional and regional roots but a modern and socially conscious musical style and message. It seeks to draw attention to the people—often the forgotten people—and to their struggles for human dignity.

Certain *Nueva Canción* performers such as Inti Illimani chose the *zampoña,* or panpipes, among other traditional instruments, to symbolize their esteem for the native traditions of the Andes and neighboring regions. It is true that panpipes are widely known outside South America. Nevertheless, the depth of the panpipe tradition in South America is remarkable. Today, we can find a huge number of named varieties of panpipes among native peoples from Panama down to Peru, Bolivia, and Chile. In Peru and Bolivia, cultures dating back fifteen centuries knew and played panpipes of bamboo or clay.

Listen to "Kutirimunapaq" (CD 4, Track 9) as performed by Ruphay, a Bolivian ensemble. They are playing *k'antu,* a type of ceremonial panpipe music from the altiplano. The word *k'antu* might be related to a widely known flower of Bolivia, the *kantuta,* or it might be derived from the Spanish word for song, *canto.* Using Western notation, we could notate what seems to be one melody line as shown in Transcription 9-6.

The entire piece is played three times. Sing the melody to get a feel for the rhythm and flow of this *zampoña* music. On a second hearing, the sound may seem richer to you than on the first; you hear a panpipe ensemble playing what seems to be the same melody at various pitch levels, one at an octave below the original pitch level, another a perfect fourth above that lower octave, or a perfect fifth below the original octave (see Transcription 9-7).

"Kutirimunapaq" (Quechua for, roughly, "So that we can return") is music of the Kallawaya people, who live on the eastern slope of the Bolivian Andes, north of Lake Titicaca, close to the Peruvian border. (In Peru and Bolivia the language is called Quechua; in Ecuador the dialects are called Quichua.) The Kallawaya *campesinos* (farmers, peasants) live at different altitudes in the Charazani Valley—from 9,000 to 16,000 feet above sea level. Those at the lower elevations speak Quechua and cultivate potatoes, barley, and beans; at the upper elevations they speak Aymara and keep llamas, alpacas, and sheep. Perhaps some 3,500 years ago, Quechua

Bolivian K'antu

CD 4/9

"Kutirimunapaq" ("So That We Can Return") (3:52). *K'antu* of Bolivia. Performed by Ruphay. Jach'a Marka, 1982. *Ruphay,* Discos Heriba SLP 2212. Heriba Ltda. La Paz, Bolivia.

Transcription 9-6

One melody line of the *k'antu* "Kutirimunapaq."

Da Capo

and Aymara were a single language. The Incas adopted Quechua as their official language, and spread it with them throughout their empire (1200–1533 C.E.). Today, from 5.5 to 8 million Andeans in Bolivia, Peru, Argentina, and Ecuador speak Quechua (or Quichua), while a minority speak Aymara (Bastien 1978:xxi). "Kutirimunapaq" is a *k'antu* from the community of Niñokorin, at 11,000 feet.

The Kallawaya musicians call these bamboo panpipes *phukuna*, from the Quechua verb *phukuy*, "to blow." The *k'antu* ensembles, for which the Charazani region is famous, each comprise twenty to thirty *phukuna*-playing dancers, who move in a circular pattern. Some of them simultaneously beat a large, double-headed drum called a *wankara*. The triangle (in Quechua, *ch'inisku*), which we hear on CD 4, Track 9, is often present as well.

The Kallawaya play the *phukunas* in their dry season, which lasts roughly from June to September; they play transverse flutes (played horizontally, like the Western silver flute) or duct flutes (played vertically, and constructed like a recorder) during the rainy season, which lasts from

Transcription 9-7
Ensemble notation of "Kutirimunapaq."

November to at least late February. The preference on the altiplano for duct flutes during the rainy season may be related to the belief that their clear sound attracts rain and prevents frost, which are both necessary conditions for growing crops.

Our ensemble consists of *phukunas* of different sizes but with the same basic construction, in terms of numbers of tubes. Each musical register is represented by one named pair of panpipes, consisting of an *ira* set of pipes (considered in the Bolivian altiplano to embody the male principle, and serving as the leader) and an *arca* set of pipes (considered to embody the female principle and serving as the follower). In our context, the *ira* set has six pipes and the *arca* set has seven; we may refer to this type as 6/7-tubed. The different-sized instruments play the same melody, which results in the rich musical fabric of parallel octaves, fifths, and fourths.

There are at least two especially interesting aspects of this music. One is the doubling of the melodic line; the other is the way a melody is produced. Doubling the melody at a fixed interval (parallel fifth, parallel fourth, parallel octave) was used in medieval plainsong. By the ninth century, plainsong (one-line Christian liturgical chant) was being accompanied either by one lower part at the octave below or by a lower part at the fourth or fifth below. Another alternative augmented the two-voice complex to three or four voices by doubling one or both lines at the octave. Thus, early medieval Europe had musical textures with parallel octaves, fourths, and fifths very similar in intervallic structure (if not in rhythm) to what we hear in twentieth-century Bolivian *k'antu.* In twentieth-century Africa, songs in parallel fourths and fifths are found among groups that have the tradition of pentatonic, or five-pitch, songs, such as the Gogo people of Tanzania; a good example of a Gogo song in parallel fourths and fifths appears in Nketia 1974:163.

Many peoples have used, and continue to use, the performance practice of *hocketing.* Performing music in hocket is a uniquely communal way of making music: You cannot play the entire melody yourself—you need one or more partners to do it with you. In Africa the hocket technique appears, among instrumental traditions, in the flute parts of Ghanaian Kasena *jongo* dance music, in the *akadinda* xylophone music of the Baganda of Uganda, and in several flute and gourd-trumpet traditions elsewhere in East Africa and in Southern Africa; for vocal traditions, hocketing can be heard in the singing of the San (Bushmen) of Southern Africa (Koetting 1992:94–97; Kaemmer 1998:703, 705; Cooke 1998:601). Certain European music of the thirteenth and fourteenth centuries had several parts but used notes and rests in a way that effectively divided the melody line between two voice parts: As one sounded, the other was silent. A hiccup effect was thus created (*hoquetus* is Latin for *hiccup* and the likely derivation of the term). Hocketing with panpipes appears closer in time and space to our modern Bolivian music. In Panama, the Kuna Indians play six-tube *guli* panpipes. Each person holds one tube, with the melody distributed among all six players. The Kuna also play *gammu burui* panpipes. Each fourteen-tube set is bound into two groups, or rafts, of seven tubes (two rafts of four-tube and three-tube size, held side by side), the melody distributed between the two seven-tube players in hocket technique (Smith 1984: 156–59, 167–72).

As among the Kuna, in Bolivian *k'antu* the hocket procedure is integral to the overall musical fabric. In fact, hocketing is actually required by the way the *phukunas* are constructed. Although there are types of altiplano panpipes with from three to seventeen tubes, a widely used type is 6/7-

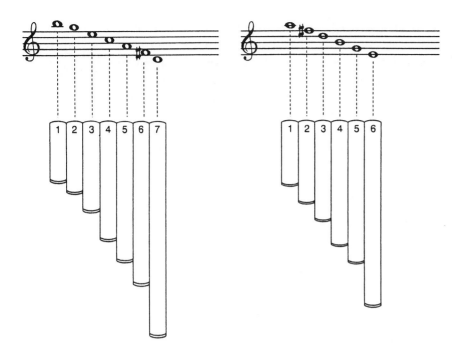

tubed—that is, the "total" instrument has thirteen tubes, consisting of one line, or rank, of six tubes (the *ira*) and one rank of seven tubes (the *arca*). This *phukuna*, or *siku* (the name used by the Aymara Indians, who inhabit the upper elevations of this same altiplano zone), may be tuned in E minor (or in another perspective, G major), as shown in Figure 9-1.

The type of *phukuna* shown in this figure has made an accommodation to European-derived scales. Not all *zampoñas* of the altiplano are tuned in this diatonic manner; many have different scales. This basic tuning is nonetheless widely found among both Quechua-speaking and Aymara-speaking peoples.

When the full instrument is combined (six- and seven-tube ranks joined together or played by two people), we have a thirteen-tube E-minor scale, over the space of an octave and a half with subtonic below (D), or a thirteen-tube G-major scale, going up to the tenth above and down to the perfect fourth below (D) (Figure 9-2).

The formal structure of "Kutirimunapaq" is ABC, each section being repeated, then the entire piece repeated twice, for a total of three times. This is a characteristic structure for the Bolivian *k'antu*, accommodating the continuous dancing that goes with the music making. Counting the number of different notes that sound in this particular *k'antu* we find that, within the octave, five notes predominate: C♯, E, F♯, G♯, and B. Then, the C♯ and E come back in the upper octave. Note that C♯, not E, serves as the tonic pitch in this case. There is one more note used (D♯), but this comes in only at the end of sections A, B, and C—once each time (see Transcription 9-6).

This *k'antu* is primarily five-pitch, or pentatonic. Many traditional dance musics in the Andes region are similarly pentatonic, though certainly

Figure 9-2
Tuning of full thirteen-tube *phukuna*.

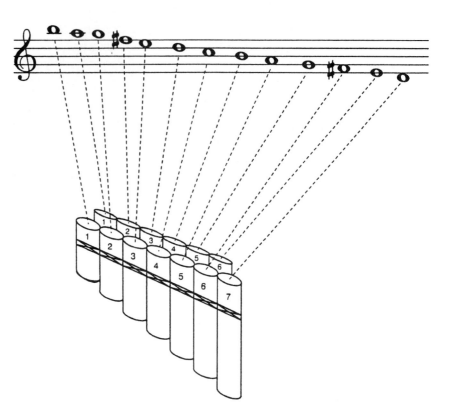

not all of them, as we shall see shortly. "Kutirimunapaq" is strongly rhythmic, with the steady pound of the *wankara* supporting the beat. Andean dance music, from Bolivia up to Ecuador, has this powerful rhythmic cast, underscoring its dance function.

Hocketing panpipes, with rhythmic melodies played in parallel fifths and octaves and with strong, steady rhythm on a large drum, begin to distinguish this Bolivian altiplano stream of Latin American music. The evocation of Native-American cultures such as this high-Andean one, through use of Andean instruments, begins to demarcate *Nueva Canción*. As we have seen, New Song is not only nostalgic but also politically committed and international. Above all, it speaks of and on behalf of the people—characteristically, the forgotten people. We now turn our attention north of Chile, Bolivia, and Peru to a nation of many other unsung (or less-sung) individuals and peoples, a country itself frequently overlooked in discussions of Latin America: Ecuador.

The Quichua of the Northern Andes of Ecuador

We can best appreciate the traditional nature of northern Ecuadorian Quichua music by knowing something of the traditional setting in which Quichua live. The musicians we shall be listening to live in *comunas*, or small clusters of houses, on the slopes of Mt. Cotacachi, one of several volcanoes in the Ecuadorian Andes. These *comunas* lie outside the town of Cotacachi, in Imbabura Province (see the map at the beginning of the chapter).

Figure 9-3
Home of Mama Ramona and Miguel Armando in the *comuna* of Tikulla, outside Cotacachi, May 1980.

John M. Schechter

The Quichua spoken in Cotacachi-area *comunas* was spoken there four hundred years ago. Today in Ecuador more than one million people speak the language.

The agriculture and material culture of the Andes around Cotacachi are also traditional. In this rich green countryside dotted with tall eucalyptus, at 8,300 to 9,700 feet above sea level, maize has been the principal cultivated crop for hundreds of years. You have already seen how Latin Americans braid natural fibers into useful objects; Cotacachi Quichua also use the thick trunks of the local cactus, *cabuya,* to make stools for the home. The harpist who plays all night in the home of a recently deceased Quichua infant sits on a *cabuya* stool.

Quichua homes typically have one room, often with a covered patio, both with dirt floor. Regional Quichua homes have been constructed this way for four hundred years. One such home is shown in Figure 9-3.

Styles of dress have also remained basically the same since the sixteenth century. Everyone covers his or her head to protect it from the intense heat and light of the near-vertical sun at midday (Cotacachi is almost precisely on the Equator). Women wear cloths, and men wear hats. Quichua women wear embroidered blouses, over which they drape shawls (in Quichua, *fachalina*). They secure their two skirts, one blue and one white, with two woven belts: a wider, inner belt, called the *mama chumbi* (mother belt) and a narrower, outer belt, called the *wawa chumbi* (child belt). You will come across this word *wawa* later, when you accompany the harpist as he plays at a *wawa velorio,* or wake for a child. Designed in this region, these belts are traditionally woven on home back-strap looms by Quichua families in various *comunas,* and they usually carry the names of Imbabura towns. Men and boys have traditionally worn a white or blue shirt, white pants, and dark poncho, though today in Imbabura you will see Quichua teenagers wearing English-language sweatshirts and jeans. Any

Figure 9-4
Three generations of Quichua men.
May 1980.

John M. Schechter

large gathering of Quichua, such as for Saturday market or Palm Sunday procession, is still largely a sea of blue and white. In Figure 9-4 we see three generations within the same family. The grandfather wears traditional dress; his adult son retains the white sandals, white shirt, pants, and hat; his grandson wears Western-influenced clothes.

Among Cotacachi Quichua, a strong sense of community arises from a common and regional dialect, a common dress, and common aspects of material culture. Quichua eat the same diet of beans and potatoes, grown in their own plots. They gather together regularly for weekly markets, for periodic community work projects *(mingas),* and for fiestas—such as a child's wake.

In 1980 few Cotacachi Quichua owned vehicles; by 1990 a few community leaders possessed new pickup trucks. In any case, Quichua homes on Cotacachi's slopes are for the most part not located on roads but interspersed along a network of footpaths called *chaki ñanes.* Without telephones, families communicate only by foot, along *chaki ñanes;* recalling Atahualpa Yupanqui's "Camino del indio," these paths bear the weight of Quichua women carrying infants, brush, and food to and from market, and of Quichua men carrying potatoes, milled grain, or perhaps a harp (see Figure 9-5).

For all Quichua, the way around the slopes on *chaki ñanes* is second nature. For example, the harpist contracted to play at a *wawa velorio,* or child's wake, can reach the home of the deceased child, one and a half hours up Mt. Cotacachi, from his own home, at night, with no illumination other than the moon. Walking (in Quichua, *purina*) is so vital in daily life that, as we shall see, it finds its way into speech and song.

Figure 9-5
Chaki ñan (Ecuadorian footpath).
May 1980.

John M. Schechter

The Musical Tradition: Sanjuán

The common language, dress, material culture, daily labor, and importance of *purina* all find a musical echo in *sanjuán.* The term *sanjuán* arose at least as early as 1860. At that time, it referred to either a type of song played at the festival of St. John (San Juan) the Baptist held in June or a type of dance performed at that festival.

Today, the instrument that Cotacachi Quichua often use to perform *sanjuán* is the harp without pedals, often referred to in English as the diatonic harp because it is usually tuned to one particular scale and cannot be changed quickly to another. Reflecting their other deep-rooted traditions, Quichua have been playing the harp in the Ecuadorian highlands for hundreds of years; in the eighteenth century, it was the most common instrument in the region. The harp's popularity in the Andes is not limited to Ecuador; recall that in the Peruvian highlands, it is so widespread among Quechua that it is considered a "native" instrument.

Of course, you have already heard the harp in Venezuelan *joropo* (CD 4, Track 7); in fact, you can hear different types of harp in various folk and indigenous musics from Mexico to Chile. Brought from Europe initially by several different groups of missionaries, especially the Jesuits, and even by the first conquistadors, the harp has been in Latin America for more than four hundred years. In Chile the tradition of female harpists is strong; this is a heritage of sixteenth-century Spain, when women were virtuosos on the instrument. Elsewhere in rural South America, including Ecuador, harp performance by folk and indigenous musicians follows the gender principle of organization in instrumental music, so that women have rarely been included. Most Latin American diatonic harpists have been and are today male. In other musical arenas, such as *Nueva Canción,* women such as Violeta Parra have been in the forefront.

Figure 9-6
Harpist Raúl, playing his Imbabura harp. Ecuador, March 1980.

John M. Schechter

Figure 9-7
Schematic diagram showing position of sound holes in an Imbabura harp.

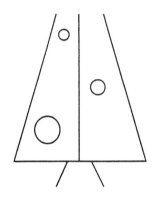

The Imbabura harp is common only in Imbabura Province (Figure 9-6). It appears as an oddity among harpists in central highland Ecuador, where musicians play a larger instrument. The type of harp Raúl plays here is made of cedar and uses wooden nails. The sound emanates through three circular holes on the top of the soundbox; they are always found in the pattern shown in Figure 9-7, on either side of the column, or pole, that connects the neck to the soundbox.

Looking at Raúl's harp, you may think that the instrument has an unusual shape, compared with Western harps with which you may be familiar. The Imbabura harp's column is straight but short, giving the instrument a low "head," or top. Its soundbox is distinctively arched, wide, and deep. On older harps in this region, bull's-hoof glue was used. The tuning pegs are made of iron or wood. The single line of strings is typically a combination of gut, possibly nylon, and steel. The gut strings—used for the bass and middle registers—used to be made by the Quichua themselves from the cut, washed, dried, and twisted intestinal fibers of sheep, dogs, cats, or goats. Sometimes musicians use nylon strings for the middle register, or range, of notes. The steel strings, closest to the performer, play the treble register, in which the melody line is articulated. Once again relying on their environment for necessary materials, Quichua musicians may use the leg bone of the sheep (in Quichua, *tullu:* bone) to turn the tuning pegs on the harp neck.

This Imbabura harp is a descendant of sixteenth- and seventeenth-century Spanish harps, as shown by shared features of tuning, construction, configuration, and stringing. The Imbabura harp has remained essentially unchanged in appearance for one hundred to two hundred years, and possibly longer (Schechter 1992).

Our first recording of a *sanjuán* is "Cascarón" (CD 4, Track 10), played in April 1980 by the Quichua master harpist Efraín on the patio of his home in the *comuna* of Saltamora, outside Cotacachi. Harpists play the higher, or treble strings (treble clef part) with their stronger hand, the lower, or bass, strings (bass clef part) with their weaker hand. Efraín, left-handed, plays treble with the left hand, bass with the right hand (Figure 9-8).

In general, the form of "Cascarón" is typical of Cotacachi Quichua *sanjuanes.* It is fundamentally a repetitive form, in which one or two different phrases are perhaps irregularly inserted into an otherwise similar phrase pattern. In *sanjuán,* the primary motive (the A phrases in Efraín's "Cascarón") predominates. These are the melodies one identifies with a particular *sanjuán.* The *sanjuán* phrase often lasts eight beats, and the rhythm of the first half of the phrase is often identical, or nearly identical, to the rhythm of the second half. Transcription 9-8 diagrams "Cascarón" in eight-beat phrases; "A" marks the primary motive, "B" the contrasting motive, and "T" the triadic arpeggiation that usually constitutes either introductory or transitional materials.

T 1/2T B B
AAAAAAAATBB
AAAAAT1/2TBB
AAAAAT1/2TBB
AAAAATBB
AAAATT chord

Transcription 9-9 on page 407 presents a notation of Efraín's "Cascarón" performance. Each transcription of Cotacachi Quichua music in this chapter begins with a small stemless pitch; this corresponds either to the pitch to which that harp was tuned by that harpist on that day or to that singer's tonic on that occasion. For comparison, all transcriptions of Cotacachi Quichua music are given in the key of D minor.

The A motive predominates in this song. The consecutive A statements are varied by a rather fixed sequence of one, one and one-half, or two T statements followed by two B statements. Most *sanjuanes* follow this general pattern, although perhaps less regularly, with A statements predominating and sometimes without any B statements at all.

CD 4/10

"Cascarón" ("thick peel, rind, or eggshell—especially a broken one") (3:26). *Sanjuán* of Ecuador. Performed by Quichua harpist Efraín. Field recording by John Schechter, outside Cotacachi, Ecuador, April 1980.

Transcription 9-8
Phrase structure, Efraín's *sanjuán* "Cascarón."

Figure 9-8
Harpist Efraín, playing his Imbabura harp.
Outside Cotacachi, Ecuador, April 1980.

John M. Schechter

Look at A_1 (the first statement of the eight-beat A phrase) and sing the eight quarter-note beats. Then sing A_2 and A_3. You will begin to sense the feeling of *sanjuán*: eight-beat phrases, usually without rests, with the consecutive statements of the primary motive slightly varied. Note that in this case A_1 differs from A_2 only in the first sixteenth note of each statement. Nevertheless, the first two notes, A and D, respectively, fall within the tonic key of D minor. The A_3 version partakes of the T phrase, with the first beat now identical to the first beat of T. Typically in *sanjuán* varied numbers of consecutive A phrases will alternate with two B phrases, and often these stress the note a perfect fourth higher than the tonic (here, G, related to D). Efraín told me that these B phrases are called *esquina* (in Spanish, "corner")

Transcription 9-9
The *sanjuán* "Cascarón" with labeled motives, as played by Efraín.

(continues)

Transcription 9-9
(continued)

Transcription 9-9
(continued)

(continues)

Transcription 9-9
(continued)

phrases: Reflecting the pattern of the *sanjuán* dance, at these B moments, dancers turn and begin to move in the opposite direction (Personal communication October 1990).

Sanjuán also provides interesting details of interval structure and rhythm. In the A statements, the three notes D–C–A and their intervallic relationships (major second and minor third) stand out. Compare this with the B statements, G–F–D, the same intervallic series, now a perfect fourth higher. Listen also to the rhythm of all the statements—T, A, and B—and note that in all cases the rhythm of the eight-beat phrase is the same (Transcription 9-10).

Also, the rhythm of the first four beats (the first half) of the phrase is echoed by the rhythm of the second half. Transcription 9-11 illustrates how regular these rhythmic features are. This collection, recorded in Cotacachi *comunas* in 1979–1980, also gives you a dozen *sanjuanes* to learn and practice singing. Note the eight-beat patterning and the equal rhythm halves; "Cascarón" is number three.

Certain *sanjuanes*, such as "Ilumán tiyu," are often sung, while others such as "Cascarón" and "Carabuela" are typically played instrumentally. You can find words for all the commonly sung *sanjuanes* in Schechter 1982:II:379–456. After singing or listening to all twelve of these *sanjuanes*, you will begin to sense that some combination of two (or all three) of the rhythmic motives shown in Transcription 9-12 characterizes most *sanjuanes*. Just as the major second–minor third pattern typifies melody in *sanjuán*, so also do these patterns typify *sanjuán* rhythm.

As for harmonic relationships, "Cascarón's" melody and Efraín's accompanying bass line illustrate the prominence of the minor tonic key

Beat number: 1   2   3   4   5   6   7   8

Transcription 9-10
Rhythmic pattern of the *sanjuán*
"Cascarón."

and its relative major key: the arpeggios (T) stress the minor key (D minor), the A sections emphasize the relative major (F major). The high B♭ of the B statements, together with the D and F in the bass, suggest a feeling of the key of B♭ major—the subdominant key, or IV, of the relative major, F. The musics of many Andean peoples reflect this close relationship of the minor to its relative major, or *bimodality.*

1. Ilumán tiyu (all but Jorge María, the oldest harpist)

2. Ilumán tiyu (Jorge María)

3. "Cascarón"

4. Ñuka llama di mi vida

5. Carabuela

6. Chayamuyari warmiku

7. Llakishamari nirkanki

8. Rusa María Kituaña

9. Segundito Muynala

10. "Llaki llakilla purini"

11. NI.5*

12. Ñ6"* (Jorge María)

Transcription 9-11
Twelve Cotacachi Quichua *sanjuanes.*
"Cascarón" is number three.

*"NI.5" refers to the fifth *sanjuán* recorded in my fieldwork with the title not identified; "Ñ6'" refers to the second variant of the sixth *sanjuán* I recorded by the Quichua blind harpist José Manuel Calapi, who was known in 1980 by his nickname, "Ñausa" (Quichua: blind).

Transcription 9-12
Characteristic *sanjuán* rhythmic figures.

Thus in Cotacachi Quichua *sanjuán* the music reveals fixed attributes, reflecting much repetition on several levels. It has a single predominating motive, often eight-beat phrases, nearly identical first-half and second-half rhythms, characteristic pitch and rhythmic motifs, and harmonic support that demonstrates the bimodal relationship of minor to relative major. These features give many of these twelve *sanjuanes* a similar sound and provide the grammar of the musical language of Cotacachi Quichua *sanjuán.* Or, as Bruno Nettl has put it, "In each . . . musical language, some style features dominate and coalesce into a mainstream," that is, a homogeneous core (1983:49).

Sanjuán and Cotacachi Quichua Lifeways

At this point you may have several questions. Do Quichua speakers throughout the Ecuadorian Andes know "Cascarón"? How is *sanjuán* performed on the Imbabura harp? On which occasions is it performed? What characteristic verse structures do sung *sanjuanes* have? How do these structures or the specific texts reflect aspects of daily Cotacachi Quichua lifeways?

For students of music-cultures, Imbabura Province and the region around Cotacachi in particular are special, even unique, sites. Writing seventy years ago, an Ecuadorian musicologist commented that the Quichua of Imbabura had "a special musical aptitude" (Moreno Andrade 1930:269); an Ecuadorian anthropologist once remarked to me that the region around Cotacachi was well-known as a "music box." A lyre on the flag of Cotacachi County confirms the central role music occupies in the region, and an author of a book on Imbabura traditions even suggests that to speak of Ecuadorian music is to speak of the music of Cotacachi (Obando 1988:155).

This feeling comes also from the Imbabureños themselves, both Quichua- and Spanish-speaking. They insist on the uniqueness of their own music in relation to that of every other region. In response to questions about the spread of a particular *sanjuán,* for example, Cotacachi Quichua answered, *"Cada llajta." Cada* is Spanish for "every," and *llajta* is Quichua for "community." *Cada llajta* is the idea that every community has its own music, or its own mortuary customs, or its own dress, or its own dialect of Quichua. *Cada llajta* extends even to the way Quichua is written in Ecuador. In 1980 representatives of various Quichua communities decided to permit the "speakers of each dialect to determine their own form of writing the language" (Harrison 1989:19). *Cada llajta* seems to operate elsewhere in Ecuador as well. In April 1980 my wife and I moved from the northern to the central highlands; I sang and played on the Imbabura harp *sanjuanes* well known in Cotacachi to Quichua speakers in this new region. Although they had never heard these songs before, they came to learn and enjoy the pieces. When *sanjuanes* are imported into other regions, the *indígenas* often name them with reference to their origin. "*San-juán* from Cotacachi," or "*Sanjuán* from Otavalo" (a town near Cotacachi).

Cada llajta also dictates the performance media and the performance practices. Cotacachi Quichua of all ages—women and men, girls and boys—sing and play *sanjuanes.* They are performed by unaccompanied voices, by vocal duos, by voice and harp—with a *golpeador* (one who beats rhythm on the harp), by solo harp and *golpeador,* by voice and guitar, by solo *kena,* by solo *bandolín* (a fretted mandolin), or by ensembles of various instruments. When you hear *sanjuán* played on the Imbabura harp, you will also see a person kneeling in front of or alongside the harp. This is the *golpeador* (in Spanish, *golpear:* to hit), who beats the lower part of the harp soundbox in rhythm to the *sanjuán.* Figure 9-9 shows Miguel Armando assuming a *golpeador* posture for César. Miguel Armando is the regular *golpeador* for his two harpist sons, César and Sergio.

All Cotacachi Quichua harpists remark that the *golpeador* and his dependable, metronomic rhythm are essential to proper *sanjuán* performance. The *golpe* is the bedrock on which the harpist's concentration rests. Without it, he cannot work. Note, for example, the prominent *golpe* in Efraín's "Cascarón" performance, by his friend Martín Mateo. This rhythmic hitting of the harp soundbox is not unique to Cotacachi, Ecuador; it also appears in diverse folk harp traditions in central highland Ecuador, Peru, Argentina, Chile, and Mexico.

Figure 9-9

Miguel Armando in *golpeador* posture, with César playing harp. Ramona, the harpists' mother, is alongside. Outside Cotacachi, Ecuador, May 1980.

John M. Schechter

The treble register of the Imbabura harp is tuned to a six-pitch, or hexatonic, scale in the natural minor key, omitting the second scale degree. For example, in our D-minor scale, the harpist will tune his treble register to the following pitches: D, F, G, A, B♭, C, and D (upper octave). This tuning permits him to play the full range of mostly pentatonic *sanjuanes* in his repertoire, as well as the occasional hexatonic one—for example, "Ilumán tiyu" (CD 4, Track 12), normally played with G minor, not D minor, as tonic. The hexatonic pitches present on the D-minor-tuned harp permit the use of A, the second degree in the key of G minor. "Ilumán tiyu" requires that second scale degree. The middle register typically is likewise hexatonic. The bass register is tuned so that the harpist may play the minor tonic triad, with upper and lower octaves, in alternation with (that is, one or sometimes two hand-positions away from) the relative major triad (Transcription 9-13). He uses four fingers of the hand (excluding the little finger), skipping one string between each finger, often two strings between index finger and thumb.

Transcription 9-13

Tuning of bass register of Imbabura harp.

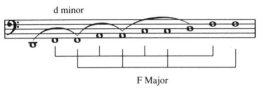

In the *comunas* outside Cotacachi, the *arpero* (harpist) and *golpeador* perform *sanjuanes* in at least three festive contexts: *matrimonio* (wedding), *misai* (private Mass), and *wawa velorio* (child's wake). Quichua in this region celebrate a five-day wedding. Within the Saturday to Wednesday cycle, Sunday or Monday sees the *ñavi maillai,* a ritual washing of feet and face, for which harp music is played. A *misai* is a private Mass held in honor of a saint. After the Mass in the church, the statue of the saint—the *santo*—is returned to its altar in its owner's home. A meal is then prepared for the Mass offerer, and a musical fiesta is celebrated through the night. In *wawa velorio,* held all night at the deceased child's home, *sanjuán* music predominates.

Sanjuán at *wawa velorio,* as elsewhere, is dance music. You can do the *sanjuán* dance step as you practice from your list of twelve *sanjuanes.* Men and women hold their hands behind their backs and stomp to each quarter-note beat. Step forward with your left foot, joining with the right foot on the next beat. Then move your right foot back first, followed by your left foot. When dancing *sanjuán,* keep your upper torso stiff, your knees bent, and your lower body relaxed, with a good bounce and stomp. The signal to turn around while dancing is (shouted) *"Tigrashpa!"* or *"Tigrapai!"*

We can view the *sanjuán* dance step as an emphatic back-and-forth walking, a stomp, to the music. At the child's wake, this stomping is performed all night as the *arpero* plays *sanjuanes* at length, sometimes several strung together without interruption. In this way *sanjuán* serves as a kinetic endorsement for both walking and the Quichua way of life that depends on it. Let us delve further into Cotacachi Quichua walking, which, as we have already observed, is vital to communication, to daily tasks—in short, to survival.

Walking in Sanjuán: The Vital-Domain Metaphor

Walking as the paramount daily activity of Cotacachi Quichua emerges in expressive culture not only in dance but in song text as well. This probably should come as no surprise, for any such distinctive facet of local ecology or behavior is bound to manifest itself in word and song. Among the Kwakiutl of Vancouver Island, for example, a person's wealth and guests were considered his "salmon" (Boas [1929] 1940:234). For the Kaluli people of the Papua New Guinea rain forest, waterway terms serve prominently as metaphors, including ones related to Kaluli music theory. In this culture, kinds of water become kinds of sound; the term for "waterfall," in particular, is the point of departure for a series of metaphors relating to musical structure (Feld 1981:26). Across the world in Spain, agricultural metaphors remain strong in Asturian deepsong—among miners, who in most cases retain some ties to the land (Fernandez 1978).

Outside Cotacachi, in the *comunas,* walking is necessary for the survival of *comunas* as well as for individual sustenance. Quichua community leaders frequently say that their particular *comuna* will succeed or fail depending on whether it can obtain outside aid. Rousing *comuna* residents to support the *comuna* and searching for assistance from provincial authorities demands footwork. Their view is that *comunas* will flourish only with persistent *purishpa* (walking) on their behalf. Moreover, on the personal level *purina* becomes to "walk" for one's educational benefit and to enable oneself to carry out family obligations. *Purina,* the inescapable daily activity of walking, becomes a positive metaphor in speech: It is behavior worthy of others' esteem because it is done on behalf of others; it is behavior leading to one's own enhanced self-respect.

In the texts of sung *sanjuán* the *purina* metaphor is "extended." In the metaphoric mechanism of extension, one takes experience from a domain where it is easily understood and uses it as the basis for more abstract and ambiguous domains. In sung *sanjuanes, purina* appears prominently in texts, notably as a verb of action. Transcription 9-14 shows *sanjuán* verse couplets, with their primary (A) motives.

a. *Kanta nishpami shamuni*   I come speaking of you
   Kanta nishpami purini   I walk speaking of you

Transcription 9-14

The Quichua verb *purina* in Cotacachi *sanjuán* couplets with their A motives.

(continues)

Transcription 9-14
(continued)

b. *Wawagumantallamari*   Indeed just because of the baby
   Wakai wakai purini   Do I walk about crying and crying
c. *Solo kampa muchitawan*   Only with your kiss
   Ayunashka purini   Nourished, do I walk about
d. *Wata wata* purini   I walk about years and years
   Kanta nishpa muyuni   I go this and that way speaking of you
e. *Wakai wakai* purinki   You (will) walk about crying and crying
   Llaki llaki muyunki   You (will) go this and that way very sad
f. *Na pimanta* purini   Not for whomever do I walk about
   Kanmantami purini   I walk about because of you

g. *Tikumantami shamuni*   I come from (the *comuna* of) Tiku
   Kanta nishpalla purini   walk about only speaking of you

h. *Ima nishpalla* purinki   Just why do you walk about?
   Mana nimanta purinki   You don't walk about for nothing

i. *Llaki llakilla* purijuni   I am walking about very sad
   Wakai wakailla purisha   I shall walk about crying very much

j. *Karu karuta* purishpa   Walking very far
   Llaki llakilla muyujun   He is moving this way and that, very sad

Purina in these *sanjuán* texts extends to emotion. The verses express either emotional release through walking ("I walk about crying and crying") or emotional involvement through walking ("I walk about because of you"). *Purina* may be traced through its various metaphoric courses—from walking along the *chaki ñan* (footpath), to walking for the benefit of the *comuna* or for one's own betterment, to wandering or going about as an outlet for love, sadness, or other emotions. Walking becomes extended to encompass the abstract—from physical movement for survival to movement for broadly social purposes or to movement for personal, emotional reasons.

You have looked at the musical character and the phrase structure of *sanjuán*, and you have seen how *purina* functions in *sanjuán* song text as a metaphor reflecting the vital domain of walking in Cotacachi Quichua daily life. Let us now learn two *sanjuanes* that, for different reasons, might be called "classics."

Two Classic Sanjuanes

In Chapter 2 David McAllester calls certain Navajo great ceremonial chants "classic." Similarly, two Imbabura Quichua *sanjuanes* qualify as classics in their highland region: "Rusa María wasi rupajmi" and "Ilumán tiyu."

"Rusa María" (CD 4, Track 11) was in 1980 one of the most beloved *sanjuanes* of the Cotacachi Quichua *comuna*. An important disc of Imbabura Quichua music, *Ñanda mañachi 1* (1977), begins side A with this *sanjuán,* and the record jacket back presents an essay, "Un país llamado Rosa María," ("A Land Called Rosa María") in which this particular *sanjuán* becomes a metaphor for the Quichua way of life in this entire region. In our field recording, Gerónimo on vocal, Sergio on harp, and his father, Miguel Armando, on *golpe,* perform this *sanjuán* at a *wawa velorio* in January 1980. You will hear noise as the microphone is passed back and forth from singer to harpist.

CD 4/11

"Rusa María wasi rupajmi" ("Rosa Maria's House A-Burning") (2:28). *Sanjuán* of Ecuador. Performed by Quichua musicians Gerónimo, vocal; Sergio, harp; and his father, Miguel Armando, *golpe.* Field recording by John Schechter, outside Cotacachi, Ecuador, January, 1980.

Transcription 9-15
Sanjuán, "Rusa María wasi rupajmi."

Text, "Rusa María wasi rupajmi"

1. *Rusa María wasi rupajmi*	Rusa María's house a-burning
Mas ki rupachun nishkashi,	So let it burn, she seems to have said,
Rusa María wasi rupajmi	Rusa María's house a-burning
Mas ki rupachun nishkashi,	So let it burn, she seems to have said,
2. *Taita Manuilpash machashkamari*	And Manuel, a father, very drunk
Manllarishkami wakajun,	Frightened, is crying,
Taita Manuilpash machashkamari	And Manuel, a father, very drunk
Manllarishkami wakajun,	Frightened, is crying,
3. *Wambrakunapash kwitsakunawan*	And young men and young women
Sirinkapajmi rishka nin,	Went to lie down together, they say,
Wambrakunapash kwitsakunawan	And young men and young women
Sirinkapajmi rishka nin.	Went to lie down together, they say.

What is it about "Rusa María" that delivers such a strong message of life in Imbabura? "Rusa María" speaks of tragedy, drunkenness, and fright, as well as courting. The first double couplet suggests resignation in the face of a disastrous house fire. Quichua homes higher up Mt. Cotacachi have thatched roofs instead of tile, with wooden support beams (see Schechter 1992:141 for a photograph). The family meal is cooked over an open hearth, and destruction by fire is an ever-present possibility. When I asked about this stanza ten years later, Imbabura Quichua musicians told me that "Rusa María's" home might well be small and old; she might be expressing both anger and the confidence that her neighbors, feeling sympathy, might build her a new home, larger and better. Quichua families are accustomed to disaster, relating both to material destruction and, as we shall see, infant death.

Alcohol can also bring about social tragedy. Much of the alcohol consumed in the Cotacachi countryside in 1980 was cane alcohol *(trago)*, brought as contraband from another region of Ecuador. Frequently, the owners of the small stores in the *comunas* would mix this *trago* with water, berry juice, or other substances, with unpredictable effects. Consumption of *trago* or other alcohol is vital in Cotacachi rituals (such as a child's wake) and in Andean rituals in general throughout Peru and Bolivia. Yet overconsumption of *trago* can produce hallucinations, strongly emotional behavior, and in the case of adulterated *trago,* even blindness or death.

"Rusa María" refers also to courting. *Wambra* and *kwitsa* may mean either young man and young woman, or boy and girl. Courting begins in the schoolyard and elsewhere at age twelve or thirteen. Quichua often marry in their mid- or late teens.

"Rusa María" speaks of the inevitable in Cotacachi Quichua life: the natural environment, ritual practice in conflict with economic exploitation, and cultural expectation and human instinct. In the final analysis, "Rusa María" is a song, danced to on festive occasions; it is a source of joy and pride to all the *indígenas* of Cotacachi.

In the case of the highly popular (both in 1980 and still in 1990) *sanjuán* "Ilumán tiyu" ("Man of Ilumán"), we know the composer: Segundo "Galo" Maigua Pillajo, a Quichua composer-guitarist-singer of the Imbabura village of Ilumán. Galo Maigua's *sanjuán* compositions are often motivated by autobiographical forces. His fame among Imbabura Quichua is attested to by wide acknowledgment of his being the composer of highly popular *sanjuanes* and by his ensemble Conjunto Ilumán's high level of demand, locally, and their having produced as of 1990 one commercial cassette.

My fieldwork in 1990 in Imbabura brought to light the fact that *sanjuán* often takes on the nature of a ballad, even in instances where that fact is not immediately obvious. The thoughts of a *sanjuán* text typically express the essence of a large story, making the *sanjuán* a highly distilled ballad form, the synoptic character of the text being in keeping with the elliptical character of Andean poetry dating back to the times of the Incas. The ballad nature of "Ilumán tiyu"—the story behind the *sanjuán*—is not at all obvious. In the village of Ilumán, in the home of a local policeman, I recorded the composer, Galo Maigua, singing "Ilumán tiyu" and playing guitar together with his Conjunto Ilumán, on October 27, 1990 (Figure 9-10; CD 4, Track 12).

CD 4/12

"Ilumán tiyu" ("Man of Ilumán") (3:23). *Sanjuán* of Ecuador. Composed by Segundo "Galo" Maigua Pillajo. Performed by "Galo," guitar and vocal, with the Quichua ensemble Conjunto Ilumán. Field recording by John Schechter. Ilumán, Ecuador, October 1990.

John M. Schechter

Figure 9-10
"Ilumán tiyu" composer, Segundo "Galo" Maigua Pillajo (far right), with his ensemble, Conjunto Ilumán, October 1990. One regular member of the ensemble, a noted harpist, could not be present on this occasion. The tradition of Quichua violinists is particularly strong today in the Otavalo-Ilumán area of Imbabura, echoing the proliferation of *indígena* violinists in eighteenth-century highland Ecuador (Schechter 1992:55).

		Text, "Ilumán tiyu"
Ilumán Tiyu cantanmi,	The man [not "uncle"] from Ilumán sings,	
Ilumán Tiyu nijunmi.	The man from Ilumán is saying.	
Ilumán Tiyu cantanmi,	The man [not "uncle"] from Ilumán sings,	
Ilumán Tiyu nijunmi.	The man from Ilumán is saying.	
Sultira kashpa paya kashpa,	Being a young (unmarried) woman, [or an] old woman,	
Ñuka tunupi bailapai.	Dance to my song.	
Sultira kashpa paya kashpa,	Being a young (unmarried) woman, [or an] old woman,	
Ñuka tunupi bailapai.	Dance to my song.	
Este es el indio de Ilumán	This is the *indígena* of Ilumán	
Él que canta sanjuanito.	He who sings *sanjuán.*	
Este es el indio de Ilumán	This is the *indígena* of Ilumán	
Él que canta sanjuanito.	He who sings *sanjuán.*	
Para que bailen toditos,	So that all [men] might dance,	
Para que bailen toditas.	So that all [women] might dance.	
Para que bailen toditos,	So that all [men] might dance,	
Para que bailen toditas.	So that all [women] might dance.	

What had never been comprehensible since my 1980 research, when I recorded numerous versions of "Ilumán tiyu" in the environs of Cotacachi, was the nature of the lyrics. When I was informed that Segundo "Galo" Maigua Pillajo was in fact the composer of this *sanjuán,* I tried, during a visit to his Ilumán home on September 30, 1990, to learn what might lie behind words that seem merely a statement that the man singing and speaking is an *indígena* from Ilumán.

Galo Maigua described the tale behind the text. He told me that before he composed "Ilumán tiyu," he had become extremely ill with tuberculosis; the condition of his lungs had deteriorated, and he believed he was about to die. Although during 1972–1973 wanderings through the *comunas* around Cotacachi he had sung the melody to a variety of words (Galo says he composes by first hearing a melody and later setting a text), he now determined that he would like everyone—be they young woman or old woman, for example—to dance to this, his song, after his death. In effect, "Ilumán tiyu" was ultimately texted as Galo's final statement of his identity to posterity: "I"—the man singing, speaking—am a man from Ilumán; remember me by remembering my music: "Dance to my song." In sum, what appeared to the uninformed listener to be innocuous words came, on greater understanding, to have profound import for a composer believing himself to be on his deathbed.

Spanish speakers will note that the intermingling of Spanish and Quichua words we spoke of early in this chapter appears prominently in this *sanjuán.* Moreover, the verse *"Este es el indio de Ilumán, él que canta sanjuanito"* is a translation of the first, critically important, verse; Galo Maigua commented to me that a major area radio station had prompted him to produce the parallel text in Spanish. Some of his other *sanjuanes,* such as "Antonio Mocho" and "Rusita Andranga," share the distilled-ballad character of "Ilumán tiyu." Both of these *sanjuanes,* along with "Ilumán tiyu," appear on the commercial cassette *Elenita Conde,* by Conjunto Ilumán; the cassette was mastered in Otavalo and mass-produced in Bogotá, Colombia, somewhat prior to 1990.

The Andean Ensemble Phenomenon

"Conjunto Ilumán" represents a now-broad phenomenon, both in the Andes and beyond: the Andean ensemble. Other Ecuadorian ensembles focusing on Quichua or *Nueva Canción* musics over the last twenty years have included Ñanda Mañachi (Quichua: "Lend me the way"; 1977, 1979, 1983); Conjunto Indígena "Peguche" (Spanish: *indígena* ensemble from the village of Peguche [near Otavalo]; 1977); and Jatari (Quichua: "Get up!"; 1978). The carefully and elaborately produced albums of Ñanda Mañachi, in particular, are notably evocative of the Quichua music-culture of Imbabura.

In the Otavalo Valley of Imbabura, Quichua ensembles date back at least to the 1940s and 1950s and began to proliferate in the 1970s (Meisch 1997:200–201). The groups mentioned earlier, such as Ñanda Mañachi and Conjunto Indígena Peguche, emphasized in their album liner notes the central role of "music as an expression of indigenous values and its role in [the 1970s indigenous Quichua] cultural resurgence" (Meisch 1997:201). The Otavalo Quichua musical-ensemble renaissance is evident from Lynn Meisch's listing of numerous long-playing records recorded from 1970 to 1986—nearly all of which were recorded in Ecuador and contained only Ecuadorian music (Meisch 1997:205–6).

In 1990, in this same broad, green valley, teenagers and young men were actively engaged in music making. In Imbabura, one radio station had an annual festival of musical ensembles, in which any and all area village ensembles could participate, each playing perhaps two songs on the radio. In July 1990 this village ensemble marathon featured enough groups to last twelve hours.

Music making provides an important means of socialization among Quichua youths who have long since ceased attending school and who find few community activities available to them, except for volleyball, which is pursued with a vengeance in the village plazas and *comunas* of Imbabura. You will hear Quichua teenagers rehearsing diligently on weekends at an ensemble member's home, performing a few traditional *sanjuanes* and, like their counterparts in the United States, often experimenting with their own compositions.

The 1990s witnessed an explosion of this music as Otavalenian musicians left their homeland to seek larger audiences throughout the world. As Lynn Meisch noted, in a comment befitting the discussion of our chapter, "Otavalo music [performed by Quichua indigenous musicians] has now become globalized, part of the world music beat influencing the music made by others, with Sanjuanitos seen as emblematic of Ecuadorian music" (1997:217). Motivated by potential economic rewards, many Imbabura Quichua ensemble members have, in effect, become "transnational migrants" (Meisch 1997:218) or "immigrants who develop and maintain multiple relationships—familial, economic, social, organizational, religious, and political—that span borders . . . [creating a] multiplicity of involvements . . . in both home and host societies" (Basch, Schiller, and Blanc 1994:7). Today's Quichua musicians are recording CDs, not LPs; those CDs are most often produced outside of Ecuador, and they include ample proportions of non-Ecuadorian, as well as Ecuadorian, Andean songs (Meisch 1997:253–55).

Not surprisingly, as the Bolivian ethnomusicologist Gilka Wara Céspedes says, "The Andean Sound is becoming a part of the sonic scene from Europe to Japan" (1993:53). Further, "Otavalo [Quichua] musicians are everywhere, playing in malls, on street corners, at music festivals, and in concert halls and clubs on six continents, and recording and selling their music at locales around the world" (Meisch 1997:243). Where Ecuadorian Andean *indígena* textile manufacturers have for some fifty years traveled the international byways, selling their home-woven ponchos, blankets, and scarves, today the entrepreneurial instinct remains intact but the product has changed: from bulky woolens to featherweight cassettes and CDs, delicate bamboo *zampoñas* and *kenas*. As one Otavalenian musician told Lynn Meisch in 1994, "'We have two ways to earn a living in whatever locale: music and the sales of *artesanías* [arts & crafts]'" (1997:187). Specifically, Otavalo Quichua ensembles have appeared at First Peoples (Native-American) powwows in Canada and the United States, in folk festivals in Poland and Washington, D.C., and on street corners, tourist thoroughfares, and subway stations in Quito, New York, San Francisco, Florence, Moscow, Montreal, Paris, Sevilla, Córdoba, and Madrid, among numerous other likely places (1997:243).

The United States unquestionably plays a vital role in this international Andean sonic scene. Amauta, based in Seattle, comprises Chilean and Bolivian musicians playing traditional Andean instruments; they have appeared at the Seattle Northwest Regional Folklife Festival. Condor, out of Corvallis, Oregon, is an ensemble of five professional, college-educated musicians from Argentina, Peru, and Mexico; the group focuses on traditional Andean musics. Andanzas (Spanish for "wanderings") performs music from a variety of Latin American and Caribbean traditions; this widely traveled, four-member ensemble includes musicians from Argentina, Bolivia, and Mexico, as well as a classically trained U.S. harpist. Andesmanta, an ensemble of Ecuadorian musicians playing traditional highland Ecuadorian musics—including *sanjuanes*—as well as other South American folk musics, has performed at Carnegie Hall and the Metropolitan Museum of Art. Among the most well-established of U.S.-based Andean groups is Sukay (Quechua for "to work furrows in straight lines" or "to whistle musically"); this group formed originally in 1974, with some eight albums by 1994, along with performances at Lincoln Center and major folk music festivals (Ross 1994:19–24). (A list of selected recordings by these and other Andean Ensembles can be found in Ross 1994:27 and, for Ecuadorian Andean ensembles, in Meisch 1997:357–65.)

One of the cofounders of Sukay was the Swiss multi-instrumentalist and instrument-craftsman Edmond Badoux. With Francy Vidal (self-described as an "eighth-generation 'Californiana' with roots in Mexico and Europe"), he formed in 1985 the gifted California-based duo Chaskinakuy (Quechua for "to give and receive, hand to hand, among many"). Chaskinakuy's husband-and-wife members, Edmond and Francy, characterize themselves as "dedicated revivalists." The two musicians sing in Quechua/Quichua and Spanish, and they play more than twenty-five native Andean instruments, some rarely heard outside their highland Andean contexts: Peruvian harp (Edmond even plays this instrument, on occasion, upside-down, in accordance with the Peruvian harp's unique processioning posture), pelican-bone flute, long straight trumpet, condor-feathered *zampoña*, and *pututu* (Quechua for "conch trumpet").

Chaskinakuy has appeared in concerts, festivals, university lecture series, and schools in eighteen U.S. states, in Canada, and in Switzerland. They return frequently to the Andes to sustain their performance research into traditional village musics and festivals. Their renditions of Andean musics reflect the musicians' wonderful blend, when singing in duet, and their remarkably close attention to every stylistic detail appropriate to the particular regional music: harmonic underpinnings, melodic lines and inflections, vocal tone qualities, phrasing, and rhythmic accentuations. Now listen to Chaskinakuy's rendition of the Peruvian *wayno*, "Amor imposible" (CD 4, Track 13).

As you listen to your third Latin American "harp-country-genre" (Venezuelan *joropo*, Ecuadorian *sanjuán*, and now Peruvian *wayno*), you will probably note four prominent similarities to Ecuadorian Quichua master harpist Efraín and his *sanjuán* "Cascarón." First, we see the use of the

Amauta is from the Quechua, *jamaut'a*, "wise"; the *amautas* were one of three types of specialists, in the Inca Empire, responsible for preserving the memory of past Inca leaders. They created brief historical stories that were passed on through oral tradition to succeeding generations (Schechter 1979:191–92).

CD 4/13

"Amor imposible" ("Impossible Love") (2:35). Traditional Peruvian *wayno*. Performed by Chaskinakuy. *Chaskinakuy, Music of the Andes: Cosecha*. CD engineered and mixed by Joe Hoffmann and remastered by Brian Walder at Hoffmann Studios. Occidental, California, 1991.

Figure 9-11
Duo Chaskinakuy. June 1992.

© Irene Young. Used by permission.

harp—now as accompaniment to the lively south-Andean *wayno,* then taking a leading instrumental role in its lively north-Andean cousin, the *sanjuán.* Second, we hear the now-familiar Andean bimodality, the use of the minor and its relative major—here, B minor/D major. Moreover, where Efraín's "Cascarón's" "B" statements explored the region of the subdominant of the relative major, likewise Edmond and Francy's "Amor imposible" employs also G major, the subdominant of its relative major—D. Third, those with keen ears will remark that the rhythm is not beaten on a drum, but rather—as in "Cascarón"—on the harp soundbox; recall that this type of percussive *golpe,* or *cajoneo,* on the harp soundbox can be heard in several Latin American countries, including Peru. Lastly, the rhythmic motifs of Ecuadorian *sanjuán* revolve around sixteenth-eighth-sixteenth notes. In Peruvian *wayno* the *golpe* involves something close to eighth-two-sixteenths; this pattern, sometimes close to three triplets, is the near-invariant rhythmic signature of the *wayno.* You can find a substantial discussion of the history, regional varieties, other musical traits, and poetic substance of the *wayno* in Romero 1999:388–89.

Again, this performance of "Amor imposible" proves particularly compelling because Edmond captures the distinctive character of Peruvian harp-accompanimental style, and Francy grasps the distinctive melodic turns of phrase, characteristic portamento, and distinctly focused and clear vocal quality of the female Peruvian singer of *wayno.*

Text, "Amor imposible"

Es imposible dejar de quererte,	It's impossible to stop loving you,
Es imposible dejar de amarte,	It's impossible to stop loving you,
Este cariño que yo a tí te tengo	This affection that I have for you
Es un cariño puro y verdadero.	Is an affection pure and true.
¡Cómo quisiera que venga la muerte!	How so, would I like death to come!
¡Cómo quisiera morir en tus brazos!	How so, would I like to die in your arms!
Quizás así podría olvidarte	Perhaps that way, I could forget you

Porque, en mi vida, todo es imposible.	Because, in my life, everything is impossible.
Ay, cruceñito, amorcito mío	Ay, dear man from [Santa] Cruz, my dear love
Este cariño te entrego y te digo	This affection I offer you and tell you of
Aunque mi cuerpo quede sepultado	Even though my body might be buried
Queda mi nombre grabado en tu pecho.	My name remains engraved in your breast.
Dicen con la muerte	They say that, with death,
Se llega a olvidar,	One comes to forget,
Quizás en la tumba	Perhaps in the grave
Más nos amamos.	We'll love one another more.
Si muero primero	Should I die first,
Yo allá te espero	I'll wait for you, over there,
Así para amarnos	In that way, to remain loving one another
Eternamente.	Eternally.

Chaskinakuy can be reached at:
P.O. Box 11421
Santa Rosa, CA 95406
Phone: (707) 571-1377
Email: chaskina@monitor.net

As you can see from the lyrics, "Amor imposible" offers one example of the poetic character of this genre: "Most *waynos* . . . are of an amorous nature. Despite the immense variety of *waynos,* many depict nostalgia for a lost love" (Romero 1999:389). The theme of nostalgia runs powerfully throughout songs that have emerged through the ages in Latin America (Schechter 1999a:2–7).

Finally, the *waynos* and *sanjuanes* of Andean ensembles—as well as *Nueva Canción* musics—have taken root in U.S. universities. For example, The University of Texas at Austin has for some years maintained an Andean ensemble, among their other Latin American groups. This began in 1976 with the *Nueva Canción* ensemble Toqui Amaru (Mapuche and Quechua for "chief serpent"), founded by Renato Espinoza of Chile, with Guillermo Delgado-P. and Enrique Cuevas of Bolivia, Néstor Lugones of Argentina, and American Alejandro Cardona. At the University of California, Santa Cruz, students perform in beginning and advanced-level Andean ensembles called VOCES (Spanish for "voices") and Taki Ñan (Quichua for "song path"), respectively.

Taki Ñan, which recorded an in-house cassette in 1992 and an in-house CD in 1998, focuses on traditional Andean musics in Spanish and Quichua/Quechua, as well as on *Nueva Canción* musics. Starting out with a single, ten-student Latin American ensemble in 1986 that focused on Ecuadorian genres, VOCES and Taki Ñan became independent of each other in 1991. Over the years, Taki Ñan has tended to follow two approaches: focusing its repertory or presenting a more varied program. When focusing in depth, during one particular quarter of study, the group would emphasize, for example, Colombian musics, Argentinean musics, Afro-South American musics; in fall 1992 they prepared six different field-recorded versions of "Ilumán tiyu." Taki Ñan has also presented programs with a variety of traditional and *Nueva Canción* musics. In nearly every one of these programs, from 1989 to the present, both Taki Ñan and VOCES have performed south-Andean *phukuna (zampoña)* musics—including the *k'antu* "Kutirimu-napaq." Over these years Taki Ñan has benefited enormously from the musical and linguistic assistance of Guillermo Delgado-P., as well as from workshops offered by Chaskinakuy and by Peruvian musician, Héctor Zapana.

The collective memory of the Taki Ñan ensemble has developed through several generations of student membership. The group has depended on the students' unquestioned commitment to the appropriate performance of Latin American traditional musics. It has also benefited from the students' initiative. They occasionally make their own musical, textual, and *zampoña* transcriptions, while at the same time mastering most melodies, harmonies, rhythms, strumming patterns, drum patterns, vocal styles and qualities, tempi, and character by ear, via aural tradition. The student musicians also frequently teach themselves new repertoire. They perform both on-campus and in local schools and libraries, and even after graduation some students remain in Taki Ñan. In short, the students' dedi-cation has helped create a rooted and ongoing music-cultural tradition, one whose constituent members share a substantial camaraderie. In this regard, Taki Ñan is an example of "affinity interculture," a phenomenon in which "musics seem to call out to audiences [or, students] across nation-state lines even when they are not a part of heritage . . . and it seems particularly the case that transmission is often of the old-fashioned variety—face to face, mouth to ear." In this way, "A given city, festival, or shop [or university musical ensemble] can create a musical world without frontiers that seems to exist across, or somehow suspended above, national lines" (Slobin 1992:48–49). A full account of the evolution of Taki Ñan appears in Schechter 1999b.

Aconcagua, at Florida State University, performs a variety of Andean musics and is currently under the direction of an alumna of Taki Ñan. Viento, in Berkeley, California, is codirected by Chaskinakuy and Duo Zapana—Héctor and Lydia Zapana, both formerly members of Taki Ñan—and comprises Berkeley resident students and community members. Fre-quently performing at the La Peña Cultural Center in Berkeley, Viento focuses on traditional south-Andean musics for *zampoña* and *tarqa* (wooden duct flute). Lydia Zapana, finally, is the founder/director of "Los Mapaches," an established ensemble of some thirty-five schoolchildren from the Berkwood Hedge School, in Berkeley, who perform Andean musics—on *zampoñas* and other instruments—locally, in concert.

Let us return now to the Andes of Imbabura, where the traditions of the Quichua of Cotacachi—the people, the language, the dress, the mate-rial culture, the character of *sanjuán* and the harp that plays it—have been preserved for hundreds of years. *Cada llajta* (individual character of the community) ensures the uniqueness of many aspects of their expressive culture. Even so, the Cotacachi Quichua share some traits with other regions and cultures of Latin America. One of these is the wake ritual for a dead child. Let us look at *wawa velorio* to see how it accommodates *cada llajta* as well as broader beliefs and practices that transcend cultural and political boundaries.

Wawa Velorio

In Imbabura as elsewhere in Latin America, infants struggle to survive. In three consecutive months in 1979–1980 I witnessed three *wawa velorio* rituals on Cotacachi's slopes. I observed a fourth child's wake there in August 1990. The infant mortality rate in Ecuador continues to be quite high; deaths are caused in large part by intestinal and respiratory diseases. U.S. history has also seen high infant mortality rates: In the era of Puritan New England (1620s to 1720s), in Boston as many as three in ten people died in infancy. The death of young children in Ecuador and throughout Latin America is a daily tragedy, one that through its very frequency ironically serves to preserve dozens of unique regional traditions of genre, instrument, and dance.

Let us now join the harpist and his family to attend a *wawa velorio* on Mt. Cotacachi. After nightfall, Sergio, the harpist contracted to provide music for the wake (Figure 9-12), his younger brother and apprentice-harpist, César, and their family leave their Tikulla home for the home of the

Figure 9-12
Harpist Sergio. March 1980.

deceased. After more than an hour's uphill winding journey on *chaki ñanes*, their father and *golpeador* Miguel Armando bearing the family harp, they arrive. At about 9:30 Sergio sits down with his harp next to the platform bearing the deceased infant. A few candles illuminate the casket and the home. After tuning, Sergio plays a strongly percussive music called *vacación* (CD 4, Track 14). The all-night *wawa velorio*—the wake for the deceased Quichua child—has begun.

Vacación (the same term is used for both the genre and the title itself) differs audibly from *sanjuán*. First, *vacación* does not require a *golpeador* but

CD 4/14

Vacación (1:23). Performed by Quichua harpist Sergio, at a child's wake. Field recording by John Schechter, outside Cotacachi, Ecuador, February 1980.

Transcription 9-16

Partial transcription of *vacación* as played by harpist Sergio, February 1980.

is performed by the harpist alone. Second, it is purely instrumental, not sung. Whereas *sanjuán* has a simple meter, *vacación* lacks the regular stresses that characterize a particular meter. *Vacación* is not built, like *sanjuán,* in eight-beat phrases but in long, descending cycles. *Sanjuán* is dance music; *vacación* is not.

Sanjuán is performed throughout the night at *wawa velorio,* accompanying the dancing of family and guests. *Vacación* is tied to two special ritual moments: the outset of the wake and whenever behavior centers on the deceased child. Harpists informed me that they play *vacación* at the beginning of the ritual in order to drive out the *demonio,* or devil, from beneath the platform supporting the deceased child. The second ritual moments include late-evening adorning of the corpse and dawn closing of the casket.

Before playing *vacación,* after playing it, and periodically throughout the night, the harpist and his family are offered food and drink—bananas, homemade bread, barley gruel, maize gruel, stewed corn, and *trago.* We have seen the central importance of *trago* consumption in ritual settings both in Cotacachi and throughout the Andes. In a *wawa velorio,* most of those present consume the drink. The man (never a woman) with the *trago* bottle and plastic cup goes around the room, offering a *copa* (cup) of *trago* to each man and woman: *"Ufyapai!"* ("Drink!"), he says; the one being offered the *copa* usually first asks him to drink—which he does—then accepts the offer him- or herself.

Until approximately midnight, Sergio performs mostly *sanjuanes.* By 10:30 P.M. he has played about five to ten *sanjuanes,* including perhaps "Carabuela," "Llakishamari nirkanki," "Ilumán tiyu," and "Rusa María." Occasionally, to keep the dancing going, he changes from one *sanjuán* to another without stopping. There is a distinctly regular and nearly metronomic sense of tempo about this father-son duo. Miguel Armando's *golpe* is solid and reliable, invariant, and Sergio's rhythm is strong and regular. Sergio's companions, Roberto and Gerónimo, sometimes serve as vocalists for the duo. One sings with Sergio. The voice-harp duo performs typically texted *sanjuanes,* including "Rusa María" and "Ruku kuskungu." To enhance the *alegre* (happy) character of the festive ritual, the harpist likes to have near-constant chatter together with his music and *golpe.*

Around 10:30 P.M., perhaps in the middle of playing a *sanjuán,* Sergio suddenly stops and shifts into *vacación.* Now the child, in its casket, is removed from the platform where it has been prominently displayed and is placed on the floor for adorning and crowning. The infant is given usually to its mother, who mourns the loss of her baby with a lament. This sobbed music uses the principal notes of *vacación:* D–C–A (scale degrees 8–7–5 of D minor). A crown of flowers is put on the baby's head. Its waist and wrists are wrapped in ribbons, and bouquets of flowers are placed alongside the body in the casket. During this entire time, Sergio plays *vacación;* he stops only when the infant and its casket are again placed on the platform.

Although dancing to *sanjuán* was slow to start, by 1:30 A.M. everyone is dancing: with the air growing colder, at 9,000 feet, the music and the festive night are warming up. The godmother and the father might begin to dance,

Figure 9-13
Harpist César. March 1980.

prompting Sergio to shout a pleased *"Achi mamaka kallarinka ña!"* ("The godmother will begin [to dance] now!"). Gerónimo shouts, *"Shinlli shinlli bailapankich' kumarigukuna!"* ("Dance really strongly, dear comadres!"). Sergio now hardly stops for small talk, immediately replenishing the musical warmth with one, then another *sanjuán*—maybe several strung together. He next begins to alternate *sanjuán* with *pareja,* a slightly faster music, also for dancing but usually without text.

Very late, at about 3 A.M., Sergio leaves the harp and asks his younger brother, César, to take over (Figure 9-13). With very few people still awake, César plays a string of short *sanjuanes.* There is no banter between César and his *golpeador*-father, as there had been between musicians of the same generation, such as Sergio and Gerónimo. This is *sanjuán* without reaction—functional dance music with little function, since no one is dancing.

By about 5 A.M. everyone is awake and shares a morning meal of boiled potatoes. Before sunrise (an hour later) Sergio again takes over the harp, tuning and perhaps playing a *pareja.* Suddenly, he shifts into *vacación* and the casket is taken outside onto the patio. Sergio stops quickly, picks up the harp, and heads outside. Our recording on CD 4, Track 15 begins with Sergio performing *vacación* as the casket is being taken outside. He then remarks, *"Sacando para afuera"* ("[They're] taking [it] outside"). He heads at once outside and there the mother begins to sing her lament.

The mother bids farewell to her child for the final time. She heard cycles of *vacación* for a few minutes just before the casket's removal outside. Now, as if on cue, and almost precisely at sunrise, she expresses her heartfelt grief in a lament that, as in the night before, uses almost exclusively the same three important pitches from *vacación:* D–C–A (in Sergio's actual tuning these pitches are G♯–F♯–D♯). Soon after she begins, Sergio, also near the casket, repeats *vacación* on the harp. Both musical expressions are *of* the

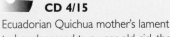

CD 4/15

Ecuadorian Quichua mother's lament to her deceased two-year-old girl, the morning after the child's wake (preceded by fifteen seconds of Sergio's *Vacación*) (3:07). Field recording by John Schechter outside Cotacachi, Ecuador, January 1980.

child: the mother's *to* the infant, the harpist's *about* the infant, marking behavior directed toward her (referring here to a January 12–13, 1980, ritual for a two-year-old girl). Because the infant is open to view for only a few more minutes, the focus of everyone's attention is on her. Although *vacación* does not "accompany" the mother's lament (they are simultaneous but independent musical expressions), nevertheless they *are* together—in time, in object focus, in musical pitch, and in structure. Like *vacación,* the lament is cyclical in form, always beginning with the G$\sharp$ and descending through the F$\sharp$ to the D$\sharp$.

The mother at this point will typically sing-sob alone. On this particular January 1980 morning, her sobs make it difficult to render most of the words precisely. Clearly she is addressing her baby daughter, whom she calls *warmiku* ("little woman"). She sobs-sings in short phrases that ultimately descend to the lowest pitch. (Respecting the mother in this moment of profound personal grief, I omit the transcription of this lament.)

Lamenting at dawn, the mother caresses her child's face or entire wrapped body one last time. Then the *golpeador* hammers on the lid of the casket, and when the child is no longer visible Sergio stops playing *vacación.* Just after 6 A.M. the godfather hoists the casket to his shoulder and everyone walks down the mountain to the town of Cotacachi, where the child is buried in the cemetery. After the burial the party adjourns to a *cantina* (tavern), where Sergio continues to play *sanjuanes* on the harp for dancing throughout the day.

Dancing, all night, at a child's wake. On Cotacachi's slopes and throughout Latin America, *wawa velorio*—or *velorio del angelito*—is a celebration. We find this surprising, perhaps. We might feel some of the confusion of a French baron, Jean Charles Davillier, who came upon a festive child's wake while traveling in the Spanish Mediterranean in the 1870s (1874:409; see Figure 9-14). He could not understand the merrymaking—in this case, a couple dancing a *jota,* accompanying themselves with castanets. One of the relatives informed him, *"Está con los ángeles"* ("She is with the angels").

The explanations are the same on this side of the Atlantic. For example, whenever certain nineteenth- and twentieth-century French and U.S. visitors to Argentina and Chile unexpectedly came upon children's wakes, they were consistently told that the gathering was a celebration in honor of the little angel, who is in the breast of God, or that the little angel has died in innocence and has gone to heaven. Therefore, there was to be rejoicing, not weeping. In our discussion of Violeta Parra, we mentioned that the great majority of Latin Americans are Roman Catholic. In Roman Catholicism, baptism confers a vital regeneration in Christ and thus an unconditional promise of salvation to a baptized child dying in infancy. In Catholic Spain and Latin America, the deceased infant is believed to dwell among the angels—to be an angel. This is cause for rejoicing.

The joyful rite is both broad and deep in Latin America. Accounts of children's wakes in this hemisphere go back to 1788 in Puerto Rico (Abbad y Lasierra 1788:281–82). In the nineteenth or twentieth centuries, *velorio del*

Illustration by Gustave Doré.

Figure 9-14
A festive child's wake in the Spanish Mediterranean, 1870s.

angelito, or *wawa velorio,* or *baquiné* (as the rite is known among African Antillans of Puerto Rico) was celebrated in Argentina, Brazil, Chile, Colombia, Cuba, the Dominican Republic, Ecuador, Mexico, Nicaragua, Panama, Paraguay, Peru, Puerto Rico, and Venezuela.

Given the joyful character of the Latin American child's wake, celebrating the ascension of the sinless infant into the realm of the angels, how does *wawa velorio* fit into the category of funeral rituals? A ritual is a formal practice or custom, and rural dwellers have both calendric rituals, tied to cycles of agriculture, religion, or national celebration, and life cycle rituals, marking significant transitional moments in the life of any individual. Funeral rites are life cycle rituals.

Within the formal practice or custom, some actions are prescribed—obligatory, standardized, conventional. At *wawa velorios,* I was struck by the precision with which certain prescribed actions were carried out. *Vacación* always began the wake; it always accompanied movement of the corpse, usually in its open casket, from one place to another; at dawn, as the casket was brought outside for closing, the mother began her lament, almost as if on cue. Interestingly, in Hungary laments are to be performed quite strictly at specified moments of the period after death and at burial; one of the specific points is when the casket is closed (Boilès 1978:130). During the period of immediate mourning, when all can view the corpse, there is always a conventionalized, dramatized outburst of grief; the corpse is usually the center of attention. There may be ritual forms of touching the corpse—the body is sometimes stroked and embraced (Malinowski [1925] 1954:49). Similarly, we saw and heard, in the Cotacachi *comuna,* the child conspicuously displayed during the night, the seemingly "cued" lament, and the Quichua mother caressing her child on the patio of their home.

Indeed, in keeping with our understanding of the prescriptive nature of ritual, most accounts of Latin American (and Spanish) children's wakes share certain prominent behaviors, regardless of cultural group or country. The child is always conspicuous by his or her presence, in the same room in which family and friends dance to the favorite music of the region (*sanjuán* in highland Ecuador, *jota* in Mediterranean Spain): This is *cada llajta* in operation. The infant is not only present but raised: lying on the elevated platform, seated on the table, tied to a ladder placed atop the casket, suspended from the roof, or pushed back and forth between poles. Each of these ritual gestures symbolizes the transformation into an angel and entry into eternity. Similarly, the infant is washed and dressed in the finest clothing available and is bedecked in ribbons, flowers, and paper or cardboard wings. Upon the child's head sits a crown of real or artificial flowers, which is both ubiquitous (in Latin American and Spanish children's wakes) and ancient (the practice of crowning dead children dates back to the time of the ancient Greeks). The atmosphere of the wake is always festive, with dancing, food, and alcoholic beverage.

Many Spanish and Latin American visual and literary artists have depicted the child's wake in paintings, novels, short stories, plays, and poems; many of these portrayals, however, criticize what the native artists view as an indefensible diminution of a life, in making its extinction the pretext for merrymaking. Nevertheless, the Latin American child's wake is a deep-rooted ritual that embodies local cultural preferences in song types, dance types, instrument types. Whether or not local artists or outsiders approve of the *velorio del angelito,* the practice serves as a reliable stamp—designed by the culture itself—of that local culture at that point in time (Schechter 1994a).

The Career Dilemma of Don César Muquinche

We have seen how vital the harpist is in Quichua children's wakes in northern highland Cotacachi. The harpist is also quite visible in the central highlands, especially in Tungurahua Province. One talented artist, Don César Muquinche, is a harpist of Illampu, a village outside Ambato, in Tungurahua (Figure 9-15). As you can see, Don César's harp is considerably larger than the Imbabura harps. It is modeled on the harps of Paraguay; these instruments are distinguished by their substantial size and by their neck shape—an inverted arch. The neck's tuning pegs are guitar-type mechanical tuning pegs, used also by the Paraguayans. The pattern of small, paired sound holes on either side of the column—holes that in fact come at the ends of (barely visible) painted S shapes—dates to Spanish harps of the seventeenth century.

An artist of national stature, Don César plays numerous musical genres, including *sanjuanito,* an adaptation of the Imbabura *sanjuán.* On CD 4, Track 16, we hear him playing an *albazo* called "Toro barroso" (Spanish for "Reddish Bull"). *Albazos* are well-known among Spanish speakers throughout the highlands and even throughout the country on the radio and at public and private celebrations.

Don César's decision to take up the harp was complicated. His father, Don Francisco, had been a professional harpist. Attending his father's performances as a child, the son witnessed the physical suffering that this career brought with it. César initially decided he would apprentice as a

CD 4/16

"Toro barroso" ("Reddish Bull") (3:32). *Albazo* of Ecuador. Performed by Don César Muquinche. Field recording by John Schechter, outside Ambato, Ecuador, 1980.

Figure 9-15
Don César Muquinche, harpist of Illampu, Tungurahua Province, at his home outside Ambato, Ecuador. August 1980.

John M. Schechter

hatmaker. But Don Francisco advised his son that whatever César chose to do, he should select something that would make him content and leave him with good memories. Ultimately these words led César back to music. His decision to be a musician also reflected Don César's great admiration and respect for his father—specifically for his father's ability to resist the temptations inherent in the harpist's career—and for his father's concern for him and his serious advice.

In fact, both father and son followed similar paths. Both had a strong business orientation. Don César speaks of Naranjo's harps and the services of Camilo Borja, Don Francisco, and himself as harpists as being "in some demand." Don César saw himself as being upwardly mobile; he disdained his own *indígena* roots. Yet both he and his father performed for both *indígena* and *blanco* (white) society, bridging this cultural gap as performers. Finally, both Don César and his father learned to play in ensemble as well as solo and to adapt to changing performance arenas, such as radio and television.

Both men appreciated playing as an art. They felt great pride in developing it both for their own self-esteem and for the satisfaction of their clients. Don César's highest compliment to artists or craftspersons was to call them "artists of quality."

In July 1980, after I had studied with him for several months, Don César Muquinche told me about the development of his artistic career. Let us look at the types of conflict he faced and how he finally resolved them, choosing harp music over hatmaking. Through his thoughts we can gain some insight into the reputation, the *fama*, of a harpist in Ecuador. I conducted the following interview of Don César Muquinche in Spanish and translated it into English (Schechter 1980).

> I was born in 1920, here in Illampu (Tungurahua). My father, Francisco, was planning to become a tailor—to make men's suits. Well, he heard Camilo Borja play—a man who lived just alongside us—and, on hearing him play the harp, my father paid attention. And he said, "I would like to learn harp from this man."
>
> My father then proposed to Borja that he teach him the harp. The man said yes and told him, "Let's make a deal: You make me trousers and I will give you harp lessons." My father told me that he had these lessons every day; he was very interested in learning quickly, taking advantage of the goodwill of the maestro.
>
> When Borja saw that my father was beginning to play the harp fairly well, the maestro, who was in great demand at that time, told him he needed to buy his own harp. . . . There was a man, Segundo Alejandro Naranjo, who made fine instruments—very special harps. They had a fantastic resonance. . . .
>
> My father told me that the harps made by this man were instruments in some demand and of very fine quality; there was no danger that the glue might loosen from the pieces. Even when the harp was hit hard, the wood would not dent or come loose, as might happen today with harps made of rough wood. . . .
>
> My father was in demand in various places—in fiestas, in *wawas muertos* [dead children, i.e., *velorio del angelito,* or *wawa velorio*]. . . . And with the rhythm of this beating upon the harp, they [the father and his *golpeador*] put on a fine show, without the need of other instruments.
>
> [At children's wakes] the *golpeador* had to stay right there, by the harpist. Then, there were other events—*matrimonio,* patron saint fiestas. Among *[indígenas],* the *matrimonio* lasts three or four days. And the harpist has to be *there.* Day and night. . . . It is the same in the fiestas—of devotion to some saint, for example. In the *wawas muertos,* some better-off people had it lasting some three days, but without doubt, one night and one day, for sure. . . . In gratitude for their having been well entertained, the people had to treat the *golpeador* and the harpist to some gifts, like *medianos,* as they call them here: a whole chicken, a rabbit, or a *cui*—a thing of great value.
>
> Yes, they made a good ensemble. And ever since I could remember, my father was in great demand—as much among the *indígenas* as among the white people. He became an innovative, popular artist who liked to entertain. [He played for] the people of society—a governor, a subtreasurer, here or beyond—in Quito [the capital], in different places. My father was very much in demand, very important: an artist of quality. He traveled to Quito, through the entire country. He became a very well known artist . . . a very distinguished artist, for every class of society.
>
> The musicians might go to their engagements in a cart pulled by a horse. At times, they went on horseback, to Quito—carrying the harp, cushioned and secured with a scarf, or something else soft. There was a person who led the horses. [My father] told me about this.

Cui: Quichua for "guinea pig." These are native to the Andes, and groups of them are kept in the house by many rural residents of highland Ecuador. Today they are raised, killed, and broiled and used as gifts for fiestas or, as here, for the harpist and *golpeador.*

Sometimes, traveling in this way was very trying. Finally my father said, "No, I won't travel like that. If we could go in those carriages . . . then I would go. I think I have been treating myself badly." And the people [provided what he requested], as they seemed to want my father's services greatly. Many times he went to Riobamba [capital of Chimborazo Province, just south of Tungurahua Province], I recall.

When I began growing up, I sometimes accompanied him, to see how he was treated, or how he might have been suffering. I saw that my father, being responsible, did not get drunk at the fiestas; he was careful to fulfill his responsibilities honorably. And wherever he went, the people paid him well. . . . But it is sad that he had to suffer a lot [owing to the extremely long hours, the demands for continuous music, and the constant pressure to partake of alcohol with the guests] because the people never tired of enjoying themselves. So I felt bad for my father, and I said to him, "Now, father, when can I learn how to play, to help you?"

I lament the death of my father. But he left good memories, as an artist—very good memories. He died while still capable, surrounded by the profits of his labors. By contrast, [another] harpist of quality [whom I knew] died poor because he was quite a womanizer. They say he squandered all he had earned, drinking with women. He died, poor, leaving his children poor. By contrast, my father said, "I have to extract a good inheritance from this profession [of harpist]. If the upper-class people occupy me well, pay me well, if the *indígenas* also pay me well, why not plant crops? Why not use [the money] for land, in things that are to serve me for life?"

My father thought about this very conscientiously. He [bought land and] worked the fields two or three days each week; he did not attend to the fields any more than that because he was in great demand in this career of music. My mother worked the fields more.

Now that I was becoming a young man, I had to think about it. There were harpists who went around poorly dressed, barefoot, dirty; I looked, and realized that my father took very good care of himself. There were other harpists, but awful ones. They got drunk and walked around looking like a mess—not even the instruments were well treated. And that's worse.

And so I said no, I do not want to be a harpist because they get very drunk. Of course, my father is fine, he takes care of me; but I see that most people put pressure on the harpist—they say, "Drink, maestro," with great fervor. "Drink." They put it into your mouth. I said to myself, "Not me . . . I won't dedicate myself to the harp." My father, when they asked him to drink, said, "Don't force me to. I must carry out my responsibilities and earn my money. After I have completed my commitment for which you have hired me, then I shall be delighted to drink. But I have to be responsible for my musical colleagues; they come with me, to earn a living. And since I made the contract, I have to charge the *patrón* who has contracted me and, in turn, pay my *compañeros,* in order to assure their accompaniment in the future. If I get drunk, I can't discharge either my contract or my agreement to pay my *compañeros,* who came along expecting me to pay them. Thus you are hurting me [by insisting that I drink and get drunk]." This retort worked very well.

Nevertheless, I still felt very suspect about being a harpist. I told my father that I did not wish to be a musician but rather a hatmaker. I liked seeing young women or men who appreciated a truly elegant hat. And there was a hatmaker of first quality, a man by the name of Segundo Villa Paredes, in Ambato [the provincial capital of Tungurahua]. I went there and learned all that the maestro had to teach—how to make hats. I was there some two years, while I was young. I think I was already hatmaking by the age of fifteen years. By the age of eighteen or twenty I was a [hatmaking] maestro.

I became independent and set up a workshop in Ambato. I worked for the "people of society," who liked my style of work. I had all the confidence of these people, and it went well for me. I had quite a nice workshop there in the city of Ambato.

When my father saw that I was a successful [hatmaking] maestro, he told me, "Son, I congratulate you. You have distinguished yourself, now, don't you see? Now, I am going to recommend to you that you take advantage, in your *youth,* of your profession. Of music, I have my fond memories. In the same way, I would recommend that you take advantage of, enjoy, your profession." I had to listen to my father, pay attention to him: He was making this recommendation for my own good.

Well, when I had become a very popular maestro, well esteemed and with plenty of work there in the city, guaranteeing me a good living, some people came to me on their own to ask that I teach them the craft of hatmaking. Others came so they might help me expedite my commitments to deliver the completed work. I accepted them as working assistants. I looked for those who already knew the craft. Others came and said, "Maestro, be so kind as to teach my son the profession." "Delighted," [I said,] and accepted them.

Soon I organized the work for those who had come to help and those who had come to learn, and I had some free time. Over there the people already knew—"You're the Muquinche—?" I said, "Yes." "Listen, and your father is a harpist of quality?" I said, "Yes." "And you don't know anything?" "I too know a little bit." "And why don't you let us hear it? Why don't you bring a harp here to your workshop and play for us? Let us hear what your style is like, or how you play."

I thought, "Perhaps, yes, I must have a harp—as recreation from work."

Since the people had requested me to play the harp for them, I had a harp made. I brought it to my workshop, and I began to play it. Every once in a while, as a rest, I would sit down and begin to play . . . [and] some people came, curious. "It sounds nice, it sounds—" this or that. "Play, maestro, play," they exhorted me. "Play the harp, maestro." "Play the harp." And I had to listen to them: "Fine, I'm delighted to. Sit down." I had them sit down in one spot, and I would do a small performance.

Meanwhile, some of the people continued talking with me: "Why not better dedicate yourself to the harp?" At times, to my good friends, I paid attention to this. But of some people, I thought, "These [people] are going to do me harm," because they said [as many had done to my father], "Look, maestro, you play beautifully; accept just one [drink]." I said, "No, I have my business—I have my workshop. I have this—how can I abandon my workshop?" When I put it this way, some withdrew their invitation; others continued asking me to play: "Play the harp, maestro." I said to myself, "Listen, this is bad; I am going to get hooked on this."

Well, as I was getting popular with my music, there came this man, I remember, from Radio Ambato, a man by the name of Villa Lobos, the manager of Radio Ambato. Juan Villa Lobos. Well, he said, "Maestro, can you do programs for Radio Ambato?" . . . I said, "Fine."

Well, then, I had to put attention into improving my art. And he said to me, "Maestro, would you be able to play together with other instruments, to make a nice *conjunto* (ensemble), with violins, *bandolín,* guitar, and flute?" I said, "Yes, sir, but only with the agreement that it is to be you who is in charge of getting these people together; if it is to be left to me to do this, then, no. I am busy." The man [did it], of course, since he liked the idea of organizing a *conjunto típico* ("typical" ensemble), as we called it. . . . A very nice ensemble was thus created, now along with the harp . . . [and] it was a great hit with the people—"Such-and-such *conjunto,* directed by . . ." They named me director of the ensemble.

We did the Radio Ambato programs Saturdays and Sundays—Saturdays in the afternoon and Sundays at midday. This was all the time, for some three years in a row. Every weekend.

This man Villa Lobos came to my hat workshop when I was about twenty-eight years old. . . . I was by then a harpist, no? By then, I had practiced my profession [of hatmaker] for some eight years. When I came into popularity [as a harpist], I was twenty-eight years old. . . .

My father visited me and said, "César, you came to like the harp?" I said yes. He answered, "Very well, between the music and the hats, I think that you are going to become a rich man—for you are accumulating money." I confided in him that I did the same as he. With the monies that I earned—as much from the music as from the hats—I bought some small pieces of land. . . .

Well, trying to maintain the workshop, trying to fulfill my commitments, I came home from work at any old hour—at dawn, practically exhausted, wasted. To get the work done, I had to dig in and work myself.

I became ill. A fever, a lung infection, or a typhoid fever. This illness was very strong. . . . It was in 1949. It was serious. I had to be hospitalized. Thank God, my hour had not yet arrived. I recuperated, my health restored. My father procured doctors to attend to me. . . .

[One] doctor said, "You have to stop practicing one of your professions. If you continue at this rate, with the hats and the music, you won't do anything, neither the one nor the other. There is a danger that very easily you could drive yourself to complete exhaustion. Continue only with the music, or continue only with the hats." Of course I had to obey him. I said, "Very well. If I try to force it—the attention to the hats, and to the music, as well—I'll be treating myself very badly." I had to pay attention to the doctor.

And so I felt myself obliged to leave the profession of hatmaking.

[Don César continues, discussing how his harp career continued to develop, to a substantial degree through his performances on radio—in Ambato, Guayaquil, Quito—as well as on television. He, too, was occasionally taken to play on horseback, in areas around Illampu, Don César himself occasionally carrying the harp on his shoulder. More typically, now, a car is sent for him and then returns him to his home—or, for performances at distant locations, he is sent the travel fare.]

African-Ecuadorian Music of the Chota River Valley

We began with the comment that Latin America was a kaleidoscope of cultural patterns, and we explored three of these. We went on to examine quite closely one region of Ecuador—northern highland Cotacachi, its Quichua culture, its *sanjuán*, and its *wawa velorio* ritual. We investigated the burgeoning phenomenon of the Andean ensemble, observing one such group from Ilumán, Imbabura, while also noting the now-global nature of this unique Andean manifestation, extending to six continents, and specifically to the United States and to U.S. universities. We met a harpist of the central highlands of Ecuador, Don César Muquinche, and became acquainted with his music and his career. Let us conclude with a look at one other culture/region of Ecuador: that of African Ecuadorians of the Chota River valley, who live approximately two hours north of the Quichua of Cotacachi.

On October 27, 1979, I was fortunate to meet Germán Congo, the excellent lead guitarist of the ensemble Conjunto Rondador (the *rondador* is a single-rank panpipe of Ecuador) at one of their performances in Ibarra, the capital of Imbabura Province. Germán invited me to visit him and his musician-brothers in the Chota Valley. Some months later, on March 1, 1980, my friend Don Valerio, my wife, Janis, and I journeyed to Chota. This was the first of several visits to Chota and Ibarra, in 1980 and again in 1990, in which my research focused on the musical artistry of the Congo brothers, their colleague Milton Tadeo, and fellow Chota musicians (Schechter 1994b).

When we think of Latin American regions that have large populations of African Americans, Ecuador does not usually come to mind. Yet as much as 25 percent of the country's population is African Ecuadorian. They are heavily concentrated in coastal Esmeraldas Province, which neighbors Imbabura Province. The first Africans arrived in Ecuador in the sixteenth century, after which Jesuit missionaries brought in large numbers of African slaves to work on plantations both on the coast and in the central highlands: Indigenous labor was hard to find in some areas and unwilling to serve as slaves in others. The relatively small pocket of approximately fifteen thousand African Ecuadorians in the Chota Valley, comprising ten to fifteen small villages, has an uncertain origin. The most widely accepted view is that the African Ecuadorians of the Chota Valley are descended from slaves held by the Jesuits on their plantations in the highlands (Lipski 1987:157–58).

The best-known musicians today in the Chota Valley are the guitarist-composer-singers Germán, Fabián, and Eleuterio Congo and their colleague Milton Tadeo. Fifteen years ago they played mostly around their home village of Carpuela; today they are regional celebrities with regular weekend performances in local villages, on the coast, and in nearby Colombia. As of October 1990 they had recorded six long-playing records within seven years. The Congo brothers are the third generation of composer-performers in their family.

Fabián and Eleuterio Congo perform "Vamos pa' Manabí" ("Let's go to Manabí" [a coastal province next to Esmeraldas]) on CD 4, Track 17. Both

CD 4/17

"Vamos pa' Manabí" ("Let's Go to Manabí") (3:01). *Bomba* of Ecuador. Performed by Fabián Congo, guitar and vocal; Eleuterio Congo, guitar. Field recording by John Schechter. Chota Valley, Ecuador, March 1980.

John M. Schechter

Figure 9-16
Fabián Congo, guitarist-singer-composer.
Ibarra, Ecuador, August 1990.

men play guitar, while Fabián sings (Figure 9-16). Notice first that, in contrast to the straight tone of the Quichua singers two hours down the road, Fabián's tone has substantial vibrato. Recall from Chapter 4 the character and importance of improvisation in African-American music. In this African-Ecuadorian song you can hear a distinctive freedom of expression in melody and rhythm—especially in the instrumental parts. Contributing to the feeling of rhythmic freedom is the fact that Fabián regularly syncopates his rhythm—that is, he seems to sing "between" the strong guitar beats instead of with them. The guitars, too, play syncopated rhythm, especially in the "instruments alone" sections. After listening a few more times, try singing along with Fabián; the text is not long or complicated. See if you can begin to feel the subtle rhythm of the syncopated song; the more you practice, the closer you will get to this relaxed feeling and the more you will enjoy singing "Manabí."

Para no sufrir hagamos así	So as not to suffer, let's do this: (repeated)	**Text, "Vamos pa' Manabí"**
Vámonos de aquí para Manabí	Let's go from here to Manabí. (repeated 3x)	
(Instruments alone)		
Por donde yo estoy, muy lejos de tí	Where I am, very far from you, (repeated)	
Siento el corazón, wambrita, por tí	I feel you in my heart, dear young woman. (repeated 3x)	

(Instruments alone)

| *Cuando yo estoy muy lejos de tí* | When I am very far from you, (repeated) |
| *Siento el corazón, wambrita, por tí.* | I feel you in my heart, dear young woman. (repeated 3x) |

Coba Andrade 1980:209.

We have been discussing the African-American character of "Manabí." One Ecuadorian ethnomusicologist has expanded this idea, referring to the *bomba* (the genre of which "Manabí" is an example) of Chota as an "*Indo-Hispano-Afro-Ecuadorian*" hybrid music (Coba Andrade 1980:185). Where, then, is the "Indo," the Native-American character? Recall from our discussion of nearby Cotacachi *sanjuán* that the accompaniment is often in the minor paired with the relative major key. In "Manabí," two chords prevail: F major and its relative minor, D. We are reminded of *sanjuán* not only by this key relationship but also by the minor-key arpeggiations of the guitar, as at the beginning of the song. Recall that this type of introductory arpeggiation also characterizes *sanjuán* when played on the Imbabura harp. The "T" motive of Efraín's "Cascarón" is an example of this.

Finally, the word *wambrita* occurs in the text of "Manabí." This word is Quichua, not Spanish. Depending on the region of the Ecuadorian highlands and on its context in a sentence, *wambra* (and its affectionate diminutive, *wambrita*) may mean either "young man" or "young woman." In "Rusa María" it means "young man"; in "Manabí" it means "young woman."

"Vamos pa' Manabí" is a rich musical expression of a border region: African Ecuadorian, close to a major Quichua cultural zone, within a Spanish-speaking nation. Not surprisingly, this piece has musical and textual characteristics associated with all three of these cultures. In this case, though, probably the sum of the parts does not create the whole: This *bomba* from Chota is unique not merely because of its several individual features but also because of the distinctive artistry of its performers, Fabián and Eleuterio—a quality that cannot be captured on paper.

Despedida, or Farewell

You have now heard examples from many different music-cultures of Latin America: the unmistakable razor's edge tempo and tension of Venezuelan *joropo*, the eloquent metaphors and profound sentiment of Víctor Jara, and the depth and richness of hocketing altiplano panpipes in ensemble. You have learned of the lifeways, harp, and songs of the Quichua of highland Ecuador, and you have witnessed the poignant Quichua ritual of *wawa velorio*—dancing at the wake of a child. Where Jara pointed to the plaiter of Lonquén and to Angelita Huenumán, we have singled out for recognition several individual "artists of quality," in Muquinche's phrase— artists who are probably among the forgotten people of Latin America, including the harpists Efraín, Sergio, and Don César himself, and Eleuterio and Fabián Congo. In their own worlds of music, these artists are highly esteemed, for they practice music-cultural traditions—*sanjuán* and *bomba*, child's wake, harp with *golpeador*—that their cultures prize highly and have preserved for hundreds of years. Finally, we have explored together the recent globalizing of the Andean musical ensemble, beginning our journey with a specific Ecuadorian Quichua group—Conjunto Ilumán—in its own cultural context, then "traveling" after Andean ensembles to cities throughout the world, and stopping along the way to take close looks at a particular Andean ensemble based in California—Chaskinakuy—and at an Andean group based in a U.S. university—Taki Ñan.

In these studies and "travels," we have discovered that our sense of community is bound up with our identification with specific musics and music rituals. In one realm or another, we all obey the dictate of *cada llajta:* Each of us, ultimately, is musically, linguistically, and certainly in many other respects, of a place—if even, at times, of a music-culturally adopted place.

References

Abbad y Lasierra, Fray Iñigo. 1788. *Historia geográfica, civil y política de la Isla de S. Juan Bautista de Puerto Rico.* Madrid: Imprenta de Don Antonio de Espinosa.

Basch, Linda, Nina Glick Schiller, and Christina Szanton Blanc. 1994. *Nations Unbound: Transnational Projects, Postcolonial Predicaments and Deterritorialized Nation-States.* Langhome, Pa.: Gordon and Breach Science Publishers.

Bastien, Joseph W. 1978. *Mountain of the Condor: Metaphor and Ritual in an Andean Ayllu.* St. Paul, Minn.: West. American Ethnological Society Monograph 64.

Boas, Franz. [1929] 1940. "Metaphorical Expression in the Language of the Kwakiutl Indians." In *Race, Language, and Culture.* New York: Free Press.

Boilès, Charles L. 1978. *Man, Magic, and Musical Occasions.* Columbus, Ohio: Collegiate.

Carrasco Pirard, Eduardo. 1982. "The Nueva Canción in Latin America." *International Social Science Journal* 94 (34:4):599–623.

Céspedes, Gilka Wara. 1993. "*Huayño, Saya,* and *Chuntunqui:* Bolivian Identity in the Music of 'Los Kjarkas.'" *Revista de Música Latinoamericana/Latin American Music Review* 14(1): 52–101.

Coba Andrade, Carlos Alberto. 1980. *Literatura popular Afroecuatoriana.* Otavalo, Ecuador: Instituto Otavaleño de Antropología.

Conjunto Ilumán. n.d. *Elenita Conde.* Ensemble directed by Segundo "Galo" Maigua Pillajo of Ilumán, Ecuador. Pre-1990. Cassette.

Conjunto Indígena "Peguche" [Ecuador]. 1977. *Folklore de mi tierra.* Orion 330-0063. Industria Fonográfica Ecuatoriana (IFESA). Guayaquil, Ecuador. Distributed by Emporio Musical S.A., Guayaquil and Psje. Amador, Quito.

Cooke, Peter. 1998. "East Africa: An Introduction." In *Africa: The Garland Encyclopedia of World Music,* vol. 1, edited by Ruth M. Stone, 598–609. New York: Garland.

Davillier, Le Baron [Jean] Ch[arles]. 1874. *L'Espagne.* Illustrated by G. Doré. Paris: Hachette.

Feld, Steven. 1981. "'Flow Like a Waterfall': The Metaphors of Kaluli Musical Theory." *1981 Yearbook for Traditional Music* 13:22–47.

Fernandez, James W. 1978. "Syllogisms of Association: Some Modern Extensions of Asturian Deepsong." In *Folklore in the Modern World,* edited by Richard M. Dorson, 183–206. Paris: Mouton.

González, Juan Pablo. 1989. "'Inti-Illimani' and the Artistic Treatment of Folklore." *Revista de Música Latinoamericana/Latin American Music Review* 10(2): 267–86.

Harrison, Regina. 1989. *Signs, Songs, and Memory in the Andes: Translating Quechua Language and Culture.* Austin: Univ. of Texas Press.

Jara, Joan. 1984. *An Unfinished Song: The Life of Víctor Jara.* New York: Ticknor and Fields.

Jatari. *Jatari!! 4.* 1978. *Fadisa.* Fábrica de Discos S.A. Quito, Ecuador. 710129.

Kaemmer, John E. 1998. "Southern Africa: An Introduction." In *Africa: The Garland Encyclopedia of World Music,* vol. 1, edited by Ruth M. Stone, 700–21. New York: Garland.

Koetting, James T. 1992. "Three: Africa/Ghana." In *Worlds of Music: An Introduction to the Music of the World's Peoples, 2nd ed.,* edited by Jeff Todd Titon, 67–105. New York: Schirmer Books.

Levy, Lisa, producer and narrator. 1988. *Violeta Madre.* 4-part series on the life and work of Violeta Parra. 2 cassettes. KAOS-FM, Evergreen State College, Olympia, Washington.

Lipski, John M. 1987. "The Chota Valley: Afro-Hispanic Language in Highland Ecuador." *Latin American Research Review* 22(1): 155–70.

Malinowski, Bronislaw. [1925] 1954. "Magic, Science, and Religion." In *Magic, Science, and Religion and Other Essays.* Garden City, N.Y.: Anchor Books.

Meisch, Lynn A. 1997. "Transnational Communities, Transnational Lives: Coping with Globalization in Otavalo, Ecuador." Ph.D. diss., Stanford University.

Moreno Andrade, Segundo Luis. 1930. "La música en el Ecuador." In *El Ecuador en cien años de independencia, 1830–1930,* vol. 2, edited by J. Gonzalo Orellana. Quito: Imprenta de la Escuela de Artes y Oficios.

Morris, Nancy. 1986. "*Canto porque es necesario cantar:* The New Song Movement in Chile, 1973–1983." *Latin American Research Review* 21(2): 117–36.

Nettl, Bruno. 1983. *The Study of Ethnomusicology: Twenty-nine Issues and Concepts.* Urbana: Univ. of Illinois Press.

Nketia, J. H. Kwabena. 1974. *The Music of Africa.* New York: Norton.

Ñanda mañachi 1 (Préstame el camino). 1977. Produced by Jean Chopin Thermes. Llaquiclla. IFESA (Industria Fonográfica Ecuatoriana S.A.) 339-0501. Guayaquil, Ecuador. Recorded in Ibarra, Ecuador.

Ñanda mañachi 2 (Préstame el camino). 1979. Produced by Jean Chopin Thermes. Llaquiclla. IFESA (Industria Fonográfica Ecuatoriana S.A.) 339-0502. Guayaquil, Ecuador. Recorded in Ibarra, Ecuador.

Ñanda mañachi/Boliviamanta: Préstame el camino desde Bolivia. Música quichua del equinoccio Andino. Churay, Churay!. 1983. Llaquiclla. Fediscos. Guayaquil, Ecuador. Onix L.P. 59003.

Obando, Segundo. 1988. *Tradiciones de Imbabura.* 3rd ed. Quito: Abya-Yala.

Romero, Raúl R. 1999. "Chapter Eight: Andean Peru." In *Music in Latin American Culture: Regional Traditions,* edited by John M. Schechter, 383–423. New York: Schirmer Books.

Ross, Joe. 1994. "Music of the Andes." *Acoustic Musician Magazine,* June, pp. 18–27.

Salvo, Calogero, writer/director. 1982. "Juan Félix Sánchez." Filmed in El Potrero, Mérida, Venezuela, November 1981 and February 1982.

Schechter, John M. 1979. "The Inca *Cantar Histórico:* A Lexico-Historical Elaboration on Two Cultural Themes." *Ethnomusicology* 23(2): 191–204.

———. 1980. Interview with César Muquinche. Illampu, Tungurahua Province, Ecuador, July 12.

———. 1982. "Music in a Northern Ecuadorian Highland Locus: Diatonic Harp, Genres, Harpists, and Their Ritual Junction in the Quechua Child's Wake." 3 vols. Ph.D. diss., Univ. of Texas.

———. 1992. *The Indispensable Harp: Historical Development, Modern Roles, Configurations, and Performance Practices in Ecuador and Latin America.* Kent, Ohio: Kent State Univ. Press.

———. 1994a. "Divergent Perspectives on the *velorio del angelito:* Ritual Imagery, Artistic Condemnation, and Ethnographic Value." *Journal of Ritual Studies* 8(2): 43–84.

———. 1994b. "Los Hermanos Congo y Milton Tadeo Ten Years Later: Evolution of an African-Ecuadorian Tradition of the Valle del Chota, Highland Ecuador." In *Music and Black Ethnicity: The Caribbean and South America,* edited by Gerard H. Béhague, 285–305. Coral Gables, Fla.: Univ. of Miami North-South Center/Transaction.

———. 1999a. "Chapter One: Themes in Latin American Music Culture." In *Music in Latin American Culture: Regional Traditions,* edited by John M. Schechter, 1–33. New York: Schirmer Books.

———. 1999b. *"Taki Ñan:* South American Affinity Interculture in Santa Cruz, California." In *Musical Cultures of Latin America: Global Effects, Past and Present,* edited by S. Loza. Proceedings of symposium, University of California at Los Angeles, May 28-30, 1999. In press.

Slobin, Mark. 1992. "Micromusics of the West: A Comparative Approach." *Ethnomusicology* 36(1): 1–87.

Smith, Sandra. 1984. "Panpipes for Power, Panpipes for Play: The Social Management of Cultural Expression in Kuna Society." Ph.D. diss., Univ. of California, Berkeley.

Additional Reading

Aretz, Isabel. 1967. *Instrumentos musicales de Venezuela.* Cumaná, Venezuela: Editorial Universitaria de Oriente.

———, relater. 1977. *América Latina en su música.* México, D.F.: Siglo Veintiuno Editores.

Aretz, Isabel, Gérard Béhague, and Robert Stevenson. 1980. "Latin America." The *New Grove Dictionary of Music and Musicians,* vol. 10, edited by Stanley Sadie, 505–34. London: Macmillan.

Baumann, Max Peter. 1985. "The Kantu Ensemble of the Kallawaya at Charazani (Bolivia)." *Yearbook for Traditional Music* 17:146–66.

Baumann, Max Peter, recopilado y editado. 1983. *Sojta Chunka Qheshwa Takis Bolivia Llajtamanta: Sesenta Canciones del Quechua Boliviano.* Cochabamba, Bolivia: Centro Pedagógico y Cultural de Portales.

Béhague, Gérard. 1990. "Latin American Folk Music." In *Folk and Traditional Music of the Western Continents, 3rd ed.,* edited by Bruno Nettl; revised and edited by Valerie Woodring Goertzen, 185–228. Englewood Cliffs, N.J.: Prentice-Hall.

———. 1979. *Music in Latin America: An Introduction.* Englewood Cliffs, N.J.: Prentice-Hall.

———. 1984. "Patterns of *Candomblé* Music Performance: An Afro-Brazilian Religious Setting." In *Performance Practice: Ethnomusicological Perspectives,* edited by G. Béhague, 222–54. Westport, Conn.: Greenwood Press.

———, ed. 1994. *Music and Black Ethnicity: The Caribbean and South America.* Coral Gables, Fla.: Univ. of Miami North-South Center/Transaction.

Carvalho-Neto, Paulo de. 1964. *Diccionario del folklore ecuatoriano.* Tratado del Folklore Ecuatoriano 1. Quito: Editorial Casa de la Cultura Ecuatoriana.

Cavour, Ernesto. c. 1974. *La zampoña, aerófono boliviano: Método audiovisual.* La Paz(?): Ediciones Tatu.

Dicks, Ted, ed. 1976. *Victor Jara: His Life and Songs.* London: Elm Tree Books.

Fairley, Jan. 1985. "Annotated Bibliography of Latin-American Popular Music with Particular Reference to Chile and to Nueva Canción." In *Popular Music, vol. 5, Continuity and Change,* 305–56. Cambridge, England: Cambridge Univ. Press.

Fuks, Victor. 1988. "Music, Dance, and Beer in an Amazonian Indian Community." *Revista de Música Latinoamericana/Latin American Music Review* 9(2): 151–86.

Grebe, María Ester. 1973. "El Kultrun mapuche: Un microcosmo simbólico." *Revista Musical Chilena* 27(123–24): 3–42.

Hurtado Suárez, Wilfredo. 1995. *Chicha peruana: Música de los nuevos migrantes.* [Lima, Perú?]: Grupo de Investigaciones Económicas ECO.

List, George. 1983. *Music and Poetry in a Colombian Village: A Tri-Cultural Heritage.* Bloomington: Indiana Univ. Press.

Mendoza, Zoila S. 2000. *Shaping Society Through Dance: Mestizo Ritual Performance in the Peruvian Andes.* Chicago Studies in Ethnomusicology. Chicago: Univ. of Chicago Press.

Olsen, Dale A. 1974. "The Function of Naming in the Curing Songs of the Warao Indians of Venezuela." *Anuario/Yearbook for Inter-American Musical Research* 10:88–122.

———. 1975. "Music-Induced Altered States of Consciousness Among Warao Shamans." *Journal of Latin American Lore* 1:19–33.

———. 1980. "Folk Music of South America: A Musical Mosaic." In *Musics of Many Cultures: An Introduction,* edited by E. May, 386–425. Berkeley: Univ. of California Press.

———. 1986–1987. "The Peruvian Folk Harp Tradition: Determinants of Style." *Folk Harp Journal* 53:48–54; 54:41–58; 55:55–59; 56:57–60.

Olsen, Dale A., and Daniel E. Sheehy, eds. 1998. *South America, Mexico, Central America, and the Caribbean.* Vol. 2 of *The Garland Encyclopedia of World Music.* New York: Garland Reference Library of the Humanities, vol. 1193.

Parra, Isabel. 1985. *El libro mayor de Violeta Parra.* Madrid: Ediciones Michay.

Parra, Violeta. 1970. *Décimas: Autobiografía en versos chilenos.* Santiago de Chile: Ediciones Nueva Universidad, Universidad Católica de Chile, Editorial Pomaire.

Ramón y Rivera, Luis Felipe. 1969. *La música folklórica de Venezuela.* Caracas: Monte Avila Editores.

Robertson, Carol E. 1979. "'Pulling the Ancestors': Performance Practice and Praxis in Mapuche Ordering." *Ethnomusicology* 23(3): 395–416.

Roel Pineda, Josafat. 1959. "El Wayno del Cuzco." *Folklore Americano* 6–7: 129–246.

Romero, Raúl, ed. 1993. *Música, danzas y máscaras en los Andes.* Lima: Pontificia Universidad Católica del Perú: Instituto Riva-Agüero.

Rush, Alfred C. 1941. *Death and Burial in Christian Antiquity.* Catholic University of America Studies in Christian Antiquity, no. 1, edited by J. Quasten. Washington, D.C.: Catholic University of America Press.

Schechter, John M. 1983. "*Corona y baile:* Music in the Child's Wake of Ecuador and Hispanic South America, Past and Present." *Revista de Música Latinoamericana/Latin American Music Review* 4(1): 1–80.

———. 1987. "Quechua *Sanjuán* in Northern Highland Ecuador: Harp Music as Structural Metaphor on *Purina*." *Journal of Latin American Lore* 13(1): 27–46.

———. gen. ed. 1999. *Music in Latin American Culture: Regional Traditions.* New York: Schirmer Books.

Seeger, Anthony. 1979. "What Can We Learn When They Sing? Vocal Genres of the Suya Indians of Central Brazil." *Ethnomusicology* 23(3): 373–94.

———. 1987. *Why Suyá Sing: A Musical Anthropology of an Amazonian People.* Cambridge, England: Cambridge Univ. Press.

Slater, Peter Gregg. 1977. *Children in the New England Mind in Death and in Life.* Hamden, Conn.: Archon Books/Shoe String Press.

Stevenson, Robert. 1968. *Music in Aztec and Inca Territory.* Berkeley: Univ. of California Press.

Turino, Thomas. 1983. "The Charango and the *Sirena:* Music, Magic, and the Power of Love." *Revista de Música Latinoamericana/Latin American Music Review* 4(1): 81–119.

———. 1989. "The Coherence of Social Style and Musical Creation Among the Aymara in Southern Peru." *Ethnomusicology* 33(1): 1–30.

———. 1993. *Moving away from Silence: Music of the Peruvian Altiplano and the Experience of Urban Migration.* Chicago: Univ. of Chicago Press.

Valencia Chacón, Américo. 1981. "Los Chiriguanos de Huancané." *Boletín de Lima* 12–14:1–28.

Additional Listening

Afro-Hispanic Music from Western Colombia and Ecuador. 1967. Recorded and edited by Norman E. Whitten, Jr. Folkways FE 4376.

El cancionero noble de Colombia. 1962. Recorded by Joaquín Piñeros Corpas. Bogotá: Ministerio de Educación-Editorial Antares-Fontón. 3 discs, 36 pp. text.

Cantan Garzón y Collazos [Colombia]. n.d. (pre-1970). Industria Electro-Sonora, Medellín, Colombia. Sonolux LP 12-104/IES-1.

Chaskinakuy. 1991. *Music of the Andes: Cosecha.* Produced by Edmond Badoux and Francy Vidal. Cassette. Also recorded at Hoffmann Studios, Occidental, California, 1993. CD. All arrangements are by Chaskinakuy.

Clásicas de la canción paraguaya: Alfredo Rolando Ortiz, arpa. n.d. (pre-1980). Industrias Famoso LDF-1015. Quito, Ecuador.

The Inca Harp: Laments and Dances of the Tawantinsuyu, the Inca Empire [Peru]. 1982. Recorded by Ronald Wright. Lyrichord LLST 7359.

Indian Music of Mexico. 1952, 1962. Recorded by Henrietta Yurchenko. Ethnic Folkways Library FE-4413. 4 pp. notes by Gordon F. Ekholm and Henrietta Yurchenko.

Mountain Music of Peru. 1966. Recorded by John Cohen. Folkways FE 4539.

Mushuc huaira huacamujun: Conjunto indígena "Peguche" [Ecuador]. 1979. IFESA (Industria Fonográfica Ecuatoriana S.A.). Runa Causay. 339-0651. Guayaquil, Ecuador.

Music of the Jívaro of Ecuador. 1972. Recorded and edited by Michael J. Harner. Ethnic Folkways Library FE 4386.

Música andina de Bolivia. 1980. Recorded with commmentary by Max Peter Baumann. Lauro Records LPLI/S-062. 36 pp. booklet.

Música folklórica de Venezuela. n.d. (post-1968). Recorded by Isabel Aretz, Luis Felipe Ramón y Rivera, and Álvaro Fernaud. International Folk Music Council, Anthologie de la Musique Populaire. Ocora OCR 78.

Perou: Julio Benavente Diaz: "Le charango du Cuzco." 1985. Recorded by Rafael Parejo and Regina Baldini. Ocora. Musiques traditionnelles vivantes. Sacem. 558 647.

Pre-Columbian Instruments: Aerophone [Mexico]. 1972. Produced by Lilian Mendelssohn, with Pablo Castellanos. Played by Jorge Daher. Ethnic Folkways Library FE 4177.

Viewing

Ayala, Fernando, and Héctor Olivera, directors. 1972. *Argentinísima I.* In Spanish, without subtitles. Featured performers: Atahualpa Yupanqui, Ariel Ramírez, Los Chalchaleros, Mercedes Sosa, and Astor Piazzolla. Media Home Entertainment, Inc., 510 W. 6th St., Suite 1032, Los Angeles, Calif. 90014.

———. 1976. *El canto cuenta su historia.* In Spanish, without subtitles. Film/video. Featured performers: Cayetano Daglio, Ángel Villoldo, Francisco Canaro, Carlos Gardel, Rosita Quiroga, Ignacio Corsini, Ada Falcón, Agustín Magaldi and Pedro Noda, Marta de los Ríos, Margarita Palacios, Eduardo Falú, Los Cantores de Quilla Huasi, Jorge Oafrune, Amelita Baltar, and Hermanos Abalos. Condor Video (A Heron International Company), c/o Jason Films, 2825 Wilcrest, Suite 670, Houston, Tex. 77042. Aries Cinematográfica, Argentina.

Benson-Gyles, Anna, producer. 1980. *The Incas.* Odyssey Series. Narrated by Tony Kahn. Michael Ambrosino, executive producer. For Odyssey: Marian White, producer; David Berenson, editor. Co-production of British Broadcasting Corporation (BBC) and Public Broadcasting Associates, Inc., Boston, Mass. Incas/Odyssey Series/Box 1000, Boston, Mass. 02118. PBS Video, 1320 Braddock Pl., Alexandria, Va. 22314.

Cohen, John, director. 1979. *Q'eros: The Shape of Survival.* 53 min. 16mm film/video. Color. Berkeley: University of California, Extension Center For Media and Independent Learning, 2000 Center St., 4th floor, Berkeley, Calif. 94704.

———. 1984. *Mountain Music of Peru.* 16mm film/video, 60 min. Color. Berkeley: University of California, Extension Center For Media and Independent Learning, 2000 Center St., 4th floor, Berkeley, Calif. 94704.

Cross, Stephen, director. 1977. *Disappearing World: Umbanda: The Problem Solver.* In English and in Portuguese with English subtitles. Peter Fry, narrator. Brian Moser, series editor. Public Media Video, 5547 N. Ravenswood Ave., Chicago, Ill. 60640-1199; Granada Colour Production, Granada UK.

Dibb, Michael, director. 1985. *What's Cuba Playing At?* (*¿Qué se toca en Cuba?*) 72 min. In Spanish, with subtitles. BBC TV Production, in association with Cuban Television. Center for Cuban Studies, 124 W. 23rd St., New York, N.Y. 10011.

Hernández, Amalia, director. 1989. *Folklórico: Ballet Folklórico de México.* In Spanish, without subtitles. Featured performers: Ballet Folklórico de México. Madera Cinevideo, 525 E. Yosemite Ave., Madera, Calif. 93638.

Rivera, Pedro A., and Susan Zeig, directors. 1989. *Plena Is Work, Plena Is Song.* 16mm film/video. Cinema Guild, Inc.: 1697 Broadway, Suite 506, New York, N.Y. 10019-5904.

Schaeffer, Nancy. 1995. "Directory of Latin American Films and Videos: Music, Dance, Mask, and Ritual." *Revista de Música Latinoamericana/Latin American Music Review* 16(2): 221–41.

Discovering and Documenting a World of Music

Jeff Todd Titon, David B. Reck, and Mark Slobin

*A*ll of us are familiar with the tale (or movie) of Dorothy and her adventures with the Tin Man, the Lion, and the Scarecrow in the fantastic land of Oz. But most of us have forgotten Dorothy's startling discovery once she got back to Kansas: Home was where her heart was, a fascinating world of people, family, neighbors, and friends, and of things that before her adventures she had overlooked. This is a familiar theme in literature the world over. The hero (representing us) travels to faraway places, sees and does fabulous things, meets incredible people, or searches for marvelous treasures. But invariably the rainbow leads home; the pot of gold is buried in one's own backyard; the princess is none other than the girl next door.

Music in Our Own Backyards

*I*n our explorations of the world's musics we—both students and scholars—are fascinated by cultures and peoples greatly separated from us in geography or time, in sound and style, in ways of making and doing music. In a sense, for every one of us there is an Oz. But there is also a music-culture surrounding us, one that we see and hear only partially because it is too close to us, because we take it for granted, as fish do water. Our musical environment is held both within us—in our perceptions and memories—and outside us—by other members of our community, only a fraction of whom we may know. It expands out from us (and contracts into us) in a series of concentric circles that may include family, ethnic groups, regional styles, geographical location, and cultural roots (Western Europe, Africa, Asia, and so on). It is available to us live or mechanically reproduced. It comes to us out of history (the classical masterworks, old-time fiddle tunes, bebop jazz) or from the here and now (the latest hit on the music charts or the avant-garde "new thing"). Our surrounding musical universe seems to us multifaceted and immensely complicated.

This chapter is all about gathering reliable information on contemporary music. We want to encourage you to seek out a nearby musical world,

to observe it in person, to talk with the people involved in it, to document it with recordings and photographs, and to present the information in a project that will contribute to the body of knowledge about contemporary musical activities. If this research project is part of a course, you should check with your instructor for specific directions. What follows is a general guide, based on the experience we and our students have had with similar projects at our colleges and universities.

Selecting a subject for your research is of course the first step in the project. Songs and instrumental music serve a great many purposes and occur in a staggeringly wide variety of contexts, from singing in the shower to the Metropolitan Opera, from the high school marching band to the rock festival, from the lullaby to the television commercial, and from music videos to computer music via the Internet. Whether trivial or profound, it is all meaningful. To help you select a subject, we shall consider a few organizing principles for imposing order on our music-culture: family, generation, avocation, religion, ethnicity, regionalism, nationalism, and commercialization. As you read through the following brief survey you may find some subjects that interest you. Here we focus on North American examples, but if you are using this book elsewhere you should apply these (and perhaps other) organizing principles to examples you think of from your own music-culture. Later we shall give you some specific suggestions.

Family

As is true of all cultures, North Americans first hear music in the context of family life (see Figure 10-1). Much of that music comes from the records on the family CD player, radio, television, or computer. This "canned" music is especially important in developing children's musical taste; people often say they were very strongly influenced by the kind of music they heard before they were old enough to have their own albums or choose the station on the family radio. Yet despite their parents' intentions, youngsters often rebel against parents' taste in music and choose to listen to what people their own age favor. Families also usually provide some live music in the family. Many mothers and grandmothers sing lullabies, for example. These can be important, because in North America, as elsewhere, lullabies not only lull but promise, praise, and teach cultural values. Sometimes lullabies are the only songs in a foreign language that North American children with strong ethnic backgrounds hear, since people (particularly grandparents) often fall back on old, familiar languages for intimate songs.

Another important family context is the automobile, where families learn songs and sing together on weekends and vacations. This is not as surprising as it appears, for the family car has become one of the basic centers of family experience, and it is one of the important places where the family gathers for an extended (some might say forced) period without outside distractions. The family used to have to choose between making their own music in the car or being force-fed by the radio, but today automobile cassette recorders and CD players allow a family to have more control over what they hear when they drive.

Figure 10-1
A sharecropper family sings hymns in front of their home. Hale County, Alabama, 1936.

Walker Evans. Courtesy of the Library of Congress.

In short, most North Americans have an early layer of songs learned in childhood in a family setting. Often they are just songs for entertaining children, with no deep cultural message to impart. What they do teach are the musical tastes and orientation of the particular social group, whether rural Quebecois, California suburban, Illinois heartland, Appalachian mountain, or New York inner-city. Children then work in harmony with (or against) this basic musical background as a part of growing up and finding their individual identity.

Generation

Much North American music making is organized along generational lines. Schools, church classes, scouting groups, children's sidewalk games, college singing groups, and many other musical situations include people of about the same age. Songs learned by these groups may stay with them as they grow older: Imagine the twentieth or fiftieth college class reunion, where the participants remember and sing the songs of their generation.

Yet the amount of generational mixing in North American musical life has grown under the influence of television and recordings. For example, much of the music thought to belong only to the young in the 1960s, such as Beatles' music, appealed to older generations as well. And today's youngsters like their parents' music better than their parents liked that of their own parents. Other styles, such as country fiddling, which not long ago attracted mainly older musicians, have been picked up by young people; in fiddle contests like the one held in Hartford, Connecticut, every year, the age spread of performers now runs from eight to eighty. In ethnic musics too, young people have taken to learning traditional songs from their grandmothers instead of laughing at the old folks' songs as they might have one or two generations ago.

Generational blurring is part of the musical homogenization we see at work in still other areas of our music-culture. For example, there are fewer gender differences regarding music than there used to be. Just as women now take up sports like race-car driving and become professional jockeys, so more women play instruments, such as the drums and saxophone, that used to be largely limited to men. A whole genre that used to be exclusively male—barbershop quartet singing—now has a parallel female style, exhibited by groups such as the Sweet Adelines. One women's bluegrass group call themselves the All Girl Boys, while a new generation of bluegrass stars includes Alison Krauss and Laurie Lewis, both outstanding fiddlers. Later in this chapter we shall see the effect of regional and ethnic blurring.

Avocation

Music as hobby is an important part of North American life. For example, one barbershop quartet program listed the wives of the singers as "Thursday Night Widows"—perhaps one reason for the formation of women's quartets. Many North Americans feel the need for a strong group hobby, and of course some of this impulse is channeled into musical organizations. A local American Legion Post, or an ethnic group such as the Polish Falcons, may have a band; here the music making affirms group solidarity. Fielding a band for the local parade or festival brings the group visibility and pride. Individual members may find performing in a fife-and-drum corps or the Governor's Footguard Band (to use Connecticut examples) a satisfying way to spend leisure time. Black youngsters in high school and college form extracurricular, informal rap groups; sometimes these groups become semiprofessional or even fully professional. Most high schools and colleges can boast a few rock bands and possibly even a jazz group, as well as cocktail pianists, folk-singing guitarists, and chamber music ensembles.

Religion

Religion is one of the better-documented areas of North American musical life. Scholars know about music's role in many religious movements, ranging from the eighteenth-century Moravians through the revival movements of the nineteenth century and the founding of new sects such as the Mormons. Much has been written about the appropriateness of certain types of music making in religious settings, such as organ playing in the Jewish synagogue or the introduction of folk and jazz elements to church services. Scholarly study focuses on the Negro spiritual, while the tent revival preacher, the snake handler, and the old-time churches also receive attention (see Figure 10-2). But the musical activities of contemporary, mainline middle-class churches, synagogues, and mosques offer equal interest, though few people study them. The songs of new, unofficial religious movements, such as small meditation groups based on Christian or oriental religious thinking, also deserve attention. These groups need to encourage

Figure 10-2
Music almost always accompanies formal rites of passage, such as this old-time baptism. Eastern Kentucky, 1990.

Jeff Todd Titon

solidarity and teach their message, but they have no traditional music. Often they change the words of well-known songs as a way of starting, just as Martin Luther changed the words of German drinking songs 450 years ago to create a body of sacred songs we know as Protestant chorales. The new unofficial groups may also work hard on developing an "inner music" of their members, through which the individual believer reaches the desired state of tranquility.

Ethnicity

Ethnicity is the oldest consideration in the study of the North American music-culture in the sense that the United States is usually regarded as a nation of immigrants. It is also one of the newest considerations because of the current interest in the public expression of ethnic identity, a trend that has gathered force since the late 1960s.

Throughout North American musical history, ethnicity has played a major role. Whether in the dialect and songs of the French Acadians in New Brunswick, the heroic *corrido* ballads sung along the Rio Grande by Mexican Americans, the retelling of the story of hard-hearted Barbara Allen by British-American ballad singers, or the singing of a Yiddish lullaby in a Brooklyn tenement, North Americans have built and maintained distinctive ethnic boundaries through music. Music's function as a sign of group solidarity and common ancestry is nowhere clearer than in the variety of songs, dances, and instrumental tunes that characterize the North American ethnic mosaic. Students in the United States whose parents or grandparents stopped public singing of Old World songs on their way to becoming "one-hundred-percent Americans" now become enthusiastic about joining ethnic music groups or studying their group's heritage. Other parents and grandparents, of course, never stopped singing their native songs. North American ethnic music has always involved transcontinental exchange. On the one hand, Greek Americans are influenced by new developments in popular music in Athens, while on the other, Polish-American records find great favor among farmers in far-off mountain villages in Poland. American jazz and country music have spread around the world, from Holland to Russia and Japan. A complicated interplay goes on between black music in the United States and the Caribbean (Figure 10-3). A single song may embody layer upon layer of musical travel. Reggae developed in Jamaica, where it represented a blend of Afro-Caribbean and black U.S. soul music. This already complicated style came to America from England, where pop groups repackaged it and exported it, and the cycle continues: Reggae is now popular in some parts of Africa.

Much of the older ethnic music of North America has changed in ways described in Chapter 5. That is, in our modern world, family- and community-based musics have become markers of ethnic identity and an older way of life. At the same time they are packaged, bought, and sold in the marketplace; this encourages originality and virtuosity, qualities that may not have been very important in the musics' traditional contexts. For example, some twentieth-century fiddle contests encourage showing off in front of the crowd. Some New England contests include young fiddle players who have classical training, or who specialize in the "trick and fancy" category of virtuoso pieces instead of the standard old-time jigs, reels, and waltzes of the Northeast. Official events such as open contests push style in directions that may be unfamiliar to older country performers, for whom fiddling meant a way to pass the time or to earn a night's pay by playing for eight solid hours of dancing. On the other hand, folk festivals in the U.S.

Figure 10-3
One of Boston's Caribbean steel-drum bands performs at a women's prison. 1979.

Jeff Todd Titon

such as the Smithsonian Institution's Folklife Festival seek out traditional singers, musicians, and craftspeople, presenting them whenever possible in traditional contexts.

Regionalism

Regionalism in North America is thought to have declined with the spread of the interstate highway system, chains of fast-food restaurants, and the spread of television, all of which began in the 1950s. But just as ethnic groups never really dissolved into the so-called melting pot, so regional homogenization never really took place in North American life. Regionalism crops up in the names of styles, such as the Chicago blues sound, the Detroit "Motown" soul sound, or even within ethnic styles, as in the distinction between a Chicago and an East Coast polka. The crisp bowing, downbeat accents, and up-tempo performance of a fiddle tune in the Northeast bears little resemblance to the same tune's performance in the Southwest, with its smooth bowing and more relaxed beat. In country music today, the Nashville sound differs from the Texas sound, reflecting earlier differences between country and country-western styles. Likewise, the same hymn tune shows considerable variation even within the same denomination in different parts of the country. One Indiana Primitive Baptist was overheard to comment on the slow, highly decorated tunes of her Primitive Baptist neighbors to the Southeast: "They take ten minutes just to get through 'Amazing Grace!'" There are also local preferences for types of ensembles. The Governor's Footguard Band, formed in Connecticut before the American Revolution, is unlikely to have a counterpart in Kansas. Connecticut's fife-and-drum corps can be found in many good-sized Connecticut towns, whereas the Midwest is the heartland of the marching band.

Like ethnicity, regionalism is coming back into fashion. There are now so many local festivals that books of listings are published. Some locales host mock battles, which are fought again and again for throngs of tourists to appropriate live or recorded music. One highly visible regional music performance is the singing of "My Old Kentucky Home" at the May running of the Kentucky Derby. In a recent year 150 thousand spectators joined in, and millions of television viewers were on hand to link the song and event to the region of its origin.

In summary, even if it sometimes seems the result of shrewd marketing to promote local cultures, regional musical diversity has not yet given way to a homogenized music. North America is still too large and diverse to turn all music into brand names or to have the entire population respond equally to all music, and the search for revival or for novelty continues.

Nationalism

As a breakaway colony that declared its independence and fought a war to preserve it, the United States long ago began seeking ways to establish a national musical identity. As we have seen, the nation developed a distinctive musical profile generated by ethnic and regional stylistic interactions. Popular national sentiment was also evoked by the frequent performance of patriotic songs, a tradition that has declined only in recent decades. Official music plays less of a part in U.S. life now than when John Philip Sousa's band and its imitators played flag-waving tunes on the bandstand for Sunday promenaders, or when schoolchildren knew all the verses of the national anthem. President Jimmy Carter's musical foray into jazz—he sang "Salt Peanuts" with composer and trumpeter Dizzy Gillespie—was a media event. President Bill Clinton's saxophone playing reflects the musical tastes of the Vietnam generation, for whom patriotic music rang hollow.

Perhaps our most obvious repertory of national music consists of Christmas songs such as "Jingle Bells," "Deck the Halls," and "Rudolph the Red-Nosed Reindeer." During the holiday season it is almost impossible to escape them. The curmudgeon who shoos away carolers from his front yard is said to lack the Christmas spirit, and he soon gains a neighborhood reputation as a Scrooge.

Commercial Music

Much of the music in North American culture is supplied by paid professionals. It is remarkable that this complex culture continues to carry on the musical situations in non- or preindustrial societies, described earlier. Though some genres, such as the funeral lament, have largely disappeared in the United States, rituals like weddings and initiations (bar mitzvahs, debutante parties, senior proms) that mark a change of life still demand solemnization by music. A wedding may take place in a park with a Good Humor truck, balloons, and jeans instead of in a formal church setting, yet music remains indispensable even if it consists of pop tunes instead of an official wedding march. Elegant yacht clubs tend to schedule dances during full-moon evenings, continuing a practice of certain ancient cultures.

A great deal of the commercial music North Americans come into daily contact with may be described as "disembodied"—that is, the listener does not feel the physical presence of the performer and many times cannot even see the original musical situation (as in Figure 10-4). Some of this music can be partially controlled by the listener who selects recordings from his or her collection to fit a mood. Choices are made from an entirely private domain of recordings over which the person has complete control; he or she can select what to hear and for how long. Although the listener can imagine the original musical situation—concert or recording studio—there is no possibility of interaction with the performers, and the music is the same each time it is heard.

One of the most significant recent developments in commercial music is the rise of the format called mp3 and the distribution of music in this format over the Internet. Musicians who think that the music industry takes too much of the profits from album sales have been able to get their recordings directly to consumers via the World Wide Web. Consumers flock to Web sites where they can download music, often for free.

Figure 10-4
Dancing to records on a juke-box. West Virginia, 1942.

John Collier: Courtesy of the Library of Congress.

"What instrument do you play?" begins an old joke. The reply: "Just the stereo." Ethnomusicologists pay attention to how people use music in their daily lives. Many young people today have become active consumers who not only select music but engineer and package it for themselves and their friends. The prototypes for this kind of musical activity were the "Deadheads" who recorded and traded tapes of live Grateful Dead concerts. Long before the Deadheads, jazz buffs were recording after-hours jam sessions and trading the results. Today, the person who downloads commercial music from the Internet, edits it, and burns custom CDs plays quite an active role in choosing music to suit a lifestyle. Music making on the computer does not require singing or playing a traditional instrument; instead, the computer becomes both the instrument and the recording studio.

At the opposite end of the spectrum from disembodied commercial music is public background music. Unlike listening to music in one's own room on a computer, there is no logical connection between buying groceries and hearing piped music in a supermarket. In offices and factories, the employer may choose to have background music that is manufactured and programmed to increase worker productivity. This of course represents a particularly powerful type of unrequested music, and there is a split among the captive audience as to whether they appreciate it. Some do not even notice it.

This brief survey should help you think about a subject for your project: a nearby musical world that you're interested in, have access to, and can gather information about.

Your aim in discovering and documenting a world of music is a *musical ethnography*—a written representation, description and interpretation of some aspect of a music-culture, organized from the standpoint of a particular topic. Your writing may be accompanied by photographs, tape recordings, and even videotapes that you make while documenting the music-culture. A major goal in doing musical ethnography is to understand a music-culture or some part of it from a native's or insider's point of view. What does that point of view encompass? Recall how in Chapter 1 we divided a music-culture into four components: ideas, activities, repertories, and material culture. Approaching a music-culture for the first time, you may feel overwhelmed, but if you use Table 1-1 (p. 20) to organize your thinking about what you see and hear, you will be able to see how you might go about gathering information on specific aspects of it.

The music in the repertory can be recorded for later study and analysis. Much of social organization and material culture can be observed. By listening to musicians talk with each other, and by talking to them, you can begin to understand their ideas about music; through interviews you can learn more about those ideas, the repertory, musical activities, and material culture. (After all, conversations and interviews formed the basis for the musicians' life histories in this book.) But discovering and documenting a world of music is not like examining an amoeba under a microscope. People will differ in how they behave, what they believe, and what they say to you. Different people will sing "the same tune" differently. Under these conditions, representing and describing a music-culture, even a single aspect of it, is a complex and subtle undertaking.

Doing Music Ethnography

Selecting a Subject:
Some Practical Suggestions

It almost goes without saying that your field project requires you to collect, understand, and organize information about music in order to present it. It differs from the usual school research paper in that it focuses on a musical situation that you seek out directly from people rather than from books in a library. In ethnomusicology, as in anthropology and folklore, this in-person witnessing, observing, questioning, tape recording, photographing, and in some cases performing is called *fieldwork:* work "in the field" rather than the laboratory or library. This is not to say that library research is useless or should be avoided. You might find background information on your topic in the library, and you should not overlook the opportunity to do so. But the thrust of your project takes you into the field, where you will obtain your most valuable and original information.

Collecting, understanding, and organizing information about music are, of course, interrelated. You will begin with certain insights about the information you collect. As you organize it, you will gain new insights as you move toward an understanding of the musical situation from the web of information you have gathered. After you organize it, you will be able to describe it and move toward an interpretation of it.

You can approach the choice of a research subject in different ways. First, you might try to chart the music you hear daily:

1. Keep a log or journal of all the music you hear over three or four days or a week. Note the context, style, and purpose of the music. Calculate how much of your day is spent with music of some sort.

2. Record, videotape, or simply describe in words several television commercials that employ music. Note the style of the music and the image it attempts to project. How is the music integrated into the message of the advertisement? Is it successful? Offensive? Both?

3. Map the uses of music in various movies or television shows as you watch them. For contrast, select a daytime serial and a crime-fighting show, or a situation comedy and a popular dramatic series, for example.

4. Survey the uses of background music in local stores. Interview sales-people, managers, owners, customers (always obtaining their permission). See what they say about music and sales.

5. Survey the contents of jukeboxes in bars and restaurants. Interview the manager about the content of the jukebox and the preferences of his or her clientele.

A second approach is to examine the music in your own background. Explore your memory of songs and music. Note how your religious and ethnic heritage influenced the music you heard and your current musical interests. How has your musical taste changed as you have grown older? Survey the contents of your CD collection or your preferences in listening to music on the radio, television, or the Internet. The same questions can be asked of your brothers and sisters, your parents, or other members of your family.

A third approach is to explore music in your community—your school community or your hometown. Here you can interview people, listen to musical performances, possibly take part in them yourself, and gather quite a lot of information. Here are several possible subject headings:

Ethnic groups
Piano teachers
Private instrumental instruction (music stores, private lessons in the home)
Choir directors
Church organists, pianists, and so on
School music (elementary, junior high, high school)
Music stores
Musical instrument makers
Background music in public places
The club scene (bars, coffeehouses, restaurants, clubs)
Musical organizations (community choral groups, bands, barbershop quartets, and so forth)
Part-time (weekend) musicians

Professional or semiprofessional bands (rock, pop, jazz, rhythm and blues, country, gospel, and so forth)

Chamber music groups

Parades and music

Disc jockeys

Symphony orchestras

A fourth approach narrows the subject and concentrates on an individual musician's life, opinions, and music. Often we focus our attention on the musical superstars, but in the process we forget the many fine and sensitive musicians, many of them amateurs, who live in our communities. Senior citizens, teachers, owners of record or music stores, or tradespeople like the local barber, school custodian, or factory worker have sometimes had rich musical experiences as professional or part-time musicians. To search out such people is not always easy. Try the musicians' union, ethnic organizations, word of mouth, school or college music teachers, radio station disc jockeys, the clergy, club owners, newspaper columnists and feature story writers, or even local police stations and fire departments. Musicians can be approached directly at fairs, contests, festivals, concerts, and dances. Many colleges and universities have foreign student associations that include amateur musicians, and they can tell you about others in the area. Ethnic specialty restaurants and grocery stores are another resource.

The musical world that surrounds you is so diverse that you may feel swamped, unable to focus your energy. But when it finally comes down to deciding on a subject for your project, two guiding principles will help you out: Choose something you are interested in, and choose something you have access to. It will be hard to succeed if you are not curious about the music you examine, and you will have to be close to it to look at it carefully.

Collecting Information

Once you have chosen a subject, your next move is to immerse yourself in the musical situation, consider what aspects of it interest you, and select a topic. Then you need to plan how to collect information—what questions to ask when you talk to the musicians or others involved, what performances to record, and so forth. Almost always you will need time and the flexibility to revise your plans as you collect the information you need. Most people will be happy to tell you about their involvement with music as long as you show them you really are interested.

Gaining Entry

Musical activities usually have a public (performance) side and a private (rehearsal) side. The performance is the tip of the iceberg; you will want to understand what lies beneath, and that is best learned by talking to the people involved. If you must approach a stranger, you may want to arrange an introduction, either by a mutual friend or by a person in authority. Protocol counts in some cases. If, for example, you want to talk with musicians in an ethnic organization, it is wise to approach the president of the organization and seek his or her advice first. This not only allows you to get good information but also to share your plans with the president, who needs to know what is going on in the group. In other situations it is best to let the people in authority know what you intend to do, and why, but to avoid having them introduce you, particularly if their authority is legal only and they do not belong to the same ethnic group as the people whose music you will be studying.

The first contact is especially important because the way you present yourself establishes your identity and role. That is one reason why you must take the time to be honest with yourself and others about your interest in their music and the purpose of your project. If you are a college student, you may find yourself being assigned the role of the expert. But this is a role to avoid. Tell the people who give you information that *they* are the experts and that you are the student who wants to learn from them—that otherwise you would not seek their help. Let them know that you hope they will be willing to let you talk with them, observe them, and, if appropriate, participate in the music.

Selecting a Topic

Usually your subject takes in several music situations, and you will find yourself having to choose among them so as not to undertake a larger project than you can accomplish. If, for example, you want to learn about Irish-American music in your community, you may find that there is so much going on that a survey of it all will be superficial. It will be easier to discover a topic if you decide to concentrate on one aspect of it, perhaps the musical tradition of one family, or the musical scene in a particular club. Remember once again to choose something you are interested in and have access to.

After you have narrowed your subject, you face the next step, which is one of the most difficult: selecting a topic. A topic is more than just a subject. It is a subject viewed from a particular angle, from a certain perspective, and with a limited goal in mind. For example, "the Jewish cantor" is a subject, something to investigate. "Musical training of Jewish cantors in New York City" is a topic. The cantor is viewed from a special perspective: his training. You want to understand what the training is and what the results are. Another example of a subject is "the Outlaws, a local country music band." A topic that involves the band might be "gender and gender roles in the music of the Outlaws, a local country music band." Here the focus is on the band members' attitudes, interactions, lyrics, social scene, and so forth. By themselves, subjects cover too much ground. Topics focus your attention on specific questions that will help you organize the information you collect.

The process of refining a topic is gradual and involves a lot of thought. To begin, go back to Chapter 1 and use the music-culture model to select aspects of your subject that you are interested in. Do you want to focus on conceptions of music, activities involving music, repertories, or material culture? Of course, these aspects are interrelated, and it will be difficult to ignore any of them completely; nevertheless, concentrating most of your attention on one of them will help you select a topic you can manage. It will also give you some initial ideas to think about as you gather your information. While doing field research you will find that some areas of your topic yield better information than others. As you assess the results of your research-in-progress you should be able to refine and refocus your topic to take advantage of the good information you have gathered, while you may have to deemphasize, or possibly even discard, other aspects of your topic that you have found difficult to research.

Your instructor can help you move from a subject to a topic. Many teachers ask students to begin their field research early in the term and to make a short, written proposal in which they describe their subject and their topic. Instructor feedback at this point can save you a lot of time later. For example, many students initially choose topics that are too broad, given the limitations on their time and the instructor's guidelines for the paper's length. Another common difficulty is a topic that is too vague. You can sharpen up your topic if you formulate it as a question or series of questions. Interpretation—figuring out what your documentation means—always goes in the direction of answering questions about your topic. If you have decided to focus on one band's repertory, a topic like "the repertory of the Accidental Tourists, a campus rock band" should be made more precise with questions like "How does the band choose, learn, arrange, and maintain songs for their repertory?" A series of questions like this can help you focus your observations and interviews. In this case you would want to ask the band members these questions and to attend some rehearsals and see how the band chooses, learns, and arranges their songs. Formulating a topic as a series of questions will help you organize your project around those questions. When it comes time to write your project up, the answers to those questions, and how the answers are related, will lead you to your overall interpretation of the topic and the main point you want to make.

In other words, gathering information is not simply a matter of recording it as a sponge soaks up water. You will want to be selective in what you document, because after documentation you will need to interpret your material. Say that your subject is music on the school radio station, and your topic has to do with the radio station's attitude toward women's rap groups. You decide to interview some of the people who work at the station, and in the interviews you try to figure out a way to approach your topic. One deejay might play a lot of women's music on a particular show, and you might find out something about this deejay's attitude toward women's rap groups by asking. As you gather information, you try to estimate how well theory is put into practice—the station people say they are in favor of women's music and women's rap groups, but you find that overall they don't play very much of it. You wonder why. Do the station people think the audience does not want to hear it? What does the audience want to hear, how do they know, and should they play what the audience wants to hear, anyway?

Questions like these will arise during the course of your research. They can help you to select the kind of documentation that you will do—whether, for example, to survey the recordings in the radio station's library—and help you to focus your interpretation so that by the end of your project you will have some answers to your questions. You will not merely be gathering material but focusing that material on a topic; the heart of your project is your own interpretation of the material in light of the topic you have chosen.

Library and Internet Research

Depending on the topic you have selected, you may want to visit the library and the Internet at this point to see if anyone has published research on your topic. Try your library's collection first. The electronic card catalog will be helpful; look under such headings as "music," "folk music," "popular music," and whatever categories and keywords are closely related to your subject. It might be useful to spend a couple of hours in the library stacks, looking at books on the shelves and opening any on your subject, for it is almost impossible to know where to look for everything in the card catalog alone.

If your library subscribes to *Ethnomusicology,* the journal of the Society for Ethnomusicology, you will find in each of its three yearly issues an invaluable guide to published research in the "Current Bibliography, Discography and Filmography" section. The most recent years' entries are available on the Society for Ethnomusicology's Web site which at this writing was located at http://www.indiana.edu/~ethmusic/. Another useful resource is *Ethnomusicology On Line,* located at http://research.umbc.edu/efhm/eol.html.

The American Folklife Center, at the Library of Congress, and the Smithsonian Institution's Center for Folklife and Heritage, both of which have extensive collections of recorded sound, can be accessed on the Internet via the following addresses:

http://lcweb.loc.gov/folklife/
http://www.folklife.si.edu/

You may find some of the following additional periodicals helpful:

American Music
Asian Music
Music Educators' Journal
Black Music Research Journal
The Black Perspective in Music
Bluegrass Unlimited
Foxfire
Frets
Journal of American Folklore
Journal of Jazz Studies

Journal of Popular Culture
Journal of Popular Music and Society
Latin American Music Review
Living Blues
The Old-Time Herald
Popular Music
Southern Exposure
Southern Folklore Quarterly
Stereo Review
Western Folklore Journal of Country Music
World of Music
Yearbook of the International Council for Traditional Music

Look in the reference section of your library or on the Internet for such bibliographies as the *Music Index* and *RILM,* as well as specialized bibliographies and reference works. There may also be discographies of recordings in music in the area you are researching. For example, Richard Spottswood's *Ethnic Music on Records: A Discography of Ethnic Recordings Produced in the United States, 1893 to 1942* is a five-volume work that lists 78-rpm recordings made during that period (Spottswood 1990). If your research topic involves a U.S. ethnic music, then this could be a valuable resource for you. The bibliographies will point you toward books and articles on your subject. The reference librarian can help you find these. Many of these music-related bibliographies and discographies are now available electronically. Some are on the Internet and others are available on CD-ROM.

The Internet has become a vast resource for information about music. Try searching the Internet for keywords that surround your topic. You will probably find that you have to refine your search greatly in order to make it efficient. You should also realize that some of the information you find on people's Web sites, such as their opinions about music, does not carry the authority of a scholarly book. Nevertheless some of these specialized Web sites offer a good deal of useful information that you may not be able to find in books.

The Internet is particularly good in gathering groups of people together to discuss a subject of common interest and share insights. For example, there are numerous bluegrass Web sites that reflect how bluegrass fans think and talk about their music. A bluegrass list, or discussion group, Bluegrass-L, is open to subscribers and might even be a good place to do research. Other interest groups involving music abound on the Internet. Look in the newsgroups listed under Rec.Music. Several discussion lists focus on musics in India, for example; there is an Arab music list, and so forth. Of course, the Internet also has a great deal of music, now available in mp3 and other audio formats, as well as in streaming audio and video.

Another good reason for visiting the library early in your project is that you may find a reference to a promising article or book that you will need to request on interlibrary loan. But avoid the temptation to read everything that looks as if it might somehow be relevant. The Internet can also take up a lot more time than it should. Remember that you will gather most of your information directly by observing a music-culture in action and by speaking with people who participate in the music-culture. Library and Internet research merely provides background information, and sometimes it cannot even do that—your subject may not have had attention in print, or the little that has been written may not be useful. But if research on your topic has been published, you will be able to undertake a better project if you are familiar with this research. Further, the people whose music you are studying often can suggest good books and articles for you to read, saving you time in your search.

Participation and Observation

Doing research in the field requires a basic plan of action. Which people should you talk with? Which performances should you witness? Should you go to rehearsals? What about a visit to a recording studio? If you are studying a music teacher, should you watch a private lesson? Should the teacher teach you? Will you take photographs? Videotape? What kind of recording equipment can you get? Who will pay for it? You have probably been thinking about these and many similar questions. One more that you should pay attention to at this time regards your personal relationship to the people whose music you will study. Should you act as an observer, as a detached, objective reporter? Or should you, in addition to observing, also participate in the musical activity if you can?

Participating as well as observing can be useful (and quite enjoyable). You hope to learn the music from the inside. Rather than hanging around the edges of the action, depending on others to explain all the rules, you will come to know some of the musical belief system intuitively.

But participating has its drawbacks. The problem with being a participant-observer is that you sometimes know too much. It is like not knowing the forest for the trees: The closer you are to a situation, the less of an overall view you have, and in order to address your project to an outside reader, you will need to imagine yourself an outsider, too. We tend to filter out the regularities of our lives. If every time we met a stranger we had to stop and think about whether our culture says we should shake hands, rub noses, or bow, we would be in constant panic; if we had to think hard whether *red* means stop or go, driving would be impossible. This filtering process means that we take the most basic aspects of a situation for granted. So if you are participating as well as observing, you must make a special effort to be an outsider and take nothing for granted. This dual perspective, the view of the participant-observer, is not difficult to maintain while you are *learning* how to participate in the musical situation. In fact, when you are learning, the dual perspective is forced on you. The trouble is that after you have learned, you can forget what it was like to be an outside observer. Therefore it is very important to keep a record of your changing perspective as you move from outsider to participant. This record should be written in your field notes or spoken into your tape recorder as your perspective changes.

In fact, you may already be a full participant in the music-culture you intend to study. Writing a musical ethnography about a music-culture in which you have been involved for some time may seem quite appealing. Although this kind of research appears easy, it is not. Your knowledge usually is too specialized for general readers. Further, the issues that matter to you as a member of the music-culture may not interest the general reader. You may feel that because of the depth of your knowledge, you do not need to interview any other members of the music-culture, but this is not so. Other participants' perspectives will be different from yours, and equally important. You may find, also, that in writing about a music-culture in which you are a full participant, you are anxious to express a particular point of view as if it is a generally accepted truth rather than a bias coming from inside the music-culture. For example, if you are writing about a chamber music group in which you are participating, your feeling that classical music is under siege might turn the project into a polemic rather than a research paper.

What if you work as an observer only and forego participation? There are some advantages to doing so. It saves time. You can put all your energy into watching and trying to understand how what people tell you is going on matches what you can actually see and hear going on. You can follow both sides of "what I say" and "what I do" more easily when you are merely observing as opposed to participating. On the other hand, you do not achieve objectivity by keeping yourself out of the action. Your very presence as an observer alters the musical situation, particularly if you are photographing or tape-recording. In many situations you will actually cause *less* interference if you participate rather than intrude as a neutral and unresponsive observer.

Ethics

Doing fieldwork involves important ethical considerations, a right-and-wrong aspect. Most colleges and universities have a policy designed to prevent people from being harmed by research. If your research project is part of a course, be sure to discuss the ethics of the project with your teacher before you begin and, if things change, as you proceed. Whether your project is part of a course or not, think carefully about the impact of what you propose to do. *Always* ask permission. Understand that people have legal rights to privacy and to how they look, what they say, and what they sing, even after you have recorded it. Be honest with yourself and with the people you study about your interest in their music and the purposes of your project. Tell them right from the start that you are interested in researching and documenting their music. If you like their music, say so. If the project is something for you to learn from, say so. Explain what will happen to the project after you finish it. Is it all right with them if you keep the photographs and tapes you make? Would they like a copy of the project? (If so, make one at your expense.) Is it all right if the project is deposited in the college or university archive? Most archives have a form that the people (yourself included) will sign, indicating that you are donating the project to the archive and that it will be used only for research purposes. If this project is not merely a contribution to knowledge but also to your career (as a student or otherwise), admit it and realize that you have a stake in its outcome. Ask the people whose music you are studying why they are cooperating with you and what they hope to achieve from the project, and bear that in mind throughout. *Never* observe, interview, make recordings, or take photographs without their knowledge and permission.

Today many ethnomusicologists believe that simply going into a musical situation and documenting it is not enough. The fieldworker must give back something to the people who have been generous with their thoughts, music, and time. In some cultures, people expect money and should be paid. Fieldworkers sometimes act not simply as reporters, or analysts, but also as cultural and musical advocates, doing whatever they can to help the music they are studying to flourish. Some excerpts from a brochure describing the now-defunct Folk Arts Program of the National Endowment for the Arts illustrate the advocacy viewpoint:

> We define our responsibility as the encouragement of those community or family-based arts that have endured through several generations and that carry with them a sense of community aesthetic. . . . We attempt to help smooth the flow of cultural experience, so that all peoples can move confidently into their own futures, secure in the knowledge of the elegance and individuality of their own cultural pasts.

Some ethnomusicologists in the United States work for arts councils, humanities councils, and other government agencies in public sector jobs where they are expected to identify, document, and present family and community-based arts to the public. Many taxpayers believe that if the government supports the fine arts, it should also support folk and ethnic arts. In fact, most European governments do more than the United States and Canada to preserve and promote their folk and ethnic music. Ethnomusicologists hear a similar kind of commercial popular music throughout the world, and many conclude that local musics—of which there are a great variety—are endangered. It is to humankind's advantage to have many different kinds of music, they believe. For that reason, they think advocacy and support are necessary in the face of all the forces that would make music sound alike the world over. This argument may at first seem remote to your project, but not when you think about your own involvement with the people and music you are studying.

Field Equipment: Notebook, Recorder, Camera

The perfect fieldworker has all-seeing eyes, all-hearing ears, and total recall. Because none of us is so well equipped, you must rely on written notes, recordings, and photographs that you yourself make in the field. These documents serve two purposes: They enable you to reexamine at leisure your field experiences when you write up your project, and they may be included in the final form your project takes because they are accurate records of performances, interviews, and observations. On the other hand, field equipment presents certain difficulties: It costs money, you need to know how to work it properly, and you may have to resist the temptation to spend much of your time fiddling with your equipment when you should be watching, thinking, and listening instead.

Fifty years ago, fieldworkers relied primarily on note taking, and today it is still indispensable. No matter how sophisticated your equipment is, you should carry a small pocket notebook. It will be useful for writing down names and addresses, directions, observations, and thoughts while in the field. In the days before sound recording, music was taken by dictation in notebooks. While this is still possible, it is not advisable except when performances are very brief and you have the required dictation skills. Dictating a song puts the performer in an unnatural context and changes the performance. However, notebooks are especially useful for preserving information learned in interviews, particularly if a tape recorder is unavailable or awkward in the interview situation. In addition, you should try to write down your detailed impressions of the overall field situation: your plans, questions, any difficulties you meet with; as complete a description as possible of the musical situation itself, including the setting, the performers, the audience, and the musical event from start to finish; and your reactions and responses to the field experience. Your field notebook becomes a journal (and in some instances also a diary) that you address *to yourself* for use when you write up your project. As such, it is useful to write in it daily.

Most university music departments and many university libraries now loan inexpensive portable cassette tape recorders to students for use in field projects. Whether you use a tape recorder, and if so what type it is (microcassette, portable cassette, mini-disc, and so forth), largely depends on the nature of your project and your instructor's expectations. Although they may be adequate for some interview situations, microcassette recorders do not record music well enough for documentation purposes. The inexpensive, portable, full-sized cassette tape recorders are best suited to recording speech (interviews, for example). Although they come with built-in microphones, the sound quality can be improved dramatically if you use an inexpensive external microphone plugged into the recorder's microphone input jack. So equipped, a portable cassette tape recorder may be adequate for recording music. Of course you need to be thoroughly familiar with its operation—*before* you go into the field—in order to make accurate recordings. But the portable cassette recorder is mechanically simple, and anyone can learn to operate it in just a few minutes. Digital mini-disc recorders are more expensive but make higher quality recordings. Digital audiotape (DAT) recorders are even more expensive and the sound is better yet, but these lie beyond the reach of most students. One thing to remember about cassette and DAT tape is that it does not age well. The useful life of a cassette tape may be as short as ten years, while a DAT or videotape may not last longer than five, depending on storage conditions. Transferred to CD or DVD format, a recording will have a much longer archival life.

The best way for beginners to improve the sound of a recording is to place the microphone in a good spot. If the sound is soft or moderate and it comes from a small area (a solo singer, a lesson on a musical instrument, or an interview, for example), place the microphone in close and equidistantly from the sources of the sounds. If the sound is loud and widely spread out (a rock band or a symphony orchestra, for example), search out "the best seat in the house" and place or hold the microphone there. Make a practice recording for a few seconds and play it back immediately to check microphone placement and to make certain the equipment is working properly. Take along spare batteries and blank tapes (see Figure 10-5).

If properly used, even the simplest cameras take adequate pictures of musical performances. A picture may not be worth a thousand words, but it goes a long way toward capturing the human impact of a musical event. An instant-picture camera is especially useful because it allows you to see the

Figure 10-5
A chief checks the quality of a recording of his musicians. Kasena-Nankani Traditional Area, Ghana.

James T. Koetting

photograph immediately and correct mistakes (such as standing too far from the action) at once. A close-up lens placed in front of the regular lens will allow you to fill up the whole picture with a musical instrument. Instant pictures have another advantage: You can give them (well, not all of them) to the people you photograph.

Using a camcorder to document a musical event offers the advantage of sound combined with a moving picture. It may be possible to focus selectively on certain aspects of the musical event, such as dancers or particular musicians, so that they can be seen as well as heard in action. Videotape footage accompanying your project should be edited down to a manageable size, and it should reveal those aspects of the music-culture that are related directly to your topic. Video formats are changing rapidly, while the quality available at a particular price point keeps improving.

Americans are in love with technology, even technology to get away from technology (backpacking equipment, for example). If you already know a lot about recording and photography, and you own or can borrow high-quality equipment, by all means use it. Some of the photographs in this book and the accompanying recordings were made by the authors using professional equipment; after all, fieldwork is a part of our profession. But the more sophisticated our equipment is, the more difficult it is to use it to its full potential. Consider the true story of a photographer who went to a rock music festival and brought only his pocket camera. In the photographer's pit in front of the stage, he had maneuvered himself into the best position and was standing there taking pictures when a professional nudged him, saying, "Get out of here with that little toy!" The pro stood there with cameras hanging from his neck and shoulders, covering his body like baby opossums. "Well," said the amateur, yielding his position with a smile, "I guess if you need all of that equipment, you need to stand in the right spot, too!"

Interviewing

Interviews with people, called consultants, whose music you are studying can help you get basic information and feedback on your own ideas. Be careful not to put words in your consultants' mouths and impose your ideas. The first step in understanding a world of music is to understand it as much as possible in your consultants' own terms. Later you can bring your own perspective to bear on the musical situation. Remember that much of their knowledge is intuitive; you will have to draw it out by asking questions.

Come into the interview with a list of questions, but be prepared to let the talk flow in the direction your consultant takes it. In his 1957 preface to *Primitive Man as Philosopher* Paul Radin distinguished between two procedures for obtaining information: question-and-answer and "letting the native philosopher expound his ideas with as few interruptions as possible" ([1927] 1957). Your consultants may not be philosophers, but they should be given the chance to say what they mean. Some people are by nature talkative, but others need to be put at ease. Let the person know in advance what sorts of questions you will be asking, what kind of information you need, and why. Often you will get important information in casual conversations rather than formal interviews; be ready to write down the information in your field notebook. Some people are by nature silent and guarded; despite your best intentions, they will not really open up to you. If you encounter that sort of person, respect his or her wishes and make the interview brief.

Beginning fieldworkers commonly make two mistakes when doing interviews. First, they worry too much about the tape recorder, and their nervousness can carry over to the person they interview. But if you have already gotten the person's consent to be interviewed, it should not be hard to get permission to tape the interview. One fieldworker always carries her tape recorder and camera so they are visible from the moment she enters the door. Then she nonchalantly sets the tape recorder down in a prominent spot and ignores it, letting the person being interviewed understand that the tape recorder is a natural and normal part of the interview. Still ignoring the recorder, she starts off with the small talk that usually begins such a visit. Eventually the other person says something like, "Oh, I see you're going to tape-record this." "Sure," she says steadily. "I brought along this tape recorder just to make sure I get down everything you say. I can always edit out any mistakes, and you can always change your mind. This is just to help me understand you better the first time." She says that once they have agreed to be interviewed, nobody has ever refused her tape recorder. But she adds that if anyone told her to keep the recorder shut off, she would certainly do so.

A second problem is that beginning fieldworkers often ask leading questions. A leading question is one that suggests or implies (that is, it leads or points to) one particular answer. Leading questions make the information obtained unreliable. In other words, it is not clear whether the person being interviewed is expressing his or her own thoughts or just being agreeable and giving the answer the consultant thinks the interviewer wants. In addition, leading questions usually result in short, uninteresting answers. Study this first dialogue to see how *not* to interview:

Fieldworker 1:	Did you get your first flute when you were a girl?
Consultant:	Yeah.
Fieldworker 1:	What was the name of your teacher?
Consultant:	Ah, I studied with Janice Sullivan.
Fieldworker 1:	When was that?
Consultant:	In college.
Fieldworker 1:	I'll bet you hated the flute when you first started. I can remember hating my first piano lessons.
Consultant:	Yeah.

The trouble here is that the consultant gives the kinds of answers she thinks are expected of her. She is not really telling the fieldworker what she thinks. She is not even giving the conversation much thought. The fieldworker has asked the wrong kind of questions. Now look what happens when another fieldworker questions the same person.

Fieldworker 2:   Can you remember when you got your first flute?

Consultant: Yeah.

Fieldworker 2:   Could you tell me about it?

Consultant: Sure. My first flute—well, I don't know if this counts, but I fell in love with the flute when I was in grade school, and I remember going down to a music store and trying one out while my father looked on, but I couldn't make a sound, you know!

Fieldworker 2:   Sure.

Consultant: So I was really disappointed, but then I remember learning to play the recorder in, I think it was third grade, and I really loved that, but I didn't stick with it. Then in college I said to myself, I'm going to take music lessons and I'm going to learn the flute.

Fieldworker 2:   Tell me about that.

Consultant: Well, I had this great teacher, Janice Sullivan, and first she taught me how to get a sound out of it. I was really frustrated at first, but after a while I got the hang of it, and she would always tell me to think of the beautiful sounds I knew a flute could make. I used to think a flute could make a sound like water, like the wind. Well, not exactly, but sort of. And then Mrs. Sullivan let me borrow a tape of *shakuhachi* music—you know, the Japanese flute?—and I *heard* different kinds of water, different kinds of wind! I knew then that I would play the flute for the rest of my life.

Compare the two fieldworkers' questions: "Did you get your first flute when you were a girl?" is a leading question because it leads to the answer, "Yes, I got my first flute when I was a girl." What is more, fieldworker 1 implies that most people get their first flutes when they are girls, so the consultant probably thinks she should answer yes. By contrast, the question of fieldworker 2—"Can you remember when you got your first flute?"—is open-ended and invites reflection, perhaps a story. When the consultant says "Yeah," fieldworker 2 asks for a story and gets a much better—and different—answer than fieldworker 1. Go over the rest of the first interview, see how fieldworker 1 injects her opinions into the dialogue ("I'll bet you hated the flute when you first started") and fails to draw out the consultant's real feelings about her lessons, whereas fieldworker 2 establishes better rapport, is a better listener, asks nondirective questions, and gets much fuller and truer answers.

If your project concentrates on a single consultant, you may want to obtain his or her life story (Titon 1980). For this purpose you truly need a tape recorder. Because the way your consultants view their lives can be as important as the factual information they give, you should try to get the life story in their own words as much as possible. This means refraining from questions that direct the story as you think it should go. What matters is how your consultant wants it to go. Come back later, in another interview, to draw out specific facts and fill in gaps by direct questioning. In the initial interview, begin by explaining that you would like your informant to tell you about his or her life as a musician (or whatever is appropriate—composer, disc jockey, and so forth) from the beginning until now. Once begun, allow plenty of time for silences to let your informant gather thoughts. If he or she looks up at you expectantly, nod your head in agreement and repeat what has just been said to show that you understand it. Resist any impulse to ask direct questions. Write them down instead, and say you will come back to ask questions later—for now you want the story to continue.

Not everyone will be able to tell you his or her musical autobiography, but if you are fortunate enough to find someone who can, it may turn out to be the most important part of your project. On the other hand, if your consultant's life story is a necessary part of your project, but you cannot obtain it except by direct and frequent questioning, you should certainly ask the questions. If you get good answers, the result will be your consultant's life *history*, a collaborative biography rather than an autobiography.

Interviews, then, with the people whose music you are studying (and perhaps with their audience) help you obtain factual information and test your ideas. They also help you begin to comprehend the musical situation from their point of view: their beliefs, their intentions, their training, their feelings, their evaluations of musical performance, and their understanding of what they are doing—what it is all about. Ultimately, because this is your project, you will combine their ideas with your own interpretations when you write the project up using the information you have collected.

Other Means of Collecting Information

Another technique, often used in social science research, is the questionnaire. Although its role in studying music is limited, a questionnaire can help you map out the general nature of a situation before moving into a specific sub-area to focus on. For example, to begin exploring the meaning of pop songs in students' lives, you may want to circulate a questionnaire to uncover the eventual sample you will study intensively. Questionnaires are most at home in studies of musical attitudes. To find out how shoppers react to supermarket background music, it would be hard to set up interviews but easy, if the store manager agrees, to distribute a questionnaire.

Aside from questionnaires, which seek out information, you might find information already gathered: autobiographical manuscripts, diaries, and tape recordings made by consultants for themselves. Clubs, fraternities, schools, churches, and various organizations often store away old materials that shed light on musical activities. At concerts, the programs handed out may be rich in information, ranging from description of the music to the type of advertisers that support the concerts. Membership lists and patrons' lists may be included as well.

Newspapers are enormously helpful. Hardly a day passes without journalistic commentary on the musical environment, in news stories, reviews, and advertisements. Feature stories provide up-to-date information on current concerts, trends, and musical attitudes, both local and national, while advertising can furnish insights into the ideals of the U.S. musical world projected by the media, ideals that influence most of us one way or another. For example, an ad for an expensive home entertainment system designed to bring music into every home offers a direct connection between musical style and the rooms of the house: "101 Strings in the greenhouse, Bach in the bedroom, Frank Sinatra in the living room, Gershwin in the den, the Boston Pops on the patio, the Rolling Stones outside by the pool." What better brief description of middle-aged, middle-class musical taste could be found?

Finishing the Project

As you do all the hard work of organizing and collecting information, always think ahead to what you will do with it. As you go along, return to the list of questions you formulated in relation to your topic—the questions you wanted to ask about the musical situation. As you gather more information you will have formulated more questions. These questions and the information you have gathered are related, and they offer a natural organization for your project. Remember that the point of your project is to document some aspect of a nearby music-culture and to interpret it based on the topic you have chosen. More advice on how to write it up and what form to present it in will be available from your instructor.

Be sure to keep in mind that you are not the only one affected by your finished project. Other people's feelings and, on occasion, social position are reflected in your work. Be clear in what you say about the people you worked with. Confidentiality may be important; if people asked you not to use their names or repeat what they said to you, respect their wishes. As is customary in many anthropological works, you may decide to change names of people or places to make certain no one is identified who does not want to be. Imagine the problems created for the member of a band who criticizes the leader if word gets back to the group, or for a school music teacher if he criticizes the school board to you in private and you quote him.

If you need to clear up research questions, check back with your informants. As you interview, collect information, and think about the musical situation you study, new questions always will occur to you. It is no different when you write up your project; you will probably find that it will be helpful to get back in touch with your consultants and ask a few final questions so that you will be satisfied with your project when you have finished it.

In our preface we wrote of our intention that our readers experience "what it is like to be an ethnomusicologist puzzling out his or her way toward understanding an unfamiliar music." A good field project inevitably provides just that experience. Valuable and enjoyable in and of itself, discovery and documentation of a world of music takes on added significance, because even the smallest project illuminates our understanding of music as human expression.

References

Radin, Paul. [1927] 1957. Preface to *Primitive Man as Philosopher*. New York: Dover.

Spottswood, Richard. 1990. *Ethnic Music on Records: a discography of ethnic recordings produced in the United States, 1893 to 1942.* 5 vols. Urbana: Univ. of Illinois Press.

Titon, Jeff Todd. 1980. "The Life Story." *Journal of American Folklore* 93:276–92.

Additional Reading

Barz, Gregory F., and Timothy J. Cooley. 1997. *Shadows in the Field: New Perspectives for Fieldwork in Ethnomusicology.* New York: Oxford Univ. Press.

Collier, John, Jr., and Malcolm Collier. 1986. *Visual Anthropology: Photography as a Research Method.* Albuquerque: Univ. of New Mexico Press.

Emerson, Robert M., Rachel I. Fretz, and Linda L. Shaw. 1995. *Writing Ethnographic Fieldnotes.* Chicago: University of Chicago Press.

Ethnomusicology 36 (2). 1992. [Special issue on fieldwork in the public interest]

Georges, Robert A., and Michael O. Jones. 1980. *People Studying People.* Berkeley: Univ. of California Press.

Golde, Peggy, ed. 1986. *Women in the Field: Anthropological Experiences.* 2nd ed. Berkeley: Univ. of California Press.

Herndon, Marcia, and Norma McLeod. 1983. *Field Manual for Ethnomusicology.* Norwood, Pa.: Norwood Editions.

Hood, Mantle. 1982. *The Ethnomusicologist,* chaps. 4 and 5. 2nd ed. Kent, Ohio: Kent State Univ. Press.

Horenstein, Henry. 1983. *Black and White Photography.* Rev. ed. New York: Little, Brown.

Ives, Edward D. 1980. *The Tape-Recorded Interview: A Manual for Fieldworkers in Folklore and Oral History.* Knoxville: Univ. of Tennessee Press.

Jackson, Bruce. 1987. *Fieldwork.* Urbana: Univ. of Illinois Press.

Lornell, Kip, and Anne K. Rasmussen. 1997. *Musics of Multicultural America.* New York: Schirmer Books.

Rabinow, Paul. 1977. *Reflections on Fieldwork in Morocco.* Berkeley: Univ. of California Press.

Sanjek, Roger, ed. 1990. *Fieldnotes: The Makings of Anthropology.* Ithaca, N.Y.: Cornell Univ. Press.

Spradley, James P. 1979. *The Ethnographic Interview.* New York: Holt, Rinehart, & Winston.

Van Maanen, John. 1988. *Tales of the Field: On Writing Ethnography.* Chicago: Univ. of Chicago Press.

Wax, Rosalie. 1971. *Doing Fieldwork: Warnings and Advice.* Chicago: Univ. of Chicago Press.

Wengle, John L. 1988. *Ethnographers in the Field: The Psychology of Research.* Tuscaloosa: Univ. of Alabama Press.

Credits

Pages 475 and 476 constitute an extension of the copyright page. We have made every effort to trace the ownership of all copyrighted material and to secure permission from copyright holders. In the event of any question arising as to the use of any material, we will be pleased to make the necessary corrections in future printings. Photos by authors of their chapters are not listed here. Thanks are due to the following authors, publishers, and agents for permission to use the material indicated.

Index